The Indiana
Jackass Regiment
in the Civil War

The Indiana Jackass Regiment in the Civil War

A History of the 21st Infantry / 1st Heavy Artillery Regiment, with a Roster

PHILLIP E. FALLER

Foreword by Lawrence Lee Hewitt

McFarland & Company, Inc., Publishers
Jefferson, North Carolina, and London

LIBRARY OF CONGRESS CATALOGUING-IN-PUBLICATION DATA

Faller, Phillip E., 1940–
The Indiana Jackass Regiment in the Civil War : a history of the 21st Infantry / 1st Heavy Artillery Regiment, with a roster / Phillip E. Faller ; foreword by Lawrence Lee Hewitt.
    p.   cm.
Includes bibliographical references and index.

ISBN 978-0-7864-7046-4
softcover : 50# alkaline paper ∞

1. United States. Army. Indiana Infantry Regiment, 21st (1861–1863)
2. United States. Army. Indiana Heavy Artillery Regiment, 1st (1863–1866)
3. Indiana—History—Civil War, 1861–1865—Regimental Histories.
4. United States—History—Civil War, 1861–1865—Regimental histories.
5. Louisiana—History—Civil War, 1861–1865—Campaigns.
6. United States—History—Civil War, 1861–1865—Campaigns.   I. Title.
E506.521st .F35   2013   973.7'472—dc23   2012044589

British Library cataloguing data are available

© 2013 Phillip E. Faller. All rights reserved

No part of this book may be reproduced or transmitted in any form or by any means, electronic or mechanical, including photocopying or recording, or by any information storage and retrieval system, without permission in writing from the publisher.

On the cover: *inset* flag presented in 1863 to the First Indiana Heavy Artillery by the Ladies of Houma, Louisiana (photograph by Victoria L. Son, Indiana War Memorials Commission); *background* detail of roster of 21st Infantry / 1st Heavy Artillery Regiment

Manufactured in the United States of America

*McFarland & Company, Inc., Publishers
Box 611, Jefferson, North Carolina 28640
www.mcfarlandpub.com*

To my patient wife of many years, for quietly reading, knitting, crocheting and visiting art galleries and museums while I searched for and studied letters, diaries, maps, images and other records at various archives, historical societies, libraries and museums around the country.

Table of Contents

Acknowledgments	ix
Foreword by Lawrence Lee Hewitt	1
Preface	3
The Formation of the 21st Indiana Volunteer Infantry	5

Part I: History

One. Indianapolis and Baltimore	9
Two. Ship Island	18
Three. New Orleans Bound	25
Four. Life in the South Louisiana Swamps	31
Five. Baton Rouge and Environs	40
Six. Baton Rouge: Battle	50
Seven. Baton Rouge: Battle Aftermath and Abandonment	75
Eight. Swamp Life, New Orleans and Camp Delights	83
Nine. Cotton and Salt	90
Ten. The *Cotton*, Port Hudson and the Teche	99
Eleven. 48 Days at Port Hudson, Starting May 23, 1893	115
Twelve. At Port Hudson, May 28–June 14	139
Thirteen. At Port Hudson, June 15–July 9	160
Fourteen. Teche, Texas, Teche	190
Fifteen. Veteran Furlough — Red River Sideshow–Garrison Doldrums	202
Sixteen. Reorganization and Action at Mobile Bay	216
Seventeen. New Orleans. Garrison Life. Mobile Campaign!	232
Eighteen. The War Is Over. When May We Go Home?	256
Epilogue	262

Part II: Regimental Roster — 263

Part III: Appendices, Notes, Bibliography, Index

A—Ship Island (The Regiment's Losses Due to Privation) — 325
B—The Battle of Baton Rouge — 325
C—The Battle of Bisland — 330
D—The Siege of Port Hudson — 331
E—Spanish Fort and Blakely — 340

Chapter Notes — 341
Bibliography — 355
Index — 361

Acknowledgments

I extend my heartfelt thanks to all the librarians, library assistants, archivists, archive assistants and historians who helped me obtain data from their archives, special collections, etc. upon which I relied in assembling this work. As memory serves, the institutions are:

Alabama State Archives, Montgomery, AL
Alexandria, LA, Public Library
Bartholomew County Historical Society, Columbus, IN
DePauw University Library, Greencastle, IN
Hill Memorial Library, LSU, Baton Rouge, LA
Illinois State Historical Society, Springfield, IL
Indiana Historical Society, Indianapolis, IN
Indiana War Memorial, Indianapolis, IN
Indiana State Library, Indianapolis, IN
Indianapolis, IN, Civil War Round Table
Jackson, MS, Civil War Round Table
Library of Congress, Washington, DC
Louisiana State Archives, Baton Rouge, LA
Mansfield, LA, Sabine Crossroads, State Historic Site
Michigan State Archives, Lansing, MI
Minnesota Historical Society, St. Paul, MN
Mississippi Archives, Jackson, MS
National Archives, Washington, DC
New York Historical Society, New York, NY
Owens County, IN, Public Library
Port Hudson, LA, State Historic Site
Tulane University, Howard Tilton Library, New Orleans, LA
United States Army Military History Institute, Carlisle, PA
University of Michigan, Bentley Library, Ann Arbor, MI
University of North Carolina at Chapel Hill, NC
University of Texas, Austin, TX
State Historical Society of Wisconsin, Madison, WI

I give a special thank you to all persons who opened their private collections or furnished copies of diaries, letters and other papers from their family archives for my use.

Foreword by Lawrence Lee Hewitt

The best way to learn about any period of history is to read the letters and diaries of its contemporaries. Ideally, these sources can be supplemented by official documents and newspapers. By integrating such materials, historians provide more reliable glimpses into the past. The foremost of such secondary works are biographies. But a dearth of primary sources can make writing an individual's story, no matter his fame, a daunting task. And what of the common man, especially the illiterate?

In the mid-twentieth century historians began abandoning the study of the "great man" and turned to investigating the masses. For Americans, the common soldier of the Civil War was propelled to the forefront of popularity by Bell I. Wiley's *The Life of Johnny Reb: The Common Soldier of the Confederacy* (1943) and *The Life of Billy Yank: The Common Soldier of the Union* (1952). Interest in Johnny Reb and Billy Yank soared during the Civil War centennial and, though waning since the 1960s, has occasionally waxed, thanks to James M. McPherson's Pulitzer Prize–winning book *Battle Cry of Freedom: The Civil War Era* (1989), Ken Burns' documentary *The Civil War* (1990), movies such as *Glory* (1989), *Gettysburg* (1993), *Andersonville* (1996), *Ride with the Devil* (1999), and *Gods & Generals* (2003), and the arrival of the Civil War sesquicentennial in 2011.

Group histories of Civil War soldiers occasionally focus on the graduates of a particular school or the residents of an individual town or county, but most often they are studied by unit. The vast majority of Union soldiers—including a few women—served in about 1,900 infantry regiments organized by state. Even though hundreds of histories have been written about these regiments, many of them have yet to be chronicled. Thanks to Philip Faller, the 21st Indiana Infantry/1st Indiana Heavy Artillery is no longer among the ignored. More importantly, his account is a worthy addition to the genre.

Any outstanding unit history requires three things: an outfit with an impressive service record for its subject; numerous primary sources written by its members; and an able author willing to spend the necessary time ferreting out sources and mastering the documents once they are gathered. If its cadre included individuals such as Eli Lilly, founder of Eli Pharmaceuticals, had a colonel who used his profits from cotton and sugar thievery to advance to brigadier general and divisional command, or was associated with the likes of Benjamin F. Butler, all the better.

Few regiments can match the record of the 21st Indiana. It served in eastern Maryland until February 1862, when it was assigned to the expeditionary force destined for Louisiana. With one exception, it served in that state for three years, participating in the capture of New Orleans, the battles of Baton Rouge and Fort Bisland, the siege of Port Hudson, and the Red River Campaign; the siege and capture of forts Gaines and Morgan, near Mobile, Alabama, in August 1864 was the exception. The regiment returned to Alabama in March 1865 for the campaign against Mobile, fighting in the siege of Spanish Fort and Fort Blakely. Following the end of the war, the Hoosiers were scattered along the Gulf coast performing garrison duty until January 1866. More importantly in regard to the 21st Indiana's service, only 33 Union regiments composed of white troops served as heavy artillery during the Civil War. While it became common in 1864 for such units to convert to infantry, only six infantry regiments converted to heavy artillery during the conflict. One of these was the 21st Indiana, which did so in February 1863, becoming the 1st Indiana Heavy Artillery and the only regiment of that branch of service from the Hoosier state.

With 2,834 mustered members, the 21st/1st Indiana had more than double the enrollment of the average regiment, which increased the likelihood of finding extant primary sources. Though Westerners were not as prolific writers as New Englanders, researching the unit for more than two decades enabled Phillip Faller to locate several diaries, memoirs, journals, and collections of letters. Samuel Armstrong's diaries cover three years of service with the regiment. A telegrapher by trade, Armstrong made comments about certain officers in Morse Code. Several newspapers published letters from the soldiers, especially the *LaGrange Standard*, which had a reporter in Company A.

Time between trips to various repositories enabled him to master the intricacies of both infantry and heavy artillery service, an awesome task seldom faced by an author. Residing in southeastern Louisiana placed the author within a day's drive of all the significant sites where the regiment served, and he spent countless days going over the terrain, especially at Port Hudson. As the manager of the Port Hudson State Historic Site (1978–1982) and the author of *Port Hudson, Confederate Bastion on the Mississippi* (1987), I know the value of *The Indiana Jackass Regiment in the Civil War*. Phillip Faller's coverage of the artillery at Port Hudson makes his book a must read for anyone interested in the longest siege in American military history.

Lawrence Lee Hewitt is a professor of history emeritus, Department of History and Government, Southeastern Louisiana University. He is also an author and was manager of the Port Hudson State Historic Site from 1978 until 1982.

Preface

The Indiana Jackass Regiment in the Civil War began as a genealogy effort to gather information about an ancestor who participated in the American Civil War. Over time this original goal evolved into a history of an Indiana infantry regiment that converted to heavy artillery. The regiment spent three and three-quarters of its four and one-half years in Federal service primarily in Louisiana. It also served in Alabama with detachments in Arkansas and Texas.

Little to nothing has been written about this regiment either as infantry or as artillery prior to this work. The soldiers served with honor, but little fanfare, as did many other regiments. Unlike many others, though, the majority of soldiers in this regiment served four and one-half years. They played an important part in securing Louisiana for the Union as infantry by capturing the railroad between New Orleans and present-day Morgan City, subduing guerillas along that railroad and fighting in the Battle of Baton Rouge. They then fought as artillery in the Teche Campaigns, without much recognition. They also participated in the Siege of Port Hudson (the other "Gibraltar on the Mississippi"). They used their artillery at the siege and reduction of Forts Gaines and Morgan at Mobile Bay, Alabama, and then again at the sieges of Spanish Fort and Fort Blakely.

I have devoted roughly twenty-five years to assembling the information in this text. The book compares the relative luxury of camp life in cities to weeks of living in tents and sleeping in the open, in sun and rain, on fence rails and in mud. I have also included their interactions with the citizens of Louisiana and their feelings about some of them. Also captured are the soldiers' feelings about some of their officers and each other as well as the effects of the war upon their lives and the lives of those back home.

The book focuses on infantry and the use of light artillery for the first nine chapters. Beginning in chapter ten the book changes focus to artillery with infantry becoming incidental. Little has been written about the art of the artilleryman, but it is included herein. This work includes unpublished maps of battlefields that explain why certain fortifications existed, where different artillery units were originally positioned (previously unknown) and where and how they moved around the battlefield showing the new locations.

Written references to this regiment were quite often oblique, such as: the siege train came up or the 21st Indiana was on the left or right as the case may be. An example of their invisibility is illustrated by my finding an unknown ordnance record stating that Company B fired 200 rounds during an action on Bayou Teche where some writers have said they were not involved or were in camp ten miles away.

I will warn the reader about direct quotes taken from letters written more than one hundred fifty years ago: the nouns and adjectives may not be politically correct in today's society, but they were commonplace and politically correct in another time. They are used herein as a reminder of the way things were.

The words "bully boys" are often used when referring to the men of the 21st Indiana

Left: John B. Yelton, 21st Indiana Infantry Regiment, USA, 1861. (Author's collection.) *Above:* Twenty-First Indiana Regiment Volunteer Infantry First National Flag (Battle Flags: Indiana War Memorials Commission).

because they were often called by that honorific. "Bully" was an expression for dashing, high-spirited, well done, good fellow; or, on occasion, as more commonly used today — loud, intimidating, or ruffian, all of which could apply to the men in the regiment at various times.

The Formation of the 21st Indiana Volunteer Infantry

In mid–April 1861, newspaper headlines in both the North and the South boldly proclaimed the news of Confederate Brigadier General Pierre Gustave Toutant Beauregard's capture of Fort Sumter, South Carolina. Fearing military action against the South, Jefferson Davis, president of the newly formed Confederate States of America, called for 100,000 volunteers to defend the new Confederacy. Men of all ages answered this call. Then, at 4:30 A.M. on April 12, the seven Confederate States of America declared their total separation from the United States of America with an artillery bombardment of Fort Sumter.

The newly formed Confederacy, especially the hot-headed South Carolinian secessionists, found the Federal controlled Fort Sumter a vexing problem. The occupants of the fort could control shipping to and from Charleston, a major southern port. Major Robert Anderson, commander of Fort Sumter, refused to surrender it to Confederate forces. Therefore, General Beauregard ordered his artillery to open fire. Ironically, Major Anderson was General Beauregard's former West Point artillery instructor. On April 13, after thirty-three hours of heavy bombardment, Anderson surrendered the fort to his former student. Now, war was a reality. Many people both North and South felt a degree of relief that the waiting was over. Both sides looked for a quick, fateful encounter on the battlefield to resolve their differences. Such an encounter would either reunite the country as one or ratify a separate southern nation.[1]

Northern reaction to Sumter's surrender was rapid. On April 15, Abraham Lincoln, president of the United States, called for 75,000 volunteers to put down the insurrection. These volunteers would serve for three months. Responding to the president's call to arms, Indiana's governor, Oliver P. Morton, requested the male citizens of Indiana to raise six regiments of volunteer infantry to serve for three months. In April this was felt to be ample time to put down the insurrection and restore the Union. These volunteers gathered at the state fairground, located about a half mile southwest of the State House in Indianapolis. The volunteers soon converted the fairground into a training camp named Camp Morton, honoring the governor. Within a few days, many Indiana communities formed volunteer companies, and they rendezvoused at the camp in Indianapolis.

On May 16, the Confederate Congress authorized the recruiting of 400,000 more men. By the 23rd of May, the eleventh (officially the last) state seceded and joined the Confederacy. Maryland and Missouri, by force of Federal arms, remained border states. Kentucky declared its neutrality and joined the Union in September 1861. Due to its small size and occupation by thousands of Union troops, Maryland was held by force of arms. By July 1, the Confederate Army, all volunteers, numbered more than 112,000 men at arms.[2]

The response to Morton's call for three months infantry volunteers greatly exceeded the number of men needed. The six requested regiments formed and designated the 6th, 7th, 8th, 9th, 10th and 11th Indiana Volunteer Infantry Regiments. (The designations of the 1st through the 5th Infantry Regiments were used in the Mexican War.) The six new regiments mustered into national service on April 25. The State of Indiana armed and equipped these regiments. After being outfitted, they moved to western Virginia where they served in General George B. McClellan's command.[2]

Governor Morton, feeling that the war would continue for longer than three months, requested the Federal government to allow the state to raise six additional regiments. These regiments would serve for twelve months, and they would use the surfeit of companies all ready on hand. Without waiting for a reply from Washington, D.C., Governor Morton had the next six regiments raised. Thus, official state action authorized the 12th through 17th Infantry Regiments on May 3, 1861. By coincidence on that same day, Lincoln called for 42,034 three-year volunteers. The Indiana government was not aware of the Federal action because the telegraph wires between Washington and Indianapolis were cut by Rebels. The 12th and the 17th Infantry Regiments formed from twenty-nine extra companies remaining at Camp Morton. The 13th Regiment formed at Camp Sullivan in Indianapolis using the balance of the excess volunteers. (Camp Sullivan was at the site of what today is Military Park, two blocks west of the Indiana State House.) The 14th Regiment at Camp Vigo, Terre Haute, the 15th Regiment at Camp Tippecanoe, Lafayette, and the 16th Regiment at Camp Wayne, Richmond, drew men from sixty-eight other companies raised throughout the state.

The 12th Regiment and 16th Regiment mustered into Federal service for twelve months on May 11. On May 21, the Federal government requested four regiments mustered to serve for three years. The 13th, 14th, 15th and 17th Regiments were asked to volunteer for three years. A discharge was allowed to any man who did not wish to serve three years. Hundreds of men took the offered discharges. The surplus of men still arriving in Indianapolis filled their places in the ranks. These four regiments mustered into Federal service during the middle of June.[3]

Patriotic fervor increased in intensity, both in the North and in the South, as the able-bodied men rallied to defend their respective causes. Due to the urgings of Indiana's warhawk governor Morton, the Indiana Legislature authorized the 18th Infantry Regiment on June 11. It authorized the 19th through 27th Infantry Regiments on June 24. Of these newly authorized regiments, the 18th, 19th, 21st, 26th and 27th organized and trained at Indianapolis.[4]

Was the North's war objective solely to eliminate slavery? Although slavery of black people (not the virtual slavery of tens of thousands of Irish and Italian immigrants laboring in the mills and manufacturing plants of New England and other East Coast states) was a major cause of the war, it is interesting to note that Indiana's Constitution, Article 13, of 1851 banned the immigration of African Americans into the state and an 1852 enactment required that resident blacks register at their county courthouses. While Indiana's earliest constitution banned slavery, an 1831 law required a $500.00 bond to be posted for each person of color brought into the state (escaped slaves or freemen fleeing the South) as a guarantee and insurance that the colored person would not become a ward of the state. Outside of this factual side-note, as to the legislative attitude of Indiana towards blacks, there will be no further discussion of this question other than to present the occasional contemporary comment germane to the story.[5]

James W. McMillan, a Republican merchantman from Lawrence County and a veteran of the Mexican War, sought to organize the 21st Indiana Volunteer Infantry Regiment. The governor so authorized and duly appointed McMillan as colonel of the new regiment. McMillan needed the usual complement of ten full companies to meet the requirement for a regiment. Men from nine southwestern and west-central counties comprised nine of the

Map of Indiana Counties of the 21st Indiana Infantry Regiment (Indiana Jackass Regiment) Company's Origins. (Note: Company letters added by author.) (Courtesy Indiana University Business Research Center.)

regiments: Clay County (Company I), Greene County (Company C), Knox County (Company G), Martin County (Company F), Morgan County (Company K), Owen County (Company B), Parke County (John Campbell raised the Parke County Rifles, Company H, and in two weeks filled the company by June 30, 1861), Putnam County (Company E, the Putnam Rifles), and Sullivan County (Company D). Local men from these counties made up 95 percent to 100 percent of their respective companies. Those not 100 percent filled by in-county residents were usually completed by men living just outside the county. Excepting Company I, only three out-of-state residents joined these nine companies. Company I had nine men who gave other states (Illinois, Iowa, Kentucky, Louisiana and Ohio) as their residence.[6]

The regiment needed one more company to be complete. After negotiations, the regiment added the LaGrange Guard (also called Tigers #2) as Company A. Captain William Roy had formed this company of men from Elkhart and LaGrange counties in the northeastern corner of Indiana. The completed regiment consisted of 980 enlisted men, 30 non-commissioned staff officers and band, 30 commissioned line officers and 8 commissioned field officers, including the chaplain, surgeon and assistant surgeon. Their ages ranged from little boys of eight years old to seasoned men of forty-four years. The regiment had the dubious distinction of having the youngest member in Federal service: Private Edward Black, Musician 3rd Class, eight years old. The regiment mustered into service on July 24, 1861. *(See map on page 7 for locations of counties and companies which formed the regiment. Indianapolis, the state capitol, is in Marion County in the center of the state.)*[7]

PART I: HISTORY

One

Indianapolis and Baltimore

The individual companies rendezvoused from around the west-central parts of the state and organized into the 21st Indiana Infantry Regiment at Camp Morton in Indianapolis. After company rolls were completed and negotiations for a tenth company from the northeast corner of the state to join the regiment were finished, they moved to Camp Sullivan for training. (Today Camp Sullivan is named Military Park between the White River and the west end of Ohio Street in downtown Indianapolis.) To keep out curious passers-by, and more importantly to keep the trainees confined, a high plank fence with one gate protected by a guard's shanty surrounded Camp Sullivan. The attractions of the big city tempted the rural trainees to go exploring and see its attractions. With leave, they visited the insane asylum to stare and laugh at the patients (a crude Victorian entertainment) and the arsenal, where they stared at one hundred pretty young women employed at making rifle and musket cartridges. Besides the cartridges, the arsenal made cannon shot, shell and case as well as many other items needed to equip and maintain troops in the field. (Arsenal Technical High School occupies part of the old arsenal grounds today.) These entertainments were safer than risking the daily fistfights inside the training camp.[1]

During their first three weeks of instruction, the trainees had no weapons or uniforms. They worked and drilled in the clothing they had worn and brought from home. Instead of muskets, they drilled with long sticks. The camp's guards carried axe-handle clubs to control the rowdy recruits. During their fourth week in camp, new Indiana State uniforms, field equipment and firearms arrived. The 21st Indiana's uniforms were made of gray denim (cotton twill) with a black collar, wide black cuffs, and black shoulder strap trimming for the jackets, and a black stripe down the outside of each trouser leg. A short brimmed gray cap topped the ensemble. Regulation U.S. belts, buckles, buttons and shoes completed the uniform. Indiana provided the regiment with all of its clothing and camp and field equipment. The boys' excitement at getting uniforms and equipment was exceeded only by receiving firearms. Skirmishers and the flank companies, A and B, received Enfield rifles. The balance of the regiment received an assortment of old smooth-bore muskets that had been converted in great haste from flintlock to percussion. All carried the usual tapering needle pointed socket bayonet.[2]

The regiment marched and drilled for three days with their new weapons before receiving cartridges and firing instructions. Officers issued cartridges, and the excited boys marched out to the firing line for target practice. The exuberant boys paid little attention to their instructors. Within minutes of taking position at the firing range, a few shots rang out before the command to fire; some shots went into the air above and to the side, a few actually made it down the firing range at the targets. The officers shouted to cease fire as they ran among the men smacking the offenders with the flats of their swords. After restoring order, the captains, lieutenants and sergeants again formed their companies on the firing line and began drilling them to fire on command.

Some of the more citified men, unused to a firearm and not understanding their instructions, fired their weapons before withdrawing the ramrod from the barrel. Ramrods spun through the air to impale trees and plow the ground. Thankfully, the officers had issued only four rounds to each man, and the spirited trainees did not shoot each other. In spite of their poor marksmanship, and after a dressing down by their officers, they marched back to quarters.[3]

The next day, Indiana's staunchest supporter of the Union, Governor Oliver P. Morton, came to their camp to watch their drill and dress parade. After his review, he congratulated the regiment on their good morale and proficiency at drill. He pronounced them fit, ready for combat, and ready to go to war. After learning of the Union defeat at Bull Run (First Manassas), he wanted to rush men to aid his friend, Abraham Lincoln. The governor's words pleased Colonel James W. McMillan and his adjutant, Lieutenant Mathew A. Latham. Both men had worked very hard to get their men properly drilled in the military formations common to the day. Out of the four regiments organized at Indianapolis on June 24, the 21st Regiment was the first designated as ready for field duty. The 21st Indiana Volunteer Infantry mustered into Federal service on July 24, 1861.[4]

On July 31, 1861, more than one thousand gray-clad soldiers and officers of the 21st Regiment Indiana Volunteer Infantry stood stiffly at attention on the platforms of the Union Depot in Indianapolis, Indiana. They had just completed a parade march from Camp Sullivan to the train depot accompanied by cheers from well-wishers. After a few patriotic tunes by their regimental band, their officers ordered the soldiers to fall out and board the cars of two trains waiting to take them eastward to the "Seat of The War." The soldiers took advantage of the time and confusion to bid loved ones farewell as they went aboard the cars. Their camp supplies, rations, and other bulky equipment previously had been taken to the station by wagons and loaded aboard the trains. Several of the soldiers clutched pies and cakes given to them by the cheering crowd.[5]

Late that afternoon the 21st Indiana began their eastward journey over the Indiana Central Railway. The regiment speculated that they could be going to any one of four areas: District of Columbia, Maryland, Pennsylvania, or the western part of Virginia. The day before, Governor Morton had telegraphed the Federal government for instructions as to where he should send the men of the 21st Regiment. The message did not go through because Rebel sympathizers had cut the telegraph wire somewhere outside of Washington, D.C. Not receiving a response, he sent the regiment to the Federal capitol at Washington, D.C. On August 1, orders to report for duty at Baltimore, Maryland, caught up with the regiment.[6]

As they traveled through Indiana and western Ohio, townspeople met the soldiers at stations along the route and cheered them on their way. Both younger and older women offered the men milk, water, cakes, pies, sandwiches, bouquets, and inspirational patriotic notes. At some stops, the older male citizens handed quarters and half dollars to the soldiers. Flirtatious young women at these stops took the attentions of several young officers. In particular, Quartermaster William Hinkle, reputedly a very handsome man, had to run after and leap aboard the train when a "pretty little witch in crinolines and curls" held his attention too long. After this happened a few times, his fellow officers tied him to a seat.[7]

Hinkle was not the only one affected by a pretty maiden's charms. At the train's midnight Dayton, Ohio, dinner stop, a young woman caught Company H's first lieutenant Thomas Bryant's attention. Bryant's captain, John Campbell, overheard her say that Lieutenant Bryant was the best looking man in the regiment. He did not pass this information on to Bryant, stating that he feared the lieutenant would request a furlough to return to Dayton "in a horn."

Continuing their travels, the men began to doze. However, each station they passed had a contingent turned out to cheer the passing trains. If the engine stopped for water, enthusiastic citizens climbed aboard the cars. The greetings interrupted the soldiers' rest; therefore, the men elected a committee to stand on the open platforms of the cars to greet and wave to the people of the towns they passed.[8]

After they arrived at Pittsburgh, Pennsylvania, they had to exit their comfortable coaches and change trains. Having ridden in the luxury of passenger cars from Indiana to Pennsylvania, the officers and enlisted men refused to board their new train's accommodations— dirty boxcars and livestock transport cars! Colonel McMillan wired Governor Morton protesting these travel accommodations. His protests fell upon deaf ears, and the regiment boarded what was available on the connecting railroad.[9]

After a few hours of odoriferous hog-car travel, the train screeched to a sudden stop in the middle of the countryside somewhere in Pennsylvania. A broken-down train blocked the rails ahead. Seeking relief from the rough-riding hog-cars, the always-hungry Hoosiers abandoned the cars and began roaming the hills looking for food. Finding a large patch of fine blackberries, they proceeded to eat. Picking and eating, they wandered farther from the cars. After gorging on the berries and napping in the warm sun for a couple of hours, their train's shrieking whistle split the air. Startled awake and realizing what the whistle meant, hundreds of Hoosiers began a wild gray scramble through the brush and briars to get aboard the train before it left them stranded in western Pennsylvania.[10]

Once safely aboard the train, their appetites filled and bodies rested, the boys were in high spirits as the train sped through the big hills. Some of the more reckless men hung off the car sides, swinging from the grab-irons and climbing from car to car. As the train rushed through a narrow cut in the hills west of Harrisburg, Pennsylvania, projecting rocks swept two men from the cars.[11]

That evening they changed trains at Harrisburg, climbed aboard comfortable passenger cars, and traveled on to Baltimore. The weary travelers fell asleep in various places in and on the cars. Company H's Zeno Rubottom slept soundly on the last car's open platform and tumbled off it onto the cinders of the right-of-way near the Maryland state line. Roughly awakened by his painful fall, he yelled a few expletives in vain at the receding train. Without much choice, Zeno saw a light and walked to it where a farmer let him sleep in his hayloft. The next morning the farm family treated Zeno to a hearty breakfast. Zeno thanked his hosts for their hospitality and directions to the nearest town and walked to the town's railroad station where he flagged down the next passing train. He begged his way aboard the train promising payment upon arrival at Baltimore. Upon arriving at Baltimore, the head of the local Union League paid Zeno's fare and escorted him to his regiment.[12]

Excepting Zeno and the casualties at the rocky cut outside Harrisburg, the 21st Indiana arrived in Baltimore, Maryland, on August 3. With flags flying and in step to their band's patriotic tunes, they marched off. As they passed near the Washington Monument, they were especially alert because rumors said that they would be attacked there. With fixed bayonets they made the six mile march to their camp without physical assault. The regiment's march drew a mixed reception from the residents along its route. Some windows displayed American flags and patriotic emblems. From other windows they received a sullen glare of contempt and a muffled cry of "Hurrah for Jeff Davis!"

The boys camped at Locust Point, between Fort McHenry and Federal Hill. At the campsite, the local Unionist citizens and their black servants gave the Hoosiers a grand welcome. An amazed Private Rufus Dooley from rural Negro–less Parke County wrote his mother: "There was about a hundred niggers there with lemonade and everything else." Most of these rural lads had never seen a Negro and only a few officers had seen one. The knowledge most of these Hoosiers had of a Negro was usually by way of a parody in a traveling minstrel show.[13]

At this time the Federal authorities held the Southern state of Maryland and its key city,

Baltimore, by force of arms. Many of the citizens of Baltimore and Maryland supported the Southern cause and favored secession from the Union. At least a dozen Federal regiments occupied the Baltimore area at the time the 21st Indiana arrived.[14]

The army lost no time in putting the Hoosiers to work. The commanding officers assigned Company A under Captain William Roy to guard the Long Bridge over the Patapsco River, which ran to the west and south of Baltimore. Another company along with Nims' 2nd Massachusetts Battery guarded the Thomas Viaduct on the Baltimore and Ohio Railroad between Baltimore and Washington. Companies E and G, commanded by Captains William Skelton and Edward McLaflin, respectively, received assignments to Fort McHenry to train as heavy artillerists. Initially, Companies E and G trained at the guns in the fort's exterior water batteries. A short time later, these two companies received assignments to duty inside the fort proper. The excitement of artillery drill and watching light batteries maneuver on the grounds outside the fort eventually caused Company E's Lieutenant Eli Lilly to resign. He returned to Indiana, where he formed and captained his own light artillery battery, the 18th Indiana Light Artillery Battery.[15]

The other companies received various guard duty assignments at points around the city. During their travels around Baltimore, the Hoosiers reported seeing some male citizens walking around the city in Confederate uniforms, and secessionist woman, when meeting Union solders walking on the street, used very vulgar language in greeting them.

Two guard details made up of seventy men and three officers each guarded the supply ships traveling between Baltimore, Washington, D.C., and Fort Monroe, Virginia. The water trip to Washington and return took about a week to ten days to make, and there were always many volunteers for guard duty aboard the ships just to get out of camp. (The same trip by rail only took one and one-half hours each way plus a day or so for unloading and reloading.) The 21st Regiment's men were honored that the district commander, Major-General John A. Dix, assigned them to these important duties.[16]

Besides the guard duties mentioned above, the regiment also provided guards for the political prisoners arrested in Baltimore and the neighboring area and some recently captured Confederate officers held at Fort McHenry. Company B had the dubious privilege of escorting thirty prisoners from their cells in Fort McHenry to Fort Lafayette and Fort Jay (aka Fort Columbus) in the environs of New York City. Among these prisoners were the former Baltimore city marshal, George P. Kane (political prisoner), and a Confederate Army officer, Colonel John Pegram (military prisoner). (Fort Columbus held Confederate officers and nearby Fort Williams, both on Governor's Island, held Confederate enlisted men.)[17]

Those fortunate Hoosiers who had guard duty aboard transport vessels took advantage of the occasion to behave like tourists. On their trips to Washington, the boys of Company H had Potomac–side views of Mount Vernon and Aquia Creek. The men were concerned about the Confederate artillery batteries constructed at Aquia Creek. Every trip bore the hazard of Rebel artillery blasting the steamers, but it did not happen.[18]

On one of their early trips as steamboat guards to Washington, the Hoosiers got into a little trouble. A Hoosier lieutenant led his men on a sightseeing trip into the city. During their tour a regular army officer stopped them to check their passes. When he learned they had no passes and recognizing stupidity when he saw it, he told them that the provost marshal heard they were in town, and he wanted to see them. Honored by such a request, the naive Hoosiers willingly went with the officer to meet the provost marshal. This officer smiled as they introduced themselves, and then he told them that they were his prisoners. After explanations, the genial provost released them with an admonishment to have passes the next time they came into the city, or they *would* go to prison.[19]

Camp life at Locust Point in Baltimore was as pleasant as camp life may be. Meals were good. A typical day's dinner might have consisted of bread, beef, rice, onions, tomatoes and coffee. Most officers hired local Negroes as cooks or to keep their quarters clean and tidy. Many of the Negroes were fugitive slaves, declared to be contraband of war by Major-General Benjamin Butler. Therefore, it was not uncommon for non-commissioned officers and groups of enlisted men to hire a cook or cleaning person for their mess or tent. Many of these servants acquired food for their employers by pilfering vendors and local farms. The result was that many of the officers and men enjoyed more and perhaps better quality vegetables and seafood than those who received rations only from the commissary. (The contrabands kept their share, too.)[20]

The soldiers' tents were pitched, staked and trenched to allow rain water to run away. Wooden pallets provided tent floors and scavenged coffee sacks or other bagging covered them to keep dust or mud at a minimum. Stray cats and dogs became the men's pets. Company C's private Thomas Ballard wrote: "We see a good deal of fun I know. Our camp-tent is in about the middle of the Regiment. I can hear every man holler, and I assure you that is all the time mighty near."

The contrabands entertained the men by imitating the officers giving orders at drill. They were very good at imitating Colonel McMillan's parade ground high-pitched squawk. They also played instruments and sang for their own amusement as well as the men's. Regarding the parodies done by the contraband Negroes, Captain Campbell stated that his prior experience about Negroes had been from traveling minstrel shows that he thought were overstated in their portrayals; now after observing them in person, he felt the shows were understated in their portrayals.[21]

The regimental chaplain, Nelson Brakeman, a Methodist minister, served the regiment's religious needs. He held Sunday services, and he held prayer meetings through the week. Only one church in Baltimore, a Presbyterian Church pastored by a Reverend Hays, opened its doors to the Hoosier soldiers. The other denominations of good Christian Baltimoreans considered the common soldiers too vile for admission to their haughty sacred edifices. Because of this, Reverend Brakeman's services had a high number of cross-denominational attendees.[22]

Medical care was poor. Two of the men died of illness before the regiment could establish a hospital. They were short on medical personnel. (Requests for medical personnel would be sent continually to Governor Oliver P. Morton for the duration of Colonel McMillan's tenure as regimental commander.) Once established, the hospital located in the St. Charles Hotel near the Locust Point camp could serve the men's needs for illness and accidental injury care.

Many of the rank and file soldiers did not consider cleanliness to be very important. As the rate of illness increased, the officers encouraged the men to bathe often. There were no private bathing facilities. Since the camp was next to the bay and open to public (female) view, the fully or partially clad men jumped into the bay, where they splashed about in the water working up a lather to wash both body and clothes. After bathing, the men ran to their camp to air dry among the tents.[23]

In late September, the regiment moved to Camp Murray near Druid Hill Park outside of Baltimore. This new camp was upon high ground with excellent spring water and a nearby hospital. The current malady making its rounds was measles. The only cure was one of bed rest and hot soups taken in a hospital. Officers could rent rooms in private homes of Union sympathizers to be nursed back to health. If a man felt like it, he left the hospital to visit camp, since it lifted his spirits. While Private Rufus Dooley was in the hospital with measles, his pard, Private John Yelton, wrote to Rufus' father. Besides reassuring Rufus' father that his son was recuperating well, he told him that the regiment received one month's pay, which amounted to $22.18 for him. Yelton further wrote that because of payday "some of the boys have been pretty tight [drunk] since, but I believe that we have the civilest [sic] company in the regiment."[24]

Camp Murray was near a horse-drawn streetcar line, and for five cents one could ride the entire route. Large crowds of Unionists came from the city by this convenient transportation to watch the regiment's parades. Much to the delight of the men, many young women accompanied their parents from the city to the camp. Back at their prior camp on Locust Point, only poor elderly women selling apples or Negroes wanting an odd job visited them.[25]

It was about this time (early October) that the regiment received new Federal–blue overcoats for the coming winter. In addition to the new overcoats, the Federal government issued Austrian and Belgian rifles to replace their smooth-bore muskets and damaged Enfield rifles. These foreign-made rifles were inferior in operation and construction to other rifles; some springs were too weak to cause the hammer to fire the percussion cap. The men demanded better firearms. The Baltimore firm of Merrill, Thomas & Company proudly and happily displayed their product, a breechloading rifle in .54-inch caliber. This breech-loading rifle opened and closed the breech (the rear of the barrel) by a toggle-lever system, which allowed for faster loading than a muzzle-loader. Company K's men opted to privately buy these rifles for themselves rather than trust their obsolete Federal–issue muzzle-loading muskets.[26]

In mid–October, the regiment, excepting Companies E and G, moved their camp again. This time they moved to slightly higher ground and Fort Marshall on Murray Hill, also called Potter's Hill or Snake Hill. Since the weather was becoming cooler, the soldiers dug shallow basements for their tents and erected sod fireplaces and chimneys at one end of them. They also constructed wooden barracks inside the fort's earthen walls. The men worked at building and strengthening the existing fortifications. Fort Marshall with its thirty-eight guns, acting together with the heavy guns at Fort McHenry and Federal Hill, could command and control an attack upon Baltimore Harbor. Further, the forts were a deterrent against rebellion from within the city itself. Across the harbor from Fort Marshall, the newly trained heavy artillerists of Companies E and G moved into the fortifications atop Federal Hill.[27]

A favorite entertainment for the Hoosiers at Fort Marshall was guard-breaking; whereby a few men would divert the attention of the guard while a larger group would run out of camp to the city. The duty guard would summon the corporal of the guard. The corporal would call the sergeant of the guard who formed a guard detail to retrieve the errant soldiers. There were always more volunteers for the detail than needed. The guard detail went into the city, usually turning down the wrong road, to catch the AWOL men. After taking more time than needed, the pursuers and their prisoners would return to camp. The prisoners spent the remainder of the night in the guardhouse. In high spirits, brought on by drinking too much spirits, the prisoners spent their time shouting and singing: "Hurrah for Jeff Davis," "Hurrah for Beauregard," "The Bonnie Blue Flag" and other songs improper for their avowed Union cause.[28]

By November new Federal–blue uniforms were issued to replace the "greasy gray" uniforms issued by the State of Indiana. On November 6, 1861, Colonel McMillan received orders for the entire left wing of the 21st Indiana Regiment to report for detached service in an expedition under Brigadier-General Henry H. Lockwood down the Eastern Virginia Peninsula. Major Benjamin Hays commanded and Captain James Grimsley of Company B acted as second in command of the left wing, consisting of companies B, G, K, E, and H.

Those who were ill or who had recently recovered from illness were excluded from duty. Handpicked volunteers from the right wing companies filled the places of those excluded from duty. If Company H (only fifty-five able-bodied men) was an indicator of the number of men available for duty from each chosen company, one would think that there would have been ample openings for those qualified from the right wing's companies. However, there were too many eager volunteers. Sergeant David Kuhn of Company H went along as a private because too many non-commissioned officers reported for the expedition. Those left behind from the right wing cursed their officers for allowing only 500 men to go. Some men vowed to desert if not chosen, and others offered two months wages for a chance to participate in the expected fight.[29]

Carrying full field packs and four-days of rations, the detachment went aboard a transport ship. Their vessel steamed across and down Chesapeake Bay to the Pocomoke River, then upriver to Newtown, Maryland. Disembarking at Newtown, they joined the 5th New York, 4th Wisconsin, 6th Michigan, and 17th Massachusetts infantry regiments, Pernell's Legion, 2nd Delaware Cavalry, the Reading Cavalry and Nims' Battery (2nd Massachusetts Light Artillery). The object of the expedition was to clean out all of the Rebels in the two counties on the Eastern Shore of Virginia (a peninsula to the south from Maryland). If the campaign succeeded, it would break a Rebel supply line using the peninsula running down from Maryland into two Virginia counties and crossing over Chesapeake Bay to Yorktown, Virginia.[30]

The Federal commanders believed that Major-General John B. Magruder, C.S.A., had entrenched about 5,000 men on the peninsula to oppose the Federal troops. Before proceeding into Virginia, couriers under a flag of truce carried a proclamation from General Dix into the Virginian counties of the peninsula. It stated that Federal troops were coming into their lands, and as long as the Virginians acted with care and did not provoke the Federals, they would not be harmed and their property would be respected.

Crossing the border between Maryland and Virginia the advancing Federals encountered only local citizens turned out to stare at them and see what a Federal soldier looked like. The soldiers, in turn, stared back at the bystanders. A wag in the 21st Indiana remarked that the local "men were small and rough-faced, with plump bellies and slouched hats;" the women were "thin and cadaverous with contracted brows and care-worn expressions."

The 5th New York Regiment (Duryea Zouaves), the 21st Indiana, 4th Wisconsin, Nims' Battery and Richard's Cavalry marched the length of the peninsula in search of someone to engage in a fight. The hottest contest in the march took place between the 5th New York Zouaves and the 21st Indiana to see which regiment could cover the most ground on a day's march. The Zouaves led off the first day and the Hoosiers kept right on their heels. The second day the 21st Indiana's bully boys led off chanting their cadence: "I left, I left, I left my wife and one little kid; I left, I left, I left my wife and two little kids; I left, I left, I left my wife and three little kids; I left ... etc." By the time to camp for the evening, the Zouave's ranks stretched out for five miles behind them. The gaily red-clad New Yorkers nicknamed the Hoosiers "The Grey–hounds," because of their speed. The race down the peninsula did not amuse the brigade's officers. The next day the 21st Regiment marched at the brigade's rear.[31]

So far the advancing army had encountered only hastily built and hastily abandoned earthworks and a few felled trees to impede their progress. The campaign resulted in the capture of seven new iron 6-pounder cannons and 100 defective muskets and shotguns. The total force opposing them was about 700 men who escaped in skiffs, canoes, and rowboats across the bay to Virginia proper with their good armaments, ammunition, and rations. The disgusted Hoosiers wondered why it took 5,000 Federals to rout only 700 Rebels. They thought the expedition was a farce — a sentiment shared by the 5th New York.[32]

The two Virginian Eastern Shore counties swore due allegiance to the Union. A small Yankee force stayed behind to uphold the forced allegiance. The main body of the Federals, including the 21st Indiana, returned to their landing point and boarded waiting steamers bound for Baltimore. The Hoosiers had liberated a large quantity of tobacco at Whitestown, Virginia. The Hoosiers crammed aboard the steamer *Wilson Small* like sardines in a can and began their trip up and across the bay to Baltimore. The bay's stormy water with its large swells and slapping whitecaps heaved the little steamer to and fro and up and down.

In a short time the tobacco gobs on the deck were one and one-half inches thick and rising. The rolling seas and the quids of tobacco combined to cause a severe epidemic of seasickness. To make matters worse, only those packed along the outside railing of the lower deck had a suitable place for their heaves. It did no good for anyone on the upper deck to yell out a warning. There was no place below to move to avoid the splash and pungent splatter. After what seemed an interminable trip, the *Wilson Small* arrived at Baltimore. The 21st Indiana, queasy, spewing, and tobacco stained, disembarked and squished their way through the muddy streets back to Fort Marshall.[33]

The troops busied themselves at cleaning up their clothing and themselves. Four companies stayed in four barracks inside the fort, and the rest of the companies stayed in temporary barracks and in their tent covered dugouts outside the fort. The barracks in the fort were spacious, each having four heated rooms (24 men to a room) and a kitchen with a cooking stove. Company H was one of the fortunate companies assigned to the relative luxury of the fort's barracks, where their quarters provided a welcome relief from the winter weather's alternation of rain, snow, sleet, hail, freezes and thaws. The depth of mud in the camp's streets increased with each change in weather.[34]

While many of the men and officers requested furloughs to visit home, only a few got the desired furlough—officers being no exception. The men passed their off-duty time by writing letters home, by visiting lewd women, drinking at gin shops and visiting local bakeries. The soldiers' devoured hundreds of cakes and pies per week. Those returning to camp late at night would occasionally put a plank across the chimney of the dug-out tent shelters. The resulting smoke-out caused a group of vehemently cursing men to erupt from the shelter into the freezing night. Of course, the smoke-out deed-doers were well hidden, and those smoked out could only hope that after their next evening turn out of camp they could pay back their prankster comrades in kind.[35]

After the measles epidemic of the past fall season ran its course, mumps began making its swollen way through the camps as the winter's primary illness. This disease slowly ran its course throughout the winter, selecting some, missing others, only to come back and infect some who had been missed at the earliest outbreak of the disease. Relatively few from the 21st Indiana Regiment used their hospital facilities during the winter. The able-bodied men engaged in drill, firearms practice and camp duties to maintain efficiency. Company K's first shipment of Merrill rifles arrived during December, and the boys proudly showed off their new breechloaders with their saber bayonets. At the next firing practice, the accuracy and rapid fire of the breechloaders impressed the entire regiment. All of the other companies clamored for these efficient weapons.[36]

The Merrill rifles complete with saber bayonet, scabbard, cartridge box, cap box, and a belt cost $45.00. Working out a private agreement to pay $15.00 per pay for three pay periods, Company H placed their orders for the Merrill rifles. Since a private's pay was about $13.00 per month, this arrangement would seem to pose a financial hardship. The basic pay plus a small enlistment bonus paid monthly, allowed the Hoosiers to make a valid offer to pay for their own arms. Private Rufus Dooley of Company H stated that out of his January 21st pay (for two months), he paid $15.00 toward his new rifle, loaned out $10.00, and had $10.00 to live on until the next pay (a total of $35.00 for two months). Some of the soldiers also received money from home with which they could pay for their rifles.[37]

About a month after the Merrill Company accepted Company H's purchase offer, the regiment's other eight companies made an offer to the Merrill Company to pay $15.00 per man per payroll until the total of $45.00 was reached. The Merrill Company, suffering from

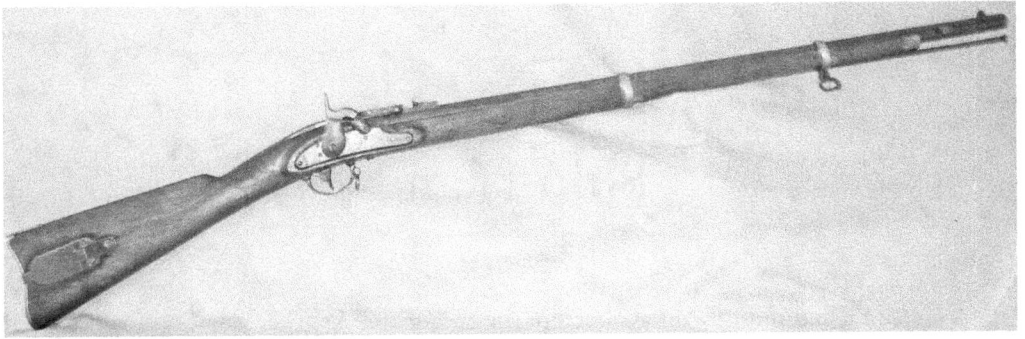

Merrill Rifle identified to the 21st Indiana Volunteer Infantry, Co. K.

slow cash flow, turned it down. Colonel McMillan wrote to his congressman, W. McKee Dunn, on January 22, wherein he asked Dunn to intercede with the secretary of war and have the War Department order the Merrill rifles for the regiment. As they received the rifles, the War Department could deduct the cost from the men's pay. Two months later, the War Department acted upon the request, and it ordered 566 Merrill rifles. The United States Quartermaster Department would receive the rifles and forward them on to the 21st Indiana. The Hoosiers eventually received about 70–percent of this order. The balance of the rifles went to sharpshooters in the Eastern Theater of war or never left the Washington and New York arsenals.[38]

Recruiting became important to replace men lost due to officers' resignations and men's transfers, illness and disability. In answer to this problem, McMillan sent selected officers back to Indiana on recruiting duty. In early February, Captain James Grimsley returned to the Baltimore camp from Indiana with forty-four recruits. Only a few of these men had any prior military training and that was with three months of service regiments. Most of them were the epitome of raw recruits. As was typical of green, country lads from rural Indiana, they spent their first few off-duty hours wandering around the camp taking in the strange new scenes of camp life. The old hands in the regiment told them plenty of colorful, highly elaborated stories and outright lies about their adventures near "the seat of the action."[39]

In early February a private from Company I, Walter Cahil, drove a wagon into the camp from Baltimore at night. As he drove across the guard lines, the guard shouted: "Halt! HALT!! **HALT!!!**" [emphasis added]. Cahil did not stop. The guard raised his musket and fired at point blank range. The hot lead ripped through Cahil's neck between the jugular veins, tearing a hole through his throat and larynx. The shot brought men on the run. Someone recognized the wounded man as one of their own, and he was carried to the regimental hospital. There was little the surgeon could do for him, except try to make him comfortable. Much of his food and water drained out of the hole in his neck when he swallowed. His Hoosier comrades came by the man's hospital bed to offer sympathy; others came only to gawk at the macabre sight. After lingering in pain for a month, Cahil died.[40]

Two

Ship Island

To ease the tedium of winter in camp, the rumor mill kept the boys' minds occupied like a rocking chair — it gave them something to do even if they did not go anywhere. Men and officers alike felt they had no other purpose in Baltimore than to eat 1,046 daily rations, polish brass buttons, and wear out clothing. What with the daily drill and polish the 21st Indiana became a fine band-box regiment. While the increased attention from the ladies at their parades was very nice, the regiment's men and officers felt they could be of better use to the government by being in combat.[1]

Late in the evening of February 18, 1862, the regiment received orders to report aboard the steamship *Georgiana* bound for Newport News, Virginia. They worked all night and most of the next day striking camp. In spite of their efforts they departed in haste, leaving behind campstools, cots, tables and corn-husk mattresses for the rag-pickers.

The news of the regiment's leaving got to the contraband camp followers almost faster than it got to the soldiers. Often, the men did not get a chance to vacate their barracks or tent before the rag-pickers entered and made off with goods and clothes waiting to be packed. Lieutenant Thomas Bryant lost his brand new $10.00 sky-blue dress pants to the scavengers. Private Rufus Dooley was among those robbed before leaving Baltimore. Suffering with mumps and his jaws "swolled like a fat hog," he wrote home describing his experience: "I left my knapsack in another room and some niggers came very coolly and took it out and that is the last I saw of my blankets and shirts and drawers and a few likenesses. So there I was stripped of nearly everything I had. I found some blankets and straps so that is all I am bothered with now."[2]

Just before they broke camp on the 19th, the men of Company H received thirty Merrill rifles from their personal orders. They gladly took them along as they marched off at 4:00 P.M. through a cold rain to the wharf. The regiment's right wing plus Company H reported in at the wharf. There, the enlisted men would stand, shivering and shaking, for a couple of hours watching their officers partake of various "warming liquids" in the shelter of local cafes, taverns, public houses, etc. Eventually, the warmly besotted officers allowed the enlisted men aboard the *Georgiana*. A wagon from the Merrill Patent Firearm Manufacturing Company arrived and delivered thirty more rifles to Company H as they were boarding. Lieutenant Samuel E. "Ed" Armstrong of Company I became hungry and tired of waiting aboard the steamer for it to depart. He went ashore to eat supper and buy a few items. Within half an hour the *Georgiana* steamed away, and Armstrong returned to an empty wharf.

In a short time, Companies B, E, G, K and the regiment's convalescent soldiers came to the wharf where they joined the unhappy and rain soaked Armstrong. These companies and Armstrong, excepting the battalion's officers who whiled away their time in warm taverns, spent a cold, shivering, rain soaked night on the wharf until another steamer arrived the next morning. The steamer's captain and crew did not allow any fires aboard the steamer, so both the sick and the well soldiers huddled together for warmth. After an overnight stop at Fortress Monroe, Virginia, they steamed to Newport News Point, Virginia. Arriving there, they disembarked into melting snow and sloshed off through the mud to seek their tents and a place to pitch them in dank Camp Butler.[3]

The weather was as miserable at Camp Butler as it had been at Baltimore. The enlisted men set up their tents in a driving rain. Their more fortunate officers sheltered in cavalry stables. After setting up their camp, the boys wandered among other regimental camps.

Previously on February 22, 1862, Major-General George B. McClellan had written to Major-General Benjamin Butler the following: "You are assigned to the command of the land forces destined to cooperate with the Navy in the attack upon New Orleans.... The force at your disposal will consist of the first thirteen regiments named in your memorandum handed to me in person, the 21st Indiana, 4th Wisconsin, and 6th Michigan (old and good regiments from Baltimore). The 21st Indiana, 4th Wisconsin and the 6th Michigan will await your orders at Ft. Monroe, Virginia. Two companies of the 21st Indiana are well drilled at heavy artillery ... I may briefly state that the general objects of the expedition are, first, the reduction of New Orleans and its approaches; then Mobile and its defenses; then Pensacola, Galveston, etc." (The thirteen regiments were all New England regiments. Because Butler was a political general from Massachusetts, he preferred to have some of his constituency witness his military ability, grant favors to and then vote him into a succession of important political offices once the war ended.)

If effective, this expedition would provide a major component of General Winfield Scott's Anaconda Plan, which would cut off cotton and sugar exports to foreign countries from the South's Gulf of Mexico ports, and it would block the South's imports of military supplies and articles of daily living from foreign countries through these same ports.[4]

On March 2, the regiment received its orders to move to Ship Island, which is about ten to twelve miles off the Mississippi Gulf Coast. They packed their baggage, but they did not strike their tents. They waited in their tents, sitting on their fully packed baggage, watching the rain fall for two more days with occasional breaks in the rain through which they could see the C.S.S. *Virginia* up the river. At last, at 5:00 P.M. on March 4, they took down their tents and marched to the wharf where they went aboard the *Constitution*. They received a good supper and dry quarters once aboard the ship. The 6th Michigan and the 4th Wisconsin shared its decks with the 21st Indiana. Once aboard the ship, they remained off Newport News until afternoon of the next day. Then the *Constitution* sailed to Fortress Monroe.

As they sailed down to Hampton Roads, the Rebel battery at Sewell's Point opened fire at them. Several soldiers climbed into the rigging to watch the battery fire. After a missile the size of a basketball with its sputtering fuse passed within a few feet of the Hoosiers aloft, they speedily descended and watched from the deck. The regiment's tow-headed 8-year-old drummer boy, Edward Black, clapped his hands and shouted to his father: "I am so glad they shot at us so I can have something good to write home to mamma." The battery fired five rounds. Two passed over the ship and three splashed into the water short of the ship. Unscathed, the *Constitution* passed on to Fortress Monroe and anchored for the night. During the night, several small craft ferried provisions and additional supplies out to the ship. Among the supplies were new rifles for the 21st Indiana to replace older and or broken weapons. This re-arming resulted in eight companies (not companies H and K) bearing a half and half mix of Enfield and Austrian rifles.[5]

Once provisioned, equipped, and upon the noon-time arrival of Brigadier General Thomas Williams, the *Constitution* put out to sea. They cleared the area two days before the C.S.S. *Virginia*'s raid. Their voyage took them south along the Atlantic coast. The next day a strong storm caught the little fleet off Cape Hatteras, North Carolina. The sixteen-hour long gale was both frightening and magnificent. Waves burst over the main deck in showers of spray and foam that leaked through onto the men below. Most men became seasick as the ship pitched and rolled about for hours in the high waves. Packed together under closed hatches as they were, the men had to lie and groan while a three- to five-inch deep mixture of sea water and their own vomit rose and sloshed around them.[6]

After the wind- and rain-churned seas and stomachs subsided, the voyage became relatively pleasant for a few days. The soldiers, allowed on deck in shifts, enjoyed watching porpoises play around the ship. At least one shark seemed to follow the vessel, likely for the garbage thrown overboard. As they progressed south, the increasingly warmer temperatures caused the shedding of overcoats. Jackets followed the overcoats, and, in turn, trousers followed the jackets. By the time the *Constitution* reached the southern coast of Florida, the men had stripped down to shirts and drawers.

The hot sun began dehydrating the soldiers. The officers had an adequate ration of water in casks, but the enlisted men's water ration ran low. To quench their thirst, they relied on distilled sea water from the ship's steam engines. Most often they drank it hot after having to wait in line for an hour or more to get a cup of the stuff to slake their thirst. All three regiments' enlisted men endured this hardship while the vessel rounded the tip of Florida and crossed the Gulf of Mexico to anchor off Ship Island on March 13. Though they had spent only three days under the hot southern sun on short water rations, the fish-belly white Northerners suffered from sunburn and dehydration.[7]

The troops' first view of Ship Island did not offer much hope that they were going ashore onto a tropical paradise with shady trees. Indeed, they said that it resembled a giant sandspit about six or seven miles long and about a half mile wide. High sand dunes and low marshes gave variety to its desert-like quality. Large chunks of driftwood lodged on top of the sand dunes bore evidence of the island's periodic inundation by the sea during severe storms. The eastern end of the island widened and supported a pine forest, but at high tide the sea washed across the island between this end and the rest of the island creating, in effect, two islands. Snakes, toads, birds, raccoons, wild pigs and alligators inhabited the woods and marshes. Brigadier-General J. W. Phelps, commanding troops already there, had not recommended Ship Island as a suitable camping and training ground for Butler's army, but that made no difference to the Federal high command.[8]

The deep-drafted *Constitution* had to anchor a little more than a quarter of a mile away from the only pier. The men disembarked the *Constitution* by climbing down ladders onto the deck of a small shallow draft river steamer, the *Lewis*. As each regiment got off, they appointed details from among themselves to help load the slings and hoists that lowered weapons, supplies, food and equipment onto the deck of the smaller vessel. When loaded, the *Lewis* steamed off to unload at the pier. The 21st Indiana was the last regiment off the ship, and it did not leave until late evening. As the sky darkened into night, the wind increased in intensity causing the waves to rise. A lot of swearing and confusion accompanied the 21st Indiana's rough night landing on the island. Lieutenant Armstrong remained aboard the *Constitution* with a detail of forty men to prepare the baggage, provisions and supplies for unloading.[9]

Once on shore, the regiment had no idea of where or in what manner they would spend the night. Their camp stuffs consisted solely of what they carried from the ship on their backs. Setting off in search of a campsite, they wandered eastward for two miles through the island's deep fine-grained white sands, scrubby grass and sea oats. Their trek was parallel to and several yards inland from the shore because they noticed how far the wind was pushing waves inland. Finally finding a semi-suitable campground, the hungry soldiers set up a temporary camp about two feet higher than the incoming waves. Their unpleasant introduction to Ship

Island was not over; the sand was alive with fleas, flies, ticks, lice, mosquitoes, and scorpions that did not enhance the boys sleep or their dispositions.[10]

The next day the wind and waves intensified. Intermittent rain squalls added to the soldiers' general discomfort. A two hundred man detail went out to the *Constitution* aboard the *Lewis* to finish unloading. Colonel McMillan and his staff went with the detail to encourage them to work harder. As work progressed, the privates overheard the officers whispering to one another that McMillan's encouragement discouraged the men more than it encouraged them. In spite of the colonel, the men got most of the supplies unloaded and ferried ashore by late afternoon.

On the last trip of the day, the commissary stores, two captains and their work details, Colonel McMillan, Chaplain Nelson Brakeman, and Quartermaster William Hinkle filled the *Lewis*. After traveling a short distance to the pier, a severe squall overtook the vessel. The little steamer bounced up and down over the waves and barely held its own against being carried out to sea by the tide. A strong wind gust slammed the *Lewis* against an anchored gunboat. The gunboat's crew threw a line to the steamer and drew her close to the gunboat where both vessels anchored and lay to all night riding out the storm.

Late the next morning the stormy weather abated, and the *Lewis* cast off from the gunboat and landed her drenched load about noon. After the Hoosiers unloaded her, the *Lewis* returned to the *Constitution* that afternoon and took on the remaining supplies, a grumbling Lieutenant Armstrong, and his forty-man work detail. The hindmost of the 21st Indiana Regiment set foot on Ship Island at nightfall on the 15th.[11]

While their comrades unloaded supplies on the 14th, the men who had spent their first night on shore moved camp to higher ground. This site was near the other newly arrived regiments on the island, the nearest regiments being the 31st Massachusetts Infantry and the 4th Wisconsin Infantry. The Hoosiers' officers assigned work details of their men to various tasks needed to make a proper camp, including marking off camp boundaries, company streets and locating men's and officers' sinks (latrines). Then they cleared and dug. Other work details brought the supplies from the landing into their camp. Firewood details brought in grass, sticks, and driftwood. Several men kindled small fires to dry their clothing. Others set up company kitchens and kindled cooking fires, but there was nothing to cook. The commissary stores had not yet arrived.

The next day, the soldiers had been without food for 40 hours. A few men purchased bread at the post bakery. Others sought a sutler or begged food from men in other regiments. As their supplies and commissary arrived, they made themselves more comfortable. The soldiers pitched their wall tents and stored their equipment. It was too late to cook; so, after dining on hardtack and water, they retired with growling stomachs. That night Mother Nature welcomed the entire regiment with storm-rolled waves crossing the sand up to the first row of tents. Wind blew down most of the tents and rain drowned out all the camp fires. Mercifully, the roaring wind changed to the west and prevented the pounding surf from sweeping across the island and taking the camps with it.[12]

After the tempest abated, the soldiers placed tents upright and repaired damage. In the morning, another firewood detail walked and waded to the eastern end of the island at low tide. They cut wood and tied it into rafts, which they poled back to the main island at high tide while looking out for sharks.

As time passed on the miserable island, the glare of the sun reflecting off of the island's white sand caused many of the soldiers to be afflicted with a disorder which caused their eyes to crust shut. Varying degrees of blindness, similar to snow blindness, occurred. Four hundred of the Indiana boys reported in sick with this malady at the same time. It took many months for some of them to recover their full vision. About a dozen men from each regiment never fully recovered from the effects of the Ship Island malady. Major-General Butler declared them to be disabled and discharged to go home.[13]

Navy transports brought casks of drinking water to the island to supply its inhabitants. Several soldiers found they could get drinkable water from shallow holes dug in the sand about two feet deep. They lined the hole with a barrel opened at both ends. The Hoosiers sometimes flavored the water with whiskey stolen from their adjutant's supply.[14]

Within a few days, the regiments were organized into brigades. The 21st Indiana was assigned to the Second Brigade, Department of the Gulf. This brigade consisted of the 21st Indiana, 26th Massachusetts, 31st Massachusetts, 6th Michigan, 4th Wisconsin, 2nd Massachusetts Battery, 6th Massachusetts Battery, and 2nd Battalion Massachusetts Cavalry (Magee's Cavalry). The Second Brigade was the largest of the three organized, consisting of more than 5,100 men of the 12,412 on the island. Brigadier General Thomas Williams, a regular army officer from Detroit but derogatorily called a "New York Yankee Barkeeper," commanded the brigade. Williams stated that he considered westerners to be uncouth and uncivilized; therefore, he was unpopular with half of his volunteers.

Williams insisted on drilling the men daily in soft sand practicing his "order of combat." This formation and movement of troops would likely give grand troop performance in a battle waged in Napoleonic style with large open fields for maneuvering. The "order of combat" involved a formation that allowed troops to shift from right to left on a battlefield so the units could provide covering fire for one another. One such maneuver called for companies or regiments to form in hollow squares. A flaw in the maneuver (as subordinate officers understood it) existed in that companies, or regiments as the case may be, crossed each other's line of march in forming the squares. They could not support each other, and got in each other's way. The daily drilling in hot sun, high humidity, woolen uniforms and full field gear did not increase the general's popularity with the Western troops. Many drills lasted eight hours. A complaining Hoosier said: "He's made of iron himself, and he thinks we are too."[15]

The martinet general, did give the brigade one good laugh, much to his chagrin. While he was drilling the brigade, he commanded them to shoulder arms. Rising in his stirrups, he called out, "Shouldah!" General Williams, after waiting a few moments and seeing that no one moved, again called out sharply, "SHOUL-dah!" Still no one stirred. Becoming more agitated, he bellowed, "Shoul-DAH!" The colonels repeated the command, but the rifle butts remained on the sand. Astounded, Williams sent his adjutant, Wyckham Hoffman, along the officers' line to instruct them to be sure to repeat the command. After the adjutant had returned, the general roared out, "**SHOUL-*DAH!***" Colonels, majors, captains, lieutenants and non-commissioned officers repeated the command, but still nothing happened. Williams, unable to control his rage, shook his fist at Colonel Halbert E. Paine (4th Wisconsin) and Colonel McMillan (21st Indiana) whom he considered to be the cause of the problem. He wheeled his horse and started riding along the line of men, glaring at each looking for a guilty reaction. After riding past half of the brigade, he remembered that he had never given the command of execution, "arms!" For a long time afterward, the western men would call out "shouldah" to start a round of laughter at Williams' expense.[16]

Finally, on March 29, General Butler gave orders to break camp and prepare to march. The 21st Indiana regiment was ordered aboard the steamer *Matanzas*. They shared this vessel with Brigadier General Williams and his staff. Each regiment could take only three tents, but they could take all their cooking kettles, mess pans, cups, plates, knives and forks. Each soldier took his knapsack, overcoat, blanket, one extra shirt, one extra pair each of drawers and shoes, one canteen and the usual forty rounds of ammunition in their cartridge boxes. They cooked and packed four days' rations in their haversacks and took all axes, hatchets, picks, shovels and spades they had in their possession.[17]

The next day the regiment had their equipment packed, but they remained in camp. They loafed about, sitting on their packs, chewing tobacco, smoking cigars, and wondering about the delay. Most of their tents remained standing, which was fortunate, because the soldiers remained in camp for the next forty-five days. (They were allowed to unpack after two days.)

The Hoosiers found that they were better off than some other regiments. These others had boarded their transports and had waited on board for four days. Sanitary reasons came to their rescue, and they disembarked to rebuild their struck camps. Their delay was due to Flag Officer Farragut's large ships not being able to pass over the sandbars at the mouth of the Mississippi River. He would not have his ships clear until April 7.[18]

The 21st Indiana again settled into their routine of grit-filled drill on the sand island. Drill plus sham battles occupied their time. In one of these battles, they charged up a sand hill directly into the fire of blank cartridges from two rifled cannon manned by Nims' 2nd Massachusetts Battery. The Hoosiers' dashing charge and capture of the cannon drew compliments from General Butler.

The Hoosiers spent some of their off-duty time engaged in card games and horseplay. A fresh infantry regiment from New England caught their attention. The regiment was composed of clean-cut, well scrubbed teen-aged boys and young men, scarcely more than green recruits and wearing their state uniforms. The day after their landing was their usual laundry day. They scrubbed their clothes clean, and they left their laundry hanging to dry on clotheslines overnight. The sun rose on empty clotheslines. After the laughter died down, the Hoosiers returned their clothes. Thereafter, the newcomers did not leave their clothes out overnight.[19]

The Hoosiers had complained about being on short rations since they had packed with nowhere to go the week before. On the 7th they received no bread from the bakery, and they were put on half-rations. They blamed their Yankee brigade commander, Thomas Williams for the short rations. Lieutenant Armstrong expressed his feelings on the short rations, writing in Morse Code: "Yankee gets plenty. Hoosier almost nothing. There seems to be some partiality shown to the blue bellies by the Yankee commander. Us Hoosiers don't stand any [chance] at all for something to eat, but Hoosiers can stand any kind of a mean treatment, after so long drilling in it by our New York barkeeper and dry goods drummer." (The last seven words were quite an insult at that time.)[20]

Their hunger increased to the point where a few wealthier men each paid a nearby sutler 25 cents for three small doughnuts—a genuine 5-cent value! Company B gained an advantage in the food department; their neighbors, the 31st Massachusetts, stored a large bowl of biscuit batter in a locked chest in the cook tent. Under cover of darkness a couple of Company B's boys broke into the chest, stole the batter and rolled a large unmarked barrel back to their camp. The Hoosiers broke open the barrel finding potatoes. Soon they dined upon baked batter-cakes and roasted potatoes.

A hard wind on the 8th blew sand onto and into everything, adding grit to the half-rations issued by the division commissary headed by General Butler's brother, "colonel" Andrew Butler. Now the Hoosiers cussed about Andrew's providing poor food and the skimming the food money into his pockets. Brigadier-General Williams got a short break from the men's curses until he issued General Order #30, which prohibited gambling and profanity in the camp of the second brigade. They could not gorge, they could not gamble, and they could not cuss. Tom-fool Yankees! On the 9th, they received fresh bread, and the grumbling focused on General Williams, again, rather than Andrew Butler.[21]

According to officers of the 21st Indiana, infighting among the military departments over which one had jurisdiction over the planned attack upon New Orleans had caused the latest turmoil at Butler's headquarters. The dispute concerned what territory made up the Military Department of the Gulf. Butler had no authority out of the Gulf of Mexico, or the Department of the Gulf. That department consisted of only Ship Island. While Butler waited for news that he had control over the area promised at the outset of the expedition he was "bellowing like a man stark mad."[22]

On the evening of the 10th, another forceful storm rolled across Ship Island. The Gulf of Mexico's waves rolled up to the 21st Indiana's camp, and at the ground's lowest places the waves rolled across it soaking everything left on the ground. The winds flattened tents and blew some a distance away into other camps. Shelterless men hastened into the storm to retrieve the canvass to cover their belongings and foodstuffs. Amid the forty-plus mile-per-hour wind and rain, lightning took its toll. In the 31st Massachusetts camp next to the Indianans, a bolt of lightning traveled down a sentry's rifle, leaning against a guard tent, and blew it to bits. The bolt also zapped thirteen 31st Massachusetts men in the guard tent and nearby tents. It killed three of the men, destroyed stacked firearms and set the tent afire. Lightning killed four men in the 6th Michigan who were in their tent. The night's lightning burned or killed thirty-two men. The guard whose rifle exploded complained of a severe headache. (It is possible that he was the injured man who died within a day or two of the lightning strike.)[23]

On or about the 10th of April the powers-that-be resolved the territorial dispute. The Department of the Gulf included Alabama, Louisiana, Mississippi and Texas. Finally on April 14, General Butler gave orders to prepare for travel and combat. Once again, the soldiery received orders to cook three days' rations, pack as they had on March 29, and prepare to leave within an hour's notice. By 10 A.M. on April 15, the 21st Indiana's Hoosiers, the 6th Michigan's Wolverines and the 4th Wisconsin's Badgers found themselves again sharing space aboard a large transport ship, the *Great Republic*, with their favorite nemesis, General Thomas Williams, who would soon board and share this ship with (as he called them) the "Western Thieves."[24]

The Hoosiers lost twenty-six men from the privation and exposure they suffered on Ship Island. Twenty-nine more men suffered from the effects of Ship Island, but the surgeon thought they would recover within thirty days; therefore, they were not shipped home. About two or three of the twenty-nine men died at New Orleans or Algiers within thirty to forty days of their stay on Ship Island, and a like number of men received disability discharges within this same period. Other regiments, such as the 12th Maine and 30th Massachusetts, suffered similar losses.[25]

(*See Appendices for a list of names of the 21st Indiana's dead and disabled caused by privation and exposure on Ship Island.*)

Three

New Orleans Bound

The *Great Republic*, a four-masted cargo vessel, would hold 2,700 men, their lice, her own crew and innumerable vermin. The transport had arrived at Ship Island fully loaded with cattle and horses. After unloading the animals and seeing them safely ashore, the troops went aboard the unswept, unwashed or deodorized ship. A Michigan Badger said that the stench from the ship could knock a man down at eighty yards as surely as a minieball. Three regiments of Western men crowded aboard on the urine and dung covered decks. The enlisted men were herded below deck to dark, cramped quarters. The soldiers were allowed only 28 inches width of space per man to sleep on the lower deck. The officers found and claimed spacious quarters in the grand saloon on the ship's upper deck before General Williams and his "Irish oafish staff" ran them out, claiming the quarters for their use. The displaced Hoosier officers found cramped space on the floor of a lower deck nearer the enlisted men. Once aboard, they all waited for two days in storm-tossed seas while tugboats and a gunboat, the *Jackson*, tried to get the overloaded ship away from her moorings.

After the tugboats and the *Jackson* broke several hawsers, the fickle weather blew in a flood tide that provided enough water to lift the cumbersome craft free of the Gulf of Mexico's bottom. Once released, she immediately set sail for the mouth of the Mississippi River to join the other transports that had sailed before. Their objective and that of the fleet that preceded them was the capture of Forts Jackson and St. Philip and then to proceed upstream to capture the major Confederate port city of New Orleans.[1]

Under full sail, the *Great Republic* made little headway. The same wind that helped her off the Gulf of Mexico's bottom now hit the *Great Republic* head on. A gale had damaged the ship's rudder on the trip to Ship Island. Without having time to repair the rudder, the wallowing craft could not steer to take advantage of the wind. Again, the *Jackson* came to the rescue and took the *Great Republic* in tow.

Two days passed while the ships traveled at about two knots per hour to the Southwest Pass of the Mississippi River. The men on the *Great Republic* had enough space to stand comfortably; however, they had to sleep in shifts. An unknown Hoosier wrote his hometown newspaper that no farmer ever saw his pigs lie closer on a winter night than the soldiers did on warm nights. Others compared their facilities and fate to those of slaves packed aboard ships bound for the New World. Meals served to all of the enlisted men consisted of some type of stew or soup ladled from large pots into whatever container the men had with them. Captain John Corden of Company F, 6th Michigan, who was a former British infantry officer, declared that the enlisted men were treated far worse than common soldiers in the English service, and the food served to them was not fit fare for a pig.[2]

For most of the journey, the enlisted men had to stay below the top deck. A lucky few managed to emerge and enjoy the sun and fresh air in shifts. Officers, however, had the run of the ship and could enjoy the luxuries of sun and fresh air. General Williams lounged in his main deck cabin enjoying the sunshine through his window until Colonel McMillan stood in front of the window blocking the general's sunlight. Williams clearly ordered McMillan away from his window.[3]

The *Great Republic* finally arrived at the Southwest Pass of the Mississippi, only to find a sandbar blocking its entrance to the river. The *Great Republic* dropped anchor. The smaller transports with the main part of the invasion force had crossed the bar two days earlier and steamed up the river to anchor within striking distance of the forts. The Western men unhappily sat aboard their pestiferous ship and picked and scratched at their gray-backs (lice). The seamen pondered how to get the transport across the sandbar.[4]

To capture the Confederate forts, General Benjamin Butler brought eight infantry regiments and three artillery batteries aboard various-sized transports to participate in a combined operation with the navy. Commander David Porter's mortar schooners had preceded Flag-Officer Farragut's larger ships up the river, where they anchored behind a shielding bend in the river below Forts Jackson and St. Philip. Flag-Officer Farragut's ships were across the bar and miles up the river in position just below Porter's mortars. The transports, minus the *Great Republic*, waited downstream from the fighting ships.[5]

Contesting the passage of Farragut, Porter and Butler were Fort Jackson on the west bank of the river and Fort St. Philip on the east bank diagonally upstream from Fort Jackson. Three thousand men, including experienced naval gunners, garrisoned the forts and manned more than 150 heavy guns. Any vessel going up or down the river had to pass by these guns. To slow the progress of ascending enemy warships and expose them to the concentrated fire of the forts, the Confederates had constructed a barrier of rafts connected by heavy chains stretched across the river. As luck would have it, debris laden floodwaters had broken the barrier. The Confederate defenders quickly replaced the barrier with another barrier made from barges and derelict schooners chained together. The debris-laden waters also broke this barrier apart. Hastily patched parts of this last effort remained to block the Yankee ships beginning their ascent of the river.[6]

When Butler began gathering his troops at Ship Island, the New Orleans shipyards had two twenty-gun ironclad rams under construction. By the time Farragut arrived off the passes of the Mississippi, the builders had mostly completed only one ram, the *Louisiana,* which had only part of its armament aboard. However, its guns could bolster the firepower of the forts. Therefore, a tugboat towed the *Louisiana* to just above Fort St. Philip where it anchored to serve as a floating heavy artillery battery.[7]

Upriver from the forts at the old Chalmette Battlefield, the Confederate defenders had constructed a line of redoubts connected by earthen breastworks. The redoubts held only a few cannons at the time Farragut began his ascent of the river. A ditch, twenty feet deep and thirty feet wide that could be flooded from the river, ran along the front of the Chalmette earthworks. Across the river from Chalmette, another line of earthworks extended from the left bank of the river into the marshes. On the upriver side of New Orleans at Carrollton, Louisiana, was another, stronger line of redoubts and earthworks with a few pieces of heavy ordnance mounted. The Confederate military was confident these works and the forts would be sufficient to defend the city against any attack from downriver or upriver.[8]

New Orleans was important to the Confederacy and the Union for many of the same reasons. It was a major seaport, it was a major population center, it had the second largest cannon foundry (Leeds & Company) in the Confederacy, it contained a major manufacturer of small arms (Cook & Brother), and it hosted large ship repair and ship building yards. The Confederacy's loss of New Orleans would give the Union a good naval base to wage war up the river and along the coast of the southern states. From this base Federal troops and vessels could cut off supplies of Louisiana salt and Texas beef from the largest geographical section of the Confederacy. The loss of Leeds & Company and other smaller foundries would severely hamper the casting of both lightweight field cannon and heavy siege and seacoast cannon badly needed by the southern states. The city's seizure would also free naval blockade vessels to intensify the blockade in other areas. However, in order for Butler and Farragut to accomplish their goals, the forts had to fall and New Orleans had to surrender to establish a Union presence in Louisiana, and eventually, a Union presence in the entire South.[9]

While Porter's mortar fleet blasted away at the forts, navy tugboats and details of soldiers worked hard to get the *Great Republic* off the bar. Most of the men remained aboard the ship while this work went on for eight days. At times, they could hear the thud of heavy artillery from upriver. At night, the flashes of exploding shells lit up the sky.

The soldiers had eaten their three days of cooked rations, and their stomachs growled again. The soldiers' available food aboard the *Great Republic* consisted of wormy hardtack, raw bacon, stale stinking warm water and the aforementioned soup. As often as they could, the men added sugar or vinegar to the water, and then they soaked the hardtack in the water to drown the worms that floated to the top where they were picked off and discarded. Afterwards, they consumed the hardtack and drank the water. The ravenous men of the 21st Indiana claimed that they came nearer to a state of starvation aboard the *Great Republic* than at any other time. Their officers fared a little better having salt pork and bean coffee to eat and drink. They all blamed their misfortune on General Benjamin Butler's brother, "colonel" Andrew Butler, in charge of the commissary. The Hoosiers' accusations went so far as to hold him to be criminally negligent in allowing others to rob the government, "if he had not swindled the government himself."

General Williams, enjoying his privilege of rank, left the *Great Republic* and traveled up the river to view the naval bombardment on Forts Jackson and St. Philip for a couple of days. He enjoyed the navy's food, drink and hospitality.[10]

Finally, the frigate *Colorado* and the ship *Fearnot* took aboard about 1,000 men from the *Great Republic* to lighten the load. Still, the bulky transport would not budge from the bar. After a couple of days in the pleasant company of their naval hosts aboard the two warships, the Hoosiers and Badgers reboarded their floating pig-pen. To make the best of a bad situation, the Hoosiers hung buckets over the ship's upstream side to catch river water to drink while imagining it was Wabash River water from Indiana.[11]

Commander David Porter's mortar schooners pounded away at the fortifications for six days without accomplishing much. At that time Flag-Officer Farragut and General Butler decided that the flag-officer's ships should run past the forts and proceed to New Orleans. The army would steam or sail behind the forts, land and cut off their garrisons from relief. This would place the forts between the naval fire of the mortar fleet and an infantry attack from the rear forcing their surrender. If this did not work, Farragut would have to return to the forts and lend his fleet's firepower to that of the mortars and the army. Farragut could not keep his fleet up the river for long without food, supplies and military targets. Also, a hostile population would surround him. The forts must fall to open the river to Federal shipping and the port of New Orleans.[12]

During the night of the 20th, two screw-propeller steamers, the *Itasca* and *Pinola*, removed their masts and steamed for the barrier of hulks and chains blocking the river. After a series of failed attempts, the *Itasca* rammed the barrier and broke it. The opening gave plenty of open water for Farragut's warships to maneuver.

Under the cover of night on April 24, Farragut's fleet built up steam pressure and headed upstream. The ship's crews loaded their broadside guns and made ready to take on the forts and the few Confederate war vessels that waited above. After a fierce battle, all but three of Farragut's ships passed the forts. The Federal fleet's broadsides had shattered the smaller Rebel

GENERAL BUTLER'S TROOPS COMING THROUGH THE BAYOU.

General Butler's troops (21st Indiana, 26th Massachusetts and 4th Wisconsin) advancing through shallow water and marshes upon Fort St. Philip from the rear as seen in *Harpers Weekly*.

river craft. Farragut detached two gunboats to cover the quarantine station and protect the army's rear as he steamed on toward New Orleans. That night Butler prepared to send his force behind the forts.[13]

On the 26th, the *Great Republic* backed off the bar and traveled around the eastern peninsula of the Mississippi River's delta. Somewhere off the east coast of the delta, the 21st Indiana and a portion of the 4th Wisconsin transferred from the *Great Republic* onto the gunboat *Miami*. The *Miami* already carried some of the 26th Massachusetts Regiment. On the 27th, the *Miami* steamed into Black Bay in the rear of Fort St. Philip where she grounded in shallow water.

The next day, as they watched from the deck of the *Miami*, the troops saw flashes of light from the direction of Fort St. Philip followed by the roar of a great explosion. At first they thought the Rebels had blown up the fort, but they later learned that the crewmen of the *Louisiana* had blown up the ship to prevent her guns from falling into Yankee hands.

That afternoon General Williams led Companies A and B from the 21st Indiana, a detachment from the 4th Wisconsin, and the 26th Massachusetts Regiment from the *Miami* aboard rowboats. Once aboard, they pulled oars for the marshy shore about five miles away. The *Miami* then steamed away with the rest of the 21st Regiment to Pass L'Outre and up the Mississippi. Unknown to the landing party, a portion of the garrison at Fort Jackson had mutinied the previous day. The mutineers spiked several guns in the fort, and offered themselves up to Butler's pickets advancing up the west bank of the river. Fort Jackson was out of action.[14]

Williams' landing party waded through the marshes in water often up to their waists and pulled the boats laden with their equipment and weapons behind them. Their objective was to take the quarantine station upstream to the rear of Fort St. Philip, and then advance on the fort from there. It was now late at night. Federal pickets had arrived near Fort St. Philip earlier in the day, only to learn that both of the forts had already surrendered to Commander David Porter. When Williams' main force arrived outside Fort St. Philip on the east bank of the Mississippi River, they spent the night on oyster shell mounds a foot out of the water. While they did not receive the fort's surrender, the soggy soldiers could dry off.[15]

Commander David D. Porter saw to it that the navy got all credit for capturing the forts, completely ignoring the part played by the infantry in surrounding them. However, General Butler, in a June 1862 letter to Secretary of War Edwin M. Stanton, praised the efforts of the army in causing the forts to surrender. Lieutenant Colonel John Keith of the 21st Indiana stated that the surrender of the forts was due to the infantry appearing in their rear and surrounding them. Flag-Officer Farragut, ever the gracious gentleman, acknowledged that he would not have steamed by the forts without Butler's assurance that he would attack by land in a combined operation.

The 16,800 mortar shells fired by Porter's mortar fleet had little apparent effect upon the forts' ability to defend themselves. The mortar shells destroyed the wooden interior citadel and barracks inside Fort Jackson. All of the wooden outer buildings burned from the exploding bombs. However, while the guns and structures of the brick forts had numerous impressions from the mortars, the guns and exterior walls of both forts suffered little severe damage. The officers' mess was damaged by a 13-inch shell coming through its thick roof, but it did not explode. Of seventy-five guns in the fort and its outer water battery, four were dismounted, none disabled. Only 10.5 percent of the fired shells found targets in Fort Jackson, and they inflicted less than fifty casualties. Fort St. Philip was in as good a condition as it had been before Porter's bombardment.[16]

The next day the gunboat *Kineo* picked up the two detached Indiana companies A and B near Fort St. Philip and took them to New Orleans. During a coaling stop, they noticed a group of Rebel prisoners wearing festive looking bright red and green patterned shirts, instead of the usual drab cloth. Engaging them in conversation, they learned that several of these prisoners claimed to have been pressed (forced) into service. A few of those men volunteered to enlist in the 21st Indiana, whereupon, they were given the oath of allegiance and released. It is very possible the local militias had forced these prisoners into Confederate service from the so-called German population — a common practice in the area. (Most communities of German extraction were loyal Unionists.) These men were among the mutineers from Fort Jackson, who refused to man their guns against the Union.[17]

Once fueled, the ship got under way to New Orleans. Acting like typical sightseers, the men admired the lush flowers and shrubbery and compared the similarity of sugar cane rows to that of corn rows. Orchards of orange and banana trees astonished them. The lazing alligators along the riverbank, the awkward splashes of pelicans, and squawking sea gulls amused them. They admired the architecture of planters' homes along the river.

After a day's journey up the river, the vessel arrived at New Orleans amid a confused spectacle. Outraged citizens, both black and white, plus their slaves lined the riverbank and levees from three or four miles below and up to the city. Behind the onlookers, nearly 15,000 bales of burning cotton sent plumes of smoke into the air. In front of them were the charred remains of eighteen vessels burned to prevent them and their cargo from falling into Yankee hands. Entire warehouses had their contents brought out and thrown onto the pyres. Nearly five million dollars of merchandise and property burned on the waterfront before the eyes of the Federal conquerors. The conflagration and destruction did not confine itself to the New Orleans side of the river; a similar smaller spectacle took place across the river in the town of Algiers.[18]

The Confederate garrison escaped with everything of military value they could carry away or ship by steamer up-river. This included most of the Cook & Brothers machinery (for manufacturing small arms), much of the new rifle manufacturing machinery from Thomas Griswold & Company, a cannon foundry on Tchoupitoulas Street, most of the machinery from Leeds' & Company (a major cannon, shot and shell foundry) on Delord Street and the Phoenix Foundry (aka M. J. Bujac's Foundry or S. Bennett's Foundry) in Gretna across the river, which manufactured various sized cannons in iron and bronze. Most of Phoenix's machinery and equipment to make Enfield–style rifles was loaded aboard a river steamer that hurriedly got underway upriver as the smoke from Flag-Officer Farragut's warships was visible coming around the bend of the river towards New Orleans. Equipment from the light cannon works of Bennett and Lurges, John Clark & Co., Jackson & Co., A.T. Patterson Iron Works and S. Wolff & Co. also made their way out of New Orleans. The militarily-purposed manufacturing equipment from New Orleans arrived at arsenals and foundries in Mississippi and Georgia.

Farragut arrived at the wharves of New Orleans and demanded its surrender. After some negotiations, the city surrendered. Sailors hoisted the Union flag over the United States Mint. However, the New Orleaneans were not bashful about shouting curses at the Union Navy. Armed citizens lined the wharves and whistled and jeered at the Federals. The women spit at the ships and marines and naval officers as they carried messages between Farragut and the mayor's office.

On May 1, the *Kinneo* with the detachment from the 21st Indiana aboard was the first ship to land soldiers at New Orleans. The other vessels docked in turn, including the *Miami* with the rest of the Hoosier regiment. While at Ship Island, the skipper of a small craft brought copies of an 1858 minstrel tune about a Negro entertainer titled "Picayune Butler Is Coming to Town." This parody version contained derisive lyrics pointedly about General Benjamin Butler. General Butler had previously offered a treat to the Hoosiers' band if they would learn the tune. The Twenty-First's Regimental Band learned it in a couple of hours.[19]

In the evening, with the gun decks cleared, the 21st Indiana's Regimental Band struck up the tune: "Picayune Butler is coming, coming; Picayune Butler's coming to town." As the melody carried over the docks and wharves of New Orleans the women jeered and called out for Butler to show himself. He did. The general set foot on the sacred soil and claimed New Orleans for the Union even though Flag-officer Farragut had done that a couple of days earlier. Enjoying the mixed sarcastic irony of the derisive tune as the New Orleaneans heard the words and melody spat back at them, Butler and his staff officers set off down the street guarded by the 31st Massachusetts Infantry Regiment to his quarters in the St. Charles Hotel. Ordered to not leave the dock, the 21st Indiana's strains of "Picayune Butler is Coming to Town" died away, and Butler had the 31st Massachusetts' band strike up "Yankee Doodle." It was repeated over and over as the general and his New England troops marched through the city. Other transports arrived later that day with the 4th Wisconsin and the 6th Michigan. These two regiments missed the honor of the parade, but they went ashore and took quarters in New Orleans. The 21st Indiana stayed aboard ship at the dock.[20]

Four
Life in the South Louisiana Swamps

Shortly after the 21st Indiana watched the Massachusetts troops march off with General Butler into New Orleans, they received orders to cross the river to Algiers, Louisiana. Their transport took the Hoosiers over the river where they disembarked. They secured a small section of the town and established their headquarters in the station and terminal buildings of the New Orleans, Opelousas and Great Western Railroad. The boys quickly converted these buildings into use as their headquarters and barracks.

After spending more than two weeks at sea or in swamps, they enjoyed the railway terminal's broad sheltered platforms and large rooms surrounded by green grass and shade trees. The rest period was put to good use in washing body and clothes and in a general cleaning up. Rumors abounded as to the possibility of an attack upon their lone regiment. After dark, a distant shot rang out. Not having brought any ammunition ashore for their rifles, the terrified Hoosiers fled the station to take shelter under the river bluff and in ditches. Much later, they crept back to the station and slept.[1] While in Algiers, the regiment's broad cross section of occupations (newspapermen, printers, lawyers, builders, railroaders, engineers, farmers, traders, merchants and others) made it very versatile in its activities. They even published their own newspaper, "The Hoosier Newsboy," edited by Sergeant-Major O. P. Hervey, from a captured newspaper office. Printed tri-weekly on brown paper during their month's stay at Algiers, its motto read: "The Union One and Inseparable."[2]

While a squad of men carried on the newspaper publishing efforts, the balance of the regiment engaged in securing Algiers for the Union. The Hoosiers mounted an around the clock guard detail at a foundry suspected of casting war materials for the Confederacy. On their second day at Algiers, Colonel McMillan found a large Rebel flag in a captured chest at his headquarters in the Algiers depot. Then the regiment received orders to secure the eighty miles of the New Orleans, Opelousas and Great Western Railroad line between Algiers and its western terminus at Brashear City, LA (present day Morgan City). Since they had several former railroaders in their numbers, the task of getting the trains at the Algiers terminal operational was theirs.[3]

The Hoosiers had the engines and cars at Algiers operational in two days. On May 4, a detachment made their first railway trip. They went out about thirty miles to Bayou des Allemands. After arriving there, the men began searching for military stores. They captured small arms, ammunition, artillery harness, canteens, etc. They also liberated eight beeves and a sheep, which allegedly were being pastured for the Confederate military. The detachment brought back the military stores, the meat on the hoof, plus some sweet potatoes and tomatoes to Algiers. The men enjoyed the fresh food, which relieved symptoms of scurvy that had begun to manifest itself among the soldiers.[4]

Those not involved in securing the railroad remained busy searching Algiers, Gretna, and other nearby towns for contraband ammunition, arms, and other Rebel paraphernalia. The soldiers dug up buried stores of weapons in citizen's yards and arrested the property owners. Among the items confiscated were kegs of gunpowder, pistols, rifles, sabers, shot, shell and Confederate flags. The boys removed a wagon-load of weapons from a plantation's ground-grain storage house a short distance from Algiers. They raided a store and took two filled-to-the-top wagon-loads of firearms, swords, and knives. The bully boys with fixed bayonets moved the heavy-laden wagons through an angry mob to safety at the depot. The local populace turned out to watch the Indianian's evening parade on the 4th. Many of the women, as in New Orleans, wore secessionist badges or small Confederate national flags pinned to their bosoms. Ragged little boys jeered the soldiers as they marched. The next day a party of picked men from the regiment and all of Companies A and B under the leadership of Captains Roy and Grimsley took part in a raid the full length of the railroad to Brashear City.[5]

Brashear City is located on Tiger Island on the eastern bank of Berwick Bay, just below the confluence of Bayou Teche and the Atchafalaya River. The Hoosiers' train left Algiers at 8 A.M. on May 5. They traveled through swamps and canebrakes, stopping only to let off details of men to guard bridges and secure depots. As their train passed plantations, slaves looked up in astonishment at the blue-jacketed "Yankee sojers" waving the Stars and Stripes from their train's cars. The train arrived at Brashear City in a few hours. The men poured from the cars, formed into details and quickly captured 8 locomotive engines, 20 passenger cars, 82 platform cars, 116 freight cars, 310 bales of cotton, 700 hogsheads of sugar, 2 brass 6-pounder cannon, ammunition, and 1,500 pounds of gunpowder. The Hoosiers' surprise arrival allowed them to carry out their search and seizure without interference. No one thought foot soldiers would avail themselves of a railroad to travel that distance and capture a town full of people and goods. Such a feat was unheard of in warfare. These soldiers were supposed to be looting Algiers and New Orleans, not Brashear City.[6]

Pressing their captured railroad cars and an engine into service, the soldiers began loading their confiscated goods aboard the two trains for a return trip to Algiers while a mob slowly gathered nearby. After loading their confiscated goods aboard the cars of the first train commanded by Company A with its captain in the engine keeping an eye on the engineer and fireman, the train departed. As the number of soldiers diminished, the crowd closed in on the remaining soldiers and officers of Company B boarding the second train for Algiers. The crowd, led by a Dr. White, began cheering and shouting "Hurrah for Jeff Davis" while cursing and insulting the departing soldiers. Doctor White then drew a small pistol and fired it. Instantly, the soldiers poured from the train and captured the doctor along with several of the more loud-mouthed citizens. A few Hoosiers fired shots over the crowd, dispersing it without injuries. The soldiers boarded the train with only Dr. White and one other man held captive and chugged away for Algiers.[7]

Louisiana rum made up a portion of the captured stores on the second train, and the officers liberated a few bottles for sampling. The captured railroad engines, cars and most of the goods had departed in the other train. After dark, the inebriated Captain Grimsley wrested the control bar from the engineer of the following train and attempted to pass the train ahead even though there was only one track. (The drunken officer afterwards claimed he saw two tracks.) The engineer applied the engine's brakes at the last minute but the captain still ran the engine into the last car of the slower moving train. The trains' crews and guard troops worked all night to place the cars on the track and clean up the mess. Finally, they rolled the most damaged car off the rails into the swamp. At sunrise the railroad opened for traffic. The men boarded the train cars, and Company A arrived in record time, well ahead of Company B's train and its hungover captain.[8]

On the 6th, a guard took Dr. White across the river to New Orleans to appear before General Butler. The General gave Dr. White the opportunity to apologize and take the oath of allegiance to the United States. However, the doctor launched into bombast against the United States, saying, in part: "I was only doing my duty to the Confederate States by firing my pistol on the Yankee soldiers. They had no business there, and the Government of Lincoln niggers had no right to disturb the liberty and property of gentlemen. If they had stayed up in New England, the pistol shot would not have harmed them."

After a long silence, General Butler asked, "Have you anything more to offer?" The doctor replied, "Nothing." Butler sentenced him to six months at hard labor repairing the fortifications of Fort Jackson. This tough action by Butler, who many western men felt was corrupt and mealy-mouthed, gained their respect. To New Orleaneans, he was "The Beast."[9]

On May 9, a scouting detachment commanded by Lieutenant William Bough, Company C, learned that a blockade runner, the *Fox*, was in Bayou Grand Caillou about 25 to 30 miles south of Terre Bonne Station. The *Fox* had sailed from Havana, Cuba, on the 30th of April, dodging blockade ships for a week before arriving in the Bayou. Bough reported the location of the *Fox* to his regimental headquarters. Colonel McMillan gathered four companies of men, a locomotive and cars, and moved his battalion over the railway to Terre Bonne Station. Getting off the train there the boys gathered several carts, mules and contraband drivers from nearby plantations to carry supplies to and to bring captured booty from the *Fox*. They formed into columns and set out on foot to capture the *Fox*.[10]

Houma, Louisiana, lay on the bully boys route. Arriving there late at night, the officers ordered the boys to break step and muffle their clinking accoutrements to not make noise to awaken the citizens. A fast riding citizen could alert the ship and enable it to escape. They passed through Houma with the only noise being the soft clopping of the mule's hooves on the soft dirt of the road and the squeak of a protesting wagon wheel. No citizen raised an alarm. A short distance past Houma, they fell into step and their pace quickened. As the sun rose, they sighted the *Fox*.[11]

Colonel McMillan divided his force into two groups, sending one across the bayou. They moved parallel to each other along the bayou to surround the vessel and prevent the escape of the crew. Upon reaching the ship, a lone guard fired one shot and ran aboard for cover. The force on the mooring side boarded by the gangplank that the running guard left in place. Some of the *Fox*'s crew jumped overboard and tried swimming away, but the Hoosiers rounded them up and brought them back aboard the ship. All hands, except the pilot and engineer, were given parole and released. At least one of the parolees told the locals what was going on with the *Fox*.

In a short time, the soldiers discovered the vessel had a leaking boiler and was aground. They also learned that half of the cargo had been unloaded and hidden in the nearby area. As they began searching for the missing cargo and working to free the ship, they placed four sick comrades aboard two mule-drawn carts. Two contrabands were assigned to drive the carts north toward the Terre Bonne Station where the sick men could catch a train bound for Algiers.[12]

After the convalescents were on their way, one company went to work freeing the *Fox* from the sand bar and repairing the ship's leaky boiler. This took three days, during which they worked on reduced rations supplemented by eating local oysters. The other companies went into the countryside looking for the missing cargo, which they found and hauled back to the *Fox*. They also located about 400 barrels of sugar, but the bayou at that place was too shallow for the *Fox* to pick it up. McMillan reported this to General Butler by sending a detachment back to Algiers from Yelton's Landing in Grand Bayou. He also requested that a U.S. Navy gunboat meet him "at the bar" at Caillou Bay and escort his prize to New Orleans.

Once the cargo was secure, the officers and men boarded the *Fox* and steamed out of the bayou into the Gulf of Mexico bound for New Orleans. As they were making their way along the coast toward the Mississippi River, a U.S. Navy patrol ship stopped and boarded them.[13]

The young naval lieutenant commanding the boarding party asked Colonel McMillan to surrender. The colonel refused on two counts: 1. The *Fox* was his prize, and 2. He had requested General Butler to have a navy gunboat sent to meet and escort his prize back to New Orleans. The surprised naval officer, who had not gotten those orders, looked at the colonel's uniform and inquired as to which navy he belonged. His proud host told him that the ship and its cargo were a prize of the 21st Indiana Volunteer Infantry. After further conversation over a brandy and a Havana cigar, the naval lieutenant departed without a capture. The *Fox* carried bills of exchange, bills of lading, invoices and letters of advice from many of the mercantile houses of New Orleans including the houses of Avendano and S.H. Kennedy & Co. The cargo consisted of morphine, lead, chloroform, sidearms, mercury, 150 tons of gunpowder, 4,500 rifles. It also carried Havana cigars, fresh food and choice wine. The wining, dining, smoking Hoosiers enjoyed the return trip. The cargo alone was worth $600,000, and because it was an army capture, the whole amount went to the U.S. Treasury. [Navy captures were shared one-half with the Treasury and one-half as prize money apportioned among the capturing officers and crew.] General Butler awarded the Hoosier seamen side arms and slouch hats from their prize. His generosity was no doubt influenced by the papers found in the ship's safe naming the New Orleans firm of S.H. Kennedy & Co. as running cotton to Cuba. The profit of $8,641 to the firm was promptly levied against them as a fine to enrich Federal coffers.[14]

While the detachment under Colonel McMillan finished loading their prize and then played navy, the four sick soldiers returning to Terre Bonne Station met with foul play. A messenger brought word to Houma that some soldiers with loot-laden carts were approaching town. A band of guerillas numbering between fifteen to twenty men rode from Houma. They hid in some bushes by the roadside about one and one-half miles south of town. The guerrillas opened fire with shotguns and muskets at the passing carts.[15]

The blasts of buck and ball tore into Sergeant Jesse Frakes, Company E, killing him, and wounding Private Josephus Morris, Company I, in the forehead and hips. The pellets killed Private Charles Geisendorffer of Company G, and they hit Private Miller, Company F, in the shoulder and thigh. The Negro cart drivers whipped their mules and tried to escape. The guerrillas mounted their horses and gave chase. In a few minutes, they caught up with the cart hauling Frakes and Morris. The cart with Geisendorffer and Miller got away and made it through Houma without being stopped. About one and one-half miles north of town, Miller had the driver halt the cart for a moment so he could abandon it, taking both rifles. The driver lashed the mule, and he and his lifeless passenger hurried off. Miller hid under a bridge until his pursuers passed by.[16]

After the band of assassins passed, Miller escaped to Terre Bonne Station. Fearing that the guerrillas would return and capture him, he turned himself over to two men who swore that they would treat him well and not turn him over to the guerrillas. They were true to their word, and they took him to General Alfred Mouton, C.S.A., at his headquarters outside of Thibodaux. Under Mouton's protection, a surgeon extracted the shot, and cleaned and dressed Miller's wounds. Miller was treated with a great amount of civility — even sharing in the same meals as his captors. He remained at Mouton's headquarters until the next evening when Captain Elihu Rose with his Hoosier Company C arrived and obtained Miller's freedom.[17]

A note from a Union sympathizer had reached Lieutenant-Colonel John Keith of the affair at Houma. After having the note translated from French, Keith had sent Captain Elihu Rose with Company C to the area to look for the missing men. Due to Colonel McMillan's absence,

Keith requested permission from General Butler to lead a general search expedition. Butler gave his permission with a verbal order stating, in part, to "not leave one stone standing upon another in Terre Bonne Parish, and hang [the perpetrators] until you have further orders." Keith called out Captain William Roy's Company A, Captain James Grimsley's Company B, Captain William Skelton's Company E, Captain Edward McLaflin's Company G, and detachments from Companies D, F and H of the 21st Indiana, plus the 6th Massachusetts Battery under Lieutenant W. C. Carruth. The avengers boarded a train and left for Houma on the 13th of May. Along the way, they met Captain Rose's detachment returning from Thibodaux with both Privates Miller and Morris. During his return trip, Rose had found Morris hiding at Terre Bonne Station.[18]

Morris related that his guerrilla captors first subjected him to an intense period of questioning. Then they accused him of killing his own comrades. This greatly offended Morris, and he plainly told his captors so. Reacting to Morris' verbal assault, his inquisitors tossed him into a jail cell with a Negro condemned for murder. After awhile, Morris' captors released him on the condition that he sign an oath stating in part "not to take up arms against the Confederate States, South America, unless my property, myself, or those depending upon me should be threatened." Morris signed. After releasing him from jail, his captors told him to leave Terre Bonne Parish within 24 hours, or he would be killed like his two comrades.[19]

After hearing Private Morris' story, the angered troops hurried to Houma. There, they learned that the two murdered men had been stripped, robbed and beaten beyond recognition. The bodies had lain in the town square near the Big Pelican Hotel. In the square, Houma's citizens, both male and female, kicked, spat on and clubbed the bodies for several hours, until they were unrecognizable as human beings. Finally, someone had a couple of Negroes dig a grave on the public ground of the square directly across from the courthouse. The Negroes rolled the bodies into the two-foot-deep grave, tossed a blanket over them, and covered them with a little earth and a lot of manure from the nearby stables.

Already angry about Morris' treatment, Lieutenant-Colonel John A. Keith, upon learning of the dead men's treatment, became thoroughly enraged at the Houma citizens. Keith first ordered the citizens to furnish proper coffins and a consecrated burial place for the dead men, and he next ordered the names of the culprits to be given to him. The citizens soon brought two coffins. Under the watchful eye of Captain Grimsley standing by a hangman's noose suspended from a tree, the more prominent citizens of Houma (under arrest) exhumed the bodies. A procession of soldiers and citizens went to the burial ground of the local Catholic Church. As Captain Rose preached the funeral sermon, the 21st Indiana laid their martyred comrades to rest in flag draped coffins with full military honors.[20]

The Hoosiers had not yet learned the names of the guerrillas and their leaders; therefore, after the funeral, Keith issued a proclamation that, in summary, stated that the Union flag was to fly over the courthouse and those who had knowledge of the names and whereabouts of the guerrillas, but withheld that knowledge, were as guilty as the guerrillas themselves. If the Union flag was not flown from that time on and the names of the guilty parties not given, the entire town of Houma would be burned to the ground. Further, he would have all the plantations in Terre Bonne Parish destroyed. Lastly, certain citizens of Houma, known to be Rebel sympathizers, would be hanged. As long as the flag flew, he would protect the ones who gave up the guerrillas and their ringleaders. To demonstrate the sincerity of his words, he ordered a detail of his men to begin building a gallows in the courthouse square, which the Hoosiers constructed with fervor.[21]

Shortly thereafter, several residents gave the names of those involved and who had hidden them to Keith. He sent very enthusiastic soldiers out who scoured the countryside, searching for the murderers but found only two for certain — the rest had fled the vicinity. Other persons, identified as guerrillas, but not as the killers, suffered great financial and personal loss due to their avowed allegiance and absence. The Hoosiers raided A. S. Hornsby's grocery, ate the food and took all of his personal property. Mr. T. A. Wood's newspaper, the *Ceres*, fell victim to a band of Indiana bully boys. They smashed the printing press and threw the type into a nearby bayou. Mr. E. N. Dutrall had his house, stable and outbuildings torn down and the contents destroyed. Dr. Jennings's home, library, barn, stables, and other outbuildings with their contents, including his buggy, went up in flames. Howard Bond's home, sugar house, more than fifty of his Negroes' houses, three stables, a steam-powered saw and corn mill, two corn storage houses, a cooper shop, a blacksmith shop, and a molasses warehouse became blazing infernos courtesy of the Hoosiers' torches. Tons of corn, sugar, molasses, hay and fodder burned within the buildings. Thirty-five mules, two yoke of oxen, six wagons, a cart and five loads of forage were taken from Bond's place before the torch was applied. Several hearty Hoosiers wielding a battering ram shattered the brick walls of the jail that had held Private Morris into a pile of rubble.[22]

Some of the troops led by Company H's Lieutenant James Connelly were too enthusiastic in their assignment. Contrary to orders, Connelly's detail also burned or seized the property of persons not identified as guerrillas and presumed innocent of the atrocities against Frakes and Geisendorffer. Family silverware, especially spoons, became the soldier's personal property. (Spoons were a favorite item because of their great utility and a symbol of being handy with the ladies. Eventually, a spoon became the regimental emblem. The 21st regiment's fascination with silver spoons helped contribute to General Benjamin Butler's nickname of "Spoons Butler.") At the rampage's end, the bully boys of the 21st Indiana had seized and destroyed property worth two million dollars. However, the Union flag waved over the courthouse.

After the destruction, confiscation, outright thefts and arrests ceased, Keith returned some of the confiscated foodstuffs and a small herd of beeves to benefit the poor, and newly poor, in Houma. Their mission accomplished, Keith formed his battalion into column and marched back to Terre Bonne Station on the 17th. In a short time, a train arrived. Leaving behind the captured property with a guard detail under Company H's Lieutenants Connelly and Thomas D. Bryant, Keith and his men with fourteen prisoners boarded the train and set off for Algiers.[23]

Another train arrived at Terre Bonne Station late that afternoon. Connelly and Bryant loaded it with the contraband goods. Arriving at Algiers, the regimental quartermaster, Lieutenant William S. Hinkle, took possession of the eighty-five mules, sixty-one cattle, eight horses, forty-three sheep, seven wagons, two carriages, two carts, and many other items aboard the train. For their good work, some enlisted men received promotions. In Company H, two of Connelly's enthusiastic spooners, John J. Spencer and John B. Yelton received sergeant's stripes and corporal's stripes, respectively. Lieutenant-Colonel Keith issued congratulatory orders to all the company captains except one.[24]

Lieutenant-Colonel Keith did not honor Captain Grimsley although he had supervised the exhumation of the bodies of the murdered men, formed the proper burial party, and encouraged the revelation of the names of the guilty parties. Grimsley refused to burn the property of a family accused of sheltering a man who may have attacked the sick Indiana soldiers. Grimsley stated that he would only destroy the personal property of a man positively identified as being directly guilty of the crime. Grimsley gave over his sword to Lt. Colonel Keith who rightly placed Grimsley under arrest for disobeying the orders of a superior officer — in this case, Major-General Benjamin Butler.[25]

After ten days of arrest, General Butler sent for Captain Grimsley, who presented his case. When Grimsley finished, Butler ordered him to take back his sword and return to his company. The matter was dropped. Lieutenant-Colonel Keith bore Captain Grimsley no ill will, making amends by going so far as to offer the services of Sergeant Jacob Sherfey, Company H, to run a personal errand for Grimsley.[26]

The boys of the 21st Indiana not involved in the Houma affair had continued their forays into the countryside around Algiers and across the river. On May 15, they captured one brass cannon, forty small arms, and two wagons full of hospital stores at Chalmette. On the 17th of May, a party commanded by Lieutenant William Bough of Company C returned from Bayou des Allemands with two 6-pounder brass cannons bearing Spanish inscriptions (Mexican War trophies). A few days later, they found one 6-pounder brass cannon. The regiment retained three of their numerous captured cannons to form their own artillery battery. They used captured harnesses and mules to pull their cannons and caissons. The mules brought forth a few cat-calls and the name Jackass Battery naturally came to apply to the improvised battery. Company F's Lieutenant James Brown commanded the new battery, and a crew composed of three or four men from each company in the regiment manned it, including Rufus Dooley from Company H.[27]

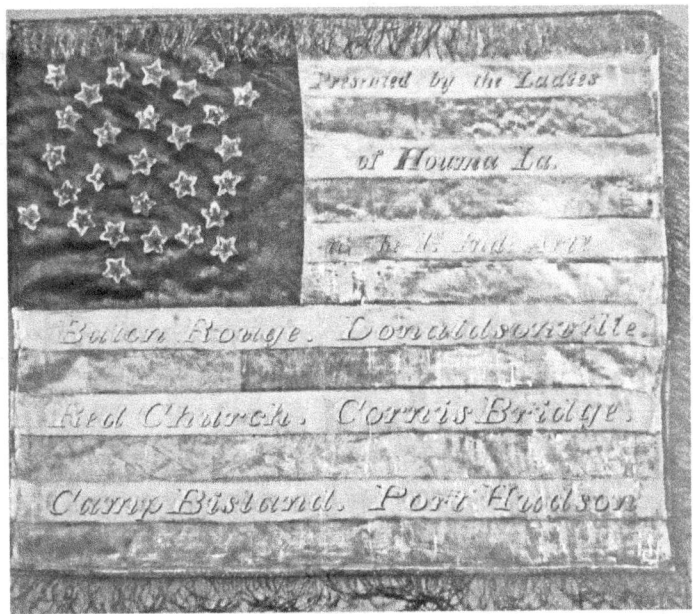

Guidon-type flag presented in 1863 to the First Indiana Heavy Artillery by the Ladies of Houma, LA, bearing the battle and skirmish honors of Baton Rouge, Donaldsonville, Red Church, Corni's Bridge, Camp Bisland, and Port Hudson. (Photograph by Victoria L. Son, Indiana War Memorials Commission.)

After returning with his prizeship, Colonel McMillan sent detachments of the bully boys on a steamship hunting foray up the Mississippi River. On the 18th, Colonel McMillan personally led a squad of seventy-five men with two guns of the Jackass Battery aboard a small, wheezing, two decked transport, the *Bee*, to capture riverboats. The colonel asked the men to distribute themselves evenly around the ship to keep it trim. If it tipped up on one side, it traveled much more slowly. To tease their colonel, the men would slowly shift to one side of the ship to hear the colonel's bellow of "Trim ship, damn you." This went on for a couple of days travel, keeping the colonel's florid face more so. Finally, after a four day journey, the *Bee* turned up the Red River, and at 4 P.M. she captured the side-wheeled steamer *Morning Light*, docked just a few miles up the Red River from the Mississippi River. This craft had a quantity of molasses, sugar, and cotton aboard.[28]

Lieutenant Ed Armstrong led a prize crew aboard the *Morning Light* to inventory their capture and to take it to New Orleans. The work aboard the *Morning Light* went well until a few of the men located the bar and began filing up their canteens and themselves. To their chagrin, the colonel sent these few to stay on the main deck in a freshly used cattle stall. The rest of the prize crew made themselves comfortable in better quarters until a Rebel cavalry unit made its presence known. It seems the locals, at whom the Hoosiers had taken a few shots when they approached the *Morning Light*, had alerted the local mounted rangers. The rangers galloped to the edge of the river and began firing at the blue-coated pirates. The prize crew increased steam on the idling *Morning Light*, and she and the *Bee* began running downstream with the cavalry closely pursuing along the riverbank. After a short chase, the cavalry gave up, and the vessels made it to New Orleans without further incident. The return trip took only one day.[29]

In five days the *Morning Light* became a Federal Army steamer. Colonel McMillan took her up the Mississippi in search of more booty. After two days' travel, McMillan caught the stern-wheeler *Louisiana Belle* about three hours north of Baton Rouge. Lieutenant Ed Armstrong took a prize crew aboard her and went to New Orleans. Colonel McMillan continued upriver looking for another prize. The 21st Indiana Infantry's privateers captured eight vessels near the confluence of the Mississippi and Red rivers before receiving other orders.[30]

As the month wore on, the citizens in and around New Orleans became more tolerant of the Yankees and the Western men. Mob demonstrations decreased both in size and spirit. Maybe the armed counter-demonstrations by the Federals and the common belief that "the Western men do fight like hell" had a soothing effect upon the more bloodthirsty members of the populace. Therefore, it seemed like pro–Union sentiment was slowly gaining, in spite of, or maybe because of, "Beast" Butler's infamous order of May 15, 1862, regarding the women of the city.[31]

Most women used their sex as a shield to cast verbal and physical insults at their Yankee conquerors. For example: Mrs. Philip Philips laughed at, jeered at, and spat on the funeral procession of a dead Yankee officer; Mrs. Hannah Larue wore a Confederate flag pinned over her bosom and stood outside of the provost marshals office cheering for Jeff Davis and daring anyone to touch her breasts to remove the flag; another woman dumped a chamber pot's contents out of her upstairs window onto Flag Officer Farragut's head. Those actions ceased when the order was proclaimed and enforced. In reality the soldiers were about to break under the women's harassment. Issuing the order defused the situation before a soldier's rifle butt was applied to a woman's jaw.

In brief, the order said that any woman insulting a Union soldier or officer by word or gesture would be considered a woman of the town (a prostitute) plying her trade and would be treated as such. Naturally, the high-class citizens of New Orleans did not receive this order with cheerfulness and good will. However, as no proper woman wanted to be considered a common prostitute, and the prostitutes could use the order to their advantage, the decent women's more offensive manifestations of southern patriotism including spitting on Federal soldiers and officers and flipping their skirts to expose their bare rear-ends (said by many soldiers to be their best looking parts) ceased. The order did not stop New Orleaneans from putting Butler's image on the inner bottoms of their chamber pots.

However, the Beast was equally harsh in punishing military offenders. In New Orleans, a gang of sailors and soldiers used the excuse of searching for contraband weapons in order to loot and steal. The provost arrested the gang for stealing $1885.00 and jewelry from a Mrs. Meisheur. Butler ordered three of the culprits hanged. He sentenced an accomplice from the 30th Massachusetts Regiment to five years hard labor at Fort Jackson. The labor to be carried out while shackled to a thirty-two pound cannon ball. Two Connecticut soldiers received shorter sentences of three to six months tethered to a cannonball then received dishonorable discharges.[32]

While the political and civil affairs in New Orleans and the nearby area were fluctuating, the Indianians kept busy. Major Benjamin Hays made a small expedition on the 25th aboard the *Bee* to Fort Livingston on Barataria Bay. They secured the fort and what stores that had not been removed by the retreating Confederates. Hays' detail returned to Algiers on the 29th with captured items, which included a twenty-one ton boat, two brass guns and some old .69 caliber muskets.[33]

About a week before Major Hays' expedition, the citizens along the length of the N.O.O. & G.W. Railroad agreed that a regular train carrying civilian passengers and goods could run each way daily. Headquarters appointed a professional civilian crew in the charge of an officer from the 21st Regiment to man the trains. More importantly, the cars would carry food from the outlying areas to the short-rationed citizens of New Orleans. All went well for a week. Then, on May 27, a band of guerrillas captured the trains with Lieutenants James Connelly of Company H and Clayton Cox of Company K, and two privates. While the guerrillas retreated towards Brashear City with their trains and prisoners, they cut the levee in six places about thirteen miles upriver from New Orleans. The Federals said the flooding from the breaks in the levee was to punish nearby pro–Union planters and to thwart Federal pursuers. The Federals put contraband laborers and local plantation slaves to work, and they soon repaired the breaks in the levee.[34]

Captain Grimsley led a detachment from Company B and one other company to recapture the missing lieutenants, but after two days of fruitless searching without any leads as to their whereabouts, Grimsley received orders to call off the search and return. Grimsley and his search party returned in time to depart with the regiment for Baton Rouge where they would reinforce General Thomas Williams' command. Company H left behind the body of a favorite sergeant, David Kuhn, who had died in the hospital on May 30. Kuhn was buried by a burial detail in the McDonald burying ground between Algiers and Gretna with services led by the regimental chaplain.

It was difficult to call off the rescue attempts for the two lieutenants and with good reason. Upon his being informed that Connelly was captured, Louisiana's governor, Thomas Moore, wrote from the temporary capital at Opelousas to Confederate president Jefferson Davis requesting orders to hang Connelly in retaliation for his "burning the property of our citizens in Terre Bonne Parish, and [because he] has exhibited a fiendish alacrity in executing the atrocious orders of Butler."[35]

While the regiment broke camp, loaded their supplies and boarded a transport, Lieutenant Armstrong and his prize crew remained tied up at a dock aboard the *Louisiana Belle*. He knew his regiment was going off to Baton Rouge to "join under the old tyrant Williams— the most disgusting & insolent being in human shape on earth." Armstrong had a comfortable berth and no orders to leave his prize vessel which contained sugar, molasses, furniture, 74 bales of cotton, and a traveling notions store. On the 3rd of June, Major Benjamin Hays arrived by steamer from Baton Rouge looking for the missing men. The next day, Hays had Armstrong and his prize crew off the *Louisiana Belle* and aboard the *Diana* bound for Baton Rouge.[36]

Five

Baton Rouge and Environs

As the sun set on May 30, the 21st Indiana Regiment boarded the ocean steamer *Mississippi* for the trip up the Mississippi River to Baton Rouge. They did not get fully loaded and under way until midnight. The 9th Connecticut Infantry, 30th Massachusetts Infantry, and Nims' battery also traveled aboard the *Mississippi* and other transports to Baton Rouge. Enjoying a tranquil night's upriver voyage, dawn's light brought lush plantations into view. The great numbers of Negroes working in the riverside fields were a continuing source of astonishment to the Hoosiers. Negroes did not inhabit rural Indiana and few lived in the Indiana cities. Even the numbers of them in Baltimore were few compared to those at work in the Louisiana fields. A pitiful handful of field hands from the plantations paddled out to the Hoosiers' transport and begged to be taken aboard. The Hoosiers laughed at their efforts and pushed them away from the steamer to go back to shore.[1]

The transport arrived at Baton Rouge at 11 A.M., June 1. The regiment was once again under Brigadier General Thomas Williams' authority. Because they had not eaten for nearly 24 hours, the always hungry Hoosiers asked permission to go ashore and prepare a meal. General Williams refused permission for the Hoosiers to land and cook, stating: "To give you permission to come ashore to cook would be a license to plunder the whole town! These headquarters do not feel inclined to let you come ashore."

The 9th Connecticut Regiment (Irish), General Williams' pet Nutmeggers, went ashore with the general's blessings. As the Irishmen went ashore, the Hoosiers expressed their feelings with cat-calls and jeers. A short time later the 30th Massachusetts disembarked. The boys of the 21st settled down to again feast on hardtack and muddy river water. Late that afternoon, Williams consented to allow the bully boys of the 21st Indiana to go ashore. They marched through town without stopping and went into camp in the suburbs on the east side of the city where they soon had their cooking fires blazing.[2]

Colonel McMillan appeared to be unaware of the orders from General Butler for his regiment to be stationed at Baton Rouge. He had been on one of his river pirating missions, and upon landing at Baton Rouge for fuel on the day of his regiment's arrival, General Williams ordered him ashore. McMillan wrote to Butler that he had "been detained by order of Brigadier-General Williams." Further, he wrote that the steamer *Mississippi* was at Baton Rouge, and he was informed that his regiment was aboard. He stated that he hoped "the necessity for sending me away *from your immediate command* will soon cease." He ended his letter by stating: "Feeling the deepest regret at being ordered away from you." Unknown to McMillan, on that same day, Butler wrote to Williams that he had sent three additional infantry regiments and Nims' battery to him, which would give him sufficient force to hold both Baton Rouge and make a demonstration against Camp Moore, a major Confederate military training center in Louisiana. Butler stated that nearly 4,500 to 5,000 poorly-armed and worse trained men were there, and he wanted Williams to capture them if it could be done quickly.

On the 6th of June, Williams replied that Butler was mistaken; there were no troops at Camp Moore.

While the correspondence as to their eventual fate was taking place, the bully boys settled into their Camp Magnolia Grove. The camp was in a park-like area of jasmine, holly, sweet gum, live oak and numerous magnolia trees draped with Spanish moss. This idyllic camp was about a mile and a half due east of downtown Baton Rouge, out present day Florida Street on the city side of Magnolia Cemetery. It was a relaxing, dry place after having been on so many long forays into the swampy areas west, south and northwest of New Orleans. The prolific lizards in camp fascinated the western troops with their antics and aptitude for running up inside an unsuspecting soldier's pant leg. No such lizards were native to Indiana. Though the location was desirable, the much-admired trees and shrubbery held a plentiful supply of ticks. These blood-sucking pests kept the boys busy daily searching them out of their hair and clothing.[3]

As at New Orleans, the Baton Rouge citizens were at first bitter toward the invaders, but soon reconciled themselves to the fact that they were likely to share the same soil, either above it or below it, for a long time. Also, as at New Orleans, the women complained that the local men gave in much too easily to the demands of the Union military might. The realistic males knew they would be arrested, tried, sentenced, and imprisoned or shot for overt demonstrations against the Union rule being forced upon them. The women received such respect as Victorian protocol dictated for their position in society—"the hand that rocks the cradle rules the world."

As in New Orleans, the Baton Rouge women wore small Confederate emblems or flags pinned over their bosoms and dared a Yankee to remove the offending item, even going so far as to carry small pistols in a pocket to defend their honor. When the soldiers behaved with gentlemanly manners and were respectful to them, many women stopped flaunting their colors and wore them discreetly. The Hoosiers were happy that they arrived after the women had calmed, and they could be engaged in reserved conversation.[4]

The Indiana officers and some of the enlisted men became acquainted with the citizens of Baton Rouge and would exchange visits. They found several substantial friends of the Union among the citizens, as well as several substantial friends of the Confederacy. The Hoosiers noticed the citizens made a major distinction in their interaction between New England troops and Western men. The Western men were more readily accepted by and related better to the local gentry than did the Easterners. Likely this was due to a similar economic backgrounds and a mutual distrust of the Eastern business establishment.[5]

The blue-coated garrison soldiers had seen or heard of only a few Partisan Rangers (called guerrillas by the Federals) operating near the city. (Louisiana's governor Thomas Moore, under an act passed by the Confederate Congress in April 1862, authorized the raising of bands of mounted men as companies, battalions or regiments of Partisan Rangers to defend local property.) Recently the bold Rangers began riding up to the Yankee picket lines, which resulted in an alarm. The hostile parties exchanged a few shots, but no serious fighting occurred. Being relatively few in number, the Rangers always fled upon seeing the approach of a company of Yankee reinforcements. Several Baton Rougeans living near the edge of town feared of being caught in crossfire between the Federals and the Rangers and left their homes to avoid the danger of being wounded or killed in the brief exchanges of gunfire. Moving from their homes was a hazard to the safety of belongings left behind. General Butler had declared that he could offer no protection against pillaging of any unoccupied house.[6]

Major-General Butler ordered General Williams to punish with the utmost severity every guerrilla attack, and burn the property of every guerrilla found murdering Union soldiers. Therefore, Williams ordered details from the Federal regiments at Baton Rouge to seize contraband property from known Rebels in the countryside near Baton Rouge. Williams felt the thieves of the 21st Indiana and the 6th Michigan would be well suited for this task. Shortly after their arrival, the Indianians received orders to go into the countryside to confiscate property belonging to identified Confederate supporters and their families.

The 6th Michigan raided the plantation of a leader of the local guerillas named Castle. Less than a week before Castle had killed a Federal naval officer. The Michigan boys disarmed and arrested Castle and three henchmen. All of Castle's property was declared contraband and carried off in wagons loaded by contraband slaves. The contrabands would be divided up and continue to serve the different regiments in Baton Rouge.

Based upon intelligence that a Mr. Bird was a captain in the Rebel army, Captain William Roy led Companies A and C out four miles from Baton Rouge to Bird's plantation. They confiscated his and his family's property under the Federal Confiscation Act. Arriving at the plantation, Roy quickly put his men to work gathering everything that could be carried off.

While the bluecoats were occupied in collecting the booty, a band of Partisan Rangers stealthily approached the plantation and commenced shooting at a sentry, Private James Howell. Howell returned fire and shouted raising an alarm. Several mounted officers, led by the regiment's adjutant, Lieutenant Mathew Latham, heard the gunfire and spurred their horses, galloping to Howell's aid. A small contingent of foot soldiers came running after the officers. After a brief exchange of shots, the partisans fled. No lives were lost on either side; the confiscation of Bird's property continued. It took a few more days to capture and load everything deemed portable. When completed, the Indianians removed two carriages complete with their harnessed teams, "400 hogsheads of sugar, 1,000 barrels of molasses, 3,000 bushels of corn, 250 head of stock, 100 head [sic] of Negroes, etc." to Baton Rouge. An early estimate valued the plunder at more than $15,000.[7]

On another early June expedition, the 21st Indiana's raiders, commanded by Adjutant Mathew Latham, surprised a company of dismounted Partisan Rangers eating and resting near the Comite River. After a brief exchange of shots, the Rangers disappeared into the woods, gifting the Hoosiers with fifty horses complete with saddles, blankets and bridles, plus assorted firearms, sheep and mules.[8]

Late in the evening of June 9, another expedition led by Colonel McMillan left Camp Magnolia Grove and went ten or fifteen miles east of town. Their search was for cotton, crops and partisans. In addition, the troops were to pick up and protect the cotton of a Union-friendly planter. The expedition consisted of about 250 men from Companies B, D, E, H and K, and a two-gun section of Nims' battery. When they arrived at their objective at 2 A.M., they found the cotton in a smoldering mass. Rather than have it taken by Yankees, partisans had burned about five hundred bales of it. The detachment arrested the overseer, posted a guard and prepared to spend the night. Company H took several chickens from the local flock and cooked dinner. They later bedded down for the night in a corn-shuck pen.

The next day the detachment began rounding up contraband cattle and pigs. They pressed several of the local Negroes into service to herd and drive the cattle and pigs. Through the help of these Negroes, the bluecoats located some buried trunks of goods in a cornfield. Many of the men wore torn clothing and worn-out shoes. Hoping to find fresh wearing apparel to replace their shirts and shoes, they broke open the trunks with a great deal of enthusiasm. When the opened trunks spilled forth only women's clothing and shoes, their mood changed. Some of the boys donned the clothing and danced to laughs and ribald comments while others angrily destroyed the apparel. That evening the raiders caught a few more chickens for dinner and again bedded down for the night in their shuck-pen. Early on the 11th, the Hoosiers set out in search of the cotton burners.[9]

Colonel McMillan, the officers, and a small party of mounted infantrymen rode slightly ahead of the foot soldiers to the home of a Mr. Roberts who informants claimed was a guerrilla. He and his two sons (one son home from Baton Rouge on a pass issued by General Williams, and the other son on leave from General Mansfield Lovell's command at Camp Moore) were at home exchanging intelligence about the troop disposition at Baton Rouge. The soldier son would take the information to officers when he returned to Camp Moore.

As the mounted Hoosiers rode up, the elder Roberts and his warrior son ran from the house firing their shotguns at the approaching officers. Five buck-shot from the Roberts' guns splattered into Colonel McMillan's left hand, arm and side. As the younger Roberts took aim on another officer, McMillan drew his .44 caliber Remington revolver and returned fire at close range. One of the colonel's shots drilled the younger Roberts through his head, killing him instantly. The distraught father dropped his weapon in surrender. The Hoosier officers quickly bound and gagged him. The foot soldiers arrived and promptly went to work burning the houses, outbuildings, cabins, stables and barns. Completing their destruction and confiscation of goods, the Hoosiers left the burial of the dead son to the women of the distraught family. The Indianians returned to Baton Rouge with cattle, horses, mules, one hundred bales of unburned cotton, the elder Roberts and his remaining son as prisoners.[10]

McMillan went to the hospital to recuperate from his wounds, two in his hand, one the length of his arm from the wrist to the elbow, one shallow breast wound and one in his side exiting from his back. The two Roberts's went on to New Orleans for military trials, where the elder Roberts received a sentence of life at hard labor in Fort Jackson for his attempted murder of Colonel McMillan. A letter to President Jefferson Davis complaining of General Butler's harsh treatment of Louisianans stated that Mr. Roberts actually was sent to Fort Pickens, Florida, for 23 years at hard labor.[11]

Feeling that the Baton Rouge area was secure, on June 20, General Williams embarked on transports with the 30th Massachusetts, 9th Connecticut, 7th Vermont, 4th Wisconsin, Nims' 2nd Massachusetts Battery and two sections (four guns) of Everett's 6th Massachusetts Battery. They headed upstream for the west bank of the Mississippi River across from Vicksburg, Mississippi. Once there, Williams endeavored to complete a canal he had begun a month earlier across a peninsula formed by a large bend in the river. The object of the canal was to allow Federal shipping and gunboats to bypass Vicksburg and its formidable array of large caliber cannons atop the river bluffs. This canal site is marked today as Grant's Canal because he also failed to complete it a year later.

At this time, Vicksburg stood alone in blocking Union control of the Mississippi River. Bypassing the city would open the Mississippi River to intense patrolling by Yankee vessels, and the vessels would greatly reduce or eliminate the flow of Confederate men, war materials, supplies and food to the Eastern Theater of the war. Instead, Federal troops and supplies could move easily and relatively quickly to most any point along the river. The Unionists still hoped that a quick victory would then result, reuniting the nation.[12]

In Baton Rouge, the 20th brought a large morale boost for the Indiana soldiers. Not only did the detested General Williams leave town for Vicksburg, but a shipment of shoes arrived. The bully boys were elated at having protection for their bare feet from thorns and blackberry briers. They had yet to receive new shirts to replace the threadbare and torn ones they wore. If they had to depend solely upon their spoiled and scarce rations for sustenance, they would be very hungry, but their foraging and berry picking supplemented their short rations. The storehouses lost supplies and rations daily, but cotton always seemed to refill the empty storage area leaving little room for additional clothing and food. The new post commander, Colonel McMillan, began moving the Hoosiers and the 6th Michigan into the Arsenal grounds.[13]

In spite of Williams' absence, Federal raids into the countryside maintained their momentum. On June 27 Lieutenant Colonel John A. Keith led a cavalry unit made up of Magee's 2nd Company, Massachusetts Cavalry, and several mounted 21st Indiana men on such a raid. The raiders rode towards the Confederate training camp at Camp Moore near Tangipahoa, Louisiana. On the way, they encountered camped companies of Vernon L. Terrell's Mississippi Dragoons and Captain Wilson Tate's Company F of Lieutenant-Colonel James H. Wingfield's 9th Battalion Louisiana Partisan Rangers on the Amite River. After a short but hotly contested fight, the Rebels fell back. The bluecoats bagged fourteen prisoners, twenty horses, three mules, and a wagon loaded with supplies and small arms. Keith then ordered his improvised cavalry battalion back to Baton Rouge with the fruits of their capture.[14]

Captain Tate rallied the remnants of his Company F. Unencumbered by prisoners and loot, they rode on back trails through the countryside to get ahead of Keith's command. About two-thirds of the way back to Baton Rouge as the Yankees came around a turn in the road, two volleys of musket fire from hidden Rangers ripped into the sides of their mounted column. The Federals' cavalry horses panicked, bucking and rearing as their riders fought for control of them. The riders tried to find cover from the whizzing bullets. Riderless horses plunged through the melee adding to the confusion. As suddenly as it began, it was over. The Partisan Rangers had disappeared into the woods after firing their two volleys. Seven prisoners made their escape with the Rangers. The gunfire killed two and wounded four of their Yankee guards. Four horses were killed, including Lieutenant-Colonel Keith's.

After gathering their scattered horses, resting a couple of hours and reconnoitering, the shaken Federals started again for Baton Rouge. A few hours later they arrived back at Baton Rouge after traveling ninety-six miles. The local Confederate commanders were surprised at the audacity of the raid by the outnumbered Keith, especially since they assumed that he was too drunk to lead raids during Colonel McMillan's disability. (In fact the opposite was true. Keith maintained a very respectful degree of sobriety as he shouldered his increased responsibility for the regiment.)[15]

The hot, humid climate continued taking its toll in sick and dead men as their unwilling southern hosts had hoped. Letters written home reflected the variety of illnesses that hospitalized some and made others feel miserable but able to report for duty. Most troops had hoped the climate of Baton Rouge would be healthier than that of New Orleans (they were justly afraid of yellow fever), but they still suffered from a variety of ailments such as ague, earaches, congestion of the brain, and typhoid. The 21st Indiana reported 304 on sick call one day in early June, and ten men died from illness during the same month. Only 350 answered the July 4 roll call. Eventually, the illnesses ran their course and by the middle of July, the sick lists indicated that the Hoosier regiment was almost back to full strength. Only fifty-seven Hoosiers reported sick on the July 15 sick list.[16]

As they were able, what with sickness, expeditions, drill, and guard duty, the men took their leisure time to frequent the town's businesses. Food prices had risen sharply in the South, and prices were almost double that paid in the North; for example: chickens were $1.00 each, eggs were $.50 a dozen, coffee was $.60 a pint, shirts were $2.22 each. These prices seemed even higher since the regiment had not been paid for six months. The enterprising Hoosiers took possession of a local bakery, and they set to work baking soft bread every other day for themselves.[17]

The bargain (for speculators) was cotton priced at $.03 a pound. The same weight would bring $1.00 in New York. Some officers were tempted by these Baton Rouge cotton prices. Captain Grimsley stated that he could clear $300.00 a month in trading through local businessmen and in Indiana. However, if he did not do it correctly, he could be court-martialed and drummed out of the service in disgrace. The risk was tempting, since he was able to send only $1,000.00 a year home to his family. He used the balance of his pay to purchase his clothing, rations and equipment. Grimsley felt the risk to his reputation too great to be caught speculating. The ever-sanctimonious Grimsley proudly admitted to sending only a few trinkets and gold jewelry home. He wrote that he came by the items that were captured from rebels by some of the boys who gave the items to him. Others did not share his feelings. A Baton Rouge post commander made $80,000 from cotton. He later went home on leave and received a promotion to brigadier general before he returned to Louisiana. (The evidence indicates the Hoosiers' own Colonel James W. McMillan was the officer.)

While the officers from both the 6th Michigan and 21st Indiana outrightly led official expeditions made up from their enlisted men to collect cotton for the Federal government or clandestinely lined their own pockets with the proceeds of private expeditions or by poor bookkeeping, the enlisted men tried to take advantage of the market. In one instance, three privates in Company B learned of a quantity of cotton stored in an abandoned home just a few hundred yards beyond their own picket lines. After offering to share with the picket on duty from Company C, the boys, carrying only pistols and knives (except for the musket-toting picket), passed out of their lines with a wagon and Negro driver for the cotton. Locating about three rooms full of loose cotton in the house, the boys set to work removing the feather stuffing from mattresses and re-stuffing them with the cotton, accompanied by loud shouts, whoops and hollers of joy at their good fortune.

Hearing the loud noises from the house, a party of Partisan Rangers resting their horses in a wooded area a hundred yards away cautiously approached the source of the sounds, dismounted and took cover in a nearby two-story frame building. The Rangers fired a few shots at the cotton loading party, which promptly discouraged the excitement and encouraged the bully boys to depart as fast as their legs would carry them. The wagon and driver shielded by part of the house started off a few seconds later from its other side. The wagon had traveled only a few yards when a pistol-toting Hoosier jumped from behind a bush in front of the wagon grabbing the reins. The driver pulled the wagon to a stop long enough for the cotton thieves to jump into the wagon. With bullets whizzing over, under, around and thudding into the tailgate and cotton packed between the rear of the wagon and the men lying low in front of the wagon, the driver jumped from the seat onto a horse's back, lay low across it and whipped the horse onward to safety. The result of this event ended individually initiated cotton thievery by enlisted Hoosiers.[18]

Early in the afternoon of July 5, the long roll sounded in the camp of the 21st Indiana. It and the other regiments formed in line of battle. A false alarm! A roving band of the 9th Battalion Partisan Rangers, Company H, had ridden up firing a few shots at the Union pickets. In the short melee that followed, the Rangers lost Private Henry Castle, taken prisoner by the pickets. The Rangers rode away as fast as they came. This was typical of the action that had been taking place near Baton Rouge for the past two months. Now, the Ranger groups were bolder, larger, and their harassment more frequent. Ever since Federal authorities had intercepted an order on June 27 from General Earl VanDorn to the citizens of Baton Rouge urging them to get eight miles back from the river to seek safety from his coming attack, the soldiers' and the pickets' nerves were on edge. During the night of July 8, picket firing caused the long roll to be sounded again. Negroes coming up to the guards caused that false alarm.[19]

General Williams' canal building project at Vicksburg failed, as would a more illustrious general's efforts nearly a year later. The deeper the troops dug, the more the river's water level receded. In addition to the strenuous labor in the ditch, the despotic general insisted upon daily drill with full packs in more than 110-degree heat. The badly weakened soldiers became very susceptible to illness, which depleted their effective numbers by about 50 percent. The sick soldiers went aboard river transports converted to hospital use. The lucky ones received transportation down river to Baton Rouge hospitals. To replace his dwindling labor ranks, Williams recruited Negro laborers from nearby plantations with promises of freedom.[20]

On July 15, the Confederate ironclad ram *Arkansas* steamed out of the Yazoo River into the Mississippi. It ran through the combined army and navy river fleets of Lieutenant-Colonel Alfred Ellet, Commodore C. H. Davis and Flag-Officer David Farragut that numbered over thirty ships. All the Union ships fired at *Arkansas* to stop her, but without avail. The *Arkansas* took more than an hour to run past the Federal fleet, returning the Federal fire in turn. She anchored safely at Vicksburg, under the protection of the heavy guns of the city. Later, two Federal vessels, *Queen of the West* and *Essex*, attacked and closely engaged the *Arkansas*, but, though they damaged her casemate armor and structure, they could not sink her. After the action in the river with *Arkansas*, the *Essex* managed to run by the guns of Vicksburg to operate in the river down to Baton Rouge.[21]

On the 24th, responding to orders from Major General Benjamin Butler, and the loss of Farragut's fleet heading back down the Mississippi to open sea to get salt water onto their hulls, Williams loaded his sick and weary men aboard river transports. They steamed for Baton Rouge to rest and recuperate in the hospitals. Williams left the Negro laborers behind to whatever fate awaited them. Farragut's fleet accompanied Williams' transports as far as Baton Rouge. Farragut then took his fleet down the river to patrol the Gulf of Mexico and season his fleet's hulls in salt water.[22]

On the 22nd of July, the Federals received reports of a large Rebel army massing at Camp Moore, about seventy miles away, to attack the Baton Rouge garrison. Colonel McMillan moved his sentinel guards from the open camp to within the confines of the Arsenal Barracks near the river. On the 25th, McMillan put about one hundred contraband laborers to work clearing a field of fire zone along Bayou Gros to the north of the Arsenal grounds. He also put men to work building earthworks atop the low bluff fronting Bayou Gros along the Arsenal yard's northern fence. Companies of infantry kept watch from guard posts set up on the main roads leading into the city. Brown's Jackass Battery and the 6th Massachusetts Battery rolled their guns into position near the intersection of Greenwell Springs Road with Jackson Road and at the intersection of Government Street with Perkins Road. The batteries functioned as heavily armed picket posts.[23]

General Williams returned with his sick and weary command on the 26th and immediately assumed command. The gaunt men and horses arrived at Baton Rouge and disembarked to enter camps and hospitals. Due to their privations, their morale was at its lowest. Williams then proceeded to lower morale among the troops that had garrisoned Baton Rouge in his absence. He ordered McMillan to move his regiment out of the fortifications they had constructed between the Pentagon Barracks and the Arsenal Powder Magazine to their previous Magnolia Grove campground. Williams ordered the 6th Michigan from their comfortable quarters in the Pentagon Barracks at the Arsenal complex to a campground about a mile and one-half east by southeast of the barracks. Williams refused to give the Michigan Wolverines any tents, even though the 9th Connecticut who now occupied the barracks had plenty of tents to spare. The 6th Michigan's lieutenant-colonel, major and two captains protested the order, which resulted in their arrest and being sent to New Orleans for court-martial.[24]

While Williams was retreating down the Mississippi to Baton Rouge, the ironclad gunboat *Essex* received repairs and orders to patrol the Mississippi River between Vicksburg and Baton Rouge. The *Essex*'s captain, William "Dirty Bill" Porter, was to warn Williams if the *Arkansas* moved downstream to where it could attack the Baton Rouge Federals in the rear with its heavy guns. As well as warning the army, Porter's instructions also called for him to engage and sink the *Arkansas* at all costs if the ram came down the river. Farragut also assigned three wooden gunboats, *Katahdin, Kineo* and *Sumter*, to support the *Essex*. Their firepower would also support troops on land if the threatened land attack materialized.[25]

With the return of Williams and his troops, the Federal infantry forces in Baton Rouge as of July 27 included the 9th Connecticut, the 21st Indiana and its Jackass Battery, the 14th Maine, the 30th Massachusetts, the 6th Michigan, the 7th Vermont, and the 4th Wisconsin regiments. The artillery consisted of Nims' 2nd Massachusetts Battery, Manning's 4th Massachusetts Battery, and Everett's 6th Massachusetts Battery. Magee's Massachusetts Cavalry battalion completed the garrison. At full strength, the regiments and batteries would number nearly 7,000 men. As it was, the other regiments were greatly reduced by disability discharges and deaths from sickness. Their numerous men in hospitals reduced the total number of effectives to about 2,500 men to defend their possession of the city. On August 1, the 21st Indiana was the larger of the regiments present, and it numbered about 850 men, including those on sick call and on special assignment. Each of Williams' other regiments could call an average of only two hundred men for review at the Baton Rouge racetrack. The 4th Wisconsin had the least of all present, sixty men, hardly enough to fill a company much less a regiment. The 21st Indiana paraded nearly four hundred for the review (half of the regiment being away on an expedition to the Duncan Kenner plantation or on guard duty at the time).[26]

Learning of the withdrawal of the Federal forces from the Vicksburg area, Confederate major-general Earl VanDorn ordered Major General John C. Breckenridge (a former United States vice-president) to move his division as fast as possible to Camp Moore, Louisiana. Once there, Breckenridge would join forces with Brigadier General Daniel Ruggles' command at Camp Moore for an assault upon the sick and weary Federals at Baton Rouge. The capture of Baton Rouge would clear the Yankees from the Mississippi River between Memphis, Tennessee, and New Orleans, Louisiana. On July 27, Breckenridge's command of about four thousand men left Vicksburg. Traveling by train, they arrived at Camp Moore, Louisiana, on the 28th. There, Breckenridge added Brigadier General Daniel Ruggles and his waiting regiments to his command. Breckenridge divided all the troops into two divisions—one commanded by Ruggles and the other commanded by Brigadier General Charles Clark. Breckenridge also sent messengers into the countryside near Baton Rouge to contact sympathizers, the Home Guard and wounded soldiers home on convalescent leave to be ready to join his army on its way to fight at Baton Rouge.[27]

On the day Breckenridge's command left Vicksburg for Baton Rouge, Lieutenant-Colonel Keith led about four hundred of his bully boys on their fourth major expedition from Baton Rouge. They boarded transports and steamed off down the Mississippi River to Ashland plantation. Ashland was the beautiful home of Duncan F. Kenner, a Louisiana representative to the Confederate Congress. He had voted for the secession of Louisiana from the Union. The prosperous Kenner grew sugar cane, and he was well known among the sporting set for his large stable of fine racehorses. If they could capture him, it would be a feather in the cap of the 21st Indiana.[28]

As the Hoosiers' steamer neared the landing at Kenner's plantation, he was riding with some friends, including his neighbor Henry Doyal (not yet identified as *Captain* Henry Doyal, leader of a local band of Partisan Rangers), along the river road. One of Kenner's Negro servants saw the bluecoats approaching and warned Kenner. Heeding the warning, Kenner changed to a faster horse from one of his riding companions and galloped off down the river road to another plantation. His wife, Nanine, watched him ride by from the front balcony of their home, but she did not recognize the rider as her husband. She would not learn of his whereabouts for more than a week.[29]

The plantation manager, one of Kenner's riding companions, rode up to the main house and alerted Mrs. Kenner of the approaching troops and that her husband had ridden to safety.

Mrs. Kenner called her family and trusted servants together and told them to hide valuable items wherever they could. After hurriedly hiding these valuables, there was a knock at the door. Opening the door, Mrs. Kenner saw her yard and porch full of blue-coated soldiers led by Lieutenant-Colonel Keith. Keith identified himself to Mrs. Kenner and told her that he commanded the expedition. Further, he was to arrest her husband and confiscate all of his and her property since the Federal government required it for its use. Mrs. Kenner truthfully replied that she did not know of her husband's whereabouts, and stated, "I am powerless to prevent you from taking what you please."[30]

Keith ordered his troops to search the house, grounds, outbuildings, and sugar mills, but he also ordered them not to destroy the buildings. Since she had cooperated in allowing his troops to search, Keith promised Mrs. Kenner that she and her household would not be molested. After searching the family's upstairs living quarters, he posted guards at the foot of the stairs to keep his men out of them. While the Hoosiers searched the main house and grounds, Keith sent details to search the neighboring plantations. Their far-flung search was not far enough because Kenner had crossed the Mississippi River into the Bayou LaFourche area near Donaldsonville and escaped.[31]

The searchers at Ashland located a hidden store of wine under the floor of one of the large brick outbuildings. The blue-coated vandals consumed the wine with gusto, although they called it "thin weak stuff." They cut paintings they liked from their frames, and pilfered all of the small household items they could cram into their pockets from the ground floor of the home. Acting upon information from one of the Negroes, the Hoosiers located a trunk of buried silverware to add to their horde of plunder. Some faithful Negroes managed to steal part of this silver back and again hid it for Mrs. Kenner.

While engaging in their looting and drinking, the soldiers, encouraged by the alcohol in their systems, got into a few fights over possession of their loot. Officers stopped most fights before they got out of control; however, on their last day at the plantation, two privates in Company G carried their differences to an extreme. Washington Cramer shot and killed Matthew Coyle. Officers ordered Cramer's arrest and immediate confinement aboard a steamer to stand trial at Baton Rouge.[32]

General Williams received information that Breckenridge's army had arrived at Camp Moore and was preparing to advance against Baton Rouge. He sent orders to the Hoosiers to return to Baton Rouge with haste. The bully boys left the Kenner home standing as promised. They also left a pony belonging to the Kenners' little boy. These two acts were all the kindness shown to the Kenners. The Indianians loaded their spoils aboard three transports and returned to Baton Rouge. The heavily laden river craft, besides containing the returning soldiers, held more than sixty racehorses from the stables of both Ashland and Waterloo plantations (valued at more than $100,000). Paintings, silver (except for eating utensils), three hundred hogsheads of sugar, salt meat, corn, 150 fat cattle, sheep, mules and eighty prisoners completed the booty crammed aboard the transports. The prisoners included all of the neighboring plantation owners, overseers, and stable boys, etc. The plantation owners included Henry Doyal, Stephen Minor, and Trasimond Landry, all prominent local men. In the evening of August 2, the raiders arrived at Baton Rouge with their booty.[33]

Since the 1st of August, the officers and men at Baton Rouge were on edge awaiting an attack. General Williams made plans to repel an attack from the north or east; however, he foolishly made no effort to erect any defenses to repel an attack. His men would fight in the fields maneuvering according to the "order of combat."

In fairness to General Williams, a couple of days earlier he had written Major-General Butler expressing his concerns regarding an attack on Baton Rouge. Butler responded on the 3rd by stating that he had planned an expedition to Madisonville, Louisiana, and the word of the expedition leaked out. This had caused Breckenridge to send four regiments toward Madisonville. An earlier report to Butler from Colonel McMillan about a reconnoitering expedition by two of his companies may have influenced Butler's response. The Hoosiers had surprised a guerrilla camp on the Amite River, captured some men and scattered the others. Butler assumed the guerrillas notified Camp Moore that a large force was moving that way, and Breckenridge had recalled his regiments marching to Madisonville and began massing forces at Camp Moore to repel a Yankee attack upon that place. Butler wrote: "This is the cause of the assembly of troops at Camp Moore.... While I would not have you relax your vigilance, I think you need fear no assault at present."

The boys of the 21st Indiana regularly went out for a mile or more beyond the picket posts to forage for blackberries and contraband chickens. They encountered no Rebels. Mounted patrols went out about three to five miles without result. Williams personally led the 6th Michigan on a midnight expedition. Relying upon faulty information, he positioned the Wolverines on a country road to intercept the expected advancing Confederate skirmishers. At sunrise, the chagrined Wolverines found themselves posted astride a road leading into a farmer's barnyard.[34]

In spite of Butler's lack of concern, the post at Baton Rouge had good reason to respond to all of the alarms. Breckenridge's command at Camp Moore rested and reorganized in only two days before he ordered it to proceed to Baton Rouge. His command of more than 4,500 men left Camp Moore for Baton Rouge on July 30 and 31. Their trip was slow and hot. By August 1, the heavy knapsacks on their backs chafed the men's shoulders raw through their sweat-soaked shirts. Clothing and personal items began disappearing from their knapsacks to lighten their load, and a few knapsacks were lost. They carried only essentials for fighting and eating on their persons. The ragged, barefoot men choked in the dust raised by their footsteps on the dirt roads. Their bodies dehydrated by the extreme heat, several soldiers staggered off the road to collapse in the shade of nearby trees and bushes. Others crushed together into every roadside well or pool of stagnant green water to quench their thirst.

By the 3rd of August, Breckenridge's command reached the Comite River. They had lost about five-hundred sick men along the way. Now, they drank, washed, pulled back from the open river, and rested. Clandestine messengers from Breckenridge alerted sympathizers in the Baton Rouge area of the coming attack. These couriers asked for volunteers to join the approaching forces, and they pleaded for medical supplies and bandages from plantation owners, who readily supplied lint and bandages.[35]

On August 4, the 21st Indiana's adjutant, Mathew A. Latham, took a mounted company eastward out the Greenwell Springs Road as far as the Amite River, where they captured a lone partisan picket. The picket told Latham that Breckenridge was "not far away." Latham reported this information to his superiors, but General Williams urged the officers not to upset their men in camp and not to erect any barricades on the roads, but to keep the pickets alert.

Patrols from other regiments reported no sign of any force assembling for an attack. That evening a second patrol from the 21st Indiana rode out a couple of miles along present-day Government Street and returned about 11 P.M. without seeing a sign of the enemy.

Under cover of a moonless, star-lit night, Breckenridge's entire command had crossed the fog-covered Comite River about 9 P.M. marching to attack Baton Rouge. At about the same time an estimated one hundred twenty-five citizens of Baton Rouge sneaked out of the town avoiding Federal pickets. One at a time or in twos and threes they made their way to a wooded area about one and one-half miles northeast of town to rendezvous with Breckenridge's army.[36]

Six

Baton Rouge: Battle

About three o'clock in the morning of August 5, Major-General John C. Breckenridge's three-thousand plus Confederates lost their opportunity to make a surprise attack on Baton Rouge. A group of troopers from the 9th Battalion Louisiana Partisan Rangers riding a little more than a mile in advance of the oncoming gray host came upon a Federal picket post a little more than a mile from Baton Rouge on the Greenwell Springs Road (present day North Street). As the Rangers approached the picket post, manned by Lieutenant Ed Armstrong and a detail from his Hoosier Company I, a picket called out for the password. Not receiving a response, the nervous pickets opened fire through the foggy night. As the flashes of light from the Hoosiers' rifle muzzles penetrated the fog, the surprised Rangers wheeled their horses and galloped back to the main body of their army. In their mad dash to the rear, they ran headlong into General Ben Hardin Helm and his staff riding at the head of his division. Helm's travel-weary men, mistaking the Rangers for charging Yankee cavalry, began firing wildly. The resulting chaos among the tangled Confederate artillery, cavalry and infantry wreaked havoc in the lead units of Breckenridge's army.

Before recognition and order could be restored, gunfire, stampeding horses, careening wagons, tumbling caissons and field pieces took their toll of human flesh. The confusing melee wounded several enlisted men in the 31st Mississippi Regiment and the Partisan Rangers. Four field and line officers, Captain Willis S. Roberts' (Company D, 4th Kentucky) and Lieutenant-Colonel John W. Caldwell's (9th Kentucky) injuries would prevent them from taking part in the coming action. General Helm's panicked horse threw him off and then fell on him causing severe injuries. Gunfire killed Helm's aide-de-camp, Lieutenant Alexander Todd. (Helm and Todd were two of U. S. president Abraham Lincoln's brothers-in-law.) Losing these competent field officers would hamper Breckenridge's forthcoming attack. The fracas also smashed the carriages of two of the three 6-pounder guns and their caissons belonging to Captain Robert S. Cobb's Kentucky Battery, reducing the number of Breckenridge's artillery pieces from thirteen to eleven, which would make him unable to engage in any intense artillery duels and keep the enemy artillery from having their way with shelling his foot soldiers. Other commanders might consider this incident a bad omen, but not Breckenridge; he got the units under control, assigned General Charles Clarke to command Helm's division and ordered his men forward to victory.[1]

Alerted by the muffled sounds of gunfire and more so by a rider from the Greenwell Springs Road picket post, the Union regiments' drummer boys beat the long roll, calling the bluecoats to arms. Men came running out of their tents, pulling on jackets, shoes, boots, caps, cartridge boxes, belts and grabbing for their rifles. The night's thickening ground fog muffled the sergeants' curses at those slower to fall into line. After the companies fell in, officers gave short speeches to their commands, exhorting them to do well in the coming fray.

The 21st Indiana's band struck up the grand march from *Norma* to cheer their comrades and arouse them to action. Their little blue-eyed, tow-headed drummer-boy, Edward Black, pounded his drum as loudly as he could to rouse the really soundsleepers among the 21st' infantrymen. As the soldiers, rubbing their eyes, fell into line, they became wide awake when they realized that this was not another false alarm. At last they were going to "see the elephant." Amid the hustle and bustle in the camps, messengers galloped back and forth between regimental headquarters, picket posts, and general headquarters to advise General Williams of the size, speed of movement and direction of the approaching force.[2]

General Thomas Williams had posted his three largest regiments on the eastern outskirts of the city in an irregular line bent sharply rearward on the Federal right by 500 yards more than the Federal left. The ends of the lines bent back toward the city along the northernmost and southernmost roads leading into the city. The perimeter ran from 300 yards north of the Greenwell Springs Road to about 200 yards south of the Clay Cut Road (present day Government Street). Williams considered these positions, about a mile from the city limits, far enough from town to spare the main civilian population from most of the stray shells and minie balls; also, the positions would give Williams' men ample room for maneuvering in the "order of combat" but no defensive works in which to shelter. The Federal regiment's and artillery batteries' battle positions were east of their camps near Dufroc Street (present day 19th Street) to contest an assault coming down the two main roads into Baton Rouge from the east, and through the fields on the north side of Greenwell Springs Road. Scattered houses with outbuildings, board fences or hedgerows sparsely dotted the main roads into Baton Rouge, with a small cluster of buildings at road intersections near the Federal camps; then the homes thinned until reaching the city proper at the penitentiary. The terrain was well chosen for an open field fight in grand Napoleonic style, but not for defense.

The units manning the front line from Union left to Union right were the 14th Maine Infantry, Everett's 6th Massachusetts Battery (under command this day of Lieutenant William Carruth), 21st Indiana Infantry, a Battalion of 6th Michigan Infantry, Captain Ormand Nims' 2nd Massachusetts Battery (commanded this day by Lieutenant George Trull), the Jackass Battery (commanded by Lieutenant James Brown) and a battalion of the 6th Michigan Infantry. To their rear were the 7th Vermont Infantry and the 30th Massachusetts Infantry. Williams positioned the manpower-depleted 9th Connecticut Infantry, the 4th Wisconsin Infantry and Manning's 4th Massachusetts Battery in reserve on the far left flank near the Arsenal grounds (a mile to the rear of the primary defenders).[3]

Messengers returning from several outposts now bore the same message: "We are being attacked!" Officers shouted orders along the one and one-half mile long front to form their men. The 14th Maine's enlisted men were eating breakfast when frightened pickets ran through the camp shouting out that the enemy was coming, and the long roll began playing. Lieutenant Ira Gardner formed his company, its captain saying he was sick. A rider galloped past the lieutenant on his foam-lathered horse yelling: "Lieutenant turn your men out, they are upon us." Gardner called to form their ranks before anyone thought to awaken their soundly sleeping colonel, Frank Nickerson, and tell him of the situation. Gardner met the lieutenant-colonel coming out of his tent and advised him of the situation before stepping into the colonel's tent to awaken him. Gardner then got his company into line of battle. Other officers followed Gardner's example with their regiments. Awake and dressed, Nickerson took charge and moved his men to the east edge of their camp, the direction from which messengers had said the enemy was advancing.

At the opposite end of the Federal lines, the 6th Michigan formed ranks, faced east along Perkins Road and waited. The 30th Massachusetts formed up in their camp near the state capitol building, and marched a short distance east to await orders. The 7th Vermont formed facing south across Florida Street. The 9th Connecticut, 4th Wisconsin and two sections of

Captain Charles Manning's 4th Massachusetts Battery moved eastward to take position at the edge of high ground on the north side of Bayou Gros across from the Arsenal. General Williams, atop his black charger (recently liberated from Stephen Minor's stables), ordered Manning's third section (two 4.62-inch rifled guns) to move across town to the center of the defensive line along Dufroc Street (19th Street) at its Florida Street intersection on the right of the 21st Indiana's camp.[4]

The wounded Colonel McMillan remained in the hospital; therefore, Lieutenant Colonel John Keith commanded the 21st Indiana. Keith, a fair-minded but feisty, small statured man, immediately mounted his magnificent white horse (recently liberated from Duncan Kenner's stable) and led his regiment from their camp eastward around the cemetery grounds along the Greenwell Springs Road (also called North Street) to meet the enemy. After marching out about 600 yards from their camp, the Hoosiers columned right and began forming in line of battle to receive the enemy in a cornfield between North Street and a dense forest to the south. (This was in the area of present-day 23rd Street.)

Taking advantage of the terrain, the seven hundred ninety-man Hoosier Regiment took their positions behind a thick hedge of Cherokee rose and a wooden fence surrounding a cornfield. Another Cherokee rose hedge on the north side of a country lane extension of Florida Street hid the Hoosiers' right flank. A dense forest of oak trees and thick brush bordered the south side of Florida Street. Major Hays took the skirmishers from Companies A and F about 150 yards ahead (near present day 27th Street) of the regiment, stopping at the far edge of the cornfield. The pickets from Company I fell in on the skirmisher left. Colonel Keith ordered the pickets back to rally on the battalion. The pickets fell back, firing as they retreated ahead of the gray-clad skirmishers coming at them down the Greenwell Springs Road. Keith positioned Company A on the right of the regiment and Company F on the regiment's left. Realizing his flanks were exposed, he moved Company C to the rear of Company A, and Company I to the flank of Company F. Companies B, D, E, G, H and K filled the line between Companies A and F.

Lieutenant William W. Carruth, commanding Everett's 6th Massachusetts Battery, moved his two rifled cannons and four 6-pounder guns about 300 yards out Greenwell Springs Road from Magnolia Cemetery. He positioned his pieces across the road and in the fields to either side of it. Nims' battery, with only eight of its red-capped and red-pantalooned crewmen reporting well enough to work their guns, Lieutenant Trull (in command due to Nims' absence in New Orleans) sent out a call for help. Twenty-five volunteers from the 9th Connecticut arrived and manned the guns in a position along a street running south from Florida Street just across from the 7th Vermont's camp to North Boulevard from where they could fire eastward from their six 3.67-inch bronze rifles. Lieutenant James Brown's 21st Indiana Jackass Battery positioned two of their 6-pounder guns on Government Street: one at the Perkins Road junction (near present day 17th Street and Government Street) and one about 200 yards farther out Government Street slightly east of some homes surrounded by wooden fences. Brown's third 6-pounder moved a short distance out North Boulevard from 17th Street. The gunners waited to load with shell, case or canister, depending upon the range to their fog-masked attackers. The fog successfully concealed the number of the attackers, their positions and proximity to the Federals; in turn, the fog masked the waiting bluecoats as well.[5]

By dawn that morning, Rebel skirmishers had driven the Federals from their outposts and the sporadic firing ceased. The Confederates could hear the bands playing, bugle calls and the beat of drums. All surprise was gone; they had to attack and quickly. In about twenty to thirty minutes, Breckenridge's First Division, led by Brigadier General Charles Clark, formed in line of battle to the east of Greenwell Springs Road. Brigadier General Daniel Ruggles moved his Second Division south from Greenwell Springs Road and formed for battle.

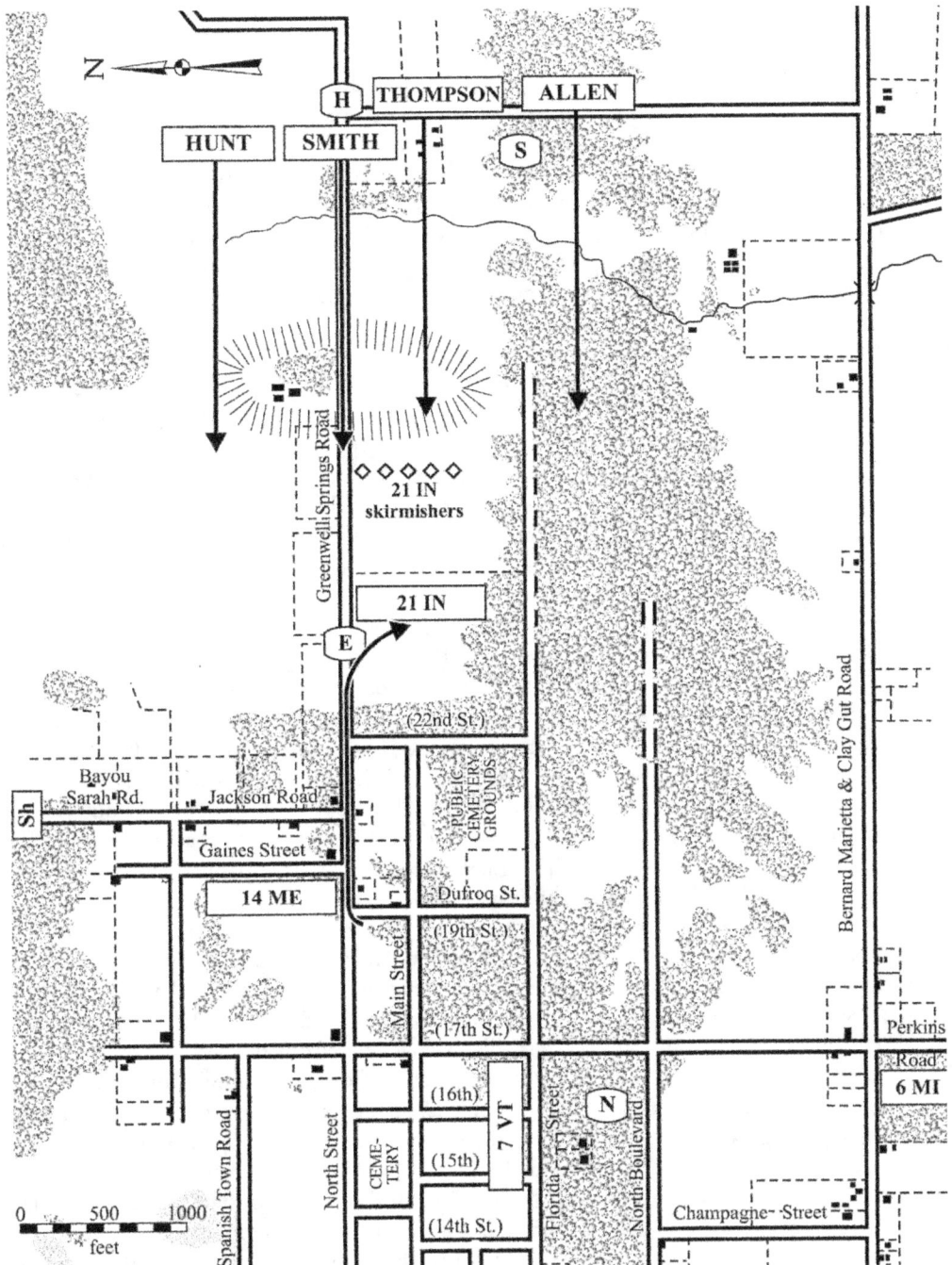

Battle of Baton Rouge, First Phase, showing infantry and artillery positions at dawn August 5, 1862. (Cartographic design by Mary Lee Eggart, based in part upon composite detail from National Archives maps RG-77-Z-293 and RG 77-Z-346-2.)

Clark split his division into two brigades, the first brigade commanded by Colonel Thomas H. Hunt on the Confederates' far right and the second brigade commanded by Colonel Thomas B. Smith in the center. Hunt was to attack along the north side of Greenwell Springs Road and Smith down the road and to its left. Ruggles also split his division into two brigades, the first brigade commanded by Colonel A. P. Thompson to cooperate with Smith in the center and the second brigade led by Colonel Henry Watkins Allen to attack from the Confederate left. The hardest punch against the Federal lines would come from the center.

(See Appendices for Confederate and Federal Order of Battle.)

As the gray-clad men moved into position, they noticed that directly overhead they could see blue sky and flying birds; however, from around fifteen feet high to within a few inches of the ground the ever-thickening fog gave only five to ten feet of visibility. Breckenridge now allowed his men a few minutes to rest. Most of his men were combat-hardened veterans of the Shiloh campaign and included the Kentucky Orphan Brigade.[6]

Breckenridge's artillery consisted of six pieces of Captain Oliver J. Semmes' 1st Louisiana Regular Battery (the only battery accepted into Regular Confederate service from Louisiana and west of the Mississippi River); one piece from Captain Robert L. Cobb's Kentucky Battery; and six guns of Hudson's Mississippi Battery (also known as "Pettus' Flying Artillery"), commanded by Lieutenant John R. Sweeney. As the infantry formed for attack, their officers made short speeches of encouragement. The Rebel artillery took position: four pieces of Semmes' battery (two 6-powder guns and two 3.67-inch rifles) on the Confederate left with Ruggles' command, four pieces of Hudson's battery on the left and center, and the rest of the cannons spaced between regiments on the center and two of Semmes rifled guns on a special detail.

The section of two 3-inch Confederate Parrott rifled cannons from Semmes' battery on the special detail accompanied two companies of the 30th Louisiana Infantry and Companies C and E of the 9th Battalion Partisan Rangers led by Lieutenant-Colonel Thomas Shields on a special night mission. Their job was to quietly flank the Federal left and get behind the 14th Maine's camp to cut off their route of retreat. Shields' force coming down the Clinton Road encountered a Federal picket post at the Clinton Road's junction with the Bayou Sara Road. The panicked pickets fled at the first fire from Shields' skirmishers, leaving their accoutrements hanging from trees and a shed. They fled into a wooded area beside the road and fired a couple of rounds towards Shields' men. Then they ran again, passing through the camp of the 14th Maine, and yelling over their shoulders to make the Maine boys aware of the coming attack as they kept running for the safety of the Arsenal Grounds by the Mississippi River.[7]

At the Federal center, the 21st Indiana's advance skirmishers waited in tight-lipped silence about 100 yards in advance of the regiment. They hid behind the thick tangled hedge of Cherokee rose. Some of Smith's and all of Thompson's troops moved into position, forming their line of advance in a cornfield only a short distance away in front of the hidden Hoosiers—Smith in line of assault (he knew there were skirmishers from Companies I and F in front of him) and Thompson in column. Hoosier skirmishers overheard a Confederate officer giving his soldiers an inspirational speech, calling for southern valor and courage to carry the day. The speaker closed by saying, "One good charge and the Yankees are ours!" Another officer responded that he would meet him in the Capitol Building for dinner that evening. The Hoosiers prayed for strength and victory. One of Company B's men prayed: "Oh Lord, be with us. If you can't be with us, don't be against us, but stand back and you will see one of the damndest fights you ever saw." The vastly outnumbered Indiana skirmishers fell on back to the very front of the regiment's line.[8]

The Confederate right and center began its advance in line; Thompson's brigade stepped off in column down a country lane to the 21st Indiana's right. On the Hoosiers' right, Company A had a board fence some 15 yards in front and chin-high corn growing between them and the fence. After passing by the skirmish line, a short and sharp-eyed drummer boy in Thompson's brigade first saw the ankles and feet of the waiting bluecoats through the thin base of the hedge. He alerted an officer, and the Rebels took position to bring their weapons to bear on the hedge.

Almost simultaneously, Smith's leading infantrymen appeared coming over and through the board fence to their left. Then one of Thompson's regiments came through the board fence to their front. The Hoosier skirmishers gave them a volley just as Thompson's men in column gave the Hoosiers a ferocious enfilading volley killing Company A's Lieutenant Charles D. Seely and killing Orderly Sergeant J. A. Bovington. The surprised Indianians reloaded and returned fire, now firing wildly to both the front and right; the foggy air rapidly filled with black powder smoke. The Hoosier skirmishers ran back from the hedge and fence to form in line with the rest of the regiment. As they retreated and tried to reform, more volleys from their front and right crashed into them, killing Corporal Isaac Knight and Private H. T. Batchelor. The entire 21st Regiment pulled back a little more than 100 yards through the corn to regroup.

As Major Benjamin Hays rode among the Hoosiers encouraging the men to form a battle line, a Rebel musket ball smashed into his foot, causing Hays to fall from his horse. Quickly remounting, Hays continued exhorting his men. Getting the men into line, he watched them get off another volley before he lost consciousness and again toppled from his mount. Two men carried him from the field to the Hoosiers' field hospital as his hastily organized line managed to hold off the enemy advance for a few minutes, losing three men from Company C in the process. Seeing Thompson's men flanking them, the Hoosiers again retreated toward their camp. Thompson's and Smith's men took possession of the cornfield.[9]

The Rebels paused for a quick rest, dressed their ranks, checked equipment and moved forward. After advancing about 150 yards, they received a thunderous volley from the 21st Indiana's new battle line. However, the Kentuckians' and Tennesseans' battle fever was up, and it caused only a slight check in their advance. Keith ordered his regiment to fall back about 200 yards and form another line. Keith hastily moved his men through more corn rows, brush and trees into another defensive line, now missing many men who in the confusion moved all the way to the rear of their campground. Keith's remaining Hoosiers got into line and fired another volley at Smith's and Thompson's brigades. The resulting return volley and continued press of gray-clads again forced the Hoosiers to break, and Company C was separated from the regiment. Company C melted into the forest and became sharpshooters for the rest of the battle harassing Thompson's left and Allen's right.

The 21st Indiana ran to Dufroc Street and their camp. John Yelton claimed that he ran so fast that the Rebel bullets could only hit the heels of his shoes. A small group of mixed Hoosier companies hastily formed a thin line in front of the cemetery and fired a ragged volley at the yelling Rebels. Then, this little line broke and fled uphill through a thinly wooded area, then through a field of corn planted in the eastern half of the cemetery and then among the cemetery's monuments and around a fence to Dufroc Street. Taking advantage of a break in fighting offered by the fleeing Federals, the Confederate advance halted to rest and dress their battle lines. Thompson's men had pushed the running Federals almost a half mile through corn and pea fields to the suburbs of Baton Rouge.[10]

Meanwhile, the Confederate right wing that had begun its advance slightly before the center met with little opposition. Hunt's men moved quickly through the fog-wet fields of sweet potatoes, peas and corn. Most of Smith's regiments formed in column and marched down Greenwell Springs Road meeting only token opposition from a few skirmishers from Companies F and I of the 21st Indiana who fell back in good order. Alerted by the exchange of gunfire between Smith's men and the skirmishers, the 14th Maine brought all companies into a battle line facing east and waited along a road bordering their camp about 100 yards west of the Clinton-Jackson Road. After firing a long-range volley at a small body of Hunt's skirmishers, a sentinel came running up to alert the Maine boys of another Confederate force marching out of the woods with artillery advancing on the left of their camp. The confused

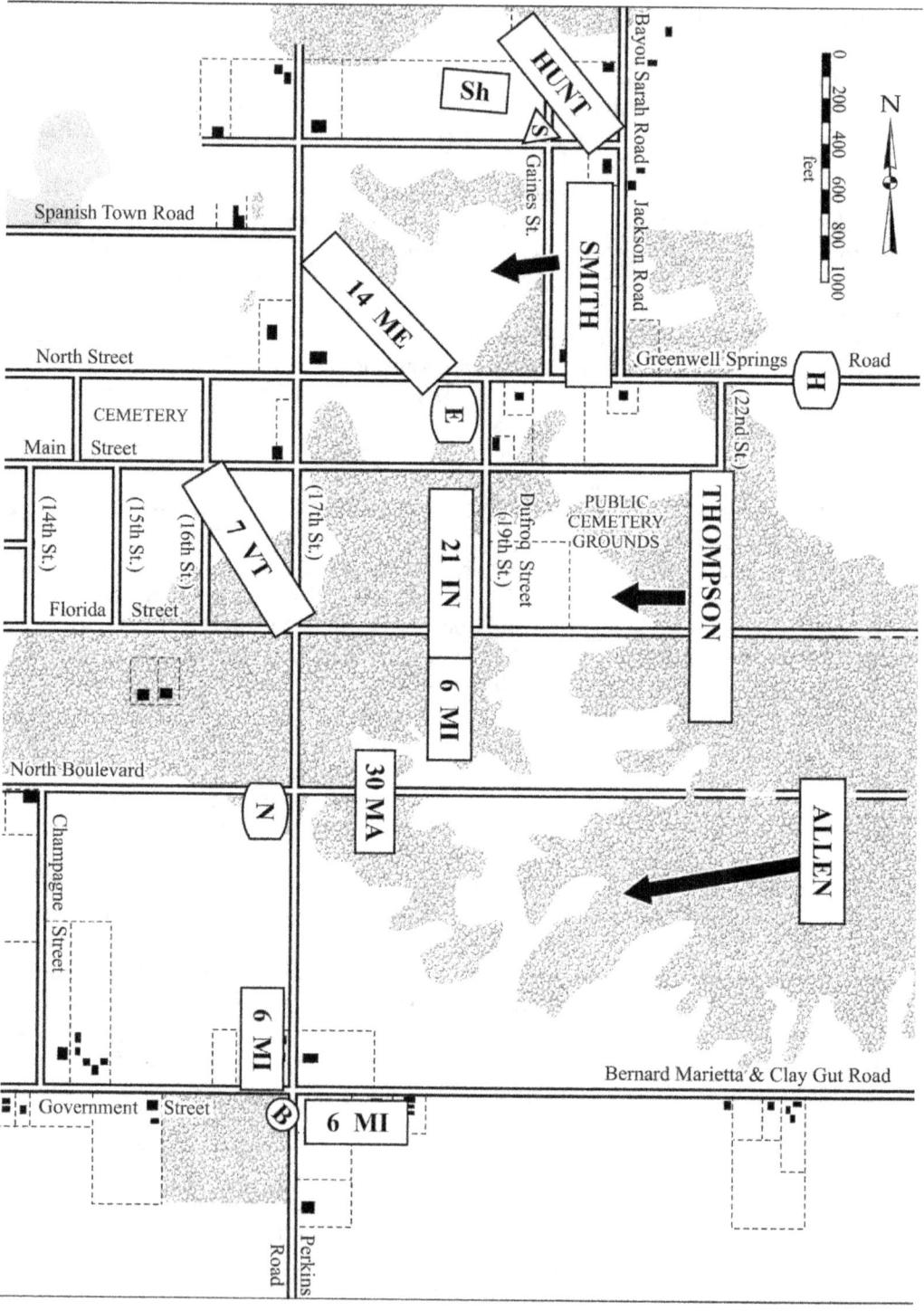

Battle of Baton Rouge, Map, Second Phase, Full Contact. (Cartographic design by Mary Lee Eggart, based in part upon composite detail from National Archives maps RG-77-Z-293 and RG 77-Z-346–2.)

Yankees watched their attackers halt about 250 feet in the rear of their left flank, maneuver into battle lines, face south, dress their lines and await orders. Shields, now aware of Hunt's advance, ordered his artillery and infantry to open fire on the 14th Maine.

Leaving a company to watch the halted enemy to the east, Nickerson ordered his regiment to turn about and march through their camp to face the more immediate threat. The section of Semmes' battery, commanded by Lieutenant T. K. Fauntleroy, and its infantry support opened an oblique fire on them as they came through camp and went into line. The opponents traded a couple of volleys and ceased fire. This new enemy force posed a very small threat, compared to the number of men now advancing from Hunt's and Smith's brigades to the east.

Again, leaving a company behind to keep Shields busy, the 14th Maine changed position to form a new defensive line against the greater threat advancing from the east through pea and corn fields and yet to keep the smaller threat on their north flank at bay. Fauntleroy lost four of his horses and feared being caught in a counter-charge without the means to withdraw rapidly. Acting quickly, he limbered up his guns and made for the rear where he would receive more infantry protection from Hunt's advancing regiments. Hunt's grayclads pressed forward and made contact with the 14th Maine. Shields again threatened the Yankees' left flank. Hit from two sides, the Yankees fell back through their camp. Colonel Nickerson restored order, detached a company as a rear guard to keep the Rebels busy, and formed the rest of the regiment in an oblique firing line from corner to corner of their camp to fire on both of the advancing Rebel lines moving on them from north and east. A breakthrough at this place would open the rear of the Federal center to Shields' flanking movement. A Rebel contingent led by "a huge Negro, armed and equipped with musket, knapsack and uniform" assaulted a house on the 14th Maine's left. The house near the rear of the Maine camp was occupied by 14th Maine sharpshooters. By seizing the house, the Rebels would have a perfect spot to lay down a covering fire for their own men. The Negro and several other grayclads fell fighting. The house remained in Maine hands for the duration of the battle.[11]

Carruth's 6th Massachusetts Battery, having been at the Greenwell Springs Road and the public cemetery when the attack began, now found itself in a precarious position. The attack on the left, which had splintered the 14th Maine sending several to the rear, had uncovered the left flank of the battery. Also, the Hudson Battery fired straight down Greenwell Springs Road into Carruth. He shifted his guns to cover his flank (and the 14th Maine) as well as to cover the retreating 21st Indiana on his right. His battery's complement of about 38 able-bodied men and officers and supplemented by men from the 14th Maine drained again as the Yankee infantrymen left to reinforce their regiment in its fight.

As Rebel bullets whistled around Carruth's guns and found fleshy targets, he tried to move his pieces to the rear while some of his guns' crewmen fled for their lives. Many of the Rebel bullets found their marks in the battery's horses, killing or severely wounding them, which greatly hindered Carruth's ability to move his cannons. Company F, skirmishing as they moved rearward, came near Carruth's guns. Seeing this body of infantry near his guns, Carruth went up to them with tears in his eyes, and said: "My brave Indianians come and man a Massachusetts Battery deserted by Massachusetts men."[12]

Hoosiers from Company F's skirmishers quickly went to Carruth's aid. With most of the company providing covering fire, the rest of them fell to the hot work of manning the guns to hold their position. They did excellent work. Lieutenant Gardner had rallied 200 plus men from the 14th Maine, which formed on the 21st Indiana's left near Carruth's battery. As the 14th Maine fired their volleys obliquely, Carruth's battery began firing double canister into the Rebel ranks at point-blank range of 30 yards, tearing and ripping bloody holes in the Rebel ranks and bringing the gray-clad charge to a halt. Colonel Nickerson now rejoined the only sizable mass of his regiment, congratulating the lieutenant for his bravery and actions in rallying the men he had.

While Hunt's men dressed their lines and Smith's men, severely punished by Carruth's canister, fell back about 50 yards to regroup, the 6th Massachusetts Battery took advantage of the brief lull to move their guns. With most of their horses dead, the gunpowder-blackened men put their shoulders to the wheels and helped move the cannons along Greenville Springs Road to the rear of the 14th Maine's camp. They left behind a couple of limbers and caissons still harnessed to their dead teams of horses. In their new position, they moved half their pieces off the road into a field to the north of the roadway. All this while, a dead artillerist lay across a retreating limber hauling one of the artillery pieces with his head flopping against a wheel, splattering his blood and brains with every bounce.

The pause in battle also gave the 14th Maine time to abandon their camp and begin to move into position to its rear and right, where they could support the 4th Massachusetts' guns and the left flank of the 21st Indiana. Everett's new position placed his guns about 150 yards to the rear of his first position. Now they faced a section north by northwest to meet Shields' gray threat near the nearly abandoned camp of the 14th Maine. From a small rise of ground north of the 14th Maine's former camp, Shields' section of Semmes' battery began blasting exploding shells into the 21st Indiana's left flank and into the rear of the maneuvering 14th Maine. Again, the Massachusetts cannoneers and their Hoosier helpers rose to the challenge. Loading with shell, they silenced Shields' section of Semmes' battery, causing it to withdraw out of sight to the rear of the hillock and then moving under its cover 200 yards back to the Bayou Sara Road.[13] Hunt's men moved into the Maine camp, and many of them stopped to eat the abandoned foodstuffs. Urged by their officers to press the battle, they grabbed what food they could carry, took weapons and ammunition from the dead to replace any of their own that were not working well and moved to re-form their ranks in the gunpowder-blackened sulfurous fog.

General Williams had not been idly watching as the Rebel assault rolled over the 14th Maine's camp. Rapidly assessing the situation, Williams ordered a battalion from the 9th Connecticut (held in reserve) to move along the river and then forward along Spanish Town Road or North Boulevard. The balance of the 9th Connecticut and the entire 4th Wisconsin with two sections of Manning's battery moved slightly forward toward the left-rear of the 14th Maine. (On this day the 4th Wisconsin fielded about 40 to 60 men, many of them sick; the rest of their men being in hospitals or in the rear helping their commissary officer remove supplies to the wharf.) The remaining two-gun section of Manning's battery hurriedly moved to the right. Upon reaching Florida Street, they wheeled left and galloped up Florida Street to support the 21st Indiana's right and add their guns to Nims' battery's firepower. All this while, several soldiers abandoned their sickbeds and moved toward the sound of battle to fall in with their regiments.

Seeing no threat to his extreme right flank, Williams ordered six companies of the 6th Michigan to the aid of the 21st Indiana, who were regrouping in the sunken roadway (Dufroc Street) at the city side of Magnolia Cemetery. Leaving three companies of Wolverines to support Brown's Jackass Battery with one company in reserve, the other six companies hurried to reinforce the 21st Regiment's right flank in the vicinity of Dufroc and North Boulevard. Seeing their Western comrades coming up, the bully boys of the 21st gave them three cheers, and then the Hoosiers passed a unanimous resolution that there would be no more breaking of ranks and running within the 21st Indiana. The Hoosiers received additional reinforcements from their own men on guard duty at the camp and men returning from scattered picket posts. With the balance of their men falling into line, the Hoosiers numbered about eight hundred and fifty men and officers.

Dufroc Street passing in the front of the cemetery on its west side was slightly lower than the ground level of the cemetery and separated from the cemetery by a board fence. Magnolia trees scattered themselves throughout the cemetery and mixed on the east and south of it with oak trees. Corn grew across the east end of the cemetery, and large family tombs were scattered in the west (city most) end of it. The Hoosiers took advantage of this shielded, sunken defensive position by lying or kneeling in the roadbed behind the board fence.

Thompson's men, Smith's men and a few of Hunt's men poured from the fields toward the cemetery. A slight rise in the ground varying from one yard to six yards high ran north to south extending from about the middle of the 14th Maine's camp along the rear of the cemetery to about two hundred yards south of Government Street. Sheltering here, Thompson's men kept up a steady fire at the Hoosiers, who returned fire from their sunken roadbed. Smith's regiments who had engaged the Hoosiers' left flank fell back and into the low ground east of the cemetery alongside of Thompson's men. After a short rest, the grayclads again received orders to charge forward and assault the resolute Hoosiers.[14]

It was here that the fiercest fighting of the day took place among and around the monuments to the dead. The shouting Confederates from Kentucky, Mississippi and Tennessee clashed with the equally vocal Hoosiers and Wolverines from Indiana and Michigan. The peaceful civilian resting place became a hellish charnel ground for blue-clad and gray-clad bodies alike as attack and counterattack moved back and forth across the hallowed ground. Minie balls whirred overhead, mixed with the swishing whine of wood plugged Enfield rounds, humming Merrill bullets and swooshing round lead balls. Chips of marble and granite peppered the Rebels taking cover behind the tombstones. Splinters from the board fence along the cemetery road gouged into the bluejackets behind it. At times, the men fired their muskets at only a few feet from each other. The chipped, shattered and gore splattered tombstones in the cemetery bore silent testimony to the ferocity of the contest. The highly-spirited death match raged in, around and through the cemetery for more than one and one-half hours before it would spill toward the river into the 21st Indiana's camp. The 6th Kentucky suffered most of its twenty-five casualties during the fighting in and around the cemetery.[15]

Hunt's brigade, now reinforced by Shields' special battalion and Smith's brigade, began another crushing advance against the rearward maneuver of the 14th Maine that again exposed the left flank of the 21st Indiana. A company of the 21st fell back from the cemetery into their camp to meet Smith's movement. Smith's men fired three volleys into the Hoosiers before being ordered to the rear. Lieutenant Carruth again limbered up his guns and moved back along Greenwell Springs Road about 100 yards toward the city. Company F went with him, still manning Carruth's guns and giving supporting rifle fire to the battery.

Hard pressed by Hunt, the 14th Maine's movement to the rear and right of their camp became a panicked rout. The 31st Mississippi took a dozen of the slower-moving Maine men prisoner during their flight. The officers worked furiously to restore order and soon managed to get about two hundred of their men to form ranks to the left and in the rear of the 21st Regiment along Greenwell Springs Road (which at the time became North Street in Baton Rouge). The rest of the Maine boys fled past the penitentiary through the town streets seeking the shelter of the levee.[16]

Still holding the Federal center, the 21st Indiana and the 6th Michigan Battalion stubbornly held onto their ground in and around the Magnolia Cemetery. The battle here had degenerated from organized fighting and maneuvering between regiments to fighting between companies and then to individual hand to hand fighting. Back and forth across the turf and roadways the gray and blue clads moved. The continued pressure from Thompson's Confederates finally allowed them to reach the board fence. Breaking through it, the defenders met the attackers with clubbed muskets, thrusting bayonets, knives, swords, pistols, fists, boots

Top: Tomb at Magnolia Cemetery dating to prior to the Battle of Baton Rouge. The base is between 18 inches and 24 inches high and shows signs of having settled inches deeper into the ground than at the time of the battle. *Bottom:* Tomb at Magnolia Cemetery dated prior to the battle. The base is roughly fifteen feet on each side and up to 30 inches high due to a slight ground curvature at its rear. Ten to twelve men easily could have sheltered behind it only ten yards from the Federal lines.

and teeth. Boards and rails torn from the cemetery's fence became clubs in the hands of the attackers and defenders alike. It was now every man for himself in a deadly free-for-all. Heads were bashed, bellies punched, shins smacked, arms cut and uniforms ripped and torn. Amid this, the Hoosiers' color guard fell back to the front (near present-day 17th Street) of the Hoosiers' camp to establish a rallying point. (The camp faced west.) Bullets tore into the back of color guard Thomas Ballard, severing his spine and sending him to the ground. Unable to move, he lay where he fell. As the crash of battle pressed forward through the camp of the 21st and over him, he feared he would be bayoneted to finish him off; instead, he heard one of the advancing Rebels say to leave him alone that he was a "deader." (Private Ballard later died on the wharf at New Orleans waiting for transportation to a hospital.)

The Hoosiers and Wolverines slowly gave way after their one and one-half hours of hard fighting in and around Magnolia Cemetery and grudgingly fell back through the Hoosiers' camp. The fighting there continued at close range. The Rebel offensive pressed on, and the Hoosiers slowly moved toward the front of their bullet-riddled camp, where they would re-form ranks. Minie balls punched holes through tents, baggage trunks, knapsacks, kettles and water buckets. The Michigan boys fell back toward the 30th Massachusetts Regiment's position, where the 30th Massachusetts boys lay flat on the ground to avoid the Rebels' high-flying musket balls.[17]

About one-half hour before the Hoosiers and Wolverines began their withdrawal, Colonel George T. Roberts moved his 7th Vermont Regiment through his camp to reinforce the Federal left flank. Marching too far to the left, they came under friendly fire from artillery shells falling short from two of Manning's 4th Massachusetts guns in their rear as well as Hunt's Rebel infantry fire from their front and right. After sending a messenger to the rear to have Manning elevate his guns, Colonel Roberts ordered his men back to their original position in front of their camp. In a few minutes General Williams rode to the 7th Vermont and excitedly and brusquely ordered Roberts to open fire at the advancing fog-clad shapes of the flanking Confederates. Roberts again moved his men left to meet the threat.

As the advancing shapes seemed to be coming from the general direction of the 14th Maine's campground, the 7th Vermont fired a volley at the advance. Amazed at the number of Rebels advancing through the powder blackened fog, the Vermonters hurriedly reloaded. Some companies changed positions to better defend against the attackers approaching from the east (the company of the 21st Indiana moving to contain the Rebels' flanking move and the rallying Hoosiers coming through their camp) other Vermont Nutmeggers held against those shapes approaching from the north and northeast (Hunt's and Smith's men advancing out of the camp of the 14th Maine). The nervous Vermonters fired a ragged volley at the oncoming shapes, and the shaken men clumsily reloaded to fire again. Hunt's men returned a murderous fire that mortally wounded Colonel Roberts and took out nearly 10 percent of the 7th Vermont Regiment's effective force.

In the confusion, Yankee bullets tore into the western men. Officers from the Indiana regiment rode into the Vermont lines and called for them to cease fire. General Williams, realizing his serious error, did likewise. The confused Nutmeggers had enough. Many of the 7th Vermont fled the field. About 150 men with Lieutenant-Colonel Fullam fled to a ravine at the rear of the State Penitentiary. (General Williams had designated the penitentiary building with its high and thick brick walls as a last-ditch rallying place and fortification.) Nearly one hundred terrified Vermonters ran through town to the Mississippi River to hide behind the levee with some of the 14th Maine and the frightened pickets. Williams tried to rally the 7th Vermont himself and succeeded in keeping about two companies of men in position. The Rebel warriors lost no time in occupying the 21st Indiana's vacated camp as they had the 14th Maine's camp.[18]

Entering the 21st Indiana's camp, the Johnnies captured a prisoner — the Hoosiers' prisoner Washington Cramer, confined to camp under arrest for murder. His guard abandoned Cramer when called to defend the camp. Cramer would probably receive no worse treatment as a prisoner of war than he would receive at his upcoming trial. The shaken but re-grouping Hoosiers moved into the now abandoned camp of the 7th Vermont and the Catholic Cemetery's grounds.[19]

An unexplained lull now occurred in the fighting. Men and officers looked at one another trying to figure out what to do next. Lieutenant Colonel Keith took the initiative and rode out to the Rebel lines. Captain Will Yerger of General Clark's staff and Adjutant Fitzpatrick of the 22nd Mississippi Regiment rode forward and met him. Keith called over to the Rebels and asked them to surrender their men. Surprised, the Rebel officers called upon Keith to surrender his. His answer was the same as the Rebels. The opposing officers saluted, wheeled their horses about, and putting spurs to their horses galloped back to their commands. Both sides resumed skirmishing, wounding the two Confederate officers. Keith escaped injury.[20]

The hard-pressed Federals' new battle lines were more compact and assumed an angular shape. One leg ran down North Street about 150 yards towards the Catholic Cemetery, and the other leg ran across a space about 350 yards to the rear of Dufroc (present day 19th) Street and over to North Boulevard. The State Penitentiary buildings and grounds were three or four blocks to the defenders' rear.

Through the smoke blackened fog, someone in Company H saw a body of men moving at a double-quick march down North Street opposite to the Indianians carrying a national flag. The men of Company H called to the other infantrymen to identify themselves. The reported responses varied from: "The 30th Massachusetts," to, "Secesh as HELL!" In either case, the result was the same. The advancing column halted, formed into a line left and gave a thunderous volley, inflicting several casualties upon the Hoosiers while they debated the others' responses. The volley brought sudden understanding to the bully boys of Company H. They leveled their fast loading Merrill rifles and gave the Rebels hell with their own volley, which was quickly followed by another and then began firing at will. Each volley took its toll among the grayclads. The Rebels' reaction to being fired upon by the 21st Indiana stopped their advance and caused them to fall back several yards and regroup with their brigade.

Company H's captain, John Campbell, bragged after the battle that his men "did wonderful execution with their new guns." Companies H and K being fully armed with these breechloading rifles fired much faster than was possible with the muzzle-loading Enfield rifle. Colonel McMillan later wrote the governor of Indiana: "My Merrill rifles went over 45 rounds and the others averaged over 30." Men in the 4th Wisconsin claimed the Hoosiers' rapid firing Merrill rifles without a doubt saved the day.[21]

In the lull that followed this terrific exchange of shots, Captain Campbell of Company H ventured farther out through the acrid, gun-smoke laden fog to the Confederate lines to see what they were doing. He soon returned and reported that it was possible to retake their camp. Returning to his company, he ordered it to advance. As he led his men forward, a minie ball tore into his right leg just below his knee. Falling to the ground, a couple of his men picked him up and carried him to the regiment's field hospital now located near 15th Street west of the Hoosiers' camp where Dr. Ezra Read tended the incoming wounded. Campbell joined two other Hoosier officers already there: Major Hays (who was wounded earlier in the first encounter with Thompson's men) and Company E's Captain William Skelton.

Skelton was having a head wound dressed. The surgeon declared that Skelton must have been holding his head right, because the ball flattened on his forehead and did not penetrate the bone. When admonished to move because of cannon balls hitting all around his tent, Read refused, saying: "It takes eighty cannon balls and six hundred musket balls to kill or wound a man. Now, when the Rebels have shot seventy-five cannon balls and five hundred musket balls at my hospital here, I shall move it, and make them begin again."[22]

Colonel McMillan, learning of the disabilities of his officers, left the Pentagon Barracks hospital to try to lead his men, but his two-month-old wounds made him too weak to mount his horse; therefore he remained in the hospital. Captain William Roy of Company A enjoyed the relative comfort of the barracks hospital where he was confined due to a severe illness. Numerous others of the 21st Indiana's field and line officers were either too ill or, by now, too seriously wounded to lead their men. Sergeant John Adams led Company G into battle because all of the company's line officers were too ill to lead. Malingering soldiers of the 21st voluntarily left the hospitals, took up their weapons, and participated in the fighting near their camp wherever they could find an enemy to shoot at.[23]

As the assault upon the compacted lines eased on the Union left and center, the Confederates maintained their presence with skirmishing and probing for weakness preparatory to launching another assault. About an hour before this lull in the fighting on the Federal left and center, Colonel Henry Watkins Allen's brigade of Ruggles' division encountered the lightly held Federal right flank. Allen's advance was delayed from engaging the enemy at the same time as the center of Breckenridge's forces for nearly an hour due to having to march through a thick oak, sweet-gum, hickory and hackberry forest. The area between the trees was choked with blackberry, honey-locust, prickly greenbrier vines and brambles. Only an occasional small cleared area for farming, surrounded by very thorny twelve-foot thick Cherokee rose hedges, broke the forested area. Only after Allen's command had advanced about three-fourths of the way toward Baton Rouge did the cut and torn brigade come out of the worst of the forest and upon a country lane extension of North Boulevard. (About one-fourth of Allen's command had no shoes; one may imagine the bad condition of their feet after the briars, brambles and thorns clawed them to shreds.) The 21st Indiana's small Company C, cut off from the rest of the defenders, fell back sharpshooting from tree to tree at Allen's men while keeping a respectful distance away from them, which also slowed Allen's advance.

Here, Allen's command first saw a gun from Manning's battery, supported by Captain Eugene Kelty's Zouave Company from the 30th Massachusetts, in a clearing to the north of North Boulevard. It was making ready to move rearward to a cut in the bluff on North Boulevard after being hammered by some of Thompson's men. Allen's men gave three cheers for the Confederacy and rapidly moved on the gun and its infantry supports. Desperately firing a blast of canister at 200 yards, the gun's crew limbered up their gun, and covered by their infantry support they hurried to the rear. They sought the relative safety of the 30th Massachusetts Infantry Regiment, Manning's previously removed gun and the lone Jackass Battery cannon about three hundred yards further to the rear. This running fight inflicted heavy casualties among those involved. It cost the Rebels the services of Captain Bolling R. Chinn, 9th Louisiana Battalion, who was carried to the rear with a leg wound, and the Yankees Captain Eugene Kelty, 30th Massachusetts, mortally wounded as well as several privates on both sides.

Allen's men now pushed forward and southward in an oblique column moving through the woods from North Boulevard. They emerged about a quarter of a mile north and west of a small detachment (one company) of infantry from the 6th Michigan hiding behind board fences and in houses to their south and the second detached gun of the Indiana Jackass Battery.

As Allen's men moved out, Thompson's brigade moved after three or four retreating companies of the 21st Indiana (those not fleeing from Smith) and six companies of the 6th Michigan with fixed bayonets. (Several soldiers in Thompson's brigade had only one or two rounds of ammunition left — many men had empty ammunition boxes.) Thompson began

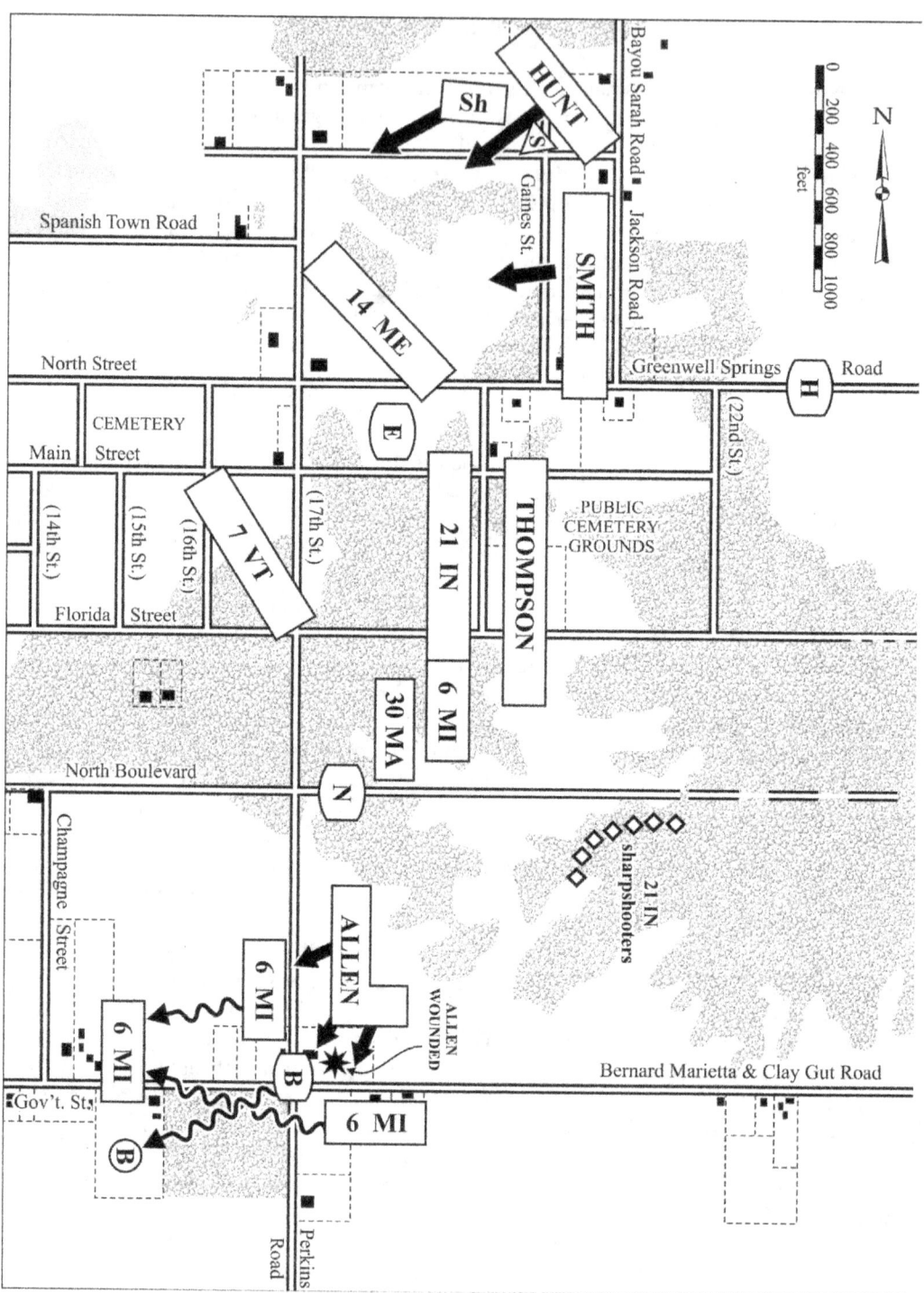

Battle of Baton Rouge, Third Phase. Henry Watkins Allen's brigade is making its oblique charge on the Federal right against Brown's Indiana Jackass Battery and 6th Michigan. The 14th Maine, 21st Indiana and 6th Michigan are holding on the Confederate right and center. The diamonds are the 21st Indiana's Company C separated from the regiment, acting as sharpshooters against any Confederate in range. On the right is a "*" where Colonel Allen was wounded. The Jackass Battery and the 6th Michigan retreated about 200 yards. (Cartographic design by Mary Lee Eggart, based in part upon composite detail from National Archives maps RG-77-Z-293 and RG 77-Z-346–2.)

extending his left, thus coming opposite a portion of the 30th Massachusetts. As the Western men rallied and formed a line of battle to the north and west through the abandoned camp of the 7th Vermont and alongside the 30th Massachusetts position, Thompson received orders to move his brigade to his right to support Hunt's brigade massing for a charge against the Vermont camp.[24]

At the far right, seeing Allen's large force advancing upon them from their left, and with only a detail from the 6th Michigan Infantry supporting them, the Jackass Battery's gun crew on Government Street rapidly limbered up and hauled their exposed piece down the road to join with their other gun at the present-day intersection of 15th and Government streets. The Jackass Battery's Michigan infantry supports helped them to move to the rear. The Wolverines' sharpshooters kept to their posts in the houses and behind their board fences along Government Street to keep the Rebels' attention occupied. Shielded by board paling fences and houses, Allen did not notice the movement of the Jackass Battery's gun to the junction of Perkins and Clay Cut roads and maintained his advance without change.

At the roads' intersection, the artillerists positioned their two 6-pounder guns hub to hub across the intersection. Three infantry companies, A, B and F, from the 6th Michigan with their Company H in reserve, held the intersection and about 150 yards of roadway north and east. The infantry and artillerists hastily erected a low barricade of carts, buggies, chairs, tables, fence boards, barrels, etc. across the intersection of Perkins and Clay Cut roads in front of the artillery where the cannons could defend against an attack coming from those roads and the fields to the north and east.

The woods that Allen's command passed through continued on the left of the defenders and extended toward the city, starting to thin near the east end of Magnolia Cemetery and ending near the rear of the penitentiary at the city limits. It effectively separated Allen's portion of the battlefield and isolated it from the antagonists fighting on the other side of the woods around the cemetery. The Jackass Battery and its 6th Michigan Infantry support, outnumbered three to one, anxiously awaited the approaching foe. The scattered men of the 21st Indiana's Company C stealthily took back to back positions as sharpshooters facing the rear of Allen's command and facing the flank of Thompson's men.[25]

Allen's infantry brigade composed of the 4th Louisiana, eight companies of the 30th Louisiana, 9th Louisiana Infantry Battalion, Company I of the 39th Mississippi, Company I of the 9th Louisiana Partisan Rangers and an odd lot of nearly one hundred partisans from Baton Rouge and vicinity moved forward until entering a clearing in the foggy overgrown woods. Allen was now nearly one and one-half hours late in beginning his attack.

Once in the clearing, the Michigan sharpshooters to the south drew the Confederates' attention. A Rebel scout promptly reported that a large body of men awaited them to the south behind the board fences shielding the sharpshooters. Allen abandoned his thought of following the now distant lone cannon and its 30th Massachusetts supports.

Allen formed his men in column and moved out of the woods, his front (4th Louisiana) to the south, and into the open field to form into a line of battle to advance southward against the Michigan sharpshooters now harassing Allen's column. About halfway through their maneuver from column into line of battle facing south across the open field, someone spotted the guns of the Jackass Battery and their infantry support to Allen's right (southwest and west) in the far corner of the field. From Allen's present position, the seemingly level field took a slow slope upward of about 9 feet leveling off again about thirty yards in front of the position of the guns and the infantry along Perkins Road. (Today, Perkins Road does not exist at this area.)

The 4th Louisiana Regiment (Allen's largest) and the 31st Mississippi, Company I, were in line to attack south. Shouting, "Boys, we must take a battery — we want one!" Allen ordered his infantry regiments (9th Louisiana Battalion and 30th Louisiana Brigade) not in line facing south to form a line facing to attack to the west. He then ordered his brigade forward in an oblique movement across the field in a reversed upside-down "L" shaped formation with the point bearing toward the cannons at the intersection of Government and 15th streets. The Ninth Louisiana Infantry Battalion closely followed alongside the Fourth Regiment. The yelling and cheering Louisianans' charge rolled toward the Hoosier battery and its Michigan supports. Federal rifles, muskets and cannons blazed forth, discharging their contents into the face of their enemy. Down went Lieutenant-Colonel Boyd of the Ninth Battalion with a wounded arm. Leading the charge, Allen again shouted: "Boys we must take those guns." Taking the flag of the 9th Louisiana Battalion, to encourage the inexperienced men in it, he put his spurs to his horse riding directly toward the cannons in the corner of the field. Wildly waving the battle flag, he repeatedly shouted for his men to follow him through the enemy lines.

A storm of case shot and musket balls tore into the massed gray wedge, but it bore down relentlessly on the thin line of bluecoats. As Allen and his first gray-clad ranks topped the slight rise in the ground, Brown's gun crews finished loading double canister into their guns. Brown's cannons roared forth a hellish hail of one-hundred and twelve 1.1-inch iron balls fired at less than twenty yards at the oncoming mass of gray-clads. The balls blasted the entire chest from Allen's horse and tore through Colonel Allen's legs, shattering one leg's bones just above the ankle and passing neatly through the other. The dead mount, its wounded rider and the flag crashed to the earth. An eyewitness said that it appeared as if the whole blast of canister struck Allen and his horse. (He fell a few yards north of the present-day 17th Street intersection with Government Street.) An unscathed Louisianan picked up the fallen flag and bore it over the bodies of his comrades forward to the cannons. Both sides closed in combat, and the battle ebbed and flowed around the Jackass Battery's artillery pieces and the houses surrounded by board fences.[26]

About a half-dozen or more of the 4th Louisiana made a stretcher of abandoned muskets, removed Lieutenant-Colonel Allen from under his mount and carried his bleeding body to the rear. Others in the 4th Louisiana stopped their charge and, gathering around Allen, openly wept at the loss of their beloved commander, while he told them to follow up their success. The 4th Louisiana did not. During the short lull in the fighting, Brown attempted moving his pieces to the rear when another gray avalanche from the 30th Louisiana and elements from the 9th Louisiana and 39th Mississippi swept up and over them, forcing them once again from their cannons.

The 6th Michigan supports began falling back and the Hoosiers ran back to catch their fleeing mules and bring them up to get their guns off the field. They were beaten back nearly 200 yards from their artillery by the Louisianans' and Mississippians' assault. They then saw the Rebels halted and milling about in confusion at 17th Street. The Confederates past that point cheered that they had broken the Federal line as they saw the Michigan flag emblazoned with "These Colors Don't Run" head to the rear. The Wolverines saw the charge halt and then, to their amazement, their triumphant foes began moving to the rear. Captain John Corden faced his three Michigan companies about and joined by the 6th Michigan's Company H (held in reserve) he led an attack with Lieutenant James Brown's Hoosiers to retake their lost position and guns.

John R. Gyles of the St. Helena Rifles Company of the 4th Louisiana placed his flag among the guns as his company swarmed forward to surround them. As the Louisianians attempted to bring off one of the guns, another soldier from the 9th Louisiana mounted the captured piece and waved the regimental flag over it shouting, "We have taken one of the damn Yankee's guns!" Rallying his Hoosiers, and followed by the Wolverine infantry, the pistol and

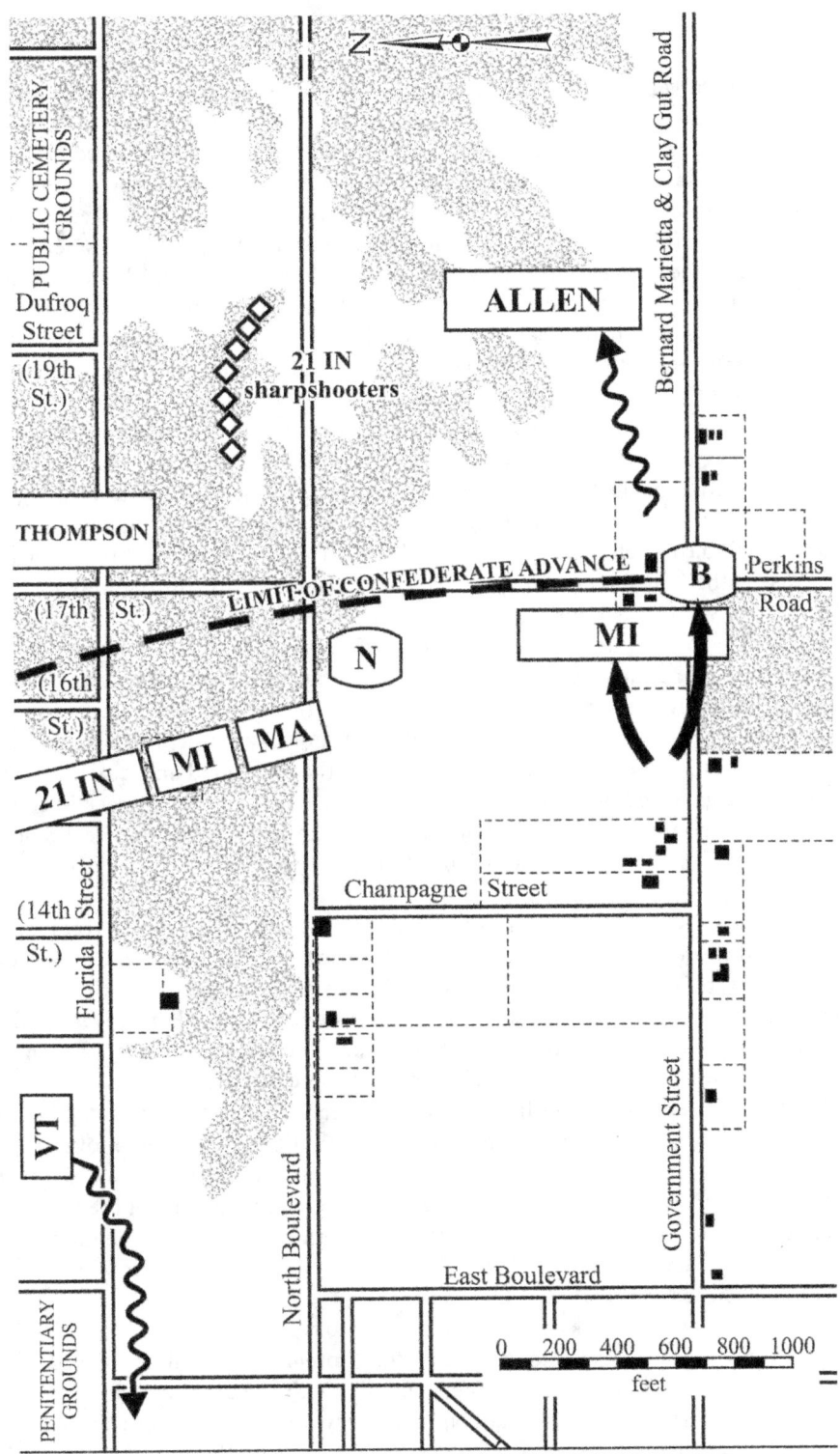

Battle of Baton Rouge, Fourth Phase. The 6th Michigan and Brown's Battery counter attack Allen's halted brigade, badly shaken by the fall of their leader, sending them into full retreat. (Cartographic design by Mary Lee Eggart, based in part upon composite detail from National Archives maps RG-77-Z-293 and RG 77-Z-346–2.)

sword waving Brown yelled, "The Hell you have!" and shot down the Rebel flag bearer as he fought for his guns. Two successive flag bearers shouting: "Hurrah, the guns are ours!" met the same fate from the muskets of the 6th Michigan. The Wolverines captured the colors of the 9th Louisiana Battalion that had waved in seeming victory over them a few minutes before.

During the turmoil, Brown's mules, held thirty yards to his rear, bolted and ran due to the combined effects of musketry, cannon fire, yelling, screaming, and the smell of blood. The running mules took cover with the wasted remnants from the 14th Maine and the cowering 7th Vermont near the penitentiary. At the crossroads, Lieutenant Brown exhorted his men to greater efforts, and using their bare hands they pushed their guns ahead to fire at the confused, demoralized southerners milling about north and east of the intersection to hasten their departure.[27]

Having heard the intense firing to their right, a company of the 30th Massachusetts, supporting a three-gun section of Nims' battery entered the contest. Lieutenant Trull, brought three of Nims' rifled guns up North Boulevard to bring an enfilading fire into the right flank of Allen's command from the intersection of present day North Boulevard and 17th Street.

Loading their 3.67-inch rifles with case and shell, Trull's guns fired obliquely across the battlefield raking the Louisianians in their right flank. (Possibly the third gun from the Jackass Battery joined with them, but the battery's record for this engagement is so fragmented it was not possible to decipher further.) The four companies from the 6th Michigan maintained a steady harassing musket fire at the foe, now 100 yards or more away from the Wolverines' front. Thoroughly demoralized by Allen's fall, faced with additional musket fire, raked with shell, case and canister from the front and flank, not having slept or eaten for sixteen hours, and having marched at least ten miles to reach the battlefield and quickly going into combat, Allen's brigade, led by the 4th Louisiana Regiment, broke and fell back in confusion. One of the hardier members of the 30th Louisiana remarked afterwards that he did not know it took an entire regiment (the 4th Louisiana) to carry one man (H. W. Allen) from a battlefield.

Under fire from Company C's sharpshooters harassing them from the trees, gray-clad comrades helped more than eighty of their wounded leave the battlefield. More than sixty maimed Confederate bodies (thirty-one of them dead) yet lay strewn across the fiercely contested battleground in front of the 21st Indiana's Jackass Battery. Only the dead, dying, and surrendered remained near the front of the battery and the 6th Michigan. The Confederate units engaged on this part of the battlefield reported 166 casualties (37 percent of *all* Confederate casualties at Baton Rouge) from this small area of combat. (Burial details interred thirty-one Confederate dead at this intersection; the wounded bodies were moved to private homes and hospitals for care.) The third and last gray-clad color bearer to fall had seven bullet holes through him. The Rebel charge had severely wounded only one of the Hoosier gunners and slightly wounded a couple of others while working their guns. The 6th Michigan had about twenty casualties during Allen's charge. The Hoosiers and their Wolverine comrades shook their heads in disbelief at the carnage.[28]

While the Rebels pulled back about a quarter mile to regroup and carry off their wounded as able, their officers tried in vain to rally them for another effort against the Federal right. However, their losses in men and top officers coupled with the continued crossfire shelling from the Jackass Battery and the section of Nims' battery prevented the disheartened soldiers from rallying for another charge. By now, the fog had lifted from the battlefield, exposing the wool-clothed men to the hot August sun. The Confederate left wing slowly withdrew further from the battlefield to search for water and shade under a covering fire from four guns of Semmes' battery. The attack on the Federal right was over. After the infantry retired, Semmes' battery moved back (east) and then to the north to support the Confederate center. Aside from sporadic sharpshooting, the battle for the Federal right was over. Droves of civilians who had not left town for fear of Federal looters now fled in any manner they could through downtown then southward along the Highland and River roads.[29]

As the Rebel left flank retired, the Confederate center and right prepared for another move forward. The bully boys of the 21st were regrouping on the left and center near the Catholic Cemetery on North Street and in front of 15th Street to take back their camp when word came to fall back. Angered at this order, they refused to obey. General Williams rode toward Lieutenant Colonel Keith after an unsuccessful attempt at rallying the 7th Vermont. Keith rode over to Williams and asked him if he had given an order to fall back. Williams replied that he had given the order, to which Keith responded: "For God's sake, General, don't order us to fall back! We'll hold this position against the whole damned rebel army." Seeing the fire in Keith's eyes and in those of his men, Williams reconsidered. Pointing to their captured camp, he asked the Hoosiers if they could retake it. Their enthusiastic response made it plain to him that they could. Realizing that retaking the camp could push the thirsty and extremely tired Rebels to the breaking point, he ordered Keith to prepare his men for an advance saying, "I will order up reinforcements, and we will yet annihilate the enemy."[30]

As the men formed in line for their charge, Clark's command of Hunt's and Smith's brigades accelerated their drive forward. Even though they were out of ammunition, Breckenridge ordered Thompson's brigade that had fought the Hoosier bully boys tooth and nail for nearly three hours to fix bayonets and move forward with Clark's valiant boys. As the Rebels' final offensive rolled forward, their muskets and cannons found several good targets among the mounted officers conferring at the left-center of the Hoosier regiment. The Indianian's adjutant, Mathew Latham, while astride his war horse, waving his sword and cheering the men, became a prime target. A combination of grape shot smashing into his face just under his nose and four bullets tearing through his torso brought instant death to the gallant adjutant. As Latham's lifeless body toppled from his rearing horse, Lieutenant-Colonel Keith lurched in his saddle and fell to the ground with a bullet-shattered shoulder. Lying on the ground with his head propped up by an aide, he continued to give orders before being carried from the field; the orders included placing Company B's Captain James Grimsley in command of the 21st Regiment and requesting General Williams to order the 4th Wisconsin to come up and reinforce the Hoosiers.

General Williams received the request and sent it on to the 4th Wisconsin. Trotting his horse up to the Hoosiers, Williams assumed direct command and shouted, "Indianians, your officers are all killed, but I will lead you. Fix bayonets!" Or, according to another source, the general shouted, "Boys, your field officers are all killed or wounded. I will lead you in a charge. The 4th Wisconsin are on the river to support you. I wish to God I had ten thousand of you western thieves!" (From this latter statement, it appears that Williams' finally appreciated the tough, brawling tenacity of Hoosiers, Badgers and Wolverines.)

At this point several companies from the 30th Massachusetts, encouraged by Williams' efforts to personally lead a charge, made their presence dramatically known by rising from their prone positions they had held most of the day and falling into line shoulder to shoulder with the Hoosiers and Wolverines. Lieutenant Trull now turned all six guns of Nims' battery leftward to the northeast, and they began an enfilading case-shot and canister fire into the left flank of Breckenridge's center. The Indianians' Company C now turned their full attention to sniping at Thompson's left flank from their hiding points in the forest.

Emboldened by the previous flight of the 14th Maine, 7th Vermont, 21st Indiana and 6th Michigan, the Confederates dressed their ranks and smartly stepped off towards the bluecoats. As the advancing line of gray approached the colorline of the Hoosiers' camp, the Hoosiers gave three cheers for each regiment now in line with them and three more for Gen-

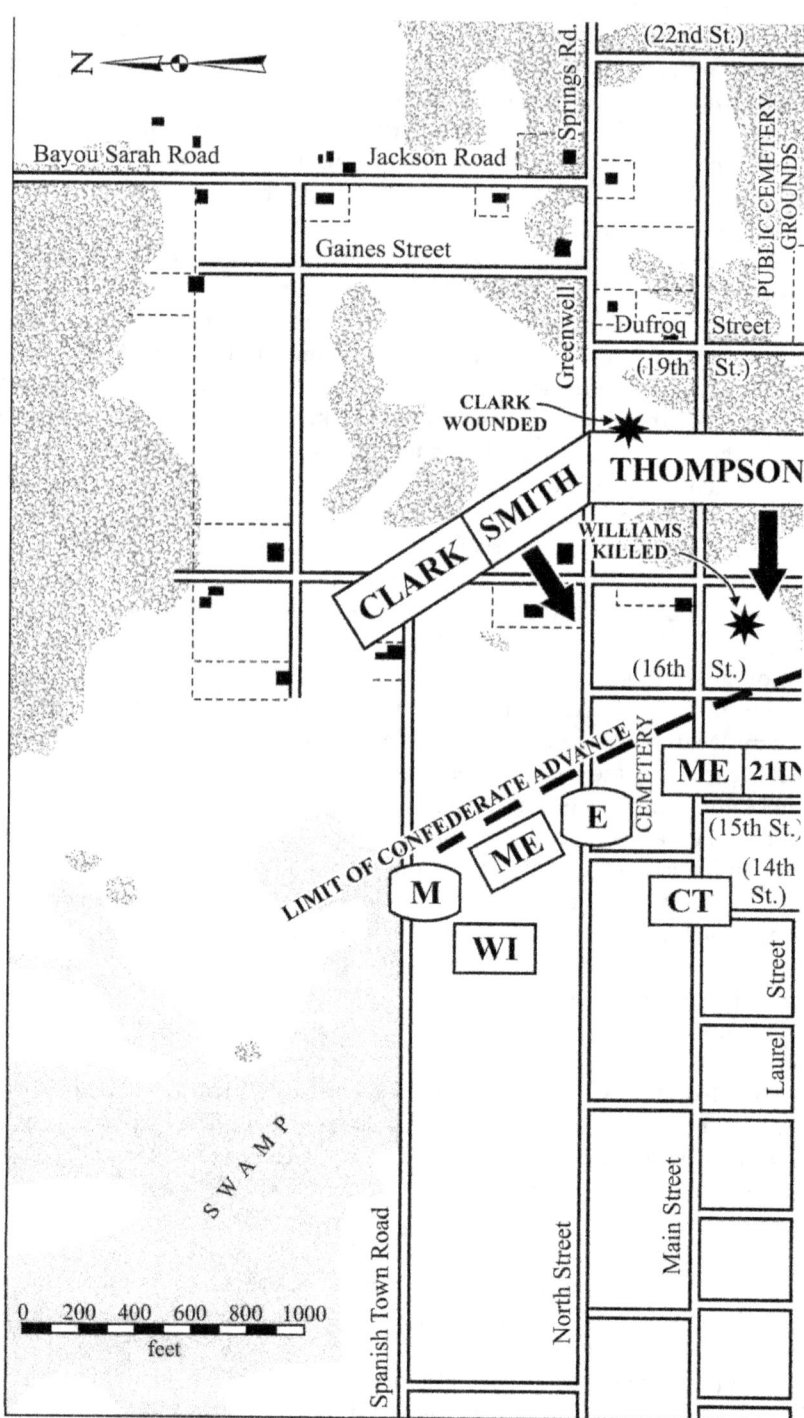

Battle of Baton Rouge, Fifth Phase. General Charles Clark's, Smith's and Thompson's assault on the Federal left. The 14th Maine, 21st Indiana and 6th Michigan fell back before the Confederate's right and center. On the left is an "*" where General Clark (CSA) was wounded; to the right is an "*" where General Thomas Williams (USA) was killed. (Cartographic design by Mary Lee Eggart, based in part upon composite detail from National Archives maps RG-77-Z-293 and RG 77-Z-346–2.)

Six. Baton Rouge

Harper's Weekly rendition of the Battle of Baton Rouge, August 5, 1862. Lieutenant Colonel John Keith, lying wounded on the ground to the left foreground, a hat-less Brigadier-General Thomas Williams, mounted, leads the final charge of the 21st Indiana.

eral Williams. They then braced for the shock of their charge smashing into the Rebels' countercharge. However, as he waved his sword exhorting leading the Hoosiers' do-or-die charge forward, General Williams became the next officer to fall. A bullet through his heart toppled him from his horse. (He fell north of the present day intersection of 17th Street and Main Street.) Corporal Daniel Pippenger from Company A and another soldier from the 21st Indiana carried Williams' body from the battlefield as the Federal battle-line pressed forward.[31]

True to his word, Williams' final messages reached the 4th Wisconsin, 9th Connecticut and the reserve section of Manning's battery. They quickly entered the battle by coming up to the left rear flank of the 14th Maine and the 21st Indiana between present-day 14th and 15th streets. As Manning's battery and Carruth's battery opened a galling fire on the Rebels' right flank and Hudson's Battery, the bully boys of the 21st Indiana and the 6th Michigan advanced in the center of the line from 15th Street.

Further to the Federal left, fire from the two hundred or so fresh infantrymen from the 9th Connecticut and 4th Wisconsin regiments plus canister from Everett's battery sent Hunt's tenacious flanking effort reeling to the rear of the 14th Maine's abandoned camp. Now the *Essex* entered the battle. The combined pounding by the *Essex*'s exploding 11-inch shells, Nims' battery, Manning's battery, Everett's battery, the hard assault by the fresh infantry on their right, a renewed effort led by the re-energized Hoosiers and Wolverines against their center, the loss of their left flank, thirst, fatigue and a lack of ammunition sapped the Confederates' final effort against the Federal left and left-center as it met the resolute Federal charge. The *Essex* ceased firing as the lines closed. The clash was furious, but it was over in about twenty to thirty minutes.

The two lines hit and hung on briefly, battering away like two tired heavyweight

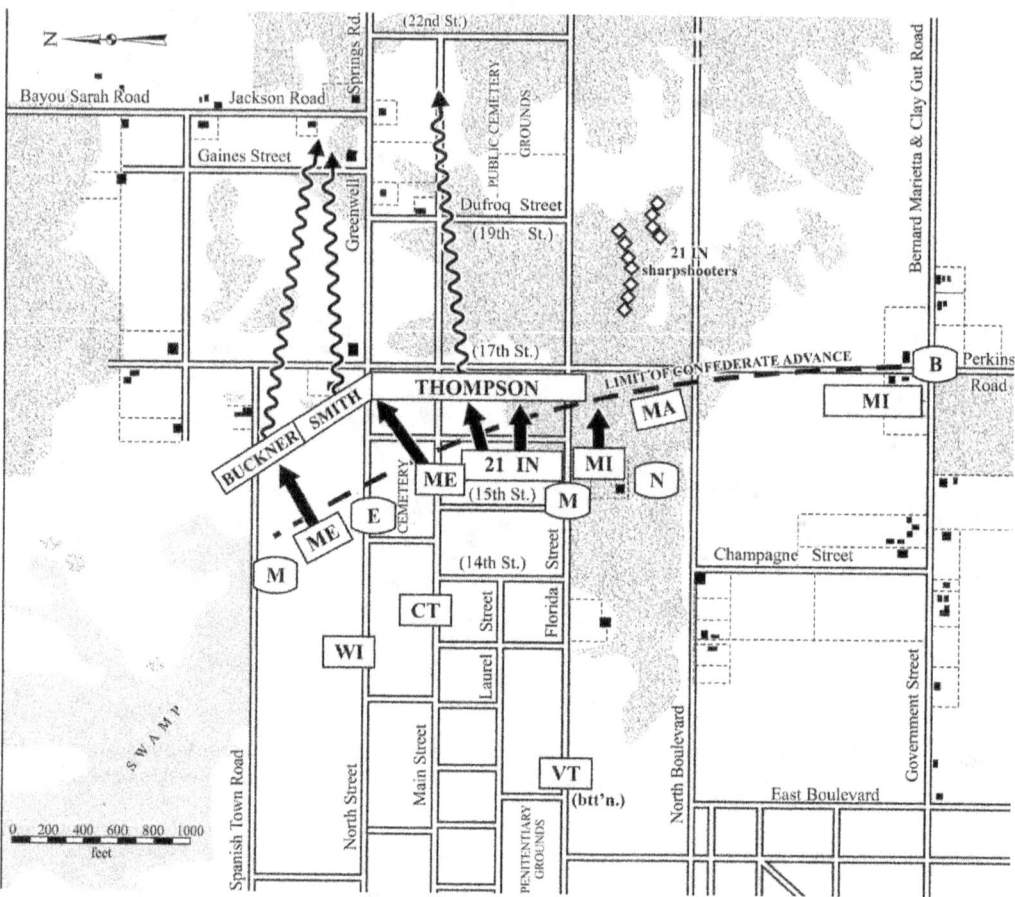

Battle of Baton Rouge, Final Phase. Federal counterattack forces the Confederates to retreat as indicated to point of original contact with the 21st Indiana; Federals advance into their ruined camps. (Cartographic design by Mary Lee Eggart, based in part upon composite detail from National Archives maps RG-77-Z-293 and RG 77-Z-346–2.)

prizefighters. Colonel Hunt fell badly wounded in a thigh. Seeing his brigade commander down, Brigadier General Clark took command, trying to rally his two brigades. Then Clark fell a few yards south of present-day 18th Street and between North and Main streets with a severe wound and ordered his divisions to fall back. Colonel John A. Buckner took over Clark's command. The Confederate and Federal antagonists again broke apart and staggered away from each other. Buckner ordered another charge, which was repelled and the exhausted Confederates retreated. The Federals drifted forward and stopped about 50 yards in the front of the 21st Indiana's camp along 17th Street as the Confederates moved backwards out of the cemetery and away into the fields east and north of town. Mutilated blue and gray clad bodies in various postures of death smeared with blood, dirt and gore covered the ground. A Michigan lieutenant recalled that they made the battle a bloody, quick, decisive defeat the Rebels would remember. After four hard-fought hours, the battle was over.

With Williams' death, the brigade's command devolved to Colonel Thomas Cahill from the 9th Connecticut and Colonel Nathan A. M. Dudley from the 30th Massachusetts as commanders of the Left Wing and the Right Wing, respectively. They were the only participating field officers uninjured during the battle.

The 21st Indiana's Company C, of thirty-nine surviving men and officers, acting as sharpshooters from behind trees, in treetops, log piles, thickets and outbuildings, took advantage of the withdrawal to come into friendly territory and add its rifle fire to the 2nd Massachusetts Battery's fire against the right rear flank of Thompson's departing brigade.[32]

Taking advantage of the stagnated battle and lull in shooting, men from the 21st Indiana began a cautious advance to the eastern edge of their camp, searching for straggling Confederates. As the two armies had separated from each other, Breckenridge had detached men to burn and destroy the food and materials in the camps as his men withdrew through them. If he could not hold the battlefield, he would demoralize the bluecoats by obliterating their supplies.

Captain Charles Jetton from the 7th Kentucky's Company H led one such squad of incendiaries into the camp of the 21st Indiana. Having fired the commissary stores, they prepared to set fire to the sutler's goods, when Jetton paused to try on a pair of pants. Rather than grab a few pairs and run, he insisted on trying them on for a good fit. Seeing the advancing Hoosiers, his men kept urging him to hurry and get away before he was captured. Finally finding a properly fitting pair of pants, he pulled them on, flung his torch on the rest and ran for the rear with bullets whizzing around him like angry bees. He and his men were untouched by the buzzing bullets and safely retreated to their regiment. The Hoosiers took possession of their demolished camp. After spending a few desultory moments sorting through the trash-heap of their former camp and picking up a few salvageable items, the boys retired to a new position where some men from the 7th Vermont and 14th Maine manned a blockade about a quarter mile to the rear of the camps and nearer to the penitentiary (about on line with present-day 13th Street), leaving the heart of the battlefield abandoned by friend and foe alike. (The city limits were at the eastern end of the state penitentiary buildings.)[33]

After the Federals occupied their new defensive line, individuals and two- or three-man groups of Confederates crept into the abandoned campgrounds of the 14th Maine and 21st Indiana — even probing as far as into the campsite of the 7th Vermont — rummaging for food, water, ammunition and clothing. The Indiana and the Maine boys lost their company records, clothing and equipment left in their camps. Federal gunboats again lobbed their shells over the city into the Confederate ranks hovering at the outskirts of the city. Navy spotters on top of the Capitol Building signaled firing directions to the Federal gunboats to direct their fire at the groups of Rebels to keep them from massing for an assault. Breckenridge listened in vain for the sound of firing on the river from the C.S.S. *Arkansas* coming to attack these gunboats, now further decimating his ranks. The only cannons firing from the river exploded their shells among Breckenridge's men — not among the Federals. The broken down ironclad ram *Arkansas* would never arrive.[34]

Knowing his men were exhausted, thirsty and nearly half of them without ammunition, he withdrew his troops about a mile to where his army had formed for their first assault. He had not achieved his plan to catch the Federals between his army and the *Arkansas*, thereby giving the Federals no choice but to surrender. His men would not occupy the castellated Capitol Building that night as previously boasted. Breckenridge pondered his soured attack — ruined by a broken down Confederate warship and a group of very stubborn Westerners. The Federals still held Baton Rouge and the bloody battlefield. Various casualty lists showed the killed and wounded as: Confederate 398 or 471 and Federal 352 or 365. Fifty-six Confederates and thirty-three Federals were shown as missing or captured. The battle resulted in a costly victory for the Federals because they would abandon the town in seventeen days. In spite of Breckenridge's claim of victory, he abandoned the battlefield, leaving the Federals in possession of Baton Rouge, therefore causing a bitter loss for the Rebels. Civilian riders carried word of the outcome of the battle, which reached all citizens of Baton Rouge and outlying homes by noon. The shouted message of "Breckenridge has lost!" stunned the local populace.

However, Breckenridge was mentally unaware that he had lost. Breckenridge boldly wrote that he had won the Battle of Baton Rouge and had driven the Federals from all points all the way back to the U.S. Arsenal Grounds and the river levee. He needed only the *Arkansas* to finish off the river fleet to make his capture of the Federal army complete. He claimed to have occupied the whole of the town and the battlefield. Actually, his army's deepest penetration was to 15th Street on his right flank. Breckenridge reportedly threw his sword to the ground in disgust, turned to the rear and angrily stomped away — hardly the attitude of a victor.

21st Indiana Volunteer Infantry Regimental flag, with the Battle of Baton Rouge honors painted on it. (Battle Flags: Indiana War Memorials Commission.)

Navy spotters atop the Capitol Building signaled the gunboats as to Breckenridge's new position and the naval gunners again had his army's range. Again, soccer-ball sized shells began dropping and exploding among his men. Late in the afternoon, after leaving Partisan Rangers and a small infantry detachment at the Pratt farm to watch the city, he moved his army a little more than a mile further to the rear, and as the navy's guns again reached him, and he withdrew further. Again the navy got his range and he withdrew some miles to the Comite River.

The facts are that Breckenridge's left wing was thoroughly demoralized, shattered, repulsed and out of the fight. Several of Breckenridge's regiments were totally out of ammunition, and the rest of his regiments were very low on ammunition. The Federals retook their camps, salvaged what little they could and moved back to fortified positions hundreds of yards in advance of the arsenal and levee. (Perhaps Breckenridge mistook the penitentiary for the arsenal.) He never occupied the town or its capitol building.

By the 7th of August, Breckenridge would move his army about twenty-five miles north to commence fortifying Port Hudson. By August 31 two companies of infantry, six batteries of light artillery and two companies of partisan rangers would garrison Port Hudson. The balance of Breckenridge's command moved to Camp Moore in Tangipahoa Parish and then to Mississippi.[35]

In summation, the battle was a battlefield victory for the Federals, because they still held the city and had beaten back a larger attacking force. However, it came to be a strategic victory for the Confederacy in that the Federals would be forced to abandon the city in two weeks to concentrate their forces around New Orleans due to a perceived threat of a major attack upon that place. The Confederacy held and began fortifying the bluffs of Port Hudson about 25 miles north of Baton Rouge. The fortifications between Port Hudson and Vicksburg would keep the Mississippi River open to the Confederacy for transshipment of food, goods and war materials from the West to the East for another year.

(See Appendices — Baton Rouge — 2 for 21st Indiana casualties by company and name.)

(See Appendices — Baton Rouge — 3 for summary of Confederate and Federal Casualties.)

Seven

Baton Rouge: Battle Aftermath and Abandonment

On August 5 several of Breckenridge's men reported that they had seen large numbers of Federals moving rearward, several going all the way to the levee, and thought they had beaten the Yankees. Actually, they had seen (A) groups of wounded going from camp hospitals to the main hospitals set up in the shelter of the levee; (B) two diversionary movements by the 30th Massachusetts to the rear to try and draw the Confederates into the open to fight; (C) the flight of most of the 7th Vermont Regiment and a few men from the 14th Maine; (D) the short retreat by the 6th Michigan and Jackass Battery before they counterattacked: and, (E) the Federals forming defensive lines at the rear of the penitentiary after the battle.[1]

After Breckenridge withdrew, the Federal officers argued as to who should assume overall field command of the brigade to replace Williams. The immediate attention for a commanding field officer turned to the 21st Indiana, but Colonel McMillan was in the hospital suffering from his previous buckshot wounds. However, upon learning of their victory, he wanted to ride out and take his men a demijohn of whiskey. He was informed that if he did that, he would be called a coward because he was too wounded to fight! He remained in bed.

For a while after being shot, Lieutenant-Colonel Keith rested in a make-shift litter on the battlefield and gave advice to his remaining line commanders (a captain, some lieutenants and sergeants) and to the commanders of other regiments. It was only when Breckenridge's army fell back that Keith finally agreed to be carried to the barracks hospital by the levee. Keith could not now command. After the remaining colonels decided who had the earliest date of his rank, brigade command devolved to Colonel Thomas Cahill of the 9th Connecticut. Cahill immediately ordered all troops to fall back and form a defensive line about one hundred yards from the rear of the camps of the Maine, Indiana and Michigan men. Getting the men in order, Cahill moved them back again to a line parallel to the river about 50 yards east of the penitentiary buildings.[2]

Cahill rearranged the regiments in this order, from left to right: 4th Wisconsin, Indiana Jackass Battery, 4th Massachusetts Battery, and 21st Indiana in the rear of the batteries. To their right for about one-half mile were two-gun artillery sections from the 2nd and the 6th Massachusetts covering each road leading east. The 14th Maine, 7th Vermont, 6th Michigan, 30th Massachusetts and 9th Connecticut infantry supported these battery sections and guarded the roads. Men from all regiments went to work throwing up barricades across the roads and fortified themselves inside the houses lining the north to south cross street in front of their new line. The Badgers and the two nearby battery sections took advantage of being on a slight rise in the ground and fortified it in a circular fashion.[3]

Army details pressed local contraband Negroes into service to gather the wounded of both sides and bring them inside the street barricades to the rear of Baton Rouge where their injuries could be better tended. Several wounded Rebels, especially, those from the Louisiana regiments, who had family in Baton Rouge, received the most loving, if not the best care in the town. Federal surgeons cared for both the Confederate and the Federal wounded. After receiving treatment by friends, family or surgeons, contrabands transported by stretcher or wagon both Rebel and Union wounded alike to the levee. There the wounded awaited transports to New Orleans and its hospitals.[4]

Several Hoosier enlisted men claimed their officers showed the "white feather" by not leaving their sick-beds to do battle as the enlisted men had done, being especially critical of their "fat Colonel Whiskey," (McMillan). The 21st Indiana was one of the more fortunate, or unfortunate, regiments (depending upon one's point of view) in that it had more than eight hundred of its men and officers available for duty in Baton Rouge on that fateful day.

The other Federal regiments had one-half or more of their men in their camp or brigade hospitals due to illness. Several of the Wisconsin and Michigan high-ranking officers languished in New Orleans under arrest pending the results of charges brought against them by Williams; in turn, they waited to resolve their complaints against Williams. The sickness and absences left the Federals' effective manpower reduced to little more than one-half strength. Even including the men who left the hospitals and helped fight, the total number of effective Union fighting men was about 20 percent less than the number of Confederates. The Confederates had an advantage of more men, including slightly more than 200 Partisan Rangers plus 125 guerrillas from among the Baton Rouge citizens.[5]

The next day (the 6th) about four hundred contrabands went to work burying the dead. The contraband Negroes buried both Federals and Confederates in shallow trenches near where they had fallen. Piles of dead artillery horses lay among the dead and wounded men. The horses' burials would wait. A soldier going out to his picket post recognized a citizen of Baton Rouge lying dead in his gray gear near the 21st Indiana's camp where he had sold milk to the Hoosier only a day before the battle. One dead Rebel's bloated body was found within the camp of the 14th Maine with his hands clutching a loaf of bread he had taken from the camp's bakery. Other mangled corpses lay blown in half by artillery; body fragments and strings of intestines splattered over the earth due to shell-blasts tearing off a man's side or abdomen, faces shot off, arms, legs and heads blown away, stretched bloated skin turned black from the sun and gunpowder and pools of dark blood everywhere on the battleground. One dead Federal soldier had his bayonet buried in a dead Confederate's body; the dead Rebel still clenched his pistol that had put a small hole in the dead Yankee's forehead.

About a dozen Confederate bodies, both dead and wounded, were recovered from behind one tomb complex in Magnolia Cemetery topped by effigies of children. Contrabands hired for the work picked up the body parts and mixed friend and foe alike. The main burial trenches were dug in the vicinity of Brown's Jackass Battery's and 6th Michigan Battalion's valiant stand at Government Street and Perkins Road and the fearsome battleground in and around Magnolia Cemetery.

The hot August sun heating up the bodies caused an awful stench. Wearing cloths over their noses the contrabands would pick up a body by its hands and feet, swinging it into their wagon, repeating the process and the motions until the wagon was full. Then they would drive the wagon to the burial trenches and repeat the process in reverse, haphazardly stacking the bodies on one another until the trench was full. Other contrabands filled in the full trench with enough earth to cover the pit and mound it about a foot high. Due to decomposition and the acceleration of odor, by the 7th and 8th of August, the bodies farther out from the main battlefield were merely covered over in roadside ditches by pulling the sides of the ditch down over them. (These bodies washed out in the next rain, making later reburial in a trench necessary, regardless of the smell.)

Sightseers and souvenir hunters from the Federal forces prowled the battlefield among the bodies. Private T. W. Gillette from Company I, 4th Wisconsin, recorded gathering a number of swords, a pistol and an old U.S. Dragoon hat with a plume in it. Gillette and some of his fellow Badgers encountered a soldier from the 21st Indiana who was looking for his company lieutenant, who fell at the first volley of the fighting in a cornfield. Venturing further away from Baton Rouge and sneaking past a Rebel picket, they arrived at a corner of a cornfield a considerable distance from the Federal lines. At the edge of the field lay the bodies of Company A's Lieutenant Charles Seely and Sergeant John Bovington. The Rebels had thoroughly scavenged the bodies of clothing, shoes, personal items and equipment. Being unable to revive the dead or drag the bodies to within their own lines because of the Rebel picket, the Hoosier and the plume-hatted Badger crept back to their lines.

Men from Nims' battery came upon four wounded Confederate artillerists: a sergeant, a corporal and two privates. They were from Semmes' battery and an exploding round of case shot that hit one of their guns had injured them. The sergeant had a piece of iron enter his shoulder and travel down his back, which he begged Sergeant Hammonds of Nims' battery to cut out. Hammonds refused for fear that he would kill the Rebel by doing so. Hammonds saw to it that the prisoners got water for which the Rebel corporal gave him a bowie knife in thanks. As Nims' men helped the wounded Confederates to a field hospital, the corporal stated that they had been told the Yankees would cut their throats instead of taking them prisoner and caring for their wounds. Days afterward, scouting parties were still finding dead and wounded Rebels in the countryside.

An 1855 tomb in Magnolia Cemetery with the sculpture of children atop it behind which dead Confederates were found.

Few Union soldiers or their families could afford the embalming cost of $185.00 and shipping cost of $300.00 to send a body back home. Identifiable dead Federals in the burial trenches had wooden markers with their names placed over them. (The dead Federals were reburied in the National Cemetery established in 1863 across Florida Street south of Magnolia Cemetery.)[6]

The soldiers continued to man the barricades and guard prisoners. Confederate prisoners asked their captors how many regiments of the Indiana troops took part in the battle. They were astonished to learn that there was only one Indiana regiment there, and they had met the Hoosiers at three places on the battlefield. One Confederate officer declared: "If it weren't for those damned Indianians, Baton Rouge would have been captured." Colonel McMillan sent a letter to the firm of Merrill Thomas and Co. in Baltimore wherein he extolled the virtues of the Merrill rifle stating: "his boys armed with the Merrill rifle fired at least 50% more shots than those armed with the Enfield or Austrian rifles during the battle of August 5, 1862 at Baton Rouge."[7]

On the 6th, while soldiers and contrabands worked to strengthen the defenses and care for the wounded, the navy proceeded upriver looking for the ram *Arkansas*. Commodore William D. "Dirty Bill" Porter led the way with his iron clad gunboat, *Essex*. Finding the *Arkansas* about four to five miles upstream, Porter opened fire. According to Captain Porter, he advanced up to within 300 yards of the *Arkansas* and holed her fourteen times, before his shells set her afire and sank her. Reports from naval officers in gunboats accompanying the *Essex* on her victorious cruise and the Confederates manning the *Arkansas* differed greatly from Porter's grandly embellished account as to the circumstances of *Arkansas*' destruction.[8]

The Rebel accounts agreed in that the *Arkansas* had engine trouble and after a series of repairs had just gotten underway when she encountered the little Federal flotilla coming upstream at about two to three miles distant. The *Essex* opened a random fire from about two miles away. Attempting to build up speed, an engine again failed, causing the *Arkansas* to lose speed and maneuvering ability. The vessel's stern swung around pointing downstream and the craft grounded on the riverbank. The crippled *Arkansas* fired her stern guns at the approaching *Essex*, which caused that vessel to slow and approach with caution. Knowing that he could not win a fight by facing the enemy with his very thinly armored stern (only boiler plate) and his two 6.4-inch bore stern rifles, Lieutenant Henry Stevens, commanding the *Arkansas*, gave orders to scuttle and set fire to the vessel.[9]

Her crewmen smashed the ram's machinery with axes, opened the magazines, and scattered cartridges, fused shells and cotton from between the bulkheads about the deck. They loaded her guns and ran them out so they would fire as the flames reached them. As the flames took hold, the men left their vessel. Going ashore, they marched off overland toward Port Hudson.

"Dirty Bill" Porter halted his cautious approach when the *Arkansas* first fired her stern guns. When she stopped firing, he very slowly came ahead again while lobbing an occasional shell at her, but missing his target. When he was within three or four hundred yards of the ram, he could plainly see she was on fire, and her crew was all ashore. The *Arkansas*' guns began discharging from the heat, and Porter backed off. As he withdrew, the *Arkansas* blew up. The Federal flotilla returned to Baton Rouge where newly arrived transports were unloading supplies and officers.[10]

Earlier, word reached General Butler at New Orleans that the Confederate forces were attacking Baton Rouge. Knowing that the ranking officers in Baton Rouge were sorely needed by their men, General Butler released the field officers of the 4th Wisconsin and the 6th Michigan from their arrest in New Orleans. He ordered them to speed to Baton Rouge. They arrived the day after the battle.[11]

Colonel Halbert Paine of the 4th Wisconsin relieved Colonel Cahill as commander of the post. Paine immediately ordered the troops to begin pulling back from their barricades to the Arsenal Grounds, leaving outposts composed of men from the 21st Indiana at the barricades guarding all the street approaches into town. Lieutenant Godfrey Weitzel's U.S. Engineers laid out plans for an earthwork fortification around the entire Arsenal Grounds. The officers named this bastion Fort Williams, after the fallen leader, General Thomas Williams, who in death was a hero— even to the men of the 21st Indiana for leading them in their final charge at the enemy. The fort encompassed the present day site of the Pentagon Barracks, Capitol Building and grounds, officer's burying grounds and the Old Arsenal Museum.[12]

Also on the 6th, the more severely wounded were carried aboard steamers for the trip downriver to New Orleans and its hospitals. General Williams' body, a military honor guard, numerous Federal wounded, three Confederate wounded and a few other passengers left Baton Rouge bound for New Orleans aboard the steamer *Lewis Whiteman*. During the trip downstream, the *Whiteman* purposely changed course to ram the sloop of war *Oneida* about fifty miles north of New Orleans. The collision sank the *Whiteman*. The *Sciota* reported that an hour before the collision with the *Oneida*, she had narrowly avoided being hit by the *Whiteman* as well.[13]

Crewmen from the *Oneida* and the gunboat *Pinola* saved most of the wounded, including the 21st Indiana's lieutenant Thomas Bryant, Co. H, and Lieutenant Thomas Grinstead, Co. K. General Williams' body was recovered from the river. A female passenger and three of the honor guard were among the drowned. The *Oneida* took the rescued men to New Orleans and its hospitals. There Lieutenant Bryant's arm was found to have "mortified," probably from soaking in the muddy river water. A surgeon amputated his arm at the shoulder to save his life, but he died in a few days despite the surgeon's best efforts. Lieutenant Grinstead, who had a leg broken by a minieball, swam to safety from the sinking ship. He, too, died of his infected wound in a New Orleans hospital.[14]

Back in Baton Rouge, Captain James Grimsley retained his temporary command of the 21st Regiment, pending the recuperation of its field officers. He sent home the bullet-torn clothes he had worn in the battle for his wife to exhibit as evidence of his bravery. Also, like many others, he picked up battlefield trophies to send back home. He proudly proclaimed that he, too, rode an imported horse from Kenner's stables (recently liberated from Ashland Plantation south of Baton Rouge). Since the 21st Indiana's and the 14th Maine's men and officers had lost most all of their camp gear to the torches, bullets and bayonet punctures of the Rebels, they had to make do with what they could find in the city. Fortunately for some, a few townspeople living alongside the street barricades invited some of the 21st Indiana's officers and men to rest inside their homes, and shared a little food with them.[15]

Finally, on the 10th of August, the 21st Indiana received orders to report to Fort Williams where they occupied the barracks and Arsenal yard. Being in close quarters with the other troops, they turned out to help with the fortifications. It did not take the military authorities long to bring in contrabands from neighboring plantations to do the pick and shovel work. In spite of a few hundred contrabands working on the earthworks, the Hoosiers heartily took on construction work, which the "drafted" contrabands did more slowly.[16]

Details from the occupying Federal regiments made forays into the nearby countryside. The 9th Connecticut's Company H found five artillery caissons full of ammunition and brought them into the Arsenal. Rebel stragglers and Rangers hovered in the area, and they made quick harassing raids up to the Federal outposts. The gunfire kept the pickets nervous, and they raised false alarms fearing another attack upon the city. Colonel Paine, commanding the brigade, was prompted to publish General Order No. 6. This order, among other things, prohibited citizens from being admitted within Fort Williams, prohibited the discharge of firearms except at the river's edge and then only with permission of the regiment's commander and prohibited officers from straying from the fort or their campgrounds.[17]

Those not working on the fortifications did guard duty in the new trenches. On the 13th of August in addition to constructing a fort, the base commander ordered a clear fire zone around Fort Williams for the river gunboats. Soldiers fell to work with gusto in razing homes and businesses a short distance east and a block south of the fort. After breaking down the home's doors, they broke into cabinets and drank whatever alcoholic potion they could find. If they could wear any clothing they found, the vandals took it. After the drinking and looting, the bully boys would gather the furniture, pile it into a room on the first floor and set it afire. The fires burned frame buildings to their foundations and gutted brick buildings. The artillery batteries shot down the brick walls. The soldiers wanted no mistake in finding clear targets for their rifles and, especially, the 11-inch shells from the fleet. To prevent accidental shelling of their own men, Colonel Paine ordered signal flags mounted by day and signal lights mounted by night to align with the ground occupied by the Federal troops around Fort Williams.[18]

It was not long before the looting spread from razed houses to abandoned houses throughout the town. Looters took what valuables they could find and items for personal comfort or luxury such as pillows, linens, candlesticks, shaving stands, razors, cooking pots, etc. The plunderers tore or cut up ladies clothing, smashed mirrors and furniture, tore books apart or threw them into fires. They smashed china wash basins, plates, cups, bowls, saucers, and chamber pots. Officers (supposedly above such base activity as looting) filled their tents with furniture from deserted houses. The Western men blamed the Yankees for the pillaging, and the Nutmeggers blamed the Westerners. Colonel McMillan wrote to General Butler complaining about the vandalism, stealing, and complete lack of discipline on the part of the Eastern troops. Lest he incur Butler's disfavor, he closed his letter by stating that the *Essex* was at Bayou Sara getting some sugar.[19]

Because General Butler had sent orders to Baton Rouge to burn the city to the ground rather than surrender it to Confederate forces, the soldiers thought they had implied consent for pillaging and vandalizing before they burnt the homes and contents. Colonel Paine disagreed with Butler's orders in the name of humanity, since carrying them out would destroy the state orphanage, deaf and dumb institute, the insane asylum and penitentiary. On August 19, Butler relented in ordering the destruction of the entire town unless it needed to be burned as a defensive action. He only ordered off the contents of the library and the marble statue of George Washington from the Capitol Building, thereby, liberating the founding father from the "Halls of Rebellion."[20]

While these events were taking place, General Breckenridge sent a message to Colonel Paine requesting that they be allowed to bury their dead. Colonel Paine informed him that that matter was being attended to by his troops. Breckenridge also wrote expressing his concerns that the Federals were recruiting Negro slaves as soldiers to be armed and used against the Confederates. He stated that if the war could not be conducted in accordance with the rules of civilized nations that the black flag would be raised and no quarter given. Colonel Paine responded: "No Negro slaves had been armed against you in this Department." Further, he stated that he would arm no Negroes: "unless in accordance with the laws of the United States."

Paine continued: "I am informed that a corps of blacks fought against us in the recent battle of Baton Rouge, and that our pickets were found tied to trees shot through the head, and I am sorry to remind you that a most barbarous system of guerrilla warfare is authorized by your officers and practiced by your troops in this department.... Nevertheless, I shall never raise that flag [black flag] which all civilized nations abhor; but I shall try to maintain the flag which you have too often promised to defend." (Several Union soldiers reported seeing their Confederate foes flying a black flag, which meant that no quarter would be given or taken. In reality this was the battle flag of the Kentucky Regiments under Breckenridge's command, The Orphan Brigade. The flag was navy blue having a dark-red Roman Cross with thirteen white stars in the cross. When damp, limp, fog or smoke shrouded, the flag looked black.)[21]

There were two other mentions of Negroes in the fighting at Baton Rouge. During a charge by the 21st Indiana near the graveyard, a Negro lying behind a tree was seen reloading a rifle he had just fired at the Rebels. When asked what he was doing, he replied that he was: "Just doin' a little picketin.'" The other mention of a Negro's participation has already been related in Chapter 6. This man could have been Peter Vertrees, who saw combat with the 6th Kentucky Regiment. About a dozen Negroes served in various capacities with the Tennessee, Kentucky and Mississippi regiments, mostly as personal servants or skilled craftsmen.[22]

"Orphan Brigade" Flag (reproduction): 3rd, 4th, 5th, 6th & 7th Kentucky Regiments.

Two weeks after the battle, orders came to leave the city. Butler decided it was better to lose this prize rather than risk losing New Orleans should the rumored all-out Confederate assault on from north and west of New Orleans prove true. Preparations began on the 18th to abandon Baton Rouge. Teamsters began loading any excess equipment in the camps of the 9th Connecticut, 30th Massachusetts, 7th Vermont and 4th Wisconsin and hauling it off to waiting steamers. By the 20th, non-essential units (sutlers, commissary stores, bands and instruments, confiscated cotton and sugar, and the 7th Vermont Regiment) left the town aboard river steamers.[23]

Emboldened by the departures observed the day before, the 9th Louisiana Battalion, Partisan Rangers, charged the Baton Rouge picket lines. Lieutenant Samuel "Ed" Armstrong had just finished giving his Company I pickets their orders for the day, when he claimed he saw more than 150 Rangers trotting toward him. Drawing his pistol, he fired, calling the guard and deployed them as skirmishers. Firing as they fell back toward town, Armstrong sent for help. Two companies from the 21st Indiana came up at the double-quick. The Hoosier battalion halted the Rangers' advance at the edge of town on the former battlefield. The U.S.S. *Mississippi* fired a broadside over the town at the Partisan Rangers, resulting in their departure at a gallop. No matter how speedy their departure the Rangers managed to take 29 head of beef and 40 horses with them. On August 21, at 1 o'clock in the afternoon, Lieutenant Armstrong brought his pickets in from the outskirts of Baton Rouge. His little detachment joined the Union forces aboard the transport steamer *Sallie Robinson* and abandoned the city to the Rebels.[24]

On the 23rd, Confederate forces again entered Baton Rouge and occupied it. However, after only three days the 4th Louisiana Infantry was ordered out and to report for duty at Port Hudson. That place was ordered to be fortified. Orders instructed the soldiery not to make contact with the enemy — by land or by river. Secrecy was of prime importance to get the fortifications established without raising Federal suspicions.

The Hoosiers traveled down the Mississippi River the entire night. Those lucky enough to have funds, secured supper and breakfast aboard the steamer for fifty cents. The next morning, they arrived at Camp Parapet behind the Parapet Line of fortifications above Carrollton, Louisiana, a little above New Orleans. Its occupants called it Camp Death due to the fevers that prevailed among its tenants.[25]

While the 21st Indiana and 6th Michigan previously had received cautious laurels for their part in the defense of Baton Rouge, the 7th Vermont, Major W. C. Holbrook, commanding, requested a hearing into their charges of misconduct and General Butler's refusal to grant them military honors for their regimental flag. The ensuing hearings and inquiry would carry on for the months of September, October and November. Butler forwarded Holbrook's request to Washington, D.C., asking for an impartial court of inquiry, noting that Major Holbrook's duties of the day kept him from the action and stated: "As there has been some rivalry of feeling, I do not think it would be best to detail a court from the officers of the regiments at Baton Rouge."

The governor of Vermont, Frederick Holbrook, leaped into the dispute with as much vigor as his office allowed. He applied political pressure by writing the secretary of war stating that the charges were grossly unjust, and by insisting on an impartial court being sent from Washington to investigate the charges. The governor's relationship (father) to the 7th Vermont's Major William C. Holbrook obviously increased the intensity of the political pressure being brought to clear the sullied name of his son's regiment.[26]

Without waiting for a delegation from Washington, Butler convened a court of inquiry. The court found: 1. The regiment was reduced in strength due to sickness; 2. They mustered only 250 effectives at the battle; 3. They fired only one volley that day; 4. The one volley was fired into the 21st Indiana; 5. Their colonel was then killed, and the regiment ran; 6. Lieutenant-Colonel Fullam led his men into a ravine 200 yards to the rear of their camp for shelter; 7. Two-fifths of the regiment never went back into any kind of action that day; 8. The balance of the regiment [about 150 men] took part in sporadic action on the right flank.

General Butler conveyed this information to Governor Holbrook. He also told him that since the regiment's colors were not lost to the enemy, and the surviving officers of those who had actually participated in the battle behaved with gallantry, and the new commander of the 7th Vermont, Major W. C. Holbrook, would doubtless lead the men of his regiment with honor, the regiment's colors would be restored to them. However, when they had their flag restored in November, Butler banished Holbrook and his regiment to duty at Fort Pickens across the bay from Pensacola, Florida.[27]

(*For text of letters lauding the conduct of the 21st Indiana Infantry Regiment during the battle of Baton Rouge, see Appendices.*)

Eight

Swamp Life, New Orleans and Camp Delights

The Federal campgrounds behind the Parapet Line covered the area from the line eastward about three miles to Carrollton. The Confederates built the fortifications to defend New Orleans from an upstream attack. A large fort anchored each end of the line of fortifications. The Rebel builders had christened the earthworks Fort John Morgan to honor the leader of Morgan's Raiders. After the Federals occupied the works, they renamed them the Parapet Line.[1]

The Parapet Line of earthen fortification stretched from the Mississippi River to a swamp near Lake Pontchartrain. The line ran roughly parallel to present day Causeway Boulevard in Metairie, Louisiana. The Main Redoubt anchored the line at the Mississippi River (near where Ochsner Hospital is today). The saw-tooth shaped packed earth parapet was nine feet high with a six feet deep and thirty feet wide ditch in front of it. Another redoubt anchored the line at the swamp. A roadway passed through the Main Redoubt over bridges placed across the redoubt's moat. The New Orleans, Jackson and Great Northern Railway pierced the line between the Main Redoubt and the swamp.[2]

After disembarking from the *Sallie Robinson,* at the Parapet Line, the 21st Indiana pitched their tents in a muddy cornfield. They camped on the Parapet Line for two days, but that was too long for the westerners. In their two days there, the western men had several quarrels with the Nutmeggers and with Brigadier-General John W. Phelps' formative Negro Brigade. In two days the Hoosiers received orders to move their camp two miles south to Camp Lewis, nearer the town of Carrollton. Rumor had it that the new campground was on higher and drier ground. Naturally, they moved in a pounding rainstorm that soaked even the supposed high ground. Those first into the camp among the new arrivals found board fences, pulled them apart and placed the planks on the ground so they could sleep off the mud.[3]

After their arrival, the higher command reorganized the brigade. Colonel Halbert E. Paine of the 4th Wisconsin was brevetted brigadier general, and he was given command of the 4th Wisconsin, 21st Indiana, its battery, and the 14th Maine. The Hoosiers cheered that Colonel Paine received command over them and not some easterner. The Indianians' Companies E and G, due to their training in heavy artillery at Fort McHenry, had detachments assigned to man the heavy guns in the Main Redoubt of the Parapet Line's fortifications. The 21st Indiana was not in the area long before they reestablished their reputation as devils. Whenever the men could get a pass, they would ride the train into New Orleans and have a high time. A New Orleans street vendor accused Private Rueben Miller from Company H of taking some articles from his stand at the corner of Perdido and Barrone streets in New Orleans. The Provost Guard arrested Miller for theft; he was tried and exonerated.[4]

Entreated by residents from Lafourche, St. Charles and Terrebonne parishes to protect their homes from raids on the west bank of the Mississippi River, General Richard Taylor ordered Colonel Edward Waller and his 13th Texas Cavalry Battalion plus an irregular Louisiana battalion made up of militia from Terrebonne and St. Charles parishes and Partisan Rangers from Rapides Parish led by "General" John G. Pratt to perform such duty (Taylor's own Fashion Plantation was raided and looted by the Yankees). Under orders from Colonel Edward Waller, Pratt's partisans ambushed the New Orleans, Opelousas and Great Western train bound for Algiers. To do this Pratt's men first captured guards from the 8th Vermont Infantry posted at Boutte Station. Then the Rebels threw a rail switch near the station to sidetrack the approaching train. A parked passenger car on the siding would serve to halt the train. The Rebels quickly hid in bushes and behind the station alongside the track.

As the train entered the sidetrack, Pratt's men rose from concealment and fired a thunderous volley of musketry, sweeping across two flat-cars carrying a guard force from the 8th Vermont Infantry and a 12-pounder howitzer being pushed ahead of the engine. Instead of braking, the panicked engineer opened the throttle, crashing his train through the empty passenger car blocking the siding. The impact sent living and dead Vermonters plus the howitzer flying through the air into the brush and mud. The train sped on through another switch and back onto the main line. The engineer fled for Algiers with his cargo of bleeding survivors. The 8th Vermont lost thirty-five men either dead or wounded. The Rebels found seven Germans among the survivors from the crash who had enlisted in the 8th Vermont at New Orleans. The militia and partisans accused the Germans of deserting from Confederate service, found them guilty at a drum-head court-martial, forced them to dig their own grave trench, and then executed them by firing squad.[5]

After Pratt's men completed their depravities, Pratt detached a guard detail to watch over the surviving Yankees. He then led his band of partisans westward down the railroad right of way to Bayou Des Allemandes. Arriving before the railroad station there, using deceit instead of force of arms, Pratt duped 138 officers and men from the 8th Vermont into surrendering. They also captured another 12-pounder howitzer and two Ellsworth breechloading cannons. After securing the area, Pratt split his command into two smaller groups to better evade capture. The larger group of infantry took the prisoners and the spoils of the Vermonters' looting and moved on west toward Camp Pratt, a prison camp on Bayou Teche. They camped a few miles away for the night, and the smaller mounted Ranger group camped near the station.

About 10 P.M., the 21st Indiana departed Camp Lewis to rescue the Vermonters. The Indianians boarded the steamer *Morning Light* and traveled about twenty miles upstream where they landed. By a fast march, they arrived at the Boutte Station at 10 A.M. They surrounded the Partisan Rangers' camp and opened fire on them. Without firing a return shot, the guerrillas abandoned their camp, horses and prisoners and fled into the swampy woods. The Hoosiers rescued eight or nine wounded Vermonters, burned the house that had held the prisoners, rounded up the horses and abandoned camp equipment, and started back to their transport. On their trek back to the waiting steamship, the Vermonters told their rescuers about their inhumane treatment at the hands of their captors. This information quickly made its way up the chain of command back at Carrollton and New Orleans.[6]

On September 8, the 21st Indiana, the Jackass Battery, the 4th Wisconsin, the 1st Maine Battery plus details from the 14th Maine and 9th Connecticut boarded four transports, the *St. Maurice, Morning Light, Laurel Hill* and *General Williams* (née *Benton*). They steamed up the Mississippi River escorted by the U.S.S. *Mississippi* searching for Pratt's mounted partisans and Colonel Edwin Waller's cavalry. About two miles below St. Charles Courthouse (present day Hahnville), the 9th Connecticut and the 14th Maine went ashore. The *Laurel Hill* and *General Williams* with the 21st Indiana and the 4th Wisconsin steamed about five

Eight. Swamp Life, New Orleans and Camp Delights

miles above St. Charles Courthouse farther upstream before disembarking their men and artillery. The Federals' objective was to bag the Rebel cavalry between their two forces.[7]

Half of the companies from the 21st Indiana, under Captain William Roy, moved into position near the river extending in line to the edge of a swamp west of the rest of the forces. A detachment from the 4th Wisconsin completed the line. The Jackass Battery moved its three 6-pounder guns into place supporting Roy and the 4th Wisconsin detachment. Captain Edward McLaflin marched the other half of the Hoosier companies into position about one and one-half miles away alongside a road running through the cane fields. The rest of the 4th Wisconsin Regiment completed this line. Captain E. W. Thompson's 1st Maine Battery rolled two 12-pounder howitzers into position to support McLaflin. Shortly, the Rebel cavalry appeared as they fled from the 14th Maine and the 9th Connecticut. They rode straight through the cane fields toward Roy's command. Rising from concealment, the infantrymen delivered a thunderous volley at the cavalrymen, which turned them back into the cane. Once in the sugarcane the riders wheeled their mounts and unknowingly rode toward McLaflin's command.[8]

Retreating through the sugarcane and rice fields from the advancing men of the 9th Connecticut and 14th Maine, Waller maintained scouts well ahead of his main cavalry force looking for an ambush. The waiting Hoosier advance scouts from Company B spotted a dismounted trooper stepping from behind a large bush, but before they could fire, another trooper pulled him back into concealment. The troopers' disappearance did not stop the Hoosier scouts from opening fire. They began shooting wildly and moving forward into the brush and overgrowth until an officer called out: "Come back here G** damn you!" Chagrined, they hastened to the rear and joined their company, concealing themselves in a ditch along the side of a north to south road running through the weed infested rice field. A lone bully-boy, ignoring his orders to remain concealed where he was, took it upon himself to move ahead through the tall weeds, rice and sugarcane to find the Texans. When he popped up from the overgrowth for a better look, three Texans spied him. They spurred their horses and rode straight for him.

Riding ahead of their comrades, they yelled and waved their fighting knives in the air as they attempted to ride down the fleeing Hoosier. As he sheathed his knife and reached for his carbine, the leading trooper shouted, "Halt, you damned Yankee!" Running toward Company B as if three demons from Hell were after him, the Hoosier tripped and fell flat about 30 yards short of his goal. At his fall, the hidden men from Companies B and G stood up and fired a single volley. The crashing blast of rifle balls struck home — toppling the three Texans from their saddles: The lead trooper fell very dead with five rifle balls through his head and seven through his chest, and the other two fell mortally wounded with numerous bullets in their bodies and died within a few minutes. At the sound of musketry, the main force of Waller's men again wheeled their horses and spurred them through the field toward the west and a heavily wooded cypress swamp, galloping hard between the advancing columns of Indiana, Wisconsin, Connecticut and Maine troops.

The Hoosiers, Badgers and Nutmeggers chased after the Texans for nearly a mile before losing them in the cane and shrubs. Waller dismounted his men, having the horses held by every sixth man and formed into a line of battle awaiting the Hoosiers. The Federal commanders called the Jackass Battery and the Maine Battery forward, and the batteries began a random shell fire into the cane feeling for the enemy. After a few rounds, the shells found targets, as indicated by screams and yells, and the Hoosiers soon heard the Rebel cavalry riding off. The Federals moved forward at the double-quick, picking up prisoners and a flag from a dead flag-bearer as they advanced. The Texans fled from the scrub and cane about three hundred yards rearward into the cypress swamp, with Hoosiers and Badgers hot on their heels. The Jackass Battery and the 1st Maine Battery blasted shell after shell into the fleeing Texans as they floundered in the swamp's churned-mud waters. Federals entered the swamp pursuing the fleeing Texans.[9] Several Texans' cavalry horses impaled themselves on cypress knees in plunging through the water, causing their riders to abandon them in such haste they could not shoot their mounts to put them out of their misery. Other troopers (to spare their mounts from injury) dismounted, cast away their equipment and fled using their own legs and arms in wading and swimming through the dark water, trees, brambles, alligators and snakes to escape their pursuers. Moving south and east through the swamp, the dismounted cavalrymen emerged from the swamp dirty and nearly naked behind General Richard Taylor's Fashion Plantation about a mile below St. Charles Courthouse. This action ended the effectiveness of Waller's 13th Texas Cavalry as a unit in Louisiana for nearly six months.

Prisoners from Waller's command reported that the encounter with such a large number of infantry with artillery came as a complete surprise to them. Waller had anticipated only a small battalion to come out looking for him in spite of a warning to the contrary by General Richard Taylor. One of the Texans' captured officers, Captain James B. P. January, confided to the 21st Indiana's surgeon, Dr. Ezra Reed, that they had expected to surprise whoever came after them and capture or kill the entire command.[10]

The Hoosiers rode the captured mounts and equipment from the swamp back to their bivouac. In describing the Hoosiers' mud soaked condition, Rufus Dooley's description of John Yelton's appearance as he came galloping into camp astride a captured mustang summed it up: "He was so muddy we could scarcely tell who he was, but it was certain that he had been to a swamp." The Hoosiers' and Badgers' captures were fifty prisoners, two hundred fifty horses, saddles, saddlebags, lariats, bridles, three flags, swords, pistols, carbines, Sharps rifles, double-barreled shotguns, hats, canteens, coats, powder kegs and knives. The victors deposited their booty aboard their transports, washed up and returned to Camp Lewis. The 9th Connecticut remained behind to search for stray Confederates. One of their officers reported that that evening they captured a lone colored well-mounted Rebel horseman spying on their camp. The next morning the Connecticut men steamed for Carrollton. For some unknown reason the Hoosiers referred to this action as "Red Church, LA."[11]

After returning to Camp Lewis, the Indianians wrote home to assure friends and relatives of their health, and in some cases, that reports of their own deaths were false. Others had the sad task of writing to friends' families describing how and under what conditions their son or husband had died. Their regiment's pride was high as indicated by Mitchel Hatten's letter home that read in part: "The old 21st fights like the devil."[12]

Those wounded at Baton Rouge began coming back into camp from the New Orleans hospitals. Overall the men's conditions in camp varied as witnessed by Rufus Dooley: "Thomas Banta and Thomas Lough were in camp a few days ago. Banta looks tolerable bad... Thomas Lough does not look as bad. He is getting along fine. John Yelton is well and enjoys himself as well as anyone in the company!" The soldiers' letters assured their families that even though they had lost much in personal effects at Baton Rouge and could not send money home at present, they would send money home as soon as they had the necessities and made themselves comfortable again.[13]

Later that month, on the 20th, Colonel McMillan set off on a reconnaissance in force with 350 of his soldiers and the Jackass Battery aboard the steamer *Laurel Hill*. They steamed up as far as Baton Rouge looking for gunboats to support their riverside expedition. Finding three gunboats near Baton Rouge, McMillan arranged for an armed escort by the gunboat *Katahdin*. Coming about, they steamed downstream to Donaldsonville, arrived across from it that evening and tied the steamer to the shore. The next morning they crossed the river and landed at Donaldsonville near Bayou LaFourche where it enters the Mississippi River.

Having heard that the Rebel forces in the area were more than 1,000 strong, the 21st Indiana left a guard at Donaldsonville and marched nearly four miles down the left side of the bayou. The Hoosiers were unopposed. The Jackass Battery fired a few shells into a sugar house and surrounding cane field that informants said concealed a body of men. The shells only flushed a few mounted cavalry from the surrounding sugarcane fields who fled deeper into them. The informants had also told the Indianians that a large number of Rebels occupied a fortified position on the other side of the bayou near the sugar warehouses of Ayraud & Koch, which the Rebels used as barracks. The Hoosiers marched back to Donaldsonville to spend the night under cover of the gunboat. During the ensuing night, Rebel scouts tested the Hoosier pickets, costing the Rebels one man killed by a picket guard from Company A.[14]

After resting for another day, early in the morning of the 24th McMillan led his forces down the right side of the bayou. When about one and one-half miles from Donaldsonville, they encountered a party of Rebel skirmishers supporting a lone 6-pounder cannon planted to contest their passage down the road. McMillan ordered up two guns from the Jackass Battery. Unlimbering, they dropped the cannons' trails and went into action. After a shell burst near the Rebel gun, the Confederates limbered up and retreated down the road. The Hoosiers gave a cheer and moved forward after their prey. The Rebels stopped about every eight hundred yards and fired a shell at the approaching Indianians, just to tantalize them. After a three to four mile chase, the Rebels took refuge in a sugar warehouse.[15]

McMillan brought up his men and ordered them into line of battle at about 900 yards from the warehouse near the St. Emma plantation. The Jackass Battery brought their brass cannons into line with the deploying infantry and commenced shelling the sugar warehouse. To their surprise, nine concealed guns including a rifled 12-pounder and two very old large bore guns stuffed with railroad iron manned by Semmes' 1st Louisiana Battery, B. F. Winchester's recruits for the Pelican Artillery, returned their fire. The Jackass Battery moved forward about 200 yards to use their shorter ranged 6-pounders with better effect. McMillan ordered his men to lie down to let the Rebel missiles fly overhead. The artillery dueled for an hour. The Hoosiers' shot and shell landed in the midst of and burst over the Rebels' breastworks. Each splendid shot brought forth cheers from the Hoosier infantry, causing the men to rise up and wave their hats, which caused the officers to yell, "Lie down, damn you!"

The Rebels' shells, shot and railroad iron sailed between and mostly over the Hoosiers, slightly wounding a handful of men. Most of the projectiles battered the supply wagons in their rear. The Rebel shells did not kill any of the 21st Indiana's men, but an exploding Rebel shell allegedly killed a Negro family huddled in a house to the rear of the regiment. Doctor Reed later estimated that the Jackass Battery fired 325 fired rounds, which he estimated must have inflicted nearly 150 casualties among the waiting Rebels. (While no official casualty reports have been found, Dr. Reed's estimate is likely inflated by more than 50 percent; even Colonel McMillan's ego only brought forth an estimate of 30 or 40 casualties inflicted on the enemy.)[16]

While the artillerists blazed away, the Hoosier bully boys fixed bayonets for a charge against the Rebel position. However, the sound of the artillery firing summoned forth Fournet's Infantry Battalion, the Assumption Parish Militia and the 2nd Louisiana Cavalry, all commanded by Colonel William G. Vincent from their camp across and a little farther down the bayou. The Louisianans fell in and hurried to cross a small bridge over the bayou to confront the Hoosiers. As they crossed the bayou, they could see the bluecoats forming into line to charge. The high-riding cavalrymen made better targets for rifle fire from the Hoosier skirmishers, which proved ineffective in hindering the troopers' movement. Fournet's infantry moved into position prepared to receive the bayonet charge from the advancing Indianians, now 700 yards away. Lieutenant-Colonel James McWaters moved his 2nd Louisiana Cavalry across the rear of the Louisiana defenses. They trotted down Sacramento Road about 400 to 500 yards north of the bayou and, screened by sugarcane, wheeled eastward and began galloping to get in the rear of the Hoosiers to cut off their way of retreat.

An alert Indianian noticed McWaters' cavalry moving parallel to and headed for the Hoosiers' rear. He quickly took the news to McMillan, who ordered a hasty retreat. The men of the 21st promptly complied to skedaddle rearward to the safety of the gunboat *Katahdin*'s guns. Captain F. A. Prudhomme's companies of the 2nd Louisiana Cavalry Regiment, providing support for Semmes' battery, began remounting to chase after the fleeing Hoosiers. Semmes' battery hastened the retreat by shooting a round of exploding shells after the fleeing Indianians sending fences crashing and dirt clods flying among them; then, the battery limbered up and followed the cavalry after the Hoosiers. The Rebel cavalry pursued and harassed the Hoosiers during their flight to the levee. McWaters' troopers passed the Hoosiers and formed in line across the road between the bluecoats and the safety of the river. The Indianians unlimbered the Jackass Battery, and prepared to load with canister to clear the cavalry out of the way. However, they observed Prudhomme's cavalry and Semmes' battery about 200 to 300 yards in their rear. McMillan pondered whether to charge blindly ahead into the waiting cavalry and the possibility of holding the levee against the infantry or to surrender. Fortunately for the panicked bluecoats, the watch officer on the *Katahdin* saw the Hoosiers' predicament and called for the gunboat to open fire on the Confederate cavalry and artillery positions.

The first cannon fire from *Katahdin* burst in the middle of McWaters' cavalrymen and sent them riding away to join their comrades in Prudhomme's command to the side and rear of the bluecoats. The gunboat fired forty-seven shells into the Confederates before they could all get out of range. The Jackass Battery limbered up and with the infantry made it to the levee under cover of the *Katahdin*'s guns. The 21st Indiana was saved by the navy from having their reconnaissance-in-force being bagged by the Rebels.

The Hoosiers had two casualties during their retreat: Lieutenant George C. Harding and an unnamed artillerist. Company F's Lieutenant Harding claimed he fell as he climbed over a fence and wrenched his back. While true, others stated his drunkenness led to his falling. After his fall, he limped after his rapidly departing men until McWaters' cavalry cut him off and captured him. Flying gravel from a shell exploding in the road near his gun splattered the face of the artillerist with gravel, but he got away to safety.[17]

The cavalrymen took their captive, Lieutenant Harding, before their regimental commander, Colonel William G. Vincent. Harding gave Vincent his promise not to attempt to escape. After giving his pledge, his captors moved him to New Iberia and then to Camp Pratt, located about six miles northwest of New Iberia. Harding soon discovered that he was in the midst of one hundred thirty-seven Nutmegger Yankees — mostly 8th Vermont captives from Bayou Des Allemandes. However, it was only a few minutes before he recognized the faces of the 21st Indiana's lieutenants Connelly and Cox in the crowd turned out to welcome the newcomer.[18]

Their captors had confined Lieutenants Connelly and Cox to a jail cell in Opelousas for more than three months before transferring them to Camp Pratt. Once in the camp, they shared an A-frame tent and three blankets with four other men. When Harding arrived, he became the seventh man in the tent. They were fed boiled beef, yellow cornmeal (from which they made mush) and sugar. Not having enough crockery plates, they ate and drank from gourds and cleaned oxen's shoulder blade bones. James Connelly succeeded in baking his cornmeal into a pone instead of boiled mush. Because he was the only one to achieve ponery he was called upon to bake pones for his tentmates. The officers and men guarding the camp had little more to eat than the prisoners and usually they shared the same poor food-stuffs.[19]

Often, the guards were local conscripts, and they were not too keen on the idea of serving in the army themselves. To keep them at their posts, more than one of these conscript guards wore chains fastened to an ankle and to a tree to keep them from wandering home. Therefore, it is safe to assume that most of the guards were not too reliable. After a little planning, the three Indiana boys tried to escape late one night. Cox and Connelly made good their escape, but Harding did not.

However, Harding was the fortunate one, because he benefited from the negotiations General Butler had been carrying on since August for the release of prisoners including Connelly and Cox. The next day he was taken by a circuitous route aboard riverboats to Vicksburg for parole and exchanged to the Federals. He had been a prisoner for only six to seven weeks. Lieutenants Cox and Connelly did not fare as well. After spending two weeks hiding in the swamps and making their way east toward New Orleans, the shoeless bloody-footed escapees were recaptured near Donaldsonville. Their captors returned them to Camp Pratt, where they remained prisoners for another month.[20]

While Connelly, Cox and Harding tasted the fruits of prison life, the rest of the regiment lolled about in camp. Captain Grimsley griped about Colonel Macmillan, because he felt the colonel acted too recklessly with the lives of the men of the regiment, a sentiment held by many other officers and the enlisted men. However, he also voiced disapproval of confiscation of property under the Confiscation Act signed July 12, 1862, just to gather cotton and sugar for one's personal profit. Grimsley's attitude had been noted previously during the May raid to Houma. When just the two of them were together, Grimsley denounced Macmillan to his face as a scoundrel and a coward and then challenged Macmillan to court-martial him for it. Grimsley relied upon the reputation he had earned as a fighter at the Battle of Baton Rouge to see him through. It worked, because nothing came of the tiff.[21]

Alcohol and association with loose women was a constant problem or requirement during the war, and the 21st Indiana was no exception to these vices. Wives and sweethearts in Indiana heard about the actions of their men, especially the officers, causing angry letters to flow southward. Captain Grimsley defended himself to his spouse by listing that whereof he partook daily stating: "He often took a glass of wine, sherry cobbler, pale ale, beer or a brandy milk punch, but he felt he had the good sense to know how much to drink." However, his men recalled seeing him so drunk he could not stand in his tent without holding onto the tent's center pole.

The fussy Grimsley also told his wife that he had many lady friends of the best families who often visited him when they came to camp. Further, he cautioned her that not every woman who came into camp was of loose character, even though many who visited were loose. He tried not to go into New Orleans so he could avoid the temptation to savor its carnal delights. He closed his defense by stating: "One thing I can say — I wish our Chaplain could say so much. No man of this regiment ever saw me in a house of bad repute in the city of New Orleans or around it."[22]

A couple of weeks later, Grimsley wrote to his wife with a twist on the "spoils of war." He bragged that he had a servant boy who looks after all his wants with the minutest care. He went on to say: "When I come home, I will try and bring you and Ma a nice Secesh girl each." This is a major change from his earlier expression of outrage at being ordered to burn secessionist property if it would result in women and children becoming homeless. What brought about such a dramatic change that caused him to feel justified to put southern women into slavery is not stated in his letters. He also sent home a few items that he acquired by "unguaranteed appropriation" with a warning not to tell anyone because a fellow officer had been severely reprimanded and punished for pilfering.[23]

Nine

Cotton and Salt

After a month of rest and recuperation, October 26 found most of the regiment aboard the steamer *St. Mary's* bound from New Orleans to Berwick Bay, Louisiana. Sick men and officers, Brown's Jackass Battery (now with four 6-pounder cannons) and the fretting Grimsley remained behind in Camp Parapet. Grimsley still worried about McMillan's wrath in spite of assurances from Generals Dudley and Paine that he had nothing to fear from official circles. While Grimsley worried about his fate, the regiment steamed down the Mississippi River and dropped anchor off the Head of Passes. There, the transport awaited gunboat escorts—the gunboats *Estrella* and *Calhoun*. Company E boarded the *Estrella* and Company G went aboard the *Calhoun*. The three vessels awaited the arrival of additional gunboats for the expedition, but after a day without any sight of them, they put out to sea.[1]

While the 21st Indiana was steaming south, then west and then north to Brashear City, newly elevated Brigadier-General Godfrey Weitzel advanced down Bayou LaFourche from Donaldsonville with 5,000 men. Fighting a rear guard action, General Alfred Mouton's Confederate forces slowly gave way down Bayou LaFourche. At Labadieville on the 27th, Mouton formed his battle lines. With only four regiments of infantry, two artillery batteries and 250 cavalrymen (about 1,392 men in all), he engaged Weitzel's superior forces.

In spite of being greatly outnumbered, Mouton managed to hold up Weitzel for several hours. Learning that his men were almost out of all artillery and musket ammunition, and after being surprised by a frenzied, cursing charge of the 12th Connecticut Infantry Regiment, Mouton ordered his men to fall back. He still tried to fight a delaying action until he could get reinforcements. Realizing no help was coming and the Federals were hard pressing him, Mouton disengaged and moved away to Terre Bonne Station. From there he marched along the New Orleans, Opelousas and Great Western Railway to Berwick Bay. As they pushed for Berwick Bay, Mouton's men burned the railroad bridges behind them to hinder the advancing Yankees. Weitzel followed, but the burned bridges slowed and all but stopped his advance. Only Federal scouting parties proceeded ahead of the main body of men. The ship-borne Hoosiers' job was to arrive at Brashear City ahead of the retreating Confederates, cut the Confederate escape route across Berwick Bay and catch them between two Federal forces.[2]

On the 29th of October, the transports and gunboat reached the mouth of the Atchafalaya River. Due to a heavy north wind blowing the Atchafalaya out to sea and holding the tides back, the convoy could not cross the sandbar at the river's mouth. The next day McMillan caused a tragedy aboard the *St. Mary's*. A small Confederate gunboat (the *Cotton*) steamed down and opened fire on the little Federal flotilla. Colonel McMillan, evidently not trusting the navy's ability to protect his command and transport, ordered a 12-pounder rifled Dahlgren on the *St. Mary's* upper deck into action. He personally directed it to be loaded with percussion-fused explosive case-shot.

Without waiting to clear the lower decks, he ordered the cannon fired at the approaching gunboat. The shell struck the *St. Mary's* smokestack's forward stay chain, which caused the shell to explode a few feet from the cannon's muzzle. The blast cut the chain, ripped shreds of metal from it, sent the chain whipping to the deck below, and showered the men and officers below with chain, flying iron fragments, burning sulfur and hot metal balls.

One piece of the shell cut entirely through Company H's Lieutenant William Wolfe's body killing him instantly. Company A's Lieutenant Eden Fisher had both of his legs mangled by the whipping chain, causing their amputation below his knees. Other flying fragments severely wounded a private's arm, killed a Negro, and inflicted cuts and bruises on many other men. Captain Elihu Rose from Company C was lucky — his coat was split down the back, but he was barely scratched. The wounded and dead were placed aboard a fast small vessel which took the wounded to the St. James Hospital at New Orleans. Surgeons at St. James amputated both of Lieutenant Fisher's legs. He remained in the hospital for about three months, when he received a reposting to Indianapolis, Indiana, as a brevet-captain on recruiting duty. He resigned at the end of 1863.

The *Calhoun's* 30-pounder Parrott rifle got off two rounds at the Rebel gunboat as it moved up the river and out of sight. McMillan's anxiety and his personal negligence in handling of the cannon cost him additional loss of respect by more of his officers and men.[3]

The vessels spent the 30th and 31st trying to enter the river. After a lot of towing, shifting of loads, depth sounding and the north wind abating to allow the water to rise, the little convoy finally made it across the sandbar on the 31st. Because the *Cotton* had removed the channel markers, the Federal ship's crews had to sound the depth of the water as their craft slowly felt its way upstream. They dropped anchor after going only two miles. About 4 P.M. on the 1st of November the way was clear and marked to Brashear City. The *St. Mary's* in company with the gunboats *Calhoun*, *Estrella* and the newly arrived *Grey Cloud* (also called *Colonel Kinsman*) slowly started upstream toward Brashear City where they arrived late that night. Mouton's Confederates had safely escaped across Berwick Bay two days before and were at Fort Bisland up Bayou Teche.[4]

Early in the morning of the 2nd, McMillan disembarked the 21st Indiana's men from the *St. Mary's* onto the streets of Brashear City. The officers maintained quarters aboard the *St. Mary's* in exchange for a fee payable to the steamer's captain. McMillan quickly had his men setting up camp in warehouses along the wharf and in buildings at the New Orleans, Opelousas and Great Western Rail Road terminus. The bully boys set about making the town Union friendly again. The departing Confederates had smashed the railroad engines and toppled cars off the tracks at Brashear City besides burning the bridges leading into town. Borrowing some tools from the navy's vessels, details from the 21st Indiana began repairing the disabled railroad engines and cars.

McMillan also sent out scouts into the countryside looking for Rebel stragglers and forage. One company marched out about five miles to the burned railroad bridge across Bayou Beouf. They returned without contacting General Weitzel's force. While McMillan established his base camp and set about getting the railroad in order, the U.S. gunboat *Diana* arrived about 5 P.M.

On the morning of November 3, the gunboat fleet coaled up preparatory to setting off in search of the *Cotton*. The Hoosiers put a company aboard each of the gunboats. Steaming a short distance up the Atchafalaya River the fleet turned up Bayou Teche. Proceeding up the Teche, the *Calhoun* came within sight of the *Cotton*. Lieutenant Thomas Buchanan, commanding the *Calhoun*, took the lead, firing his 30-pounder Parrott rifle at the *Cotton*. The crew had fired only three shots from the 30-pounder Parrott when the breeching ropes gave way putting it temporarily out of action. The *Calhoun* stopped for repairs. The *Estrella* proceeded on and soon came bow to bow with the *Cotton*.

Harper's Weekly **rendition of loading confiscated cotton aboard steamers at Brashear City.**

The *Cotton* had backed up the bayou so she could fight head-on with her heaviest armor and four 32-pounder guns facing the Federal vessels. The *Cotton* was in a good position behind obstructions placed in the bayou and alongside an on-shore battery of four light artillery guns. A section of the Pelican Light Artillery (Faries' battery) with two 3-inch rifled guns (Parrott pattern) and a section of the 1st Confederate Regular Battery (Semmes' battery) with two captured 12-pounder James rifles were on the right bank of the bayou.

After a short time fighting, the *Cotton* put a shot through the *Estrella*'s bow, splintering it, killing three men and wounding five others. The *Estrella* pulled to the side of the bayou allowing the *Diana* and *Grey Cloud* to pass and engage the enemy. The *Diana* and *Grey Cloud* fired shot and grape at both the *Cotton* and the field batteries. The *Diana* took three hits, damaging her stern. The *Grey Cloud* steamed up closer to the *Cotton*, and at 1,000 yards began pouring close range fire into her and the field batteries.[5]

Buchanan's crew finished repairs to the *Calhoun*'s Parrott rifle, and he steamed closer to the *Cotton*. About halfway to her, he nosed in to the bank and let Captain Edward McLaflin lead his Company G ashore to try to get opposite the *Cotton* with his riflemen. The *Calhoun* then proceeded up the bayou. McLaflin's objective was to get close enough to the *Cotton* to fire into the open gunports in the armor plate of the ship. The ricocheting lead inside the armor plate could cause numerous casualties among the crewmen resulting in either retreat or surrender of the vessel. McLaflin and his company floundered through the swampy land to get within range of the *Cotton*.

While the *Grey Cloud* kept the *Cotton* engaged with its rifled cannon, it saluted the Rebel field artillery with blasts of 32-pounder grape shot. Now the *Calhoun* came up and turned broadside to the *Cotton*. The battered *Grey Cloud* withdrew. The Rebel field artillery, unsupported by infantry, ripped by the rounds of grape, and threatened by McLaflin's troops, withdrew. The *Calhoun* brought her port broadside guns to bear on the *Cotton*. The *Cotton* was now out of powder cartridges, and began backing up the bayou.

McLaflin got to his pre-determined position in time to see the *Cotton* disappearing up the Teche. Determined to keep fighting even as he backed upstream, some of Fuller's men cut off their pants' legs. Binding the material at one end, they filled the resulting bag with cannon powder and then tied off the other end making a cartridge bag. The makeshift cartridges enabled Fuller to keep the enemy well away as the *Cotton* backed up the bayou out of harm's way. After two hours, the engagement ended in a draw. The worn detachment from Company G made their way to the rear and again boarded the *Calhoun*; all the Union vessels returned to Brashear City for repairs.[6]

The *Grey Cloud* received fifty-four shots through its upper structures and hull, mostly from the field artillery, killing one seaman and wounding four. The *Calhoun* received eight rounds which wounded five seamen (one mortally) and killed Cornelius Wilson from Company G. The *Diana* received three shots injuring no one. The *Estrella* received three rounds taking their toll among the Hoosiers manning *Estrella*'s guns. The exploding shells killed Privates Staneshlow Jarboe and Francis Mathews of Company E and wounded one other man from Company E. In total, the navy had ten casualties aboard the gunboats, the 21st Indiana reported three killed and five wounded, and Captain Fuller reported three casualties aboard the *Cotton*: one killed, one mortally wounded, and one wounded. This would not be the regiment's last engagement with the *Cotton*.[7]

On the 5th, the gunboats *Calhoun* and *Estrella* again went up the Teche looking for the *Cotton*. By this time the Confederates had built two earthwork fortifications, one on each side of the bayou above the obstructions and in front of the *Cotton* that held some infantry and light artillery. Again, the *Cotton* and her comrades-in-arms were victorious. After fighting for two hours and losing three men, the Federals retired to Brashear City.[8]

Back at Brashear City, the Hoosiers continued work on repairing the railroad and had one engine running by the time the gunboats returned from their expedition of the 5th. Many of Brashear City's secessionist citizens fled at the initial approach of the Federals; their abandoned homes were seized by both commissioned and senior non-commissioned officers and quickly turned into their housing. A couple of houses became hospitals for the officers and men. Foraging parties had caught a few Rebel stragglers and brought them into town where the Johnnies were put into makeshift prisons.

The Hoosiers thought the area's supply of sweet potatoes, corn bread and lean beef rather poor fare after the plentiful supply of fruits, fresh baked pies and cakes available at New Orleans. At a later date, they would yearn for those sweet potatoes, corn bread and lean beef.[9]

On November 7, a train on its way to Brashear City from Algiers, loaded with ammunition for the gunboats, exploded near LaFourche Crossing. The blast killed and wounded sixteen officers and soldiers from regimental details guarding the train and working on the railroad. Among the dead was the 21st Indiana's sergeant Everet Delameter of Company F; injured was Bugler Benjamin Culbertson from Company A. Immediate rumors blamed the explosion on partisan sabotage; however, no proof of sabotage was found. It was just an untimely accident, probably caused by a cigar smoking soldier. Surviving troops repaired the train and salvaged all they could. The train arrived at Brashear City the next day. Much of the ammunition was lost, but a small amount survived to partially resupply the gunboats. Also on the 7th, units from the 8th Vermont arrived to reinforce Brashear City. General Weitzel had holed up in Thibodaux after clearing the LaFourche. Knowing by the end of October that further pursuit of Mouton was futile, he sent out regiments to hold the railroad and make repairs.

On the 9th, the 21st Indiana's scavengers brought in railroad ties from Berwick City (across the river from Brashear City) to repair damage to the railroad track. The army and navy went about the countryside looking for cotton and sugar. Lieutenant S. E. Armstrong negotiated for eighty-seven hogsheads of sugar at $20.00 per hogshead from the Vinson plantation. Armstrong noted that the soldiers complained about having to labor at loading cotton and sugar and of mounting guard over it for the benefit of high ranking officers. In a few weeks the privates would get their revenge on several officers.[10]

Even though the railway was open, the telegraph lines were still down between Brashear City and Algiers. If no train was handy, communications between Brashear City and the nearest telegraph at Bayou Beouf were carried between these places by mounted messengers. On the 16th, at 2 o'clock in the morning Lieutenant Armstrong walked to the railroad picket line, commandeered a handcar, and pumped his way to Bayou Beouf. From there he sent a dispatch from Colonel McMillan to General Butler. He returned to Brashear City without waiting for an answer.

At 9 o'clock that same morning, McMillan sent Armstrong back to Bayou Beouf to wait for a reply. At 2 P.M. the reply arrived at Bayou Beouf. That evening Armstrong found himself in company with McMillan, most of the regiment's field officers, Companies A, C and D plus detachments from other companies all aboard the *St. Mary's* steaming down Berwick Bay to the Gulf of Mexico, accompanied by the gunboat *Grey Cloud*.[11]

Their current objective was to destroy the salt works owned by J. D. Avery up Bayou Petit Anse from Vermilion Bay. This salt works was not an evaporative salt works like many others. It was a mine with two shafts sunk into solid rock salt where the salt was blasted out with gunpowder. At that time, the Confederates knew the salt dome measured some 400 yards across and at least 30 feet down. Salt sold at the mine for $9.00 per 200 pound sack. It resold in Jackson, Mississippi, for $15.00 per 100 pound sack. Cutting off the supply of this vital item would strike a heavy blow against the salt-poor Confederacy. It would also drive the price of salt to prohibitively high prices when it was available.[12]

Arriving in Vermilion Bay on the 18th, they found the gunboat *Diana* at the mouth of Bayou Petit Anse waiting for them. That evening McMillan led about 135 men and his officers from the *St. Mary's* onto the *Grey Cloud*. They steamed over to the *Diana* and McMillan sent half of his detachment aboard her. The gunboats steamed for the bayou and began working their way into it. The next morning they were still in sight of the *St. Mary's* trying to get up the bayou. These shallow waters formed the salt works' defense against seaborne invasion.[13]

The Rebels soon learned of the expedition and at 1 A.M. on the 19th dispatched two 3-inch banded rifles and two 12-pounder howitzers from T. A. Faries' Louisiana Pelican Light Artillery to Petit Anse Island with a small detail from Waller's Texas Cavalry to support the artillery. After a difficult journey, complicated by the causeway to the island being washed out, the artillery arrived on the 20th. Lieutenant Oscar Gaudet moved his two 12-pounder howitzers to the seaward side of the island where a band of scrubby trees masked his guns. From there Gaudet could see the two Federal gunboats hard aground in the bayou about one and one-half miles away. Lieutenant B. F. Winchester got his two 3-inch rifles into position atop a small knoll on the island the next day.

St. Mary's Captain Tolbert sent off a ship's boat with messages to row over the sandbar and up to the mired gunboats. The light boat hit the bar and stuck. Another boat rowed to the bar from one of the gunboats. Captain William Roy from Company A and Adjutant Henry McMillan, bearing dispatches, climbed out of one boat, sloshed across the bar, and boarded the boat sent out from the *St. Mary's*.[14]

On the morning of the 21st, Captain Roy and Captain Tolbert took a small boat from the *St. Mary's* and passed over the bar at high tide. They took a supply of whiskey, cigars and coffee to the gunboats for Colonel McMillan and the officers. Arriving at the gunboats, they saw that the *Grey Cloud* was afloat, but the *Diana* was still hard aground. As the officers enjoyed their little luxuries, men from the 21st Indiana and some sailors from the gunboats rowed up the bayou to the island.

Nine. Cotton and Salt

The men landed and prepared to scout the island. As they formed their squads, two 12-pound rounds of spherical case burst around them. The thoroughly surprised Hoosiers and sailors scattered and ran back to their landing place. The Federals rearguard fired a few wild shots at the woods in the general direction from where the howitzers had roared. Three more rounds of exploding case shot chased the full rowboats down the bayou. Seeing that his men had safely returned to the gunboats, Colonel McMillan departed and went back to the safety of the *St. Mary's*.

The next day the *St. Mary's* got under way for Brashear City taking Colonel McMillan and Adjutant Henry McMillan with it. Lieutenant S. E. Armstrong went aboard one of four boats of supplies left by the *St. Mary's* and rowed up the bayou to the gunboats. After the small boats passed over the bar, and drew nearer to the gunboats they heard cannon fire which grew louder as they approached the gunboats. They could see an occasional shot splashing into the water from Winchester's 3-inch rifles which were visible on a low hill. They also saw a gunboat fire one of its cannons, and they watched its shell with its sputtering fuse fly over the hill. In a short while, the men and boat crews went aboard the gunboats and settled in to watch the artillery duel from their decks. After firing thirty-three shot and shell without effect, Lieutenant Winchester ceased firing and began moving his light guns from their exposed position. The larger naval guns reached his position better than his guns could reach the gunboats; in spite of this advantage, the gunboats' shot and shell flew high over Winchester's guns. As Winchester safely moved away, the naval vessels got the range. The next round of shells exploded directly on his vacated position.[15]

Later that day the *Diana* got afloat, and the two gunboats worked their way back down the bayou to the sand and mud bar at the entrance to the bay. After waiting more than a day for a high enough tide, the *Diana* made it over the bar at 3 A.M. on the 24th. She steamed off to Brashear City leaving the *Grey Cloud* stuck on the bar with her compliment of irate Hoosiers. When it was clear the Federals had had enough and skedaddled, Faries' Battery abandoned the island at 5:30 A.M. that same day.

The stuck *Grey Cloud* sent out a few foragers armed with shotguns into the nearby marshes. They brought back ducks, gulls and snipe for dinner. Two days later, the Rebels set fire to the marshes, which drove off the wild game supply. Captain Roy took out a well armed thirty-man party in small boats to high ground, and they brought back fresh beef and pork. Plentiful oysters were still available for those brave enough to wade into the chill waters against the cold north wind. The Indianians without blankets and overcoats suffered from the sudden onset of cold, windy weather. The walls of the ship protected only those within them from the wind, which meant officers, seamen, and rotating shifts of infantrymen.[16]

While his command was stuck in the mud, Colonel McMillan telegraphed General Butler from the comforts of Brashear City that while he could not get salt, he did know of a place to get cotton. Butler telegraphed McMillan with the following message: "Your business is to make war, sir, and not to steal cotton."

Upon learning of this exchange between Butler and McMillan, the Hoosier officers at Brashear City had a hearty laugh. One of the officers estimated that McMillan had made between $40,000 to $50,000 from the trade in cotton and sugar up to that time. The response from Butler was likely generated by Colonel McMillan's use of a written message requesting Butler's approval for the appropriation of cotton, or it could have been because the message was intended for General Butler's brother Andrew and misdirected to Benjamin. McMillan had engaged in speculation with Andrew Butler for some time.

While it has not been proven that General Butler personally profited from cotton or sugar, he often looked the other way when his subordinates did profit. Butler's use of money from cotton and sugar went to pay for expenses of operating his department at a savings to the Federal government. McMillan's men stuck in Vermilion Bay did not know why McMillan made such a hasty return to Brashear City; they surmised his departure was due to cowardice.[17]

Finally, on the 30th of November, the *Diana* returned with mail for the men and coal for the *Grey Cloud*. The infantrymen transferred to the *Diana* by small boats, and that afternoon they steamed off for Brashear City. Misfortune struck again. The *Diana* ran onto a shell reef between Vermilion Bay and Grand Cote Bay.

While the men got off and pushed and pulled with the seamen, Captain Elihu Rose from Company C took out a hunting party aboard a small sloop. They sailed about five miles to the nearest land and bagged some fresh beef for dinner. The next day Lieutenant Armstrong set out in the sloop accompanied by a rowboat with fourteen soldiers and sailors to find water. After searching about all day and finding no fresh water, Armstrong tied the rowboat up to the sloop several miles from the *Diana*. A sudden gale blew the sloop and rowboat toward the relative safety of the shore. The storm abated about 11 P.M. A lookout spotted *Diana*'s lights, and Armstrong's group reached her about midnight. The same gale that had sent Armstrong's party into shore had lifted *Diana* off the reef. She made full speed for Brashear City with all soldiers and sailors aboard.[18]

Finally, on the 4th of December, after more than sixteen days of working on grounded ships the men of the 21st Regiment were all ashore at Brashear City. The officers again took room and board on the *St. Mary's* for $1.50 per day. The officers' Negro servants cost them an additional $.50 a day for their room and board aboard the *St. Mary's*. To add insult to injury, the officers later learned that the owners of the *St. Mary's* received $900 per day from the Federal government to transport, house and feed them.

The enlisted men living in Brashear City warehouses now watched as their living areas filled with bales of cotton and barrels of sugar for shipment to New Orleans by rail and sea. The soldiers added sheds and lean-tos onto the warehouses to provide living quarters as the goods forced them out of the main buildings. Besides repairing the railroad, enhancing the warehouses, and rounding up cotton and sugar, they helped with the work on building two forts. One fort protected the upper approach to the town by the Atchafalaya River, and the other fort protected the middle of the town and warehouses.[19]

Shortly after the bully boys returned from their wild salt chase, Company E went aboard the gunboat *Estrella*. Their expedition set out up the Atchafalaya River to gather cattle. Landing at the Dorsino Rentrop plantation, the Indiana raiders went about their task of rounding up animals for food. The mistress of the estate left the bedside of her dying husband and ran out to the marauders, entreating them to go about their business quietly and to leave the house alone.

Of course, this caused the Hoosiers to be more than interested in the contents of the house, and what may be hidden therein. While some of the men opened fire on Rebel chickens, others invaded the house and the deathbed chamber like barbarians. The ruffians taunted and jeered the dying man, while rummaging for hidden silver and valuables. They left after finding nothing of great value and killing more than they could reasonably take away to eat.

The next day the *Estrella* brought them back for more. By now Mr. Rentrop had died and the grieving family gathered in the house. The Hoosiers came ashore and began shooting more chickens, geese and cattle to take back to Brashear City. Lieutenant Hamrick entered the house and arrested the two sons mourning their late father. The young men were taken away on suspicion of being active in the Confederate Army. One had been in the Confederate service, but he was out on disability. The two were later released, and they both became active members in the Confederate forces. The Hoosiers came back a third day to finish carrying off the livestock. During this pillaging episode, they noticed the family's orange grove and picked all the ripe oranges for their larder.[20]

A much less harmful, but humorous, event happened about the same time. It seems foragers from Company C caught a hog that supposedly had escaped from its owner's pen. The men brought their catch to camp for dinner; however, the unidentified owner secretly followed the group to camp.

The owner located Colonel McMillan and filed a formal complaint that the men stole the hog from his pen. McMillan dutifully took the owner out to the camp of Company C with a promise to find and punish the thieves. The quick thinking foragers put the newly-deceased pig onto a cot in their quarters, covered it with a blanket and set a small table with a cup of water by its side. One of the guilty parties got into a cot adjacent, pulled up a blanket and commenced fanning himself in the forty degree weather. When Colonel McMillan and the owner looked into the tent, they saw the obviously fevered pair and moved on. McMillan and Company C enjoyed roast pork at the next day's dinner.[21]

While the men brought in wild ducks with their other game from the countryside, a few domestic ducks also became table food. Some of Company B spotted a flock of ducks nesting under an old Frenchman's house. The house was perched atop pilings to keep it dry at flood times, and the space under it was lightly lathed to keep large animals out, but the ducks could get in. A soldier crawled under the house and fetched a couple of ducks. However, the ducks raised a great amount of noise, and the Frenchman and his wife quickly descended the stairs cursing the thief. The old woman began hitting the duck thief with a broom, forcing him to throw his catch at his attackers and run off empty-handed. His partners in crime stood a short distance away laughing.

Life in Brashear City did not remain countrified and rustic for long. The thriving military community attracted cotton and sugar speculators, sutlers, professional money lenders, gamblers and associated riff-raff joined the inhabitants in the town's businesses. A New Orleans business woman arrived and purchased a house. She imported a bevy of soiled doves from New Orleans to staff it. Her house provided the finest food, cigars, beverages and entertainment in Brashear City. This pleasure palace quickly became the local gentlemen's and officers' club, much to the ire of the enlisted men.

After bearing this discrimination for a few weeks, the bully boys waited until late one night when their colonel and a few other officers were pleasantly sated and comfortable in the house. The privates gathered around the house and began throwing rocks at it, while shouting and beating on the outside walls with clubs. Shortly the windows broke and the enraged soldiers began stripping off the wooden siding of the house.

The angry prostitutes shouted curses at the soldiers and began throwing things out of the windows at the men. Some of the women wrested a club or two from the men, and by hanging out of the windows, they began bashing them back — tit-for-tat. McMillan and the other patrons poured out the door and ran as fast as their legs would carry them for the *St. Mary's* or any other place to hide from the rocks thrown by hooting and howling Hoosier privates. The house's first floor was reduced to a skeletal framework, and the contents trashed. The women of pleasure fled to the second floor and locked the doors. Their mission accomplished, the privates returned to their quarters by round-about ways staying out of sight of guards and officers. The next day the first train from Brashear City carried the madam and her girls back to New Orleans.[22]

News that General Nathaniel P. Banks had replaced General Benjamin Butler as commander of the Department of the Gulf reached the men at Brashear City in the middle of December. Butler wrote a farewell address to the soldiers of the Army of the Gulf wherein he complimented them for their perseverance in enduring Ship Island, wading to Fort St. Philip to force its surrender, fighting an enemy force of double their numbers at Baton Rouge, contributing nearly $500,000 in contraband goods to the Federal Treasury, and costing the government less by four-fifths than any other Federal expedition to date.

The 21st Regiment received this news with mixed emotions, since many former scoffers had grown to admire Butler for his firm-handedness. Some, like the New Orleaneans, were overjoyed at the news of Butler's departure. Some feared Banks would be a repeat of Butler. (Banks would be a far poorer administrator and a worse military commander.)

However, Banks was officially in command as of December 15, 1863. He brought additional troops with him, and promptly sent a force up the Mississippi River to occupy Baton Rouge. The occupation took place on December 17 without opposition. The news of this latter event caused some of the Hoosiers to regard Banks as a man for military work, and to regard him as not coming to Louisiana for cotton and sugar speculation. The additional regiments (all easterners) that Banks brought with him more than doubled the number of soldiers and officers in the Department of the Gulf.

The *St. Mary's* steamed away from Brashear City on the 20th. The displaced officers took rooms in Brashear City at $9.00 to $10.00 a week. This was a slight savings over the *St. Mary's* rates. The plenitude of available Negroes put the officers' servants on their own to find a place to stay. Colonel McMillan left for Indiana around Christmas. He departed amid hisses, name calling and three groans (instead of cheers) from the men. Officers made no attempt to quiet the soldiers.

On December 31, long-awaited tents, camp equipment from Camp Parapet and the Jackass Battery from Bonne Carre arrived. The reunited regiment celebrated. They set up a tent camp about 300 yards from the waterfront just out of the town proper. Pay arrived for the past four months. Their joy dropped somewhat when they discovered that thieves had broken into the storehouse at Camp Parapet and stolen a large portion of the men's clothing and belongings worth hundreds of dollars. The men made do with what they received and already had. Any surplus from raids was shared among one another. Receiving anything was a cause to celebrate. The bully boys got a morale boost when they learned that Lieutenants Connelly and Cox had been released, and the lieutenants had enjoyed Christmas at home in Indiana.[23]

Ten

The *Cotton*, Port Hudson and the Teche

On January 5, by order of President Abraham Lincoln, all of the troops that made up the Department of the Gulf as of December 14, 1862, became the XIX Army Corps. General Nathaniel Prentiss Banks reorganized his new corps to properly apportion troops as needed for combat and to suit their commanders.

Realizing that the *Cotton* posed a major threat to the safety of the numerous Federal vessels operating in the bayous and rivers near Brashear City, General Banks' planned a joint army and navy action against her. In addition to the *Cotton*'s threat to the Federal river and bayou vessels, she blocked Federal naval access to Bayou Teche and the towns upstream. Especially sensitive to the Confederate war effort were the salt works and the arsenal and foundry at New Iberia. Therefore, Brigadier-General Godfrey Weitzel began strategizing with Lieutenant-Commander Thomas Buchanan, commander of the local naval forces, about how to take the *Cotton* out of action.[1]

In January Weitzel reorganized and marshaled his forces at Brashear City for an attack upon the *Cotton*. Fresh troops arrived between the 8th and 12th of January. Weitzel's new contingent of infantry included the 12th Connecticut, 23rd Connecticut, 21st Indiana, 6th Michigan, 75th New York, 160th New York and 8th Vermont. Weitzel's artillery included: the 1st Maine Battery, 6th Massachusetts Battery, two pieces from the 4th Massachusetts Battery and four pieces from the 1st U.S. Artillery Battery A. One company of Louisiana Cavalry (USA) accompanied the infantry and artillery. Weitzel ordered the Indiana Jackass Battery up to Donaldsonville to guard the troops working on Fort Butler at the confluence of Bayou LaFourche and the Mississippi River.[2]

At 3 A.M. on January 10, Weitzel ordered the 21st Indiana's Companies F and H across the bay to secure and guard the landing at Berwick with orders to shoot anyone coming across their picket line. The bully boys crossed over with an artillery battery and secured the landing area. While waiting for the brigade's artillery contingent to cross over, a squad of Hoosiers smelled a cooking fire and went looking for something to eat. They found an old Negro woman in her hut and talked her into making them a cornpone. After enjoying their feast, they hurried back to their assigned position just in time to meet the artillery vessels crossing the bay. After the artillery shoved off from Brashear, the infantry crowded aboard all the remaining vessels. The infantrymen so badly overloaded their vessels that one could hardly see the vessel's structure. The 23rd Connecticut remained in Brashear City to guard against an attack from the rear.[3]

The boys of Companies F and H escorted the artillery as far as Pattersonville, Louisiana. The vessels jammed with infantry put ashore and unloaded at Pattersonville, a short distance up Bayou Teche from the Atchafalaya River. After unloading, General Weitzel drew his brigade up in line of battle with the 75th New York, 160th New York and 12th Connecticut in the advance, followed by the artillery and the 8th Vermont, 21st Indiana and 6th Michigan in reserve. They marched up the Teche bayou road until dusk when they were ordered to sleep with their muskets at hand in a vacant field. The tentless men slept with their weapons, all rolled up in their blankets, which provided marginal protection from that evening's rain.

The next morning, Weitzel's force continued their advance in columns up the left (west) side of the bayou. General Weitzel gave orders that once fighting started no one should leave the line to carry off the wounded; there would be time for that after the battle. The 8th Vermont crossed the bayou and advanced along the right (east) bank of the bayou. Four light-draft Union gunboats steamed up the Teche in single file to clear the way with their heavy guns.[4]

Federal scouts soon encountered the *Cotton* and Mouton's advance pickets. The Federal artillery rolled into position on the roads alongside the bayou and began firing into the sides of the Rebel ironclad while the Union gunboats pounded it head on with their heaviest guns. The 21st Indiana acted as infantry support for the artillery batteries on the left bank of the Teche. While they tried to keep the Rebel infantry busy to protect their artillerists, they came under a heavy return artillery fire from the *Cotton* and the Confederate land batteries. Two men in the 1st Maine Light Artillery were wounded.

The 8th Vermont encountered little resistance on the east bank and drove off the men firing on the advancing Union fleet. The Nutmeggers captured forty-one prisoners, and its sharpshooters soon came within easy range of the *Cotton* and opened fire on her. On the west bank, sharpshooter volunteers from the 75th New York crept up within close musket range of the *Cotton*. Caught between two infantry fires, the gunners on the main deck and crewmen in the pilot house suffered casualties. The New Yorkers and Vermonters killed at least four and wounded several aboard the gunboat. Men from the 75th New York attempted to board the ship, but a blast of grape and canister from one of the gunboat's 32-pounders immediately took eight of the New Yorkers out of action. The New Yorkers rapidly retreated from the *Cotton*. In the process, they suffered sixteen additional casualties.[5]

By noon, having taken a severe amount of punishment to his vessel and crew, Captain Fuller ordered full reverse speed. The sharpshooter's bullets had badly wounded Captain Fuller in both arms and he steered his damaged vessel with his feet. In spite of his handicap and pain, Fuller guided his craft upstream safely away from the barrage of musketry and artillery against it. Barriers placed in the water slightly downstream from the *Cotton*'s original position halted the Union fleet and prevented it from following the crippled gunboat. Hot and heavy Confederate infantry and light artillery fire held off any attempt to follow the gunboat by the Federal infantry and artillery. The *Cotton* escaped.[6]

Night fell, rain fell, and the Federal army camped on their arms in muddy fields. Company B of the 21st Indiana went out on picket duty. The rest of the Hoosiers and other infantrymen tore down fences and stole fodder to make pallets so they could rest out of the mud. After a supper of raw bacon and crackers, they bedded down using their blankets to keep the raindrops off their faces and tried to sleep. Their rest was broken about 4 o'clock in the morning by an explosion and a gusher of sky-searching flames rising above the tree tops from up the bayou.

General Mouton, knowing that his outnumbered force could not hold its position, burned the damaged *Cotton* to prevent it from falling into Yankee hands. Mouton withdrew his army northward toward New Iberia. Federal scouts reported to General Weitzel that the roaring flames came from the burning *Cotton*. His mission accomplished, Weitzel ordered his forces back to Brashear City. The Confederates hailed the battle as a victory for their side, since the Billy Yanks had withdrawn after learning of the total destruction of the *Cotton*. The

Ten. The Cotton, Port Hudson and the Teche

bluecoats, likewise, claimed a victory, because the Johnnies withdrew and the *Cotton* rested in charred pieces on the bottom of the bayou. The Confederates called this action the Battle of Cornay's Bridge. The Federals misspelled it as Corni's bridge.[7]

Upon his return to Brashear City, General Weitzel telegraphed news of his victory to Major-General Banks. The official Union losses reported six killed and twenty-seven wounded in the infantry with the 75th New York having borne the brunt of the losses. Lieutenant-Commander Buchanan, commander of the local Union naval flotilla, was among the navy's casualties. Confederate sharpshooters on the east bank of the Teche had killed Buchanan early in the engagement.[8]

The 21st Indiana's men went back into their tent camp at Brashear City where they marveled at the abundance of mosquitoes during winter. They enjoyed the plentiful supply of sweet potatoes and fresh beef available at their camp even if they stole it. One soldier related: "I saw an old darkey planting potatoes. After he departed, I went out quietly and got the potatoes he had planted. Some six weeks after, he was looking over the fence, but he didn't see any potatoes that had come up."[9]

Also in January, Major-General Banks relieved Colonel McMillan from duty with the 21st Indiana while he was on furlough. Resting in Indiana, McMillan received a promotion to brigadier-general. Upon his return to Louisiana, McMillan received a brigade command with the XIX Corps, which command did not include the 21st Indiana Infantry. Thereafter, the regiment had little contact with McMillan until the Red River campaign in 1864.

John A. Keith received his promotion to colonel of the regiment, but because he was still recuperating from the wounds he received at Baton Rouge, Major Benjamin Hays assumed temporary command of the 21st Regiment. The men again grew lax in personal hygiene. An inspection of the post revealed that the Hoosiers were dirty, unkempt, long-haired, beards untrimmed, uniforms dirty or partially non-existent and the campgrounds not properly maintained. However, the men's weapons, accoutrements, harness and animals were in very good condition. Therefore, Major Hays ordered a company officer to sleep in each company's camp and to attend all of the drills as often as was practicable. He failed to define what was practicable. Four days later, Major Hays issued a clarifying order that no officer would be permitted outside the campgrounds after Tattoo, and all officers must attend drill unless on other duty. Further, one officer of a company must remain within the Guard Line at all times.

Banks began planning a major campaign up the Teche and now referred to the affair with the *Cotton* as "a reconnaissance in force." The Hoosiers heard a rumor that Banks planned to reorganize them into a regiment of heavy artillery. They felt that this rumor was unfounded.[10]

Early in February Lieutenants Connelly and Cox, after a prisoner exchange and a resulting furlough, returned to the regiment at Camp Hays, Brashear City. As soon as they reported in at New Orleans, the lieutenants were ordered back to duty with the regiment currently en route from Brashear City to New Orleans.[11]

Shortly before Connelly and Cox arrived in New Orleans, the heavy artillery rumor came true, and the regiment officially became the First Indiana Heavy Artillery. It took some time for the men to get used to this new appellation, and they referred to themselves as the 21st Indiana Heavy Artillery for several months thereafter. The change meant that while they would have batteries of heavy cannon for each company of men, and the companies would still be referred to as company, not as battery. In addition, two more companies would be formed to raise the strength of the regiment to twelve companies. Their regiment was the only heavy artillery unit from the state of Indiana. On February 7, the men moved from Brashear City to New Orleans where they took up quarters in the Louisiana Cotton Press Number Two. There, they would be equipped as heavy artillerists and refreshed in their training as such.

Also, they had stable call added to their daily "Order of Exercise" for the entire afternoon between dinner and supper.[12]

The reorganization plan was for the regiment to be armed with 30-pounder Parrott rifles. By February 11, they had received eight of these large siege cannons. These Parrott rifles had barrels about eleven feet long and a 4.2-inch diameter bore. A heavy band of iron encircled the breech of the rifles to strengthen them. The solid projectile they fired weighed about thirty pounds, therefore, the designation of thirty-pounder. The shells and canister fired by these weapons weighed less than 30 pounds. In time, the regiment also would use twenty-pounder Parrott rifles, eight-inch bore siege mortars, ten-inch bore siege mortars, eight-inch bore siege howitzers, 24-pounder iron siege guns and two heavy 12-pounder brass guns (rifled in the James fashion). Shortly after receiving their Long Tom 30-pounder Parrotts, the Hoosier bully boys received two heavy 12-pounder brass rifles from the 4th Massachusetts Battery. The 4th Massachusetts Battery was re-equipped with four 12-pounder Napoleon guns and two 3-inch Ordnance rifles.[13]

The bully boys shared mixed feelings about the change. Some felt that they would not be involved in the more active campaigns, because of the slow speed with which they would have to move with the heavy guns. Others were relieved by the prospect of not being sent on daily forays into the swamps. Six men evidently wanting more action applied for transfers to the 2nd U.S. Artillery, Company C. The regular U.S. Artillery accepted their transfer requests.

As usual, many of the men grew bored with camp life. Mitchell Hatten wrote that he wished something would happen to make things a little livelier. It was tiresome to laze in camp with nothing to do except to think about being discharged in sixteen months. However, he believed that before the war was over every man in the United States would be in the field. To ease their boredom, they got their hands on a large ball and played a rough game of football similar to either rugby or soccer that caused bruised and battered shins.[14]

Life in New Orleans was an improvement over that at Brashear City. They were dry and under roof again at the Louisiana Cotton Press #2. However, the western men still feuded with the eastern Nutmegs. On one occasion, the field officer of the day, a nine-month Nutmeg major, came around to check the 1st Indiana's camp; he haughtily displayed a better-than-thou attitude to show off

Top: Regimental flag of First Indiana Regiment of Heavy Artillery. (Battle Flags: Indiana War Memorials Commission). *Bottom:* Thirty-pounder Parrott rifle on siege carriage like those used by several companies of the 21st Indiana / 1st Indiana Heavy Artillery.

his eastern superiority over the western men. The 1st Indiana's officer-of-the-day told the Easterner that he was an ass and threatened to kick him out of camp if he didn't shutup. Further, the Hoosier told the Yankee officer that the stupidest private in the regiment knew more than he did. The Easterner went off threatening to prefer charges, but nothing came of it.[15]

Although Cotton Press #2 had a large yard for exercise, it was also surrounded by brick and wooden fences some twelve feet high. Heavy wooden doors, barred from the outside, kept the men inside and away from the city's diversions. Several of the 1st Indiana's men, led by the mischievous rowdies in Company H, would scale the fences or pick holes through the eighteen inch thick brick walls with their bayonets and knives to crawl out into town. (The 6th Michigan Infantry Regiment did the same thing.)

The Hoosiers made so many escapes from the cotton press that they were moved to another cotton press which proved just as easy for the "sojer laddies" to escape. The men would sneak out in small groups and stay together just to vex the guards who were usually from the Irish 9th Connecticut Regiment. The 1st Indiana's Company H's sergeant Cyrus Hunt called the 9th Connecticut "a set of foolhardy, raw sons of the sod as ever left their 'mither' land." The bully boys would often sneak out of camp just to look for a Nutmeg patrol to taunt and start a fight. Occasionally, the patrol won.

The ballgames, theater, guard breaking and fights were not always enough to satisfy the men or non-commissioned officers. The camp's guardsmen were not immune from trouble. It seems that the colonel went looking for a corporal of the guard because none had answered his summons for one. Upon visiting the guard quarters he found no non-commissioned officers there, except for a lone sergeant. The corporals were likely hiding somewhere nearby sharing a bottle of "Oh, be joyful." The resulting consequences were that Corporals John B. Yelton (Co. H), Stuart [William Stewart?] (Co. I), William Elliott (Co. K) and Nathan P. Calvin (Co. F) were arrested, reduced to privates and released to duty.[16]

By mid–February the general commanding, Nathaniel P. Banks, completed his plans for a campaign to capture and secure for the Union the main avenues used to transport goods by the Confederacy through Louisiana. This included taking the Bayou Teche, Atchafalaya River, Grand Lake, the lower Red River and the Mississippi River. The expedition was delayed due to rising water on the rivers and bayous and the presence of five mile long log jams blocking the channels. A direct attack upon Port Hudson, a Confederate fortress that controlled traffic on the Mississippi River one hundred twenty-five miles below Vicksburg, was impractical at the time.

Port Hudson and Vicksburg were the two strongholds between which a Confederate Mississippi River flowed. At this point in time, General Ulysses S. Grant was trying to find a way around Vicksburg, and completing the canal project begun by Brigadier Thomas Williams during the summer of 1862. Again, if Vicksburg could be bypassed by the canal, only Port Hudson would block full Federal control of the Mississippi River. Many of Banks' New England regiments he brought with him into the XIX Corps were recruited for a nine-month term of service and poorly trained. The delay caused by the log jammed waters would give time to train them.[17]

On March 7, General Banks began moving his forces to Baton Rouge. The 1st Indiana Heavy Artillery boarded the transport *Laurel Hill* and steamed off to Baton Rouge. By March 13, Banks had his army advancing on Port Hudson in a joint operation with Admiral David G. Farragut's river fleet. The Hoosiers remained behind in Baton Rouge where they guarded the waterfront and manned the guns in Fort Williams. This first attempt to take Port Hudson by General Banks and Admiral Farragut would be a Federal failure.[18]

At Port Hudson, Major-General Franklin Gardner had slightly more than 15,000 troops fit for duty out of nearly 20,000 men stationed there. Gardner also had plenty of artillery to keep an attacking force at bay. On March 14, Banks' army arrived in the rear of Port Hudson, but they were too far away to be of any help to the navy. Banks' more advanced troops encountered a few pickets from Rust's brigade. These men engaged in sporadic skirmishing for a few hours, until Rust's pickets fell back to stronger positions. The Federals did not press the matter. The 4th Louisiana Infantry and Miles' Legion rushed to man the outer battlements in expectation of a land attack.[19]

Late that night Admiral Farragut made ready to run the gauntlet of guns at Port Hudson like he had passed Forts St. Philip and Jackson nearly eleven months prior. Feeling sufficient time had been spent for the army to have drawn off units of light artillery and infantry from the bluffs, Farragut ordered his fleet at full steam up the river. Except for the U.S.S. *Mississippi* (a side-wheeler), all of his sloops of war had a smaller gunboat lashed to their side to provide greater power against the current.

The defenses at Port Hudson included between eleven to thirteen light artillery batteries manning fifty to sixty light guns. The river batteries, by this time, mounted nineteen heavy guns, which ranged in size from a 4.62-inch bore Gibbon and Andrews banded rifle (called a 30-pounder by the Port Hudson garrison) to 10-inch Columbiad smooth-bore guns firing from behind twenty-foot thick emplacements.

Confederate engineers had plotted the distances from the heavy gun emplacements to landmarks on both the east and west banks of the river. They had placed signals including piles of brush and a train engine's headlight at these points to ignite in anticipation of a night attack. The fortress' entire complement of heavy and most of the light artillery (a two-mile long gauntlet of cannons) awaited the fleet.[20]

(*See Appendix for the Confederate Engineering Department's list of ranges from the River Batteries to different target zones along the river.*)

The leading ships first came under a scathing fire from the 6-pounder and 12-pounder light guns of Point Coupe Batteries A and C as well as Lieutenant J. Watts Kearney's 20-pounder Parrott rifle located in improvised earthworks on a low part of the bluff just south of River Battery XI. The fleet responded with blasts from its 24-pounder howitzers in the crow's nests atop its stepped masts and their 9-inch cannon. With the high water level of the river, the howitzers were almost even with the gun emplacements atop Port Hudson's bluff. Commander David Porter's mortar schooners joined in from below Port Hudson and the burning fuses of 13-inch shells arched through the night's air toward Port Hudson's defenders.

As the fleet proceeded upstream, it came under fire from the heavier guns atop the bluffs. The seamen worked their broadside guns feverishly to counter the Confederate fire. The pivot guns could be used only with effect at the more distant targets due to the target's elevation. The opposite problem held true for the Rebels manning the heavy guns on the bluff. Their choice targets were those at an angle and not broadside to them.

Confederate riflemen peppered the Yankee gunners trying to work their guns on the ship's decks below. The leading vessels, *Hartford* and *Albatross*, their commanders and pilots blinded by the smoke, turned too soon and ran aground on a large sandbar opposite the heaviest batteries. The Alabamians,' Louisianians' and Tennesseans' eight- and ten-inch Columbiads, seven-inch guns and a rifled 6.4-inch gun inflicted heavy damage on the ships. The Yankees fought back as well as they could — unleashing hundreds of rounds of exploding shells and stands of grape shot against the fortified bluffs, but it was nearly impossible to elevate their broadside guns to fire at the Rebel guns atop an eighty-five foot tall bluff. In due time, the *Hartford* and her consort got off the mud flat and proceeded upstream, around the river bend to the left and dropped anchor to fire their stern guns at Port Hudson.

The U.S.S. *Mississippi* went aground. A hot-shot battery of two 24-pounder guns, commanded by Lieutenant E. C. McDowell, was dug in about fifteen feet down from the bluff's top. A small brick furnace in the battery heated the cannonballs to nearly white heat before they were loaded atop a wet wad, rammed home to sit on the gunpowder and very quickly fired. A red-hot shot set fire to the *Mississippi*.

A 4.62-inch rifle shot from the 1st Alabama's Battery at position #1 knocked one of *Mississippi*'s foretop howitzers from its mount into the river. A sitting duck, the Rebel gunners sent round after round into her. The *Mississippi*'s officers and crew abandoned her, and watched as the flaming hulk slipped from the sand bar and drifted downstream. Near Profit's Island, her loaded guns fired a last broadside salute as the flames touched off the primers. Eventually, she disappeared beneath the muddy water a few miles below Profit's Island and north of Baton Rouge.

The *Richmond* and her escort, *Genesee,* nosed into a mudbank near the bend of the river at the north end of the bluffs. Now she and her stalled companion came under more intense fire. The *Richmond* received major damage to the machinery of her steam engine from the shot of an "80-pounder rifle" (in this case, a 32-pounder gun rifled at 6.4-inches). The *Genesee* received her only hull wound from this rifle. The same rifle damaged the *Monongahela*'s reversing gear as she followed the *Richmond*. Getting free of the mud, they turned back downstream letting the current bear them out of harm's way. In comparison to the *Hartford, Mississippi,* and *Richmond,* the other vessels received light damage before they broke off the engagement and steamed downstream. The Port Hudson defenders fired more than six hundred heavy shot and shell during the three hour engagement with Farragut's fleet. The thunderous cannonade was heard as far away as Fort Pike, Louisiana (about 120 direct miles away), where an unknown Massachusetts diarist recorded hearing the bombardment.

Admiral Farragut's flagship, *Hartford*, and her gunboat escort, *Albatross*, were now isolated between Port Hudson and Vicksburg. Consequently, the crews devoted their time to making repairs and in re-establishing contact with Federal forces below Port Hudson and near Vicksburg. Farragut would also block Confederate shipping coming down the Red River, thus partially accomplishing one of the objects of the expedition.

When the thunder of the guns ended and the *Mississippi* exploded in great spectacle, General Banks stated that the object of the expedition was accomplished and the army returned to Baton Rouge. Admiral Farragut later traveled by small craft down the Atchafalaya River to Brashear City and then by rail to Algiers where he crossed the Mississippi River to New Orleans, arriving on May 8, 1863.[21]

While the naval forces engaged in refitting and repairing, General Banks took time in Baton Rouge to review his options. On the 19th of March he reviewed and inspected the 1st Indiana Heavy Artillery. The new artillerists harnessed their mule teams and proudly paraded through the streets of the city. Crowds of citizens and soldiers stared, admired, cheered or jeered the passing men, officers, 58 drivers and 116 jackasses pulling eight 30-pounder Parrott rifles, two rifled heavy 12-pounder guns, caissons and limbers. Many soldiers yelled: "Good for the bully 21st Indiana Artillery." (Their companion regiments took a while to get used to the new regimental designation, too!) The Hoosiers no longer had a Jackass Battery; they were all the Indiana Jackass Regiment. After the parade, Banks requested that the artillerists form along the waterfront for a firing demonstration.[22]

The 30-pounder Parrott rifles of Companies B, G and H plus the 4.62-inch bronze rifles of Company K lined up along the bank of the Mississippi River upstream from the vessels crowding the wharf. After firing at a mound of earth about 1,300 yards distant, Banks asked the 30-pounder Parrott rifle crews to test their accuracy on two brick chimneys across the Mississippi River about one mile away. The chimneys were about 6 feet across at the base and tapered to 3 feet across at the top.

First Indiana Heavy Artillery Company A with their 20-pounder Parrott rifles at the Baton Rouge Arsenal grounds, 1863. (Andrew Lytle Collection, Mss. 893, 1254, Louisiana and Lower Mississippi Valley Collections, LSU Libraries, Baton Rouge, Louisiana.)

The cannoneers aimed and fired. Four shots were placed into one hole about three feet across near the base of a chimney; another shot chipped its right corner; another shot chipped its left corner and a final shot placed higher and dead center toppled it. The gunners then leveled the remaining chimney. General Banks complimented the artillerists saying: "Bully! Bully! That was the best firing for the distance I have ever seen."[23]

The demonstration must really have impressed General Banks, because on March 29 he ordered the Jackass Regiment back to Brashear City to join General Godfrey Weitzel's command. Weitzel was planning a major expedition up the Teche. The bully boys met up with Weitzel about seven miles to the rear of Brashear City at Bayou Beouf. Captain Grimsley, who loved Baton Rouge, called Bayou Beouf "a God–forsaken spot of swamp, alligators, mosquitoes, Negroes and Cajuns." For five days after they arrived, the Hoosiers' 30-pounder Parrotts and equipment remained on the railroad either in boxcars, platform cars, hog cars or else piled alongside of the track.

While Weitzel waited and the reinforcements arrived, the Union gunboat *Diana* made a reconnaissance run up the lakes and river looking for the Rebel army. Disobeying orders, the *Diana* turned up Bayou Teche for some sugar. Waller's newly remounted and equipped 13th Texas Cavalry Battalion and the Valverde Battery engaged her near Pattersonville. After a hot engagement lasting nearly three hours, the *Diana* surrendered. The Confederates quickly repaired her smashed steering wheel, ropes and machinery. The addition of the *Diana*'s five heavy guns to his waterway defenses greatly pleased Major-General Richard Taylor, CSA.

Meanwhile, Weitzel assigned the Hoosiers to defend Brashear City against any attacks by the gunboats *Diana*, *Hart* or *Queen of the West* coming down the Atchafalaya River or Bayou Teche into the bay. General Weitzel, not wishing to expose his infantry and light batteries to the heavy guns on these gunboats and fearing the Rebels would cut off his supplies and reinforcements by burning the bridges across Bayou Beouf to the rear of Brashear City moved his army to Bayou Beouf while awaiting the arrival of heavy artillery. Now, what with twenty-one infantry regiments and six light artillery batteries under Brigadier-Generals Cuvier Grover and William H. Emory present or scheduled to arrive within a day, and with the Indiana Jackass Regiment's Long Toms to ward off the enemy gunboats at long range, Weitzel moved back into Brashear City.[24]

On the 6th, newly promoted Brigadier-General Richard Arnold, now in charge of the artillery for the XIX Corps, ordered four 20-pounder Parrott rifles removed from the Parapet Line and prepared for field service. He rushed these rifled cannon to the Jackass Regiment at Brashear City where Company E received them.

While waiting for everything and everyone to get into place at Brashear City, General Richard Taylor placed Brigadier-General Henry H. Sibley in command of the Texas troops and General Mouton in command of the Louisiana troops. Taylor sent a battery of small guns to harass the Federals from the Berwick side of the Atchafalaya River. Company B brought two of its Long Toms to bear on the landing at Berwick and sent the Confederate artillery running.

Major General Nathaniel P. Banks arrived on the 8th to direct the overall operations. On April 9, Weitzel and Emory began crossing Berwick Bay with their armies. The crossing took the better part of a day and night. Grover's command boarded transports for a long-distance amphibious operation around the enemy to land several miles to their rear to cut off their retreat.

Contrary to their expectations, the commanding general called upon the Jackass Regiment's Companies B, E, G, and K to participate in the field with the rest of the army. This countered the boys' previous feelings that they would not be invited to participate in the coming field action because of the weight of their heavy guns. Those who remained behind vied to catch the biggest fish and develop their tans into the "darkest a white man can get."[25]

The selected companies of Hoosier bully boys soon had their guns across the bay and rolling along the road to Pattersonville with the rest of the army. Reaching Pattersonville, they moved through the town and pitched their camp on the north side of town.

The next day, April 12, the Federals resumed their march about 11 o'clock in the morning. They moved along both sides of the bayou toward Camp Bisland. Weitzel's skirmishers encountered General Sibley's skirmishers about three to four miles northwest of Pattersonville. The Yankees formed their battle lines and began advancing toward the enemy. By ten o'clock the Federal army with its flags flying formed a line from the marshes to the right of the Teche and to the railroad embankment left of the Teche. The Teche made a wet gap in the offensive and defensive lines. The Confederate defenders displayed their colors in an equally long line opposite. It was a splendid site to behold: the contrasting colors of the lines of men, bright banners fluttering in the wind, sun glinting off rifles, sabers and bayonets, all silently awaiting orders to kill each other.

However, it was not until between four and five o'clock in the afternoon that the Federal skirmishers drove the Rebel skirmishers inside of their fortifications. The 1st U.S. Artillery, Battery A, under command of Captain Edmund Bainbridge, came up, went into position, and began an artillery duel with two Confederate batteries: Semmes' 1st Confederate Battery and Cornay's St. Mary's Battery. The gunboat *Diana* came down and joined in. Cornay, furious at the Yankees occupying his plantation and home about 2,000 yards away, ordered his guns to fire at his own property. Additional light Federal batteries came up to assist Bainbridge and were met by the fire of thirty-nine Confederate guns. Under cover of darkness, the Yankee batteries fell back while Federal infantry probed Dick Taylor's defensive line for weak points and then fell back. Quiet reigned.[26]

Taylor's defenses at Bisland consisted of a line of low earthen fortifications stretching from the swamp at Grand Bay across a neck of land to Bayou Teche. On the west side of the Teche, the fortifications continued parallel to and behind a small bayou used as a water-filled moat until they terminated at the unfinished New Orleans, Opelousas and Great Western Rail Road's elevated rail embankment. The embankment became an earthwork shielding the Confederate right flank.

In the rear of the first line of Rebel defenses on the east bank was a second line of defenses.

On the east side of the bayou, it began at the eastern end of the first line and angled to the rear to reach the bayou about three-fourths of a mile to the rear of the first line. This rear line continued on the west side of the bayou, crossed the railroad embankment, and ended in an impassable swamp about a half mile farther. Taylor's men had constructed a redan by the bayou about halfway between the front and rear parapets. Another redan filled the angle at the eastern end of the parapet.

This well chosen site crossed the only easily traveled land at its narrowest part, and it enabled the Confederates to concentrate their limited manpower for the best firepower effect. The former Union gunboat *Diana* took position on the Teche slightly to the front of the downstream Confederate fortification. From there its large caliber guns could bear upon both banks of the Teche and enfilade the approaching Federal regiments.[27]

General Mouton, commanding the east bank's defenses at Bisland, placed all six guns of Faries' Pelican Light Artillery (5th Louisiana Battery) and a two gun section of Cornay's St. Mary's Cannoneers (1st Louisiana Battery) in position behind the earthworks on the east bank of the Teche. The Pelican Light Artillery's lieutenant B.F. Winchester positioned his section of two 3-inch banded rifles near the redoubt at the extreme left of the line of earthworks; Lieutenant Oscar Gaudet positioned his two 6-pounder guns in the center of the line of earthworks and Lieutenant J.R. Winchester positioned his two 12-pounder howitzers at the right of the line of earthworks near the bayou. Two 12-pounder howitzers from Cornay's Saint Mary's Battery commanded by Lieutenant Oscar Berwick manned the redoubt on the extreme left. Berwick would move his guns on the 13th to the west bank of the bayou to reinforce the defenses against the greater pressure of Yankee infantry and artillery there.

General Sibley, commanding the forces on the west bank of the Teche, placed the three 6-pounder smoothbore guns and two 12-pounder howitzers of the Valverde Battery, Semmes' 1st Regular Confederate Battery, with four 3.67" brass rifles and two 3-inch rifles, and one section of Cornay's Battery into position along the line of the fortifications. Semmes' two 3-inch rifles, commanded by Lieutenant J.A. West, took position about midway between the bayou and the swamp on the right of the line. A 24-pounder gun on a siege carriage commanded the road approaching the defenses where its 5.8-inch bore full of canister or iron trash or both could blast swaths through any force foolish enough to approach it by way of the road.

The dismounted 5th Texas Mounted Regiment, dismounted Waller's 13th Texas Battalion, and the 28th Louisiana Infantry Regiment manned the eastern defenses. Fourney's Yellow Jacket Battalion (10th Battalion, Louisiana), the Crescent Regiment (24th Louisiana), and the 18th Louisiana Infantry Regiment manned the western defensive line. The 7th Texas Mounted Sharpshooters dismounted and manned an outer line of rifle pits on the west side of the bayou. The 4th Texas Mounted Regiment and the 2nd Louisiana Cavalry Regiment plus a two gun section of Cornay's battery made up the Confederate reserve.[28]

A thunderous crash of artillery fire broke the stillness of the early morning on the 13th as the battle began in earnest. Federal infantry moved forward through fields full of uncut sugar cane, the troops taking cover from the rifle and cannon balls in the numerous drainage ditches. All of the defenders' artillery was brought into position and opened fire on the Yankees. As planned, the *Diana* opened an enfilading fire of grapeshot down the Yankees' ranks.

Captain Edward McLaflin's 1st Indiana, Company G, moved its two 30-pounder Parrotts to where they could fire obliquely at the *Diana* from the Federal far left and sweep the earthworks on the left bank. The range was about 2,000 yards distant. McLaflin's Parrotts would fire 250 rounds at the enemy that day. General Banks ordered Company B positioned at his command post in Cornay's sugar house near Cornay's bridge to open fire at the *Diana* with its two 30-pounder Parrotts. At 9:30 A.M. the Hoosiers' third and fourth shots disabled the ship by piercing its armor and exploding in the engine room, killing two engineers and wound-

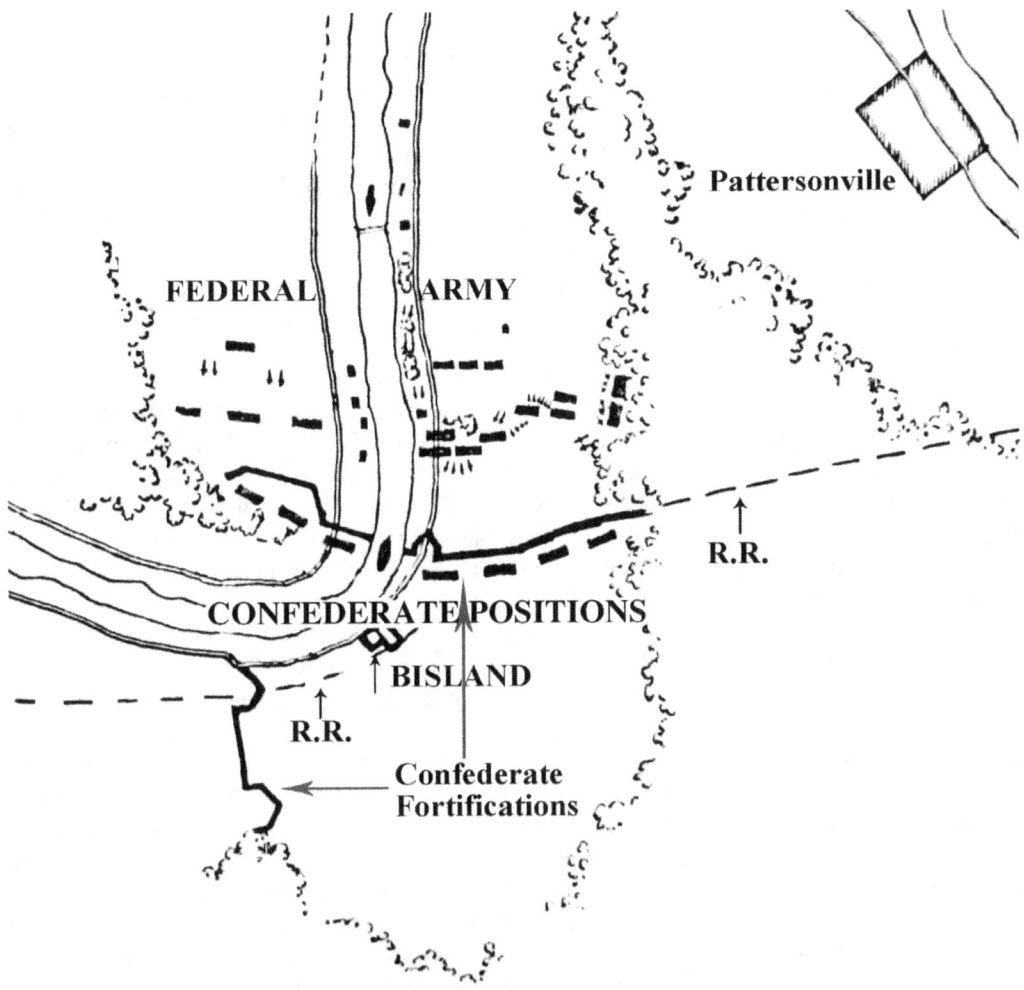

Battle of Bisland — Infantry and Artillery Positions. (Detail of map from National Archives, RG 77-M-111.)

ing five crewmen. Observers reported a large cloud of steam rising from the stricken vessel. Within one-half hour's firing, the Hoosiers had put six of twenty shots into her and taken the *Diana* out of action. Rebel soldiers along the banks of the bayou hauled the *Diana* up the Teche out of harm's way by pulling ropes attached to her stern.

With this assignment finished, all four 30-pounders then turned their attention to the Rebel land fortifications and joined the light batteries in hammering them for the rest of the day. Company B reported hitting a brass 12-pounder in the earthworks and permanently taking it out of action. (This was a piece from Cornay's battery.) While the Hoosiers were occupied with the *Diana*, they became special targets of Rebel artillery. Round balls flew overhead; one narrowly missed the head of a Hoosier artillerist mounted on one of the battery's limber mules as he watched it go by. A 24-pounder shell exploded between Company B's two Parrotts, digging a hole as large as a grave. Another round ball expended its flight, dropped to the ground and rolled after another artilleryman walking to the rear for ammunition; his companions called for him to turn left which he did, keeping his leg from being taken off by the fast rolling ball.[29]

Captain Cox's Company K took position with their two rifled guns in the left center of the heavy artillery and reserve infantry line. Later in the afternoon, he moved his guns forward to within four hundred yards of the enemy works to assist Bainbridge's 1st U.S., Battery A, and Captain William Carruth's 6th Massachusetts Battery that were running low on ammunition. Bainbridge's battery had already lost fifteen of its horses and two gun carriages from the Rebel cannon-fire during the thick of battle. Cox's artillerists here performed excellent service. They fired more than one hundred rounds, driving the enemy gunners from their guns, upsetting a caisson and killing several artillery horses. Captain James Hamrick's 1st Indiana, Company E, held position in the road near Company B and the sugar house used as Banks' headquarters. The Rebel 24-pounder and several light guns across the bayou constantly engaged Hamrick's position.

Mack's 18th New York Black Horse Battery divided its four 20-pounder Parrotts into two 2-gun sections. It worked along the center and the right of the Federal line. The section on the bayou-side road had to change its position several times because of intense enemy fire. The 1st Maine Battery worked its way up the east bank of the bayou to engage the enemy's artillery behind a line of low earthworks on that side of the bayou. Colonel Oliver P. Gooding's brigade of infantry advanced along the east bank ahead of the 1st Maine Battery and captured the advanced enemy rifle pits. At this point the Yankees reformed their lines and kept up a steady fire at the distant entrenched enemy.[30]

Until noon, the battle had been one primarily between the artillery. The Federal infantry mostly maneuvered on the east bank to move in closer to the Rebel earthworks by taking advantage of the cover afforded by using the drainage ditches that crisscrossed the fields. Those on the west bank maneuvered in an open field, going to ground a lengthy distance from the Rebel parapet as the defenders splashed some artillery shells among them. The 1st Maine Light Battery having held on both sides of the bayou, crossed two sections over to the east (right) side of the bayou about 1 P.M. joining a third section, where they fought a heavy engagement from about 3 P.M. until dark. During the afternoon, the artillery continued firing at a slower pace and at more selective targets. The Federal infantry on the east side of Bayou Teche attacked by advancing in short charges, and going to ground, only to rise in a minute and rush forward a few paces before dropping flat again to discourage enemy volley fire. On the west side of Bayou Teche, Colonel Halbert E. Paine's and Brigadier General Godfrey Weitzel's men advanced in two lines of battalions. Captain Richard C. Duryea's 1st U.S., Battery F, advanced between Paine's and Weitzel's men. Bainbridge's 1st U.S. Battery A, and Carruth's 6th Massachusetts Battery, now resupplied with ammunition, moved forward on the left flank.

Weitzel, on the left, tried to gain an advantage against the enemy's works nearest to the railroad embankment. The attack on the left flank halted in a nearly impassable thicket of bushes and briers. The men from the 75th and 114th New York Infantry fired a few volleys through the brush in the direction of the Rebels' works. The return fire from Taylor's Texas and Louisiana troops plus canister and case-shot from Semmes and the Valverde battery dropped 1-inch balls like rain around the New Yorkers. The Yankees hugged the ground until after dark when they safely could pull back. The rest of the Yankee force went to ground a hundred yards or more to the rear of the 75th and 114th New York — a long way from Taylor's ramparts.

Receiving word late in the day that Grover had landed in the enemy's rear at Irish Bend, Banks sent out orders not to press the attack, but to hold position. Banks would allow his men to rest. He would not move until the next morning with the object of crushing Taylor's army between his forces. Therefore, the battle ended at dark with neither side gaining a clear advantage.[31]

After the battle, Faries' battery reported two men killed, nine men wounded, thirty horses killed and eleven horses wounded; they had expended five hundred and fifteen rounds of shot, shell, case and canister during the battle. Faries' center section of six-pounder guns had borne the brunt of Mack's 20-pounder Parrott's fire and from some of the 1st Indiana's Parrott rifles along the bayou. This fire killed Joseph Landry (acting gunner), wounded three other men and shot off the right wheel of a gun carriage. The wheel was replaced while under fire, and the gun continued firing canister until dark.

General Taylor, having been alerted previously to the troop laden transports steaming up Grand Lake in his rear, received confirmation that the Yankees had landed in his rear. Furthermore, the bluecoats were moving to cut his line of retreat from Bisland. That night Major-General Taylor and Brigadier-General Sibley argued over the continued defense of Bisland. Taylor won the argument, placed Sibley in command of the retreating wagon train and ordered the wagons on their way. Taylor placed Colonel Thomas Green in command of Sibley's former brigade. Taylor ordered all of *his* divisions from Bisland's parapets. Taylor's troops began a forced night march to reinforce the infantry regiment, cavalry regiment and two sections of Cornay's battery already waiting outside of Franklin, Louisiana, for the Yankee advance.

Early the next morning, Yankee pickets alerted by the sounds of moving men and equipment sent back word to bring more men forward. Skirmishers cautiously advanced toward the shadowed breastworks and found them abandoned. Three full regiments followed and poured over the earthworks on both sides of the bayou almost simultaneously. Planting their colors on the abandoned fortification, the Yankees declared a victory.

General Richard Arnold congratulated the Hoosier artillerists for "the fire of the heavy artillery...directed at all parts of the enemy's line...for seven hours with accuracy and effect, as the number of dead horses, dismounted guns, in the rear of the enemy's works and the number of wounded with cannon shot in the hospital at Franklin attest." After the battle, the victorious Federals found the Confederate 24-pounder siege gun abandoned in the works. They also found a 12-pounder gun from Cornay's battery with a graze in the barrel lying amid the wreckage of its smashed carriage. The Federals reported losses of forty men and officers killed and 184 men and officers wounded. The Federal artillery had six men killed, 27 men and officers wounded, fifteen horses killed, 12 horses wounded, one cannon carriage lost and four cannon carriages damaged.[32]

Brigadier General Cuvier Grover disembarked his division of Billy Yanks from the steamers on Grand Lake and moved toward Franklin. His men arrived at Bayou Teche a few miles north of Franklin. At this place, the Teche runs in a large loop (called Irish Bend) to the east just above Franklin, Louisiana. There were two bridges across Irish Bend located at the northern and northeastern parts of the loop. Grover's troops crossed over and camped the night of the 13th in the northeast section of the loop. Only Colonel William Vincent's 2nd Cavalry Regiment and a section of Cornay's battery stood between Grover's divisions and Taylor's escape route.

On the morning of the 14th, Lieutenant-Colonel Franklin H. Clack's infantry battalion arrived from New Iberia to reinforce the Confederates. Taylor, now on the scene, ordered Colonel James Reily's 4th Texas Mounted unit into Nerson's Woods, which ran across the neck of Irish Bend. Reily's men dismounted and formed a battle line. Colonel Vincent moved to Reily's left into the northern end of the woods with two guns. Clack's men and two guns from Cornay's battery moved up the road along the Teche and took cover behind sugar cane. The *Diana*, now partially repaired, backed up the Teche into position alongside the infantry forces. Taylor concentrated on moving his army arriving from Bisland to safety behind the screen of Nerson's Woods, relying upon the havoc his hidden soldiers could bring to keep Grover's men from capturing the his entire army.[33]

Grover's forces marched down the road along the bayou and directly into the concealed Confederates. A sharp firefight ensued. The Federal left fell back, and Grover shifted the weight of his advance to the center of the Rebel line. The Rebels lost the ground gained on their right by having to fall back and reinforce the center. Federal musket fire killed Colonel Reily and wounded Colonel Vincent. Command was uncertain until Brigadier-General Alfred Mouton arrived on the scene and assumed overall command of the resistance. The outnumbered Rebels held off Grover's vastly superior force until mouton received news that the main part of Taylor's army had passed to their rear and was marching to New Iberia. Mouton ordered the defenders to fall back upon Taylor's rearguard. The cavalrymen were told to "get your horses as quick as hell will let you." The mounted troopers rode off while the infantry covered them.

The retreating Confederates put the *Diana* to the torch. As she burned in the bayou above Franklin, the supply boats *Gossamer, Newsboy* and *Era No. 2*, anchored at Franklin, likewise, burned to their waterlines. The *Cornie* was spared because she housed nearly one hundred of their wounded comrades.[34]

The Johnnies retreated north, following Bayous Teche, Carencro, Courtableu, and Boeuf to Alexandria, Louisiana. Major-General Banks consolidated his forces, and the Billy Yanks slowly followed Taylor's army. As they advanced along the Teche, the Federals passed several scuttled transports and gunboats. Minor skirmishes took place at Jeanerette and at New Iberia. At the latter place, the triumphant Federals captured the foundry and arsenal.[35]

The Federal army moved on to Vermilionville (Lafayette, Louisiana), where the Yankee juggernaut halted on the banks of the Vermilion River. Taylor's men had burned the bridges across the river and set a small rearguard to harass and prevent an attempt to rebuild the bridges. The Hoosiers' artillery shelled the Rebel positions on the other side. Federal skirmishers opened fire on Taylor's rearguard, which was comprised of Colonel Thomas Green's Texans. Green eventually fell back, and the Federals began building a bridge over the river.[36]

Being short on rations, the advancing Yankee horde gathered forage from plantations along their march. Banks gave orders to post guards to protect the property of persons living in homes with more than one chimney. This left the only the poorer residents as ready prey for the Yankees. However, some of these took advantage of the situation and shared in the invaders' largess. Others (described as Frenchwomen) gave hominy and cold meat to those who asked. One bluecoat guard posted at a large home loaded with provender complained that a year prior he was a Rebel prisoner, and now he was protecting them. Protecting the assumed enemy may have cost Banks some votes on the home front, but it may have pacified the people so treated.[37]

By the 18th of April, large numbers of hungry troops began disobeying Banks' orders against foraging. They plundered Vermilionville of sweet potatoes, chickens, beef and blackberries before they marched to Opelousas. Reaching Opelousas on the 20th, Banks commandeered the most splendid residence in town for his headquarters and ordered his army to encamp in the fields surrounding the town. While revising and discussing his campaign plans with his officers, Banks implemented measures to prevent looting. He ordered a surgeon to be posted in the rear of each regiment during their marches to give sick passes to any one dropping out of the marching column. Cavalry assigned in the rear of each brigade and division had orders to pick up anyone without a written permit and arrest that person as a straggler and looter.

Banks ordered the Jackass Regiment's companies B, G and K's 30-pounder Parrott rifles and rifled model 1841 12-pounders back to Brashear City because they were too heavy for the rapid travel expected of them over soft muddy roads.) Banks retained Company E's lighter-weight 20-pounder Parrott rifles with the expedition in pursuit of Taylor.

Banks' army moved rapidly toward Alexandria; however, orders notwithstanding, some men left their companies and looted nearby homes. Brigadier-General William Dwight personally caught a man from the 131st New York carrying clothing from a private home. Dwight instantly judged and had him shot by a firing squad in front of the whole brigade as an example. The plundering stopped, and the troops moved along faster. As the army neared Alexandria, Banks learned that Taylor's army had retreated up the Red River to Shreveport, more than one hundred miles distant. The army halted at Alexandria, and occupied it and the nearby area for the next two weeks.[38]

The 1st Indiana's companies made their return trip to Brashear City enjoyable by staying intoxicated most of the way. Loosely riding their mules and swaying from the barrels of their cannons they partook of bottles and jugs of "Oh, Be Joyful" while singing bawdy songs to while away the hours as they rode towards Brashear City holding onto one another to keep from falling. Officers were no exception to the festivities. In spite of their besotted condition, they all made it back to Brashear City and into their camp.

As the main body of Banks' army occupied Alexandria, they began constructing a few fortifications at easily defended areas. Companies of detached infantry occupied towns and critical points to hold the conquered territory along the Teche. The 1st Indiana had five companies garrisoned in Brashear City, two garrisoned in New Orleans, two garrisoned in Baton Rouge and one in the field with Banks. At New Orleans, they manned 8-inch siege howitzers on the Parapet Line. At Baton Rouge they occupied the U.S. Barracks and manned the 24-pounder and 32-pounder siege and garrison guns in Fort Williams. At Brashear City, two companies were stationed in the town, one company at Fort Buchanan, one company at Bayou Boeuf, and Company H at Camp Connelly, which was at the edge of a swamp to the northeast of the town.

Those at Brashear City enjoyed an abundant supply of fresh fish from the waters of Berwick Bay. The woods were full of juicy wild blackberries. Because they had liberated plenty of sugar, the men made jam from the blackberries, and they enjoyed an ample supply of it with their rations. Wild game such as duck, turkey, pigeon, and chicken was also plentiful. A nearby flock of sheep (originally fifty in number, now only twenty) provided mutton. Some of the boys in Company H shot an alligator and tried it. John Yelton told that "we boiled the damned thing for a week, and it was still tougher than shoe leather."[39]

After a month of this sumptuous fare, the *New Orleans Era* newspaper reported that a concerted move soon would be underway upon Port Hudson. Unknown to the men at this time, General Banks was writing to Major-General Henry W. Halleck that he had ordered his army at Alexandria to move on Port Hudson. His generals there already had their divisions in motion toward the east and their new objective. This left General Richard Taylor's replenishing and resupplying army far to their rear at Shreveport, Louisiana. Unknown to the bully boys at Brashear, Baton Rouge and New Orleans, Banks planned to include them in his Port Hudson campaign.[40]

(See Appendices for artillery engaged at Bisland and Irish Bend.)

Eleven

48 Days at Port Hudson, Starting May 23, 1863

[Author's note: While the next three and one-half chapters contain information about the Indiana Jackass Regiment during the Siege of Port Hudson, Louisiana, they also describe artillery used by both sides and the work involved in protecting artillery, location of batteries and changes of artillery position, much of it previously not described. It involves the Federal advance upon Port Hudson to its surrender and retaking the LaFourche District and Brashear City. These chapters exclude much of the usual infantry activity contained in other descriptions of the siege to focus on artillery.]

During the first week in May 1863, Major-General Ulysses S. Grant crossed his Federal army over the Mississippi River at Bruinsburg, Louisiana, just south of Port Gibson, Mississippi. From there, he began a campaign through west-central Mississippi that swept Confederate opposition before him. Within the next two weeks, Grant captured the Mississippi state capital of Jackson and turned his army towards Vicksburg, Mississippi, and (depending upon one's viewpoint) fame or infamy.

The Confederacy's president, Jefferson Davis, ordered Lieutenant-General John C. Pemberton (commander of the area along the Mississippi River including Vicksburg, Mississippi, and Port Hudson, Louisiana) to *hold Vicksburg and Port Hudson at all costs* (emphasis added). On May 8, Pemberton wired to General Franklin Gardner (previously ordered to evacuate Port Hudson) to "return to Port Hudson...and hold it to the last. President says both places must be held."[1]

On May 13, 1863, while Grant moved through Mississippi, Major-General Nathaniel P. Banks ordered his generals to move their troops against Port Hudson. The twin bastions of Vicksburg and Port Hudson held 125 miles of the Mississippi River open between them. This long length allowed plenty of area for Confederate river transports and small boats to bypass Yankee patrol boats and bring greatly needed materials and food from Texas across to supply armies in the Confederate East. Cowboys swam herds of Texas cattle across without any interference from Yankees. The Federals had to close this opening to cut off the flow of food and war materials to the eastern Confederacy. Banks intended to have his share of glory in doing this. The Confederacy ranked Port Hudson second only to Vicksburg in strength and importance.[2]

By the 17th, Grover's division had moved from Alexandria to Simmesport, and Emory's division camped only seven miles away. Weitzel's division remained near Alexandria until Grover and Emory reached the Simmesport area. After Grover reached Simmesport, Weitzel moved a few miles south of Alexandria to Bayou Huffpauer from where he could cover the rear of Grover's and Emory's divisions. Weitzel's southward movement also covered the rear of a long wagon train bound for Opelousas and Brashear City loaded with "surplus supplies"

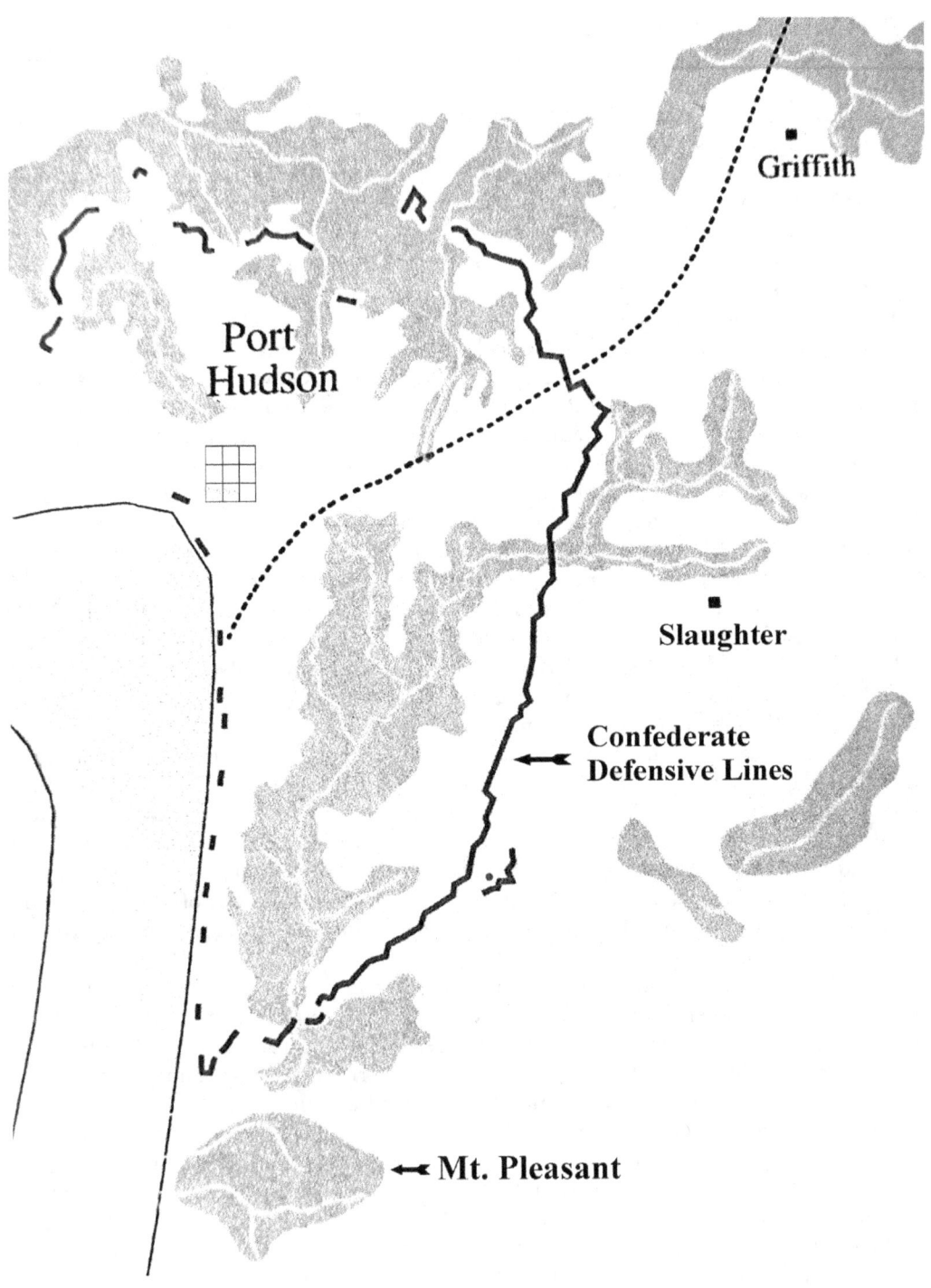

Map of Port Hudson showing Confederate defenses. (Based upon National Archives map RG 77-M-107.)

(cotton and other spoils of war). The warehouses at Brashear City already bulged with 200,000 bales of stolen cotton, and more bales in creaking overloaded wagons were on their way from Alexandria.

Banks ordered Brigadier-General Christopher Augur's division from Baton Rouge to the rear (east and northeast) of Port Hudson on the 18th. Once there, Augur would rendezvous with Banks' forces scheduled to cross the Mississippi River at Bayou Sara north of Port Hudson. Banks' divisions from Alexandria would then march southeast from Bayou Sara to join with Augur. The order to Augur requested that the Indiana Jackass companies stationed at Baton Rouge be left behind.[3]

Banks, from his Simmesport headquarters, relieved the ailing General William Emory from field command and transferred him to New Orleans to take charge of its garrison. At the same time Banks ordered Brigadier-General Thomas W. Sherman from New Orleans into the field to replace Emory. While these orders were in transit, Grover's command was slowly being ferried over the Atchafalaya River by rafts and the wheezy old steamer *Bee*. After carrying over the last of Grover's men, the *Bee* gave up the ghost and rolled over on her side next to the levee. Details of men from Emory's division went to work and turned her top-side-up.

Fortunately, the steamer *Laurel Hill* arrived as the *Bee* turned turtle. The next morning the *Laurel Hill* began ferrying over Emory's division, now under the provisional command of Colonel Halbert Paine of the 4th Wisconsin. The *Bee* was made operational, and she and the *Laurel Hill* made quick work of ferrying Paine's troops across. After crossing the Atchafalaya, Paine moved on to Morganza. On the 22nd, Weitzel arrived, and on the 23rd, he began crossing his troops. With the ironclad gunboat *Pittsburgh* providing river picket duty at Morganza, the steamers *Empire Parish* and *St. Maurice* soon completed ferrying Grover's men across the Mississippi River. As Weitzel's division approached Morganza, the steamers were finishing the job of taking Paine's men across the River. Weitzel was next.[4]

Admiral Farragut had his river fleet, including the iron-clad *Essex*, the *Monongahela*, the *Richmond*, the *Genesee*, and Porter's mortar fleet anchored in the Mississippi River just south of Port Hudson and out of range of the defenders' heavy guns. Since May 8, the mortar fleet had engaged in periodically lobbing 13-inch shells into Port Hudson. The ships *Hartford* and *Albatross* prowled the Mississippi River waters between Port Hudson and Vicksburg. The gunboats *Estrella*, *Arizona* and *Sachem* arrived above Port Hudson by way of Berwick Bay and the Atchafalaya River. They added their guns to those protecting the right flank of Grover's and Weitzel's advance.[5]

While these maneuvers took place, other orders went out that affected Banks' infantry regiments in the southern part of the state and included the rest of the Jackass Regiment. An urgent message to Brashear City on the 19th ordered four companies of Hoosiers to move with "the utmost dispatch" all eight 30-pounder Parrott rifles, two 12-pounder rifled bronze guns, all field equipment, and all ammunition on hand and in storage at Brashear City to Algiers where they would board river steamers to travel upstream. A fifth company of Hoosiers would move to Algiers and take over a four piece, 20-pounder Parrott rifle battery being prepared there. Once equipped, they would board river steamers for travel upriver. General Richard Arnold ordered the quartermaster at Algiers to have steamers ready at the Algiers landing to transport the men, guns, 100 mules for the guns and 50 four-mule wagons with their mules upon their arrival at the docks.[6]

While the Hoosiers packed and moved, Augur's troops had departed from Baton Rouge bound for Port Hudson. On the 19th, an advance scouting party sent by Colonel N. A. M. Dudley went out to check Plains Store and the roads from there to Port Hudson, about four miles to the west of Plains (a.k.a. Plains Store). A few miles from the little crossroads hamlet of Plains, Dudley's scouts encountered Captain Thomas R. Stockdale's Mississippi Cavalry Battalion. A short skirmish followed in which Dudley's men easily pushed Stockdale's cavalry back to Plains and disengaged. That evening, Colonel Frank Powers, chief of cavalry, moved his command of several cavalry battalions forward to reinforce Stockdale.

Upon being warned of the encounter at Plains, Major-General Franklin Gardner sent an infantry force of three hundred men from various regiments and Abbay's battery (Company K, 1st Mississippi Light Artillery) to reinforce Powers on the 20th. Dudley waited as Federal reinforcements approached. Augur's full force of fourteen infantry regiments, three light artillery batteries and a two-gun section of the 18th New York Battery arrived near Plains Store at 6 A.M. on the 21st. At about 10 o'clock that morning Augur's advance clashed with Powers' defense. Abbay's battery blocked the road and unleashed a hellish fire into Dudley's men. Dudley called up Captain Pythagoras Holcomb's 2nd Vermont Battery with six 3.67-inch Sawyer rifles to engage Abbay's guns (six 12-pounder howitzers). In the artillery duel that followed, one of Abbay's pieces was crippled and removed from the field, Lieutenant Erwin Pierce killed, twenty-one enlisted men killed or injured and most of the battery's horses killed.

In spite of the unequal odds, the small Confederate force held off Augur's attack for two hours until the Mississippi battery ran out of ammunition. Abbay's artillerymen withdrew their cannons and empty limbers, attached those they could to their few remaining horses, applied whips to hurry them rearward to their newly arrived caissons parked on the Jackson Road about a mile to their rear. Arriving at the caissons, the artillerists quickly began replenishing their ammunition. Those gun crews not having horses pulled and rolled their howitzers to the rear by hand and determination. Without the canister and case shot to hold the Yankees, Powers ordered his dismounted cavalry and infantry force to pull back before the superior numbers.[7]

Reacting to reports that the Federals had forced his defenders back, Gardner sent out Miles' Legion (400 infantry plus Boone's battery) shortly before noon to reinforce Powers. Miles' skirmishers met the enemy skirmishers on their flank and promptly drove them back about a mile. About this time, the resupplied Abbay's battery fell into line with Powers' men. Powers, hearing Miles' firing, turned and advanced against their now surprised adversaries. Abbay's men attached special ropes (prolongs) and pulled their guns along with Power's men. They fired canister when the cavalrymen fired a volley. After each firing, the artillerists reloaded and rolled their pieces forward keeping pace with the advancing cavalry on foot. In a short time the Yankees were checked. Very shortly after the counterattack rolled forward, Miles' main infantry force and Boone's Battery fell in with Powers, adding their numbers to his counterattack.

Augur sent in Colonel Edward P. Chapin's 1st Division to face Miles' men, but a surprise attack by two Louisiana companies threw Chapin's command into confusion. Rallying his men, Chapin then charged the Louisianans. This attack sent the two companies reeling backwards.

About this time Brigadier-General William Beall (C.S.A.) arrived on the field. Seeing Miles' men were about to be encircled, and Powers' men were severely fatigued, Beall ordered the grayclads to fall back. To cover their withdrawal, Miles moved two guns from Boone's battery up the Plains Store road where they opened an enfilading fire on Chapin. The surprise and disorganization caused by Boone's guns checked Chapin's men and any thought of pursuit. Powers safely withdrew his cavalry north. The Confederate infantry and artillery fell back to Port Hudson in good order. Augur remained at Plains, consolidating his position in the event that the enemy should attack the next day.[8]

Colonel Miles' Legion had eighty-nine casualties among whom were Captain J. B. Turner, Lieutenant Crawford and Lieutenant J. B. Wilson. Captain George Abbay lost four men and Lieutenant Pearson as well as having sixteen men wounded in the fight at Plains Store.

That evening General Gardner placed all of his troops both inside and outside of Port Hudson's main line of defense on alert and ordered one-third of his available men into the breastworks at the eastern and southern breastworks, even though the Yankees' main body was coming from the north. Early the next morning, Gardner ordered several fatigue details to work on strengthening existing breastworks to the east and south as well as to begin constructing breastworks along the northern ridges in addition to the existing rifle pits. Grover's advance, though nine miles away, threatened to penetrate the seemingly impenetrable tangle of valleys, briers, brush, and swamp on the north side. Gardner would take no chances on leaving open holes in his fortifications for Grover's division to use to their advantage. He also needed to keep an eye out for Augur's advance coming down the Plains to Port Hudson road from the east. Would Augur strike his northeast line, or would it turn south and make a grand charge across the open fields to the south?

The Confederate engineers had planned their defenses well. The engineers had marked off a perimeter about one-quarter mile or less from the breastwork and redan defenses to establish the range for their guns and riflemen at different points around their perimeter. Where groves of trees grew within that perimeter, the engineers marked the nearest trees to establish ranges. This provided a defined killing zone for sharpshooters and cannoneers. A couple of masked batteries and unfinished redoubts within the breastworks provided additional firepower and refuge in case of a Yankee breakthrough.[9]

Grover finished crossing the Mississippi River on the 21st. The next day his advance units skirmished with Lieutenant-Colonel J. H. Wingfield's 9th Louisiana Battalion of Cavalry a few miles from Bayou Sara. Wingfield determined that a general movement was underfoot by the Yankees to encircle Port Hudson and prevent any possible means of escape. (Banks had already put two infantry regiments and a section of artillery from Carruth's 6th Massachusetts Battery to patrol the west bank of the Mississippi River across from Port Hudson).

Also late in the afternoon of the 22nd, Brigadier-General T. W. Sherman arrived with his division and positioned his men to the south of Augur. Sherman's troops occupied the area from the center of the earliest built (and impractical) exterior line of detached Rebel redoubts and rifle pits around to the river. (These early detached redoubts and rifle pits were a mile or more distant from the final defenses.) Later that night, scouts from Augur's and Grover's divisions met in the rear of Port Hudson completing its encirclement.

Gardner had placed Colonel I.G.W. Steedman of the 1st Alabama Infantry Regiment in command of the northern defenses on the 22nd. Steedman sent out four companies of skirmishers from the 1st Alabama Regiment to cooperate with Wingfield in delaying the enemy. For two days Steedman's and Wingfield's men scouted and harassed the enemy advance. Steedman also brought up a 5.82-inch rifled siege gun from one of the river batteries and planted it to sweep a ravine approaching his center.[10]

On the 23rd, five companies of the 1st Indiana Heavy Artillery (Companies A, B, G, H and K) arrived with their caissons, equipment, limbers, mules, men, guns and 200 rounds of ammunition for each gun. They reported in to General Augur and parked their artillery along Plains Road about one and one-half miles from the enemy's works. Once their equipment was parked, they pitched tents and slept.

Company E of the 1st Indiana Heavy Artillery, commanded by Captain James W. Hamrick, had arrived with General Grover's command. On May 24, Company E claimed to have fired the first artillery rounds into the defenses of Port Hudson. A Rebel gun firing by the corner of a white-painted house filled with sharpshooters kept General Grover's leading unit at bay by maintaining a heavy fire. Captain Hamrick's 20-pounder Parrotts opened a brisk fire on the enemy gun and house. After two hours, Hamrick's rifles had silenced the Rebel gun, forced its withdrawal and set the house afire. As it burned to the ground, the sharpshooters fled to the rear. Grover's men pushed forward to camp on the enemy's former territory. That night Company E moved their Parrotts into park and awaited further orders.

Other Federal brigades had pushed forward and south around Port Hudson until there was no place for the defenders to escape. The advance dislodged the defenders from the outer defenses of scattered rifle pits and lunettes, which made tidy camping places for some Federals. The Confederates had built about a dozen of these outer works with high thick parapets and a six-foot deep ditch in front, which were large enough to hold 200 men and capable of mounting six to eight guns. Scattered areas of dense forest hid these outer works from the main defenses.

By the 25th of May, General Weitzel's division arrived on the north side of Port Hudson. Weitzel held the Federal right from the Telegraph Road to the Bayou Sara Road. General William Dwight's brigade was on Weitzel's right. General Halbert Paine's brigade was on Weitzel's left. General Grover held the right center by the Jackson Road and north of the Clinton Railroad extending left to Paine. General Augur held the left center with the Plains Road running through the left of his line. General Sherman held the left wing along the Baton Rouge Road. Nearly 29,000 Federal men and officers encircled Port Hudson as follows: Weitzel's, about 5,500; Grover's, about 5,800; Augur's, about 9,200; and Sherman's, about 8,500. All commanders pushed their skirmishers closer to the enemy works, except for Grover who could not advance without encountering the enemy's main defenses.

From the 24th through the 26th of May, Federal skirmishers and sections of light artillery batteries probed the enemy defenses. During the night of the 25th a two-gun section of the 1st Vermont Battery advanced on Sherman's front to within 1,500 yards of the Rebel lines on the southern part of the eastward facing defenses. The Vermonters commenced a probing fire. Rebel gunners answered by firing at the flashes of Hebard's guns. When the sun rose, the gray-clad gunners got the range of their target and shattered the trail of one of Hebard's guns, wounding two men (George E. Allen and Thomas Ritchie) with flying splinters and mortally wounding another (Corporal J. H. Sendell). In a few minutes more Rebel shells disabled the second of Hebard's guns, wounding one man and two horses. The battery called for help to get the guns to the rear and withdrew to repair the guns and treat their men's wounds.

Inside the earthworks, Confederate general Franklin Gardner and about 6,500 fighters, both sick and able-bodied, awaited the coming attack. (Port Hudson also held about forty female residents and their children, camp-followers and washerwomen.) The anticipated attack did not come. General Banks' delay in pushing forward would allow General Gardner a much needed day to strengthen and make some physical changes in his defenses and in his defensive strategy.

Until the 21st of May, except for lines of rifle pits the defenses on the northern portion of Port Hudson were non-existent. The numerous ravines and wooded areas had been thought impregnable. What with most of Banks' army approaching from the north, the gray-clad soldiers received orders to begin erecting breastworks along their lines of rifle pits. Suddenly insecure behind their ravines, brush tangles and felled trees, Gardner's engineers and men fell to work with a strong will and hastily began erecting nearly two miles of low breastworks.

Gardner had divided his defensive lines into three divisions, placing Colonel I.G.W. Steedman in command of the left (northern) defenses, Brigadier-General W.N.R. Beall in command of the center and Colonel W. R. Miles in command of the right (southern) defenses. They bore the responsibility for their defensive works. On the 26th, Gardner's engineers, directed by Colonel Steadman, used 200 Negroes and squads from each regiment to erect a line of these works nearly one-half mile long from Commissary Hill westward to Bennett's by using only a few stacked fence rails in front of a shallow ditch with the ditch's dirt thrown on top. Not having additional time to build them higher and thicker and dig the ditch lower, they would have to do. Work also proceeded on reinforcing and extending the breastworks of a detached lunette in front of the 15th Arkansas. Federal skirmishers made it hot here for the semi-exposed 39th Mississippians working with the Arkansans deepening the ditch in front of the lunette that formed a salient point in the defenses. Elsewhere along the line, workers had cut down the trees within 100 to 200 yards of the breastworks forming a clear field of fire. The workers dragged the downed trees to place in front of the defenses with the base toward the defenses and the tangle of upper limbs pointed outward forming an abatis. Federal skirmishers hiding in the woods, shooting at the workers, prevented construction of an abatis in front of the 15th Arkansas lunette. An abatis would have been a godsend for the Confederate defenders because the lunette extended across a road atop a narrow ridge, which the attackers had to come down to assault the Arkansans and gain access to Port Hudson.

Observing the Federal engineers and Corps d'Afrique busily erecting a bridge across Sandy Creek, Gardner realized his entire left flank was in the air, and the enemy had a clear approach up the low water Telegraph Road along the base of the bluffs and the Graveyard Road atop the bluffs to its junction with Telegraph Road and the town of Port Hudson. He ordered Colonel W. B. Shelby to bring his 39th Mississippi Regiment from the detached Arkansas lunette to the far left of the line and dig in. Shelby's 550 men and Wingfield's dismounted 9th Louisiana Cavalry Battalion began constructing rifle pits along the top of the bluffs along the river and facing to the north connecting a series of light gun emplacements. From Shelby's left to his right the guns were positioned as follows: one breechloading Hughes 2-pounder gun (firing canister) at a mound by the sally port down Telegraph Road, commanded by Lieutenant J.D. Dalliet and a detachment from Wingfield's battalion; three guns from Captain A. J. Herod's Company B, 1st Mississippi Light Artillery Regiment, one gun posted on a hill a short distance from the bluff (position III), another at the sally port of the Graveyard Road and the third one atop the bluff near the Port Hudson Graveyard. These guns commanded the approaches from the willow flats and cane breaks at Sandy Creek up to the edge of the town of Port Hudson.[11]

To further strengthen their landward defenses the southerners moved two smoothbore 24-pounder guns from the Hot Shot Battery on the river to General Beall's defenses near where the Clinton & Port Hudson Rail Road tracks and the Jackson Road passed through the breastworks. Captain F.J. Weller and Lieutenant Lahey of the 1st Tennessee Battalion commanded those guns. Beall also had a smoothbore 32-pounder moved from the river batteries to his lines near the Slaughter's Road sally port at position XXII. Steedman had an additional 5.82-inch rifled siege gun commanded by Lieutenant Asa Harmon of the 1st Alabama Company A, sent from the river batteries and mounted on his lines near Bennett's house. Two 3.5-inch Blakely rifles commanded by Captain Jesse Sparkman of the 1st Tennessee Battalion moved from the river to a position atop Commissary Hill in the rear of General Beall's command and to the rear of Fort Desperate. Again, the engineers went to work and hastily erected earthworks atop the hill to protect the Commissary Hill gun position. (The author indicates this position as IX, which was omitted from period maps.) A 5.82-inch 24-pounder rifled gun commanded by Lieutenant John Sanford, 1st Alabama Infantry Company A, moved to the Commissary Hill battery. A 5.82-inch rifled 24-pounder gun commanded by Captain W.N. Coffin of the 1st Tennessee Battalion moved from the river to the Slaughter's Field lines at position XXIV.

The 4.62-inch "Parrott" rifle was prepared to move from river battery #1 downstream to battery #11. To replace it, a 24-pounder gun was prepared to move from river battery #2 to river battery #1. Quaker guns (peeled logs about eight to ten inches in diameter, hastily shaped on one end into the semblance of a cannon and painted black) replaced the heavy artillery moved out of the river batteries. Work details got busy thickening the ramparts at

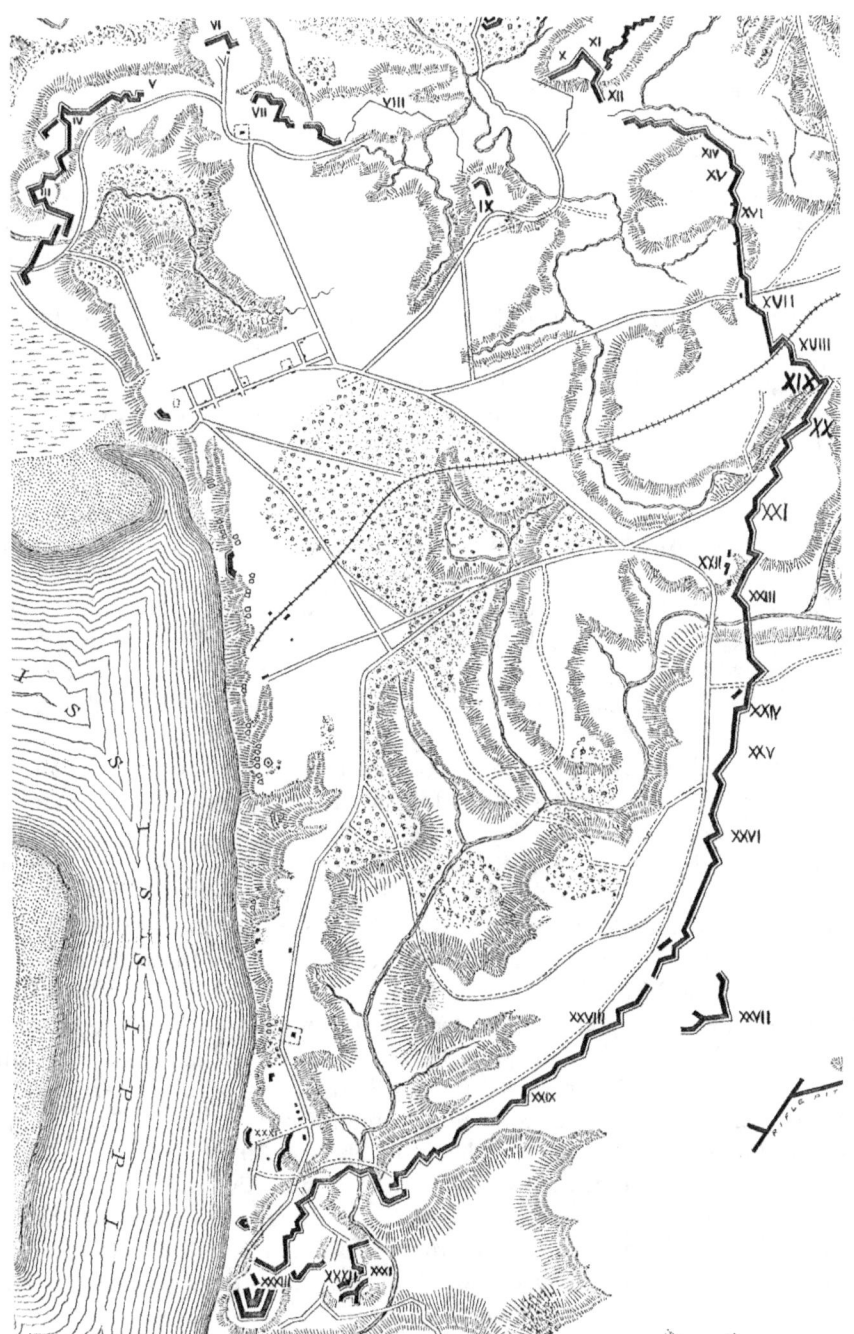

Confederate land batteries at Port Hudson (Roman numerals). (National Archives, RG 77-M-107.)

the heavy artillery positions on the northern and eastern defenses as well as at the Citadel at River Battery XI.[12]

On the 26th of May, Company E reported for duty to Colonel John Keith, commanding the 1st Indiana Heavy Artillery. General Banks ordered Brigadier-General Richard Arnold to take command of all heavy artillery that was not assigned to a division or brigade. General

T. W. Sherman had only two batteries of light artillery to support his attack, and he asked Arnold for additional artillery support. Arnold ordered the 1st Indiana Company A from Augur to report in to Sherman and that evening Company A did so.[13]

That same evening Banks called his generals together for a final council of war. Weitzel was to attack from the north to take advantage of the assaults going on from the east and southeast on the enemy works. Grover would support Weitzel and cover the right flank of the heavy artillery while Augur was occupied. Sherman was to attack the southeastern defenses. As soon as Sherman's attack was under way, Augur was to launch his assault against the middle. All infantry operations were to begin "at the earliest hour practicable."

The Federal commanders gave orders for the posting of their batteries and infantry for the next morning's assault on Gardner's defenses. Banks ordered Augur's and Sherman's light artillery to begin firing at daybreak on the 27th, and the heavy artillery to open no later than 6 that same morning. The attack was to begin simultaneously on the right and left flanks with a final rush in the center as the enemy's flanks collapsed.[14]

(See Appendices for a list of artillery engaged on May 27, 1863.)

About one o'clock in the morning of the 27th, Colonel John Keith began moving his heavy guns into position on Augur's front. Captain Clayton Cox's Company K positioned its two rifled heavy 12-pounder guns on General Augur's right flank about 975 yards from the Rebel parapet. Cox's guns were partially protected by being at the edge of a point of woods in Griffith's fields. Captain Edward McLaflin's Company G moved its three 30-pounder Parrott rifles into a hastily built thinly walled cotton bale and earth emplacement on Cox's left in the center of Griffith's field. McLaflin was within easy field gun and rifled-musket range of the defenders.

Captain James Grimsley's Company B positioned their three 30-pounder Parrott rifles about 2,200 yards from the enemy works and 1,225 yards to the rear of McLaflin on General Augur's right flank. A crude earthwork protected Grimsley's Parrott rifles. Captain James W. Connelly's Company H moved its two 30-pounder Parrott rifles into an open position almost directly opposite the center of the Rebel earthworks and to the right of Company B. Company E waited with its four 20-pounder Parrott rifles along Plains Road to the left of Company B. Both of Keith's lines of artillery had easy access to their positions by way of country lanes running northward from Plains Road.[15]

All three sections of Captain Albert Mack's 18th New York Black Horse Battery moved its six 20-pounder Parrott rifles into position in the field off the north side of Plains Road and alongside of the Jackass Regiment's Company E. Augur's two light batteries, Rawles' and Holcomb's, limbered up and waited for action. Captain Jacob Rawles' 5th U.S., Company G, took position with its six 12-pounder Napoleon guns about 1,250 yards from the enemy breastworks to the right (north) of the Plains Road. A thicket and hedges shielded the battery from the defenders' view. Captain Pythagoras Holcomb's 2nd Vermont Battery took position with its six 12-pounder 3.67-inch Sawyer rifles across Plains Road from Rawles' Battery.

While Augur's and Keith's artillery moved into attack positions, General Sherman positioned his artillery. One two-gun section of the 1st Indiana's Company A 20-pounder rifles took position about 850 yards from the Rebel works behind the smoldering ruins of Slaughter's house at the northeast end of Slaughter's field. The other section took position about 1,500 yards from the breastworks at the south end of Slaughter's field near Gibbon's house. Captain George T. Hebard's 1st Vermont Battery at the north end of a moderately forested area near Slaughter's and Captain James Barnes' 21st New York Battery at the south end of the forest near Gibbon's house waited to move into action when the infantry advance began. An area of brushy woods to their rear sheltered the Yankee army camps whose occupants were being roused from their slumber for breakfast in preparation for the day's coming assault.[16]

Eleven. 48 Days at Port Hudson, Starting May 23, 1863

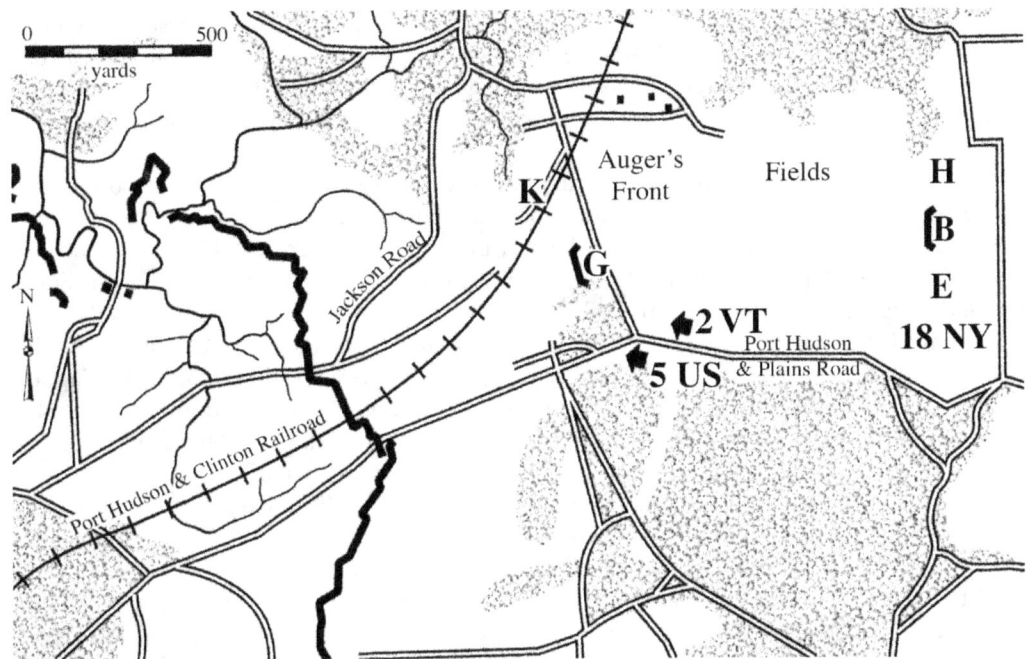

Positions of the Indiana Jackass Regiment's Companies B (3 30-Pounder Parrott rifles), E (4–20-Pounder Parrott rifles), G (3 30-Pdr. Parrott rifles), H (2 30-Pounder Parrott rifles), K (2 4.62-inch rifled Model 1841 [heavy] 12-Pounder Guns), and the guns of the 18th New York (2 20-pounder Parrott rifles), 5th U.S., Co. G (6 12-Pounder Napoleon guns) and 2nd Vermont (6 3.67-inch Sawyer rifles) at the opening barrage of Port Hudson on May 27, 1863, on Augur's Front. (Cartographic design by Mary Lee Eggart, based in part upon National Archives map from RG-77-M-109.)

To the north with Weitzel and Paine, the 1st Maine Battery, the 2nd Massachusetts Battery, two sections of the 6th Massachusetts Battery and the 4th Massachusetts Battery, and Companies A and F of the 1st United States Artillery hitched their draft animals and checked their ammunition. On Grover's front, Company L of the 1st United States Artillery and Company C of the 2nd United States Artillery made ready to advance with the infantry.

During the night of the 26th, thirty-nine regiments of Federal infantry cleaned their weapons, making sure they had forty rounds of cartridges and caps prepared. Some men tried to sleep and others visited with friends. A great number of men wrote letters to their wives or parents and instructed comrades to mail them if they should not survive the assault. Several ran to the bushes to relieve their watery bowels.[17]

Under a flag of truce, Nathaniel Prentiss Banks, major general commanding, sent a brief letter into Port Hudson to Frank Gardner, major-general commanding, C.S.A., offering him a chance to surrender Port Hudson and avoid further bloodshed because Banks had an entire army corps, consisting of several divisions and a great amount of artillery outnumbering that at Gardner's disposal. Further, Port Hudson was effectively circled and his communications entirely cut off. Gardner's response was succinct: "General N.P. Banks, Sir, you demand the surrender of this post, which I decline to do. As you have such an army and immense park of artillery, you must take the post by force, but no other way you can have it. I am Sir, very respectfully yours, Frank Gardner, Major General Commanding, C.S.A."

Gardner's defending artillery from the left to right was a 2-pounder breechloading Hughes gun, the 1st Mississippi Light Artillery Regiment, Company B (Herod's battery of six guns) and Company F (Bradford's battery with one section of two 12-pounder howitzers) and a two gun section of 6-pounder guns of the Watson battery. Supplementing these pieces along Steedman's line were two 5.82" rifled siege guns (manned by detachments from the 1st Alabama Infantry—one at Bennett's house, one at Commissary Hill) and two 3.5" Blakely rifles (manned by a detachment from Captain James M. Sparkman's 1st Tennessee Battalion Heavy Artillery) atop Commissary Hill.

Along Beall's front artillerymen with the 1st Mississippi Light Artillery's Company F (Bradford's battery—one section of two 6-pounder guns), and the Watson battery (two 6-pounder guns and two 12-pounder howitzers), manned their pieces. A 12-pounder bronze rifle ("The Baby"), manned by a detail from the 1st Alabama Company K, Lieutenant Frank commanding, two 24-pounder smoothbore siege guns commanded by Captain Weller and Lieutenant James Lahey, a 32-pounder siege gun manned by a detachment from the 1st Alabama Company D, a 5.82" rifled 24-pounder siege gun ("Virginia") commanded by Captain Coffin with a detail from Company D, 12th Louisiana Heavy Artillery Battalion and six 12-pounder howitzers of the 1st Mississippi Artillery Company K commanded by Captain George Abbay, filled out Beall's artillery compliment. (Abbay's battery shared space on the line with some of Boone's and Roberts' guns from Miles' Legion.) At Miles' front on the right flank were the light guns of Boone's and Roberts' batteries (a mixture of 6-pounder guns, 12-pounder. howitzers, 3-inch banded iron rifles, and a 3.3-inch bronze rifle), plus Lieutenant J. Watts Kearney's (Miles' Legion) 20-pounder Parrott rifle, which had been captured in Virginia from a New York artillery unit and marked "S.N.Y." (The rifle was sent to Port Hudson by order of Jefferson Davis along with the 24-pounder rifle named the "Virginia.")

Within the Confederate lines, nineteen infantry regiments and battalions (some regiments had scarcely more strength than did a full Federal company) waited for the enemy. The men deepened their trenches and threw the dirt on top of the breastworks to their front. They checked their weapons, stockpiled ammunition nearby, and wrote letters to loved ones and friends and, if possible, settled debts. The pensive comrades shared a chew of tobacco or a cigar or pipe with the thoughts that this might be the last time they would engage in this ritual of friendship with one another.[18]

By four o'clock in the morning (by today's Central Standard Time), as the first silver-gray glow of pre-dawn light brought the outlines of nearby objects into a black on dark gray view, Federal preparations for the opening shot into Port Hudson were complete.

As it dawned the defenders' earthworks changed from black to brown in the sun's pinkish glow, when the sound of the signal round's explosion was heard and all of the light artillery opened fire. The signal round was fired by the 1st Indiana's Company A stationed to the rear of Slaughter's house. Brigadier-General Thomas W. Sherman and his staff watched the first rounds fired at the enemy works by these 20-pounders. After watching the shells effects, Sherman retired to his camp with his staff to rest, drink whiskey, eat, drink whiskey, enjoy his staff's company, drink and wait to attack while having a whiskey. (Because he did not believe a frontal assault from all quarters at the same time could take Port Hudson, he would disobey Banks' orders and malinger in his camp. Sherman missed his flank attack's time by several hours.)

For the better part of an hour, the light batteries shot and shell played upon the breastworks to demoralize the enemy and silence their artillery. Showers of flying dirt and debris covered the defenders staying hunkered down behind their earthen walls. Soon the sound of the barrage reached the ears of the crews aboard the U.S. Navy vessels lying in the river both above and below Port Hudson. The navy opened with their long-range rifles and mortars. Now the sun rose above the horizon shedding its full light upon the scene, and the more distant targets became clearly visible to the artillerists.

Now the Hoosiers' heavy rifled cannon and Mack's 20-pounder Parrott rifles on Augur's front pierced the dawn with flaming thunder from their guns' muzzles. Sputtering time-fused shells and solid shot roared across the breadth of Captain Griffin's and Mrs. Loudon's fields. The shots plowed the earth and the shells exploded around the distant Confederate cannons located at Commissary Hill. Shot and shell smashed and blasted at the Priest Cap, the Jackson Road redan, sally ports at the Clinton–Port Hudson Railroad, the Plains Road and the line of earthworks in between.[19]

To the northwest, Weitzel's assault got under way about six o'clock. He seems to have been the only commander to comply with Banks' orders. Dwight's division and Paine's division moved forward along the lanes leading to the northern edges of Port Hudson. Dwight's men, including the Native Guards, moved the farthest to the west, and Paine moved forward across open fields to their right. Within a few minutes after Weitzel's command lined up on the roads for their charge, Grover's division began moving toward Steedman's lines and Fort Desperate.

A section of the 2nd Massachusetts Battery (Nims) and the 6th Massachusetts Battery (two sections) moved with Dwight's advance. The 1st Maine Battery (Healy), the 1st U.S. Companies A (Bainbridge) and F (Duryea) moved into position with Paine's infantry. The Yankee infantry formed their lines in the last level land before a tangle of felled trees, deep ravines, briars and tangled vines. The artillery moved along a narrow road into clearings and went into battery where they prepared to open fire upon their readily visible enemy about 600 yards away. The Confederates ducked for cover behind their breastworks. The Yankee artillerists had a good view of these defenses opposite them that lined the crest of a hill beyond the deep valley of Foster's Creek.

The Confederates had as good a view of the Yankees as they of the men in gray. As the Yankees prepared to open fire on the defenders, the Southrons' guns opened the ball with a murderous cannonade. Surprisingly accurate Rebel cannon fire from near Bennett's house, various places along Steedman's defenses and from Commissary Hill fell among the men and horses of Healy's 1st Maine and Bainbridge's Company A 1st U.S. Artillery batteries. A hissing 24-pound bolt from 1st Alabama Lieutenant Asa Harman's 5.82-inch rifle near Bennett's house smashed through a tall tree, cutting it off about 30 feet above the ground. The toppling mass of timber crushed one of Healy's limber horses, smashed the limber and slightly injured some infantrymen supporting the battery. More Rebel shot and shell quickly took their toll—dropping Healy's horse from under him, killing a private and wounding two more. A corporal and nine privates received mortal wounds within a short time, and thirteen horses in Haley's battery were killed. To their great credit, Healy's men hunkered down at the far side of the opening and held their position, stubbornly throwing up earthworks to their front while returning fire.

The same Rebel barrages killed two men, maimed Lieutenant Humphrey, eleven men and fifteen horses in Bainbridge's 1st U.S. Company A as they prepared for action with Healy. Even as Bainbridge brought his guns to bear on Lieutenant Harman's rifled gun, Harman's well-aimed shot and shells disabled two of Bainbridge's guns in quick succession. Bursting Rebel shells and case shot flung shreds of human and horse flesh onto the trees, bushes and ground. The Federal artillerists and their infantry supports kept to their posts as human and horse body parts along with blood-soaked clothing, hair and skin from Bainbridge's and Haley's two batteries hung and dripped from tree limbs and trunks onto the ground and men below.[20]

Duryea's Company F, 1st U.S., coming into view of the chaotic scene taking place in Bainbridge's unit halted and managed to turn around and move back and left to an elevated opening in the trees a few hundred yards from Bainbridge. They unlimbered and went into action at Federal Position #6 alongside a road leading directly into the Rebel works. Taking heed of the intense Confederate artillery barrage, General Cuvier Grover sent Closson's 1st

U.S. Company L, into action a few hundred yards to Duryea's left (near Federal Position #8). The Rebel batteries on Steedman's lines that had taken such a heavy toll on Company A and the 1st Maine Battery turned their attention to Closson and his infantry supports by pouring an enfilading fire into them. While Confederate artillery paid their welcoming compliments to Closson's Company L, the 1st U.S. Companies A and F and the 1st Maine Battery managed to open a counterfire from all three batteries on the Rebel cannons. Two sections of Nims' 2nd Massachusetts Battery came forward and roared into action between the 1st U.S. Batteries F and L. Nims' rifled guns were slightly farther from the enemy works than Duryea and Closson, but the Massachusetts rifled cannons carried the distance. The combined fire from six batteries or sections eventually silenced the defenders' cannons.

Eventually Nims' cannoneers worked one section to their left and within 700 yards of the enemy. They concentrated their fire upon an advanced detached work across and blocking the country lane they were on while holding the end of a ridge leading into Port Hudson. This vital work was the lunette held by the 15th Arkansas Infantry, under Colonel Ben Johnson, which would soon earn the name Fort Desperate.

The two 12-pounder howitzers of Herod's 1st Mississippi, Company B, in the 15th Arkansas' fort became caught between a blistering fire from Nims' battery's advance section and Closson's guns. A Yankee shell smashed into the wheel of one of the howitzers, exploded, and killed the gun's commander, Lieutenant J.B. Edrington. Two other gunners were wounded as a storm of shot and shell descended on this target, smashing the other wheel, shattering the axle, denting the howitzer's base-ring, and pounding the muzzle into the semblance of a puckered mouth. Within a few minutes, Nims' advance guns came under a flanking fire from Sparkman's Blakely rifles on Commissary Hill and Bradford's nearby 6-pounders. Nims' artillerists limbered up their two guns and withdrew from action. Nims' second section had spent the day working with 1st U.S., Battery L.[21]

While both sides' artilleries worked against each other on this section of the lines, Weitzel's Federal infantry stepped off against the Port Hudson works. Marching down into the ravines and creek valley between the high ground occupied by both armies, the Yankees came under a murderous fire from muskets, shotguns and .69 caliber flintlock muskets loaded with buck and ball. Still they came on and pushed the scattered Confederate skirmishers back into their main breastworks. Southron cannons sent blasts of canister into the blue-coated ranks. Soon the Yankee charge ground to a halt in the tangle of felled trees, vines and briars. The hail of Rebel iron and lead pinned the bluecoats down. Every tree, rock and log had a full complement of huddled bluecoats behind it. Some lay still and dead, others writhed in bullet pierced agony, and others, unscathed, shuddered and wondered when their turn would come as they heard bullets thunk into dead comrades and logs.

The men of the 4th Wisconsin found they were caught between two ravines where enfilading canister would sweep them away. However, as the day wore on, hostilities ceased. Even some friendly banter took place between the Badgers and the 12th Arkansas and 1st Alabama companies. An Arkansas Razorback called out, "What regiment mout [sic] we call you, stranger?" The Badger replied, "The 4th Wisconsin, sir; how do you like our shooting?" The Razorback: "Ye shoot mighty well—no fault t' find, sir." The Badger: "When are you going to give us the fort?" The Razorback: "When you take it, I reckon."[22]

As Weitzel's assault came to a standstill, Brigadier-General William Dwight ordered Colonel John A. Nelson to attack the far-left flank along the riverside bluffs. Nelson ordered the 1st and 3rd Louisiana Native Guards into column. Free men of color composed the 1st Regiment of Native Guards, which had colored officers. Contraband blacks formed the 3rd Regiment of Native Guards, which had white officers. Dismounted cavalry troops formed in the rear of them. Crossing Sandy Creek on a pontoon bridge erected the night before, the Native

Eleven. 48 Days at Port Hudson, Starting May 23, 1863

Twelve-pounder howitzer, disabled by artillery fire from Closson's Company L, 1st U.S. and Nims' 2nd Massachusetts that also killed Lieutenant J.B. Edrington who commanded the piece. The opposite side of the cannon's muzzle is smashed flat against the muzzle side in this image. It was located in the eastern Salient of Fort Desperate. (Courtesy of Military Order of the Loyal Legion of the United States, housed at USAMHI, Carlisle Barracks, Pennsylvania.)

Guards marched forward along the narrow road toward the towering bluffs ahead. The road provided the only dry ground between the creek and the bluffs as it cut through marsh and swampy backwaters from the Mississippi River. The assaulting columns came under fire from Company B of Colonel W. B. Shelby's 39th Mississippi infantry and fifteen men from Wingfield's Battalion, making a total of sixty sharpshooters. Shelby's keen-eyed riflemen manned advanced rifle pits atop knobs projecting from the farend of the bluff's ridge top.

In a matter of minutes, three 6-pounder guns from Herod's Mississippi Battery, a rifled 24-pounder from River Battery #1, one small rapid-fire breechloading cannon and two small mountain howitzers began hammering at the closely packed Native Guards' columns. Lieutenant Sorrel's 6-pounder gun at the sally port at the head of the road loaded with solid shot and drove off the Federal's two supporting 12-pounder howitzers crossing the bridge to unlimber. Sorrell's fire was so accurate that the two howitzers pulled back across the bridge, taking up flanking positions in the rear of the bridge. Undaunted by the lack of artillery support, the Negroes pressed on. Filing out to their right, they formed into line of battle and moved toward the Rebel works. Five more companies of Shelby's men came up and moved into a trench line running along the crest of the bluffs. More rebel heavy artillery fire rained down upon the Native Guards as a 42-pounder in river battery #2 swung its muzzle around to the north and opened fire.

The Native Guards charged the Rebel positions. At a distance of two hundred yards from their goal of entering Port Hudson, point-blank discharges of canister from the light guns, bursting shells and foot long pieces of railroad rail fired from the 10-inch Columbiad at Battery #4 tore huge holes in the Guards' rank and file. A sheet of flame burst from atop the bluffs as the 39th Mississippi fired a volley and then followed it with as rapid a fire as possible into the climbing Negroes. Three times the Native Guards reformed their ranks and charged, but the defenders' fire was too much. The Native Guards fled leaving about 200 dead and dying behind. A Federal rout!

A few of the surviving Native Guards crossed the bridge to safety, most dived onto the willow marsh and took cover where they could find it in the muck and grasses and wished they could sink deeper into the soft earth as shot and shell shattered the willow trees and plowed mud near them, throwing sharp splinters into them and gobs of mud onto them. General William Dwight refused the pleas of Colonel Nelson to allow his depleted regiments of Native Guards to retreat; Dwight ordered them to "Keep your negroes charging as long as there is a corporal's guard of them left.... When there is only one man left, let him come to me and report."[23] The colored soldiers had to remain in the morass for four hours more, trying to keep up a desultory fire at the bluffs. The 39th Mississippi and 9th Louisiana Battalion defenders had no casualties. Some Confederates swore a Yankee regiment fired into the rear of the Negroes to halt their retreat, thereby causing many of their losses. Dwight ordered them to charge as long as there was a "Corporal's Guard left of them." Several Mississippians crawled over the breastworks and took armaments and souvenirs from the bodies nearest to them. They found commission papers in a breast pocket of a mulatto captain (Andrew Cailloux) dated September 20, 1862, and eight greenback dollars.[24]

In the northeast bend of the defenses, another wave of Federal blue, under command of General Cuvier Grover, moved against an outer-work called Fort Desperate. Due to the heavy blasts of artillery fire towards Colonel Benjamin Johnson's 15th Arkansas' position, cannon smoke concealed the three regiments of Yankees until they were within one hundred yards of the Rebel earthworks. Johnson let his prey advance to within 60 yards of his works when he gave the command to open fire. A storm of musket fire and blasts of 12-pounder doubled-canister caught Grover's men coming down the narrow causeway (a forty to one hundred-foot wide ridgeback). Many of the bluecoats trying to dodge bullets tumbled down steep ravines to the side and tried to scramble up them. A small tangle of felled trees and a lot of briars and brambles tore at the men's clothing. Again, minie balls and buck and ball took their toll among the Yankees. The main body of Grover's assault broke at its center, fell back, drew in its flanks upon its center and rested.

An hour after the first assault, Grover's men charged again. This time Johnson's men held their fire until the Yankees got within 40 yards of their parapet. Again, they unleashed a massive volley, but only one howitzer on the left flank could fire canister at the Yankees. This time the 160th New York pressed forward getting more than one hundred men into the ditch in front of the earthworks, which gave the defenders a break from any Federal artillery fire. In the ditch, Yankee officers gave rousing speeches to urge their men to go up and over the parapet and take the enemy. After challenging his men to do so and getting a chorus of "ready," the officer yelled "charge." As he rose atop the parapet with eight men, they were all felled by musketry and fell into the ditch. The Yankees were trapped. They threw rocks, sticks dirt clods and trash over the parapet at the defenders. The defenders tossed it back. Some defenders stuck the muzzles of their guns loaded with buck and ball over the parapet and blindly pulled the trigger hoping to hear a Yankee cry of pain. After some time of this unequal standoff, the devious Yankees in front of Steedman raised a white flag; and Steedman complied with a cease fire. While the white flag was raised, the double-crossing Yankees calmly marched out of the ditch back to where they started — a clear violation of the white flag in the Rules of War.[25]

It was now past 11 o'clock in the morning and all remained fairly quiet on the Federal Left, except for Rebel sharpshooters shooting at any exposed bluecoats. What had happened to the coordinated attacks? The Confederate defenders on their left flank had fully repulsed some of the attackers and brought the others to a standstill, pinned down in the abatis, brush, stumps and logs. The battle against the north end of Port Hudson was over for the day. Banks waited in vain for the sound of an assault coming from his left flank. After waiting more than a modest amount of time, Major-General Banks mounted and rode to Brigadier-General T. W. Sherman's headquarters. Banks found his subordinate, Sherman, and his staff at lunch and quaffing copious quantities of spirits, well to the rear. Banks (a volunteer officer) raised hell with Sherman about his inability to follow simple orders and left determined to replace the West Pointer and regular army officer. Reaching his headquarters, Banks ordered Brigadier-General George L. Andrews to take over Sherman's command and lead the troops into battle. Andrews mounted and rode to Sherman's camp. Arriving there, he found a contrite but besotted Sherman and his staff officers all mounted and ordering his men into action. Andrews prudently decided not to interfere and to let Sherman begin his assault.[26]

At 2:15 P.M., six hours late, Sherman led his division into action with Brigadier-General Neal Dow's brigade on the right and Brigadier-General Franklin S. Nickerson's brigade on his left. Roy's Parrott rifles intensified their fire as the infantry came up. Captain James Barnes' 21st N.Y. Battery and Captain George Hebard's 1st Vermont Battery raced out from their cover, unlimbered and went into fighting positions—Hebard to the right of a wooded area about 550 yards from the enemy parapet, and Barnes' to the left of the same woods at about 800 yards from the enemy. The batteries went to work providing covering fire as the infantry formed their battle lines and began moving out of the woods for their charge. The 15th New Hampshire supported Hebard's guns.

The Federal batteries opening fire brought about a surprise response from a masked Rebel 24-pounder. Captain W. Norris Coffin sat a few yards to the rear of his primed and loaded gun waiting for the Yankees to show themselves before they went into action when the gun roared flame and smoke. Coffin looked over and saw smoke still rising from its vent and muzzle, and he began looking for a careless gunner to cuss out. An officer of a nearby light gun called out that it had fired itself. Sure enough, the battery position was empty of men; the port-fire was propped against the side of the earthwork. An examination of the piece showed it had been grazed across the top of the barrel and across the vent. The friction of the enemy projectile had ignited the powder train and fired the piece. The Confederate friction primers were very unreliable so the gunners resorted to the old-fashioned method of pouring a powder train into the vent and then lighting it with a port fire (a stick with a slow burning fuse cord wrapped around it and a bracket at the end holding the burning part.). The force of the projectile had also moved the gun's aiming slightly so it had fired directly at the enemy battery. The accidentally aimed cannon ball forced the Federal artillerists to change their position.

The Federal infantry's right, led by the 6th Michigan Infantry, forced its way around the remains of slave cabins and through four board fences around the burned Slaughter family's residence. Rifled minie balls smacked into the 6th Michigan as they destroyed the fence and emerged through its gap-toothed cover of board palings. The Sixth Michigan lost a third of its men in this charge.[27]

The accurate barrage of pre-assault Federal artillery fire had forced Captain George Abbay's 1st Mississippi Artillery Battery to pull their cannons back from their embrasures. Along the Confederate defenses, Abbay's six 12-pounder howitzers spread over an area covering a quarter mile long front between positions XXV and XXVII. Captain Abbay's officers and sergeants, R. Abbay, Kell Shaifer, Wheelis, Mimms, McDonald, Girault and R. Love, each commanding one of five 12-pounder howitzers and two 6-pounder guns in barbette positions, waited for their turn at the Yankees. Captain Abbay smoked his pipe with Shaifer, Wheelis and Mims. They waited squatted down with their men behind the breastworks in a three gun position in the center of Dow's approach across the fields. To the south, a detached lunette guarding a badly needed water well held one of Abbay's howitzers to bring a flanking and enfilading fire upon the Yankees. Two more light guns manned by men from Boone's and Roberts' battery occupied the breastworks to the lunette's rear at Nickerson's approach against them.

Due to the long wait between attacks, reinforcements arrived from the northern defenses where the assaults had stopped. Colonel Miles' sent over reinforcements from his river end of the line. A mixture of Arkansas infantry regiments and a battalion made up of odd companies and squads from Louisiana and Texas held the line from Slaughters' past Gibbons' fields to Miles' Legion's area. The anxious defenders placed their extra ammunition on the yellow clay breastworks in front of them to facilitate reloading and ducked below the breastworks to wait. In a few minutes, Rebel sharpshooters opened sporadic fire as the Yankees stepped out of the woods. A couple of pieces of Rebel light artillery opened with solid shot. The Federal advance had moved forward but about fifty yards when a shot brought down Sherman's horse. Dazed, the now-sobered Sherman rose to his feet and continued forward urging on his men.

Dow, on the right of Sherman, led his men down a shady lane among magnolia trees leading to Slaughter's house. The 6th Michigan men tore down a board fence in the grove of magnolias, advanced through the ruins of Slaughter's house marked by assorted scorched debris and two tall chimneys. Ahead was another solid board fence. Pushing it over with enthusiasm they discovered directly in their front cannon muzzles aimed at them that no one knew were there. The bluecoats' lines now in full view and less than 800 yards away began taking casualties from exploding case shot and shell fired from a couple of 6-pounder guns. In a minute the concealed 24-pounder at position XXIV opened on them with shell. On came the boys in blue, filling in the gaps in the front rank with men from the rear ranks, after advancing a few more yards, the Confederate gunners switched to grapeshot.

As the bluecoats got within 150 yards (considered point-blank), Captain George Abbay ordered his 1st Mississippi gunners to run out their double canister charged howitzers from hiding, yelling: "Now, boys, I want you to stick to the pieces and give the Yankees hell!" (Double canister from a 12-pounder would fire either forty-eight 1.5-inch iron balls or ninety-six 1-inch balls at a time, giving a weight between fifty-five to seventy-five pounds of iron to rip through flesh and bone with each barrage.) In about five minutes, the 6-pounders and the 24-pounder to Abbay's left switched to grape and canister.

As Abbay's artillerists sprang their trap, the entire confederate infantry line blazed a volley of musket and shotgun fire into the bluecoats. Sherman, leading his men forward on foot advanced only a short distance when a blast of canister shattered one of his legs below the knee. Along with dozens of his men, General Neal Dow also went down, wounded in the left thigh. Great gaps appeared in the lines as the canister-balls and massed volleys of minie-balls and buck and ball (buckshot and round shot packaged together) smacked into flesh and bone — felling scores of Yankees. Pushing forward into the hail of death flying among them from a crossfire of cannons, a fifty-man Forlorn Hope carrying fascines and long planks to bridge the ditch and the 128th New York's skirmishers pushed to within 110 yards of the Rebel parapet, where the enemy fire forced them to take cover in a six-foot deep gully filled with tree limbs and blackberry briars. The regiment's colonel lost his life in the charge. Most of Dow's men now bogged down upon abatis of felled trees with their spiky upper branches pointing into them and in an abatis-lined gully. In a short while they would flee to better shelter.[28]

Eleven. 48 Days at Port Hudson, Starting May 23, 1863

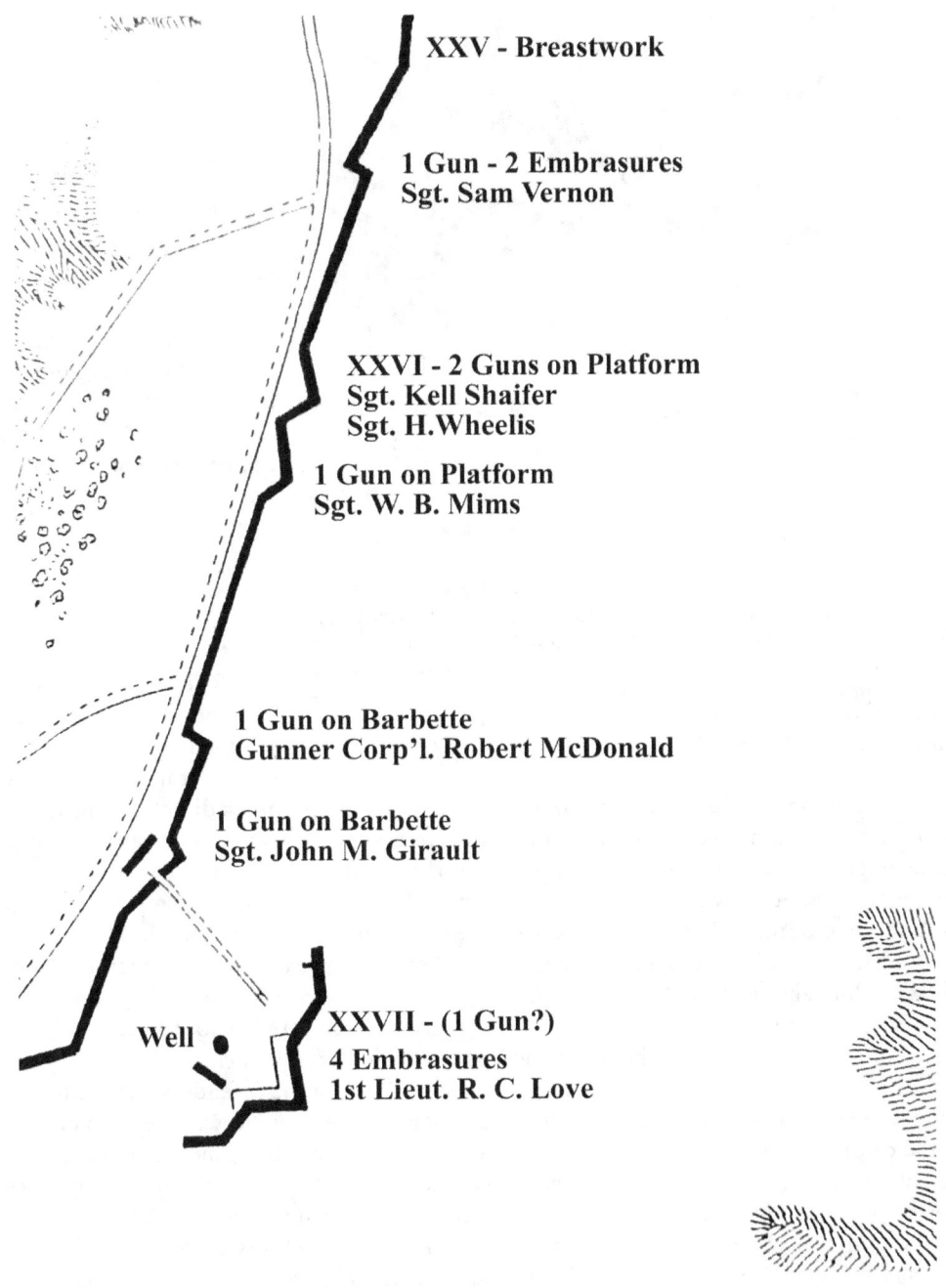

Slaughter's Field, showing Captain George Abbay's battery, First Mississippi Light Artillery, Company K's positions at the breastworks. Slaughter's and Gibbon's fields are in front of Abbay's guns. The Federals attacked from the right of the map. The individual Confederate gun commanders' names in Abbay's battery were written on a map by Sgt. Kell Shaifer. Kell was later promoted to lieutenant. An important well is represented by a round dot in the detached lunette holding Lt. Love's cannon. The site of the detached lunette is on private property, but the owner has placed a marker at the site and it can be viewed from the Port Hudson National Cemetery. (Geographic detail is from a map in the National Archives, RG-77-M-107. Names added from a copy of Kell Shaifer's map provided courtesy of Mrs. Elizabeth Shaifer Hollingsworth of Mississippi.)

Thirty-two-pounder gun (in background) disabled by 1st Indiana Heavy Artillery, Company A, and 2nd Vermont Light Artillery. Unscathed 3.3-inch Leeds rifle in foreground belonging to Boone's battery, Miles Legion. Located at north end of Slaughter's Field defensive position XXIV and opposite Federal position #15. (Courtesy of Military Order of the Loyal Legion of the United States, housed at USAMHI, Carlisle Barracks, Pennsylvania.)

Now in command of the division but unaware of it, Colonel Nickerson pressed on, waving his sword and urging his brigade forward across the south end of Slaughter's fields and north and central portions of Gibbon's fields. In spite of Nickerson's brave encouragement, many Yankees faltered and went to ground. In the detached lunette guarding a well and held by the 4th Louisiana, one of Abbay's howitzers packed with home-made canister of scrap iron, chains, nails, etc. bound in cut-off shirt sleeves or pant legs, waited to fire at point-blank range.

The 165th New York, a red-pantalooned Zouave regiment, advanced on the Confederate defenders as if on parade and was repulsed. Now, it came on again at the double quick directly at the lunette. The lunette's cannon fired, a section of Roberts' artillery on a rise about 400 yards to the rear of the lunette fired, a mass of .58 and .69 caliber rifles and 8- and 10-gauge shotguns within the lunette fired. A few volleys brought the red pantalooned Zouaves to a complete halt. They dived to the ground at 70 yards or less from the 4th Louisiana's lunette taking cover behind anything they found that looked like shelter. The Zouave flag bearer defiantly planted the regiment's colors ahead of the lunette. Bullets brought the colors down, and they were picked up only to have the bearer shot down. The flag rose and fell three or four times until it fell finally for lack of a bearer. All the while, the Zouaves' colonel, stood nearby, waving his sword and exhorting his men to rise up and charge forward. Most of the defenders refused to shoot at the colonel because of his bravery. After the last flag-bearer went down, the colonel picked up the colors and stood firm. A little while later, a Confederate sharpshooter put a bullet in the colonel, bringing down the seemingly charmed officer. As one of the defenders started over the breastworks after the flag, a red-panted soldier ran up, snatched the flag from the ground and bore the colors to the rear. Soon the brave colonel was carried off the field by stretcher bearers without incident. The defenders held their fire at the stretcher bearers out of respect for the officer's bravery. One of the defenders later commented that the Zouaves' charge made here was the finest charge of the war.

In a few minutes, there was another charge, and Abbay's howitzers to the Federal front and left plus exploding shells from a 3-inch banded Parrott rifle to their far left with an enfilading fire brought another charge to a halt. Again, the 4th Louisiana defenders in the lunette brought their rifles and shotguns into action and the Zouaves, again, fell back or dropped to the ground faking injury or death until nightfall, again, leaving their flag behind. The Zouaves had not realized, until they were caught in a deadly crossfire, that they mistakenly focused their attack on a detached lunette with flank extensions on each side, while the main Rebel line of breastworks lay several yards behind it. A section of Roy's 20-pounder Parrotts to the Zouaves' left covered their retreat. The Louisianians' took the Zouaves' flag for a trophy. The defenders took at least nine of the wounded Zouaves prisoners.[29]

Dow's men were now subject to flames caused by exploding shells in the brush and trees in which they hid. Dow's shattered brigade, throwing caution to the wind, hastened to the rear or melted away into a ravine to their right. The ravine led to safety in the rear of Slaughter's place. As they moved away from harm into the ravine, the 20-Pounder Parrotts of Company A near the Slaughter house's remains once again opened fire covering the retreat. The 6th Michigan Regiment lost seventeen men killed and one hundred eleven wounded in the aborted assault. Later that afternoon, now supported by the 15th New Hampshire Infantry, the first section of Company A's Parrotts dismounted the enemy 24-pounder gun that had inflicted several casualties among Dow's men. The second section of Company A dismounted a 3.3-inch bronze rifle. (This occurred after Augur's assault got underway.) Company A had two men, Privates Thomas Cole and T. B. McConnell, wounded in the day's fighting.[30]

After sunrise, the long-range rifles of the Jackass Regiment opened fire against artillery targets on Commissary Hill, the Jackson Road redan, the Clinton and Port Hudson Railroad, the earthworks between the railroad and the Plains-Port Hudson Road, a corn mill, repair shops, food storage and ordnance storage buildings inside the defenses. These targets occupied areas in front of Weitzel, Grover and Auger. When Captain Edward McLaflin's Company G guns first opened, Confederate rifle fire and light artillery fire took a heavy toll upon the crews in their exposed position. Amid the minie balls ricocheting from his guns and carriages, McLaflin yelled to his infantry support: "For God's sake, hurry up, boys, they are shooting us down!" The 50th Massachusetts Company E's riflemen hurried into action and contained the enemy sharpshooters' fire.

Six-pounder shot and shell from a section of the Watson battery and from Bradford's battery punched into Company G from their right front and right flank. Heavy shot from two 24-pounder smoothbores and a 4.62-inch brass rifle ("The Baby") came from their front and right. While the shot and shell battered Company G, several riflemen from their infantry supports dropped their packs, haversacks and rifles and helped man the guns. Exploding Rebel shells broke off the sponge in one of the guns, blew the lanyard away and knocked the handspikes from the hands of the crewmen. Flying Rebel shell fragments killed Privates Harrison Grey and George Morris of Company G.

Round shot repeatedly struck around the center gun and eventually blew off its right wheel. The Indianians and the Massachusetts boys got a spare wheel from the limber, rolled it into position, jacked up the three ton gun and carriage, and replaced the wheel while under fire in an open field. Company K (to the right of G) took up the fight, and after an hour they silenced the light guns, dismounting one of them. The Hoosier Company K's infantry support was the 50th Massachusetts Company K. The determined McLaflin, now supported by fire from his fellow Hoosiers in Companies B, E and H to his rear, and by a two-gun section of Captain Pythagoras Holcomb's 2nd Vermont Battery, silenced the 24-pounders after an hour of intense artillery dueling. During this exchange, an exploding shell broke the axle of one of Holcomb's guns. The gun's crew moved the disabled gun and its companion to the rear for repairs.

Captain James Connelly's Company H, working a little more than one-half mile to the rear of Company G, reported that as they helped Company G they, too, dodged shot and shell from the formidable 24-pounders. However, the 24-pound shot did not worry them too much. Private Rufus Dooley in Company H reported that while reading a letter he received that morning, he would move to dodge a cannonball, read another page and dodge again as another 24-pound ball came bouncing toward him. His casual attitude changed when the cannonballs came faster, and they had to man the guns and return fire to silence the 24-pounders for a while. Mack's 18th New York Battery, to the Hoosiers' left, reported that while the enemy targeted Connelly's 30-pounders, they left their battery alone. Mack's battery had different problems. After they opened fire, some of their shells exploded prematurely or stripped their sabots over Holcomb's gunners. Mack's battery ceased firing until either Holcomb moved or Mack acquired targets in a different area.

Shortly after 8 o'clock that morning, the enemy artillery's fire stopped as Weitzel's and Grover's assaults ground to a standstill. After a brief wait to resupply, the defenders again opened with slow and deliberate artillery shelling for half an hour then ceased.[31]

The Federal heavy batteries worked during most of the morning to keep the enemy guns silenced. The combined fire from Connelly's, Cox', Grimsley's and McLaflin's rifles dismounted two of the heavy guns and one light gun in the center of the enemy works. The Parrotts silenced the four pieces of Rebel artillery on Commissary Hill, wounding Captain J. L. Bradford and mortally wounding Captain James Sparkman. A Parrott shell exploded at Sparkman's feet, mangling his lower body and driving some of his own accoutrements into his groin and shredding it. He died after a few days of horrible pain and suffering. Bradford and Sparkman commanded two 3.5-inch Blakely rifles, one 24-pounder rifled siege gun and one 6-pounder gun.

During a short break in the firing, the 1st Indiana's quartermaster passed out buckets of whiskey to the thirsty men manning the rear line of Parrotts. Those Hoosiers on the front line of rifles were too exposed to the enemy for the quartermaster to ladle out his "Oh, be joyful" to them. The business of dodging rifle, musket, and artillery fire kept McLaflin's and Cox's men too occupied to think about what they were missing. Once they silenced the enemy artillery, their front row of heavy guns slowed to a timed maintenance fire for the rest of the morning; then, the foremost heavy batteries partook of the whiskey.

That afternoon after Sherman's assault got under way, in obedience to orders to move only when he heard the guns of Sherman's assault, Major-General Christopher Columbus Augur, now ordered his men into line of battle across a front less than one-half mile wide. Augur's front ran from the ravines north of Slaughter's field across Plains Road to the edge of a ravine just north of the Jackson Road. As Augur's infantry formed their lines of battle, the two rows of artillery prepared to open again upon the defenses. Light artillery of Captain Jacob Rawles' 5th U.S., Company G, Lieutenant Frederick W. Reinhard's 4th Massachusetts Battery, and Captain Pythagoras Holcomb's 2nd Vermont Battery galloped into positions in line with the front row of heavy guns. The reinforced front row of heavy artillery and the rear row opened fire with a ground-shaking barrage against the Confederates to their front. (Rawles' Napoleon guns were several yards to the left of McLaflin's 30-pounders, and Holcomb completed the line to the left of Rawles.) A mixture of thirty-eight light and heavy guns fired 720 pounds of shot and shell against the defenders every two minutes.

Rebel artillery responded at once. Rawles' battery came under a flanking fire from a 3.3-inch rifle, a 32-pounder and another large rifle gun. The Confederate fire was very accurate and Rawles' was ordered to move 200 yards to his right where a thicket would screen his battery from the enemy. Rawles accomplished the move in good order and opened fire for a short time. A two-gun section of Rawles' Napoleons under Lieutenant Craft moved 300 yards forward to a strip of woods and opened fire, which the enemy returned vigorously causing the section to move again. Holcomb's battery moved forward as did Rawles' sections. The two batteries opened fire from 1,000 yards and continued firing until their ammunition ran out. The enemy fire that had began at a rapid pace slowly diminished. One by one the Federal tor-

Eleven. 48 Days at Port Hudson, Starting May 23, 1863 135

Blakely rifle in working order positioned atop Commissary Hill, one of two positioned there. (Courtesy of Military Order of the Loyal Legion of the United States, housed at USAMHI, Carlisle Barracks, Pennsylvania.)

rent of flying iron systematically silenced the Confederate cannons. Holcomb and Rawles limbered up and moved to the rear.[32]

His lines formed, Augur ordered his men forward. The storming party, carrying bags of cotton and fascines to fill the ditches, moved out with the front ranks of riflemen. The front row of artillery fell silent as the soldiers marched through and to the front of them. The rearmost line of artillery slowed its fire. Only an occasional shell flew over the advancing infantrymen's heads as the gunners tried to keep the enemies' heads down and prevent their shooting at the oncoming blue infantry lines. Augur's men came upon hedgerows of Osage orange which slowed their advance. Once through the hedgerows the Yankees dressed their lines and pressed forward. Advancing about 50 yards farther, the attackers ran into an abatis that slowed their movement to the advantage of rebel sharpshooters. Some yards past the abatis, the Federals came upon shallow gullies filled with tree limbs forming a deep gauntlet of fast tangled obstructions, which brought the Yankees to a dead stop. The blue-bellies went to ground on their bellies.

The Confederate commanders shifted men from the northern and far southern lines to reinforce the new point of attack. General Thomas Sherman's drunken refusal to follow orders gave the defenders plenty of time to maneuver to the next hot spot. The reinforcements from the north end of the Confederate defenses arrived in time to fire a devastating volley into the stalled blue-bellies. Free from pounding by Federal artillery, the 24-pounders fired bags full of fragments of railroad rails, spikes, broken chains and nails, at Augur's regiments, which

Lieutenant Lahey's blasted 24-pounder smoothbore gun. Located at Plains Road sally port. (Courtesy of Military Order of the Loyal Legion of the United States, housed at USAMHI, Carlisle Barracks, Pennsylvania.)

scythed gaping holes through the blue lines. The Yankees took refuge behind tree stumps, the logs of the abatis and even lumps of earth thrown up by exploded shells. The fascine and cotton bag bearers dropped their useless items and fled to the rear.

Again the heavy guns began firing. Company H sent a man high into a nearby pine tree to observe the enemy and report the results of their fire. The Federal heavy batteries had worked during most of the morning to keep the enemy guns silenced. Now, the combined fire from Connelly's and McLaflin's Parrott rifles dismounted the two 24-pounders and one light gun in the center of the enemy works. Lieutenant Lahey of the 1st Tennessee Artillery Battalion, commanding a 24-pounder opposing Augur, saw his gun not only dismounted but pounded into scrap metal by 30-pounder shells fired from Company H. Federal shells also blew holes in the Rebel parapet unmasking a few Confederate light guns ready to fire into Augur's infantry.

After a short rest under cover, at 3:30 P.M. the colonel of the 48th Massachusetts, James O'Brien, ordered his men up, to fix bayonets, and charge. They moved forward, and in less than a minute, a minie ball killed O'Brien. Colonel Edward P. Chapin, leading the 116th New York, collapsed after a bullet entered through his nose and tore apart his brain. One-legged Colonel William F. Bartlett, riding his horse because he could not walk and lead the 49th Massachusetts Infantry, toppled from his saddle as a bullet smacked home. Bartlett lost an arm from this wound. This, the third phase of the assault, fell yards short of its goal, as had all the attacks. Lieutenant J.B. Briggs of the 4th Massachusetts Battery took one 12-pounder gun and hurried across the open field to the right flank. From there, he opened a partially successful fire to draw some of the enemy's attention from the storming party.

Rawles' and Holcomb's guns also moved from cover to draw off the musket fire from the Rebel ramparts and to cover the retreat of the able-bodied. Firing at a distance of 1,000 yards from the enemy lines, Rawles' and Holcomb's gunners emptied their ammunition chests. While waiting for more ammunition to come up, they received orders to withdraw. Then the heavy guns from the 1st Indiana's Batteries E, G and K withdrew from the front and went into park a little more than a mile to the rear. By six o'clock, Augur's batteries had all moved into park.

Fires started by the flash of bursting shells and muskets' muzzle flashes ignited dry grass and timber in some abatis. Flames caused wounded Federals to move from cover, which exposed them to sharpshooters. General Christopher Augur, unlike General Sherman, was not wounded; he had urged his men onward from the rear of a large gum tree.

Some have criticized General Augur for not advancing when he heard the attacks of Dwight, Grover and Weitzel; however, Augur followed Banks' orders, which called for him to attack *after* Sherman attacked. The day's failure must be placed squarely onto the shoulders of General T. W. Sherman for disdaining to follow orders from a Volunteer commanding officer and not advancing with Grover and Weitzel.[33]

As the firing ceased around the lines, the fatigued Rebels stood and stared over their earthworks and the heaps of bodies before them. Not a word was spoken or a cheer given. The wounded Yankees that were able to do so crawled off the battlefield to the rear without harassment. As night fell, stretcher-bearers moved out and carried off the wounded and dead near the Federal lines. In the rear, fatigued surgeons who had been hard at work during the day kept at it. Severed limbs and gore piled higher around their operating tables.

Similar scenes on a smaller scale took place behind the Confederate lines. By virtue of being behind fortifications, most of Gardner's men's injuries were relatively few, but they were head and shoulder injuries of varying severity. The Rebel artillery had taken a major pounding. Federal cannoneers had blown the muzzle off Lahey's 24-pounder gun totally disabling it. Masses of hurtling Federal iron had dismounted all of the light guns on Commissary Hill. Several other cannons scattered along the defenses met a similar fate. A lucky shell from the fleet, fired more than two miles distant, knocked a 10-inch Columbiad cannon from its carriage in river battery #5 at the same time tearing apart a private from Company G, 1st Alabama, who was standing on the gun's carriage. Except for Sergeant W. L. Ellis, exploding shells and sharpshooters bullets had killed or wounded every man and officer in the 1st Alabama Company K's detail, manning the "Baby" (4.62-inch brass rifle) at the Jackson Road redan opposite Augur's front. While moving the "Lady Whitfield" to battery #11 through the camp area, more than a mile to the rear of their breastworks, an exploding shell killed a 1st Alabama private. Observers estimated the Confederate casualties as 200 for the day.

Federal casualties reached 1,995: 15 officers, 278 men killed; 90 officers, 1,455 men wounded; 2 officers, 155 men unaccounted for. For individual regiments, the 165th New York Zouaves had the highest percentage of losses and the Negro troops the second highest percentage of losses during the day's fighting.[34]

The artillery on Augur's and Sherman's front had performed admirably. A few statistical reports gave the following information: the 1st Indiana's Company A fired more than 650 rounds before, during and after Sherman's abortive assault; Company G fired 450 rounds from their three 30-pounder Parrott rifles. Company B did not report the number of 30-pounder rounds it fired or if it hit anything.

Company H, consisting of two 30-pounder Parrott rifles firing percussion shells dismounted one Rebel gun and silenced two others in General Augur's front. Company H fired between 200 and 250 rounds from its two Parrotts. Company H had received heavy return fire from 24-pounder siege guns (the only ones with range to reach them), without damage. (Having witnessed the folly of other men who had a foot torn off by placing it in the way of a slowly rolling cannonball to stop its progress, Connelly's men stepped aside from rolling

24-pound balls and kept their feet.) Company K, with two heavy 12-pounder rifled bronze guns, fired 300 Schenkl rounds, dismounting one enemy gun during its eight hours of engagement. Enemy return fire severely wounded two men in the battery.

Rawles' 5th U.S., Battery G, fired 180 rounds—mostly exploding shell and case shot. Lieutenant Briggs' section of the 4th Massachusetts Battery fired only 16 shells during his one and one-half hours in action on Augur's right flank. Holcomb's 2nd Vermont Battery fired 202 Sawyer shells and canister.[35]

That night the Hoosiers' Company A joined its two sections into one battery positioned near the remains of Slaughter's house. After reuniting its pieces, it began a timed fire of one shell at fifteen-minute intervals throughout the night to ruin the enemy's sleep. Companies H and B remained in their positions, where they, too, maintained a timed fire . Both of these companies reported no casualties for the day other than some dust in the men's eyes and the loss of a mule in Company B.

In spite of a heavy rain, the Confederates began repair work began on artillery carriages and remounted the dismounted guns. Soldiers stealthily crawled over their breastworks and confiscated Enfield rifles, Springfield rifles and ammunition nearer to their works dropped by dead, retreating or wounded Federals. The Confederate defenders happily added the prized Enfields and Springfields for "long taw" shooting to their personal arsenals and kept their buck and ball charged flintlock muskets for close shooting. That evening, Banks having failed to carry Port Hudson by storm, summoned his officers and engineers to lay plans for taking it by siege. Banks had to satisfy himself with the fact that he had advanced his lines forward a mere hundred yards or so all around the fortifications.[36]

Twelve

At Port Hudson, May 28–June 14

Neither the officers nor the fighting men could have known the coming siege would become the longest total siege of the war. Banks sent out a flag of truce about 10 A.M. on May 28 that lasted long enough for the Federals to gather the wounded and dead from the battlefield; however the burial details left many of the Negro soldiers where they fell. Men from the 39th Mississippi tied rags over their noses to block the terrible fetid stench of rotting bloated black bodies that were strewn across the road and the face of the bluff in front of their trenches and rifle pits. Even though Banks sent out letters extolling the virtues of the Negro soldier's fighting abilities, he did not honor them with proper removal and burial. He let the Negro enlisted men's bodies lay and rot in front of the 39th Mississippi's breastworks. Banks, a typical Massachusetts politician who said one thing and did another, reserved burial for only the dead Native Guard officers, who were either free men of color or white. The 39th Mississippi thought in common that Banks could not drive them out; therefore, he intended to stink them out. The compassionate Mississippians felt it was a shame that the Yankees had buried all the white men and left the poor black creatures to melt in the sun to be a larder for birds, beasts, bugs and worms. The rebels asked Banks if he would remove and bury the Negroes. Banks replied that he had no troops over there. (Six weeks later several decomposed Negro and "free men of color" bodies, skeletons and bones scattered by dogs, feral pigs, coyotes, etc. still remained.)

During the cease-fire, Banks ordered his engineers to begin constructing a series of offensive earthworks, including battery emplacements and trench approaches (saps) to Gardner's lines. Most of the Native Guards (now renamed the Corps d'Afrique) from the failed attempt of the 27th were pressed into the Pioneer units as laborers for the engineers. They would wield spade, axe, saw, pick and shovel, instead of rifle and bayonet, to construct a series of disconnected rifle pits, trenches and artillery emplacements that would stretch almost six miles roughly parallel the Confederate works. From these earthworks the Yankees would slowly dig toward the Rebel parapet.

Banks' military telegraph department began stringing wire. It was nearly impossible for couriers to gallop through the thick, vine-covered woods surrounding Port Hudson. The same trees prevented signal towers from being effective means of communicating by signal flags, excepting across the open river between the navy and cavalry patrols on the west bank. The telegraph people nailed their wires to trees and poles set in clearings between the trees. In a week, fifteen miles of wire and five operators at Grover's Headquarters (HQ), Banks' HQ, Augur's HQ, Dwight's HQ and Springfield Landing saw to it that messages and new developments were quickly made available to all of the Federal commanders.[1]

Banks sent mounted couriers galloping to Baton Rouge to have all available infantry regiments that could be spared from defending Baton Rouge, Brashear City and New Orleans to move to Port Hudson to reinforce his besiegers. Banks' orders concerning artillery were to General Emory, in command of the defenses of New Orleans. The orders required moving four 9-inch guns from the fort at English Turn, Louisiana; four 8-inch siege howitzers from Fort Parapet; five 24-pounder siege guns, four 10-inch mortars and four 8-inch mortars from New Orleans; plus two Billinghurst-Requa battery guns stored at the Vicksburg Cotton Press in New Orleans to Port Hudson. (Due to defective primers, these 24-shot guns were not fired at Port Hudson.) He also requested that Emory in New Orleans send him three additional light artillery batteries. From Admiral David G. Farragut, Banks requested 500 hand grenades.

Banks ordered Brigadier-General Richard Arnold, chief of artillery, to call up all available siege artillerists and all of the guns manned by the 1st Indiana Heavy artillery. Arnold complied by calling Company C with their four 8-inch siege howitzers from Camp Parapet and Company D with five 24-pounder smoothbore siege guns from Brashear City and Baton Rouge. Getting the 9-inch guns at English Turn was a problem. The army turned to the navy for assistance. They had 9-inch guns aboard their ships at Port Hudson. Admiral Farragut agreed to help.

The Federal supply officers had their main supply base and depot at Springfield Landing on the Mississippi River a few miles below Port Hudson. A road (currently being improved upon) led north to the Federal camps for teamsters to haul the wagon-loads of ammunition, food and clothing to Port Hudson. The medical corps established a hospital at the landing to hold the injured awaiting the next vessel going to New Orleans. General Arnold appointed Lieutenant S. E. "Ed" Armstrong from the 1st Indiana Heavy Artillery to duty at Springfield Landing as the acting ordnance officer with the responsibility for receiving and distributing all army stores.

Responding to Banks' call for infantry, eight regiments left behind in the Teche country to occupy various towns captured during that spring's Teche Campaign packed up and hastened by road to Brashear City, then by rail to New Orleans and by steamer to Port Hudson. The result of this withdrawal of Federal soldiers left the territory along Bayou Teche wide open to be retaken by General Richard Taylor's Confederates.[2]

Banks also set to work realigning his divisions and brigades. General Dwight assumed command of the wounded General T. W. Sherman's division. General Dow's brigade came under the 6th Michigan's Colonel Clark and was assigned to General Dwight. General Grover assumed command of the entire right wing with Dwight's former brigade assigned to General Weitzel. General Paine commanded a brigade between Grover and Augur. General Augur retained command of his former division and assumed over-command of Dwight. Newly promoted to brigadier general after making his famous foray from Tennessee through Mississippi into Louisiana, Benjamin Grierson assumed command of all Federal cavalry in the area. His cavalry not only had the responsibility of guarding the rear approaches to Banks besiegers, but also to guard the supply depot at Springfield Landing and the supply roads from that remote point up to the offensive lines.[3]

Violating a white flag, Yankee engineers dragged in some chopped bushes to screen their activities and began digging a sunken battery position for Healy's 1st Maine Battery. Later, after the white flag expired, engineers began fortifying and building emplacements near where the 1st U.S. Companies F and L had occupied on May 27. Bainbridge's 1st U.S. Company A moved into position next to Duryea's Company F on the 28th. Both of these companies and the 1st Maine Battery maintained a very slow fire during the day, and at precisely midnight every night they sent a brief flurry of solid shot arcing high overhead at maximum elevation in the general direction of the Rebel encampments. The 1st Maine lost two men wounded by a cannon's accidental discharge.

After a few days, the Confederates reconstructed a 10-inch Columbiad river emplacement so that it could fully turn 360 degrees to bear on the landward side. The 10-inch piece became so effective at its inland fire that the Yankees called it Old Demoralizer. Her gun crew affectionately called the piece Lady Davis. At midnight it returned the Federals' midnight fire. The range from the Columbiad was close to two miles, but their aim was on line with their target. The 1st U.S. artillerists watched as a bright flame erupted upwards from behind distant trees followed by a spark that grew larger as the 128-pound shell approached and exploded over riflemen in front of them or swooshed over their heads to explode in camp to their rear.

While Banks waited for more men and artillery and prepared siege works, Gardner was not idle within his defenses. Gardner had the other 10-inch Columbiad and the 8-inch Columbiad mounted on center-pintle carriages, and he ordered an 8-inch shell gun (named Lt. Col. DeGournay after the commander of the left end of the river batteries) remounted in a higher position and on a center pintle carriage that fired inland as well as covering the river. Moving the shell gun took about a week. The defenders in the trenches dug them deeper and threw the dirt higher atop the breastworks in front of the trenches. Soldiers rolled stout headlogs atop their breastworks. (So named because they had a small hole cut out of the dirt or logs under them to shoot through so that the top-most log protected the head of the shooter.)

The defending infantrymen constructed traverses across their trenches perpendicular to the face of the trench to block Federal enfilading fire from sweeping the length of their trenches. They placed sharpened stakes in the ground in front of their breastworks. At the Priest Cap, its defenders dug a maze of pits, planted sharp stakes pointing upward and covered them with brush—calling the pit and stake defense the Rat Trap. They filled additional bags with dirt and sand leftover from deepening their trenches and piled the bags in front of their earthworks to strengthen them against light artillery fire. Spacing the bags with small gaps between them and laying another bag on top bridging the gap also gave the defenders the same advantage as a headlog. The spaces were large enough to look through and pass a rifle barrel through to shoot but narrow enough usually to protect the shooter.[4]

On the 28th the Confederate engineers constructed a siege carriage for a 32-pounder smooth-bore gun. By the 29th they completed the carriage, mounted the gun and moved it from its river battery to the siege lines near Slaughters' field. Another 24-pounder moved from its river battery to the land defenses. The 32-pounder rifle moved from river battery #III to river battery #X; a 42-pounder moved from river battery #III to river battery #I.

By the 28th of May, Lieutenant Pratt had his 4.62-inch Parrott rifle (Lady Whitfield) in position at the Citadel. Also in the Citadel was a 5.82-inch 24-pounder rifled gun (the Virginia) from River Battery VIII commanded by Lieutenant L.A. Schirmer of the 12th Louisiana Artillery Battalion. Both pieces had taken much longer than planned to make the trip to the Citadel because of having to fill numerous shell holes blown in the narrow road atop the river bluff by the mortar fleet. About 6 A.M. the two guns opened fire on the mortar boats and the *Essex* anchored about a mile downstream. After a few rounds the mortar boats backed off to a safer distance. The *Essex* lobbed three nine-inch shells at the battery position in the Citadel. The shells exploded on the gun platform knocking a canteen off the cascable knob of the Parrott and slightly wounding a Private Tunnel—he being hurled through the air to land on his face. He got up, dusted himself off and wiping blood from his face said, "Well, boys they liked to have got me." While his wounds were not disabling, he was relieved from further duty that night. Lieutenant Pratt then helped to serve the gun.

A little later, as Lieutenant Pratt stood atop the parapet observing the effect of his gun's firing, a 9-inch naval shell exploded as it plowed into the parapet under Pratt. The explosion hurled the lieutenant through the air to land in back of the battery. Lieutenant Schirmer then assumed command of both heavy guns, while Pratt, literally shell shocked but not shell-struck, rested. Battery XI's projectiles struck the *Essex* several times. After a shell from the Lady Whitfield flew through an open gunport on the *Essex,* she closed her gunports and backed down the river. The Parrott rifle had fired forty-nine 4.62-inch shot and shell, and the 5.82-inch 24-pounder rifle had fired fifty shot and shell at the *Essex* and the mortar boats.

Late that night between 11 P.M. and 12:30 A.M., the mortar fleet came back up the river and a brief engagement took place between them and the two heavy guns. A mortar shell burst behind the Citadel and wounded three men of the 12th Louisiana Battalion. Lieutenant Schirmer commanded the 4.62-inch rifle, and after firing nineteen shells, the mortar fleet moved downstream out of range.[5]

The Federal light artillery, being more maneuverable than the heavy artillery, began moving into siege positions within a couple of days after the 27th of May. They could move their pieces into places initially protected by a couple of felled trees and screened by brush. The 6th Massachusetts moved a section of 12-pounder howitzers into Federal position #2 commanded by Lieutenant John F. Phelps, and Healy moved his six 3.67-inch bronze rifles a little farther to his right into Federal position #5. Work on position #4 had not yet begun, but work on position #3 was nearly finished. Work on two other positions began farther out the ridge opposite Bennett's house, but they would not be occupied for three weeks.

On the evening of May 31, Captain Edward McLaflin's Company G with its three 30-pounder Parrotts moved to General Grover's front where it occupied part of a shallow, unreinforced emplacement recently vacated by the 1st U.S. Artillery's Company F. One 30-pounder Parrott from Company B, under Lieutenant William Blankenship, was detached from that company and assigned to McLaflin on Grover's right wing.

By June 1, McLaflin's four guns occupied the semi-exposed position #7 only 400 yards from Steedman's defenses. They commenced firing and received only a moderate amount of return fire from sharpshooters. Perhaps the sharpshooters were too good, because Private Vincent Powers deserted from Company G in the face of the enemy on June 1. Lieutenant Blankenship, firing in conjunction with a section of Lieutenant Phelps' 6th Massachusetts Battery in position #2, nearly opposite him, succeeded in dismounting a 24-pounder rifled gun on their first day of firing. Phelps' shot knocked spokes out of a wheel and Blankenship splintered the trail. The Rebel gunners jacked the piece up on blocks to keep it from falling, but Blankenship's shell sent the blocks flying and the gun collapsed to the ground. A 30-pounder shell explosion killed two men, Sam Hagan and Bob Bailey in Company H, 1st Alabama, near the 24-pounder. Most of the guns on Commissary Hill and on the line of the 1st Alabama had been dismounted during the last week, causing John A. Kennedy of the Alabamans to declare, "They were the best artillerists I ever saw."[6]

On June 1, the four 8-inch siege howitzers of Company C, commanded by Captain Elihu Rose, and five 24-pounder guns (one gun borrowed from Company I) of Company D, commanded by Captain William Hinkle, arrived from Baton Rouge at Springfield Landing. The men of the companies proceeded directly to report to General Arnold and Colonel Keith at Port Hudson. Their weapons remained at Springfield Landing awaiting teams to haul the heavy guns and equipment to their positions at Port Hudson. Colonel Keith assigned Company C into a position under construction on the left of the center of the besieging lines. Company D received orders to place three of its five guns, under Lieutenant Jesse Haddon, in Federal position #13 under construction on General Augur's left and two guns, under Lieutenant William Harper, to the right of General Dwight, who had assumed General Sherman's command, in Federal position #15 under construction.

Company E moved one section of 20-pounder Parrotts under Captain James Hamrick to the rear of Federal position #15 on June 1. The position was to the right of General Dwight. When the position was completed, Company E would share the battery with the two newly

McLaflin's Company G, 1st Indiana Heavy Artillery, with two 30-pounder Parrott Rifles in position #7 when photographed. (Courtesy of Military Order of the Loyal Legion of the United States, housed at USAMHI, Carlisle Barracks, Pennsylvania.)

arrived 24-pounder guns of Company D under Harper. Harper's guns still sat at Springfield Landing awaiting transportation. Once in position they would maintain a regular fire at the enemy for the next two weeks and succeed in dismounting a 32-pounder smoothbore. Eight companies of the Indiana Jackass Regiment had joined with the fourteen light batteries surrounding Port Hudson to provide covering fire and to destroy the enemy's buildings and guns. Batteries from the Indiana Jackass Regiment's Companies F and I did not participate in the siege. Company I remained in the defenses of New Orleans, and Company F, while training many recruits, manned the artillery defenses at Brashear City.

The light artillery batteries moved around as well as the heavies. A two-gun section of 3.67-inch Sawyer rifles from Captain Pythagoras Holcomb's 2nd Vermont Artillery Battery moved to the far right of the Federal line. It occupied Position #3 on June 1, and it opened fire a few days afterward. The move placed their Sawyer rifles within 400 yards of Bennett's House and in easy range of Whitfield's 9th Louisiana Cavalry (dismounted), the 39th Mississippi Regiment and a portion of the 1st Alabama Infantry. The Confederate guns at the knoll overlooking Telegraph Road, Slaughter Pen and Bennett's Redoubt received the Sawyers' attention as well as the men in the ridge-top rifle pits on the far left of the defenders' lines. This battery fired several bolts and shells across the town of Port Hudson while targeting the heavy artillery (especially the 10-inch Columbiad) on the river by aiming at the clouds of smoke they made when firing. However, the gunners fired too short and showered the buildings in the town with iron and lead. General Gardner's headquarters was hit several times, one projectile missing him by a few inches. In the next few days, the Sawyers' missiles riddled Gardner's headquarters and many buildings and dwellings in the town. Two soldiers standing in the roadway visiting with each other lost their heads to one of the 2nd Vermont's missiles.[7]

On June 2, General Banks requested the 1st Louisiana Engineers to construct a road between Dwight's Headquarters and Springfield Landing in order to transport heavy artillery. This would include the six heavy pieces for Companies C and D of the Indiana Jackass Regiment, which arrived there on June 1 and the anticipated 9-inch Dahlgren guns being loaned by the navy. Also that day, Lieutenant Benjamin Harrower of the Jackass Regiment's Company G, commanding one 30-pounder Parrott rifle now in position #4, received instructions to depress his gun's firing in aiming at strategic buildings on his left that were deep within

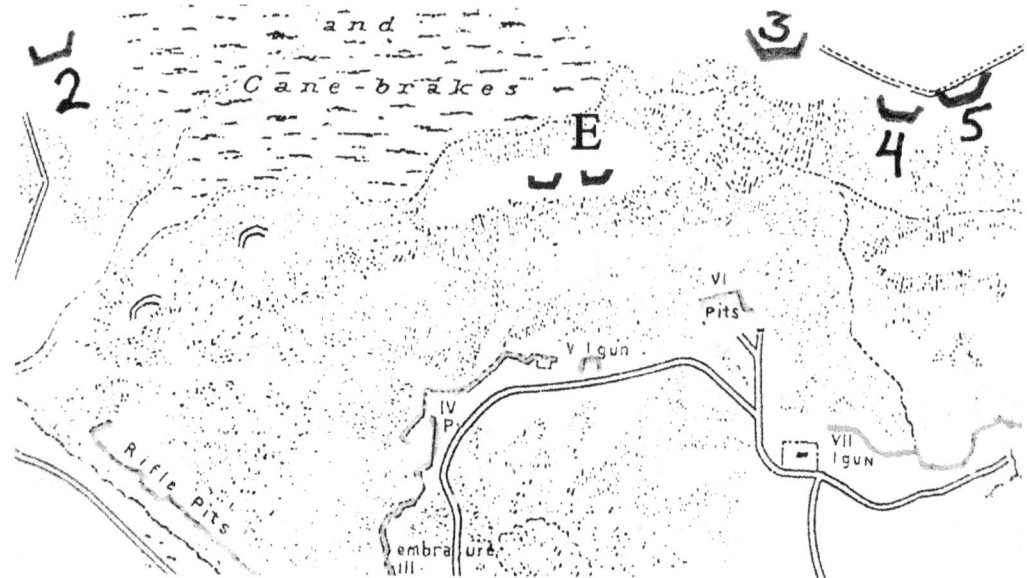

Federal artillery positions 2 through 5 and previously unidentified Jackass Regiment Company E on the North End of Port Hudson siege lines. Confederate positions are the lighter single lines facing the Federal lines. (Detail from map in the National Archives, RG 77-M-107.)

the enemy fortifications. His high-flying shells carried entirely over the enemy works and hit just in front of the Federal lines two miles and more to the southeast. Overshooting was not an uncommon occurrence. Confederate reports indicated that once the land-based siege batteries were in place, several of the Parrott projectiles would come over the eastern front, pass over the river batteries and either splash into the Mississippi River or clear it and land far in the fields across it.[8]

On June 3, Banks requested Captain Barnes of the 21st New York Battery, Lieutenant Harvey Hall commanding the 1st Indiana Company A, Captain Hebard of the 1st Vermont Battery and the commander of the 2nd U.S., Company C, to report to Captain Harwood of the Engineers to superintend the construction of battery positions. Also that day, Captain William Roy received his muster as major, a post to which he had been commissioned since March 10 when Benjamin Hays received his commission as lieutenant colonel and John A. Keith received his colonel's commission. (Both officers had been acting in their newly commissioned capacity for about four months.)

Lieutenant Harvey Hall received orders to move into position much farther to the left (south) of the besiegers' lines. It moved its four rifled cannon to a temporary location just off a road and partially screened by trees in front of the road. It came under fire from seven Confederate guns, including two of Boones' battery's 3-inch Confederate Parrott rifles, Lieutenant Watts Kearney's 20-pounder Parrott rifle, two 24-pounder rifled guns and two 6-pounder bronze guns of Captain Calvit Roberts' 7-stars Battery. After a long artillery exchange, Hall drove the defenders from their pieces, giving his company some rest and quiet. For five days after that, it fired one round every fifteen minutes at targets of opportunity (this was at anything that moved or an object that caught their fancy). The sole purpose of this was to harass the enemy and keep him uncomfortable.

Company K moved into position #9 on June 3 in front of Colonel Dudley's brigade in hastily prepared earthworks between 100 yards to 200 yards west of its original unprotected position of May 27. This battery was within 700 yards to the north of two large double salients

Company K, 1st Indiana Heavy Artillery, at Port Hudson. (Courtesy of Military Order of the Loyal Legion of the United States, housed at USAMHI, Carlisle Barracks, Pennsylvania.)

in the Confederate defensive line known as the Priest Cap. From its new position it blew up a small powder magazine during its first day's firing of twenty-three Schenkl rounds. This battery continued its harassing fire at fifteen minute intervals for the next ten days in an effort to prevent the defenders from strengthening their defenses.

McLaflin reported that by the 5th of June, he had his guns fully emplaced in their battery at position #7. While at work improving their battery position by strengthening and raising their front parapet and adding gun platforms for the three-ton Parrott rifles, Rebel sharpshooters' fire killed Private George Sackett on June 3. With all four Parrott rifles properly emplaced, all his guns commenced firing the morning of the 5th. During the day's firing, McLaflin's gun dismounted a heavy rifled gun. Sergeant Fuller's gun dismounted two light artillery pieces, one having its carriage broken into several pieces. Fuller's gun also destroyed the defenders' steam engine that powered the corn mill. Lieutenant Blankenship's gun dismounted a light artillery gun, and his exploding shells set fire to a storehouse, destroying about two thousand to three thousand bushels of corn. Lieutenant Harrower's gun also dismounted two light guns. Some of the battery's shells also hit the Quartermaster's storage buildings.[9]

By June 6, workers had built up the gun emplacements on Augur's front enough to begin bringing in sharpshooters to their adjoining rifle pits and begin bringing equipment and ammunition to the magazines. Banks admonished General Augur to make all necessary preparations to protect the heavy guns going into battery on his front in battery positions #10 and #11. In battery position #10, Lieutenant-Commander Edward Terry, Ensign Robert P. Swann with fifty-one men from the U.S.S. *Richmond* and Ensign E. M. Shepard with seventeen men from the *Essex* worked to get their emplacements ready for the three anticipated 9-inch Dahlgren cannons. The navy loaned these guns from their ships, off-loading them at Springfield Landing. After waiting for the road improvements to be finished, they began transporting their 9,200 pound guns (not including the weight of the carriage) to position #10. It would take three more days to prepare platforms and sling and mount the guns on their carriages in their battery position in Griffith's field. A fourth 9-inch Dahlgren would arrive on

Shot-up Confederate Quartermaster storage buildings at Port Hudson. Notice the artillery caisson, battery wagon and battery forge parked nearby. (Courtesy of Military Order of the Loyal Legion of the United States, housed at USAMHI, Carlisle Barracks, Pennsylvania.)

June 8 to be placed into position by Lieutenant Terry's work crews. The 161st New York Infantry working on Terry's emplacement completed their assignments on the 8th.

Moving into his new but not fully completed battery Position #4, Lieutenant Benjamin S. Harrower sent a few shells from Whistling Dick over the earthworks held by the 1st Alabama Infantry and into their camp. (Whistling Dick was the name given to this Parrott rifle by its Confederate recipients due to the peculiar whistling noise its shells made in flight.)

Lieutenant Harvey Hall received orders to move his four 20-pounder Parrots out of the woods and into position just off the Mount Pleasant-Troth's Road on the far south. However, the position was incomplete. Hall held his guns in the woods and reconnoitered the construction site for a view of the terrain and field of fire. It would be two or three days before his position was actually ready for occupancy.

On June 7 near the Citadel and Devil's Elbow, the Confederate infantrymen worked hard in digging bombproofs to shelter from the fleets' mortar shells and other exploding shells in general. Digging deep pits about fifteen feet deep and ten to twelve feet wide, with a ramp or earthen steps to enter the pit, the soldiers covered the pits with stout logs supported by thick upright timbers and covered by several feet of dirt. Some of these were dug more hastily under enemy fire and were not as deep and had thinner roofs.

Various reports indicated the Rebels' light guns in front of the Federal right wing had withdrawn rearward to an inner line of defense. The Federal reports erred; instead, the guns had been cleverly hidden in shallow pits dug behind the newly strengthened and heightened

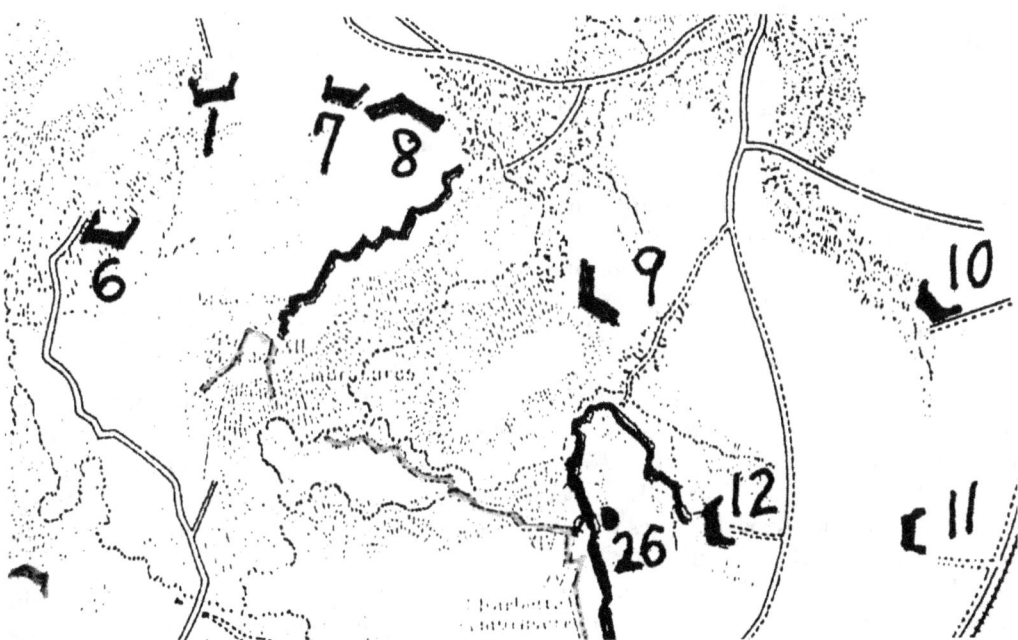

Federal batteries 1 and 6 through 12. They fired at Fort Desperate in left center, the Priest Cap lower center opposite #26, which is the trench Cavalier protecting the upside-down "U"-shaped sap running from #12, and at Commissary Hill at far lower left corner. NOTE: Position #9 is a final position; the artillery was moved here from a position near where the road forks in the rear of its final position. Position #12 was not constructed until near the end of the siege. (Detail from National Archives map RG 77–M-107.)

earthworks. The light guns could be run up a ramp to their embrasure ready to fight in a couple of minutes when needed. Federal mortars were in the process of being moved to Position #3. The 161st New York Infantry had been busy digging rifle pits and strengthening the parapets at these batteries.

Also, the industrious Yankee engineers began expanding rifle pits at #7 to include an earthwork for battery position #8. Lieutenant Taylor from Closson's 1st U.S. Company L who was scheduled to command the mortars in position #8 would, instead, command the same mortars in Position #3 for a few days. Position #11 for Mack's 18th New York Black Horse Battery was nearly finished, and Mack would move his six 20-pounder Parrott rifles into it by 7 o'clock that night. Position #13 on the Plains Road for the 2nd Vermont Battery was supposed to be completed, but it was not.[10]

June 8 saw additional battery positions on the far northwestern end of the Federal lines completed and ready for the guns to be run in. Under cover of darkness on the 7th, flatbed wagons hauled a mixture of 8-inch and 10-inch mortars toward Position #3 as the 2nd Vermont pulled its two Sawyer rifle section out, heading towards Position #14, nearly halfway around the siege lines.

Early the next morning Lieutenant F. E. Taylor of 1st U.S. Company L and his battery's crew arrived at Position #3 to mount their mortars behind a large wall of earth and cotton bales about eight to ten feet high in front of the position. Because mortars shoot upward at an elevation of about forty-five degrees, the crews could stand up behind the mound in great safety — a comfort not available to a cannoneer behind an open embrasure of a siege or field gun emplacement. Taylor's mortars test fired at 1 o'clock A.M. on the 9th and later fired for effect after dawn. At this time, the Federal artillery along the northwestern most end of Port Hudson consisted of Lieutenant Taylor's 8-inch and 10-inch mortars, Lieutenant Harrower with his 30-pounder Parrott rifle in position #4 and Lieutenant Healy in Position #4 with his 1st Maine Battery of 3.67-inch bronze rifles in position #5.

John D. Austen, the Confederates' chief telegrapher at Port Hudson, calculated the following artillery statistics for the 13-inch mortars fired from the mortar fleet below Port Hudson from their first shells fired against the fort on May 8 up to June 8. The mortars had fired at least 3000 shells or 600,000 pounds of iron that had killed and wounded only six men, or one casualty per every 100,000 pounds of iron thrown; all of this at an expense of $75,000.00 in material, exclusive of labor, etc., or $12,500 per casualty. Austen speculated that it seemed to be a horrible waste of economy. At that cost, not counting the value of a life, how can war be economically justified? It is a good question, even today.

June 9 saw more major changes in positions by the Federal artillery. Most of the batteries were completed or would be completed in a few hours and ready for occupancy. The Jackass Regiment's Company A finally advanced its four Parrott rifles 300 yards into battery a little north of the Mount Pleasant Road, set up shop and commenced firing. The battery fired as needed to silence Rebel batteries whenever they opened fire against Federal working parties advancing trenches and rifle pits.

The two remaining 30-pounders of Company B and the two 30-pounders of Company H moved under cover of darkness behind the lines into the newly constructed Position #21 astride the Baton Rouge alternate road on the far left wing. (Company A would eventually move into Position #20 to the right of Companies B and H.) Companies B and H were now 700 yards away from the Devil's Elbow and 900 yards from the Citadel or River Battery XI. At 8 A.M. on the 9th, they commenced firing at the Rebel works, spacing their shots at five-minute intervals without response. On the northeast side of the siege lines, the two-gun section of the 2nd Vermont Battery completed its journey to camp on the Plains Road where they waited with the rest of the battery for their new position to be completed.

In the same general area, along the northern defenses, a sortie against the Rebel works was made early in the morning, and as usual, it was repulsed with only one casualty among the defenders. Whistling Dick continued tearing the 1st Alabama's nearby camps and storage facilities to pieces. One of its shells tore into the 1st Alabama Company H cooking shelter, blowing up and wounding two men as well as blasting the shelter to pieces. The regiment moved its sick men to the safety of a ravine at the camp's rear. Exploding shells also burnt the 1st Alabama's commissary.

The 1st Vermont Battery (now commanded by Lieutenant Rice due to Captain Hebard being appointed acting commander of artillery for General William Dwight) moved during the night from its position near Slaughter's house going about a mile to the south where it moved into battery position #19. This position, built of sandbags and earth, was about 800 yards from the enemy works. From here it could fire upon two Confederate salients behind which the upper story of Gibbon's cotton gin was plainly visible. The battery occasionally sent a spiteful shell at the gin house for the rest of the siege, but they never saw that they hit it. That night it commenced raining again and did not let up until 8 o'clock in the morning.[11]

The 1st Indiana's Company D had moved into Federal position #13, and it first opened fire on the 9th. It reported dismounting six guns over the next five days. They continued shelling the same positions during the day to prevent repairs being made to the dismounted guns, which were usually repaired overnight by the superhuman efforts of the Confederate engineers and ready to fight the next day. The 1st Indiana's Company C commanded by Captain Elihu Rose moved into Federal position #17. With one 8-inch siege howitzer in place and another being emplaced, the battery commenced an enfilading fire into Colonel W. R. Miles' positions causing his men a great amount of worry.

Captain Rose ordered his left 8-inch siege mortars to fire with reduced powder charges, causing his shells loaded with shrapnel made of copper balls to roll along the enemy trenches a considerable number of yards before exploding. Upon receiving word of this new tactic and the fact that Rose's howitzers enfiladed nearly 800 yards of his lines, Miles ordered four-foot deep ditches dug across the trenches with the dirt piled on the side toward Rose's battery forming strong traverses. The traverses trapped the exploding shells fired from Captain Roses' 8-inch Bounding Betsy, and prevented the shells from bouncing along the bottom of the trench wrecking wooden braces for the trench walls, smashing boxes of supplies, rifles, feet and ankles in its path before exploding. The defenders here and elsewhere also dug gopher holes at an angle to their trench in which they sheltered from exploding shells and rain.

Two 8-inch mortars commanded by Captain R. M. Hill of the Ordnance Department moved into position #18 and commenced firing. The battery would eventually hold an additional two 10-inch mortars. On the northern side of the lines, bursting shells fired from Federal Battery positions 1, 7 and 8 set fire to General Beale's headquarters building.[12]

June 10 and 11 saw an abortive general night-time assault on Port Hudson's northern defenses fizzle out almost before it began. All day there was land and river based artillery fire to try to force the Confederates to unmask their hidden guns to return fire, which would reveal their positions. The Confederates did not respond to the Federals' probe and held their cannon fire. They replied only with sharpshooters' bullets. Into the rain-soaked night the Federal artillery played on the defenses without causing concern among the Rebel batteries. However, Federal artillery shells flying too high and missing their targets landed in the Confederates' Provost Compound housing prisoners of war. One such friendly shell mortally wounded Theophilus S. Bousley from the 48th Massachusetts Infantry Regiment who had been captured at Plains Store on May 21. The shell blew off one of Bousley's legs on the 10th. After an emergency amputation by the post surgeon to save his life and stop his bleeding, he died on June 12.

The Federal men under arms had been slowly closing in as best as they could under cover of the rain and undergrowth, but most units halted short of the breastworks. However, the Twelfth Maine and the Twenty-second Maine regiments accidently got within Steedman's lines. These two regiments blundered through the underbrush, their noise covered by the sound of the heavy rain, into the offal pit in the ravine by the slaughterhouse on the hilltop above. Covered by the putrid mess they climbed up the low bluff and took shelter in the slaughterhouse. At dawn twenty-five Maine boys, a lieutenant and a captain found themselves surrounded by one officer and eight men from the 39th Mississippi who took them prisoners; a few Maine boys escaped back the way they had come and sheltered in the brush and abatis to the rear of the pond of rotting blood, bones, feces, guts, heads, hooves, etc. A little farther to the right in Steedman's lines the Alabamians discovered an entire company of Yankee skirmishers 100 yards in front of a 24-pounder. Promptly loading it with a double charge of canister, the gunners fired into the bluecoats. The survivors threw down their firearms and ran as hard as they could for the rear. The defenders added these Enfield rifles to their armament.[13]

Also on the 10th, the Hoosiers in either Company C or D dismounted a 24-pounder gun in the works near the Clinton and Port Hudson Railway killing its commander, Captain Weller of the 1st Tennessee Artillery Battalion, when the exploding shell tore out his breast as it knocked the cannon barrel off its carriage.

A few Federal supply problems surfaced about this time. Captain Hill telegraphed that he had only eighty 10-inch shells left and needed a resupply, which caused a flurry of activity at Springfield Landing. Lieutenant Armstrong responded to Brigadier-General Richard Arnold, chief of artillery for the 19th Corps, that no ammunition of any kind had arrived since he had sent all he had to the front the day before. Later that day, Armstrong telegraphed both Generals Grover and Arnold that the steamer *St. Mary's* had arrived with a shipment from Key West consisting of 418 boxes of 30-pounder projectiles a lot of cartridge bags for the 30-pounders, kegs of powder, friction primers and fuses with a sealed invoice from Captain Shunk (chief of ordnance at New Orleans). Later yet, Armstrong telegraphed Arnold that the promised wagon trains had not arrived at Springfield Landing. He had no wagons to carry 9-inch powder cartridges, and he had no cartridges for a 24-pounder gun.

On the 11th General Arnold received communiqués that the battery positions #13 and #14 were still incomplete — #13 being about three-fourths complete and #14 about one-half complete. Haddon's Company D battery of three 24-pounder guns had already moved into position #13, and between shots they worked on reinforcing and raising their parapet. Their heavy guns battered the Confederate earthworks in their front between the Plains Road and Jackson Road. In spite of the daily shelling, the Confederates had remounted the 24-pounder at the Jackson Road sally port. Engineering lieutenant James Freret, in charge of the center of the Confederate works, had his engineers valiantly working at night as hard as they could. Engineering lieutenant Stork commanded the Confederate engineers doing yeoman's work on the extreme right and river defenses. Engineering lieutenant Frederick Y. Dabney had his engineers at work on the northern portion of the lines. Dabney would soon take over the work at the far south end of the lines as well.[14]

On the 11th of June, a 20-pounder Parrott shell fired from Hall's position #20, mortally wounded Captain Richard M. Boone of Boone's battery while atop the parapet near the Devil's Elbow observing the effect of shot against Position #20. The shell tore off his right leg just below his hip and the left leg of a washer-woman who was near him. The surgeons amputated at his hip, stitched him up and added one more leg to the pile of severed limbs outside the surgery. After the anesthesia wore off, the mortally wounded Boone ordered his men to retrieve the limb from the surgeon and fire it back at the enemy. (The author could find no record of that happening.)

The 12th of June brought a little excitement to the members of Company D of the 1st Heavy Artillery. A sharpshooter's bullet wounded 2nd Lieutenant Jesse Haddon in his right arm while he was in the battery's lookout tree calling the effect of their rounds to his gunners below. His wound was not severe, and he recovered to eventually become the captain of this company. Haddon was not alone in the wounds received in this company: Privates George McCormick and Marshall Lauder also received some special attention from the Confederate sharpshooters. McCormick would receive a disability discharge in January 1864.

Farther around the besiegers lines to the north side of the battlefield, Lieutenant Harrower's 30-pounder Parrott at position #4 created harrowing experiences among the men of the 39th Mississippi causing W. S. Turner to declare that the Parrott's shells bursting over his head made his place in the breastworks the worst position he had ever been in. Parrott shells knocked down the 39th Mississippi's breastworks in several places. One shell came into the head of their trench, exploded in the dirt and threw two pieces of shell and a large quantity of dirt to nearly bury an orderly and private stationed there who received only small bruises and cuts.

Company H in position #21 on the 12th of June, while repairing their parapet came under a heavy fire from Rebel sharpshooters. The Hoosiers' Brevet-Major William Roy, now in command of all the batteries on the Federal left, gave the bully boys permission to counter the sharpshooters, saying, "If that is their game, we might help them play it." About half of the men in the battery grabbed their Merrill rifles and quickly moved along the trench connect-

Twelve. At Port Hudson, May 28–June 14

A 4.62-inch Gibbon & Andrews rifle located in the Citadel, also known as River Battery XI. Disabled by 1st Indiana Heavy Artillery, Company H.

ing their battery to the rifle pits to their left. (The Jackass Regiment had 181 Merrill rifles at Port Hudson: Company A had 48, Company H had 65 and Company K had 68. Companies H and K owned their rifles and Company A had government issued rifles. They snaked into position in rifle pits alongside their comrades from the 6th Michigan about 175 yards from the Citadel where they came in plain view of the Confederate 4.62-inch rifle pointing down river at the Federal fleet below. They commenced an accurate fire, which made the Rebel sharpshooters keep their heads down and unable to shoot back with any accuracy. Company H suffered only one casualty during their adventure: a Confederate sharpshooter's bullet found its mark in one of Private James Coleman's thighs as he forgot to keep his rear end down as he returned to the battery position with his comrades.[15]

While half of Company H's boys entertained themselves as sharpshooters, General Banks rode up to the battery position and asked Captain Connelly if they could dismount a rifled gun (the 4.62-inch rifle Lady Whitfield) that had severely annoyed the fleet below by putting seven or eight shells into the *Essex*. Grinning as he replied that he could if so ordered, the fiery red-headed Connelly ordered his men to wheel number one gun into an exposed position in an open field about 200 yards in front of and to the left of their earthworks where it could fire into an opening on the western side of the Citadel. While the gun's crew was busy rolling it into position, Connelly ordered the newly returned sharpshooters to return to the rifle pits and cover their comrades now fully exposed to enemy fire as they worked in the open field.

Under cover of their sharpshooters, the crew of the lone Parrott opened fire. The first round fell short of the target; the next round went over; the following round struck the Lady Whitfield, but did no damage. Several more rounds fell around the big rifle, but did not strike it. During this time of near misses, Lieutenant L. A. Schirmer, 12th Louisiana Artillery Battalion commanding the piece, ordered his men to move the gun into position to return fire. The Hoosier sharpshooters had the Rebel gunners ducking and covering as they tried to move their rifle rearward and then swing the muzzle to bear on the 30-pounder in the field. The Rebel sharpshooters could not mount a sufficient return fire against the Parrott's gun crew to drive them away because they, too, were ducking Merrill bullets. However, the cannoneers could not get their heavy rifle (weighing almost a ton more than a 30-pounder Parrott) into firing position fast enough to get an effective counterfire at the Parrott. In less than an hour from the first shell fired, Company H's gun disabled and dismounted the Lady Whitfield with five consecutive rounds.

It is interesting that while the Federal and Confederate accounts vary as to the type of the gun, their description of the damage done to it and the sequence of damage is identical. Rufus Dooley of the 1st Indiana H.A., Company H, wrote: "One shot struck it in the muzzle and knocked a piece out, one glanced the axle, another the top of the wheel, the final shot came, it struck the center of the axle close to the hub, and down she went amid the yells of the sharpshooters." Confederate lieutenant colonel P.F. DeGournay, commanding the Left Wing, Heavy Batteries, wrote: "The shot struck the gun near the muzzle, cutting off a piece and splitting the gun. Two other successive shots broke the axle and a wheel, making the gun a complete wreck." None of the Confederate or Federal gunners were hurt. Their job completed, Company H moved its exposed piece back into the safety of its earth and cotton-bale works.

The official Union accounts erroneously call the rebel gun either a 42-pounder or a 68-pounder. Lieutenant-Colonel P.F. DeGournay, commanding the left wing of the Confederate river batteries, erroneously records this dismounted gun as being a 30-pounder Parrott rifle. While not a Parrott rifle, the correct projectiles for the Rebel rifle did weigh between 27 to 35 pounds. The Confederate rifle weighed about four tons with its carriage as compared to about three tons for a 30-pounder Parrott rifle and carriage.[16]

The same day that the 1st Vermont Battery moved to a permanent position, the 2nd Vermont Battery moved forward from its camp into position #14. The battery had an easy run down the Plains Road into its new emplacement adjacent on the south of the road. This placed the battery about 300 yards from the enemy breastworks.

A few of the light batteries continuously moved in and out of positions, never going into a fixed position. These batteries were kept ready to go out as entire batteries or by two-gun sections to accompany the cavalry on foraging parties to guard the wagons. The Confederate cavalry was always a threat to the rear of Banks' lines as well as to threaten his supply depot at Springfield Landing. For example, there is no mention of the 1st Indiana's Company E as occupying a permanent position until after June 22, and Nims' battery, the 2nd Massachusetts, seems to have never occupied any position for more than a couple of days. Nims' battery also fought by two-gun sections, adding firepower where needed. After being detached a few weeks back to guard Barre's Landing on Bayou Teche, Nims' center section arrived at Port Hudson.

By now the Federal artillery occupied all battery positions from numbers 1 through 21. On the Federal left, the 128th New York made a demonstration about 11 o'clock the morning of the 12th against the Citadel to draw out their cannons from hiding. After three hours of taunting the Confederates with various maneuvers and receiving no artillery fire, but plenty of rifle fire, the bloodied 128th returned to camp and filled their hospital with wounded. The demonstration failed to reveal any cannons.

On the 13th, the general bombardment began with its slow fire from all heavy artillery around the fortifications. Within a short time the vent burned out of Company H's number two gun, disabling it. A little later, a shell burst prematurely in the muzzle of number one gun and destroyed the Parrott rifle, which Edward Bacon of the 6th Michigan described happening as: "The breech of the piece only backed a little and rolled off the carriage, while two or three large fragments flew up about twenty feet in the air and fell, giving everybody a chance to get out of the way." Fortunately, the cotton bales in their front of the battery bore the brunt of the explosion. The artillerymen received only minor scratches and bruises from it. Captain Connelly and his gun's crews moved both of his disabled Parrotts to Springfield Landing, leaving Company B. Two 12-pounder Napoleons from Lieutenant Theodore Bradley's 2nd U.S., Battery C, moved into the spot abandoned by Company H.

The next day, Connelly had the two siege rifles loaded aboard the next steamer bound for New Orleans, and he and some of his officers accompanied the guns to New Orleans. Once there, the Ordnance Department replaced the number one gun and repaired the vent bushing on the number two gun. The guns' crews remained at Springfield Landing where they went to work at the supply depot helping with artillery supplies and filling shells with gunpowder.

June 13 also saw the 1st U.S. Companies F and L (Duryea's and Closson's batteries) and Nims' battery (2nd Massachusetts) pulled off the lines and moved under cover to the rear to participate in the next morning's assault with Augur's division and Paine's divisions. Captain R. C. Duryea had six 12-pounder Napoleons and Captain H. W. Closson had four 3-inch Ordnance rifles. Captain E. C. Bainbridge moved his 1st U.S. Company A with four 12-pounder Napoleons into position #8 alongside a two gun section of 1st U.S. Company L's 3-inch Ordnance rifles commanded by Lieutenant H. P. Norris. The 6th Massachusetts Battery, commanded by Captain William W. Carruth, also had four 12-pounder Napoleon guns in this position. This large battery was collectively called Bainbridge's battery. (Sometimes writers have enlarged the position to include McLaflin's two 30-pounders that were a few yards away in position #7.) On the extreme left of the Confederate lines a Federal battery tried to go into position, but the 39th Mississippi on the ridge made it too hot for them to set up. The battery withdrew. Mack's 18th New York Black Horse Battery moved its right and left sections under cover of darkness from nearly a mile away from the Rebel ramparts between Plains Road and the railroad into a newly constructed position about 1000 yards from the ramparts. They placed only the right and left sections into it, because it was pierced for only four guns, not six. The center section's two guns remained parked a mile away.[17]

After playing musical chairs with the artillery pieces at the last moment, a general bombardment from all of Banks' land batteries in conjunction with Farragut's mortar boats began about 11 o'clock A.M. and continued for two hours. About 1:00 P.M. General Nathaniel Banks sent in a flag of truce with a request that in order to avoid further bloodshed, General Franklin Gardner should surrender his post. Gardner politely refused, and sent out orders for all to prepare to repulse an assault. That night the mortar boats began a terrific bombardment that lasted about three hours. From position #13, Company D, 1st Indiana fired the signal rockets to begin the barrage from the land batteries. The mass of shells tearing up the sod confirmed to the men in gray that something was definitely coming their way.

Messages rapidly flowed to and from Federal Headquarters and outlying commanders to locate artillery targets and plans for additional siege work. General Grover, in overall command of the assault forces against the Priest Cap that day, requested that on the 13th Terry's navy battery focus their fire on two casemates in his front that might contain guns that would hold up his assault of the 14th. Headquarters ordered a detachment of the 1st Louisiana Engineers to report to General Grover with entrenching tools and sandbags to take position near Cox's 12-pounder rifled battery on the 13th (position #9).

Banks' chief of artillery, Richard Arnold, sent the commanding officer of the 1st Indiana Heavy Artillery and General William Dwight this message for firing on the 14th: "Have the heavy batteries fire one gun from each battery at ten minutes at irregular intervals until midnight. The intervals will then slacken up to one gun in half an hour until to 2:45 A.M., when the fire will be increased to one shot from each gun in eight minutes up to the time of the advance of the skirmishers of General Dwight and Augur about 3:15 A.M., when the fire will be increased to five minute intervals or as fast as the guns will bear for a continued action of two hours.

"The fire will first be directed about 100 yards over the parapet of the enemy and as the skirmishers advance the range will be increased to ensure a fire that must prevent the enemy making a determined stand in the works. This fire will continue until orders from General Banks or Generals Dwight or Augur are given to cease. You will enjoin upon all the officers the importance of firing with great care and accuracy and let their attention be particularly called to the heavy guns of the enemy which must be silenced."

Late that night, in River Battery #VI a strange happening occurred. The battery held two 24-pounder rifles in barbette positions, which means they could pivot 180 degrees around a pintle or pivot attached to the very front of the carriage. Both guns were located in sunken gun pits dug down into the bluff bordering the river: one gun being in a pit several feet below the other. Accounts vary as to the triggering cause, i.e.: a six foot high wave coming upstream, or a mild earthquake, or, more likely, giving away due to the discharges of the cannons shaking the earth loose, but the bank collapsed under the upper gun, carrying it down into the river. The lower gun survived and Confederate engineers quickly went to work to remove it and place it into river battery # VIII.[18]

At half-past three o'clock in the morning of Sunday, June 14, one could still hear the thunderous roar of the Federal artillery attempting to breach the Rebels' earthen walls or disable any opposing artillery that would dare shell the assaulting columns. From the Priest Cap southward to the Citadel, bluecoats came out from camps and formed their columns. As previously ordered by General Banks, the men would advance in columns of 2,000 men. In the front of each column were to be 300 skirmishers and 70 pioneers with axes, handsaws, hatchets, picks and shovels. Following them were 300 men carrying three-foot long bags of cotton, supports and planks for bridges. The infantry followed. Again, the cotton bag carriers' function was that when in front of the Rebel parapet, they were to throw the bags into the outside ditch to fill it, then place the supports and lay the planks across them to bridge the gap, so the soldiers could charge across with enough momentum to scale the earthworks behind. The infantrymen thought the bags may slow down a bullet, so it would only slightly kill the bag carrier.[19]

Shortly after 3 A.M., his artillery having failed to unmask the enemy artillery, Augur sent his five remaining regiments and a light battery forward in a feint to draw the Rebels' attention to the center. His light artillery and skirmishers advanced against the Rebel line along a ravine near the Slaughter house ruins. His ruse was quickly discovered and repulsed. His part in the assault was finished; he withdrew his brigade to the rear, except for sharpshooters. They remained along his front to continue harassing the enemy.

On the Federal right of center, in accordance with General Cuvier Grover's battle plan, regiments left their camps and marched to a staging area. General Halbert Paine was to lead his columns forth from a staging area on the Jackson Road. General Weitzel was to simultaneously step off on Paine's right with him. General Dwight, far to the south, upon hearing the sound of the firing was to throw his men forward against the Citadel.

Paine's regiments formed in their camps and marched off to the staging area through a light fog. They had covered their accoutrements, such as canteens, dippers, cups, etc. with cloth or cotton to muffle any clanking the items may make during their march. Marching down the road, they crossed over a bridge with its roadway covered in cotton to muffle their footsteps as they crossed and continued down the Bayou Sara-Jackson Road behind a thick hedge. Halting at their jumping off place that was still concealed from the enemy, they hunkered down and waited for nearly two hours for the fog to lift.

A brief but brisk Federal artillery fire again raked the enemy lines. As soon as the artillery ceased fire, Paine's men moved against the enemy fortifications still shrouded by a light fog, pushing against the right of the Confederate center and the southern Priest Cap's breastworks. Paine accompanied his men, encouraging them forward.

Paine led from the front and his men spiritedly followed him onward. A few men fell on the open field extending about 500 yards from the breastworks. Then the charge encountered a ravine choked with abatis and thicker fog about 100 yards from the enemy parapet. After climbing into the ravine, picking through the abatis and climbing out of the ravine, the assaulting line moved forward at the quick and then the double-quick. When within forty yards of the Rebel lines, a sheet of flame atop the breastworks lit up the morning. Musket balls, buckshot and homemade cannon canister (bags of picked up minie balls and military trash) crashed into the Federal ranks with sickening thuds and thumps. Dead and maimed men fell to the earth. (A three-inch piece of a broken bayonet was later removed from the upper palate of a Massachusetts captain.)

General Paine, accompanying his beloved 4th Wisconsin Regiment and the 8th New Hampshire Regiment at the front of the division, fell in the first fire with one or two bullets in his left thigh. Other officers went down, followed by scores of enlisted men. However, keeping their promise to Paine to do their duty, several men of the 4th Wisconsin and 8th New Hampshire made it to the Rebel parapet and twenty-two from the 4th plus a handful from the 8th made it over. One or two from the 38th Massachusetts got on the parapet and fell wounded, later taken prisoner. The 53rd Massachusetts had a similar fate, having a handful of men making it over the parapet. Seeing no support immediately behind them, the few Federals inside Port Hudson wisely surrendered and were imprisoned or sent to the Post Hospital.[20]

Outside the breastworks, bodies from the 8th New Hampshire, 53rd Massachusetts and 4th Wisconsin regiments filled the ditch before it — no cotton bags came close to it. The Yankees' three- and five-pound Ketchum hand grenades failed because their percussion strikers did not hit with enough force to ignite them. Their intended victims caught them and tossed them down the Federal ranks in the ditch before the breastworks where many exploded killing and wounding the Yankees. One-third of the 38th Massachusetts and the 53rd Massachusetts lay wounded or dead from the returned grenades, cannon, rifle and shotgun fire alongside and behind the Badgers and Granite Staters. Most of their bodies lay between the ditch and the 100-yard distant ravine. The 31st Massachusetts, at the ravine, threw their cotton bags onto the ground and took shelter behind them for the rest of the day. They would still suffer more than thirty casualties from the affair.

The bulk of the Federal casualties were from the first volleys to reach them. The fire from the 16th Arkansas (one of the regiments called up to reinforce the defenses) at the attackers was so severe the shooters later complained of having bruised shoulders from their firearms' numerous recoils. Those who tried to get off the battlefield usually went singly or in small groups of three or four. They were easy targets for the sharpshooters. The 4th Massachusetts had gone to ground early, not reaching the ravine. The 133rd New York halted in the open field before reaching the ravine after the death of its colonel early on in the assault. They, too, went to ground or fled to safety in the rear. Sharpshooters would continue searching for movement among the bodies lying on the ground during the next three days and their bullets would put an end to the movement. Rebel sharpshooters detailed from the 16th Arkansas had all the targets they could handle.

Colonel Paine had managed to fall into a furrow in the field. He lay between two small ridges of earth heaved by the plow that had made the furrow, which kept him from being seen by the enemy sharpshooters, and no doubt saved his life. Not all moving wounded or able bodied became sharpshooters' targets; some of the 4th Wisconsin and the 8th New Hampshire reported that a Confederate soldier came over the parapet and asked if they wished to surrender. They did not; so, after taking one of the Federal officers' broad brimmed hats, he departed. Later in the heat of the day, the wounded officer called out that he wished to surrender and was removed to a hospital behind the Confederate lines. That night under cover of darkness, Federal stretcher bearers brought Paine off the battlefield. He would be shipped to Hotel Dieu in New Orleans where his leg would be amputated nine days later.

During the dark hours survivors from the 4th Wisconsin, 8th New Hampshire, 31st, 38th and 53rd Massachusetts stealthily crept off the battlefield as best as they could without getting shot. If possible, they pulled their wounded comrades behind them to safety. Once safe in the rear, the wounded went to the field hospitals. Many men blamed the 4th Massachusetts and 133rd New York for the assault's failure due to their failure to move out promptly, lagging far to the rear away from Paine's eye and then hiding in a gully behind the other regiments when they should have been charging forward.[21]

About an hour after Paine's assault began, Weitzel's division began its assault against the northern portion of the Priest Cap. Weitzel's division moved off the Jackson Road and into a deep, wide ravine near battery position #9. They moved forward and came under fire from two Rebel light artillery pieces just run out of hiding at the Priest Cap. Company G's 30-pounder Parrotts in position #7 had the range and bearing and forced the Rebel cannons back into hiding and out of action. The 9-inch Dahlgrens at the naval battery fired a last land-locked broadside at the Priest Cap, the huge shells flying over Weitzel's advancing regiments.

Weitzel's men advanced down the main ravine cut by the South Fork of Sandy Creek also known as Fosters Creek, which was easily swept by fire from Fort Desperate, Colonel Steedman's right flank and the left end of the Priest Cap. A smaller ravine bore off to the south from the main ravine in front of and roughly parallel to the Priest Cap becoming the barrier which had both trapped and saved the men in Paine's assault. The bulk of Weitzel's division avoided it and continued on down the main ravine; however, the 24th Connecticut climbed up a low mound dividing the two ravines and charged forward and down a dip into a shallow gully and then up again climbing steeply up to the crest of the ravine to find they were only 30 yards from the Priest Cap.

As the Connecticut boys came over the crest of the mound carrying their two thirty-pound bags of cotton, they came within view of the carnage taking place ahead of them to the assaulting columns. Weitzel's left and center had gained the crest of the ridge upon which the Priest Cap rested, but the defenders had moved in reinforcements. As the assaulting mass came out of the valley shouting huzzahs, a scythe of rifle and musket fire cut through the blue-bellies. In the face of the defenders' intense fire, the assault came to a halt at the ditch in front of the earthworks. In went the hand grenades; back came the hand grenades, reaping death and maiming injuries among those in the ditch. (It seems some clever Rebels used blankets to catch the grenades then toss them back.)

Stopped in the ditch, the Yankees looked rearward for support. Several of the supporting soldiers lay paralyzed by fear just forward of the ravine; other men remained in the ravine being urged forward by their officers. In spite of this, several hardy souls made it up to the ditch in front of the steep northern face of the Priest Cap. The Yanks hugged the ridge and the ditch side nearest the parapet all day, and those who were able tried to make their way to the rear. Those who fled did so at great peril from Rebel sharpshooters looking for them. The smarter Yankees crawled away after dark.

The 24th Connecticut threw their bags of cotton down along the ridge top, using them as instant cover and unslung their rifles going into action to support those on the ground in their front. In a short while, their muzzle-blasts set the cotton filled bags on fire, which they put out by flinging handfuls of dirt onto the flames. They had to remain and hold the ground gained where they lay, unlike the other regiments that crawled to the rear after dark. The 24th lost 8 killed and 20 wounded during the day's fighting.

All along the Priest Cap's interior, the rifle, shotgun and musket-toting defenders breathed a sigh of relief at the repulse of the blueclads. Many defenders had fired so many shots that they had used up their supply of firearm caps. Resorting to scavenging, they had taken caps from fallen comrades' cap boxes until runners could fetch more from the supply depot. Several Federals wounded at the Priest Cap got medical care at the Confederates' Post Hospital; treated were: 4th Wisconsin — 12, 8th New Hampshire — 7, 110th New York — 5, 28th Connecticut — 2, 4th Massachusetts — 2 and 74th New York — 1. Once again, another effort failed to capture Port Hudson.[22]

To the south on Dwight's front was the Rebel Citadel or River Battery XI. The Citadel anchored the south end of the defenses of Port Hudson where the land lines reach the river. Some Yankees called an earthwork facing south and east and covering the hilltop along the west side the road to the south Citadel #1, and they called River Battery XI Citadel #2. A line of earthworks extended along the top of a bluff from the east side of the aforementioned road and ran to the northeast and then turned north by northeast forming a set of salients called the Devil's Elbow. (Hereinafter, Confederate River Battery XI, Citadel #1 and Citadel #2, will be called collectively the Citadel. The works to the east of the Citadel and across a road are the Devil's Elbow.)

On the far left of the Yankee lines, Dwight's assault against the Citadel and Devil's Elbow did not get under way until broad daylight, after Weitzel's and Paine's assaults failed. Four brigades made up Dwight's assaulting division. In order of advance, the brigades were Colonel Wilkinson's, Colonel Nickerson's, Colonel Charles Clark's and Colonel Benedict's. Lieutenant-Colonel Edward Bacon led the 6th Michigan Regiment from Clark's brigade forward along the Mount Pleasant Road. Passing a ravine he saw Colonel Clark's horse tied to a sapling, and then he saw the colonel squatting in some bushes busy with dysentery. Bacon moved the regiment onward as he wondered if he was now in charge of the brigade or the regiment. Before he could turn around to ask the question, a courier rode up asking Bacon where he was going. Bacon replied that he was following his orders as part of the main assaulting columns. The courier told him that was wrong and to follow him to the river from where he would launch a direct assault straight upon the Citadel. General Dwight had another drunken inspiration. Bacon turned his regiment around and found he was following, not leading, the 14th Maine toward the river.

Arriving at the river, the two regiments went over the bank to dry ground between the river and the high-water riverbank, re-formed their columns and advanced toward the Citadel under the shelter of both a woods and the riverbank to their right. Further away to their right on the opposite side of Mount Pleasant, The main body of Dwight's assaulting columns advanced steadily forward, passing the 30-pounder Parrots in position 21, until they broke the cover of a point of woods to the left front of the battery.

Coming out of the woods, Clark's command began hearing a few rounds of rifle fire from Miles' Legion of Louisianians pattering into the ground amongst them as well as hearing a few solid thunks hitting some men. Colonel W.R. Miles, defending the Citadel and Devil's Elbow, allowed only two regiments to approach the valley when they commenced firing upon them, taking the second regiment first with artillery fire from Roberts' Battery and a light gun manned by Miles' infantry. Taking a cue from the light guns, the 1st Alabama, Company K's Lieutenant M. E. Pratt turned the Virginia to the southeast and sent 5.82-inch shrapnel shells mowing down the blue line. The Federals charged along the roadway across two hundred yards of cleared ground and then downward into an abatis, a blackberry bramble, chaparral and broken tree lined valley before them. As they descended into the valley, the patter of minie balls changed to a hailstorm of bullets. Lieutenant Thomas, commanding Boone's battery, added to the explosion of artillery shells and flesh-rending volleys of case and canister with his guns. The charging Federals in the lead went from quick-time to the double-quick, forded the narrow and got off the roadway swept by the 24-pounder. They tried to climb the up the nearly perpendicular bluff against the Rebel works.

Even though the Jackass Regiment's Company A and B and the light battery next to them provided covering artillery fire, the Confederate artillery had an advantage over the Federal infantry due to the layout of the land. The red-coated fascine bearers from the 165th New York, advancing behind the skirmishers of the 128th New York threw their fascines to the ground and sought shelter behind them as an exploding shell knocked sixteen men to the ground in various stages of maimed life and death. The 48th Massachusetts advanced through the prostrate red-coated Yankees and jeered at them. Then the hurricane of lead and exploding iron returned, tearing into the 48th Massachusetts' ranks, and they, too, went to ground or ran pell-mell to the rear. The fire was too much. Swept from the open roadway by the maelstrom of enemy fire what was left of the assaulting regiments either hugged the ground, taking such shelter as they could find, or took a chance to out-run the Louisianians' bullets as they ran to the rear. After dark, the men and officers, who were able to do so, used darkness as cover to get to the rear and safety.

On the left of Mount Pleasant, Bacon's command, sheltered by the riverbank, came to where the creek in the valley of death emptied into the Mississippi River. At this point in time, the creek was a wide sea of muddy ooze in a cut lower than the river flats the Wolverines had advanced on. Across the brown mire, directly ahead about 400 yards, the muzzle of a 24-pounder gun (the Virginia) and a light gun faced Bacon and his officers. They immediately fell back to the shelter of the riverbank to ponder their next move. Fortunately for them, an aide to General Dwight rode up and ordered the 6th Michigan and the 14th Maine to the rear to pass around to the east of Mount Pleasant where the assault on that side began. The return march was interrupted briefly as they passed a small clearing in the trees, and a rapid firing small caliber artillery piece, probably a Hughes gun, opened fire on them as they passed the clearing. Once past the hazardous opening, Bacon's men formed in good order and marched to join with the balance of his regiment that had made it to the other side of Mount Pleasant.

With most human targets now well hidden or out of range, the Rebels turned their rifle fire on Company A's and Company B's Parrott rifles. Bacon quickly dispatched two companies to support the batteries. That afternoon, the remnants of the 128th New York relieved the Wolverines supporting batteries 21 and 20. So that the battle would not appear as a total loss, the gaining of the entire hill of Mount Pleasant by driving off a handful of enemy skirmishers stationed near the river early on was touted in the Union-controlled New Orleans newspaper, *The Era*, as "an important result." Again, too many men died so that the ravine and its lip held by the 24th Connecticut in front of the Priest Cap could be called an "important result." Once again, all of the massed assaults against Port Hudson failed. The Federals suffered 1,805 casualties, which far exceeded the Confederate casualties of only 47. That evening the 6th Michigan and Jackass Regiment's western men pondered why it was that if two companies of the 4th Wisconsin and some 8th New Hampshire soldiers could go into the Priest Cap that 2,000 more soldiers in the Badgers' and Granite Staters' rear could not support them by going in and holding it. It was a good question.[23]

A major contributing factor to failure, in addition to improper planning, lack of coordination of the attacks, again, and lack of leadership in the Nutmeg regiments (as regiments from east of Ohio were called by the western men) by many of their officers, was the morale of the nine-months soldiers. These poorly trained nine-month men were a constant disciplinary problem, and to the delight of the western men, these problem nine-month men were all so-called Nutmeggers from Connecticut, Massachusetts New Hampshire and Vermont. Their terms of enlistment would expire in a matter of days or weeks, and not one of them wanted to be the last casualty of the siege. Three of the Massachusetts regiments would attempt mutiny before the siege ended, but they would be unsuccessful. Of these reluctant regiments, the 4th Massachusetts had been in Paine's attack upon the Priest Cap. The Western men felt that if the 4th, 31st, 38th, and 53rd Massachusetts regiments had held their ground, the Federals could have taken Port Hudson that day.

This rumor was only partially true. A handful of men from the 53rd Massachusetts' skirmishers had reached the Rebel breastwork, but were captured. The rest of the regiment lay dead or dying in the ditch or within 100 yards of the breastworks. The 38th Massachusetts Regiment had gotten mixed up with the 53rd Massachusetts, and only a few men got into the deadly ditch in front of the breastworks. Many went to ground or fell coming out of the ravine about 100 yards from the Rebel earthworks. Nims' battery in the rear could not assist with covering fire because of the stalled supporting regiments and pioneers (a brigade and a half of men) in front of them. The adjutant of the 16th New Hampshire stated: "Sunday ... brings us to the second unfortunate and unjustifiable assault on Port Hudson. It was at best a reckless Sunday adventure which many of our New England men engaged in without heart, or enthusiasm."

Among the Hoosier "artillerists," Company A expended 400 rounds while providing covering fire to Dwight's assaulting columns. Company A lost Privates Manius Braugher to the bullets, shot and shell from the defenders in the Citadel and Devil's Elbow. Company B lost Private Alexander Stines (killed) and Private Charles Myers (blinded) due to the failure of one of the crew to properly keep his thumb on the vent hole while the piece was being loaded. The cannon discharged prematurely causing Stines' death and Myers to be forever blinded by the powder blast burning both of his eyes out of their sockets. Company B's Captain James Grimsley was so callous about the loss of these two men that he wrote his wife on June 30 denying *any* losses except for his "young and best horse ... badly cut on its shoulder" by a piece of artillery shell.

While the Federals ended the day on a sad, dreary note, the Confederates took time to clean up, strengthen their works with sandbags and put poultices or liniment on their sore, recoil-bruised shoulders. After dark, they enjoyed church services in their camps, trenches and behind the walls of their strong points. Hymns were sung and short sermons given for nearly an hour at the Citadel, while shells from the mortar boats burst overhead.

Unbeknown to the Confederates, the Federals were very low (about out) on artillery ammunition. Urgent telegraph messages to Springfield Landing from General Richard Arnold asking for more ammunition were answered by Lieutenant "Ed" Armstrong that there was not a round of any light or heavy artillery ammunition at the supply depot, except for 120 rounds of 12-pounder Sawyer rifle shells which did not fit any cannon at Port Hudson. Company K's ordnance officer had informed Armstrong that these Sawyers could not fit their 4.62-inch rifles. Armstrong then telegraphed Arnold stupidly asking if he must forward to headquarters all other ammunition as fast as it arrived at the landing. The response was emphatic: "Yes!"[24]

(*See Appendices for the artillery engaged on June 14, 1863.*)

Thirteen
At Port Hudson, June 15–July 9

After the grand plan of June 14 to take Port Hudson failed, Banks, in complete denial, took no action to bring his wounded and dead off the battlefield where they had lain since the morning of the 14th. On the 15th Banks asked leave of Gardner to send medical supplies to him to attend to the needs of the wounded of both sides. Gardner readily accepted the offer, and he called Banks' attention to the dead and living Federal bodies in front of his lines. Banks' responded to Gardner that he had no dead there (in front of the Priest Cap). He issued a general order to his men proudly proclaiming: "We are at all points on the threshold of his fortifications." He then continued with a two paragraph call for one thousand volunteers for a storming party (a forlorn hope) to take Port Hudson. Late on the 16th, Gardner asked General Beale to send a flag of truce to General Augur to allow them to bring off the Federal dead. Augur replied that he was unaware of any dead there, but he would grant a cessation of hostilities to review the situation.

Late on the 16th, and during the morning of the 17th, a flag of truce went into effect to bring off the dead and wounded. Those few living who the stretcher bearers brought off were fly-blown and their wounds full of maggots (the maggots may have saved some men from the ravages of gangrene). At the Priest Cap, the Confederates could not let the Yankees get close to their earthworks; instead, using body-hooks, they pulled the dead out of the ditch and took 135 dead and 2 wounded off about thirty to fifty yards (depending upon the terrain) where they laid them out for the Yankees to pick up for burial. One hundred thirty dead men and two Newfoundland dogs were laid out for burial in front of the 52nd Massachusetts and hundreds more brought out from the ditches and fields along the Priest Cap. On the northern most part of the Priest Cap and on Colonel Steedman's front, the dead Yankees who had strayed off course from their regiments during the assault would lie for at least three more weeks.

The few dead carried off the night of the 14th, if identifiable, were buried by surviving members of their regiment and crude boards with the names of the dead written thereon marked the burial places. By the 17th the bodies could not be identified and were piled into burial trenches. Many of the men wounded on the 14th had died from exposure: either dehydration or sunstroke due to Banks' apathy.

While the burials took place, a 42-pounder from river Battery #II or III was dismounted and moved to vacant Battery #I and remounted to replace the 24-pounder previously moved to the land lines. Perhaps it could reach Whistling Dick and put that irritant out of action.

While Banks indulged in a self-pity party and confined his regard for humanity within his politician's shriveled black heart, he began plotting with his surviving generals and colonels on how to best capture Port Hudson. The resulting plan called for regular siege tactics of saps, trenches, covered ways, mines and continual artillery bombardment. General Dwight convinced Banks that if a large enough battery were constructed on the shoulder of Mount Pleasant just 300 yards or less from the Citadel, it would blast the Citadel off the face of the earth and open a clear way to drive into the center of Port Hudson.

Because the Citadel was a heavily fortified position located on a high bluff by the river at the southernmost end of the Rebel lines from where it could command all approaches by river and land, it made sense to put time and effort into removing the obstacle to both land and river attack. Across a valley and roughly 300 yards away (the distance varied with the curve of the bluffs and valley) was a hill (Mount Pleasant) now in Federal control. Across from it, the Confederate engineers had worked night and day to strengthen the earthworks of the Citadel and construct inner works in the event the Federals would get into the original works. The Citadel was so fortified that if the main defensive line were broken, the defenders could fall back to secondary and newly constructed tertiary lines within it to continue their hold upon the river.[1]

In addition to approving construction of the large battery position on Dwight's front, Banks ordered several wide zigzag approach trenches called saps to be dug toward the Rebel earthworks. These works would approach as follows: 1) from battery #8, along the edge of a valley to enter the ditch at Fort Desperate; 2) about 300 yards south at battery #12 and going north by north west about 100 yards into a shallow valley with a country lane at its rear, then forming an elbow by turning almost due south to run parallel to the east face of the Priest Cap and the breastworks south almost to the Jackson Road; 3) a zigzag approach from the valley just north of Slaughter's house, crossing the road and stopping at battery #16; 4) from the valley in front of battery #18 leading toward the advanced lunette in Gibbon's field just south of Slaughter's field; 5) from behind Mount Pleasant along the river to the riverside corner of the Citadel.

The rifle pits leading from the left of battery #20 to the right of battery #21 were deepened and lengthened to provide better cover for their occupants and to allow the free passage of individual men to threatened points. As firing steps were completed, the trench deepened and extended from #21 at a forward left oblique to the edge of the valley in front of Mount Pleasant and then along the front of Mount Pleasant to the Mississippi River. Work on this trench along the brow of the valley began at night on the 16th.[2]

Opposite the valley from the extending rifle pits, the Confederates busily repaired their battered earthworks every night, which gave the Federals a measure of rest from sharpshooters' fire while they dug their extended rifle trench to the river. The Federal pickets were scattered out about 110 yards forward and left of the trench. The Yankee pickets slowly drove the enemy pickets back so the trench could advance toward the river, which put the Federal pickets within sixty-six yards of the enemy pickets. The driving in of the Confederate pickets was not limited to Dwight's end of the line.

Skirmishing went on all around the siege line as did sharpshooting. In a few places the skirmishers moved up to the defenders' breastworks before being discovered. An unpleasant choice awaited those skirmishers when discovered: either get shot in the back while running away, or surrender into captivity as a prisoner of war.

As the Federal line of connected rifle pits neared the river in front of the Citadel, work began on the great battery at position #23. The initial moving of cotton bales into position to provide protection for the workers leveling off the hillside began after dark on the evening of the 16th. This battery's plans called for it to have embrasures for 17 guns of various calibers. Dwight's acting engineer, Major Joseph Bailey, from the Fourth Wisconsin, now a cavalry regiment designed the battery, which included a bombproof log and dirt room in its center-rear slightly elevated above the floor of the battery with very thick walls and a series of small loopholes for General Dwight to safely observe the firing of the battery and his infantry's operations against the Citadel.

Bailey supervised a group of Negro Pioneers who built the battery a little to the rear of and along the line of the 6th Michigan's rifle pits within roughly 175 to 250 yards of the Confederate defensive works. About 200 contrabands and members of the Pioneers hurriedly constructed a parapet from cotton bales laid end to end, side by side and atop each other during the moonless night. A course or two of sandbags topped off the layers of cotton bales.

Daylight came and the workers received only sporadic rifle fire from the Citadel; therefore, they hauled more cotton bales into position to thicken the walls and construct traverses to counter enfilading fire. Details from the 6th Michigan assisted in working on the position as well as providing fire support for it. As night fell again, they called over to the Rebels that they were ceasing fire, and the Rebels ceased, likewise. The mutual cease fire continued during the day of the 17th as well, and that night a few of the adversaries came out of their pits and trench, sat down and talked with each other.

One man from the 6th Michigan calling over to the other side agreed to meet a Rebel in the middle of the valley and exchanged a chew of tobacco for a newspaper. The Rebels had an abundance of sugar and molasses, which they were willing to share or trade for other food items. Later on that month the Yanks would tease them about eating mule meat and rats. The 6th Michigan would playfully toss dirt clods at their Rebel counterparts and vice versa. Each side would warn the other when they had to shoot. It indeed made for a strange kind of warfare. The situation distressed commanding officers to the point where orders were issued for the subordinate officers and men to cease fraternizing.[3]

Both sides conserved precious ammunition by not firing at one another. The shortage of artillery ammunition continued to hamper the requisite timed artillery fire at the Rebels. On the 15th, the assistant ordnance officer at Baton Rouge, Lieutenant E. W. Leymour, telegraphed General Arnold that he had no Parrott ammunition nor any eight or ten inch shells. He had only 400 solid shot and 286 cartridge bags of powder for 24-pounders on hand. From Springfield Landing, Lieutenant Armstrong wired Arnold that the steamer *Sallie Robinson* had just arrived with 320 rounds of 20-pounder Parrott projectiles, 2,578 12-pounder projectiles, 2,700 3-inch projectiles, 4,500 10-pounder (2.9-inch) projectiles, 552 rounds of 6-pounder (3.67-inch) Sawyer shells, 780 12-pounder (4.62-inch) rifle cartridges, 500 6-pounder (3.67-inch) rifle cartridges, 43 barrels of 3-inch rifle cartridges, 14 barrels of 20-pounder (3.67-inches) Parrot cartridges and 93, 24-pounder solid shot. Banks' headquarters requested the navy to furnish 20-pounder and 30-pounder shell, case and shot to his command for use by his artillery.

An unusual order went out by telegram on the 16th from Richard Arnold to General Dwight. It authorized Dwight to take boiler iron from any sugar house, and went on to state that he was to utilize the navy to help procure it. The heavy iron sheets used for boilers were nearly impervious to rifle fire. A blacksmith could make them flat so that they would provide mantelets to cover the gun openings in the new seventeen gun "Cotton Bale" battery being constructed on Dwight's front opposite the Citadel. The mantelets would be closed while the gun crews reloaded their pieces and opened while aiming and shooting.

A few days prior to this and presumably during the cease-fire period, the Federal Engineering Department made a series of compass readings and estimations of distance to various Confederate targets sighting points around the lines from the Federal battery positions. *(See Appendices for a copy of this table.)*

The heavy artillery batteries resumed their slow-timed fire to harass the Confederates, and Federal sharpshooters continued their shooting at the Rebel sharpshooters and vice-versa, resulting in a boring, tedious and deadly standoff. Intermittent rain squalls kept the rifle pits and trenches muddy. A Mississippi soldier wrote that he fired his rifle about four or five times a day. Several men from the 39th Mississippi were lucky to have an abandoned house to shelter from the frequent summer rain squalls; however, exploding Federal shells sent it up in flames on the 16th. The Mississippians had parched corn for breakfast.

Farther to the right, Colonel B. W. Johnson, commanding the 15th Arkansas in Fort Desperate, had Captain Louis J. Girard of the Ordnance Department fix some unexploded 13-inch mortar shells fired from the Federal mortar boats as land mines. The Ordnance Department fixed cannon friction primers to the mortar shells so they could be triggered by a man inside the breastwork pulling a lanyard attached to the primer in the touch hole of the shell. The huge shells were planted outside of Fort Desperate's fortifications where they would do the most damage to a charging enemy. A few days later, Captain Girard placed fourteen additional 13-inch mortar shells just outside the Priest Cap.[4]

June 17 was fairly quiet around the battlefield. The stench was so bad from rotting Yankee carcasses that Confederate general officers raised a white flag and asked Banks for permission to bury the Federal dead, since he would not do so. Banks gave in and had the dead men removed and buried. While the truce existed, no firing took place. On Weitzel's and Paine's front, the dead were laid out in rows of one hundred along the burial trenches before having a few words said and the bodies tumbled into the trenches.

The 4th Massachusetts Battery under Lieutenant Trull received orders to withdraw to Plains Store and report to Colonel Dudley for an unknown mission. The movement was one of many made by selected light artillery batteries during the siege. Sections of the 2nd Massachusetts Battery, 4th Massachusetts Battery, 1st U.S. Company L and the 2nd Vermont Battery were used as flying artillery to hasten to various areas that needed covering fire, to guard wagon trains of foragers, to reinforce a weak point from an anticipated attack in the rear by Rebel cavalry, or provide covering fire for the cavalry on its many raids. The 2nd Massachusetts had one section detached for much of the siege accompanying cavalry on the west bank of the Mississippi River.

Banks ended a little squabbling among his generals on the 17th by sending a telegram to General Grover stating that he would not order General Auger to withdraw his lines to give up what little ground he gained; instead, Grover should order his artillery to either reduce their powder charges so their projectiles would not reach Augur's lines, or Grover should order his artillery to fire in another direction.

Grover also requested from General Richard Arnold permission to move a 10-inch and one 8-inch mortar from his right and position them near Bainbridge's battery in an unconstructed position. If and when he received the permission, he would have the holes completed to emplace the mortars. The Federals continually maneuvered their artillery to come up with a way to blow Port Hudson open so the infantry could march in with flags flying high. Dwight's drunken visions seem to be infecting the entire Federal command.

Back at Gardner's headquarters area, his telegrapher reported that the commissary was out of meal, rice, bacon and lard. Fresh beef and hominy were still in supply. At the Hoosiers' headquarters, William Roy received his official commission as major.[5]

On the south of the lines, General Dwight was well known to frequently over imbibe of strong spirits and any available Negro wenches. Allegedly being a West Pointer, he chronically cursed volunteer military units and their officers as inferior to regular army men and officers. This was enigmatic, because Dwight had flunked out of West Point. Dwight called Captains Cordon and Stark before him to be judged for disobedience of orders in the presence of the enemy on June 14 and to be summarily executed, Dwight yelled: "'you — you — hic — hanged — hic.' He holds onto the tent pole, 'hanged — hic' 'Gentlemen, 'ep yur-selves.'" The two officers took the cups from the table by Dwight, drank up and speedily departed before the sot changed his mind. (The two officers had wisely made the decision to not attack the enemy Citadel from the riverside. For some reason Dwight did not include Lt.-Colonel Bacon, and Dwight seems to have disregarded *his* ordering the companies these officers commanded to the other side of Mount Pleasant.) When Dwight was sober he was a mediocre commander; however, he was seldom sober.

These were not the only subordinate officers who were fed up with Dwight and the Federal Army in general. The 6th Michigan's Captain John Cordon complained about the army's poor treatment and lack of care the enlisted men received. He stated that the privations of all were far worse than any he had to live under in South Africa while in Her Majesty's service. They had no tents and were exposed to all kinds of weather, insects and reptiles. They could not remove their boots without getting their feet chewed on by something. Unfortunately, this was true of the men on both sides of the siege lines and even worse within Port Hudson.

The siege steadily ground on. Saps continued to be lengthened and deepened, the artillery maintained a monotonous timed fire, sharpshooters kept up their sniping and men were sporadically wounded or killed. The Naval Battery, position #10, removed one 9-inch Dahlgren gun, assigning Ensign Swann to take charge of the piece. The navy men prepared it for travel to the far left of their lines.

Ammunition for the siege guns had arrived in the days between June 15 and June 20, keeping the wagoners busy transporting the shot, shell and case from Springfield Landing to the Ordnance Depot at Port Hudson. Armstrong dutifully reported the off-loading of artillery projectiles and ammunition in the thousands of rounds and tons of cartridges and barrels of gunpowder. No one, especially the officer in charge of it, wanted the supplies to remain too long at the landing, which was lightly guarded and vulnerable to raids by guerrillas or cavalry.[6]

Around June 20, a foraging party of one hundred fifty-four army wagons, including some wagons from the 1st Indiana, went into the countryside accompanied by a two gun section of Battery L, 1st U.S. Artillery, the 52nd Massachusetts infantry, and a battalion of Grierson's Illinois Cavalry to bring in cotton and food from nearby plantations. The loaded caravan was attacked by Rebel cavalry who shot the mules of the lead wagons, thereby blocking the road. The Rebels found easy pickings among the wagons as their teamsters applied their whips, maneuvering wildly in any direction that looked open in order to escape. The infantry tried to form a line of battle, but they were impeded by the Rebel horsemen milling among them. They fired at the horsemen, but without good results since they couldn't get into a battle line, and being nine-months men did not have the training to fight by squads, in a square or at will.

The artillery section moved onto a low hill and fired upon the attackers, which signaled the Federal cavalry, Grierson's Illinois, which was in the rear that something was amiss. The Federal cavalry charged the rear of the wagon train. The Rebels fled with at least eighteen captured wagons and fifty prisoners from the caravan, including Zeno Rubottom from Company H, four men from Company K of the 1st Indiana and a wagon with its six mule-team and driver from Nims' battery. A few wagons overturned in the melee and were complete wrecks to be left behind. The remaining supply wagons and troops returned safely. The event was duly noted by a telegram to General Banks' headquarters that reported the most essential details of the loss: "About one-half the wagon train captured, 62 wagons." "Commissary has no Whiskey either."

At Springfield Landing, the Hoosier artillerists from Company H continued sorting the ammunition coming in by its intended destination and filled artillery shells with powder, while they hoped their hearing would improve because they were away from the roaring of their thirty-pounders. The boys from Company H had availed themselves of an abandoned house in which to sleep soundly on the floor past sunrise.

The bully boys also took advantage of every opportunity to poke fun at the poorly performing Easterners who came around. Naturally, the Easterners, especially the nine-month Massachusetts, Vermont and Connecticut soldiers bore the brunt of the Hoosiers' jokes. These men's poor discipline, attitude and morale caused them to become the butt of the western men's humor. The Hoosiers delighted in asking them if they were soldiers or nine-month men. Rufus Dooley said "it makes them very 'wrathy,' but that is all the good it does them; they know the Hoosiers too well to fool with them."

The Hoosiers' Captain Connelly claiming to have been a witness to the performance of the assault of the 14th, stated that many of the Eastern troops (men enlisted for only nine months) made a rapid reconnaissance to the rear and could not be found until the battle closed for the day. The 6th Michigan also engaged in taunting the eastern Yankees. However, both regiments acknowledged that most of the New Yorkers and a couple of long-term eastern regiments were pretty good at fighting.[7]

Inside the earthworks of Port Hudson at the northern lines another Federal infantry probe began and ended against the 39th Mississippi's defenses. As usual, the Federals gained nothing in this abortive attempt. (The Federals had made and would continue to make similar probes all around the lines testing the defenses day and night as long as the siege lasted.) However, to shore up the defenses in that area, Colonel I.G.W. Steedman ordered Lieutenant J. P. Caldwell to move a 6-pounder brass gun from the arsenal to a gun pit being prepared in the center of the 39th Mississippi's lines.

Orders again went out to the siege guns to fire at least twenty rounds a day. Quite often military targets were not readily available, in which case shells were lobbed at whatever target was handy. Lieutenant-Colonel Edward Bacon of the 6th Michigan, while visiting Captain Hamrick's two 24-pounder siege gun section of the Jackass Regiment, Company D, in Position #15, asked the captain what they saw to shoot at. Hamrick in turn asked the chief of piece of one of the 24-pounders. The chief answered that he saw nothing. A cannoneer said that he saw an old cow inside the fortifications. The officer said to let her have it. The blast echoed in the gun pit while the shell flew toward the cow and burst, with a large puff of smoke, about 100 yards short of the cow, which ran into the woods. Company D had fulfilled their required duty and would not need to waste ammunition for twenty more minutes.

Meanwhile, deep within the Confederate defenses, improvisation became the order of the day. Beginning on the 20th, the engineers sent details of men passing through every encampment, trench, rifle pit, gopher hole and the more troubled places along the fortifications to recover spent bullets, non-exploded artillery shells and solid shot. Ten-inch and eight-inch shells were very desirable, because they could be fired back at the Federals from the eight and ten-inch guns on the river. In the rear, men melted the scavenged lead bullets and cast them in molds to fit the muskets used on the firing line. They made between 4,000 to 5,000 new bullets a day, which kept the men on the firing lines well supplied.

Some of the recovered 12-pounder shot and shells were recycled for their howitzers, and the rest used with other spent artillery ammunition to which the engineers could affix fuses. With the fuses and fresh powder, the shells would be used as hand-grenades against the sappers working in the advancing saps and against assaulting infantry. (Recycling is not a new idea.) The large bore rifled ammunition and 9-inch balls would be used as torpedoes (land mines) planted in front of the breastworks or rolled down a slope into the advancing saps or defensive ditch. The engineers rigged some novel ways to place cannon friction primers as triggers for the torpedoes so that the tug on a wire leading to the shelter of a trench would fire the torpedo in the face of an advancing enemy. Similar firing mechanisms were used to explode smaller caliber shells and rifled cannon shells as torpedoes or thrown grenades. The latter could be as dangerous to the thrower as the intended victims.[8]

On June 22, the usual infantry skirmishers made probes against the south and the north sides of the defenders lines. During time out periods of firing, the soldiers exchanged newspapers, hardtack and tobacco as the antagonists met between the lines. The Yankees were "perfect gentlemen" declared some 39th Mississippi boys. That evening found the same men engaged in heavy skirmishing with each other.

Far to the south, the seventeen gun battery and its attendant two mortar pits reached a state of completion that allowed heavy ordnance to be brought in. This battery was called either Battery Bailey after its designer and constructor or the Cotton Bale Battery after its chief structural component. (On the maps accompanying this book, it is Position #24.) Orders had already reached the heavy artillery units around Port Hudson to tell them what armament was to be removed from their present position and prepared to emplace in the Cotton Bale Battery. The artillerists had been moving cannon around for the last couple of days, and they would soon receive their assigned places within the great battery.

Accompanied by scattered rain showers but not much action from Rebel sharpshooters, the 1st Indiana, Company A, moved from Position 20-OLD into Position #20. Company B under Captain James Grimsley moved from Position #21 into the Cotton Bale Battery (Position #24), Company C in Position #17 moved one 8-inch howitzer under Lieutenant William Bough into Position #22, which was a heavily reinforced salient point in the line of rifle pits and trenches running from the river to Position #20. Company D moved two 24-pounder guns from Position #13 and one 24-pounder gun from Position #15 under Captain William S. Hinkle into the Cotton Bale Battery and Company E moved two 20-pounder Parrott rifles from the reserve park under Lieutenant Samuel Hartley into the Cotton Bale Battery. Lieutenant Theodore C. Bradley, 2nd U.S. Company C moved his remaining two 12-pounder Napoleons into the space in #21 vacated by Grimsley. Ensign Robert P. Swan commanded two of the navy's 9-inch Dahlgren guns, but only one went into the Cotton Bale Battery at this time. The 1st Vermont under Captain George T. Hebard moved into Position #19 with six 3-inch Ordnance rifles.[9]

After the 1st U.S., Battery L, moved two 12-pounder Napoleons and two 2.9-inch 10-pounder Parrott rifles into Battery Bailey, the largest and heaviest gun went next. Mule-drawn sling carts carried the 9-inch Dahlgren gun into the works, and unloaded. Using levers, its crewmen alternately lifted one end and inserted a block, stacking the blocks atop each other until its naval carriage could be slipped into position under the 9-inch monster and then lowered it onto the carriage. Once done, the crewmen rolled it into position on a planked platform. The other heavy pieces rolled in on their own carriages, which allowed for road travel, which the naval carriage did not.

The line of artillery going into the battery let the Confederate commanders know exactly what was about to happen at that end of their defenses. In less than an hour, there were as many Confederate officers peering over the Citadel's parapets as there were Federal officers in the Cotton Bale Battery watching the armament process going on. For some reason the Rebels were more interested in observing what was taking place than in shooting away at it.

Work carried on at saps pushing forward from near Positions #8 and #12. Here too, cotton bales pushed ahead by the diggers protected them from sharpshooters. Men of the 53rd Massachusetts constructed fascines (large baskets made of interwoven brush and tree branches then filled with dirt and cotton) and placed them along the top of the ditch, thereby, raising the sides of the ditch by two to three feet to give more protection to the workers in the sap. This was critical when the northerly running sap from Position #12 to the Priest Cap made a

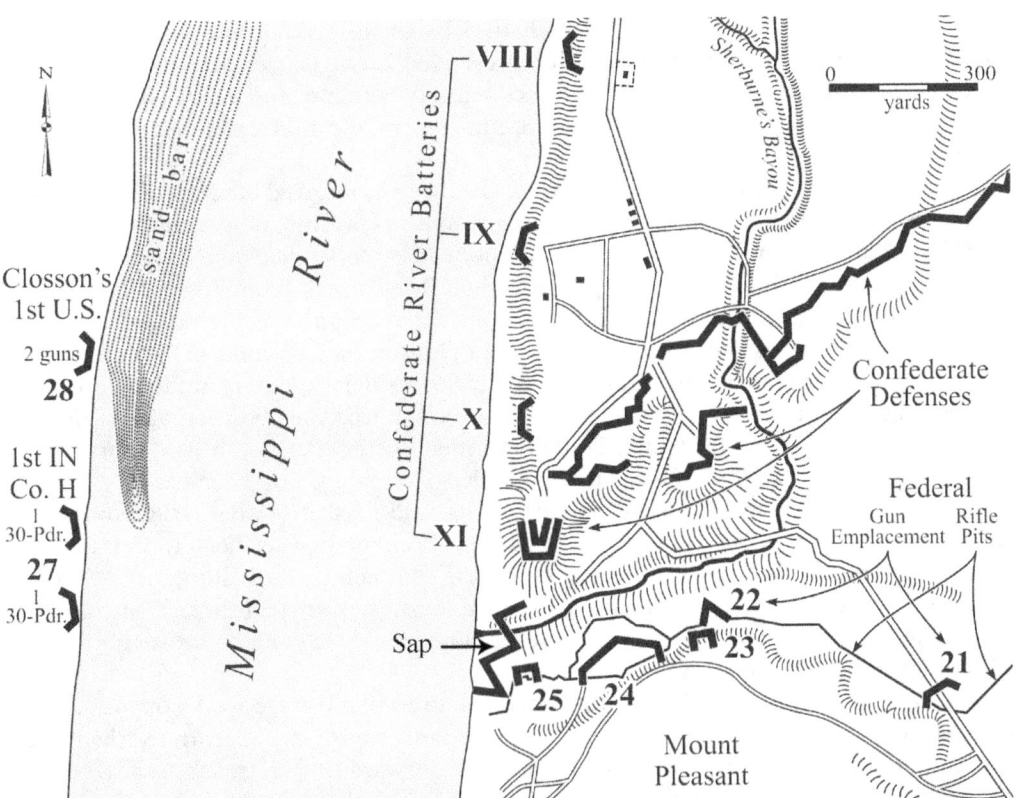

Confederate River Batteries VIII through XI (the Citadel). Federal Batteries 21 through 28 as corrected by the author. The Jackass Regiment's Company H was on the west bank of the river in position #27 for a week at the end of the siege. Company H's targets were the river batteries where they disabled guns in VIII through X. A two-gun section of Nims' battery occupied #28 for two days; afterwards a detachment from Captain Closson's 1st U.S., Company L, had two 12-pounder Napoleon guns there. (Cartographic design by Mary Lee Eggart, based upon a National Archives map, RG 77-M-107.)

U-turn at the edge of a ravine and began going southerly parallel to the face of the Priest Cap and only a few yards from it.[10]

The next day, the 23rd, Captain Connelly returned from New Orleans with one repaired and one replacement 30-pounder Parrott for Company H. The Hoosiers at Springfield Landing joyfully left the supply depot as teams of mules hauled their Long Toms to the Cotton Bale Battery. Once there, they unhitched the mules, and a detail took the teams to the rear and stabled them. The rest of the company attached ropes and pulled and pushed their guns into their places in the battery. Once they had the guns emplaced, the men set up their shelters from rain and sun, spread their blankets, set up their cooking equipment and became as comfortable as possible.

The walls of Battery Bailey were more than head high and had swinging mantlets of boiler plate in the embrasures to stop the occasional sharpshooter's bullets from finding human targets working around the guns. (The mantlets covered the embrasure and could be swung up out of the way when the gun's crew put the gun in battery, aimed and fired. The mantlets were swung shut after the gun fired and recoiled back for service.) The remnants of the 14th Maine Infantry moved into the rifle pits adjoining the Cotton Bale Battery and positions #20, 21, 22 and 23.

In addition to Company H going into Battery Bailey this day, an additional 8-inch howitzer from Company C, commanded by 1st Sergeant William B. Glover, also moved into Position #24. The First Indiana's Company K received orders to move to a new position, but as usual it was not completed. It was just more miscommunication and failed coordination among the Yankee brass.

Lieutenant F. E. Taylor from the 1st U.S., Company L, received orders to leave his mortar battery taking 3 privates with him and report to his company. Another task awaited this capable artillery officer. He took command of four 12-pounder Napoleons and their crews, and they headed south to the vicinity of the Cotton Bale Battery. From Taylor's old position a 10-inch mortar was loaded on a wagon and transported around the lines to go into Battery Position #23, which was higher up Mount Pleasant's hillside than Position #22 but on the same level as Battery Bailey. The 13th Massachusetts Light Artillery's lieutenant Ellis Motte commanded the mortar. Two additional 10-inch mortars moved into Position #25, which had been constructed to the left of and slightly lower than Battery Bailey. The two mortars were under command of the 13th Massachusetts Artillery's captain C.H.J. Hamlen.

During the past two days 1000 pounds of rifle and musket powder, 1394 powder cartridges for siege guns of various caliber, 88 barrels of cannon powder, 1600 rounds of 3 inch rifle projectiles and 3185 rounds of solid shot, case-shot and shell of all the large siege gun and mortar calibers arrived at Springfield Landing. A partial shipment to the front was made using fifteen wagons on hand, and a request for more wagons to come to the supply depot to pick up more siege materials sent with them.[11]

When work drew to a close on the Federal batteries and siege works opposite to the Citadel and its left side's flanking works on the 23rd, the engineers concentrated their attention on constructing a zigzag sap from the end of the forward rifle pit trench at the river bank toward the Citadel. Strangely, the Confederate response to the great amount of shovel, pick and spade work going on across from the Citadel was lackluster. The defenders fired only a few bullets at the besiegers. They seemed content to watch the sap's progress and the strengthening of the Cotton Bale Battery and wait. Colonel Miles attributed the lack of shooting and fraternization of the past week to his men's trying to conserve their scarce ammunition.

With the addition of the two flanking mortar pits, Battery Bailey was often referred to by the recipients of its wrath as the "nineteen gun battery" as well as the "seventeen gun battery" or that "big damn battery."

On the 25th two flags (symbols of two different causes or ideologies as to the relationship of the rights of an individual to either the individual's state, or to a national overseer of all states, thereby, suborning the individual), flew only 175 yards from each other at the Citadel and Battery Bailey. Among the Hoosiers, Rufus Dooley worried about the two flags flying with no lead flying—"There is something very strange about this." It just was not right. Why were both flags allowed to fly? Why did the Confederates not attempt to shoot the Union's flag down and vice-versa? The answer came later that day, when Confederate officers observed the new sap begun on the riverside of Battery Bailey and directed at the Citadel. Rebel sharpshooters opened a brisk fire upon the sap and the Cotton Bale Battery. The now blasé Dooley "thought it was tolerable heavy." It was suicide to show one's head above the sandbag topped parapets.[12]

The sap at the Citadel was not the only sap being watched. The boys in gray also watched the progress of the four saps underway on the east and northeast sides of the earthworks. No saps approached on the north or northwest end of the defenses. The Federals kept the Confederates busy with continual skirmishing and (with exception of mortars and one 30-pounder) fire by light artillery all along the portion of the line held by the 10th Arkansas, 9th Louisiana and 39th Mississippi.

The sap extending from near battery #18 was soon close enough to the defenders that action needed to be taken against it. During the night of June 26, a squad of thirty men and officers from the 16th Arkansas led by Lieutenant Arch S. McKinnon went over their parapet and walked silently in single file to the sap. When within 20 yards of it, they charged the saphead and sent the diggers and their guards running to the rear without firing a shot. The battalion destroyed what they could of the sap. As minie balls began whistling about them, the Arkansans hurried back to their lines with three prisoners: two privates and a first lieutenant from the 25th Maine Infantry.

The sap running from the ravine by Slaughter's ruins to Position #16 was far enough away from the Confederate breastworks that it drew little attention from the defenders. It appeared to be more of a covered way for the artillerists at #16 to come and go from their artillery pieces and a firing trench for the battery's infantry support rather than a sap.[13]

The saps near Battery Positions #8 and #12 caused a great deal of concern to the 15th Arkansas at Fort Desperate and the 1st Mississippi at the Priest Cap. As the saps got nearer to the Priest Cap, Company B from the 53rd Massachusetts along with details of Pioneers filled hogsheads with dirt and maneuvered them into the sap at Battery #18. They rolled them along the sap, rounded the U-turn at the valley and started pushing them up atop the edge of the sap closest to the Rebel lines. Other hogsheads began rising along the sap's parallel to form a stack which become the base of a trench cavalier (a tower rising above the trench and enemy defensive parapet, which allows marksmen to shoot into an enemy's defensive works).

At the Priest Cap the defenders dug traverses, gopher holes to hide in and an additional inner defensive trench. They filled the first trench with sharply pointed wooden stakes angled towards the breastworks in front. Piled brush camouflaged the death pit called the Rat Trap. Dirt piled in front of the new trench made a new breastwork. From the Priest Cap to Slaughter's Field across from General Augur's front, traverses went up and the breastworks thickened as the trench widened and deepened. On the 25th, a corporal from the 1st Mississippi crawled out of the Priest Cap's defenses to the head of the approaching sap. Using an artillery port-fire he set the cotton bales ablaze, which halted the work and exposed the workers to rifle fire. The corporal made it back to his lines unscathed; progress on the sap halted until the damage could be repaired. Then the defenders made crude bows and arrows and shot flaming arrows at the cotton bales, again halting work.

Frederick Y. Dabney ordered his engineers to move a 24-pounder siege gun from the redan near the Clinton to Port Hudson Railroad's entrance through the breastworks. They moved it a little to the left and a considerable distance to the rear to occupy a position on a spur ridge relatively protected from the Yankee artillery. From this position it could shoot at the head of the Yankee sap at the Priest Cap and the trench cavalier. The 1st Alabama began digging a sunken position behind their redan at the railroad to emplace The Baby to fire at the cavalier. Most of the light guns inside Port Hudson were now in shallow pits to better preserve them from destruction. Replacement parts were running low, and The Baby already had two to three sets of wheel replacements made. Due to Yankee sharpshooters and artillery, the Alabamians could work only at night and did not get The Baby into the reinforced emplacement in time to be of much use against the trench cavalier.

Countering the sap at Fort Desperate, Colonel Johnson had tunnels dug under his parapet to connect with the ditch in front from which his men could use the ditch as a forward rifle pit to snipe at the Yankees. A semi-detached sunken rifle pit was constructed on the left of the parapet so as to be nearly invisible to attackers making their way into the fort's ditch. Johnson also had an earthen version of a trench cavalier built from dirt mounded behind and atop his parapet, thick enough to be proof against artillery and high enough for his sharpshooters to shoot down into the enemy sap.

At the southern end in the Citadel and Devil's Elbow, the defenders had constructed gopher holes and an inner line of trenches. At the Citadel, engineers constructed a third inner line of defenses. Also, in this area and in the Devil's Elbow, they mounted two disabled 10-pounder Confederate Parrotts on large pieces of wood, poured in a couple of pounds of gunpowder and topped that with a bag of rocks, nails, nuts, bolts, spent minie balls, buttons, broken crockery, anything that could inflict a wound when the Yankees charged their earthworks.[14]

Top: Confederate living quarters near the Citadel called gopher holes by their occupants. Notice the disabled 3-inch Confederate Parrott rifle from Calvit Roberts' Seven Stars Mississippi Battery. (Courtesy Military Order of the Loyal Legion of the United States, housed at USAMHI, Carlisle Barracks, Pennsylvania) *Bottom:* Interior of Devil's Elbow. Confederate 3-inch Parrott rifle from Calvit Roberts' Mississippi 7-Stars Battery. Located at embrasure on southeastern face of parapet. The barrel's muzzle was shot off, and a tube was affixed to a beam so it could be filled with powder and improvised canister to be fired once as the Yankees came over the parapet. (Courtesy Lawrence Lee Hewitt.)

As if the bullets, cannon balls and saps weren't enough for the Confederates to withstand, their rations (limited from the beginning) had failed. Large quantities of sugar and molasses existed, but supplies of meat and vegetables had gotten very low by mid–June. The defenders went on quarter rations with molasses to stretch what little they had.

General Gardner's Commissary Department had commandeered a new but not yet fully completed and dedicated Methodist Episcopal Church before the siege began for storage. The church's location near the river and the Plains Road was centered between the ends of the line along the river. The commissary used it as a storage building for shelled dried peas. Due to the visibility of its steeple and roof, the Federal artillery, except for the guns in Positions #2, #5, #6, #8 #12, #16 and Mack's 18th New York Battery, used it as an aiming point for their guns. Because broken glass from shot-out windows and splinters from the wooden walls and roof had mixed well in the peas, the peas took special care to eat. The defenders easily picked out splin-

Port Hudson Methodist Church, used as a granary by the Confederate defenders. (Courtesy Military Order of the Loyal Legion of the United States, housed at USAMHI, Carlisle Barracks, Pennsylvania.)

ters but had to examine their peas in bright sunlight to see glints of light from the glass particles to pick out of their peas. Once the peas were glass-free, the men ground them and made bad-tasting, but edible, bread from them.

The men also consumed dried boiled or parched corn on the cob after Federal artillery blew apart their corn mill's power supply. Ground corn came back onto the menu in limited quantities after engineers set up the mill stones and a drive mechanism in the train shed. They jacked up a train engine and used it to power a belt attached to its drive wheels and to the mill's stones. Often the corn meal was mixed with ground peas for a loaf of not-so-tasty bread. A parched mixture of corn and peas could even be used to make ersatz coffee.

Due to the corn being needed to feed the men, their cattle supply was turned free to roam for subsistence. The cattle became rangy from a grass-only diet, and they had to be caught to slaughter, which could be a dangerous task for the cowboys. Also, farther ranging cattle weren't safe from Federal cannonballs. In time, cattle inside of Port Hudson's defenses became extinct and no longer included in rations. Thereafter, by utilizing most officers' and couriers' horses, horse meat next appeared on the rations menu. When that meat supply ran out, mule meat would supplement the daily fare, with a side of rat meat. Captain J. M. Bailey, 16th Arkansas, stated that barbequed rat meat did him once; after that experience, he had a vegetarian diet. The strict rationing extended to officers as well as enlisted men.

As usual, soldiers everywhere can be inventive in their ways to acquire fermented beverages to slake their thirst. Those in Port Hudson desiring to make their corn more palatable began brewing corn beer made from corn and sugar or corn and molasses, or just molasses. Barrels of the stuff were kept at the lines to drink instead of their muddy water. Many engaged in this pursuit, but it seems to have been a prized specialty among the 15th Arkansas Regiment.[15]

Back at Battery Bailey on June 26, the first round was fired at Battery XI, which flew over it, landing in the river. The next round did better, but the riflemen's return fire flew so thick no one dared to look over the parapet and see the effect of the shot. Other rounds from the Federals began playing against the Citadel as well as the parapet works to its east and across the alternate road to Baton Rouge at the Devil's Elbow. The noise of the firing became like a percussion concert. Confederate rifle fire played a lengthy staccato alto prelude until 4 o'clock P.M. A bombastic counterpoint of tenor and baritone Federal cannon blasts then resounded from the Cotton Bale Battery accompanied by the bass section from the navy's 13-inch mortars. The concert rose in crescendo until five o'clock P.M. and held until the sun began to set, when the percussive tones diminished and stopped at night. Thereafter, a baritone or bass burp erupted every fifteen minutes until the next day's dawn, when all sections came into the grand movement and performed a cacophonous crescendo that lasted until high noon — then ceased.

At the bombardment's height, the guns hurled hundreds of pounds of iron a minute toward the Rebel parapet. Often, the guns of the great battery would fire all at once. The thundering roar at such a broadside shook the earth around the battery. The pounding by the guns tore the Rebel parapet to pieces and knocked their cotton bales and gabions all over the place. The Citadel's fortifications opposite the Cotton Bale Battery were in ruin, but the determined garrison within it held on and kept down. From the bastion to the Citadel's left (Devil's Elbow), a few shots from a 3.67-inch Parrott rifle and from sharpshooters let the Federals know that they had not been intimidated into surrendering.

As all fell still, a Hoosier observer peeking through a small opening in the sandbags, noted that the Rebel parapet looked like the ruins of an ancient city. No more symmetry of sandbags, cotton bales and stacked hogsheads and gabions filled with dirt; it was a mixed jumble of wood, dirt, remnants of cotton bales, fluffed batches of cotton, and iron, the iron being the remains of the massive barrage of Federal projectiles recently fired into the Rebel parapet. Engineer Fred Y. Dabney gave the same description of the Citadel, adding that the Citadel was no longer defensible to protect its lone piece of siege artillery, the Virginia, and its crew. Dabney ordered the siege gun removed to the rear of the Citadel into the third line of defense that had been under construction for a few days where it could be defended and still be used against the enemy. From there it could be rolled back farther or nearer if it was needed. The Citadel's primary defense fell to riflemen in the pits before it and dug into its interior and to the guns in the projecting earthworks to its left along the Baton Rouge Road.

Except for the sharpshooters, the primary battery was virtually abandoned except for fatigue parties working at night to strengthen the rifle pits and repair daily damage done to them. To thwart the advance of the sap against the Citadel, the riflemen had orders to use volley fire against anyone showing a body part to increase the chances of hitting the target. Engineers kept busy at strengthening the secondary and tertiary defenses immediately behind the smashed walls of the primary Citadel.

Being so close to the Citadel, the Federal artillerists needed to dodge blowback from their own exploding shells. Bits and pieces from their bursts flew back and struck or dropped into the battery due to its close proximity to the Citadel. Captain Grimsley's flag, handmade by the ladies of Gosport, Indiana, and proudly hoisted that morning had nineteen holes torn through it by nightfall. The Cotton Bale Battery's flag was shot down once and the pole immediately repaired and the flag being raised so it waved at dawn's light.

(Confederate hospital records show that Private Samuel Cordy [Conley] from the Hoosiers' Company B was captured June 26 and treated in the Port Hudson Post Hospital for a head wound. Confederate records list his date of death as July 1, 1863. Conley was just another casualty not reported by Grimsley.[16]

The next morning on the 27th, dawn's light also shone on another red, white and blue flag from Miles' Legion flying in the Citadel. Lieutenant Louis A. Schirmer of DeGournay's 12th Louisiana Artillery Battalion having no artillery piece to command for the time being, stayed with the Confederate colors in the Citadel. During the intense firing from Battery Bailey and the navy's mortar boats on the 26th and the 27th, the flag fell three or four times due to shell pieces shattering the flagstaff. A mortar round penetrated the roof of a small powder magazine in the Citadel, exploding it and knocking down the flag. Each time it fell, Schirmer grabbed the flag, affixed it to another pole, waived it at the enemy and then planted it firmly atop the parapet to the cheers of the riflemen. Later that day, a Federal sharpshooter's bullet killed Schirmer as he sought to restore the flag that was again knocked down. About five defenders were killed and wounded about a dozen during the Federal barrage.

The next morning a second 9-inch Dahlgren was pulled from its home in Position #10 and began its way to Battery Bailey. Traveling over improved roads, it would be placed in position #24 that night under Ensign Terry's command. This action left only two 9-inch Dahlgrens in Position #10, where they were commanded by Ensign E. M. Shepard from the *Essex*. Lieutenant Commander Edward Terry would retain overall supervision of the navy's guns and seamen and visit the commands daily. As the Federals opened fire again on the Citadel, it was answered by an 8-inch Seacoast Howitzer and 10-inch Columbiad guns in the river batteries mounted on a center pintle.[17]

All the way across the defenses more than two miles to the north, the 39th Mississippi lost Private Ashley of Company F due to a bizarre accident. The soldier was leaning on his shotgun, loaded with the usual buck and ball, with his hands clasped on the muzzle and his face resting on his hands. The shotgun discharged, and the buck and ball passed through both hands and ripped off his face, shredding blood vessels, brains and other organs. The soldier describing the event noted that "he must have cocked his gun with his foot." The officers and men nearby determined that from the deceased's stance prior to the shot, it was most likely an accident caused by extreme fatigue and exposure.

General Gardner reputedly ordered the government papers burned or buried at this time. He evidently was preparing for the end of the siege, feeling they could not hold out for much longer due to their short rations, increasing sickness and low supply of gunpowder. To ease the strain on his commissary, Gardner offered to parole all of his Yankee prisoners and release them to General Banks. The next day Banks turned down the parole offer by replying that if they were sent over to him, he would put them back in the ranks immediately. Banks' action not only lowered the moral among the prisoners inside Port Hudson, but it had a negative effect upon the fighting men outside of Port Hudson. Those soldiers in the trenches outside of Port Hudson felt Banks' actions of not burying the dead on the 14th of June and not allowing parole for those held prisoner pointed to his lack of regard for his soldiers, and he was "using them up."

The work on the sap by the Cotton Bale Battery moved on toward the Citadel's remains and allowed for a rifle trench to be dug at an angle from it toward the rifle pits in front of the Citadel. This rifle pit manned by men from the 6th Michigan now approached as close as 50 feet from the enemy rifle pits and 100 feet from the parapet. They were also under the enemy guns and safe from them. Only the Rebel sharpshooters could threaten the Federals in the advanced rifle pits, but Federal sharpshooters in an upper trench could usually keep them pinned down. To protect his troops working on this sap and rifle pits, Lieutenant-Colonel

Bacon of the 6th Michigan borrowed Merrill rifles from his friends in the 1st Indiana (probably from Company A) giving them a receipt for the loan. He said, "The new arms would make one man equal to six men with muzzle-loading guns."

Major William Roy, Indiana Jackass Regiment, now commanded all the non-naval guns and non–U.S. Regular Artillery in the Cotton Bale Battery, as well as the 1st Indiana's Company A, the 1st Vermont, and the 21st New York batteries outside and to the right of the huge battery. While the major was personally directing the fire of one of the guns, he received a slight wound in his right arm. The force of the bullet was lessened by its passing first through the body of a marine visiting the battery. The marine died. Major Roy remained at his post.[18]

The 28th of June. The defenders wondered as to what great things the Yankees would attempt today. Being as it was a Sunday, the Confederates, remembering Banks' ill advised assaults of Sunday the 14th, considered a sacrilege by many on each side, remained ready for anything to happen on a Sunday. General Gardner sent a message around the lines asking all the men to be awakened at daylight and to be ready. Nothing special happened. Only the usual timed artillery fire and tired skirmishers making half-hearted probes. The Hoosiers' Whistling Dick's shells tore down a large portion of the 39th Mississippi's parapet, but Colonel Steedman still had eleven pieces of light artillery (two 3.5-inch Blakely rifles, seven 6-pounder guns and two 12-pounder howitzers) and one 24-pounder rifled siege gun in service along his defenses.

Company K's new battery position was finally ready including a magazine that had been forgotten earlier. Limbering up, the battery moved forward into a position made from tightly stacked cotton bales less than 375 yards from the Priest Cap on June 28. Once established in their new position, they provided covering fire for the workers in the sap. Also, they received a new assignment to disable the Confederates' 24-pounder that had been moved a few days earlier. The 24-pounder was knocking holes through the top of the Yankees' trench cavaliers at the Priest Cap taking a heavy toll among the Yankee sharpshooters firing from up there. Immediately after Company K vacated their old battery position, engineers went to work demolishing it and beginning another approach sap along the side of a gully leading to the first sap at the Priest Cap.

From the Federal left came word that the work on the sap was progressing well. Skirmishers had taken up a trip-wire from immediately in front of the enemy parapet that connected loaded cannons filled with shrapnel fixed in an abandoned rifle pit to blast an assaulting column. The skirmishers also dug up a torpedo planted there and carried it back to General F. S. Nickerson's headquarters.

Lieutenant Taylor, 1st U.S., Battery L, received orders to take four of his battery's guns (taking some out of Battery Bailey) and report to Springfield Landing where he would join a brigade commanded by Brigadier General Strong and board a waiting steamer. The next morning at daybreak the steamer arrived at Donaldsonville, Louisiana. There the brigade formed in line outside of Fort Butler. The day before, the fort had repelled an attack by dismounted cavalry from Major-General Richard "Dick" Taylor's corps now busy retaking the lightly guarded Teche and LaFourche country from the Union. Strong's force engaged the enemy for an hour and a half. After leaving a two gun section inside Fort Butler, Lieutenant Taylor returned to Port Hudson that night with his remaining two guns.

Down at Springfield Landing, the usual steamers landed bearing munitions of war, except this time the steamer *St. Mary*'s arrived with 16 boxes of fire balls in addition to 1,005 rounds of assorted 3.67-inch rifle ammunition and 1,005 cartridges for same.[19]

On June 29, General Dwight, his mind fogged more than usual with alcohol, decided to assault the grossly battered Citadel with infantry. He called for two regiments to go against the place in a like manner as his failed attempt of June 14. He was convinced this attempt would be successful because his artillery had pounded the enemy's front gun positions and rifle pits into a muddy pulp. Following Dwight's whiskey fortified orders to "Charge, and keep on charging as long as you have a corporal's guard left," two regiments, the 6th Michigan and 165th New York (Zouaves), made the charge. Led by the 6th Michigan, they threw scores of Ketchum hand grenades as they neared the top of the bluff and the enemy works. Those men in front heard the Rebel officers telling their men to hold their fire and "let the damned Yankees get into the ditch." The gray-clad riflemen, not content to wait, opened fire, which immediately made the advancing men hit the ground on the face of the bluff in front of the defender's ditch. A slight curve in the front of the bluff sheltered the blue and red jacketed Federals from the returned grenades and whizzing bullets. A few 12-pounder and 24-pounder shells with sputtering fuses came bouncing down the bluff amongst the Ketchum grenades. The bouncing shell's explosions caused wounds where bullets sailed overhead without effect. After an hour, at dusk, the firing greatly slackened to almost nothing.

As daylight came, the Wolverines and New Yorkers, realizing that the curve only partially sheltered them, and they were now excellent targets, chose the lesser of two evils and ran for the safety of their forward trench in the rear, leaving their dead behind and ending the Whiskey Charge. The two regiments had fled, but not to safety. Dwight, still drunk, had another mission for these two regiments; they were to charge through the sap along the riverside and assail the heights of the Citadel at its end.

At six o'clock the evening of June 30, led by the 165th New York this time, the regiments advanced against the Citadel by the riverside sap. The sap by now had gone up the two outer mounds of the Citadel's extended bluff, and it had reached the base of the nearly perpendicular true bluff. Heavy skirmishing had taken place there the past couple of days. For this night's greeting, the defenders had made a trough and extended it over the edge of the bluff to empty directly into the end of the sap. The silently advancing Zouaves came to the end of the sap and began to climb the bluff. A few gained the exterior ditch and drove off the few riflemen in it. Alarmed by the shouts and gunfire, the dining defenders dropped their plates, grabbed their firearms and opened fire on the handful of Zouaves coming over the parapet, dropping them all. The grayclads ran to their parapet and opened a merciless fire on the Yankees in its ditch and coming out of the sap. Confederate reinforcements came up at a run.

As yelling Arkansans, Alabamians and Louisianians poured an intense fire into the ditch and the sap, others lit a few fuses of the prepared 24-pound shells and began rolling them down the trough into the mass of Billy Yanks, which caused a rapid dash to the rear and over its sides as the shells began exploding. Many Yanks remained in the rear while others held their ground by hiding behind large dirt clods and tried sharpshooting. Behind the New Yorkers came the 6th Michigan. The Wolverines now in the sap tried to get a noose around the trough to pull it out of the enemy's hands. Lieutenant John S. Kendall, 4th Louisiana Infantry, cut a fuse very short on a 9-inch shell, lit it and let it burn down to the shell before he gave it a push down the trough. Rebel riflemen cut loose with a hellish fire on the trough ropers, driving them away. The huge shell exploded just as it came off the end of the trough, bringing the matter to an end. The Feds abandoned their assault. The defenders then set fire to the Yankee cotton bales at the sap and watched as they burned to cinders.

The first assault made by using a sap at Port Hudson came to an end. Dwight prepared the two tattered regiments to make another charge by cursing them soundly; however, General Banks intervened, sparing the Wolverines and Zouaves more slaughter. Afterward, Dwight was not much heard from. He disappeared from the area.[20]

Dwight's Whiskey Charge had not been the only Federal activity on the 29th and 30th. Duryea's 1st U.S., Battery F, from #6 moved into a brand new Battery Position #12 where he had a direct line of fire against the Priest Cap. A 20-pounder Parrott rifle from either the Jackass Regiment, Company E or from the center section of the 18th New York moved into the same position alongside Duryea's 12-pounder Napoleons. (Neither company's record mentions such a move, but each unit had two 20-pounder Parrotts in park from which to choose.) Seven cannons now bore on the Priest Cap and the Jackson Road Redan from less than 500 yards away in a reinforced position with boiler iron mantlets hung across the embrasures just like at the Cotton Bale Battery. Two tall poles with bags of cotton fasted to their tops marked the ends of Duryea's Battery so the Navy Battery and Mack's Battery to their rear would not shoot into them.

A pair of Parrott rifles from the Jackass Regiment's Company E moved into a couple of recently constructed battery positions atop a ridge between Federal Positions #2 and #3. The Parrotts opened fire against the guns at Bennett's stables, about 200 yards distant. These Parrotts' position and parapet fully protected them from nearby Confederate sharpshooters, thereby enabling the gunners to work in relative ease. Before the surrender, the Parrotts' shot and shell struck a light 6-pounder gun near Bennett's and cut the gun's barrel in half. This piece was a trophy at West Point Military Academy until it disappeared during the 1920s. The nearby 24-pounder commanded by Lieutenant Asa W. Harmon, 1st Alabama Company A, was hit by musketry but not hurt.[21]

Back at the Federal left, the besiegers decided that sharpshooters in an outer rifle pit to the left of the Citadel had a flanking fire at the sap and needed to be eliminated. The pits were dug very near to the edge of the cut into the hill for the Baton Rouge Road with only a couple of feet of earth between them and open air. The guns in Battery Bailey swung to the right and in a relatively short time succeeded in destroying the rifle pits.

Company H received orders to move out of Battery Bailey to Springfield Landing. Picking up their hand spikes, the bully boys moved their 30-pounders out of battery, hitched up their mules and proceeded to Springfield Landing. On reaching the landing at 11 P.M., they got themselves, their mules and their equipment aboard a waiting steamer. It transported them and their guns across and up the Mississippi River a mile or two for a special assignment. While the steamer made way, the Hoosiers slept. Engineers were already busily cutting embrasures in the levee in two places for the Indianians' two Parrott rifles and building up earthen ramps under the embrasures for gun emplacements.

The steamer landed at a point opposite and a little below the Citadel and the river batteries, where they unloaded. The *Richmond* came upstream and provided extra covering fire at the Confederates' river batteries as the Hoosiers and their gear got ashore and behind the levee. Once behind the shelter of the levee they moved their guns north to their two pre-prepared Battery Positions #27. Getting into position, filling the magazine, arranging sandbags to better suit their activities and pitching tents filled most of their time during the rest of the night. After breakfast, on July 1, Captain James Connelly had his guns open fire in mid-morning at a battery two to three hundred yards behind the Citadel. Eight Confederate guns from several positions across the river returned fire with shells varying from 5.82 inches to 10 inches in diameter.

After firing continuously for range and bearings until noon, the Hoosiers took a lunch break, and the Confederates ceased firing. After lunch the bully boys in Company H resumed a slow testing fire lasting all afternoon. The river batteries seldom replied. At nightfall they ceased firing and cooked and ate dinner. Guards were posted, and the gunners went to sleep.

At least the bully boys had enjoyed a good breakfast, lunch and dinner that day. The defenders in Port Hudson did not have that luxury. Corn bread, molasses, peas with ground glass and fried rat mystery meat provided three meals a day for those in the trenches. The siege was causing a great amount of hunger, if not near starvation in some remote positions. Not surprisingly, morale widely fluctuated among the defenders, as evidenced by the increasing number of deserters coming into Federal lines. A staunch Mississippian wrote that he would last two or three weeks longer on the corn bread, molasses and pea diet, even if a shell from Whistling Dick had just killed the best man in his company (Patrick Ryan) by tearing off an arm and a large chunk of his abdomen before exploding to tear up the nearby breastwork. The same day one of the post's telegraphers deserted because he did not care for mule meat. This man's taste was not shared by the post's main telegrapher, John Austen, who found mule steak to taste "good, tender and nutritious."[22]

Across the river Lieutenant Theodore Bradley moved a two gun section of 12-pounder Napoleons of the 2nd U.S., Battery C, past the Hoosiers into a position (Position #28) about a quarter mile north of them. Like the Hoosiers, he had embrasures cut in the levee to position his guns behind. His assignment was likely similar to that of Nims. However, Bradley himself spent a great deal of time watching the effect of the firing from the Cotton Bale Battery and the firing of the Hoosiers, which he communicated through the signal corps from one side of the river to the other. Lieutenant F. E. Taylor assisted the signal corps in coordinating the Cotton Bale Battery's firing against the enemy's river batteries.

Early in the morning of July 2, Company H opened fire on the guns across the river and received a reply from the rifled 32-pounder in River Battery #X. The rifled 32-pounder almost directly across from the 30-pounders got the Hoosiers' range and disabled number 1 gun with a solid shot damaging its carriage. Pulling it out of action, its crew assessed the damage and requested a new carriage, which was sent through signals and telegraph to General Arnold. Number 2 gun carried on the work. In about forty minutes a shot from it made the timber, dirt and dust fly and down went the rifled 32-pounder. The bully boys' shot and shell had cut down the cheeks of its carriage. (The Federals thought that this gun fired the first shot at the river fleet when Admiral Farragut had tried to run past the Port Hudson batteries in March. The gun had also inflicted severe damage several vessels at that time.) The Hoosiers' shells also slightly wounded the rifle's commander, Captain W. N. Coffin. The cheering bully boys climbed atop the levee to better see the results of their work when they saw four big round balls flying their way. Hurling themselves off the levee, they were covered with bushels of dirt as the balls plowed across where they had just been celebrating and bounced a few hundred yards past before coming to rest or exploding. As the return fire flew overhead, the boys in Company H took a dinner break. After dinner, they again began a slow fire from number 2 gun, which they kept up until dark.

Up the river from Company H, the U.S. Battery got a shell into the remaining counterscarp rifle pit at the Citadel, which killed three men and wounded five more. That night the counterscarp pit was abandoned, and engineers dug pits and four traverses to the shell blasted parapet's rear to provide cover and to trap rolling balls from both Battery Bailey and across the river. The repair crews rebuilt works every night, and the Yanks' artillery tore it up during the day.

That night a transport unloaded a new carriage for number one gun, and a supply of ammunition. The men worked at mounting number one's tube on the new carriage and filling their magazines. The morning of the 3rd, the rifled 32-pounder was up and "looking as saucy as ever." However, Company H was too busy re-mounting number one gun, making other repairs and hauling ammunition to fire more than a couple of shots before sunset.[23]

The cannons in the Cotton Bale Battery roared on filling the air with projectiles. It was a routine job designed to keep the Rebels' heads down and to try and suppress return cannon fire from their large guns on up the riverbank while the Federal sap moved forward. The Citadel's defenders had burned the cotton bales used by the sappers as a sap roller to push ahead of the workers as they advanced the sap. Therefore, the clever sappers made a true saproller from a sugar hogshead filled with wooden staves that was impregnable to bullets. As it rolled ahead, the sap advanced to the base of the Citadel in spite of lit 8-inch and 10-inch fused shells being rolled down to it. The blasted earth often bounced the shells away from the sap to explode harmlessly.

The men working the sap tossed hand grenades into the Citadel; the grenades usually did not explode. As a company from the 15th New Hampshire worked the sap and tossed grenades at the Rebels without much effect, the defenders caught the grenades in blankets and tossed them back into the sap, which exploded in the sap, killing a few and wounding several Yankees. To counter the effect of rifle fire and grenade returns the Federal engineers ordered a trench cavalier begun atop a mound (abandoned river battery #XII) in front of the Citadel to get a line of fire behind the ruins of the Citadel. (The trench cavalier was not completed by the end of the siege.)

Another sap branched from the main one and worked its way along the riverside by the Citadel. At the head end of the original sap, miners worked on a tunnel under the works above. Their objective was to dig several yards under the Citadel and then begin packing the tunnel with barrels of gunpowder. When ready, a lit fuse would explode the gunpowder, blowing the face of the bluff into the air and elsewhere. Federal infantry would then charge in through the open pit, climb its far end and secure the fortress.

The work of the sappers and miners continued in front of Fort Desperate and at the Priest Cap. At Fort Desperate the sap had slowly inched to within 30 yards of the fort's ditch. The expert Arkansan sharpshooters in their sturdy earthen mound-tower controlled the sap's advance, making it extremely dangerous to be a sapper at that location. Colonel Ben Johnson, commanding in Desperate, made plans to take the sap and turn it to his use as a rifle pit when it got closer to his ditch.[24]

Dawn the next day brought a surprise raid down at Springfield Landing. Colonel John L. Logan led his Confederate cavalry troopers against the Federals' main supply depot for Port Hudson. Logan reported that his troopers burned the commissary and quartermaster's stores, destroyed 100 wagons, killed and wounded about 140 men, took 35 prisoners and paroled 22 of them. His men engaged a brigade of Yankees and held them in check until the destruction was done. He then retired with a loss of 4 killed and 10 wounded. Only the day before, a party of Logan's scouts captured Brigadier-General Neal Dow from a private residence in the rear of Port Hudson where he had been convalescing from his wound of May 27.

Federal reports differed greatly from Logan's. Lieutenant-Colonel Blanchard with the 162nd New York Infantry reported that his command and some Negro soldiers had engaged Logan at Springfield Landing. The brunt of the attack was against the Negroes who retreated, which allowed the Rebels to set fire to and destroy most of the commissary stores. His regiment then came up and engaged Logan's troopers driving in Logan's left flank, right flank and his center, thereby, repulsing his brigade. Logan lost three or four killed, a number wounded, and had two men taken prisoner. Blanchard lost two wounded, the Negroes lost three wounded and one killed. Somewhere between the two reports lies the truth, namely: the commissary stores were destroyed, both sides had a few casualties, Logan retired, the Yankees prevailed and still held the supply depot. The Negroes bore the brunt of the attack.

At the Priest Cap, a Rebel soldier accidently dropped a lit hand grenade into a full box of grenades. The explosion blew tons of dirt, wood and a lot of iron into the air, killing two grayclad soldiers and wounding one.

Also at the Priest Cap, the 24-pounder kept the Federals' trench cavalier from rising to its full height as planned. Yankee sharpshooters climbed to man the tower at great hazard to their lives. When the Yankee sharpshooters were unable to fire, the defenders rolled lit 10-inch fused shells across the short distance between their breastworks and into the sap as well as throwing hand grenades into the sap. Engineer Captain L. J. Girard supervised the digging of a deep tunnel from inside the Priest Cap directly out to and under the Yankee sap. Upon reaching the Yankees' sap, Girard's miners turned their tunnel at a right angle and ran it a short distance under where the Billy Yanks were digging. Shortly after midnight of July 3, the gallery was finished. The tunnel under the sap was filled with kegs of gunpowder, a powder train laid and blocked off at the right angle turn. The miners heard the tapping of Yankee picks through the earth. The Confederate officers at the Priest Cap decided to give the Yankees a special Fourth of July and set fire to the powder train at 9 A.M. on the Fourth.

The Federal sap across from the Priest Cap violently exploded. The ground heaved upward, and a black column of dirt rose high into the air as did shovels, picks and spades. Then all descended both outside the Confederate lines and inside. It took several minutes for the dirt clods to quit falling and the dust to settle. The Yankees had been caught unawares. The explosion killed two Yankees and severely wounded many others, mostly Negroes. The sap's breastworks were blown away and the ditch filled with rubbish. There could have been more killed, but just minutes before the blast the Yankee sappers had broken through into the counter-mine gallery and, seeing the powder kegs, they began running away.[25]

Elsewhere around the lines it was business as usual — only scattered shots and mostly random firing. Most of the Confederate diaries mention the artillery dueling at the left of the defenders lines on the river and scattered skirmishing (no less deadly) by riflemen elsewhere around the defenses. It was unusually quiet. The Confederates dined on pea bread, pickled mule, molasses and fried squirrel (rat). Seven Yanks and thirty-seven Rebs escaped or deserted from Port Hudson on July 3.

The Glorious Fourth of July! After the Confederate counter-mine explosion, only the usual sharpshooting, and a Federal blank cannon salute of one gun for each state including those in the Confederacy occurred. There were no assaults against the Confederate works. Common feeling among the defenders was that most of the western men in Banks' army had been killed or wounded (except for the Hoosiers). That left only the Eastern men to charge them. The Rebel defenders stated that the Eastern men never charged near enough to get hurt. Overall it was a quiet day except along the riverbank.

Captain Connelly's instructions to his gun crews was to fire a shotted salute, not to use blanks, at whatever they saw for a possible target across the river, which included Confederate soldiers hunkered down below the bluff to eat a meager meal. A 30-pound Parrott shell hurled across the river to land in a cooking fire, scattered ashes and a pot all around the little ledge below the bluff top. The severely startled and shocked soldiers soundly cursed the damned Yankees for spoiling their meal as they ran for cover. Across the Mississippi, Hoosiers laughed. The next morning, Federal artillery fire intensified, and it was answered by an 8-inch Seacoast Howitzer and 10-inch Columbiad guns in the river batteries.[26]

A section of Nims' battery commanded by Lieutenant Hall had moved its guns into position behind a cut in the levee on the west side of the river. Banks ordered the battery across, guided by a Zouave who had escaped from the Port Hudson prison. The Zouave knew the location of the current corn mill, housed in the Port Hudson & Clinton Railroad station. The battery's assignment was to take out the mill and add to the food shortages inside the defenses. After positioning their two guns behind the levee, they cut away part of the levee using the dirt to elevate the position behind it. The Zouave pointed out the storage buildings and railroad station to the gunners; then he climbed atop the levee to call out the effect of the guns firing. Hall's gunners aimed and fired their guns. The Zouave reclined on his side holding the upper part of his body more or less upright to watch the fire which fully exposed his head and shoulders.

After two or three good line shots, Lieutenant Hall, peering through his field glasses as he ordered the elevation reduced so the next percussion shells went into the railroad station,

Thirty-two pounder gun rifled to 6.4 inches. Located in River Battery #10. Gun disabled by 1st Indiana Heavy Artillery, Company H, from across the Mississippi River. (Courtesy Lawrence Lee Hewitt.)

noticed a puff of smoke from one of the river batteries. A 42-pounder solid shot plowed a furrow across the levee, cutting the poor Zoo-Zoo in half. After burying the pieces of the Zouave, Hall took the section of Nims' battery away by the same route as they had come. They arrived back at Port Hudson in time to join the victory procession into Port Hudson.

Farther downstream, one of the Rebels' river guns got a shell into one of Lieutenant Bradley's embrasures and blasted off the left wheel and broke the axle of a gun. His guns had not been able to reach any buildings with shell to set them afire. He withdrew both guns, while repairing the one. He sent word to Richard Arnold that incendiary shells (fire balls) did not work well in either his guns, or in Company H's guns. The Confederate gunners manning the 8-inch and 10-inch Columbiads reported that they had silenced Bradley's guns.[27]

Things were quickly coming to an end at Port Hudson. On July 5 from across the river, the Hoosiers in Company H renewed their fire in the morning without much effect. They were unable to hit the machinery of the mill in the railroad station any better than either Bradley's gunners or Hall's gunners had. However, things changed later that day when the 32-pounder rifle reappeared at Battery #X.

Top: Eight-inch Sea-Coast howitzer, formerly mounted en barbette in River Battery #8; the right trunnion was shot off by 1st Indiana H. A., Company H. This gun is displayed at Port Hudson State Historical Area, Louisiana. *Bottom:* River Battery 24-pounder rifled gun mounted en barbette, located in River Battery #10. Disabled by 1st Indiana H. A., Company H, from across the river. Note the cascable knob is shot off. The damaged right trunnion is not visible in this image. (Courtesy Military Order of the Loyal Legion of the United States, housed at USAMHI, Carlisle Barracks, Pennsylvania.)

After working away at it, a 30-pounder shell disabled the gun. Upon receiving word of the permanent disabling of the rifled 32-pounder, General Banks' clapped his hands and exclaimed: "Bully!" Company H's bully boys greatly appreciated hearing about this very high compliment from the commanding general.

The next day, Company H's Hoosiers were at it again, this time bringing their guns to bear farther upstream on Battery #VIII housing an 8-inch Sea-Coast howitzer (shell-gun). (It was called a howitzer or a shell-gun, because it held a lighter powder charge in a chamber at the rear of the barrel, and it fired shells which were lighter than a solid iron ball.) After a couple of hours of being battered by thirty-pounder shot and shell making a couple of nicks in its muzzle and grazing its barrel, it was disabled by a one-two punch of 30-pounder muscle knocking off its right trunnion and tearing away the elevating screw under the rear of the piece. The tube dropped down into its carriage and would not be fired again. A name painted in white paint around its breech read: "Lt-Colonel DeGournay."

After the bully boys had a bite to eat, they went back to work in the afternoon and met with further success. They turned their attention back up-stream to Battery #IX, which held a rifled 24-pounder. That evening, they hit it a couple of times, disabling it by shooting off a trunnion, and also breaking off its cascable knob.

Seven guns remained in the Port Hudson river batteries. The guns dug into the bluff down from its top had brush piled in front of them to mask them from the Federals, while the upper guns engaged the Parrotts. Fortunately, for the defenders, the upper guns were the smoothbore long-ranged heavyweights, one 8-inch and two 10-inch Columbiads throwing 65 and 120 pound shot, respectively, at a range of nearly two miles. The three Port Hudson 42-pounders were out of range to reach the 30-pounder Parrotts and vice versa. The Parrotts had nearly the same range as the Columbiads, but their projectiles were lighter and would not carry the impact to take a ten-thousand pound cannon out of action at a two mile distance; however, their shell and shrapnel bursts could play havoc with the gun crews. To return the Hoosiers' compliments, Rebel gunners burst their last shells over the Hoosiers, who took the big incoming rounds in stride. Whenever they saw a 10-inch ball or shell coming at them, they would drop to the ground and call out, "How are you, 10-inch?" as it swooshed overhead (hopefully) without exploding. (Because solid shot were plentiful in relation to the Confederates' supply of shells, chances were pretty good that the round would not explode.)[28]

While the boys in Company H had their sport with the river batteries, the Federal sappers continued working on two trench cavaliers in front of the Priest Cap. The engineers and sappers had been unable to make headway with constructing a trench cavalier of a large earthen mound like the one the 15th Arkansas used against their sapping efforts. A clever cavalry officer, Colonel Edward Prince, 7th Illinois Cavalry, said he had seen several empty hogsheads in a sugar house. (A hogshead is a large wooden cask or barrel capable of holding between 63 gallons up to 140 gallons being between five feet to eight feet high.) During the night of July 4, his troopers brought up the empty hogsheads by carrying them on a pole stretched between two riders. The sappers rolled in the casks, placed them into position atop the low mound and then filled them with dirt. A second tier was added in a like manner, and topped with sand bags to shelter one or two sharpshooters. By morning the left trench cavalier was finished and manned, and the right one was half finished.

In the light of morning the defenders saw the trench cavalier rising several feet above them. Lieutenant Bledsoe with the 1st Tennessee Artillery Battalion ordered his gunner to open fire upon the trench cavalier; his 24-pounder smooth-bore gun with 5.82-inch round balls fired repeatedly, knocking the barrels apart and gouging large holes through the dirt filling. Cox's Company K in its new position only 500 yards away opened on the 24-pounder with two guns firing 4.62-inch Schenkl shells and silenced it. This took place on July 5. The

Baby, in its new sunken redoubt, opened fire at the trench cavalier; however, its embrasure was not positioned to allow the gun to fire without the muzzle blast knocking away some of the embrasure's side and caving it in. After three shots, the gun could not be moved enough to bring it to bear on the trench cavalier. Because of Yankee sharpshooters, repair work could not be made until after dark.

Mack's battery, near the Priest Cap area of the lines, received orders on July 5 to either redirect or hold their fire because their 20-pounder Parrott shot and shells sabots stripped during the projectile's flight and landed among the Yankee soldiers holding forward positions. The flying sabots (iron or brass rings attached to the Parrott projectiles to impart their spin) breaking off the projectiles hit the soldiers on their heads or backs doing the same damage as if they were exploding Confederate shell or shrapnel rounds. (Based upon current archaeological evidence, Mack's battery had a small supply of Schenkl shells that used paper-maché sabots, which would not hurt men in front of them. Probably, they were brought up after the complaints.)

Under cover of darkness, to counter the sap that ran from Cox's old position down into a ravine and then cut into its side to meet up with the original sap running northwest from near Duryea's battery, the Rebels moved the 24-pounder rifle commanded by Lieutenant John Sanford from Commissary Hill to the rear of Fort Desperate to defend against this coming threat.[29]

On July 7 at the Priest Cap, the Yankee miners' finished digging their mine, having extended their galleries to just under the defenders outer trench at its salient point, and began filling it with gunpowder. Having had several inches of rain fall over the past few days, the bottom of this mine's gallery and sap were wet and had puddles of standing water, as was the sap on Dwight's front. Banks had requested materials from the navy to make 1-inch tubes to fill with gunpowder with which to pack the mine or lay as a powder train. Banks also requested the navy to furnish fresh dry fuses. While workers filled the tubes and brought up powder filled kegs, others very carefully began bringing in the explosives until it was packed with 1,200 pounds of black powder and back-filled with sandbags. It was to explode on the morning of July 9 so that his Forlorn Hope could rush in, hold the opening and seize Port Hudson.

Banks' volunteer Forlorn Hope of 67 officers and 826 men was commanded by Colonel Henry W. Birge of the 13th Connecticut. Many more had volunteered, but Banks turned away 91 non-commissioned officers and men from the 1st and 3rd Louisiana Native Guards who wanted a chance to fight, not dig. The white men accepted had a special camp in a grove to the rear of the naval battery (position #10). The Forlorn Hope's job would be to charge and take the works at the Priest Cap after the mine exploded, or to die trying. Therefore, they received a little special treatment like favored Roman gladiators. To keep their spirits up, their mess had good food and drink, and the soldiers did not have to rotate on and off the firing line. They carried the best firearms and fighting gear available and they had clean clothes. They rested and wrote what may be their final letters home; they made arrangements with comrades on who to contact with news of their death and to whom to give prized personal items and any money they may have with them.

On the Yankees' left wing, the mine's gallery extended several yards under the Citadel's parapet, but due to the damage inflicted on the parapet by the Cotton Bale Battery, a lengthened gallery was dug under the damaged parapet far enough to reach the second line of inner defenses. The sappers and miners had the mine packed with 1,500 pounds of powder by the 7th, back-filled with sand-bags and a powder train laid.[30]

However, things were about to change. On July 7, the ironclad *General Price* brought word downriver to Commodore Palmer, on board the *Hartford*, lying just above Port Hudson, that Lieutenant-General John C. Pemberton had surrendered Vicksburg to Major-General Ulysses S. Grant on July 4 in hopes of receiving more favorable surrender terms. The news reached Banks' headquarters about eleven o'clock that morning. Banks immediately had his adjutant-general, Richard B. Irwin, telegraph the news around the lines to the various commanders. The message to General Dwight from Irwin read: "Vicksburg fell. Closson's Battery on the left and 30-Pounders on the right (in Battery Bailey) are to fire a 100-gun blank salute."

Meanwhile the feud at the Priest Cap between Bledsoe's gun and Cox's guns continued. The trench cavaliers were both completed and repaired that morning, and Bledsoe was trying his best to tear them apart again. Evidently, he was coming too close to accomplishing his task, because 20-pounder Parrott rifles from either Duryea's 5th US Battery or from Mack's 18th New York Battery joined in the action. It was only a matter of time before the 20-pounders found the range and zeroed in on the target. A 3.67-inch percussion-fused Parrott shell struck the muzzle and blew up. The explosion sent pieces of the shell flying around causing damage to the gun and tearing off Lieutenant Bledsoe's head, spraying the cannon barrel with gore. Additional shell blasts followed and damaged the right wheel, stripped off its iron tire and cut down the right cheek, thereby causing the barrel to tip sideways, fall to the axle and again disable the gun. It could not be repaired. Bledsoe had the dubious honor of being the last officer killed among the defenders. He was the last of four of this gun's commanders killed in the line of duty during the siege. The dead commanders in order of death were Captain F. I. Weller and Lieutenants T. B. Cooke, John Penix and W. Bledsoe all of the 1st Tennessee Battalion.

As the news of Vicksburg's fall speedily traveled around the lines, the defenders of Port Hudson wondered what all the cheers, yells and bands playing the "Star-Spangled Banner" were about. A Yankee officer tossed a dirt clod with the message of the surrender of Vicksburg wrapped about it into the defenders' lines near the Priest Cap. Again, the word quickly spread but without joy. Among many there was utter disbelief. The Arkansas officer who first received the written message yelled back: "This is another damned Yankee lie!" Most firing around the lines died away even in violation of orders to keep it up. In spite of commands to the contrary, several of the men on both sides called over to the others and agreed to meet and relax in between the lines. Jibes, stories, coffee and corn beer were freely exchanged between many of the enlisted men.

Unknown to the Yankees, dispatches from General Joseph E. Johnson made their way into the works carried by Captain R. S. Pruyn, 43rd Louisiana Infantry, who had earlier escaped from Port Hudson, met with Johnson and had traveled back on the other side of the river, then swam and floated across the Mississippi River holding onto a wooden watering trough. He landed below one of the river batteries and came to Gardner's headquarters with the dispatches. Among them was one giving Gardner the sad news that he could expect no help from Johnson; instead, Gardner was ordered to cut his way out through the Yankees or flee across the river and join General Richard Taylor in the field against the Yankees.

During the 8th Gardner mulled over his choices. Late that afternoon as he and his staff smoked dried magnolia blossoms in their pipes and watched the river flow by in the rear of his headquarters, he sent for General Beal, Colonels Johnson, Miles, Shelby, Smith and Steadman to come to his headquarters. He laid out the facts before them as to Joseph Johnson's last order, the lack of aid, the lack of food, and increasing prevalence of disease (nearly 1,000 on the sick list) and the generally debilitated condition of the men. A decision was made.

That night around midnight, General Gardner sent an officer with a small escort under a white flag on a long pole with a lantern fastened to the pole above the flag to make it visible to all Yankees who saw the lantern and party of men. A bugle sounded "Cease Fire" as the little party approached the Plains Road sally port. The Confederate officer handed a sealed dispatch to Lieutenant Orton S. Clark of the 116th New York Infantry.[31]

Disabled 24-pounder smoothbore on land defenses. Lieutenant Bledsoe's blood smears are on the barrel by the damaged carriage cheek. (Courtesy Military Order of the Loyal Legion of the United States, housed at USAMHI, Carlisle Barracks, Pennsylvania.)

Gardner's dispatch requested confirmation from General Banks that Vicksburg had indeed fallen. If true, Gardner wanted a cessation of hostilities while considering terms. Banks replied and attached a copy of Grant's dispatch relating to the capitulation of Vicksburg. Banks also told Gardner that he could not agree to an unconditional truce for an unspecified time. Banks' adjutant general, Richard Irwin, and General Charles Stone and Lieutenant Clark first went to General Augur's quarters to give him the news and to get a bugler to accompany them as they made their way to the Plains Road sally port. A bugle blast brought back the party of Confederates who took Banks' dispatches to Gardner. Now the Federals sat and waited. Unofficial word to cease firing, but stay low, traveled north and south around the Federal picket lines.

Gardner met with several of his officers and further discussed the situation. Nearly half of their artillery pieces were out of action, and little or no defensive ammunition remained in the magazines for the remaining guns. They had nobly done their duty greatly above and beyond that which was required to defend Port Hudson with the relatively few resources in men and materials they had. Gardner made his decision. Just before dawn, Gardner's reply reached the waiting Yankees at the sally port.

Gardner stated his willingness to surrender and would send three officers to act as his commissioners to meet with a similar commission from Banks to agree upon and draw up the surrender documents. The meeting was to begin at nine o'clock in the morning outside of his breastworks. Gardner appointed Colonels J. G. W. Steedman, W. R. Miles and Lieutenant-Colonel Marshall J. Smith to act as his commissioners in drawing up the terms of surrender on his behalf. These officers arrived about nine o'clock at the Plains Road sally port and met with Brigadier-General Charles Stone, Brigadier-General William Dwight and Colonel Henry W. Birge on July 8 to discuss the terms of surrender. Moving to the shade of some nearby trees the men visited for a while, took liquid refreshment, studied the articles of surrender submitted by Banks, and after making only one change, they all affixed their signatures to the document.[32]

The one change made was to change the time of the occupation of the works by the besiegers. Their pleasant conversation for nearly four hours caused the time to be changed from 5 o'clock that evening to 7 o'clock the next morning so all due preparations could be made for the surrender ceremony.

Word quickly passed around both Confederate and Federal lines that the surrender document was signed. Almost as if a signal had been given, most men from each army laid aside their enmity and met in a cordial manner. Howard Wright, a lieutenant in the 30th Louisiana and judge advocate of the district around Port Hudson, wrote after the siege that he was especially surprised at the chivalric consideration and studied politeness at the hands of the enemy, from General Banks down to the least private. Instead of being treated as captives, the Federals acted as if the prisoners were their honored guests. He stated that one of the best Federal generals (William Weitzel) told him and other officers visiting together: "Gentlemen, you are the victors—we claim no laurels here." Late that afternoon, a Federal surgeon entered the works with a supply of medicines and helped dose the patients who suffered from intermittent fever and chills with quinine. Two wagons loaded with commissary supplies came into the Confederate lines that evening.

The morning of the 9th was clear. The Confederate defenders had left their dugouts, rat holes, gopher holes, other shelters, etc., packed their meager belongings and moved to the long road from the village of Port Hudson that ran along the bluff top by the river. Those men not in the hospitals formed their ranks beginning at the intersection with the Plains Road near the railroad station and then stretched across an open prairie up the road towards the village. As General Gardner rode down the grayclad lines one last time, the cheers from the men resounded across the prairie from railroad station to the village of Port Hudson.[33]

About nine o'clock, blue-clad columns with flags flying came marching up the Plains Road. The leading columns surprised the assembled Confederates by marching past them and down the road to the riverboat landing. Their destination was Donaldsonville, Louisiana.

At the intersection of Plains Road and the river road, General Gardner and his staff awaited the arrival of the Federal officials and the conquering army columns to accept his surrender and perform the final ceremonies. Brigadier General Andrews and his staff rode at the head of the Federals all with flags flying. He was followed by an honor guard of the Forlorn Hope, the 75th New York, the 116th New York, 2nd Louisiana (white), 12th Maine, 13th Connecticut, 6th Michigan, 14th Maine, 4th Wisconsin and 8th New Hampshire. Duryea's battery and a detachment of sailors from the naval battery.

Gardner stepped forward with his drawn sword reversed in his hands and presented it to General Andrews. Gardner is reported to have said: "Having defended this position as thoroughly and as long as I deemed it necessary, I find myself compelled to surrender to you my sword and with it this post and its garrison." Andrews replied: "I return your sword as a proper compliment to the gallant commander of such gallant troops—conduct that would be heroic in another cause." Gardner, as he slammed his sword into its scabbard, rebuked Andrews saying: "This is neither the time nor the place to discuss the cause!"

The Confederates grounded their arms, then stood in line while the Federals marched from left to right and formed in line in front of and facing the grayclads. As bugles called, the garrison's Stars and Bars came down the post's flagpole and navy tars hoisted the Stars and Stripes up the flagpole. The "Star-Spangled Banner played and Duryea's battery fired a salute. The surrender was official! The brief ceremony and the longest siege of the Civil War were both officially over.

Depending upon who is relating the story, everyone had a position of honor in the Federal procession into Port Hudson. Banks' adjutant general, who was in charge of who had the honors and when and where, does not mention who was first in line. The 1st Indiana Heavy Artillery marched into Port Hudson about noon with its colors flying. According to Colonel Keith, the 1st Indiana was given a conspicuous position for the occasion — the last regiment to enter. As the largest and longest unit in the procession, the now correctly termed siege train occupied last place. Evidently Keith felt the best came last![34]

After the ceremonies and celebrations ended, details of Federals loaded wagons with the surrendered small arms to take to a safe area for discharging and storage. Several wagons loaded with supplies and food rolled into Port Hudson for the surrendered soldiers. The Yankees escorted them to a new camp area away from the roads and helped them set up tents and their commissaries. Food was issued, fires lit and all of the soldiers set about making themselves comfortable and filling their stomachs. There were 6,340 Confederate prisoners of war including nearly 1,000 sick or badly injured. An estimate of Confederate losses at Port Hudson was put at 176 officers and men killed and 447 officers and men wounded, including those that died in the hospitals, for a total of 623 casualties. While exact losses by each unit are generally unknown, a few units reported their losses. Captain George Abbay's Company K, 1st Mississippi Light Artillery, lost two guns, six men killed and ten wounded. The 1st Alabama Regiment, both infantry and artillerists, listed 48 killed, 70 wounded (1 mortally) and 16 dead from disease. Shelby's 39th Mississippi Infantry Regiment reported 11 killed and 12 wounded. The 9th Louisiana Battalion had 7 killed and 12 wounded. The 12th Louisiana Artillery Battalion had 9 killed and 17 wounded; the 1st Tennessee Artillery Battalion had 15 killed and 12 wounded.

Federal losses were shown as 45 officers and 663 men killed, 191 officers and 3,145 men wounded and 12 officers and 307 men captured or missing for 4,463 total casualties. The Hoosiers had 22 casualties.

The Feds and the Rebs fraternized like old acquaintances during the short time they were together. There was very little outright animosity shown. Within a couple of days the enlisted men among the Confederate prisoners began receiving their paroles and started for home. Within a week the able-bodied enlisted men had melted away from Port Hudson like butter under a hot sun. The officers were transported to New Orleans where they had comfortable quarters in the Customs House Prison at 21 Rampart Street. They remained there for several weeks before being transported north to Johnson's Island Prison in Ohio.

Not generally mentioned, a few women and children had remained in the village of Port Hudson sharing in the soldiers' privations. Several of the women served as nurses or did laundry for the men. A few of the women and children were family members of the defenders. Two or three old men who lived there did odd jobs repairing things and patching buildings for the defenders, but no mention was made of them taking up arms. One of the women and a child were injured when an unexploded percussion shell the little boy was playing with exploded, wounding both him and his mother.[35]

The Hoosiers had fought well. Perhaps the greatest compliment can be made by one's former opponent. Colonel Keith wrote: "In a well written history of the siege of Port Hudson, by a Confederate officer, he says: 'To the Indiana regiment of artillery, which had many batteries of Parrott guns, we attributed the most of our misfortunes. Some of our guns were dismounted over and over again, the wheels knocked to pieces and the carriages shattered into splinters. The enemy's artillery fire was very severe from the commencement, and many of their guns were fired with the accuracy of a rifle.' Again, he says: 'The Parrott shot, from the accuracy of the fire, appeared to be the most effective.'" Besides sharing in the regiment's laurels, Company H received its own compliment from the 30th Louisiana's Lieutenant Howard C. Wright. In writing about the disabling of Port Hudson's river defense guns by Company H, he concluded by stating: "This artillery practice was probably equal, if

Top: First Regiment Indiana Heavy Artillery national flag with battle honors inscribed thereon. (Battle Flags: Indiana War Memorials Commission.) *Bottom:* A portion of the Confederate light artillery captured at Port Hudson. (Courtesy Military Order of the Loyal Legion of the United States, housed at USAMHI, Carlisle Barracks, Pennsylvania.)

not superior, to anything which has ever been accomplished of the kind, the distance being from one thousand to fourteen hundred yards."

Details of Hoosiers performed guard duty, watching while prisoners waited for parole. Yet, they had plenty of time to wander around the premises and inspect the siege works. Many of the boys speculated in amazement and in doubt of their own eyes as to the poor quality of the Rebel fortifications and how the Rebels had held out so long; they ignored the fact they had been pounding them to pieces for the past seven weeks.

The Federals at Port Hudson, having a good supply of quinine, freely dosed those who complained of "chills" and liberally administered the curative to the hospitalized prisoners. Quinine and whiskey had a good effect upon the ill men. The few severely wounded Hoosiers received discharges and travel pay for the journey home. Captain Grimsley finally mentioned Charley Myers when he wrote his wife on July 11.

Overjoyed by the victory at Port Hudson, J Ferguson in the Jackass Regiment's Company A dashed off an untitled song. The words were sung to the tune of "Happy Land of Canaan." Only the first verse is reproduced here. The rest of the verses are much the same in sentiment.

> The rebels are enraged,
> To think we are engaged
> In trying to put down this cursed rebellion;
> We will show them that we can
> Turn out to a single man,
> To drive them to the happy land of Canaan.
> Oh! Oh! Oh! Confeds, don't you know
> A good time for us is a-coming?
> We will show you that we're right,
> That you rebels cannot fight,
> And drive you to the happy land of Canaan.[36]

Company A received orders to move to Baton Rouge. The balance of the regiment at Port Hudson received orders to haul all of the surrendered guns not mounted on the river and from the field-works and to put them in park near their own heavy artillery park. They also had to catalogue the guns, equipment and ammunition and describe the condition of the items so catalogued. On their own, they collected several samples of various types of Confederate artillery ammunition.

Now Banks had to retake Bayous LaFourche and Teche from Major-General Richard "Dick" Taylor's Confederates. Thibodaux, Vermillionville, New Iberia, Brashear City and the N.O.O.&G.W. Railroad had all received attention from Taylor's men. His army had retaken most of these places and threatened New Orleans as it advanced along the N.O.O.&G.W. R.R. from Brashear City. Generals Weitzel and Grover had gotten their divisions on the move just after the surrender. The Hoosiers' Company A now at Baton Rouge received orders on July 12 for them to report to General Grover at Donaldsonville.[37]

(See Appendices for a correct list of the Federal artillery battery positions at the end of the siege; most published maps list the positions in the wrong places. Also see Appendices for captured Confederate ordnance and munitions; for a listing of cannons taken to West Point, New York, as trophies; and for a listing of buildings surviving the siege.)

Fourteen
Teche, Texas, Teche

In early June 1863 most of Major-General Banks' 19th Corps was engaged in besieging Port Hudson. Confederate major-general Richard "Dick" Taylor, reinforced by General Sibley's Texas Brigade, gathered his army and set out to relieve Port Hudson. Taylor would take back the territory along Bayou Teche and Bayou LaFourche. Once he secured those places, he would turn his army eastward to capture New Orleans. If the Yankees abandoned Port Hudson to chase him, the Port Hudson garrison could escape northward to join General Joseph Johnson's army at Jackson, Mississippi. Banks was aware that his withdrawing more than ten thousand men from this area to reinforce his army at Port Hudson would give Taylor the opportunity to retake the Teche and LaFourche districts, but it was a risk he was willing to take. He relied on Brigadier-General William H. Emory commanding the defenses of New Orleans to deal with such a maneuver by Taylor.

Taylor moved down the Red River to Alexandria, where he picked up three small regiments of Texas cavalry (about 650 men), commanded by Colonel James P. Major. Taylor ordered Major's troopers to Morgan's Ferry on the Atchafalaya River. Taylor rode down to Bayou Teche and met with Major-General Alfred Mouton and Brigadier-General Thomas Green, giving them instructions to proceed with the utmost secrecy to gather sugar coolers, small boats, skiffs and flat-boats for the coming mission. Taylor returned north to Morgan's Ferry on the Atchafalaya, where he met up again with Colonel Major. Taylor and Major moved down Bayou Fordoche and Bayou Gross-Tete, working their way eastward to False River, where Taylor visited a friend's home to gather intelligence on the situation at Port Hudson, within easy hearing distance of the cannon fire at Port Hudson.

During a conversation at the friend's home, Taylor learned that fewer than 1,000 Federals occupied Brashear City and Berwick City, and only a small garrison in Fort Butler at Donaldsonville stood between him and Brashear City — a little more than 100 miles travel. Haste was necessary; therefore, Colonel Major's command moved rapidly down Bayou Grosse-Tete to Rosedale and at dark pushed on to Indian Village arriving at 2 A.M. on June 18. Major detached a regiment commanded by Colonel Joseph Phillips that rode on to Plaquemine, Louisiana, at the junction of Bayou Plaquemine and the Mississippi River. Phillips' regiment took 87 prisoners, burned three supply steamers, two small sailing vessels, 100 bales of cotton and captured a goodly amount of commissary stores. Reuniting his brigade and upon finding a place to cross Bayou Plaquemine, Major crossed the bayou late that afternoon and after a forced march arrived at daybreak the next day at the town of Bayou Goula.[1]

Colonel Major moved on towards Bayou LaFourche, and he made a feint against Fort Butler at Donaldsonville that panicked the garrison. Free from pursuit, he detached Lane's and a portion of Phillip's regiments, commanded by Colonel W. P. Lane, to move through swamp and fields by the most direct route to take Thibodaux, cut the telegraph wires and seize the railroad a few miles south of there at LaFourche Crossing. Major's main force moved down the winding roads alongside Bayou LaFourche. Colonel Major's forces encountered a small Federal force on June 20, at LaFourche Crossing on the N.O.O. & G.W.R.R. Major detached a 206-man unit under Colonel C. L. Pyron reinforced by three battalions from Terre Bonne Station to scout out the Federal position. Lieutenant J.A.A. West with Semmes' battery accompanied Pyron's men. Their scouting was delayed by a torrential rainstorm until nearly nightfall. Instead of a probe against the Federals, Pyron ordered a full-scale assault.[2]

The Federal forces were made up of small detachments and convalescents of five infantry units, one cavalry unit, and two artillery units, including 23 men and Lieutenant James Brown of Company F, Indiana Jackass Regiment. A short but fierce fight soon took place between the opposing forces. The Federals had the advantage of having part of their line sheltered behind a levee and two-foot high earthworks on the flanks. The Hoosiers from Company F manned a light gun in the action. The 25th New York manned two 12-pounder howitzers. It was not until 7 P.M. that the yelling Rebel troops charged the lines.

Due to the close range of the fighting, the artillerists expended their entire supply of canister and improvised by filling cloth bags with rifle balls to fire at the charging Rebel who ran directly into the blasts of canister to take the guns. Even though they suffered that body-shredding fire a few feet from the cannons' muzzles, several Rebels passed the guns to where they were met by a line of Billy Yanks with fixed bayonets. Throwing themselves at the bristling bayonets, the heroic Rebel infantry engaged defiant Federal defenders in hand to hand fighting around the guns.

As one of the defending artillerists attempted to push a cannonball down the tube of his cannon, he felt a Rebel bayonet at his throat. The Rebel ordered him to drop the ball. Instead, the gunner threw the ball into the face of his attacker, caving in his skull and killing him. Another Rebel had his hands around the neck of a gun captain, choking him, when a defender thrust and twisted his bayonet through the attacker's body. Artillerymen drew their revolvers and sabers and waded into the hand to hand fray. After an hour of combat, the Federals forced the attackers back. Eighteen dead Confederates lay in front of and under the cannons. The Hoosiers' Company F lost two men — Peter Sears killed and one man wounded. Total Federal losses were 8 killed and 16 wounded. Richard Taylor reported a total loss of 55 men killed and wounded.

Late that night, three hundred Federal reinforcements arrived from New Orleans. The battle was not rejoined. The Federals burned the bridge behind them as they hurried toward Bayou Beouf and Brashear City. In their haste they left the three cannons behind. Colonel Major's command sidestepped the Federals and moved his men on toward Brashear City, which was actually on Tiger Island.[3]

Across Berwick Bay, General Thomas Green began his feint against Brashear City, which was garrisoned by three hundred hospitalized convalescents, four companies of the 23rd Connecticut, two companies of the 176th New York, one company of the 42nd Massachusetts infantry, fifty-two men and Captain F. W. Noblet of Company F, one man of Company A, one man of Company B and forty-six unassigned recruits designated for Companies F and L of the Jackass Regiment. Lieutenant Jacob Sherfey from Company H commanded the raw recruits. The Confederates fired their cannon from Berwick, across the bay, to attract the attention of the garrison in the city. Unknown to the Federals, Major Sherod Hunter, C.S.A., had secretly crossed the Atchafalaya River the night before in forty-eight small boats, sugar coolers and skiffs. Aware of the approaching threat from Berwick, Captain Noblet suggested arming the 2,000 Negro contrabands camped around town. The Rhode Island post commander turned down Noblet's suggestion.

After crossing Grand Lake and the Atchafalaya River at night, Major Sherod landed his men on Tiger Island in a palmetto swamp. Finding a narrow trail through the palmettos, his command of picked troops marched to within 800 yards of the rear of Brashear City. They rested a short time and moved 400 yards closer where they formed into line of battle. At dawn of the 23rd his men stood ready to attack Brashear City from the rear. Being discovered in the backlight of dawn, Sherod immediately ordered a charge at the Federals who had the sun directly in their eyes.

From across the river General Green's artillery opened fire and a company or two of sharpshooters opened fire from Griffin's Island in the Atchafalaya River. The rapid artillery fire and the lowering of boats into the water from the Berwick side of the river to ferry Green's men across coincided with the rush of Hunter's men to the rear of the defenders.

The garrison at Brashear had been expecting an attack to be made, possibly from their rear, and they had moved a 24-pounder gun mounted on a siege carriage to the railroad water tank at the rear of the city to where it could bear on the railroad bridge crossing from the mainland to the island. On hearing the roar of the cannon from across the river, the men moved the 24-pounder from the water tank to a new position to bear upon the Rebel guns at Berwick. Ten other heavy guns in a waterfront star fort were manned in the belief that the attack would be made from across the bay, and the infantry positioned themselves to repel it. Around 6:30 that morning, they heard rebel yells from their rear.

The garrison at Fort Buchanan could do little but watch the events unfold around them because the fortifications in the shape of a redan with pan-coupé faced northeast to defend against an attack from the water. The cannons all faced the water. The rear of the fort facing the land-side of Tiger Island was little more than a low wooden stockade and piles of trash. The men were never called to arms. Even though the Hoosier artillerists later proclaimed they could have held the fort, it was highly unlikely they would have lasted longer than a few minutes.

Major Robert Anthony, 2nd Rhode Island Calvary, surrendered it to the Confederates. The enraged Captain Noblet quickly mounted his horse and rode toward Fort Buchannan to persuade Major Anthony to not surrender. His horse was shot from under him before he got there, and Noblet became a Confederate prisoner of war before he could contest the surrender. The Rhode Island major came under sharp criticism by the Hoosiers for his hasty surrender to the Confederate forces. (The 2nd Rhode Island Cavalry was not known for its good behavior, nor its military conduct. Two months after their shameful conduct at Brashear this regiment would be court-martialed for open mutiny. Two enlisted men would be shot and the officers mustered out of service.)[4]

A Hoosier private, Thomas Burt, of Company B, claimed that the 42nd Massachusetts had hidden their arms and surrendered to Major Hunter's troops when they first appeared. The Rebel troops told their Hoosier prisoners that they first found the weapons and then the men of the 42nd Massachusetts. Major Hunter's surprise was complete. He had come between the town and a small fort to its rear, causing the men in the fort to only fire one shell at them before being surrounded. The stubborn Indianans refused the initial request to haul down their flag, but eventually conceded. Brashear City fell at 7:30 the morning of June 23. The Confederates captured a large quantity of goods, including eleven heavy guns ranging in caliber from 24- to 32-pounders, several 30-pounder Parrott guns, 5,000 rifles, 2,000 Negroes, 300 wagons, quartermasters' stores valued at over $2,000,000 and all of the Indiana Jackass Regiment's clothing and personal items stored in a warehouse at Brashear City.

After the fall of Brashear, General Thomas Green pushed onward to Bayou Beouf with 435 officers and men and four pieces of heavy and light artillery. At Bayou Beouf he encountered a Federal force of 275 men and officers. Among the Federals was Lieutenant Jacob Sherfey, Company H, with 10 men from Company H and 30 recruits manning two pieces of light artillery. The Hoosiers were successful in repelling their attackers on the 23rd, but on the 24th, they found themselves trapped between the Rebels under Colonel Major who had come down the LaFourche and General Green who had advanced from Brashear. Sherfey and his men being outnumbered by at least 20 to 1 wisely surrendered with the rest of battalion. All of the men captured here and at Brashear City received paroles as prisoners on the 27th of June and allowed to leave for New Orleans. The commissioned officers boarded wagons for transportation to prison in Camp Ford at Tyler, Texas.[5]

Southerner newspapers cried out at the atrocities of the Yankees toward the 2,000 contrabands in their camp outside of Brashear City who "were dying in squalid filth, or living in abject misery." It was also alleged that the Yankees had poisoned the ill, aged and infants. The Northern press carried stories that directly contradicted the Southern ones. For example: "Those who remained were slaughtered by the Texas cavalry in the most shocking manner. The cry of the sucking babe, the prayer of the aged and the shrieks of the mother had no effect."

A more truthful account is found written by a captain of the 18th Louisiana Infantry (Confederate) who traveled down the road from New Iberia to Brashear City and Tigerville a few days after the action at Brashear City. He described seeing a group of about 50 Negroes covered by maggots, some of them still alive, lying in a group by the roadside a few miles east of Brashear City at Bayou Ramos. The roads from Franklin to Tigerville (present day Gibson) were lined with nearly a thousand half-starved, nearly naked, sick Negroes, no longer fed, sheltered and cared for by the Yankees and wondering if their old masters would come to take them back. Their former masters saved an unknown number of the slaves.[6]

Dick Taylor's forces moved to within 20 miles of New Orleans driving the Yankees before them, but by now Port Hudson had fallen. Thousands of Federal troops hastened to the aid of their beleaguered comrades. Generals Weitzel and Grover moved down the Mississippi River to engage the Rebel forces. Meanwhile, the reinforced garrison at Donaldsonville, consisting of the 28th Maine, the 7th Vermont (brought from Pensacola, Florida) and some of the United States Colored Troops (U.S.C.T.), formerly the Corps de Afrique, had repelled an attack by General Thomas Green on June 28.

The encounter at Fort Butler began in the afternoon of the 27th with a flag of truce from General Thomas Green to the commander of Fort Butler (still under construction) at the intersection of Bayou LaFourche and the Mississippi River, allowing the women and children to be removed three miles from Donaldsonville. This being accomplished, at 1:30 in the morning of the 28th Colonel Joseph Phillips led his men forward. Not really being aware of the contour and shape of the ground in front of him, Phillips men blundered into the ditch going around the fort. This big mistake was discovered when musket balls began raining down from the top of the wall above them. Phillips climbed the wall, urging his men upward; upon reaching the top, his dead body slid down into the ditch. Three river gunboats, anchored just offshore, heard the firing and opened on the ground around the fort with grapeshot and shells. The combat was so close between the attackers in the ditch and the defenders that bricks were thrown back and forth between the combatants. The Confederate force lost 120 men and officers (mostly in the ditch), while the Federals lost five or six killed and a few wounded.

The Rebels withdrew due to their uneven losses from a relatively few men and the cannonade from the gunboats. The Federals continued to hold Fort Butler at the confluence of Bayou LaFourche and the Mississippi River. The forces of Weitzel and Grover landed here and began their march down both sides of the bayou. Two companies, A and E, of the Indiana Jackass Regiment accompanied General Weitzel.[7]

Weitzel's forces encountered General Green's forces at Koch's Plantation on the right bank of the LaFourche and were repulsed by General Green's Texans. After conferring with General Banks, it was agreed between he and Weitzel that no further attempt would be made to wrest control of the LaFourche from the Confederacy until gunboats could enter Berwick Bay. The gunboats *Estrella* and *Clifton* entered it on July 22, and General Taylor began withdrawing his troops from the area. Taylor's retreating men burned the railroad bridges behind them, and then they ran the steam engines into the bay at Brashear. General Weitzel's troops arrived on July 25, but Dick Taylor's army escaped.

On July 29, Capt. Edward McLaflin's Battery G, now at Donaldsonville and the Indiana detachment at New Orleans were ordered to Port Hudson to rejoin their regiment. The 6th Michigan Infantry was reorganized into heavy artillery and was assigned to be trained by the Indiana Jackass Regiment at Port Hudson. The 26th Indiana Infantry traveling down the river stopped at Port Hudson and visited their fellow Hoosiers. This was the first Indiana regiment that the boys of the Jackass Regiment had seen since leaving Fort Monroe in March of 1862, and they eagerly sought and received first-hand news from home.

Capt. Grimsley wrote his wife to come visit him now that the Mississippi was open to traffic. He noted that there was no fit house in Port Hudson for her to stay, but he was homesick, writing: "As we are not very large, we might make my little camp cot answer for sleeping purposes. But come on down and see me. The food is not too great, my man of color, Joshua Giddings, is a clean cook, to say the least, and he may surprise you with his ingenuity."[8]

Major Hays, who had missed the siege of Port Hudson by being in Indiana on recruiting duty, rejoined the regiment with the news of successfully recruiting an entire company, which would be joining them soon. Captain Isaac Hendricks commanded this new company and was at Indianapolis with the recruits.

The new company traveled by train and river steamer to Louisiana to join the Nineteenth Corps in August 1863. Arriving at Port Hudson, it received orders to move on to Baton Rouge because the regiment had moved there on June 3. The regiment moved into a different camp located a little more than two miles southeast of town, once again named Magnolia Grove. The regiment parked its artillery in a large semicircle, muzzles outward, and pitched their tents inside of the guns.

They found the city of Baton Rouge had changed since they had left it nearly a year before. There was more business being transacted in the town, and the stores carried more items than before — both in quantity and type. However, many families had not returned to live in the former battleground.

Once in a garrison mode, more restrictive orders took effect governing the rambunctious Hoosiers and their officers. Effective August 9, first sergeants of each company would report the names of all men absent for roll call to the regimental headquarters. No non-comm or private could leave camp on any mount. No commissioned officer could leave camp without written permission from the commanding officer. No non-comm or private could leave camp without a pass signed by the company commander *and* the regimental commander. All company commanders would turn over to the regimental quartermaster all horses and mules in excess of those allowed by military regulations. This meant no more joy rides by the officers and men. On August 10, Corporal James Jerome (Company H), who had distinguished himself with his gunning abilities at Port Hudson, was reduced to private at his request. John Yelton received a promotion to corporal to replace Jerome as of that day.[9]

On August 25, orders were received for a battalion of three companies from the regiment to report to New Orleans for duty with General Godfrey Weitzel. By August 30, Companies A, G, and H had reported to New Orleans under command of Major William Roy. Also at this time, the Hoosiers' Colonel John Keith was placed in command of the entire post of Baton Rouge and Captain James Grimsley of Company B had command of the regiment's companies present there. The regiment moved into Fort Williams, the old U.S. Barracks, the Arsenal grounds and its buildings.

General Banks ordered a combined operation to invade Texas by sea and land led by Major-General William B. Franklin. Franklin's orders included an admonition to disembark his troops only *"if you find that the Navy has succeeded in making the landing feasible."* Seven thousand infantry from Maine and New York plus the Hoosiers' Companies A, and H, mounting four 20-pounder and four 30-pounder Parrott rifles, respectively, participated in the seaborne invasion aboard river steamers. Company A traveled aboard the steamer *St. Charles* and Company H traveled aboard the steamer, *I.C. Landis*. They departed on September 4.[10]

After a series of misadventures involving missing rendezvous points and missing Sabine Pass at night because of no blockading vessel present to show a signal light, the thirty-odd vessel fleet steamed back and located Sabine Pass late on the night of the 7th. Hoisting all the lights they could aboard their rocking vessels, the gathering Federals made a festive show to the entertainment of the Davis Guards manning the guns in Fort Griffin. The leading transports had trouble getting over a large sandbar at the entrance to the pass, and only seven transports with a total of 700 infantry, a battery of field artillery and eight heavy guns, including Companies A and H of the Jackass Regiment, made it inside the bar by the next morning. Some transports did not cross the bar until 3 P.M.

The first seven transports and the gunboats *Arizona*, *Clifton*, *Sachem*, and *Granite City* anchored in the river. The largest of the four gunboats, the *Clifton* anchored near the lighthouse after firing a few shells at it to chase away any would-be defenders. The *Clifton* then turned its long-range guns on Fort Griffin and fired at it until 7:30 A.M. Twenty-six shells passed over the fort landing in its rear and disturbed a group of men cooking breakfast. No fire was returned at the *Clifton*, and it then returned and anchored near the bar with the transports inside the pass. The armament of the gunboats was as follows: *Arizona*: four light 32-pounders, one 30-pounder Parrott rifle and one 12-pounder Rifle; *Clifton*: two 9-inch Dahlgren guns, four heavy 32-pounder guns, one 30-pounder Parrott navy rifle and one 20-pounder. Parrott army rifle; *Granite City*: six 24-pounder howitzers and one 12-pounder pivot-mounted rifle, *Sachem*: one 20-pounder Parrott rifle and four heavy 32-pounders. These shallow draft gunboats could throw a broadside of sixteen rounds against the fort's six rounds.[11]

The next day, the gunboats split into two groups and cautiously felt their way forward up the two channels of the pass. A large bar of oyster shells covered by only eighteen inches of water split the pass into two channels about five feet deep and two to three hundred feet wide. Pilings driven into the water at openings large enough to admit a ship closed the few alternate routes up the pass. The gunboats opened fire on the little stair-step-shaped fort on the west side of the pass and the battle was joined. The fort mounted six heavy guns (from nearest to the water to the landward side, there were two 32-pounder iron and two 24-pounder iron siege or naval guns and two 32-pounder brass howitzers. (Some accounts say the howitzers were 24-pounders.)

The Davis Guards, consisting of roughly forty hard-drinking, hard-fighting Irishmen from the docks and wharves of Houston, commanded by Lieutenant Dick Dowling manned the fort's guns. About 200 Texas infantrymen waited in the bushes and marsh grass near the fort for any Federal infantry to advance up the muddy road along the water's edge from the salt marshes only eight hundred yards south of Fort Griffin and in the rear of abandoned Fort Sabine. General Weitzel had orders to land about 500 men and light artillery at the road's end in the rear of the old fort (Fort Sabine) where a sandy beach provided a good landing place for rowboats loaded to the gunwales with infantry from the transport *General Banks*.

In the morning the Yankee gunboats advanced. The gunboats *Clifton* and *Granite City* advanced up the Texas channel and the *Arizona* and *Sachem* advanced up the Louisiana channel. The *Sachem* opened fire from directly opposite the fort, and the Davis Guards returned

The Battle of Sabine Pass as drawn by Private James Ferguson, Company A, 1st Indiana Heavy Artillery. The vessels from left to right are: gunboats *Granite City* and *Clifton*, transport *General Banks*, gunboats *Sachem* and *Arizona*. Fort Griffin is located under the cloud of gun-smoke above the *Clifton*.

the *Sachem*'s cannon fire with great intensity. The infantry aboard the gunboats opened fire at the forts. However, the cannon fire from the fort drove the infantry into the gunboats and forced the gunboats to close their gunports unless firing. The accurate cannon fire hit the *Sachem* amidships and blew up her steam equipment, taking her out of action. The *Arizona* went partially aground and worked to back into the channel. The *Granite City*, in the Texas channel and aground, turned her broadside to the fort. As she worked to get free, she fired on the fort with her broadside. Fort Griffin returned her fire and after about twenty minutes of intense punishment, with no more help than a few long-range shots from the *Arizona*, now retreating down the Louisiana channel, she surrendered.[12]

Some reports stated that barkeeper Dick Dowling with forty drunken Irishmen held the fort and drove off the entire Federal fleet. Regardless of the men's sobriety or lack thereof, they stopped the Yankees' invasion attempt of that part of Texas cold in its tracks.

The *Arizona* ran aground again on the way out of Sabine Pass and held up the fleet's retreat while her crew worked to get her off the mud and sand. The transports had been unable to get close enough to shore to land their troops in the salt marshes on either side of the pass, and at least one steamer ran hard aground trying to do so. After throwing 200 mules and 200,000 rations overboard, the steamer was once again afloat. All the vessels then withdrew to the open sea where they were joined by the two surviving gunboats. One of the officers in the 14th Maine Infantry observed that his men got as close to the fort in Sabine Pass as Moses got to the Holy Land. "We could see it, but was [sic] not permitted to enter."[13]

Mother Nature made the trip back to New Orleans as bad for the soldiers and sailors as the abortive attempt against Fort Griffin. Heavy seas and gale-force winds forced the fleet to anchor behind some shoals for twelve hours. The steamer *Laurel Hill* lost her smokestacks, another lost a paddlewheel and several other vessels (including the Hoosiers' *Landis*) had their sides bashed inward by the waves. Drinking water rations ran short, and the men relied on condensed steam just as on their trip to Ship Island. On the 12th of September, the battered and fatigued fleet and men arrived back at New Orleans. The soldiers feelings about their bluewater adventure were summed up in Rufus Dooley's letter to his mother: "If I were ever to be upon the blue water again, I hope it would not be on such a frail worthless craft as it was the last time. I love to ride on the sea with the right kind of a vessel under me, but in such vessels as the old *Landis*, I would rather be excused."[14]

Meanwhile, at Baton Rouge some of the officers' wives had come down the newly opened Mississippi River to visit their husbands. The wives liked the town of Baton Rouge, but disliked paying $18.00 per week room and board. Fearing the expense if his wife were to come to Baton Rouge to visit, Lieutenant George Harding admonished his wife to "bring your grub along as that amount, with what I pay for my own board, is a little more than I can stand." He and a few other officers looked forward to the time they could honorably muster out, because they thought they would not be in combat again, and they did not care for garrison duty. Captain Grimsley, miffed at being passed over for a promotion to major, thought about applying for a colonelcy of a colored regiment.

On September 22, the regiment again received orders to move to New Orleans. Grimsley's wife and the few other wives who had come down to visit at Port Hudson and Baton Rouge traveled to the big city with their husbands and stayed with them for a few weeks. The reason for the move to New Orleans was to be nearer fast transportation to western Louisiana to reinforce the infantry divisions, light batteries and cavalry moving across land toward Texas. The Hoosiers' Companies A, G, and H were already on the move with General Franklin's army up the Teche.[15]

The batteries of the Indiana Jackass Regiment, most of the XIX Corps and the entire XIII Corps composed the invading army. The quartermaster issued the bully boys new clothing and accoutrements on September 19 before they left New Orleans. The boys of Company H even received six new canteens full of whiskey from their quartermaster among their new accoutrements for the trip. The XIX Corps artillery for the second Teche Expedition consisted of Companies A, F and L of the First U.S. Artillery, three companies of the Jackass Regiment, Second, Fourth and Sixth Massachusetts Batteries, First Maine Battery, Eighteenth New York Battery and First Vermont Battery. Total guns were twenty-two Napoleon Guns, four 3-inch rifles, six 6-pounder rifles, two 10-pounder Parrotts, eight 20-pounder Parrotts and four 30-pounder Parrotts.

Their journey took them by rail to Brashear City, by boat across the bay to Berwick, and by foot, mule, caisson and limber to encamp on October 1, at Bisland, Louisiana. From there they moved on through New Iberia, and they arrived on the banks of Vermillion Bayou on the 8th.

Their 20-pounder and 30-pounder Parrotts, acting in conjunction with the light artillery batteries, assisted the infantry in a brief skirmish with the Confederate forces along the banks of Vermillion Bayou. The Confederates retreated, and the bayou was crossed. The army moved on through Vermillionville [present day Lafayette] and camped just north of it. The next day the army moved northward to Carrion Crow Bayou, eight miles south of Opelousas. The bully boys were again called into action to flush out Rebel guns thought to be hidden across the bayou. After the artillery fired one round each from their 20 and 30-pounders without any response, the XIX Corps crossed Carrion Crow Bayou and went into camp, on its north bank the 11th of October. The heavy artillerists fortunately went into camp a few miles in the rear of the corps nearer to Vermillionville.

The main army remained on Carrion Crow Bayou for several days, sending out skirmishing parties and being harassed by Rebel cavalry. Finally, at dawn on October 15, the Federals encountered General Thomas Green's 4th, 5th and 7th Texas Cavalry Regiments at Chretien Point plantation on Bayou Bourbeux. The XIX Corps promptly turned out with General Weitzel's division in front, and General Grover's division following. The battle lines were almost a mile in length as the troops moved across Buzzards' Prairie from Camp Carrion Crow towards Bayou Bourbeux. However, instead of a fierce charge, the Federals advanced slowly, and coming under heavy artillery fire from Semmes' and the Valverde batteries and Confederate infantry fire, their advance stalled. Suddenly, Texas cavalry burst from a gully parallel to Weitzel's lines and charged into the Yankees firing shotguns and slashing their way through them. The Federals panicked and ran. As another Confederate charge rolled forward, the Yankees managed to re-form and meet the attack supported by their own artillery fire. The Confederates withdrew. This back and forth dance went on until about 10 A.M., when a division of the Federal XIII Corps arrived.[16]

The Vicksburg veteran westerners of the XIII Corps entered the battle with vigor. They were eager to show the Nutmegs of the XIX Corps what western men could do, and do it they did. Supported by the combined batteries (both light and heavy) of three divisions, their charge caused the Texans to retreat. The Johnnies' withdrawal took them across Bayou Bourbeux and two miles up the other side, but not before they ambushed and stopped the westerners' advance at a coulee just across the bayou, ending the Battle of Buzzard's Prairie.

The Chretien mansion was spared total destruction even though the battle had raged around the house for several hours. The owner made Masonic distress signs to the Federals and a Masonic officer ordered the home spared. The lower floor and outbuildings were used by the Federal army for officers' quarters and hospital wards. Rows of tents sprang up on the grounds as the soldiers made camp. The Indianians were very happy to see the westerners of the XIII Corps join their army. Company H's Corporal Cyrus Hunt wrote: "Western men, and especially Hoosiers, are as abundant here as ever nine months' men were; and we feel much relieved to know that we have fighting men with us—men who came out to fight for their country, instead of playing off for money, and who carry hardtack and bullets, instead of blankets and ginger bread."[17]

Besides enjoying the company of comrades from Old Hoosier, the men of Companies A, G, and H received 124 pairs of new cavalry boots on October 16. They had a good diet of foraged fresh beef, sweet potatoes, and pumpkins. During searches for forage for their mules and officers' horses, foraging parties gave out receipts for corn taken during the last 17 days of October as follows:

"3,584 pounds of corn taken from a rebel plantation, Carrion Crow Bayou, to Martha Guidry of St. Landry Parish.

2,240 pounds of corn, Carrion Crow Bayou, deserted plantation, receipt given to Placide Guilbeau of Lafayette Parish.

1,762 pounds of corn from rebel plantation, St. Landry Parish.

1,300 pounds of corn from deserted plantation, St. Landry Parish.

3,000 pounds of corn from deserted plantation, St. Landry Parish.

3,500 pounds of corn from deserted plantation, St. Landry Parish, receipt made out to 'Sugar Sastrapes' [Ludger Lastrapes]."[18]

The Federals continued probing for a good route to Texas, but without boats the Sabine River thwarted their plans. Their supply lines ran from Berwick to Washington, Louisiana. Because of constant raids by fast moving Texas cavalry, they feared to stretch their supply lines any longer or thinner. The fast moving horsemen of General Thomas Green's and Colonel Major's cavalry posed a constant threat of a mad dash to seize Federal supplies from the caravan for their own use. General Banks already had earned the nickname of "Commissary Banks" in Virginia because he lost his entire supply train to Major-General Andrew Jackson's men. Also, Federal commanders were concerned about the lack of or super-abundance of water and limited forage for the men and animals should they turn west toward Texas. As winter approached, there would be too much water and the roads would be impassable mud flats.

General Banks decided to make another assault by sea on the lower Texas coast, and on October 26, he sent the second division of the XIII Corps to land at the mouth of the Rio Grande. General Franklin moved his XIX Corps from Opelousas, and Washburn moved his XIII Corps from Washington. Both were to occupy camps on Carrion Crow Bayou. The division remaining of the XIII Corps, commanded by General Washburn, was to camp on the north side of the bayou, and the XIX Corps, Generals Weitzel and Grover, plus the Indiana siege and Reserve artillery were to camp on the south side of the bayou.

Intermittent rains began the latter part of October, and the roads got so muddy that the heavy artillery's 30-pounders frequently sunk nearly to their axles in the soft muddy roads. Rufus Dooley wrote his mother that it appeared the road to Texas had proved a failure from some cause that privates could not understand. General Franklin was hesitant to send the heavy guns back to Brashear City because he felt they would be needed if he ever encountered a major Confederate army; therefore, he kept them with his command. The XIII Corps had not all withdrawn to Camp Carrion Crow, and General Burbridge's command was attacked at its temporary camp on Bayou Bourbeux, a few miles north of Carrion Crow Bayou near the town of Sunset, Louisiana, on November 3, 1863. This engagement was sudden and furious, and it resulted in a full-scale rout of Burbridge's command. When the battle was over, the Johnnies had captured a 10-pounder Parrott rifle, more than six hundred prisoners (including thirty-two officers), the entire 67th Indiana Regiment, plus a large number of small arms, ammunition and supplies.[19]

The XIX Corps moved to Vermillion Bayou, where they remained until November 15. Then they moved south to New Iberia where they camped until January 1864. They had nothing to do except entertain themselves and eat. Food was plentiful, the duty light, they had plenty to wear, and the weather was pleasant. Companies G and H received new jackets while at New Iberia. Foraging for their food was good as Rufus Dooley described: "We crossed the bayou the other night and suddenly came upon a large flock of sheep of about 50 and now they only number 20." They enjoyed their mutton and even tried cooking an alligator. Since shooting the beasts was a sport among the troops, it was in due course that they should try to eat an alligator.

While three companies of the Jackass Regiment were in the western part of the state, the rest of the regiment remained as garrison troops in Baton Rouge and New Orleans. It came as a surprise to the officers there to learn that the regiment was to have completed quarterly quartermaster reports on all the ordnance and stores. This had not been required by and followed up on by Colonel McMillan with his officers, because he had done it himself. As a result, no report had been rendered since the regiment was changed to heavy artillery. The reports for the second and third quarters of 1863 were incomplete and only two companies were mentioned. The commanding general stopped the pay of the officers until the reports were done, and they were completed before the end of the fourth quarter.[20]

What with Companies L and M being authorized in the spring of 1863, recruits for these companies had been reporting to New Orleans over the past few months for assignment to Company L with excess recruits going into other companies with vacancies. On November 9, the final recruits authorized to fill Company M, commanded by Captain Samuel E. Armstrong (formerly lieutenant of Company I), traveled by railroad and riverboat from Indianapolis to

Memphis. At Memphis they boarded the steamer *Emerald* and proceeded to Baton Rouge. As they steamed past Hog Landing just south of the Red River, Rebel artillery opened fire on them. The Rebel cannoneers fired twenty-one shots, and three shots hit the vessel. Lieutenant Henry McMillan, adjutant of the 1st Indiana, organized such men as had rifles and returned fire at the battery. None of the Hoosier men were injured. The steamer escaped without further damage, and on the 18th, it arrived at Baton Rouge. The recruits were sworn into Company M at Fort Williams, added to the muster rolls as soldiers and drew muskets for drill and garrison duty.

On December 17, both Companies L and M moved to New Orleans. On the 19th of December, Company L turned over its three 12-pounder brass guns, its two 20-pounder Parrott rifles, and its 46 mules to Company M. Company L received four 30-pounder Parrott rifles and other equipment it needed from Company B and boarded the *Clifton* bound for Matagorda, Texas, assigned to General Cadwallader Washburn's new command at Fort Esperanza, Texas.[21] At the close of 1863, the regiment was stationed as follows:

> Company A at New Iberia, Louisiana; Company B at New Orleans, Louisiana; Company C at Baton Rouge, Louisiana; Company D at Baton Rouge, Louisiana; Company E at Baton Rouge, Louisiana; Company F at Baton Rouge, Louisiana; Company G at New Iberia, Louisiana; Company H at New Iberia, Louisiana; Company I at New Orleans, Louisiana; Company K at New Orleans, Louisiana; Company L at Matagorda Island, Texas; Company M at New Orleans, Louisiana.[22]

Heretofore, this chapter has dealt with the activities of four companies: A, F, G and H. The majority of the regiment remained at Baton Rouge. After Roy left, Colonel John Keith, post commander, temporarily assumed command of the regiment as well as the post until he appointed Captain James Grimsley as regimental commander. It was the usual routine: clean weapons, groom, feed and water the animals, drill as infantry and drill with artillery on a daily basis. The horses and mules were kept in a line on the west side of Uncle Sam Street and on a line north of the hospital building; none were to be kept east of Uncle Sam Street or south of the line north of the hospital.

In October, work continued on strengthening Fort Williams' earthen walls and artillery platforms. Sergeant George James of Company I and Private Beck of Company F were detailed to take charge of the contrabands and superintend the work on the fortifications. Sanitary conditions around these earthworks and behind buildings within the confines of Fort Williams became a problem. Typhoid fever appeared among the men. Commanding officers of companies and non-commissioned officers in charge of detachments were ordered to inspect the company quarters once each day for cleanliness. These same officers were held responsible for the sanitary conditions of the quarters. Also, all persons found defecating, urinating or vomiting inside the walls of the fortifications or in the ditches or trenches outside them were required to clean up such nuisances themselves besides receiving other punishments as deemed necessary by the commandant of the fort. All those within the garrison had to use the sinks and privies, and if more were needed, they were to tell the officer of the day. This order applied to everyone in the fort, especially contrabands.

These orders reflected the presence of Brigadier-General Philip St. George Cooke, a spit-and-polish general officer, who on October 8 had assumed overall command of the Baton Rouge Military District. This military district consisted of Baton Rouge and all territory within a twenty-five mile radius thereof with the exceptions of Port Hudson and Donaldsonville. Within the military district were two sub-districts with headquarters in Baton Rouge and across the Mississippi River at Plaquemine, Louisiana.

In September Captain Grimsley was ordered to take his two 30-pounder Parrotts and one 30-pounder Parrott from Company I (this Parrot to be commanded by Sergeant Sibert of Company G), his men of Company B, all equipment complete and mules to New Orleans by the first available transportation.

In early October, Captain Richard Campbell, Company I, took a detachment from his company consisting of one sergeant, one corporal and sixteen men to Port Hudson to retrieve and transport back to the regimental headquarters at Baton Rouge four 8-inch mortars and four 10-inch mortars, which had been stored at Port Hudson since the siege ended. Also, Lieutenant John Adams of Company G at Baton Rouge was ordered to take command of all men from Companies A, G and H on detached duty, guard duty and convalescents fit for duty at Baton Rouge, accompany them and report them in to their company commanders in the field.

In late October orders were given to issue arms and accoutrements to all men and officers. Also, instructions were given on the proper situations when to salute or not to salute to both the men and officers. Officers were to always return a salute. Men were not to casually wave at an officer and call the officer by his first name; instead, they should give a proper salute and face the officer when doing so.

On November 2, Companies I and K were ordered to move their batteries to the defenses of New Orleans. December was a quiet month.[23]

Fifteen

Veteran Furlough — Red River Sideshow — Garrison Doldrums

The Jackass Regiment's boys at New Iberia had a merry Christmas; they got paid on the holiday. Everyone had ideas about doing something and spending their money, but there was not much to do. Therefore, they reminisced about Christmases past in Indiana, speculated on what the folks back home were doing this day, and wrote letters home to their family and female secret correspondents.

The Hoosiers along the Mississippi River had a better Christmas. The steamer *City Belle*, loaded with supplies from the people of Indiana for her troops along the Mississippi River, docked at Baton Rouge. The Jackass Regiment's boys there received forty barrels of potatoes, ten barrels of onions, twenty barrels of fresh apples, five barrels of dried apples, five barrels of corn meal, and ten barrels of turnips. The hospital was supplied with fruits, fresh cabbage, potatoes, onions, turnips, a case of bottled whisky, four boxes of clothing and two boxes of reading matter. The Indiana men at New Orleans, received 441 barrels of potatoes, 320 barrels of fresh apples, 118 barrels of dried apples, 121 barrels of onions, 148 barrels of turnips, 13 barrels of crackers, 112 boxes of canned fruit, 23 cases of bottled spirits and 160 boxes of clothing and reading material.[1]

The men at New Orleans celebrated Christmas far differently than at New Iberia. Major Grimsley described his Victorian Christmas as follows: "The day has passed with the usual rounds of high glee, good cheer, and merrymaking over sumptuous dinners, numerous punchbowls, and numerable potions from the stores of the god of Bacchus.... It is generally conceded as privilege to all to get genteelly boozy at Christmas and no one has a thought of it. Drinking in the army is carried on to fearfully dangerous extent at all times and under all circumstances, but on Christmas and the 4th of July, officers and men consider it not just privilege, but duty to get tight."

In January 1864, General Nathaniel P. Banks began planning another expedition into Texas by an overland route. The War Department ordered Banks to bring all Louisiana back into the Union, hold a constitutional convention and free elections. President Lincoln wanted and needed the votes, and generals, too, followed orders. Banks' new route to Texas would be up the Red River, which would give the army and navy many opportunities to seize Confederate cotton. Abundant cotton speculators in New Orleans approached all they thought might be involved in the forthcoming campaign with purchase offers. A leading firm in New Orleans offered up to $40,000 for a military officer to invest on the business' behalf in western Louisiana or eastern Texas to purchase cotton or sugar. The participating officer could reap a small fortune from his share on the sale of the goods.[2]

On January 1, Batteries G and H received orders to move from New Iberia to Franklin, Louisiana, for winter quarters. Being ordered to move was cause for celebration — better than sitting around a camp whittling whistles and toothpicks. The weather was rainy and the shortcuts across the bends of the bayou were now marshes full of cold water. On moving day, the weather was clear and cold, and the mules were fresh and frisky. They moved rapidly, and while cutting across country to avoid a flooded shortcut one of Company G's gun carriages in bouncing across a ditch caught its limber pole on the far side of the ditch and broke. This caused a merry series of jeers from the other members of the artillery battalion as they safely bounced past. The pole was soon mended, and the boys moved on. They cracked jokes all along their way.

Unlike some of the infantry who made their shortcuts along the bayou by stealing rowboats or canoes and floating with the current down to Franklin, the artillerists contented themselves with their version of chariot racing. In two days as they passed through Franklin, Louisiana, to their camp, they noticed some good-looking women, who had looked "sour" to them as they had passed through three months before, standing in their doorways smiling and watching the laughing artillerists go on their way. Rufus Dooley wrote home: "I was tempted to call for a drink, but was not in the least dry." These smiling women did so because they thought the Federal army was retreating.[3]

The men of the First Indiana's Companies A, B, F, G, H, I and K that had not reenlisted for three more years received orders on January 7 to report to General Franklin at New Iberia to man the 20-pounder Parrott rifles and the 30-pounder Parrott Rifles from Companies A, G and H under his command. These men were to be formed temporarily into provisional Companies A and G to replace the men who had reenlisted and were to be granted veterans furloughs. Company M at New Orleans turned in their guns and departed on the 18th for garrison duty at Baton Rouge. They would remain at Baton Rouge until July 6, 1864, under Major James B. Grimsley. Grimsley, finally getting his wish to be a major and have a big command, was placed in command of the non-reenlisting men and Company M on February 8.

On January 15 Company L at Fort Esperanza detached a section of one 30-pounder Parrott rifle under the command of Lieutenant Robert Rhea, and sent it to Indianola, Texas. The gun and its crew reported in for temporary duty as part of the 3rd Division of the XIII Corps and were attached to the light artillery units of the 3rd Brigade. Because the 30-pounder could shoot a heavier projectile a longer distance than the light field guns, its function was to protect the supply depot at Indianola from attack by Rebel cottonclad gunboats.[4]

In Louisiana, Companies A, G and H moved from Franklin to Brashear City, where they boarded the steamer *Red Chief #2* and steamed to New Orleans. Arriving there on January 15 they took quarters in one of the cotton presses. Their reenlisted comrades arrived daily from Baton Rouge to join them. When all assembled at New Orleans the reenlisted men received their veteran status. Their socializing reunion was sometimes subdued because several of the men had smallpox, and two of the comrades in Company H died from the illness. However, several bottles of "Old Reunion" or "Oh Be Joyful" loosened the men up while they waited for transportation home. Some of them expressed mixed feelings of shame at not being in a more active army group even though they had reenlisted. Several officers expressed similar thoughts and were hoping to muster out as soon as they could.[5]

The veterans had received pay for some months' past service. They also were allowed $40.00 for reenlisting plus a bounty of $100.00. The healthy veterans had an easy way to spend their money on drink, gambling and ladies of easy virtue during their leisure hours in the Crescent City; however, most men saved for the family back home. Some expressed money back home to keep themselves from spending it all before they got back home. The artillerists had their pictures taken, and many had albums made up with their comrades' pictures. These were highly prized items, and the men would not take a small fortune for them and the memories contained therein.

The leave amounted to sixty days and began when they boarded the river steamers on the 9th of February for the long trip north. They traveled up the Mississippi River for several days to Cairo, Illinois. From there, they traveled by railroad to Indianapolis, Indiana, where they arrived safely on February 19, 1864.[6]

(In the middle of February, the XIX Corps was reorganized. The Indiana Jackass Regiment was detached from the corps and made a part of a separate brigade of heavy artillery [siege train] along with the 6th Michigan.)

After arrival in Indianapolis, the Veteran Volunteers of the 1st Indiana Heavy Artillery (old 21st Regiment Indiana Volunteer Infantry) proudly led a parade from the Soldiers' Home through the streets of downtown Indianapolis to Metropolitan Hall. The boys were dressed in clean new uniforms and showed off their three captured 6-pounder brass cannons used by the original Jackass Battery. At Metropolitan Hall the bully boys of the Jackass Regiment found the best seating reserved for them at a grand reception. Speeches by Governor Morton, General Hovey, Colonels Slack and Keith and Indianapolis mayor Craven entertained and honored the veterans. With great ceremony, the 1st Indiana reenlisted 503 men, which was the largest number of reenlistments for *any* three year Indiana regiment. After the official festivities, the comrades took leave of each other to visit families and friends. Those having purchased their own Merrill rifles took them home. From now on they would use only government issued firearms and accoutrements. (It appears that they presented their three cannons as trophies to Governor Morton where they were displayed at the State House Museum until fifty or sixty years ago. One may still survive in the Eli Lilly Civil War Museum.)

Most (451) of the reenlisted veterans were from the 7th congressional district, which consisted of Clay, Greene, Owen, Parke, Putnam, Sullivan, Vermillion and Vigo counties. What is surprising about this is the fact that Copperheads, Knights of the Golden Circle and Sons of Liberty were most active in Greene, Parke, Putnam and Sullivan counties. Sullivan County was a veritable hot-bed of pro-secessionist activities. (Copperheads, the Sons of Liberty and the Knights of the Golden Circle were pro-secessionist activists and often violent.) For example, in Parke County, Salmon Lusk, a Parke County patriarch and outspoken Republican, had forty yards of bleached muslin curtain material stolen from his two-story home and his haystacks burned by Copperheads. Other loyal Unionists had their haystacks, barns and houses burned. Other secessionists threatened the lives of the citizens, and many loyal unionists were beaten and robbed by members of the pro-secession groups. Recruiting soldiers and draft workers received threatening letters, were maimed or killed. Several attempts were made to assassinate Indiana's governor, Oliver P. Morton; his closest brush with death came when an assassin's rifle ball grazed his head as he was leaving the State House after dark. The would-be assassin escaped.[7]

During 1863 and early 1864, many of the counties in the state, especially those in the above paragraph, held public meetings that resolved: "There should be a cessation of hostilities ... and not another soldier and not another dollar ought to be furnished for the further prosecution of the Negro emancipation." At least twenty-four Indiana counties had already passed similar resolutions when the 1st Indiana set about recruiting to fill the ranks of those who had not reenlisted. This made the Federal draft and recruiting for Federal service illegal in those counties—illegal, yes, but it was not enforceable insofar as the Federal authorities and the governor were concerned. Indiana was not recruiting to fill the ranks of U.S. soldiers—these men were asked to fill Indiana regiments. A band of soldiers of the 33rd Infantry Regiment home on leave were attacked in their hotel ballroom by a mob of citizens; one soldier was shot, others clubbed. Copperheads robbed military payroll trains and depots storing the payroll. A recruiting officer had his home riddled by more than 60 bullets while he was reading. To enlist or to reenlist was a very difficult decision for a man to make, especially so since it meant that he must leave his family exposed to violence at home while he was hundreds of miles away in another hostile area.[8]

The visit home was too brief, as is usual for visits of this kind. The men rendezvoused at Indianapolis on March 23. They conducted a final recruiting drive and then introduced the recruits to a sampling of army drill and preparation before returning to Baton Rouge. The regiment left Indianapolis on April 3 and traveled by train to Cairo, Illinois.

From there they traveled by river steamer down the Mississippi River to Memphis. At Memphis they changed to another steamer, the *Jatan*, which took them to Vicksburg. A couple of miles above Vicksburg two rebel cannons opened fire on the steamer and exploded a barrel or two of eggs, splattering the 1st Indiana boys hunkered down behind the barrels. A few shells also penetrated the hull and the *Jatan* sank shortly after it docked and discharged its passengers. The Hoosiers transferred to the steamers *Henry Ames* and *Gray Eagle* which took them to Baton Rouge where they landed late on the 11th of April. There they found the post under the command of General Philip St. George Cooke. The next day, as the regiment settled into Fort Williams, they received orders to be armed as infantry and sent to reinforce General Banks on the Red River.[9]

After delaying two weeks, Colonel John Keith wrote to General Richard Arnold, chief of artillery, on May 1 listing arguments as to why the 1st Indiana should not be sent into the field as infantry: mainly because of defective weapons and too many new recruits with lack of training. At the time Colonel Keith wrote the letter he had not received word that Major-General J. J. Reynolds on April 22 had already countermanded the order for the Jackass Regiment to move to the front as infantry to reinforce General Banks. The 24th Indiana Infantry departed for the Red River battlefront in place of the 1st Indiana.[10]

Major-General Banks had begun his dismally tedious Red River Campaign on March 8. The gunboats of Admiral David Porter steamed up the Red River. Brigadier-General Andrew Jackson "A. J." Smith and his XVI Corps left Vicksburg by river steamers to join with Porter's river fleet for a combined army-navy operation from the Mississippi River up the Red River to Alexandria, Louisiana. Around March 10, the XIX Corps under Brigadier-General William B. Franklin was ordered to move north towards Alexandria, Louisiana, to rendezvous with the XVI Corps and the fleet. Also, a part of the XIII Corps had been ordered back from Texas to become part of the new effort to capture Texas by land.

(Unfortunately, there is very little information available regarding the activities of the First Indiana Heavy Artillery's provisional companies A and G during this time. Therefore, this narrative of the Red River Campaign involves the 1st Indiana's two companies in actions rather than battles. The author suggests that for more detailed accounts of the Red River Campaign, one should obtain a copy of Dr. Gary Joiner's *One Damned Blunder from Beginning to End* or Ludwell H. Johnson's *Red River Campaign*.)

On March 14, Fort DeRussy at Marksville, Louisiana, fell to A. J. Smith's XVI Corps and Admiral Porter's gunboats. Smith's men rounded up about 250 prisoners and captured ten heavy guns. (One of the guns, a rifled 32-pounder, was taken as a trophy by Porter. It is displayed at the Washington Naval Yard.) The gunboats proceeded on to Alexandria where they waited for the army's arrival. Smith's XVI Corps occupied 15 transports and 5 vessels of the Marine Brigade. Also on this date, the reserve artillery, including provisional Companies A and G of the 1st Indiana Heavy Artillery, started from Franklin to Alexandria, Louisiana. By the 24th, Major General N. P. Banks and his entire army made up of part of the XIII Corps, XVI Corps, Red River Division of the XVII Corps and the XIX Corps numbering about 31,000 men were gathered at Alexandria ready to march up the Red River into Texas. Admiral Porter's gunboats and transport steamers for men, mules, guns, ammunition, food and medicine filled the Alexandria waterfront. Many of the steamers and the Navy gun-boats already held stolen

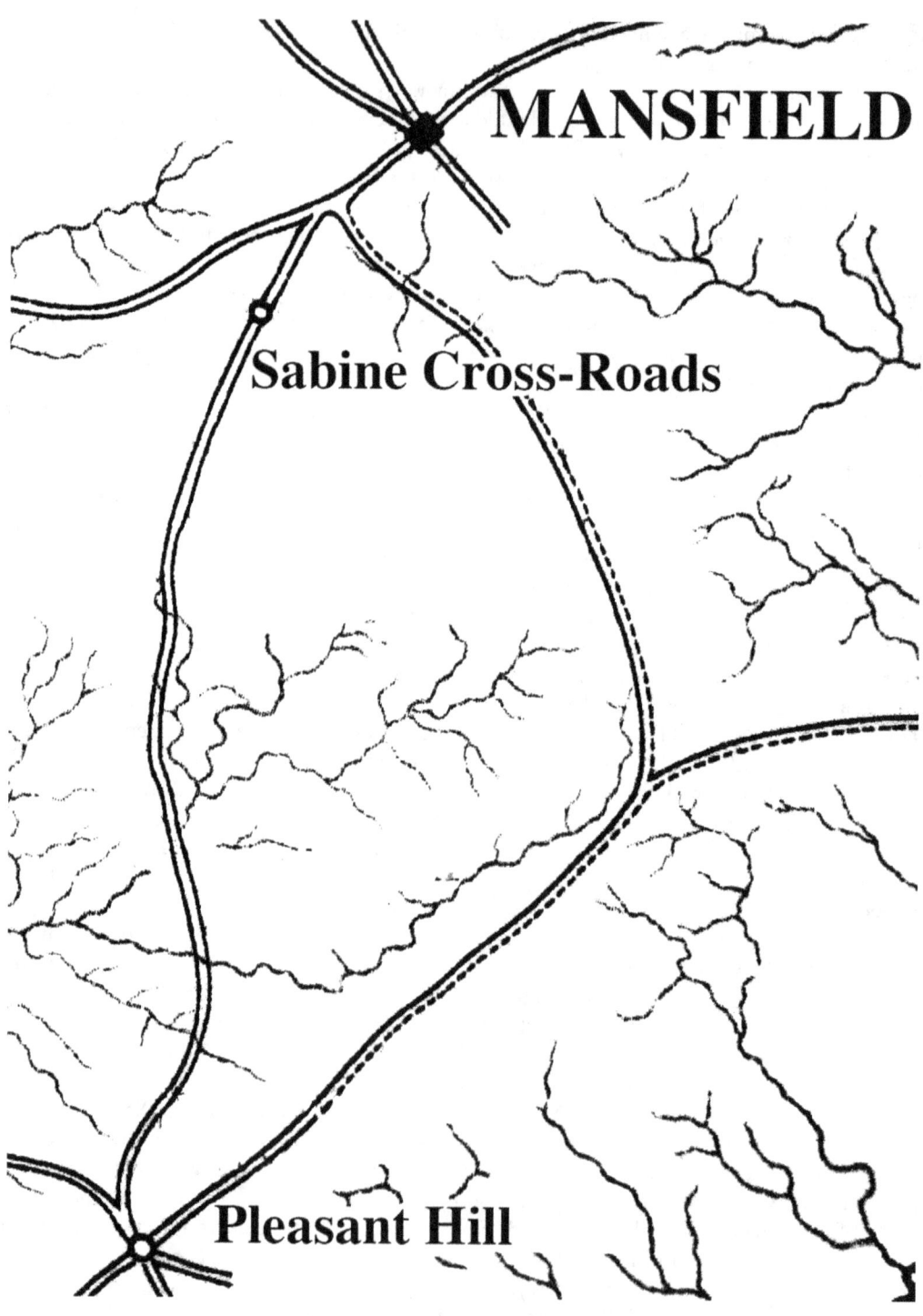

Red River Campaign map of the northern portion of Louisiana showing the location of the Battle of Sabine Cross-Roads and the Battle of Pleasant Hill. (Composite map derived from National Archives maps and a map in the collection of Lawrence Lee Hewitt.)

cotton, much of it taken by the navy without regard as to the loyalty of the owners. The 1st Indiana Company G with four 30-pounder Parrotts went aboard the steamer *Rob Roy* at Alexandria. The 1st Indiana Company A had the jackass teams of Companies F and G added to their jackass teams and could easily haul their 20-pounder rifles, wagons and field forge.[11]

The army marched from Alexandria, following the road along the banks of the Red River. They reached the Cane River at its confluence with the Red River on the 31st. (The Cane River is the former main channel of the Red River and flows parallel to it from its divergence north of Grand Ecore until it rejoins the Red about ten miles north of present day Boyce, Louisiana.) Taking the shortest and driest road to Shreveport, the XIX Corps and XIII marched on the road to Natchitoches alongside the Cane River.

When the army arrived at Cane River, Captain John Day of Company B and 83 men of Companies A, B, and F were relieved from artillery duty with the XIX Corps. They returned to Baton Rouge to strengthen the garrison in Fort Williams. Company D's Captain William Hinkle assumed overall command of the two provisional companies of the 1st Indiana. The main body of the army with its cavalry scouts out front continued to Natchitoches where they remained a day or two. The Hoosiers in Company A took over the local newspaper for a day and issued a special edition called the *Natchitoches Union*. It was a red-hot, definitely pro–Union edition intended to give the "greasy, yellow-haired, snuff-dipping Yahoos of that God-forsaken town some new ideas as to loyalty and patriotism." The fleet lay over a day about four miles upstream from Natchitoches at Grand Ecore.

Banks' main force moved west out of Natchitoches a few miles to a junction with the road from Grand Ecore. There, General A. J. Smith's XVI Corps coming from the landing at Grand Ecore joined the rear of the column. About eight miles west at a cross-road junction (near present-day Robeline), Banks' army turned right taking the Shreveport Road north through Pleasant Hill to Mansfield. From Mansfield, General Banks could continue to Shreveport.

Banks marched through Pleasant Hill and moved on toward Mansfield. The army passed through about twelve miles of pine forest. Very few clearings existed and few houses, and tilled land stood at the road-side. On April 7, Porter's fleet of six shallow-draft gunboats and twenty transports with Brigadier-General Thomas Kilby Smith's provisional Red River Division of the XVII Corps and military stores of all kinds set out for a landing about 110 winding river miles north of Grand Ecore.[12]

On April 8, just a mile or so south of Mansfield, Louisiana, near Sabine Crossroads the advance parties of Banks' army encountered their first sizable opposition. Banks' cavalry, commanded by Brigadier-General Albert Lee, was in front and had been having minor skirmishes with enemy cavalry for the past few miles. Banks' command had cavalry in advance and a couple of light batteries and limited infantry at its front, followed by a large wagon train of supplies, followed by the XIII Corps and cannon followed by more supply wagons, etc., followed by the XIX Corps, more wagons, etc., followed by the XVI Corps suddenly halted. (Banks' column of cavalry, infantry, artillery and transport wagons extended roughly ten miles along the road from Pleasant Hill to Mansfield.)

As Brigadier General Albert L. Lee's leading cavalry came into an exceptionally large clearing in the piney woods and moved up a small hill, they spotted a large Confederate force before them and to their right at the far edge of open ground behind a fence. A forest to the rear of the fence hid additional infantry and cavalry. Lieutenant-General Richard Taylor had 16,000 infantrymen and cavalry, commanded from their left to right by Brigadier-General Hamilton Bee (cavalry), Lieutenant-General John G. Walker (infantry), Brigadier-General Alfred Mouton (infantry) and Brigadier-General Thomas Greene (cavalry), looking across the field at Lee's cavalry. Lee sent his troopers forward to skirmish and he called for infantry and artillery to come up at the double-quick.

The skirmishing continued for a couple of hours as the Federals bought time for reinforcements. Bee's cavalry probes against Lee were repulsed. After a couple of hours with both armies essentially standing in lines facing each other, General Mouton ordered his brigade commanders to charge. With blood-curdling yells the Confederates made an all-out assault against the Federal center and right flank, driving the skirmishers and Lee's cavalry off the high ground and across the field to a line of fences. The Federals here at the fences were Brigadier-General Thomas E. G. Ransom's XIII Corps infantry on the left and Colonel Thomas J. Lucas' First Brigade, Cavalry Division, Department of the Gulf, on the right, about 3,500 in all, supported by Nims' battery on the left.

Taylor's army hit them with nearly 10,000 men. Two additional light batteries came up on the Federal right, the Chicago Mercantile Battery and Klaus' 1st Indiana Light Battery, and immediately opened fire on the advancing gray horde with little effect. Ransom's and Lucas' lines, hit very hard by Mouton's men, broke. General Mouton fell, shot to death, leading the attack. General Franklin galloped up to assess the condition of the Federal line and was at once shot from his horse by Walker's infantry. The Federal line gave up ground, firing as it moved backwards. Nims abandoned three guns due to his horses all being killed and was driving his remaining guns to the rear when he came to a huge roadblock made by the cavalry's supply wagons being mired in a muddy slough at the base of two hills.

The wagons blocked not only the road, but also the small clear area by the road and parts of the forest's bottom land to each side of the road. Nims left his last guns behind as he got his men to the rear. The Chicago Mercantile Battery and Klaus' Indiana Battery abandoned their guns at the giant roadblock. Two other batteries each had to leave a two-gun section behind. Things got worse as the frightened horses began plunging around churning up more mud, breaking free and plowing the ground with parts of broken wagons dragged behind them. The wagon train was lost. Those in the rear first learned of the disaster taking place at the front when a cavalryman riding a foam-covered horse road up yelling that the whole damned Rebel army was in front and our troops were being cut to pieces.

Major-General Emory, XIX Corps, now came up from a few miles back with his division. It advanced with bayonets fixed, swords drawn and muskets cocked. He ordered Dwight to hold the road, McMillan to hold the right, Benedict to hold the left and Kinsey to put his command out as skirmishers in front to try and keep the retreat from becoming a route. He met the victorious Confederates about three miles back from where they had soundly beaten Lee, Ransom and Lucas. After twenty minutes of the most intense fighting that Emory had ever been in, the Confederates stopped, pulled back a few yards and waited. Emory offered no more fight. He blocked the road for a time while the rest of the army retreated to Pleasant Hill and then pulled back. The Rebels advanced and secured the hill that Emory had formerly occupied, thereby gaining the stream at its base. The grayclads needed the water and rest; therefore, they made camp for the night. The Federal losses that day were 2,186 men, 20 pieces of artillery (six 3.67-inch rifled bronze guns, eight 3-inch wrought iron [Ordnance] rifles, four 12-pounder Napoleons, two 12-pounder mountain howitzers and sixteen caissons of ammunition), nearly 200 wagons of supplies and thousands of small arms. Taylor claimed to have lost 1,000 men, but he gave no details.

About four miles to the rear of where Lee's cavalry had first met Taylor's army, Company A of the Jackass Regiment, manned by one-hundred-twenty-three men from Companies A, I and K, rolled their four 20-pounder Parrott rifles to the east side of the road into a cane field where they awaited orders to move forward. They occupied this position from 3 P.M., when Lee first engaged Taylor. They listened to the firing and remained in this position until midnight when, without firing a shot, they received orders to limber up and return to Pleasant Hill.

Companies of Bee's and Greene's cavalry rode around the flanks of Emory's blockade and made harassing forays against Banks' rear in its chaotic retreat. The Hoosiers reached Pleasant Hill at daybreak. They had scarcely finished breakfast and a cup of coffee when they received orders to move to the rear and join the supply train already retreating to Grand Ecore.[13]

On the morning of the 9th, General Banks anticipated another attack and ordered the XVI Corps and the XIII Corps to be alert to repel the enemy. That afternoon, shortly after the last wagon had gotten on its way to Grand Ecore, the Rebels charged the Federal lines. The Rebels attacked first on the flanks to cut off retreat over the road to Blair's Landing and to Grand Ecore. The ensuing battle lasted several hours during which Captain Chambers B. Etter's Arkansas Battery lost one gun and Captain James M. Daniels lost two guns. The XVI Corps' general A.J. Smith, hatless, with his gray hair flowing in the wind, bravely charged with his men into battle at Pleasant Hill saving the day. The blue-bellies chased the grayclads a short distance into the woods and up the roads toward Sabine River and Mansfield. After his questionable win, Banks hastily abandoned the battlefield, giving the Confederates the victory honors. Major-General "Commissary" Banks' army began a dismal retreat to Grand Ecore.

Not only the enlisted men were bitter and disillusioned; the feeling extended all the way up to the corps commanders. A. J. Smith (of whom Banks had said, "God bless you, General; you have saved the army.") expressed his displeasure with Banks' willingness to flee in the face of victory. The campaign was an ignominious failure. The Federal losses were estimated at 4,000 casualties, loss of 25 pieces of artillery and 5,000 stands of small arms. The dead and wounded were left in the hands of the enemy. (Private Joseph Horner of the Jackass Regiment's Company K died at Pleasant Hill, Louisiana, April 9, 1864.)[14]

On April 12, about 4:30 P.M., General Thomas Green's cavalry had ridden around Banks' retreating column to attack the Federal transports on the Red River. The boats were withdrawing down the shallow river since they had learned that the army was in full retreat. The army was to have acted in mutual support with the navy. Without their infantry advancing, there was no need for the navy to continue onward. Also, the water in the river was dropping exposing more sandbars and offering less water on which to float. While turning around, some of the boats ran into each other and onto sandbars, but with repairs they traveled downstream.

The gunboat U.S.S. *Lexington* collided with the transport *Rob Roy* in the narrow channel damaging its wheelhouse and smokestacks. Five hours later after its crew finished repairing the *Rob Roy*, it and the other transport steamers, *Hastings,* and *Black Hawk*, plus the gunboats *Osage* and the *Lexington* got underway. They trailed behind the main flotilla. After traveling for more than an hour, the vessels heard the sound of gunfire coming from ahead at the Blair Plantation's landing. All of General Greene's cavalry and a howitzer section of Captain John A. West's Horse Artillery had attacked the steamer *Alice Vivian* and the gunboat *Osage*, both aground against the east bank of the river, as well as the steamer *Blackhawk*, trying to pull off the grounded vessels. The gunboats *Osage* and *Lexington* were returning fire at the dismounted cavalry lining the west bank of the river.

As the *Rob Roy* came steaming downstream around a bend in the river, her bow turned to face the southwest bank of the river. As the bow faced the Texans, Captain Hinkle's four 30-pounder Parrotts lined up around the bow unleashed a thundering blast of canister at the massed Texans on the red clay riverbank. General Kilby Smith's soldiers aboard the gunboats and transports opened fire with their muskets from behind cotton bales and Smith's transport, *Hastings*, added the fire of her howitzers to the melee. Exhorted on by General Greene riding up and down the riverbank the Texans returned a punishing rifle fire at the vessels,

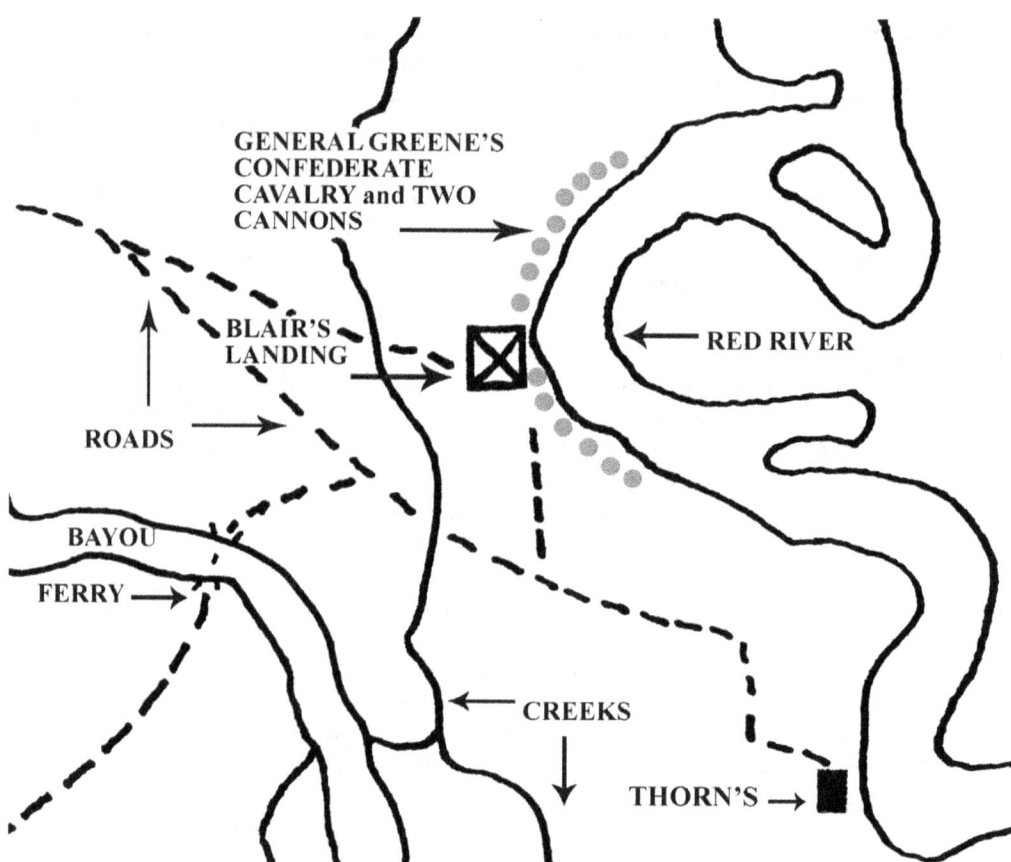

Map of Blair's Landing on the Red River in Louisiana. Dotted lines are roads. Gray dots on the bank of the Red River are the positions of General Greene's cavalry. Parallel lines with dashes between them indicate Bayou Pierre. (Modified detail to map in the collection of Lawrence Lee Hewitt.)

forcing the infantrymen behind wooden planking to lie prone. One Texan's bullet aimed at the *Rob Roy* ricocheted off one of the 30-pounder Parrott's iron tires and struck Zeno Rubottom in the right thigh just below his groin as he was reloading the cannon. The bullet halted its travel with its nose bruising his thigh bone.

After half an hour, a direct hit from canister or grapeshot tore off General Greene's head. Seeing their beloved general's headless body topple to the riverbank, the hollering hard-fighting Texans lost their spirit and left the riverbank for the cover of bushes, trees and levee. The Texas cavalry suffered more than 200 casualties, including General Greene. They left behind many of their muskets, knapsacks and rum-filled canteens.

Like the navy, the bully boys' Captain William Hinkle reported that Greene had fallen, headless, from a discharge of canister. Hinkle did not say it was his Parrott rifles' canister or naval canister or grapeshot; but he worded his report so it could be implied that his Parrotts' grapeshot did the deed. Hinkle went on to explain that his guns had exhausted their supply of the 30-pounder canister aboard the *Rob Roy* at the Texans, therefore, they resorted to the use of doubled charges of 20-pounder canister, which they had stored on board the *Rob Roy*. The effect of the doubled 20-pounder canister was just as effective as the 30-pounder canister.

As they steamed on downstream that night, the Indianians aboard the *Rob Roy* assisted the U.S.S. *Cricket* in shelling the woods along the river as they fought off bands of marauding Rebel cavalry. The day's action had damaged the *Rob Roy*'s rudder, and that night she was towed downstream to Grand Ecore for repairs.[15]

The army rested and recuperated at Grand Ecore for a few days. During this time, Lieutenant-General Kirby Smith, C.S.A., ordered Churchill and Walker's divisions away from Taylor's army, which left Taylor with only Brigadier-General Camille Armand Jules Marie Prince de Polignac's infantry (about 2,000 men) and the remnants of Greene's cavalry now commanded by Major-General John A. Wharton. Banks' army, instead of advancing against its greatly weakened foe, again began a weary trudge retracing its route in coming up the river. The Indiana Jackass Battalion was assigned to Brigadier-General William H. Emory's First Division of the XIX Corps for the trek. The XIX Corps burned occasional buildings along their line of march from Natchitoches and then burned every building but one after leaving Cloutierville. By April 22, Banks' army arrived near Monett's Ferry.

At the ferry, the army halted in its retreat as it encountered two brigades of cavalry with artillery commanded by Brigadier-General Hamilton P. Bee and Brigadier-General James P. Major holding the bluffs and the crossing on the Cane River. Bee's and Major's artillery, commanded by Major Oliver Semmes with William Moseley's battery, M. V. McMahan's battery, J. A. West's battery, and the rifle section of Timothy D. Nettle's battery held the heights of the bluffs with two of their batteries at the crossing. To bypass the crossing meant a retrograde movement of Banks' army to an undesirable crossing onto a poor road that would slow his retreat by days. Therefore, a head-on conflict resulted, beginning with Captain Benjamin Nields' 1st Delaware Battery of six 3-inch rifles and a two-gun section of Company A's 20-pounder Parrott rifles going into action against a six-gun Rebel battery atop the bluff to their front while infantry maneuvered forward through a forest on the artillery's left.

After a relatively short duel, the Rebel battery ceased firing and moved away. Besides driving the enemy artillery away, the Federal artillery fire drew attention away from a flanking attack by Brigadier-General Henry W. Birge's XIX Corps, Second Division, that had crossed the Cane River two miles upstream and was coming down hard upon the Confederate left flank.

Birge opened his attack and rushed toward a little sandy hillock, quickly overran it and sent the small force of dismounted cavalry holding it running to a higher hill in their rear. However, Bee had spotted Birge's movement and had moved most of his troopers around the hilltop to face the Yankee attackers. After a sharp contest, the Rebels gave way and retreated to the bluff top forming a new left flank for Bee's lines. Birge gave his men a short rest while he reconnoitered the area in front of him. Finding a crossing over a small creek valley to his front, he formed his men to advance on the new Rebel left flank. McMahan's artillery took position there and stopped Birge's movement, saving most of Bee's left wing.

The Hoosier and the Delaware batteries moved forward to the end of the woods across from the bluff being attacked by Birge and wheeled left. Moving forward a short distance, Captain Nields' cannon and the Heavies, two Parrot rifles, began firing into a section of artillery on the Federal side of the river. The bursting 20-pound shells made it too hot for the Rebel gun section. They limbered up and fell back across the river to go into line with the other Confederate artillery at the river. A two-gun section of Jacob Rawles, Battery G, 5th U.S. Artillery, moved forward to where Nields and the Hoosiers had been to cover Birge's advance.[16]

Captain Henry Closson, 1st U.S. Artillery, ordered Captain Hinkle, 1st Indiana Heavy Artillery with the remaining section of two 20-pounder Parrotts, Captain George T. Hebard, 1st Vermont Battery with one 3-inch rifle, Lieutenant Thomas A. Porter, 1st Delaware Battery with one 3-inch rifle and Lieutenant John O. Flanders, 25th New York Battery with one

3-inch rifle to advance through the woods and take a position directly across the river crossing from two six-gun Rebel batteries on the south bank of the Cane and one Rebel battery (six guns) atop the bluff to their right (Bee's center) of the crossing. After a difficult trek, the rifled artillery battalion, commanded by Captain Hinkle, emerged into an open area across from the Rebel artillery. A skirmish line from the 2nd New York Veteran Cavalry went out about two hundred yards to protect the Federal artillery. Four rifled cannons set up to engage the massed artillery across the Cane at the river crossing and one rifle moved into position to take on the battery atop the bluff.

The Rebels occupied densely wooded hills flanking both sides of the road to Alexandria across the river. The battalion of mixed guns began to shell the Confederate cannons as the more remote battery had been doing. The 20-pounder shells exploded on a Rebel battery wagon, killing its driver and all of the horses. Other shells kept the Rebel artillery ducking and covering. Bee ordered a troop of cavalry to charge the Federal guns in his front.

After having fired only ten minutes, the artillerists saw Rebel cavalry dashing across the low water crossing, coming directly toward them. The artillerists, having next to no canister, ceased firing and began moving back into the forest. The artillery's supporting dismounted cavalry skirmishers, reinforced by the rest of Colonel Morgan H. Chrysler's 2nd New York Veteran Cavalry, who were waiting at the edge of the forest, charged and beat back Bee's cavalry.

Once again pressed by artillery fire making his position untenable, General Bee, seeing his men about to be encircled by Birge from his left and his center crumbling due to Churchill's cavalry and artillery, ordered his entire force to mount up and withdraw down the road toward Fort Jesup. Federal cavalry pursued the retreating Confederates, crossed the river, secured the crossing, and chased the Rebels a short distance away. Generals Bee and Major beat a hasty retreat to Beasley's Plantation eighteen miles away on the Fort Jesup Road. Bee's losses were about 50 men and one battery wagon. The Confederate artillery had expended 533 rounds against the Federals.[17]

Banks' army crossed the Cane River and made haste to Alexandria where it would remain until May 13, when the boats could safely get over the falls there. The Red River had fallen so low that the river fleet was trapped above Alexandria. A couple of dams were constructed by the infantry, acting under the direction of Lieutenant-Colonel Joseph Bailey. In honor of its designer, the lower dam at Alexandria was named Bailey's Dam. Made of logs and sunken barges filled with dirt and rocks it did the job. Another similar dam was constructed upstream at the upper falls to force the water to flow more deeply into the channel. Parts of the dam could be seen at low water until late in 1988, when the Corps of Engineers closed the gates at its latest lock and dam on the Red River, thereby flooding Bailey's dam under 18 feet of water.

While construction of Bailey's dam was going on, the troops not working on it constructed and manned a line of earthworks stretching around Alexandria from Bayou Rapides on the west running east to the other side of Smith Smith's Railroad on the eastern side of town and followed it north to the Red River, surrounding the town with a fortified line reinforced by redans and lunettes, especially at road entrances. Abatis of fallen trees lay in front of the redans. A small bayou flowed along the outer side of the line of fortifications for much of their length acting as a moat. The boys in Company A were amused at doing picket duty with 20-pounder Parrott rifles in the redans at the roads entering Alexandria. They stated that General Dwight "did not feel safe unless we were out there."

From daylight until dark the sharpshooters on both sides sniped away at each other from points along Bayou Rapides and Bayou Robert. Minor cavalry skirmishes and small-scale infantry clashes occurred on expeditions from Alexandria out along Bayou Robert toward

LeCompte, and Cheneyville, Louisiana. Rebel cavalry made constant probes of Alexandria's defenses.

Safe in their camp, Privates Hillis and Shoemaker of Company E had built a bed of fence rails to keep them off the wet ground. Hillis had bedded down, but Shoemaker and some other soldiers went foraging for food at a nearby plantation. There they found an old colored preacher. The pranksters told him that they needed a preacher to go and pray for a man down sick at camp and going to die. Private Hillis told this story of his awakening: "There was that old nigger down over me praying and saying, 'Oh Lord, bless the Linkum soldier.' Well, that was enough for me, and I grabbed my saber, and I can tell you the old colored brother got out of there pretty lively."[18]

To lighten the boats to get them over the rocky rapids and falls, Admiral Porter ordered the artillery, ammunition, sugar barrels and cotton taken off and moved into the town for storage. Finally, the water was deep enough. One by one, the boats cautiously moved forward and shot the narrow gap of rushing water through an opening in the dam. After the boats were safely over the falls through the dam's spillway, they loaded their guns, cotton, etc. and got underway on the 13th. The army again took up its retreat parallel to the river.

Behind them the town of Alexandria was burning. The flames destroyed an area from Smith Smith's Railroad about eight blocks long by the Red River and five blocks away from the river along the railroad. The area of damage shortened the farther away from the river it burned, burning only two blocks at its furthest from the river. The finger of blame for starting the fire usually is pointed at soldiers from the XVI Corps, often called Smith's Gorillas, or at a local group of murderers and plunderers living in the forest and swamps not far from the town. No one really knows who started it.

Below Alexandria the river craft proceeded downstream in a convoy headed by five or six gunboats; the center of the convoy consisted of thirteen transports with various army regiments and artillery aboard, and the rear of the convoy consisted of four or five gunboats each escorting a transport. An amusing little ditty (partially shown below) sung to the tune of "When Johnny Comes Marching Home" brightened the marching soldiers' days as they marched towards Simmesport.

> But Taylor and Smith, with ragged ranks,
> For bales, for bales;
> But Taylor and Smith, with ragged ranks,
> For bales, says I;
> But Taylor and Smith, with ragged ranks,
> burned up the cotton and whipped old Banks,
> and we'll all drink stone blind,
> Johnny fill up the bowl.

As the army crossed the Plains of Mansura, just outside of the town of Mansura, it again encountered General Dick Taylor's Confederates. Taylor's army, Commanded by Wharton, Polignac and Major blocked the road. The Confederate lines extended for a significant distance to either side of the road, making a splendid display in grand Napoleonic formation. The Confederates had positioned their artillery between regiments and brigades. The Federals lined up much the same way. The two armies drawn up in splendid formations faced each other across the flat plains with flags waving. The Rebel artillery, consisting of two 30-pounder Parrotts and twenty-two pieces of light artillery, including captured 3.67-inch bronze rifles, captured 3-inch ordnance rifles, a captured 12-pounder Napoleon, 6-pounder guns, 12-pounder howitzers and 3-inch Confederate Parrotts, opened the ball. They had plenty of captured ammunition to expend on the Yankees and the ensuing artillery duel lasted for four hours.

The artillery had roared for some time when the Federals ordered up their reserve artillery brigade to reinforce the line. The Hoosiers' Company A passed through seven lines of waiting infantry before they unlimbered, dropped trail and added the fire of their guns to that of the light guns. After firing for about half an hour, Company A received orders to limber up and advance about 600 yards to the farthest reach of Rebel musket range and engage the enemy, who threatened a Federal supply wagon train. As they unlimbered, moved their guns into firing position and prepared to load and fire, a general officer rode up to Company A and ordered them to turn their guns to the right to blast an enemy column. A sharp-eyed Hoosier saw Stars and Stripes flying over the so-called enemy column and passed the word to his lieutenant, who in turn passed it on to the general. The general turned his glass on the flag and countermanded his previous order to fire, saying, "Yes, that's our flag. Now, turn your guns straight to the front and let those fellows have it!"

In a minute Company A became a prime target for the Rebel artillery. A Rebel shell struck between the two center 20-pounders and covered the guns and the crews with a prodigious amount of Louisiana dirt. The Federals finally made a general advance turning the Confederates' flanks; the Rebels, being flanked and running short of ammunition, withdrew to the general area of Simmesport to resupply. Two days later, the armies would meet again along Yellow Bayou on the way to Simmesport.[19]

Banks' army resumed its retreat to Simmesport, and on the 18th, the main body of Banks' army began crossing the Atchafalaya River on a bridge, courtesy again of the ingenious Colonel Bailey, constructed of river transport boats lashed together, the bows covered by planks connecting them. As the last train of supplies was passing over Yellow Bayou on its way to Simmesport, Rebel forces under General Polignac and Colonel Major attacked the wagon train and its rear guard. The XVI Corps Infantry Division, commanded by Brigadier-General Joseph A. Mower, Klaus' 1st Indiana Battery and Company A's Heavies turned and rapidly moved to the rear to save the wagon train. Confederate cavalry from Wharton's command dismounted and moved forward across an open field blocking their own batteries. Shortly, the cavalrymen dove into a drainage ditch running across the field as their own artillery opened fire. The ditch saved many of their lives. The roar of cannon from the Louisianans' St. Mary's and Pelican Batteries and Benton's Texas Battery filled the air as they shelled the wagon train and the arriving Federal infantry.

Klaus' Battery and Company A went into action. It did not take but a few shots before the boys of Company A knew they had defective ammunition. Their first shot tumbled end over end and fell halfway to the Rebel line, The artillerists elevated their cannon, reloaded and fired; the shot flew straight but passed a half mile over the Rebels' heads. An officer rode to General Mower and explained the problem. Mower ordered the Heavies to the rear as soon as a replacement battery arrived.

Their replacement battery arrived, the Heavies withdrew and the fight continued. After nearly an hour, General Wharton's men fell back and General Polignac's infantry division entered the fight. Heavy canister fire from the Federal guns and the hot flames of a brush fire kindled by their own muzzle blasts in front of the Rebels forced them to fall back. This allowed the Union troops to continue to withdraw to the Atchafalaya River and safely cross over it on Bailey's bridge. The steamers cut loose from each other and moved away to prevent capture by the Confederates. General Taylor reported about 500 casualties. The Confederates buried 50 dead at a brick church near the bayou and buried several more at Moreauville.

When the Federals were safely across the river, Companies A and G's Heavies moved on to the fort at Morganza, Louisiana. Arriving there on the 21st, they "rejoiced with great joy" celebrating that they were through with Banks' Red River Campaign.

The XVI Corps and the XVII Corps proceeded to Vicksburg. The men of the XIII and

XIX Corps remained at Simmesport and expressed their feelings about Banks by cat-calls, hisses and groans whenever they saw him. Threatened with physical harm, Banks took refuge in a gunboat on the Atchafalaya lest one of his soldiers shoot him. Major General Edward R. S. Canby arrived at Simmesport to assume control of the army, now in the Military Division of West Mississippi, which included the Department of the Gulf. When the new commander arrived and addressed the men, ill feelings toward Banks subsided as Canby informed them that General Banks' duties in this department would be civil duties only from now on. As of May 7, 1864, the XIII and XIX Corps worked for General Canby.[20]

Sixteen

Reorganization and Action at Mobile Bay

During the month of May, uncertainty and anxiety filled the Jackass Regiment's men and officers. On May 23, General Banks sent orders that the Jackass Regiment temporarily be outfitted, equipped as infantry and be attached to the Nineteenth Army Corps, Third Division, Second Brigade. The regiment shared this fate with the 6th Michigan Heavy Artillery and the 4th Wisconsin Cavalry. (The portion of non-reenlisted men scheduled for discharge from the regiment and serving in the field was to remain as artillery.) Colonel Keith contested these orders that were in direct conflict with orders to the opposite effect given the first of May. (Several orders from Banks read by the author appear to have been outside his civil jurisdiction and interfering with Canby's military authority.)[1]

Previously on April 25, Colonel Keith had ordered Lieutenant Robert H. Crist of Company L to Pass Cavallo on Matagorda Island, Texas, with a layover in New Orleans. During his layover, Crist was to remove the crates of Merrill rifles, accoutrements and other small arms stored at the Vicksburg Cotton Press and send them all to the regimental headquarters at Baton Rouge along with an inventory. After doing that, he was to proceed on to Texas. On the same date as Crist received his orders, Keith released a new list of non-commissioned officers for Companies A through K, including John Yelton's and Rufus Dooley's promotions to second and seventh corporals, respectively.

A Baton Rouge Methodist church sponsored a large rally where the boys listened to inspirational temperance messages from their regiment's Chaplain Brakeman and "Ervin of Company F" who blamed the loss of an arm to Louisiana rum. After the rally, nearly one-third of the regiment at Baton Rouge signed temperance pledges to abstain from strong spirits.

Rather than have his Hoosiers perform fatigue duty in Fort Williams and Baton Rouge, Keith ordered one hundred men, two commissioned officers, two sergeants and four corporals from the 62nd U.S. Colored Troops to be furnished with shovels and report to Lieutenant George Curtis, street commissioner, for fatigue duty.

The artillerists at Morganza seemed to be enjoying themselves without the worries of those men at Baton Rouge. An unsigned letter written from Morganza to "Betsy Jane" in Baton Rouge on June 13, 1864, made references to the shenanigans of some of the bully boys of Company H at Morganza. The "Betsy Jane" letter stated that "George" and the writer had been running a game of chuck-a-luck. The guard detail arrested two of the boys, Lough and Mater, for gambling on Sunday. As punishment, the two stood at attention in the rain the rest of the day until dark. The letter also mentioned that the boys caught plenty of fish to supplement their rations. It seems these boys liked their gambling and fishing.[2]

On June 14, Major-General E.R.S. Canby firmly resolved the status of the bully boys— they would remain as heavy artillery. General E.R.S. Canby ordered Companies A and G to

Morganza for the relief of the two provisional batteries there. Canby ordered the rest of the Jackass Regiment stationed outside of Baton Rouge to report in at Baton Rouge. Company L returned to New Orleans from Matagorda Island, Texas, by the end of June. The XIX Corps was then re-organized with the First and Second Divisions being ordered to report for duty at Washington, D.C. The Third Division was incorporated into the re-organized XIII Corps. The Indiana Jackass Regiment remained behind. Lieutenant-Colonel Richard Irwin, A.A.G. of the XIX Corps, in his narrative of that corps, praised the Jackass Regiment by stating: "Some of the best regiments of the corps were left behind.... Among the troops thus cut off [from the XIX Corps] were the ... 1st Indiana Heavy Artillery."[3]

The Jackass Regiment quartered in the old, clean and comfortable two-story brick barracks (Pentagon Barracks), or in tents surrounding it, all being inside of Fort Williams. On June 17, John Yelton was promoted to sergeant due to James Reddish's death from illness. On June 25, to standardize the armament and ammunition of the regiment, Colonel Keith ordered Companies B, H and I to retain their Merrill rifles. Companies C and K transferred their Merrill rifles to Company B, Company E transferred their Merrill rifles to Company H and Company F transferred their Merrill rifles to Company I. As usual, the men complained about duty inside the fort, but the boys welcomed picket duty outside its earthen walls. They could roam through the woods and brush, picking blackberries, scaring snakes or being scared by snakes. On the 28th of June they received orders from General Canby organizing them into a siege train.

The new recruits that had come down in April and May suffered from homesickness. Some of the recruits would stand on the riverfront and blankly stare upstream towards home. The recruits who were hospitalized with diseases, such as scurvy, chronic diarrhea, swamp fever, typhoid, yellow fever or smallpox, couldn't stare up the river towards home; their deaths were recorded nearly every day. One has to pity the men who had recruited their brothers and close friends, and who now sat by their beds as they died.[4]

On July 3, Colonel Keith ordered Captain Edward McLaflin, Company G, to New Orleans to reserve the proper accommodations for six companies being ordered to that place. Colonel Keith placed Lieutenant-Colonel Benjamin Hays in command of the detachment of Companies C, D, E and I to remain at Baton Rouge. Keith accompanied Companies B, F, H, K, and M aboard the steamer *Nebraska* bound for New Orleans. Not only the colonel and his artillery battalion of men, but also their 200 mules and horses, 25 wagons, baggage, the 22nd Iowa Regiment and their 80 mules and horses crowded aboard the steamer. There was standing room only. The *Nebraska* first landed at Algiers and let off the 22nd Iowa and their baggage, mules and horses. The steamer then crossed the river and let the Hoosiers, mules, etc. off on the 8th.

The artillerists moved to take quarters in the Steam Cotton Press building; however, it was already occupied. After waiting around in the street for a few hours, the Hoosiers moved into a run-down tobacco warehouse opposite a foundry near to the Saint Mary's Market. Colonel Keith established his regimental headquarters nearby. Other officers roomed in hotels like the Louisiana Hotel (75 cents a day) or boarding houses. On July 10, Company I received orders to move to Brashear City. Companies A and G were still at Morganza, Louisiana, but in the XIII Corps. Companies C, D, and E remained behind to garrison Baton Rouge. Companies B, F, H, K, L, and M now quartered at New Orleans.[5]

The men at New Orleans did not at all like being confined to the old, dusty, smoke-scented nearly windowless tobacco warehouse, especially, during days when temperatures reached nearly 100 degrees in the shade. The men wished they were in more open quarters or outside in tents. Some of the men regularly got outside to attend church, Sunday school and prayer meetings. Rufus Dooley visited a nearby Baptist church which he described as having "very few persons there, and what there was seemed to take but very little interest in the services." The building for the church was the plainest church in the city — more like the churches in Indiana. Another church that he visited on Canal Street he described as "the most beautiful I ever saw, impossible for me to describe ... but it seemed as if there was more style and pride than religion." The churches in the city were not one-third filled on Sunday, but the theaters were filled to standing room only. (Some things have not changed.)

On July 21, the boys moved from the old tobacco press to Steam Cotton Press #2 on the levee. The cotton press had been vacated the day before by XIX Corps cavalry and some USCT soldiers. Its former occupants left the place dirty, which required a week of fatigue duty to get in proper order. Naturally, the cleaning took place while the soldiers occupied the press. During their cleaning and organizing, some of the men thought back to what they had seen and heard during their veterans' furlough. Many of their wives, sweethearts and sisters back home were doing men's work in the fields and trade-craft work repairing furniture, harness, equipment and outbuildings. They thought about what might take place when the war was over and they arrived back home. Would they be welcome in their own homes? Would the women still have a need for the men's agricultural, home repair, building and livestock tending skills? More secure men, who knew their crafts and abilities would blend with the newly learned skills of the women back home, thought that it was very practical for the women to be doing this kind of work. In a way they felt relief; these toughened women would be more than able to withstand and share the rigors of moving West and establishing homesteads in new land.[6]

While the Hoosiers settled in, requests and orders flowed through official channels requesting that siege batteries and light artillery batteries be put into readiness to move at a moment's notice. Specifically requested were Company A of the 2nd Illinois Heavy Artillery and Company L of the Jackass Regiment for the siege batteries. Both mounted four 30-pounder Parrott rifles. Further, five 30-pounder Parrotts were to be removed from Forts Jackson and St. Philip and brought to New Orleans to be assigned to the Indiana artillerists. The light batteries selected to be ready to move at a moment's notice were the 17th Ohio with six 12-pounder Napoleon guns and the 2nd Connecticut with six 3-inch rifled guns.

Colonel Keith on July 25 ordered Company M to turn over thirty-eight serviceable mules to Company E, Company C to turn over all of its harness to Company E and for Company L to turn over its four 30-pounder Parrott rifles, ordnance, ordnance stores, horses, mules and harness to Company H.[7]

On July 29, Company H, drew four 30-pounder Parrots, equipment, mules, forty Enfield rifles in addition to their seventy Merrill rifles and stored them aboard a little two boiler steamer, the *Tamaulipas*, also occupied by Company A, 2nd Illinois Heavy Artillery, with their four 30-pounder Parrots, horses, equipment, etc. With mixed feelings because they thought they thought they were bound for a short stay at Ship Island, the bully boys steamed down the Mississippi River. They lay over for the night near Pilot Town at the Southeast Pass. The next day, August 1, they steamed at first light out into the Gulf of Mexico and headed northeast toward Ship Island. A gale blew up after they left the Mississippi River and turned to cross the Gulf. The winds and seas abated as the *Tamaulipas* came within sight of Ship Island late that afternoon. Instead of landing, the *Tamaulipas* steamed around the western end of the island and turned east.

Steaming up the channel between the mainland and the barrier islands off the coasts of Mississippi and Alabama, the boat ran out of drinking water. The men aboard brought out their oilcloth rain blankets and caught rainwater to fill canteens and buckets. For fear of running aground on some sand bar or in shallow water, the *Tamaulipas* dropped anchor every night. Meeting one of Admiral Farragut's gunboats as they neared the northwest end of

Sixteen. Reorganization and Action at Mobile Bay

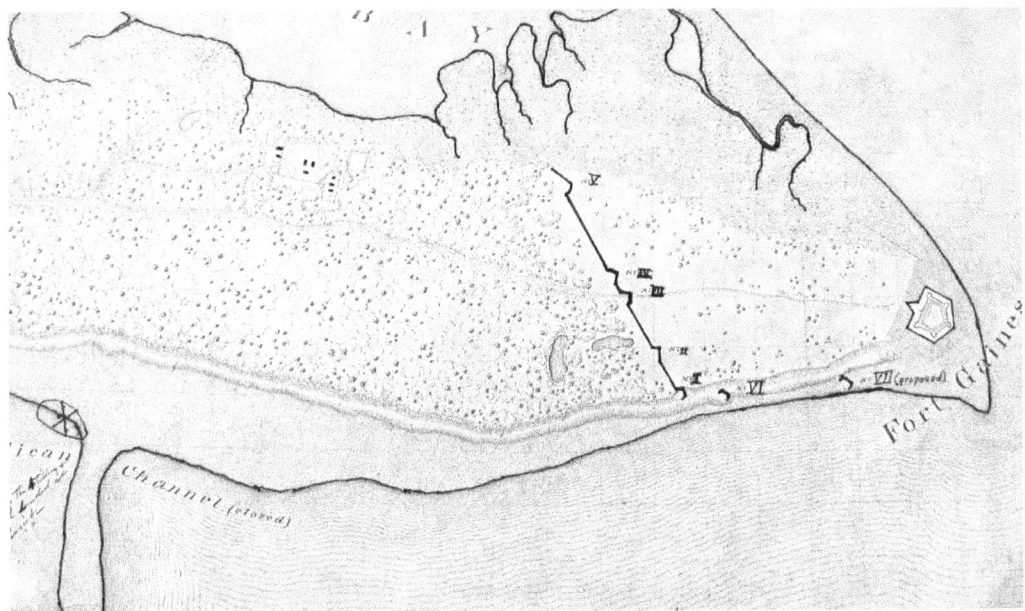

Dauphine Island, Alabama. Fort Gaines is at the right end of the image. Left of the fort and at points along the beach are the Federal artillery and infantry positions. Pelican Point (now Pelican Island) is the land jutting downward into the Gulf of Mexico at the bottom left. (Detail from map at National Archives, RG 77–121–5.)

Dauphin Island, the *Tamaulipas* dropped anchor for several hours as other transports arrived. Many of the men aboard the *Tamaulipas* took the opportunity to go swimming and have a bath. Rebel newspapers gave little chance for Federal success in this expedition or campaign. They felt Admiral Farragut may be dangerous, but as for General Canby the *Richmond Whig* wrote: "What we learn is by no means as well fitted for the conduct of siege operations as General Gilmore. General Canby is a mere routine soldier, entirely without the knowledge of artillery, fearful of responsibility, and, at bottom, a man of slow, shallow intellect."

Canby knew how to command and placed the expedition into the capable hands of Major-General Gordon Granger. The evening of August 4, the little fleet with infantry and light artillery steamed ahead to land on the north side of Dauphin Island out of range of the guns in Fort Powell, an earthen fort located on a mud island toward the Alabama mainland side of the channel. Naturally, a squall blew in as the infantry off-loaded into rowboats to make their landing. Under oar power the little boats bobbed and rolled around in the choppy water until they grounded a few yards from the shore. Then the infantrymen jumped into the water and waded ashore. A light artillery battery experienced a similar process in getting ashore. The next morning found the heavy artillerists still aboard ship and staring at Confederate Fort Powell. In the morning's light, the Hoosiers watched the gunboats lob an occasional shell at the fort, and the infantry march off the beach heading east as they disappeared into palmettos, pines and brush.[8]

The transport raised anchor and steamed around the island's west end and headed east. The steamer stopped just off the rear of Pelican Island. (Sometimes the island is a sand peninsula jutting from the south shore of Dauphin Island, depending upon storm tides and currents.)

The *Tamaulipas* pushed a barge lashed to its bow until the barge grounded about fifteen or twenty feet from the shore and dropped anchors at the bow and stern. With the help of a

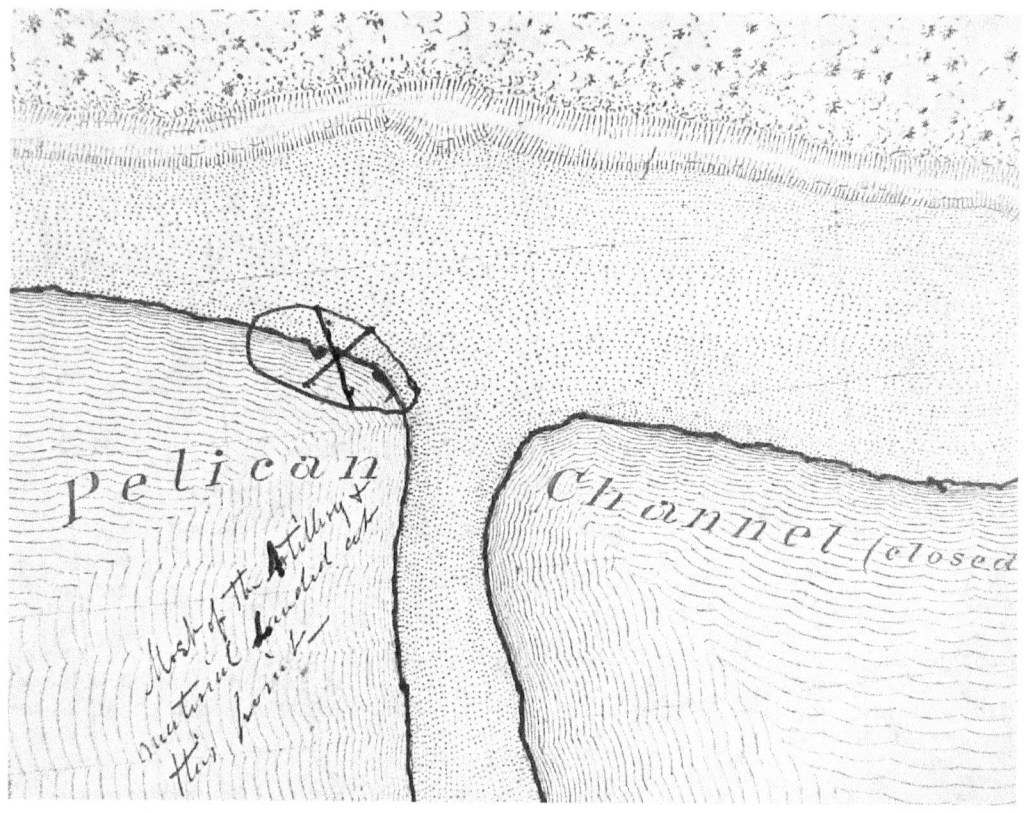

Close up of Pelican Point (now Pelican Island). Most of the Federal artillery, materials and munitions landed here and moved overland through the sand to the assault positions on map 58. (Detail from map at National Archives, RG 77–121–5.)

small boat the bully boys carried a rope to the shore and made it fast to a tree. Then by fastening the ship-end or barge-end of the line to a hawser (a thick heavy rope), they pulled the hawser to shore and fastened it to the same tree. Several of the men now climbed hand over hand, monkey style, along the rope from ship to shore. The boys strung additional hawsers from barge and ship to shore. By using a system of ropes, pulleys and rollers, they hauled their four two-ton rifle barrels suspended from the navy's hawsers to the barge and then to shore. Then the gun carriages followed using the same system. Next, they worked the ammunition and equipment ashore on swings hung from the hawsers. The mules brayed loudly as they swung from booms lowering them to the water to swim ashore. After working several hours in waist-deep water and waves breaking over their heads, the boys got their equipment, guns and mules off the ship and barge onto dry land by sundown. Company H had coffee on the beach, and then they worked for four to five hours moving two of their guns through more than 2 miles of soft sand along the beach next to the sub-tropical growth-lined inner part of the island. At midnight they arrived at a position about 1,200 yards from Fort Gaines dug in the dune line between the beach and scrub forest.[9]

While the offloading of the heavy artillery was going on, a much larger show took place to the east of their position. Admiral David G. Farragut ordered his fleet to proceed into the lion's mouth of Mobile Pass to occupy the bay. In a double line of seven sloops of war each with another ship lashed to their sides in the left line and four ironclad turreted monitors in the right line, Farragut's fleet steamed into the bay.

The ironclad monitor USS *Tecumseh* became the first and only victim of the bay's defenses. The monitor veered off course to the right to go straight at the ironclad CSS *Tennessee*. The *Tecumseh* hit two torpedoes (mines) and went to the bottom with her captain and 170 crewmen. Aboard Farragut's flagship, the *Harford*, the sailors could hear the clicking of firing mechanisms on defective mines as she passed over them. Farragut, standing in the rigging, yelled his famous words: "Damn the torpedoes, full speed ahead!" Fort Morgan and its water battery blazed away at the passing fleet; the ironclad CSS *Tennessee*, lightly armored gunboats *Gaines*, *Morgan* and *Selma* sent their shotted greetings to the Yankee vessels entering the bay. The propeller driven USS *Oneida* had both of its boilers punctured by Confederate shot and was out of combat

As the Federal vessels got out of range of Fort Morgan's main batteries, the wooden vessels cut loose from each other. A brawl on water soon ensued between the Federal and Confederate vessels. In this uneven fight (seventeen Federal ships against four Confederate vessels) the *Tennessee* valiantly stood her ground while as many as seven or eight ships surrounded and attacked her at a time. She gave better than she received in that she did more damage to the U.S. Navy than did all the guns in Fort Morgan. Finally after an hour or more of fighting, having her rudder chains blown apart and her tiller shaft (stern-post) shot off rendering her unable to maneuver, a cannon shot from about fifteen yards away entered one of the *Tennessee*'s open gun-ports and tore off one of Admiral Buchannan's legs. The CSS *Tennessee* surrendered. This humanitarian act was at odds with Admiral Buchannan's orders to "Sink her, but never give her up." Captain Johnson wishing to preserve her crew and to save the badly bleeding admiral's life surrendered the battered *Tennessee*.

The U.S. Navy chased the CSS *Selma* into shallow water near Navy Cove and she surrendered. Intense cannon fire disabled the CSS *Gaines*, and she ran aground on Mobile Point protected by the guns of Fort Morgan and got her crew onto shore as she sank into the shallow water. The CSS *Morgan*, supported by the guns of Fort Morgan, fought until dark and then ran without lights up the bay for Mobile and escaped. Admiral Farragut's fleet controlled the inner bay. Now he needed to wait until the army captured the forts on Dauphin Island and Mobile Point, Alabama, to fully cut off supplies entering the Confederacy from abroad.[10]

Back on Dauphin Island, the 67th Indiana and the 5th Iowa Infantry had been at work digging a gun emplacement for the Parrott rifles at the south end of their infantry trench. It was a welcome relief to the Hoosier artillerymen to finally get two of their guns into it. They promptly fell asleep and slept until well after the sun was up the next morning. Their supplies came up while rebel sharpshooters' bullets dug into the sand around them making Company H's boys kept their heads down. After a hardtack breakfast, they dug a little deeper, until they could get a lot of sand piled in front reinforced by a stacked-log backing. They then built a proper magazine and cut firing embrasures. The Federal infantry had good positions on the Hoosiers' left and returned rifle fire at the fort. However, the Rebel sharpshooters kept on firing from behind sandbags atop the fort's parapet and through rifle ports in the fort's brick walls. The Federals often heard the whine of bullets passing over their heads.

A Federal light artillery battery opened on the fort with six 3-inch Ordnance rifles. Navy gunboats having scared the commander of Fort Powell into blowing up his magazine and abandoning the fort began shelling Fort Gaines from the rear with impunity. The heavy guns atop Fort Gaines had little protection and between the gunboats and the light battery were silenced by the 7th of August. On the 7th the Heavies opened fire. They had fired one shot from their guns when orders came to cease fire. After Major-General Gordon Granger and Admiral David Farragut finished arguing over who should receive the official surrender, Farragut accepted Fort Gaines surrender honors from Colonel C.D. Anderson, commander of Fort Gaines, at 10 A.M. on the 8th. With surrender of the fort, about 800 men (including boy

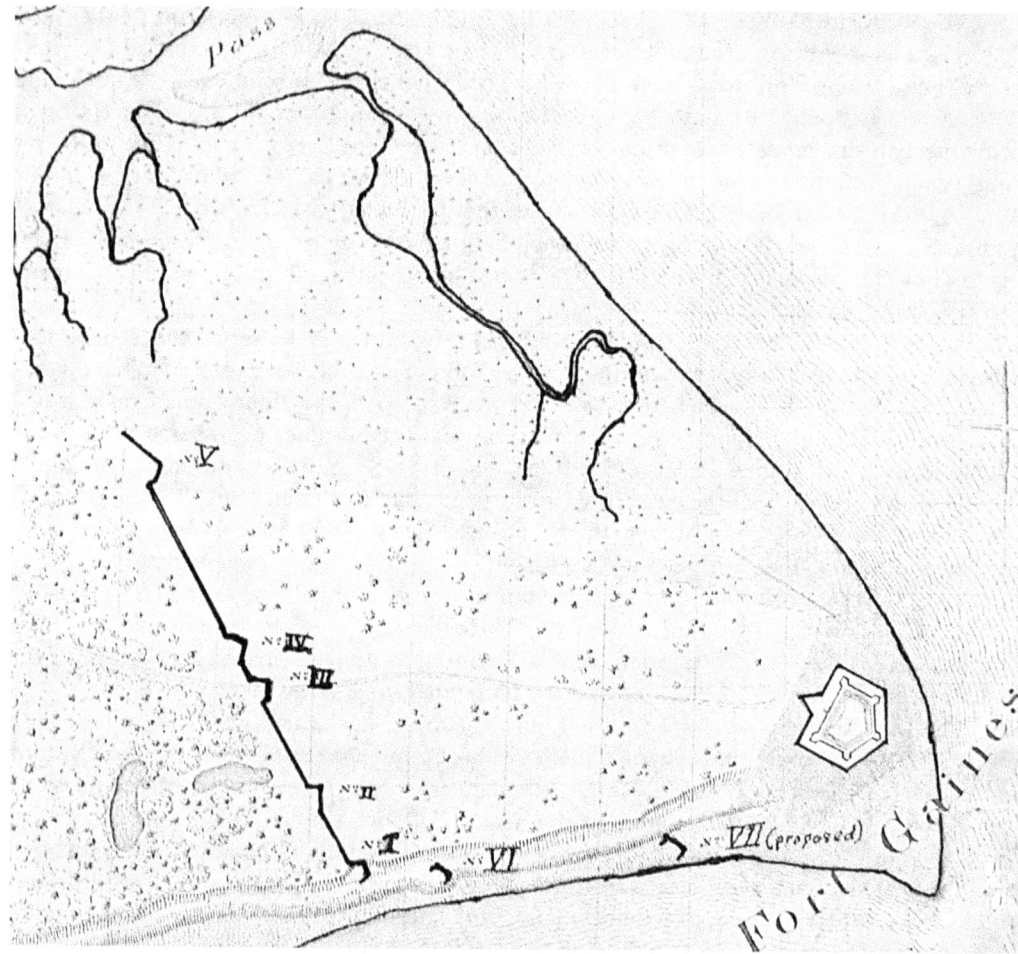

Close up of Federal siege lines before Fort Gaines on Dauphine Island. (Detail from map at National Archives, RG 77–121–5.)

cadets from Mobile) and 46 officers became prisoners of war. Four 10-inch Columbiad cannons, two 7-inch Brooke rifles, twelve or fifteen 24- and 32-pounders (some rifled but not reinforced), five or six 24-pounder flank-defense howitzers, ammunition and rations for two to six months fell into Federal hands.

(Colonel Anderson received severe criticism from Confederate officers stationed at various points around Mobile Bay. Especially angry at Anderson was General Page, commander of Fort Morgan and environs, who accused Anderson of violating a superior officer's direct orders. In Richmond, Virginia, a newspaper article about the fall of Fort Gaines called its commander a traitor. A court-martial was ordered. However, on March 14, 1865, as the Confederate High Command debated the fate of Colonel Anderson, a letter from an imprisoned soldier captured at Fort Gaines, which outlined facts of the situation that had hitherto been unknown, was published in a Richmond newspaper. Among the details of the letter as to the indefensibility of Fort Gaines was a petition to Colonel Anderson signed by forty-two subordinate officers on August 6, 1864, urging the surrender of the fort to the Federals lest the broadsides of the Federal fleet and army cannons surrounding them completely destroy the fort and kill all within, including the boy cadets from Mobile.)

Later that day, the boys of Company H joyously marched into the fort and shot a national salute of thirty-five guns—bragging that they used Rebel cannon filled with Rebel powder. They then moved into wooden Rebel barracks outside the fort a few yards to the northwest of it, where they sat in Rebel chairs, slept in Rebel beds and ate Rebel food. Rufus Dooley described Fort Gaines as "the best little fort I ever saw." Among the captured foodstuffs were large stores of corn meal and bacon. It did not take the men long to cook a hot meal of bacon slabs and cornbread baked in the fort's ovens.[11]

While Company H was enjoying some action, the other companies in Louisiana were suffering from the usual garrison boredom. Seven officers were under arrest at Baton Rouge and confined to the guard house. One of them, Captain John Day, was to appear before a court-martial on the charges of embezzlement and fraud, which seemed to please Major James Grimsley that his enemy was in trouble; on the other hand, he asked his wife to tell no one about the charges, especially Day's wife, because Captain Day had not told her about his arrest. (Day was exonerated.)

Several officers, like the enlisted men, had not reenlisted. Majors Grimsley and McLaflin would take their veterans' furlough and then not reenlist. They were advised that their receipt of the benefits of furlough constituted acceptance of a full term reenlistment. Also, they were advised of a recent War Department order that prohibited officers from mustering out, but they would be allowed to resign their commissions. However, General Canby issued an order in August that would allow officers having served three years to resign or be mustered out. Majors Grimsley and McLaflin promptly mustered out. They would be replaced within two months by Majors John W. Day (formerly captain of Company B) and James W. Connelly (formerly captain of Company H). Other officers who left the First Indiana Heavy Artillery that summer were Captain William S. Hinkle, Company D, discharged; Capt. James W. Hamrick, Company E, honorably discharged; Captain Francis W. Noblet, Company F, discharged; and Captain Clayton Cox, Company K, mustered out.[12]

Many of the non-veterans who were mustered out and a ship's guard detail drawn from the garrison troops saw more action on the transport steamer *Empress*' return trip to Indiana than they had in the previous eight months in the Department of the Gulf. At Gaines' Landing near the junction of the White River with the Mississippi River in Arkansas, an eight gun Confederate artillery battery with infantry support opened fire upon the steamer *Empress* on August 10. Five hundred passengers, including two hundred discharged soldiers and sixty women and children were aboard. Sixty-three cannonballs and shells punctured the vessel killing five persons, including the steamer's captain, and severely injuring nine others. Four of the casualties among the Jackass Regiment were: Private Cornelius Kinney, on active duty with Company M, "died"; 2nd Lieutenant Joseph Siddons of Company E, "killed on steamer *Empress*," William H. Anderson II, formerly of Company B, "severely wounded and given up"; and Greenup Gott, formerly of Company D, "fractured radius and ulna, right arm." Several ladies on board the boat tended the wounded, and their prompt attention and ministrations very likely saved several lives among the passengers (civilian and military).[13]

On August 9, Federal engineers and 2,000 soldiers arrived on the northern shore of Mobile Point. A reconnaissance quickly discovered a deserted line of excellent Rebel entrenchments stretching across the peninsula of Mobile Point. The engineers had put infantrymen to work moving the raised breastworks on the east side of the trenches to the west side making a fighting parallel against the fort. Then they began work on adding gun emplacements along the line facing the fort. The diggers then dug an approach toward the fort along points A to A. Then they turned northward and dug a parallel from points B to B on the map. Next, the engineers added gun emplacements north of shoreline B and at the railroad. Next they began extending the approaches on both the north shore and south shores from C to C.

Company H came across the bay on a barge from Ft. Gaines on the 12th. At noon their barge grounded at low tide about 100 yards from shore near Pilot Cove (not shown on the map). While waiting for high tide to move their equipment laden barge closer to shore, they rowed ashore in small boats and began work building a short pier out to where they hoped the high tide would float their full and heavy barge. They cooked and ate a good dinner and went to sleep until the high tide would come in about 2 o'clock the next morning. The anticipated high tide did not help them much. It took two more hours of hard work in calm waist deep water to move the barge to the wharf. The Hoosiers got their guns ashore at sunrise.

The waterlogged artillerists ate a hearty breakfast of hardtack and lots of coffee. No time to rest after eating this time. The teamsters brought the mule teams into place, hitched up the guns and supply wagons and moved off toward Fort Morgan. The artillerists followed in the wake of their guns along A to A until they arrived at a prepared emplacement between 1,400 to 1,500 yards distant from the fort's ramparts about 100 yards north of map position B along the south beach where they mounted a section of two Parrott rifles. Then the other section moved on up B to B into a position alongside a railroad near the center of the peninsula.

The guns by the railroad were among low sand dunes. The guns near to the shore were dug into the main dune line, which at that point was between fifteen to twenty-five feet high. The tired Hoosier artillerists began work constructing firing platforms from split logs on the floor of their emplacements. By sunset, the emplacements were complete and the guns properly positioned. Now that they had burrowed deeply into the dune, they slept soundly in spite of Rebel sharpshooters' bullets zipping overhead. Two 9-inch Dahlgren guns borrowed from the navy came ashore in scows, hidden from the fort by sand dunes on the northern shore. They would have to wait a couple of days before taking position in emplacements under construction along the north shore of approach B to B. A mortar battery outside the dune line on the south beach between B and C would be occupied by four mortars, currently being moved into position, but without gun crews. The 2nd Illinois Heavy Artillery Company A moved their four 30-pounder Parrotts into a battery position 250 yards north of the railroad where B to B turned into an approach rather a parallel.

On August 13, Major-General Canby issued Special Order #72 ordering Companies B and F to report the next day to Lakeport Landing. Company L received orders to take 30 men to Forts Jackson and St. Philip and remove all the 30-pounder Parrott rifles, siege carriages, implements and equipments complete, but they did not go anywhere. Companies B, F and K with their guns, equipment and mules boarded steamers bound for Mobile Point.

The morning of the 16th, the Hoosiers from Companies B, F and K arrived at Navy Cove wharf on Mobile Point and unloaded their artillery pieces and equipment at the wharf. Company B received four 10-inch mortars; Company F received two 8-inch and two 10-inch mortars and Company K received four 10-inch mortars. These batteries would be emplaced along a line about 700 to 900 yards away from Ft. Morgan. Two additional two-gun batteries of 10-inch mortars were manned by men from the 38th Iowa.[14]

The day before, on the 15th, the Navy's three remaining monitors took positions in the bay off the northern shore of Dauphin Point opposite Fort Morgan. The monitors and some light artillery batteries on shore had opened fire against the fort at thirty-minute intervals. One of the USS *Manhattan's* 15-inch shells skimmed the fort's glacis and dropped enough to penetrate a flank casemate and explode within it. The casemate was used as living quarters by some of the 1st Tennessee Heavy Artillery. Fortunately, the Tennesseans had vacated the casemate, but its flank defense howitzers were dismounted. One of Company H's batteries opened fire at the fort to try the range and elevation, then ceased firing.

On the 16th the two 30-pounder batteries of Company H opened fire against Fort Mor-

Sixteen. Reorganization and Action at Mobile Bay

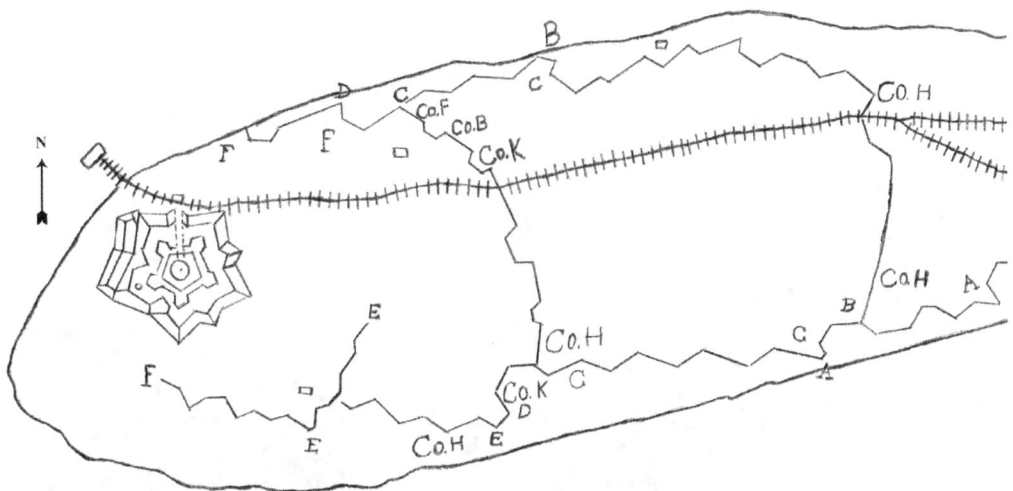

Map of the Siege of Fort Morgan. (Sketched by Bonnie Faller and the author based upon maps in the National Archives, Record Group 77-F-82.)

gan about one o'clock in the afternoon. Prior to that time, the only firing that day was between sharpshooters on both sides. By 2 P.M. the mortars and light artillery opened on the fort. All guns tried to dismount the exposed cannons in the fort. The fort's cannons were mounted on barbette carriages and fired over the top of the fort's walls and not through protective embrasures. Sand bags piled atop the walls protected the cannons and their crews from rifle fire.

Field officers studied the effects of the firing as they debated where to better place the 30-pounders, mortars and light guns. Also, they were determining the feasibility of advancing infantry to form an advanced sharpshooting line against the fort. During the day's bombardment, a lookout on the fort's rampart called out the direction of the incoming rounds so that those nearby and below would know when to duck and run. He had just shouted "Look out below!" when a 30-pounder shell tore off his head and shoulders. The 30-pounder shells hitting the bastion holding two heavy guns caused enough damage that the Rebel artillerists felt that much more similar firing would breach their wall. The Federal artillery fire filled the air with shrieking shells, which limited the Rebel artillery's return fire.

The Federal officers reached their decision and the infantry received orders to move forward. Advancing in groups of three with one man carrying a wooden box about eight inches by four inches at one end and tapering to four by four inches at the other end, and two men carrying two sand bags and a shovel, they ran forward to about 700 to 900 yards from Fort Morgan. At this distance the infantrymen stacked the sand bags in their front and dug furiously into the sand. In five minutes they were deep in the sand. During the infantry advance, the fort's guns changed from counter-battery fire to shelling the hell out of the charging infantry. Because the infantrymen had not advanced in line or column formation, but instead at a dead run with every trio for itself, their casualties were far less than normal. The infantrymen placed their boxes with the four by eight opening toward the fort and covered it with sandbags and piled additional sand on top of it making a sharpshooter's rifle pit. Then the infantrymen began digging trenches toward each other

That night's sleep was disturbed by the fort's artillery fire at Federal artillery emplacements. In turn Company H returned the fort's fire to disturb the Rebels' sleep. During the

S.E. bastion of Fort Morgan. The rebel cannon is a 42-pounder (7-inch) naval gun. Note the heavy hawser rope wrapped around the breech of the cannon. This rope served as a makeshift mantlet to protect the gun's crew. (The Federal tents in the background were not pitched there until after the fort surrendered.) (National Archives, RG 77-F-82-69.)

night several artillerists atop the fort's walls and bastions facing the landward side wrapped heavy hawser rope around the chase of their cannons to form a mantelet ring to protect the gunners from sharpshooter's bullets.

The veterans of the Port Hudson siege were not too bothered by this harassing exchange, but the inexperienced recruits looked about in wonder of what would happen next. The old hands played upon the fears of the "greener than owl-shit" recruits, but the new men quickly learned to keep their heads and rear ends down. Company H maintained its fire from its positions over the next five days, and it disabled at least three of the barbette mounted guns atop the walls of Fort Morgan eight-tenths of a mile distant.[15]

By now Federal artillery fire and incendiaries had reduced the fort's outbuildings, including two hospitals and the main supply depot, to ashes and cinders. Some of the fort's barbette guns had been dismounted but few disabled. At night the defenders remounted the guns. The fort's parapets began showing their vulnerability to rifled cannon and larger than basketball-sized round naval shot.

The Federals established supply depots by the landing and immediately to the rear of their lines in the former Confederate Eastern Battery and Battery Bragg near the gulf shore. Navy scows could bring supplies up to the shore line where the dunes hid them from the fort's guns. Supply lines pushed forward along C to C on each side connecting to the entrenchments begun by the infantry on the 16th at D to D. Extension trenches and covered ways advanced from E to E on the south and F to F on the north. Then work began on an approach to the fort and a small fortified sally port in its south side at E to F. The small door in the sally port allowed the men to exit the fort at night to bathe in the Gulf of Mexico and to tend to nearby outbuildings. (During the siege there were almost daily rainstorms that allowed fresh water to be easily obtained from cisterns in and near the fort. The rain also obscured the defenders' outdoor activities.)

On August 17, the battery position at the rear of the north approach was finished and received two 9-inch Dahlgren guns. All gun positions from C to C were completed and had cannons mounted therein. The Federal engineering headquarters and ordnance depot were along the rear end of the north approach, hidden behind tall sand dunes. On August 18, the engineers and digging infantrymen partially completed the fourth parallel from E to E to connect with the sharpshooters. The engineers then scouted ahead for the location of an emplacement for a western trench to house two light 12-pounder Napoleons at F on the south shore. Construction began on a mortar battery emplacement at D on the south shore. Platforms for twelve mortars were completed at south C and between north C and the railroad. Companies B, F and K of the Jackass Regiment took position in their assigned mortar batteries between north C and the railroad. Company B manned four 10-inch mortars, Company F manned two 8-inch and two 10-inch mortars and Company K manned two 10-inch mortars by the railroad and two 8-inch mortars on the south shore near D. Additional lumber for more magazines and emplacements came up on a navy scow that night.

On August 19, construction began for batteries at E and F on the south shore for two 3-inch rifles and two light 12-pounders, respectively. Near E and on the parallel above D on the south shore positions were plotted for 30-pounder Parrotts to be occupied by Company H. These positions were the most exposed to Rebel sharpshooters.[16]

The artillerists received orders to refrain from targeting the lighthouse on the opposite side of Fort Morgan. Some of the bully boys in Company H took exception to this order but did not say anything about it within their officers' hearing. They knew that Rebel spotters with binoculars or telescopes looked out over the fort from the lighthouse to direct the fort's artillery fire at opportune targets, and that a couple of sharpshooters always fired from the top of it.

While the officers were away attending to other matters, Frank Abbot accepted the order as a personal challenge. On the fort's eastern parapet, a rifled cannon stood in line with the lighthouse. Abbott adjusted his sights, adjusted the trail of the rifle and fired; Abbott's 30-pounder shell flew over the fort's parapet missing the cannon and by chance put a hole in the lighthouse. The other gunner in the battery copied Abbott's success and made bricks fly from the lighthouse until Captain Connelly returned from headquarters. All the fun stopped immediately as the captain chewed out the gunners up one side and down the other for their poor aim in taking out the enemy cannon atop Fort Morgan's parapet. The navy's officers as well as the army's general and field officers all saw the need for an intact and usable lighthouse to guide ships and transport vessels through the mouth of the bay, even if the Hoosier gunners did not quite grasp the concept.

A heavy storm rolled in late on the 19th and continued through the 20th nearly stopping work on the trenches and advanced emplacements. The ditches retained water in a few places making transport and work in those areas difficult but not impossible. The artillerists sheltered from the rain under canvas awnings or in tents pitched in the emplacement, if the emplacement was large enough. Otherwise, they ducked behind a nearby sand dune and put up tents. All of the Federal heavy batteries were manned and ready to fire.

On the morning of August 21, the Rebel cannons began roaring forth grapeshot, canister and shells in all directions at the advancing trenches and batteries. In an ironic twist, the newly repaired Federal USS *Tennessee* test fired her 7-inch rifles at the fort she had fought to protect less than two weeks earlier. The navy's monitors also replied to the fort's challenge. The federal batteries commenced returning fire and an exchange of shot and shell kept up for more than two hours until the fort quit firing.

During the day's firing an 8-inch shell from one of the fort's Blakely Rifles penetrated the sand and wood of one of Company H's emplacements and spewed sand over the men as it plowed under the muzzle of a Parrott rifle. The sand-covered Parrott's crew froze as they watched the sputtering fuse, which ceased sputtering. Expecting to be blown to kingdom come and their eyes wide with fear, the crewmen waited, waited and then exhaled. No explosion. The crew went back to work stepping easily to avoid the shell that they later removed. After the cannons ceased firing, only the sharpshooters kept busy at each other for the rest of the day. The artillerists rested under their tent shelters. The defenders could not stop the advance of the Federal trench approaches toward the walls of the fort.[17]

At 5:00 A.M. on the 22nd, the fort's defenders had their worst fears come true. The Federal artillery opened upon them with a devastating fire from

Fort Morgan (Mobile Point) Lighthouse after the fall of Fort Morgan. (National Archives, RG 77-F-82-59.)

eight 30-pounder Parrotts, four 9-inch Dahlgrens, twelve 10-inch mortars, four 8-inch mortars, two 3-inch Ordnance rifles, and four 12-pounder Napoleons. The navy's monitors and the USS *Tennessee* at about 1,100 yards north of the fort and the rest of the Farragut's fleet at about 1,800 yards out joined in the bombardment. The naval ammunition ranged in size from 7-inch Brooke rifles to 15-inch smoothbore Dahlgren guns. The concussion from the exploding shells and the pounding recoil from the army's guns made the very sand of the peninsula dance across it from the Gulf of Mexico to Mobile Bay. The mortars maintained their fire for twenty-five hours and forty minutes with nearly 90 percent of their missiles landing in or on the fort's walls. Observers reported seeing six mortar shells arcing towards the fort at the same time. The mortar batteries of the Jackass Regiment fired 779 mortar shells at the fort, and better than 93 percent of the shells fell inside the fort; this was very good shooting for anyone and especially for the Hoosiers due to their limited practice with mortars.

By noon on the 22nd, Company H had fired 200 rounds when they were ordered to change their positions to two new and much closer positions located about 300 to 500 yards from Fort Morgan's ramparts near E and north of C. Upon arriving, they found the engineers had not fully completed the breastworks. The boys settled down behind a sand hill to wait until they could move in. The sun had set before the emplacement's embrasures were ready. As the artillerists moved their Long Toms into their new positions, they watched the arcing trails of fire from the mortar fuses ascending and then descending on the fort.

The burning fuses from all the types of shells flying through the night sky made "brilliant fireworks never to be forgotten." Against that backdrop, flames began licking into the air from the middle of the fort. The flames grew into a gusher of fire, described as "the most beautiful sight ... the mortar shells had set something on fire in the fort which made a terrible light!" The light came from the burning three-story barracks or citadel in the center of the fort. The occupants of the fort sheltered in the bombproofs away from the flames and some brave souls tossed barrel after barrel of gunpowder into a water-filled cistern to keep from being blown up. About midnight the fort fired off signal rockets in a series of red, white and red — a distress call! The land batteries increased their efforts at this sight, and the roar of the flames and the thunder of the guns again shook the sand to the water's edge.[18]

The Rebel artillery hardly had been able to return any fire at all during this tremendous battering. Since most of the landward pointing guns within the fort were mounted en barbette and only protected by a low brick wall and sandbags, it was almost certain death to man them in such an exposed position especially being backlit by the burning citadel. In addition, several of the Rebel guns were disabled or dismounted and could not shoot at anything. The boys in Company H had, after the novelty of the fire wore off, slept until sunup on the 23rd. As the sun rose, so did the boys in Company H. The army and navy cannonade against the fort continued; so, the Hoosiers loaded and sighted their Parrotts on their targets and opened fire. The Parrotts had let fly with only nine rounds when a small towel-sized white flag went up in the fort. The Hoosiers sent up a wild yell at the sight. Captain Connelly told his bully boys that if that little flag was all the better the Rebels could do, they could give them another round. The sanguine Hoosiers promptly obeyed the command. In a minute a large white sheet or tent-half rose up the pole. The bombardment had lasted for twenty-six hours.

The surrender of the fort being formalized at two in the afternoon on the 23rd of August, the victorious artillerists would enter the fort that afternoon and help with the prisoners. The Indiana Jackass Regiment's men had many remarks called to them by the Confederate sharpshooters and pickets about the jackasses used to haul their heavy guns. The Rebel's favorite taunt was in comparing the likeness of the Hoosiers to their mules — either end. The length of the animal's ears compared to the men's ears was a favorite jibe. Now the boys of Company H returned the jibes as they mounted guard over 500 prisoners assigned to their care.

East Wall of Fort Morgan showing the effects of cannon fire in vertical lines used to cut away the bricks to cause their collapse and expose the interior to direct fire. (National Archives, RG 77-F-82-64.)

The sad prisoners looked more bedraggled than the Hoosiers' asses. The bantering participants all took it in a good-humor.[19]

With the fort and its garrison secure, it was time to move the camps closer to the fort. They accomplished the move within a day or two. Shortly, the men would begin constructing wooden cabins or barracks around the fort to house the troops left to garrison the fort. When not guarding the prisoners, the artillerists and soldiers explored the fort and examined the effect of their handiwork. Photographers from New Orleans arrived to take photographs of the damage. The fort had been extensively damaged by the artillery bombardment not only on the exterior, but also on the interior. The three story citadel (main barracks) in the center of the fort was a fire-gutted ruin, and falling pieces from it kept men dodging them. The conquerors began tearing down the hazardous remains. Not five square feet of the walls existed that did not show the effect of a cannon hit. At least twelve of the barbette guns were disabled, some having had their trunnions knocked off and carriages broken to pieces by the 30-pounder Parrotts. Many of the guns in the fort had been dismounted by the shot and shell fired by the besiegers. Like soldiers everywhere, the Hoosier Heavies picked up souvenirs and trophies from their battle. One such trophy was a ring that someone had made, perhaps for a wife or sweetheart, but it found its way north to Rufus Dooley's "Martha."[20]

Company B received orders to turn its mortars over to the post ordnance officer on the last day of August 1864. On September 1, the First Indiana Heavy Artillery received a commendation from the chief of artillery for their superior performance at the siege of Fort Morgan. It read in part: "Although entirely uninstructed in the use of mortars, through the high order of intelligence of the men, and the interest and intelligence on the part of the officers, coupled with the personal instruction of the officers on my staff, they seem to have acquired

Photograph of Fort Morgan showing the rear of the northeast bastion, the north curtain wall and the main entrance from the north. All of this is protected by a high earthen wall upon which the photographer took this photograph. Please note the Jackass Regiment's parked mortars in the ditch, next to the bastion's wall. Also, there are a few glancing artillery pockmarks on the wall. There were no good direct points of fire at this wall from the army's guns. (National Archives, RG 77-F-82-63.)

a perfect knowledge of the use of the mortar, which accuracy of their fire, during the bombardment, most conclusively proves. Captain Connelly, commanding Company H, 1st Indiana Heavy Artillery, exhibited the same skill and accuracy in the handling of his Company, which characterized him at Port Hudson, and is deserving of special mention for his services." After receiving their commendation, they received orders to move to New Orleans.[21]

Seventeen

New Orleans. Garrison Life. Mobile Campaign!

On September 1, the Hoosier artillerists took their siege guns and equipment, except for eight 10-inch mortars of the old pattern, and returned to New Orleans. They left the old 10-inch mortars behind in care of the ordnance officer at Fort Morgan. This meant that the battalion returned with four 30-pounder Parrotts, two 8-inch mortars, and two 10-inch mortars. They also displayed a captured battle flag of the First Alabama Artillery among their souvenirs. (Three companies of the 1st Alabama Infantry-1st Alabama Heavy Artillery were at Fort Gaines. Men from four companies of the First Battalion, Alabama Artillery, were at Fort Morgan.) Company A of the 2nd Illinois returned with the Hoosiers, and upon arrival at New Orleans, they were ordered to keep their draft-animals and harness, but to turn over their four 30-pounder Parrotts to Company K of the 1st Indiana. Company M, which had remained behind in New Orleans, was ordered to draw four 30-pounder Parrotts and harness for its mules and then wait for further orders. In the meantime, the dirty, weary veterans of Fort Morgan went into quarters in the Steam Cotton Press #2. They took baths and put on clean, sand-less uniforms, looking forward to some relaxing time in the city. Because officers had orders to confiscate or destroy any and all civilian clothing found in camp or garrison, the men had to wear uniforms in or out of garrison or camp.

Rufus Dooley received a letter from William Phillips at Baton Rouge telling him that Rufus' brother Atelus "Tell" Dooley had died of a fever in the Baton Rouge hospital and that he had gotten head and foot boards for his grave. Rufus wrote to his mother promising he would collect on all of the notes his brother had held on small loans that he had made to other members of the company, but the collection would have to wait until the next payday. Among the notes was one on his "pard," Sergeant Yelton. The notes were not much, but they would provide a little relief for Tell's widow and two children.[1]

Anticipations of duty in the form of various regimental orders kept the men enthused for a while after their arrival back in New Orleans. In September, Company L received orders to turn over two 30-pounder Parrotts with complete implements to Company F; Company H received orders to turn over two 30-pounder Parrotts to Company F with all implements; Company F received eighty brand new Springfield rifles with full accoutrements; Companies B and H were ordered to turn in all of their Merrill rifles and Merrill accoutrements and receive eighty brand-new Springfield rifles with full accoutrements for each company. Then on October 4, the regiment received orders to have nine companies fully equipped for effective siege and field purposes; therefore, the regimental commander drew up artillery assignments as follows: Company A, four 20-pounder Parrotts, Company B, four 8-inch & four

10-inch mortars, Company C, four 8-inch siege howitzers, Company F, four 30-pounder Parrotts, Company G, four 30-pounder Parrotts, Company H, four 30-pounder Parrotts, Company K, four 30-pounder Parrotts, Company L, four 30-pounder Parrotts, and Company M, four 30-pounder Parrotts.

The companies were to be so equipped without delay, and only the very finest draft animals would be selected for the companies. This news lifted the men's spirits as they anticipated action. They now had the finest of equipment, the finest mules, finest harness and were thoroughly drilled, but they did not move out as anticipated. They remained impoverished, bored, depressed, and garrisoned in New Orleans. No pay had come for six months. Enlisted men commonly exchanged personal notes for cash to those (usually officers) who had it.

Without any money, the few free attractions and observances drew the comrades' attention. Church services occupied many of the men on Sunday, Tuesday and Friday nights. An unnamed brigadier general preached on many Sundays and became the men's favorite speaker. Political rallies attracted a great deal of attention from the soldiers. A well attended Union Lincoln meeting was held at the Opera Hall on October 19. The orators gave political speeches for the Lincoln reelection campaign and on the deeds of Admiral Farragut, "The King of the Modern Seas." The Hoosiers noticed that the attendees consisted of men and women of all types and classes.[2]

During October the only order received was for Company A and its four 20-pounders to be placed on detached duty with instructions to travel up the Mississippi River to the mouth of the White River in Arkansas and report in to Major-General J. J. Reynolds. For the time being, it would garrison a fort guarding the mouth of White River to control Rebel shipping past that point. The reason for Company A's new assignment was due in part to Major-General E.R.S. Canby's being shot by a guerilla with a nasty sense of humor. Canby was aboard the gunboat *Cricket* near this location on October 6, when a guerilla put a rifle ball through the general's thigh, scrotum, and nicked his penis. While the wound missed the main artery in the thigh and was not mortal, it caused a terrific amount of pain, which caused the general to abort his inspection trip to Little Rock. The steamer made full speed back to New Orleans. At New Orleans, he received the best of loving, tender care from Mrs. Canby who would not allow any nurses to attend the general.

The War Department sent orders to General Canby not to move at this time against Mobile. On November 7, the War Department ordered the remaining units from the old XIX Corps in Louisiana to be officially dissolved and the units therein reorganized as the general commanding saw fit. Therefore, on November 9, Company A received an affirmation of its assignment to the White River, but reassigned to the Department of Arkansas. The official reassignment to the VII Corps, First Division, Department of Arkansas, would take place on February 3, 1865. (Unfortunately, that is the last information available on that company until the end of hostilities between North and South.) Company G at Morganza received reassignment to the Reserve Corps of the Military Division of West Mississippi.[3]

Colonel Keith returned to the regiment bringing with him bonus money for the reenlisted veterans amounting to $200.00 each. Several of the veterans expressed part of their money back home, and they asked that it be used to purchase bonds to finance the war effort. The recruits had yet to receive pay. The veterans used their money to repay debts, purchase personal items, purchase civilian style shirts for their uniforms, and gain entrance to local entertainments, such as the race track, circus, theaters, the 1,165 rum establishments, or one of several houses of ill-fame where shameless business went on day and night. Even though photography was still in its infancy, erotic photographs were available in New Orleans and many made their way north through the mail. A Massachusetts soldier mailed one to his wife in a letter telling her that he wished he was with her the way the man and girl were in the photograph. The amusement places were only open Monday through Saturday, because by official military order all amusement houses, liquor serving establishments, and gambling parlors were closed on Sunday. However, not all could enjoy the diversions, since fevers of various types were rampant, which the authorities tried to keep out of the newspapers. In early December, smallpox killed Barton Rumbaugh and James Huff of Company H.[4]

The Hoosier Heavies were again called upon to form details to act as cargo guards on various river steamboats and as prison guards on steamers to Ship Island. This desolate island made an excellent prison camp. Other details did guard duty in the city where they arrested soldiers on the streets without passes. The regimental courts-martial stayed very busy deciding absent without leave cases between January 19 and February 21, 1865. The life of a garrison soldier, even though relieved by various guard duties, was still boring; however, Company H celebrated their "Capting" being promoted to major of the regiment.

Under the impression that they had enlisted for only one year, forty or more men in Company L mutinied claiming that their enlistment time was up. The officers and guards promptly placed them under arrest and explained that they had enlisted for two years offering them proof of the enlistments, which quelled the unrest.

The Regimental Commissary Department tried to vary the menu to help the men's disposition. The Hoosiers' menu constantly changed: one week they ate hardtack, the next week fresh bread, then hardtack, and so on. One week they dined on salt horse (pickled beef) and the next on codfish. The week of codfish tested the cooks' ingenuity: fried, boiled, stewed, and codfish balls. Everyone within a couple of blocks of the camp knew what was on the menu that week by its smell. A particular delight was "Compressed Vegetables" a two-foot square by six inch thick dry mass of "almost anything that grew on land or water." They used it as a soupbase. Pickled pork and bacon completed the meat on the menu. Strangely, army hogs did not have hams or shoulders. However, the men received a supply of coffee, tea, sugar, rice, beans, potatoes, onions, cabbage, etc. Overall it was not too bad a menu, discounting a week per month of codfish and compressed vegetables.[5]

Parades and reviews were held to keep the men on their toes and occupy their time and minds. One such review took place on December 30. Dooley described it as "a long train of heavy artillery. It was led by our little Colonel [John A. Keith] who only weighs 98 pounds." The regimental parade displayed their cannons, mules and all the trappings passing by some three or four generals' headquarters, including those of Canby and Totten, who all agreed that Company H "lifted the rag from the bush." The Hoosiers held out hope that these compliments would help to get them out of New Orleans.

The regiment's favorite colonel, John A. Keith, resigned his commission due to aggravation of the severe shoulder wound he had received at the Battle of Baton Rouge on August 5, 1862. Colonel Benjamin F. Hays assumed command of the regiment.

A little scandal accompanied Colonel Keith's departure. The veterans accused him of making a fortune off of their re-enlistments. They heard that he supposedly drew $400 bounty for each reenlisted man from the state. The men were paid $200 by Colonel Keith. Since there were over 450 remaining veterans, they figured that the colonel had kept the $90,000 difference. The colonel disagreed, and publicly stated that "he obtained local bounties and credits, which, prorated among them, netted to them each $205.10; this in addition to their Government bounty, receipts from whom were taken by him in duplicate, one deposited in the office of the Adjutant General of the State, the other retained by him." This accounting seems to have squelched the scandal, because no more was heard of it. It seems that Keith had collected only the local bounties for the men. The Federal Government bounty would have to come to the men from the Federal paymaster.

February 14 was a red letter day for the comrades of the Indiana Jackass Regiment. St.

Valentine had nothing to do with making their pulses race and morale rise. Major-General E.R.S. Canby issued Special Order No. 45 relieving Companies B, C, H, I, K, L, and M from garrison duty in New Orleans and ordered them to report to General Totten, chief of artillery and ordnance, for further orders. The Jackass Regiment's colonel, Benjamin F. Hays, and his regimental staff also received orders to report to General Totten for duty with the siege train, which consisted of the above mentioned companies of the Jackass Regiment, two companies (A and K) of the 6th Michigan Heavy Artillery and the 18th New York (Mack's Black Horse) Battery.

There was no more guard duty or leisure time for the Hoosier bully boys. Another regiment was requested for guard duty in New Orleans to replace the 1st Indiana, with the stipulation that to do the job properly, it should be a large one. Evidently, the Hoosiers had performed well on guard duty even if they had not cared for it.[6]

The XIII Corps and XVI Corps had already moved to Mobile Point, Alabama. For about a week, thousands of infantrymen and light artillery came down river, took the Pontchartrain Railroad across to Lake Pontchartrain and boarded steamers bound for Mobile Point. The Jackass Regiment's siege train was to follow, but it took a while to get it all in motion. On February 17, Company B drew two 6-mule teams, wagons, harness, covers, etc. from the regimental quartermaster. On the 25th and 27th orders to company commanders requested that all personal items, surplus camp equipment and the like be boxed, properly marked and turned in to the Quartermaster Department of the Gulf for storage and take receipts for all items. The 1st Indiana's men loaded their guns, wagons, harness, mules and other equipment, plus themselves aboard six steamships and a barge. Between February 26, and March 3, the transport ships were kept busy carrying the siege train.

Just before the Heavies steamed away from New Orleans they received special orders that divided them into siege train battalions. The first battalion consisted of Companies K, L and M under command of Major James Connelly. The second battalion consisted of Companies B, C and H, under command of Major John Day.

Companies K, L and M loaded their mules aboard the steamer *Iberville*. They loaded their equipment and themselves aboard the steamer *J.D. Swaim*. Steaming from Hickock's Landing on Lake Pontchartrain on the 28th, they arrived at Dauphin Island on March 1, where they stayed until ordered out on April 1. Company I, on detached status, arrived at Dauphin Island on March 3 with the 18th New York Battery.

Companies B, C and H loaded their mules and artillery aboard a barge. The barge was constructed of two old river steamer hulls about 200 feet long spiked together and reinforced by struts and braces. A top of planks reached across the breadth and length of the hulls forming a flat platform about 100 feet wide and 200 feet long. The mules occupied the center of the barge, the guns, wagons, supplies and equipment surrounded the mules forming a fence. The men of companies B, C and H went aboard the steamer *J.M. Brown* and one other. The steamers, tied together, pulled the barge like a seagoing train. They slowly steamed to Ship Island where they anchored for the night. After spending the night aboard ship and not among the mosquitoes on the island, they steamed the next morning for Mobile Point and arrived that evening. Upon arriving, they took their camp gear and personal equipment off the ships, but the guns and ammunition remained on the barge for later offloading.[7]

The 2nd Battalion, in spite of speculation that their barge would be towed to another place, received orders to get the barge unloaded at sun-up the morning after they landed. After getting enough of their equipment unloaded to make room to get the hungry and thirsty mules off, the men hobbled the mules in pairs and brought them off in teams of six. The mules smelled food and fresh water coming from among a large group of Sibley tents housing officers. The mule teams broke free from their handlers and in spite of their hobbles, made a rush through the officer's camp. When the mules finished their dash, not a tent remained upright. The officer's camp was a mess. The Hoosiers heard the most cursing and profanity from officers and gentlemen they had heard to date. Eventually, the Hoosiers got the mules rounded up, properly fed, watered and corralled. Then the boys pitched their tents away from the officers and near to the positions they had occupied the previous August. Companies A and K from the 6th Michigan Heavy Artillery were already at Fort Morgan having become part of the fort's garrison on August 22, 1864.

The 2nd Battalion Heavy Artillery headquartered on Mobile Point at Fort Morgan. The 1st Battalion headquartered at Fort Gaines across the mouth of Mobile Bay from Fort Morgan. Three weeks of drill and more drill occupied the time of the artillerists at their two stations. When allowed, the men traveled between the two forts by way of transports ferrying supplies. Not too many made the trip because of the wet, windy weather and rough seas.[8]

On the 16th of March the XIII Corps, 3rd Division with the 2nd Division, 1st Brigade, at Dauphin Island received orders to board steamers and cross the bay to disembark at Navy Cove on Mobile Point. From there they would march to Dannelly's Mills on Fish River by following the telegraph road between Fort Morgan and Blakely. On the 17th of March, the XIII Corps, First Division, received orders to leave Dauphine Island and cross over to Mobile Point. The XVI Corps, received orders to detach a brigade from the 3rd Division and a light artillery battery to proceed from Fort Gaines by steamer directly across Mobile Bay to land and hold Cedar Point on the eastern shore. On the same day, the XVI Corps ordered each division commander to see that each division was provided with 300 spades or shovels, 300 axes and 90 picks for entrenching purposes. An extra wagon was allowed to each brigade to carry these additional tools. Each division had a company of pioneers assigned to it. Obviously, Canby was preparing to besiege the strong points on the eastern shore of Mobile Bay.

The XIII Corps' line of march took the army eastward along the Mobile Point peninsula and then north along the east shore of Mobile Bay towards Spanish Fort. The weather turned from mild to mildly nasty. Daily rain showers gained in intensity. Later in the day of the 17th, Veatch's division steamed over from Fort Gaines between gales, and it landed at Navy Cove two miles in the rear of Fort Morgan. From there Veatch followed the same route as the rest of the XIII Corps. The heavy rainfall made the marching difficult. The pioneers (engineers) were kept busy cutting trees to corduroy roads for the wagons and guns to follow. Often, they had to repeat the process in some places due to the increasing rain washing out sections of logs as marshy places became streams. Many wagons bogged down to their axles in the mud, and their teams churning the mud to pull their wagon dug themselves in up to their chests and bellies. Infantrymen came to the rescue and by using ropes pulled both team and wagon from the muck. The poor weather would delay the XIII Corps from reaching their rendezvous with the XVI Corps for several days.[9]

The main body of the XVI Corps, infantry and light batteries, received orders on the 18th to board steamers and land up the Fish River near Dannelly's Mills on the west shore of the river. At Fish River the XVI Corps would strongly fortify an area large enough for the forces to concentrate upon arrival of the XIII Corps. The XVI Corps would also construct a pontoon bridge across the river for the XIII Corps to cross over. The XVI Corps arrived at Dannelly's Mill on the 20th of March and immediately set about carrying out their orders. Meanwhile, the XIII Corps was still slogging on through the mud and muck. The wagon trains and artillery were just crossing the east fork of the Fish River at Magnolia and heading for the north fork of the river to meet the XVI Corps.

On the 21st General Canby ordered all members of the XVI Corps still at Fort Gaines, Dauphin Island and Cedar Point to board steamers bound for Fish River. After a few miles, heavy winds blew two of the transport ships ashore, and a third transport ship had both of her smokestacks blown off. The troops from the disabled vessels had to make their way as best as they could to their rendezvous sites. The turbulent weather also prevented additional transports carrying additional men, rations and wagons from leaving port to ferry these supplies to the Fish River. The next day the weather broke and the first sunshine of that month appeared. The transports steamed off for Fish River.

Unlike Banks, Canby had provided for triple lines of guards extending out from the camps. The first line was at least one mile distant with the other two inside it nearer the camp. Also infantry patrols roamed the perimeter. These precautions prevented Rebel scouts and cavalry from kidnapping the Federal skirmishers on the picket lines.

The two corps met on the 23rd, and the bands played "Oh, Ain't You Glad You're Out of the Wilderness." The tail-end of the XIII Corps took another three to four days to arrive. The first units from the XIII Corps to arrive had two days in which to dry out. The 25th saw lead elements from the XVI Corps and the rested men from the XIII Corps on the move towards Spanish Fort to rebuild bridges and guard them from being burned behind them by Rebel cavalry. A day later the army was still moving out of camp at Fish River while the last of the XIII Corps was still arriving at Fish River, resting a while and then moving on.

Canby placed his wagon trains in the center of his divisions with an infantry brigade behind and one on each side to protect the supplies from Rebel cavalry. Brigadier-General Joseph F. Knipe's cavalry division, detached from Brigadier-General George H. Thomas' Army of the Cumberland, had arrived at Navy Cove. Canby ordered the cavalry to come up as fast as they could and in no less strength than 1,500 to 2,000 strong for each column. Because of the poor roads they brought along only the supplies they absolutely needed for the fast journey. Transport steamers carried all other cavalry supplies to meet the overland cavalry expedition at Point Zeb.[10]

With the fair weather aiding them, Canby's lead elements arrived near Spanish Fort on the 26th. The officers began visually surveying the ground to locate positions for an attack against the Confederates' defenses. The army and navy secured wharves along the coast so their supplies would be delivered to them by water, rather than having to rely on the longer and more treacherous overland route.

The skirmishers of Brigadier-General Liddell, C.S.A., engaged the Federals along the last few miles to Spanish Fort. A few casualties were inflicted by both sides during the constant push forward by the Federals. The Confederate skirmishers withdrew inside of their defenses at Spanish Fort. A detachment of troops from Fort Blakely that had assisted Liddell in keeping the advancing Yankees in check returned to Blakely. As the Confederates in the Spanish Fort defenses watched the movement of the Yankees, the Federal engineers began laying out the first in a series of siege trenches opposite the Rebel lines. The pioneers began digging.

A detachment of 400 Confederates went out the next morning to determine the strength of the Federal line. With a loud yell they attacked the front of Veatch's division. They broke through the first regiment they encountered sending the Yankees running. A few yards past this point, the Rebel infantry came into easy range of the riflemen in the new breastworks and received heavy rifle fire. Forced to retreat, the Johnnies carried off their wounded through the storm of minie balls back to their fortifications. The Federals in this fracas had three men wounded. Skirmishing between full regimental sized forces occurred during the entire day along the slowly encircling siege line. The light artillery batteries were brought up and positioned opposing the Rebel fortification's strongest places. They commenced firing at Red Fort, a large redoubt in the center of the Rebel line.[11]

The men deepened their trenches and pioneers began work on digging saps from selected points toward the enemy defenses. The Yankees began building bombproof shelters of logs and piled dirt along the trenches to protect themselves from Rebel mortar fire. Pioneers constructed breastworks and magazines for the placement of the heavy artillery, which could now land at Starke's Wharf, Point Zeb or Deep Hole. The generals began sending out questions as to when the siege train would arrive.

The chief of artillery and ordnance, James Totten, at Navy Cove received orders to send a mortar battery and a 30-pounder Parrott battery to Spanish Fort. Another order received later that day requested the 8-inch howitzer battery and an additional 30-pounder battery. The whole Second Battalion, Jackass Regiment, mobilized.

Since they had remained so long at Fort Morgan, the 2nd Battalion had unloaded their guns and equipment from the barge for gunnery practice. Now they struggled in wind whipped rain to load it again. Remembering their struggle in chest deep water to unload their equipment during their landing on Dauphin Island last August, they were thankful that they had a dock from which to load the barge this time. Company C's four 8-inch siege howitzers and Company H's four 30-pounder Parrotts moved aboard the barge. The mortars of Company B plus the mules and men of Companies B, C and H went aboard the transport *Laura* and another vessel from Fort Gaines that also held Company K and its guns, etc. The barge was roped to the *Laura* and towed behind. At Fort Gaines Landing, Company I put its 30-pounder Parrotts, equipment, mules and men aboard the steamer *Iberville*. The vessels ventured out into the stormy bay, staying far enough from the shore to avoid being blown upon it, but hopefully near enough to the shore so the men and mules could swim to it if the craft should capsize.

By the 29th, they had landed at Belle Rose wharf near Point Zeb about five miles south of Spanish Fort. Companies B, H and K were ordered to unload and go ashore at once. Initially, General Canby felt the mortars would be more effective against the Rebel gunboats than the Parrott rifles, and he felt the Parrotts would be more effective against them than the howitzers. Therefore, Company C was held aboard until all of the other batteries were unloaded and moved off toward Spanish Fort.

The *Iberville* landed the next day and unloaded all of Company I; then the *Iberville* steamed back to Dauphin Island. On April 1, it picked up Company M and all of their ammunition, guns, equipment, wagons and supplies. The *Iberville* arrived at Starke's Landing later that morning. With several steamers waiting ahead of them, Company M unloaded about 4 P.M. After unloading, they reported in to Major-General Gordon Granger's headquarters.[12]

Companies H and K had previously gone to look over their position under construction on the far northern end of the siege lines near the shore of Minette Bay. Their primary task would be to keep Rebel gunboats and transports from coming down the rivers behind Spanish Fort to assist it with their heavy guns and landing men and supplies. Their secondary task was to neutralize Forts Huger and Tracy located 2,800 yards and 3,300 yards away, respectively, on marshy islands across a river behind Spanish Fort from the planned emplacement for the Hoosier's 30-pounders. (This river was called the Appalachee River as well as the Blakely River in this area on both Confederate and Federal maps. Herein it is called the Blakely River.)

Multiple rows of pilings driven into the river channels and rows of torpedoes prevented deep-draft U.S. Navy vessels from using the river. The navy tried sending vessels up the Blakely River, but a torpedo blew up the monitor *Milwaukee*. Those observing in Spanish Fort said the explosion's water and smoke obscured the gunboat for a minute like a big smudge on an artist's canvas. As the smoke and vapor cleared, the bow reared up into the air and went down stern first with the stern hitting bottom in three minutes about eight to ten feet down; the bow remained afloat for nearly an hour, which allowed the crew to get off safely. The next day the USS *Osage*, a double-ender (pointed at both bow and stern) steam-powered gunboat, moved into the Blakely River. As she dropped anchor, an explosion tore off her

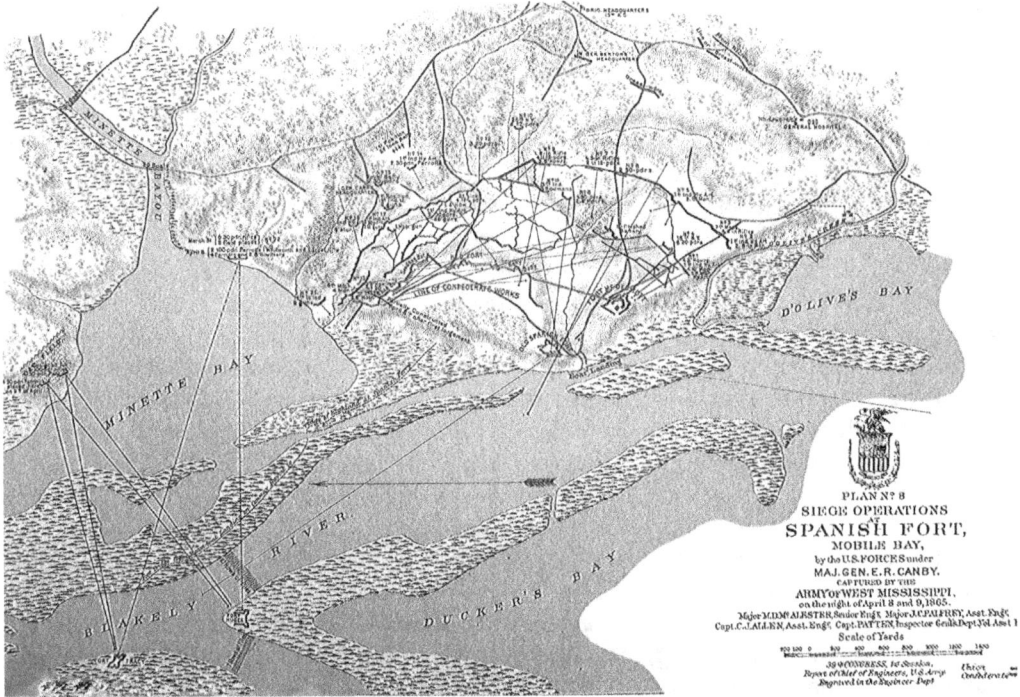

Map of Spanish Fort, April 1864. Batteries Huger and Tracey are on the swamp islands to the right of the Blakely River. At the single conjoining lines of fire to and from the forts are Companies H and K. (National Archives map, RG 77–121–16–1.)

bow, and she went down in a few minutes in twelve feet of water. Her crew lost five men killed and twelve men wounded.

The forts on the islands were relatively small but well armed. Fort Huger had one 8-inch double-banded gun on the northeast bastion, one 6.4-inch Brooke rifle and one 10-inch mortar on the east face, one 7-inch Brooke rifle on the southeast bastion, one 10-inch double-banded Brooke smoothbore on the south face, one 7-inch rifle on the southwest bastion, one 6.4-inch Brooke rifle on the west face, two 12-pounder howitzers in the open north side, and two 10-inch Columbiads on center-pintle mounts on top of a twenty-five foot high bombproof structure in the center of the fort. These 10-inch guns could be turned to bear on a target in any direction. Fort Tracy mounted five 7-inch Brooke rifled guns. These forts guns outclassed the 30-pounders of Companies H and K. The distances of one and one-half miles and one and three-fourths miles to the forts were an extremely long range for a line-of-sight weapon. The 30-pounder shells could carry a mile or more farther than their targets, but seeing the target, and especially hitting it, were two entirely different things.[13]

On the 30th Company B began moving its four 10-inch mortars, under Captain William Blankenship, into position on Brigadier-General Eugene A. Carr's, 3rd Division, XVI Corps, front at 900 yards distant from the main redoubt, Red Fort, on the Spanish Fort line. The four 8-inch mortars of Company B, under 1st Lieutenant Thomas Raper, took position in an emplacement on Brigadier General William P. Benton's 3rd Division, XIII Corps, front at 800 yards from Fort McDermott (Fort Alexis). Fort McDermott, at the far south end of the Spanish Fort defenses, held fifteen guns: six 6-pounder guns, two 24-pounder howitzers, six coehorn mortars and one 6.4-inch Brooke rifle mounted on a center pintle so it could turn 360 degrees. McDermott's lunette shaped southeast bastion had 12-pounder shells fused as land mines buried all around its base. The gun embrasures could be closed by mantlets of 1-inch thick steel plates. Fort McDermott was separated from the main lines of Spanish Fort by a creek-carved steep-sided valley that emptied into the Blakely River by Old Spanish Fort. After the rifled guns of Companies H and K were on the move to their emplacements on the far right of the siege lines, the 8-inch howitzers of Company C were brought up and placed in General Benton's area on the brow of a low hill 800 yards from Fort McDermott.

Behind the defenses of the Spanish Fort lines, Captain Cuthbert H. Slocomb's 5th Washington Artillery with one 8-inch Columbiad, three light guns and two coehorn mortars occupied the Confederate left center in two redans called Red Fort. To the left of Red Fort the breastworks came to four blunt-pointed lunettes that housed eight guns and two mortars manned by Phillip's battery. The breastworks then turned west running a hundred more yards or so where three guns of Lumsden's battery defended before the earthworks ended in a marsh near Bay Minette. A five-foot deep and eight-foot wide ditch went around the outside of the breastworks. More 12-pounder shells fixed as land-mines protected the ground in front of the breastworks from Slocomb's position to a little past the blunt headed lunette at the defenses' left. Like Fort McDermott all artillery embrasures along these defenses could be closed by steel mantlets.

On the 30th, General Canby had ordered a general bombardment of the Confederate defenses to begin late in the day of the 31st. However, General A. J. Smith complained to General Canby about the intense cannon fire from forts Huger and Tracy and the injuries it caused among his troops along his right flank. Smith requested permission to have the eight-gun 30-pounder battery on his right open fire on these two forts as soon as the guns were in finished emplacements. Canby agreed with Smith and Companies H and K received orders to open fire on the two forts as soon as the battery was fully emplaced and the targets visible.[14]

As the boys from Companies H and K moved themselves and their guns, etc. around the outside perimeter of the Federal lines, the Confederate artillery commenced firing a few shells their way. The Rebels' fuse shells had their fuses cut too long so they exploded after they flew over and past the Hoosiers. Reaching the freshly made lane to their position, the bully boys turned onto it and moved through a pine woods while Rebel shells cut off tree limbs around them. About two hundred yards from their emplacement, they paused and rested while the workers at the emplacements labored on.

Early in the afternoon, the waiting Hoosiers got word that their emplacements were ready, and they needed to bring their guns up. As two of the men rose from behind a pine tree to get to their mules, a 7-inch shot from Fort Huger hit the tree about twenty feet up shattering it to pieces and splitting the trunk to its roots. The falling debris missed the Hoosiers. They got their Parrotts into position without mishap and walked the mules back about 200 yards to a picket rope stretched from tree to tree and tethered them to the rope. Their eight-gun emplacement atop a bluff overlooking Minette Bay gave them a slightly plunging fire toward Forts Huger and Tracy.

Due to rebel sharpshooters' fire from across Bay Minette, light artillery fire and the heavy guns' fire from the forts, General Smith ordered all of his men to get under as much cover as was possible, especially, the bully boys of Companies H and K. The A.A.G's. office had reported to General Canby that the artillerists needlessly exposed themselves to enemy view.[15]

The morning of the 31st dawned, and a heavy haze hung over the water and low in the ravine between Forts McDermott and Spanish Fort. A lighter fog shrouded Spanish Fort and the besiegers. Companies H and K commenced firing ass the fog lifted. Their targets were two gunboats and two transports in the channel between them and forts Tracy and Huger coming toward Spanish Fort. The transports, a regular steamer and a white painted side-wheel steamer built on the lines of a blockade runner received the bully boys' immediate attention. Shrapnel from exploding shells tore through the vessels, and three direct hits to them took place within the first twenty minutes of firing. After receiving so much abuse in such a short time, the ships' captains had enough and backed their vessels upstream out of range. Next the Hoosiers engaged the gunboats *Nashville* (a large side-wheel double-ender ram) and the *Huntsville* (a heavily armored turtleback ram). The *Nashville* mounted two 6.4-inch Brooke rifles and two 7-inch Brooke rifles; the *Huntsville* mounted four 32-pounder guns.

The gunboats had fired a few shots back at the Hoosiers when the forts joined in with a brisk fire. The *Nashville* carried 2-inch thick iron plates only on the end shields of her gun and works casemate. The sides of the casemate had no armor plating. The pilot house atop the casemate had 2-inch iron plate on the front and sides below the windows. It soon withdrew after being struck at least eight times broadside where the hits could do the most damage. She made way for Mobile where she would lay up two days for repairs. The turtleback ram remained in position until nightfall when she could be removed under cover of darkness. Both of these ironclads had underpowered engines and could move the vessels at only four knots under the best conditions. Due to its defective engines, the *Huntsville*, originally planned as a powerful companion to the ironclad ram *Tennessee*, was of little more use than a floating gun battery. It could not take action against the Federal Navy due to its lack of power, slow maneuverability and weaker guns. Company H had hit the gunboats at least twelve times out of forty-eight fired. One shell from Sgt. William H. Wilkey's number one gun hit a gunboat "fair and square." The *Huntsville*'s gunpowder must have been defective, because her shot and shell barely reached the bully boys' gun emplacement.

Early that afternoon another transport, the *Jeff Davis*, attempted the passage to Spanish Fort but it, too, reversed up the river after twelve rounds splashed around it and two direct hits exploded in her. One round from Sgt. John B. Yelton's number two gun and one round from Sgt. Cyrus Hunt's number three gun scored the hits on the *Jeff Davis*. So far, the 30-pounder battery was doing its job of keeping the gunboats from lending their fire to that of the forts, and it had prevented the transports from landing supplies and reinforcements.[16]

As soon as all of the vessels except the turtleback ram were driven off, Company H and Company K's Parrotts turned their attention to the distant forts and the buildings outside of them. The bully boys then fired fourteen rounds at Fort Huger, hitting it or putting shells into its interior five times. Company H fired 165 times that day. Company K, alongside Company H, had similar success in its shooting. The thirty pound bolts and shells caused a lot of damage to a building inside Huger. One shot entered the officers' dining room and scattered the diners; its passage through the air concussed a sentry's head standing near the magazine before it plunged into earth. Company K fired even more shells at the forts with equally good results. The return fire from the fort's Brooke Rifles and 10-inch guns made the dirt from the Hoosiers' earthworks fly—penetrating through four to six feet of earth and splintering the wooden supporting braces at the rear or these works. The men were constantly exposed to the flying clods of dirt, shell fragments and wood splinters as they worked their guns. In spite of this, Company H reported only one casualty that day: Private Randolph A. Smock, slightly wounded by flying splinters. That night a transport tried to make a run to Spanish Fort. The boys in Company H opened fire at the moving lights going downstream. They fired twenty-two times at the vessel, but due to the darkness they could not tell if they ever hit it.

After seeing the splendid performance done by the First Indiana's 30-pounders, General Canby rescinded his order to have mortars brought up into the same position as the 30-pounder battery to fire at Forts Huger and Tracy. Instead, he ordered the remaining mortars and their crews brought up and placed into position to shell Spanish Fort and Fort McDermott (Alexis) instead.[17]

Company B had opened on Red Fort with its 10-inch mortars at 8 A.M. on the 31st, and it had battered the fort severely. B's bursting shells dropped directly into the trenches behind the fort's ramparts, scattering the troops within to seek shelter in the bombproofs. However, here as at Port Hudson, they were not totally proof from bombs (the name given to mortar shells). One 10-inch mortar shell plowed through the seven foot thick roof of such a bombproof at Red Fort. The mortar shell's explosion and shrapnel killed or badly maimed fifteen men within the confined area of the shelter. Company B's 8-inch mortars and Company C's 8-inch howitzers had opened fire that morning on Fort McDermott. They maintained a steady and accurate fire while being raked with shell fire from both Red Fort and McDermott.

During the evening of the 31st, Company L arrived from Ft. Gaines. One section of two 30-pounder Parrotts was sent into position about 1,000 yards from Red Fort. The other two gun section was placed into position 600 yards from Red Fort. The two Parrott batteries were fairly close from side to side, but one a significant distance ahead of the other. Both of these positions were on the right wing of the encircling lines. That same evening Company H spotted a transport's lights as it came down the foggy river. The men fired nineteen 11-second fuse shells and two percussion shells at the transport with great success. The steamer was badly damaged, and another vessel came and towed it upstream out of harm's way.[18]

That night the muffled sounds of men moving around and working were heard coming from the woods across Minette Bayou to the north of Companies H and K. Suspecting an attack of some sort on their position, Captain William P. Wimmer of Company H alerted his men to be prepared for an assault from the direction of Blakely, and they grabbed their Springfield rifles to fight it off. No assault came.

On the morning of April 1, as the battery prepared to open fire against the forts, it was raked from right to left by an intense cannon fire of shot and shell from across Minette Bayou. The activity heard the night before had been men led by Captain John B. Grayson, C.S.A., bringing a light battery of two 10-pounder Parrotts and two 12-pounder howitzers into position, probably from Winston's battery. Trees had effectively masked the movement of the Rebel guns until they opened fire about 1,200 yards away from the Hoosiers across Minette Bayou near where it empties into Minette Bay.

The right and left sides of the breastwork returns on the Indiana battery's gun emplacement were lower than the one in front and left the men and guns partially exposed to rifle and cannon fire from the sides. The magazine full of black powder had its entrance facing to the north, which dangerously exposed its contents to the incoming shells. Because they were closer to the breastworks on the north side where the incoming shots went over them before landing at the farther end of their earthworks, guns number one and two got off two shots each, and number three gun got off one shot before the crews sought shelter. Going to work with shovels and spades, a detail of the boys began elevating and thickening the north side of their works. Another detail was busy building a protective rampart of logs and sand in front of the magazine's exposed entrance, and covering the top of the magazine with additional sand, logs and dirt. A third detail went to work digging a new gun emplacement to the left and forward of the present position.

While the repairing and repositioning took place, Grayson's battery kept the Hoosiers under a constant fire as well as did the guns of the forts and the gunboat *Morgan*, an open deck sidewheeler. Guns number one and two being the more protected of the Parrotts went back into action after a few hours and their flank defenses were strengthened and heightened. They resumed a slow fire for the rest of the day. By 4:30 P.M. the new gun emplacement was completed and gun number four moved into place, where it could bear upon the battery across the bayou. However, the commander at Blakely ordered Captain Grayson to return to

Seventeen. New Orleans. Garrison Life. Mobile Campaign!

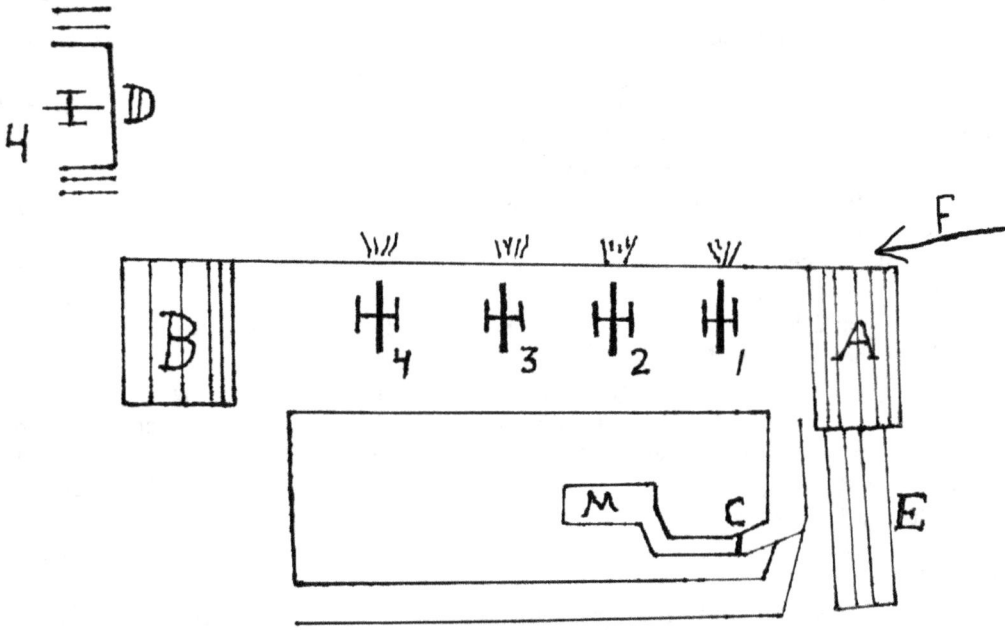

Sketch map of the gun emplacement for Company H, showing direction of enfilading fire from the enemy battery and relocated position of gun number 4 by Captain William Wimmer, Company H, Indiana Jackass Regiment. (Courtesy Indiana Historical Society.)

Blakely to defend it from Major-General (USV) also brevet Brigadier-General (USA) Frederick Steele, commander of the District of West Florida, Department of the Gulf's columns advancing from the north. Grayson began limbering up as the Hoosiers moved their 30-pounder into place to bear on his battery. Due to lack of ammunition, the *Morgan* could not help Spanish Fort anymore that day and backed up the river to be resupplied.[19]

In spite of the enfilading fire, the men of Company H had had only one major casualty that day, and that was suffered by Private Samuel Pollom, who was severely injured by a falling tree limb shot off a nearby tree. The men of Company K, being located nearby to Company H, received a similar battering by cannon fire from Captain Grayson's guns. Company K suffered two casualties, severity unknown. As a precaution against the Rebels returning to the bayou, Company H held its number four gun in its new position for the night.

Further left on the besieging lines, that morning, the second section of Company L opened fire from their 30-pounder Parrotts for the first time against Red Fort. Company B's 8-inch mortars opened fire at Fort McDermott causing a great deal of damage to that place. Company B's 10-inch mortars opened on Red Fort in the afternoon and lobbed 47 shells into it, dismounting a gun and killing two men. Company C was intensely engaged as well, and it suffered from having too thin a front parapet to withstand Rebel rifle fire. A sharpshooter's rifle ball killed Company C's private William Hogue. Company M with its 30-pounders reported for duty late in the afternoon. The batteries kept up a sporadic fire against the Rebel forts until nightfall.

During the day the 6th Michigan, Companies A and K, arrived with eight 10-inch mortars and General Totten. The pioneers finished the emplacements for Mack's 18th New York's six 20-pounder Parrot rifles, and the battery moved into the positions. The pioneers began a position for some of the Michigan mortars behind Company B's mortar battery.[20]

After leaving a strong guard at Pensacola, General Steele, cooperating with Canby, moved his forces from Pensacola, Florida, westward to help reduce the defenses of Mobile. To confuse the enemy, he had marched northward of the Mobile route. The Confederates thought he was going to attack points north of Mobile to cut off supplies coming down the river system that flowed into Mobile Bay and then take Selma, Alabama. The ruse worked for several days during which his army encountered the same stormy weather and muddy road conditions that held up Canby's army. As the weather had cleared, he turned his command southwest toward Fort Blakely. The Confederate forces at Blakely, already outnumbered by Canby's forces, asked for reinforcements.

Brigadier-General R. L. Gibson, commanding at Spanish Fort sent requests to Major-General Dabney Maury, district commander at Mobile, and to Brigadier-General St. John R. Liddell, commanding Fort Blakely, for additional men to hold Spanish Fort. Liddell at Blakely refused, stating that he had a Federal corps advancing toward him that was larger than the two corps before Spanish Fort. Further a large number of the forces coming against Blakely were Negroes who would not spare any of his defenders if they should surrender. Liddell and Gibson, having been turned down by Maury for more men, agreed to defend their posts with all honor (2,100 men garrisoned Spanish Fort, 2,600 men garrisoned Fort Blakely). Most of the men under Maury's command felt he was a gallant and efficient leader; however, because he was short, his men joked that he was every inch a general, only there were not many inches of him.[21]

April 2 dawned without any surprises for the Indiana artillerists. During this day, Company L engaged the artillery in Red Fort for a short time. The 5th Washington Artillery turned their guns from Company L to Company B's mortars in an attempt to relieve Fort McDermott from the intensity of the mortar fire. Some of Slocomb's guns could get a slight enfilading fire at Mack's battery and at Lieutenant Raper's sections of Company B. Exploding mortar shells had begun crumbling McDermott's south parapet, and the bombs had completely disabled the 6.4-inch Brooke rifle inside the fort on a pivoting mount. Mack also disabled a 24-pounder howitzer. Mack's 18th New York Battery was parallel to and on the right of a 6th Michigan company of four 10-inch mortars about four hundred and fifty yards from McDermott. Two-hundred yards behind them was the 7th Massachusetts Battery with 3-inch rifles flanked on each side by two of Raper's mortars. General Canby, seeing the good effect the heavy guns were having upon the Rebel forts, sent for another four gun battery of 30-pounders and for two 100-pounder Parrotts to be brought to the front.

There were no weapons of this caliber or artillerists trained in their use nearby. Because of this, an order went out to New Orleans, for Company G. However, this battery was on duty at Morganza, Louisiana, and the commander there could not spare them because they were the only experienced battery he had. In addition to their garrison assignment, Company G trained men from other regiments in both field and garrison artillery duty so they could be re-assigned to garrison Unionized towns in Louisiana. Baton Rouge, on the other hand, had three batteries of heavy artillery. Therefore, the Jackass Regiment's Company F, a 30-pounder Parrott unit, received orders to move from Baton Rouge to Spanish Fort. The company also received orders to pick up two 100-pounder Parrotts from Fort Jackson or Fort St. Philip and bring them to Spanish Fort.[22]

On the far right of the siege lines, following their curve to the Blakely River, another company of the 6th Michigan with four mortars went into an emplacement behind a small ridge only 200 yards from the garrison's works. Nine hundred yards farther to the right from the 6th Michigan's mortars were Jackass Regiment Companies H and K.

On April 2, Company H opened fire with guns number one, two and three. The first two or three shots fired from Company H's Long Toms were at a gunboat, which being hit twice, moved off. The rest of the day was spent in firing at the forts. (Gun number four did not fire because it still bore on the woods across the bayou in case the Rebel artillery moved back there. This day only Federal infantrymen busily building up breastworks from which they could defend against another surprise attack were seen across the bayou.) Company H fired 78 rounds at Fort Tracy and its outbuildings, hit it directly 19 times, hit a large gun in the fort 3 times, and showered the fort with fragments from 8 time-fused shells bursting over it. Corporal Thomas J. Lough and number three gun had Fort Tracy's number and scored most of the hits in, on and around it. The boys fired at Fort Huger 40 times and hit it 4 times. Sergeant John B. Yelton on number two gun made two of these hits, and Corporal John Bishop scored the other two hits with number one gun. Most of the shells fired at Huger flew high and passed over it. The forts did not return any of the fire this day. Number one gun's accuracy improved after making a repair to its bent breech sight. Corporals Lough and Bishop attracted the attention of General Totten because of their excellent shots at Fort Tracy. Most of the poorer shots fired were poor due to the poor quality of the Hotchkiss bolts and shells furnished to the battery.[23]

The Hotchkiss 30-pound solid shot and exploding shell were known to tumble in flight and fly off target. Besides being inaccurate, the tumbling movement caused the percussion shells to explode prematurely. This posed a great amount of danger to any friendly infantrymen in pits or trenches in front of the guns. The shells were made somewhat better in accuracy and much safer by pouring out the gunpowder bursting charge within them and re-filling them with sand. The sand was heavier than the gunpowder and helped change the center of gravity making the shells fly straighter. The problem with this procedure was that the shell had to be used as solid shot, and it could not be used to burst over personnel or to ignite wooden buildings with its bursting flame.[24]

The day of April 3 saw additional artillery of four 24-pounder coehorn mortars brought into action. These little mortars were great for harassment and when properly handled could be quite deadly. The coehorns were commanded by Lieutenant Thomas Sibert, the First Indiana Regiment's acting adjutant, and manned by a detail of men from Company B. The small mortars went into place in the advanced approaches of the siege saps where they would be most effective. Company C moved its guns 200 to 300 yards to their right to a new position on a plateau still on the Union left. They were a short distance from the bluff overlooking the bay and about 450 yards from the southeast angle of Fort McDermott. Company M's emplacement in front of the XIII Corps was now finished, and Captain Armstrong moved two 30-pounder Parrotts into it.

Company B maintained a steady fire from its heavy mortars all night long. They lobbed over 125 shells during the night and day at the garrison. However, the men in the forts had dug their bombproofs deeper, and the pieces from the exploding shells did little harm to them.

The night before, the Rebels had given the men of Company B a taste of their own medicine. A shell from one of the Confederates' coehorn mortars dropped into a campfire surrounded by a group of Company B's men. With its fuse gaily sputtering, the shell scattered the blazing embers or the campfire to the four winds, the artillerists jumped in as many directions, dropped to the ground and rolled downhill away from their fire. The shell then exploded scattering iron fragments as it had scattered the embers. None were injured.

The fort had fourteen coehorn mortars with ten in use on the land defenses. The Confederate artillerists of the 5th Washington Artillery occupying the Red Fort portion of the Spanish Fort lines were good shots with their coehorn mortars as well as with their heavier guns. For sport, the crews of one 2-mortar section of coehorns watched for the results of shells fired from their two coehorn mortars, named Louise and Peanuts. The men placed bets on what the results of the shell's explosion would toss into the air—coats, hats, pants, body parts, etc.

Louise was the first coehorn in the battery to "kick a Federal soldier higher than a kite," and she had to prove her reputation daily. The Louisiana artillerists also bet on the height to which Louise or Peanuts would blast her next victim. Louise was named after a coquettish waitress in a Mobile hotel. This was unlike the 8-inch Columbiad in the battery, which was named Lady Slocomb in honor the wife of the battery commander, Captain Cuthbert H. Slocomb. Other guns in the battery were named Lady Vaught (after the battery's Lieutenant Vaught), Cora Slocomb (after Captain Slocomb's daughter) and General Gibson (commander of Spanish Fort).[25]

The Confederate defenders referred to the 30-pounder battery on Bay Minette, as "*That* Battery!" or "That *Damned* Battery!" The battery continued its daily task of effectively preventing supplies and reinforcements from landing at Spanish Fort and Fort McDermott. It also kept blasting away at Forts Huger and Tracy. The signal corps built a lookout post at this battery, and they reported that a ram and two transports had withdrawn up the Tensas River early that morning. Having no ships to chase away, the guns of the Companies H and K opened on the forts, and pounded away at them the entire day. Company H also fired three shots at some men in a skiff for fun. (The bully boys did not realize it at the time, but the oar-powered skiffs and floating or poled flatboats hauled supplies in to Spanish Fort and Forts Huger and Tracy. After dark, the skiffs took the wounded out for treatment in Mobile.) The rest of the day they fired at Forts Huger and Tracy.

The defenders at Fort Huger did not take the shelling with good humor. Its men worked feverishly to add additional sandbags to their parapets to shield the pivot gun and the parapet guns. In the afternoon of the 3rd, Huger responded with a furious barrage from its mortar and three heavy guns, one of which annoyed the Hoosiers greatly. The boys in Companies H and K maintained a spirited fire, hitting the fort several times. They got a few shells to burst above the guns in the fort, making the Rebel gunners duck for cover. The last shot from gun number three landed right in the embrasure of the Rebel gun that annoyed the bully boys the most and disabled it.

Company H's cannonading permanently disabled Fort Tracy's 7-inch Brooke rifle, and broke the traverse circle of a 10-inch Columbiad in Fort Huger, partially immobilizing the gun. The Hoosiers had not escaped injury from the fort's guns. Private Joseph Holt, a member of number three gun's crew, was seriously wounded in the thigh by a fragment from a shell that exploded over number two gun. Privates David B. Gray and William B. Newman were slightly wounded by splinters from the shell shattered supports of their works. A Rebel shell fragment shattered one of the men's Springfield rifles propped against a tree to their rear.

A few high-flying Confederate shells landed in the boys' camp two hundred yards to the rear of their battery. The flying shells cut the rope tethering the mules and horses in several places, wounding some of the animals and allowing other to run away. The Rebel shells demolished two supply wagons. One shell exploded near one of company's black cooks and buried him, his fire and kettles with sand. The cook quickly took leave of his employers and ran off to anywhere safer.[26]

That night the men busied themselves putting up shields against the flying shell fragments, and they moved number four gun back into position to defend against the expected renewal of the attack upon them from Huger and Tracy. They did not fire that night. The next day, April 4, did not bring a renewal of the severe shelling by the forts that they had given the Bay Minette battery the day before. Only a few shots were fired by either side.

Special Field Orders No. 24, issued on the 4th of April by General Canby, general in chief, directed that a general bombardment of the fortifications take place from 5 to 7 P.M. that evening by all of the light and heavy guns and mortars. Therefore, to conserve ammunition for the evening's work, the siege pieces were fairly quiet during the day. The Johnnies saw this as

Lady Slocomb. The eight-inch bore Columbiad is at the Civil War Museum, New Orleans, Louisiana. Note the sight mounting hole on the left trunnion base. This piece was cast at Tredegar Foundry on October 13, 1863, and has foundry #1932.

an opportunity to have a little fun, and they directed a slow, careful fire at the Federals. Towards dinner time they placed a shell through the tent of Captain William Blankenship, commander of Company B. The blast of the shell smashed the dinnerware (a cup and saucer) and the dinner. The captain wasn't hurt, but he was upset. That night Blankenship's 10-inch and 8-inch mortar batteries outdid themselves by hurling 160 shells into Fort McDermott and Spanish Fort during a furious two-hour bombardment.[27]

At 5 P.M., all the guns opened as ordered. The first section of Company M opened for the first time on Spanish Fort and blew up a magazine in the fort. As the gun crew was cheering and celebrating their good work, the Confederates concentrated their fire upon them and did not let up until after dark; 6.4-inch shells fired from Old Spanish Fort and some 8-inch shells from Red Fort exploded over and all around them. Captain Armstrong considered it miraculous that they had not been hit by the flying shrapnel. The men of Company M fired back, but they could not regain their lost initiative.

Lieutenant George James of Company I arrived with a detachment of men from that battery, and they took over the job of firing the 24-pounder coehorns from Company B's detail. The intense mortar and cannon fire disabled a Parrott rifle in the Fort McDermott defenses. The Rebels' greatest artillery losses were due to a combination one-two punch from two different batteries.

Company L's first section had commenced firing for the first time that evening. It worked in conjunction with the second section of Company L. Their target was Red Fort, and the 8-inch Columbiad of the 5th Washington Artillery. These elite Rebel gunners had just fired the Lady Slocomb at the second section of Company L. As they started to close the gun's embrasure, Company L's Corporal James Busby fired a solid shot. At nearly the same time, a 20-pounder Parrott shell fired by Mack's battery flew toward the Lady Slocomb. Company L's shot tore through the bottom of the embrasure, traveled between the cheeks of the gun carriage and tore off the elevating screw supporting the rear of the cannon barrel. Simultaneously, Mack's shell coming from the gun's right rear struck it, blew up and broke off the right trunnion of the Columbiad. A crew member placed an iron hand spike across the cheeks of the carriage under the breech, which held the gun up in a threatening position, but an idle threat. After the smoke and dust from the blast cleared, three of the Lady's crewmen's bodies were on or around their doubly-disabled weapon. The intense firing that evening from all

Federal guns seemed to concentrate on the area of the Lady Slocomb eating away at the Rebel parapet. Both sections of Company L kept firing at the parapet hiding the Lady Slocomb. The parapet there became more of a low mound rather than a definite shape. Late that night the Lady Slocomb was removed and tossed to one side. A fresh 8-inch Columbiad took her place on another carriage. During the night, the Washington Artillerymen worked hard to rebuild their parapet and restore the embrasures. (The Lady is now displayed at the Museum of the Confederacy in New Orleans, Louisiana.)[28]

At the Bay Minette battery, Captain Wimmer of Company H reported that three large steamers loaded with troops had come across from Mobile, but rather than face the guns of his battery they had turned towards Blakely. The gunboat *Nashville* lay up the channel from Fort Tracy, and it was making fairly good shots at H and K's battery. Fort Huger joined in by firing its remaining rifled gun and two small mortars that bore on them. Company H had gotten off three Hotchkiss shells at the transports without effect before the ships steamed out of sight. The rest of the day's fire was directed at Fort Huger trying to hit its mortars. There were a few good shots that burst over the target, but of the 39 shots fired, most tumbled off course or didn't burst because of defective fuses.

A two gun battery of naval 30-pounder Parrotts had been off-loaded from the USS *Milwaukee*, remounted on siege carriages and moved into position by their gun crews near the center of the siege lines. On the 4th, these siege rifles opened fire against Red Fort.[29]

The siege wore on, and the large guns maintained a slow fire during the 5th. Not much would happen on this day. The siege batteries were under orders not to provoke a general engagement due to a shortage of ammunition. Because of these orders and the heavy activity of the night before, the men were able to get a little rest. Company B, under Captain Blankenship who had missed his dinner the evening before, fired only six rounds. Companies H and K did not fire. Company M, under Captain Samuel Armstrong, being under orders not to bring on an engagement without direct orders from the corps commander, fired only a couple of shots.

April 6 was not much more active even though the Rebel gunners shelled Company M out of its position for a while. General Gordon Granger then ordered Company M to open fire on rifle pits in front of Red Fort. None of Captain Armstrong's embrasures would allow such a fire; therefore, he removed one Parrott from his emplacement and had it rolled a few yards to the left. He opened fire with this gun and after fifteen rounds of case and shell into the rifle pits, the sharpshooters fled. The besiegers concentrated on advancing their saps to the walls of the forts. Company H received orders to move out of the Bay Minette battery and move all of their guns, equipment, etc. to join General Steele's army besieging Fort Blakely about two to three miles north of Bay Minette. The Hoosiers spent the day packing and moving to the rear.

The Confederates were trying to extend the parapet on their left flank to the end of the bluff at the water's edge. They were relying on the swamp and the dense brush below their hillside to slow an attack, but they knew that it wouldn't stop a determined effort against them. The Rebels placed additional mines made from 12-pounder cannon shells in front of their parapet to further discourage an assault.[30]

Captain Richard Campbell, Company I, came up with the remainder of the battery. He and his men took charge of two 30-pounder Parrotts, and they also took charge of three 20-pounder Parrotts. Now that Company H had left the Bay Minette battery, Company K, having the party all to itself, opened fire against the gunboat *Morgan*. The *Morgan*'s shells harmlessly chased Company H's men as they moved to the rear.

The *Morgan* was a wooden sidewheeler and lightly armored with boiler plate, but she mounted four 32-pounder broadside deck guns and two 7-inch pivot guns, one each on her exposed bow and stern decks. Company K fired ten shots at her, hitting her twice in a wheelhouse, and the rest coming so close as to force the ship to retreat a few miles up the river where she joined the *Huntsville* and *Nashville* at work assisting in the Rebel defense of Blakely. A 100-pounder Parrott rifle barrel arrived and was sent into Company H's old position. It was not of service to the Federals because it needed to be mounted on a proper sized carriage, but Company K went to work on that problem. A 1.8-inch breechloading Whitworth rifle, a Steel gun (Wiard?) and two 8-inch howitzers also moved into the Bay Minette Battery.

At midnight, Company H, led by a company of infantry, began crossing a new pontoon bridge across Bayou Minette. The narrow bridge wobbled under the weight of the Parrott rifles making the men and their mules very nervous and skittish. By moving very slowly the wobble decreased and the artillery train inched over the bayou. By 2:30 P.M. Company H, and their infantry escort, had crossed the pontoon bridge and were on the road north to Blakely.[31]

Having been notified that a heavy battery was on its way, the Federal engineers at Blakely began constructing a large battery north of Blakely on the far right of the Federal lines. This work was on high ground and could command the Blakely and Tensaw rivers at the rear (west side) of Fort Blakely.

The battery's assignment here was to be much the same as it had been at Spanish Fort, namely, to drive off the gunboats and prevent resupply of the garrison. It would also bombard the Rebel defensive lines of the fort itself. The newly built earthwork for the 30-pounders went by a three names: Battery Wilson, Battery Drew and the 30-pounder battery. The engineers could not find any thick planks to build the minimum 16 by 16 foot platforms for each heavy gun to rest upon. When the guns were not in place on the 7th, a discussion took place between the major-general commanding, E.R.S. Canby, and General Steele wherein the ranking general pointed out that corduroy log platforms for the Parrott guns had worked quite well at Spanish Fort. General Steele readily agreed with Canby's wisdom, and the guns of Company H would run into place as soon as the engineers corduroyed the platforms.[32]

While the platform construction project took place at Blakely on April 7, at Spanish Fort the 100-pounder Parrott rifle went up on its new carriage. Lieutenant Thomas Compton with twenty of his men from Company K and Lieutenant John Parker of Company L with twenty men from companies C, L and M took charge of the 6.4-inch Parrott rifle. Another 100-pounder Parrott rifle was ordered to move into position alongside the first 100-pounder rifle. Lieutenant Richard Stamper, Company B, selected a new position for his 8-inch mortars, and moved them about 1,000 yards to the right of his former position for a more effective concentration of fire against Red Fort. He would receive a commendation for the selecting of this position and for the effectiveness of his firing from it. Company K, still working its 30-pounders, dismounted a 12-pounder howitzer and disabled the 10-inch Columbiad in Fort Huger.

The Hoosier artillerists were pleased by the skillful way in which their talents and guns were being used against the well defended forts. An officer noted in his diary: "The siege progresses splendidly. How different from Port Hudson. There it was charge! charge! charge! Here a little more good sense is shown, and a regard for human life; and the end approaches more rapidly." Ammunition had arrived for all, and General A. J. Smith asked to open with all of his guns for one hour at 5 P.M. on April 8. General Canby's response was to oblige General Smith's request for "playing a tune with his guns," but he suggested an intense two hour general bombardment all along the line with the guns' tune to be called: "The Spanish Fort Dead March."[33]

At 5:30 P.M., Saturday, April 8, fifty-three siege guns plus thirty-seven field guns began playing their tune against Spanish Fort and Fort McDermott. The fire was heavy, sustained, and murderous. The second section of Company M had just moved into position about 1,500 yards from Spanish Fort, and this bombardment was its first exposure to fire. This battery fired a round every thirty seconds from its 30-pounder Parrotts. Its location at the right of the XIII Corps near the center of the siege lines made it a prime target for many of the guns and rifles in Spanish Fort. A Red Fort sharpshooter's minie ball struck Company M's Private William H. Sparks in his forehead, severely wounding him, during this evening's work. He survived and would be mustered out in 1866.

Company K, now firing two 100-pounder Parrotts, four 30-pounder Parrotts, a Whitworth, a steel rifle and two 8-inch howitzers, commanded by Captain Chambers Cox, had four men wounded. Company L, commanded by Captain Isaac Hendricks had one man wounded. Captain Blankenship's battery of mortars were doing splendid work this evening, firing one hundred twenty 10-inch rounds; however, they did not equal the number fired when the captain's dinner was ruined.

The men in the forts were driven from their guns by the battering they received, and they were forced to seek cover from the exploding shells. They watched the descending mortar balls and played a deadly game of dodgeball with them. The 5th Washington Artillery's P. D. Stephenson was known for his accuracy in gauging where the incoming missiles would land, and the 5th Washington's officers often shouted: "Sing out, Stephenson, and tell us which way to run." The defenders often sought the open ground to the rear of their parapet's walls just to have room to dodge the mortar shells. It was better now to stay out of the shelters, even if the 10-inch bombs blew a 15-foot wide by 5-foot deep hole in the ground.[34]

Late on the 8th, General Carr ordered his men forward through the marsh, thickets and felled trees on his far right to establish an advanced picket guard about 100-yards from the enemy position at the northern end of the Rebel defenses. After 6 P.M. the 8th Iowa Infantry began moving two companies forward from behind gabions about 400 yards distant from the Texans defending that part of the defenses. The companies advanced straight through the marsh toward the weakest part of the defenses. When about 100-yards away, the Texans opened a heavy fire on the bluecoats. The colonel of the Iowans ordered more companies forward to press the attack lest they be killed by trying to make a stand in the marsh and felled logs.

The Iowa regiment rushed their attack and carried the defenders' line, pushing the defenders to slightly higher and drier pine-tree land. Now in the dark, the Federal infantrymen waved their colors in the bright moonlight to halt the mortars that unknowingly were dropping their shells among their own infantry inside of and holding the western end of Spanish Fort. The mortar batteries noticed the flags and shifted their aim. Headquarters did not learn of the successful assault for some time; therefore, reinforcements did not arrive to bag the Confederate defenders. As a result, many of the defenders had ample time to make good their escape. Brigadier-General Mathew D. Ector's Brigade of the 9th, 10th, 14th and 32nd Texas Regiments and the 29th and 39th North Carolina regiments reformed and made a stand against the Yankees. (These regiments each had the strength of about one Federal company.)

At 10 P.M. the artillerists in the Spanish Fort defenses had placed the last spike into their guns' vents and bent them back inside the guns by shoving the rammer down the tube. With most of the infantry they silently moved off down a ravine to their rear. They came out of the ravine on the shore of the bay, and were ordered to silently remove their shoes and boots. Confederate engineers had completed a narrow wooden treadway, about 18 inches wide, mounted upon short pilings a few days earlier. The treadway led through the marshes and tidal flats. A narrow water passage at Bay Minette was bridged by floating flatboats. Across the passage the wooden treadway continued through tidal flats to a point opposite Fort Tracy. The boardwalk could be accessed by the men from Fort McDermott by leaving its rear, going down into the valley, crossing the creek and wading through the marsh to the walkway.

As the men made their way out of the fort, the mortar shells bursting around them caused a few casualties, mostly minor, among the retreating Confederates. Making his way out of the fort, a shell fragment struck Tony Barrow of the 5th Washington Artillery knocking him to the ground. He asked his friend P. D. Stephenson, "Tell my mother I died for my country." A quick examination by Stephenson did not reveal any blood, but it did disclose a badly cut up bedroll on his back caused by a shell fragment. Recovering his dying breath, Tony jumped to his feet and proceeded away from Spanish Fort.[35]

The retreating men's pathway along the treadway took them directly past the guns of what Stephenson described as "that stupid battery!" The men could hear the pickets and gunners voices carried over the water as they talked with one another. An occasional shot from the Bay Minette battery passed over the Confederates' heads toward Fort Huger, but these were only to harass the fort. They made their escape past Fort Huger to a place opposite Fort Tracy to where gunboats and other small craft without lights showing waited in the dark for them. When the men filled the watercraft, they got up steam and moved away upstream. Alerted by the sound of steam engines, the Bay Minette battery commenced firing at the sound of the rescue boats. In moments the vessels passed out of range. Nearly one thousand of the escapees following a guide made their way through the marshes to Blakely. Some men remained behind to reinforce Blakely and others boarded steamers there going to Mobile.

Late that night, the balance of General Carr's troops entered the earthworks of the abandoned fort. The besiegers slowly advanced through the fort expecting to be fired upon from an inner defensive line at any moment. Scattered firing from a few sharpshooters in the fort took place to keep the Yankees confused as to the true status of the retreating defenders. Most of these surrendered after being surrounded. Others refused to surrender until a musket was placed at their head. The fort's torpedoes planted between the outer rifle pits and the main breastworks waited for victims. A muffled whump would tell of some poor soul who discovered one of these devices with his last step. Before dawn the fighting was over. The Federals possessed Fort McDermott and Spanish Fort. Estimates were that five hundred Confederates went missing in action or became Federal prisoners of war.[36]

Up at Blakely the defenders staunchly held their fortifications against another superior force. The cautious besiegers worried about the heavy artillery fire that gunboats in the river off Blakely Landing would bring against any attack they launched. (At Spanish Fort the navy had been able to reach Fort McDermott and the Old Spanish Fort with their mortars.) The water here ran in much shallower and narrower channels rivers than at Spanish Fort. Ten rows of pilings across the Blakely River and seven rows of pilings across the waterway to the west side of Fort Huger blocked the channels.

Fort Blakely, supported by Confederate gunboats to the east and north of them and by Forts Huger and Tracy south of them, could hold out under conditions that Spanish Fort could not. Blakely could easily receive supplies and men by ship from Mobile. It was to cut off their supply line and their avenue of escape that Company H had moved to Blakely. Their new position was in a low-walled emplacement atop a bluff about 900 yards north of the Confederate defenses; 1,700 yards away were Blakely Landing and the gunboats. The Hoosiers did not open fire as ordered on the morning of the 8th. The major-general commanding inquired as to why they hadn't commenced firing. They replied that while they now had gun platforms, the magazine for the safekeeping of the ammunition had not been completed.[37]

By 1 P.M. the engineers completed the magazine. By 2 P.M. several infantry officers assembled near Company H to witness the marksmanship of this splendid battery, and the cannoneers commenced firing at the gunboats near Blakely Landing. These vessels were Company H's old nemeses from Spanish Fort: the ironclad turtlebacked ram *Huntsville*, the sandbag protected, open-decked *Nashville* and the *Morgan*. The day before, these craft had poured a

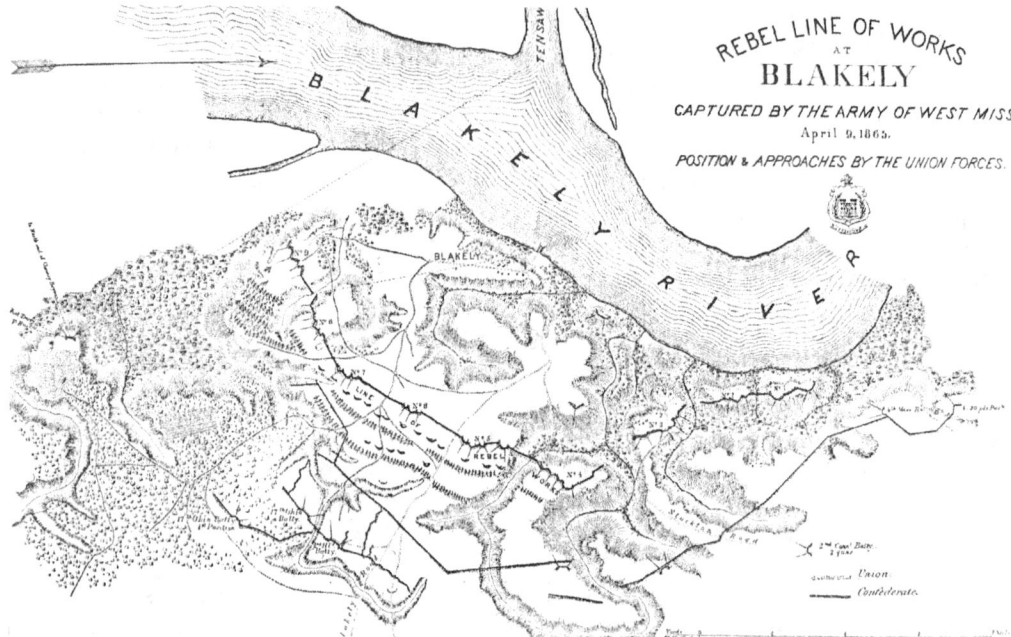

Map of Fort Blakely, Alabama. Position of Company H is at the far right of this map at the very end of the Federal lines. The gunboats they chased away were directly under the L in Blakely River. (National Archives RG-77-121-17-3.)

steady fire into General Steele's right flank making it hell for the Federal infantry and light artillery. Again today, the gunboats poured a steady fire of exploding shells into the right of the besieger's lines, which had prompted that morning's inquiry as to the lack of response from the 30-pounder battery. A forest between Company H and the river concealed its presence from the gunboats.

When Captain Wimmer gave the order to commence firing, Sergeant John Yelton had his #2 gun ready to go. Corporal Eli Robbins took careful aim. He pulled the lanyard, and a percussion shell hurled toward the *Morgan*, blowing a small hole in its middle. Sergeant William Wilkey's #1 gun was next to open fire. Corporal George Scott fired, and his shell smacked into the *Morgan*. The gunboat's crew set to work locating the source of the incoming rounds, all the while working very quickly at readying their guns to return the fire. Soon the gunboat's shots began to hit near the bully boys' earthworks. However, the Hoosiers had soon put seven shots into the *Morgan*. Sergeant Cyrus Hunt's gun #3 with Corporal Thomas Lough's deadly aim put a solid shot through her starboard wheelhouse, smashing it.

After one and one-half hours of fighting the *Morgan* had expended her starboard broadside and fore and aft pivot guns' ammunition when Lough's shot tore a non-repairable hole through her hull at the starboard waterline. To keep her from sinking, the Confederate States Marines on board and the *Morgan*'s crew moved her deck guns from the starboard to the port side and shifted all weighty items to the port side. The Marines stayed on the port side to add weight so as to lift the hole out of the water. Being seriously damaged and in danger of sinking, she slowly steamed away up the Raft River getting out of range and made her way to Mobile for repairs.[38]

The *Nashville* had received little attention from the battery until now, since they had concentrated their fire upon the *Morgan*, but the *Nashville* had exhausted her supply of 12-pounder ammunition, and had blown the bushing out of the vent of the 7-inch Brooke rifle mounted on its stern, thereby, disabling it. Coming under heavier fire now that the *Morgan* had withdrawn and not being able to fight with all her armament, she slowly moved downstream to seek shelter under the high bluffs of Blakely.

Finally Company H's emplacement was extended and corduroyed so #4 Parrott could move into position. Corporal Andrew Loudermilk fired exploding shells at the departing *Nashville* to hasten her on her way. The more heavily armored *Huntsville* stayed in position and fought it out with the battery until she was hors de combat. Ninety fused shells and solid shot were fired at her, striking her repeatedly, penetrating the *Huntsville*'s armor and smashing the skiff (lifeboat) at her stern. A small steamer and rowboats towed her away that night.

The boys of Company H had suffered two casualties that day. Sergeant William H. Wilkey was severely injured in his face by dirt and debris thrown by an exploding shell. Private Johnson Darrock was slightly wounded by debris also thrown by a shell. The infantry officers, present to watch the activity, had not been disappointed. Captain William Wimmer, commanding Company H, thought that his men could have done even better work if the battery emplacement had been built with higher walls between the embrasures to protect his men. He also complained that the intervening trees should have been cut down so the gunners could have had a clearer view of their distant targets. The matter of the trees was a mixed blessing. The gunboats could not see the battery well either and had fired at puffs of gunsmoke. Otherwise, their fire may have been more destructive. The large guns in Blakely did not fire against the battery for the same reason, and the small guns did not have the range to reach it.[39]

On the 9th another emplacement for heavy guns was prepared on the north side of Bay Minette to the left of Blakely for Companies K and L. A detail from Company K would man two 100-pounder Parrotts to keep Forts Huger and Tracy occupied. Companies K and L 30-pounder Parrotts moved in and opened fire at Fort Blakely. Companies B, C, and M were ordered to Blakely on the 9th.

Captain Rice's 17th Ohio Battery, Mack's 18th New York Battery, Captain Lowell's 2nd Illinois Battery and Ginn's 3rd Indiana Battery came up from Spanish Fort and took position in the center and the right of Steele's lines encircling Blakely. These four batteries added six 20-pounder Parrott rifles, eight 10-pounder Parrott rifles and three 12-pounder Napoleon guns to the ring of fire facing Blakely's defenders.

From its earthworks on the right of the lines, with the help of spotters atop tall pine trees, Company H engaged targets all day in Blakely. For a more effective line of fire at Blakely's fortifications, Company H rolled gun #1 out of its protective emplacement onto open ground and opened fire. One other gun fired from a flank embrasure at the fortifications while another gun covered the river waiting for a gunboat to come into range. No gunboat entered the fight.[40]

General Steele ordered for probes in force against portions of the Blakely defenses at 5 P.M. on the 9th. The messages got confused and some regiments did not receive them; other regiments thought it was for a general advance. The light guns began firing at the Blakely artillery emplacements. However, early in the afternoon the Confederate sharpshooters in front of a division of USCT stopped firing. A company of the USCT went forward to investigate the cause. The sharpshooters opened fire causing several casualties. In spite of this, the colored troop company kept advancing in spurts of running forward to cover and opening fire so another group could repeat the maneuver. By this unlikely manner the USCT men and officers reached the defenders far left flank near the river bluff, but they could go no farther. Only 65 men and 19 officers remained — not enough to rush a garrison. Rebel bullets and artillery fire tore overhead of the USCT company hunkered down in a shallow depression. Additional companies of USCT came up and they all moved forward into the last line of Rebel rifle pits. As they lay in the captured pits they could hear the 30-pounder shells from Company H whistle overhead and cry out, "Another through train to Mobile."

The USCT heard firing from their left and discovered the Second Division (white) assaulting the Blakely lines. This diverted the defenders' attention from the USCT and with fixed bayonets they rushed into the defenses. Confederate soldiers threw down their muskets and ran to surrender to the white soldiers. A Confederate officer commanded his men, "Lay low and mow the ground — the damned niggers are coming!" Some reported atrocities occurred of surrendered men without weapons being shot or bayoneted to death by the colored troops. Others received kindness; a former slave shared his canteen with his former youthful master. However some USCT from Louisiana attacked the surrendered prisoners as they huddled in groups fearing their black captors. The Louisianians were forcefully restrained. The USCT had 371 casualties; the defenders in their front had about 125 casualties.

Now the assault became general. As the Federals swarmed forward all along the lines they met a hail of cannon fire and rifle fire. A Confederate officer yelled: "No quarter to the damned Yankees!" Even when asked to surrender the Rebels grabbed up dropped rifles and tried to shoot those demanding surrender. One Rebel officer tried a succession of three muskets against a Yankee officer asking him to surrender until he was shot by a soldier. Finally, the defenders surrendered, even if they had to be dragged out of the Blakely River or from the beach, which included the commanding officer, General Liddell.

Afterwards, some of Blakely's captured defenders told the Jackass Regiment's boys that their aim had been good, and they had done a considerable amount of damage to the fort and to the troops inside. Only a coehorn mortar had returned any fire at Company H, and that had not done any damage. Captain Wimmer congratulated his bully boys on the excellent job they had done, especially on their having successfully manned a weakly built work that was relatively unprotected against return artillery fire from the land and river defenses of Blakely.[41]

Company M got lost in the woods on its way to Blakely. During the night, they had wandered close to the Confederate pickets, but discovering the Rebels in time, the cannoneers quietly and safely made it away from them and continued searching for Blakely. When morning came on the 10th, they discovered that they were within a mile of where they had started their journey. They had caused more damage to their equipment during their stumbling around in the dark than they had received from the Rebel artillery at Spanish Fort. A gun's limber pole broke, and the peripatetic artillerists abandoned the gun and a field-forge. Next, they upset one of the ammunition wagons, but they managed to get it upright and reloaded. Shortly thereafter, the blunderers drove another wagon against a tree and broke it. This wreck, too, was left behind. Arriving at the wrong place long after the battle was over, they were ordered back to Bay Minette to go into camp alongside the 100-pounders at the old Minette Bay battery site formerly occupied by Companies H and K. They arrived with their three remaining guns, and being exhausted from their travels, they went into camp and to sleep directly as ordered.

Companies B and C returned to Spanish Fort and went into park inside the fort. On the morning of April 11, a shotted salute was ordered to be made by the 1st Missouri's Company F, now manning three 6.4-inch captured Brooke's rifles in Old Spanish Fort, the 6th Michigan's four mortars, the Hoosier's 100-pounders and Company M's 30-pounders at Forts Huger and Tracy in honor of the surrender of Richmond, Virginia. From their positions south of Blakely, Companies K and L joined in the fun and opened fire on the island forts. After Company M had fired several shots of the salute, the guns in Forts Huger and Tracy opened return fire of great intensity, which tore up the earthwork and showered the men with clods of dirt from exploding shells. There was only one injury, Lieutenant Theodore Markle's horse. Company M kept firing until it ran out of ammunition. Then they worked until 10 P.M. repairing their works and in getting ammunition. The battery again opened fire against the forts from ten o'clock until midnight.[42]

Later that night, there were several signal lights seen from Forts Huger and Tracy, and the general feeling among the Federals was that the forts were being abandoned. The 114th Illinois Pontoniers rowed out to the forts and found them totally abandoned. In true Kilroy fashion, they wrote their company identification on the guns and the time of night — 11:00 P.M. It was ironic that lowly Pontoniers and not an elite infantry unit officially claimed the forts.

The next day some Federal officers rowed out to these troublesome forts and inspected them. In Huger, a 100-pounder Parrott shot had completely demolished the carriage of a 10-inch Columbiad. A 30-pounder shot had carried away the elevating screw of the other 10-inch Columbiad, thereby disabling it. Most of the guns in the fort bore signs of having been hit by the 30-pounders but not permanently disabled. All of the buildings inside and outside of the forts had been riddled by the 30-pounders, and the fort's ramparts and embrasures badly torn up by the shot and shell.

On the 12th, Company F arrived from Baton Rouge. It and the four batteries at Spanish Fort received orders to go into park inside of the fort. Companies H, K, and L went into park at Blakely, and the Indiana Jackass Regiment's Headquarters moved there. On the 14th, Major John Day was ordered to collect and catalogue all captured ordnance and ordnance stores at Spanish Fort and Fort Blakely. He also had responsibility to gather all such stores left by the U.S. forces.

The battles were over. Lee had surrendered at Appomattox on the 9th. Blakely was the last sizable battle of the Civil War. Now it was time to seek the remaining Confederate armies surrenders and administer the peace. The Jackass Regiment had incurred only twenty casualties among men and officers during these last twelve days of battle. Company H had seven injured, Company K had six injured, Company C had one killed, Company L had one injured and Company M had one injured. The other two injuries were not identified as to their name or company.[43]

The Jackass Regiment's major James W. Connelly commanded the batteries on the right of the siege lines in front of the XVI Corps, and Major John Day commanded the batteries on the left of the lines in front of the XIII Corps. The batteries had fought against forty-six siege and field pieces at Spanish Fort (300 artillerymen), forty cannon at Blakely (350 artillerymen), and sixteen siege and garrison guns at forts Huger and Tracy. The regimental commander, Lieutenant-Colonel Benjamin F. Hays, expressed his thanks to all of his officers and men for a job well done. He extended special thanks to the officers and men of Companies H and K writing: "Captains Wimmer of H and Cox of K deserve special and honorable mention for their courage and skill in manning their guns and the accurate fire and splendid gunnery of their men when in position on Minette Bay and when under orders of General Steele [at Blakely]."[44]

Eighteen

The War Is Over. When May We Go Home?

Eight companies (B, C, F, H, I, K, L and M) of the Indiana Jackass Regiment began making themselves at home in their camps at Spanish Fort and Blakely. On April 15, the City of Mobile surrendered to arriving Federal forces. At Spanish Fort the artillerists fired a 100-gun salute from captured guns to celebrate the capture. On the 16th news arrived at Spanish Fort and at Blakely of the surrender of Lieutenant-General Robert E. Lee. The next day the 1st Missouri, Company F fired a 200-gun salute commemorating the surrender of General Lee and his army. On the 20th the men received the news of President Abraham Lincoln's assassination, and their exhilaration quickly changed to mourning.

On the 21st, in Spanish Fort a mourning gun fired every half hour until about one P.M. Then the guns fired once a minute for an hour in honor of the deceased president. A mourner wrote that the gods seemed to join the mourning because the sky darkened with black clouds, and wind blew very hard bending and twisting the tall pine trees around the fort as torrents of rain fell.[1]

General Dabney Maury had ordered the works at Mobile to be dismantled and abandoned on April 10. On the 11th what remained of his army was moving north. By the 15th of April, General Maury was in Meridian, Mississippi, and the city of Mobile, Alabama, was in Federal hands.

Orders came on April 23 for the Jackass Regiment to move across the bay to Mobile. Companies B and C boarded transports bound for Mobile on the 25th. The men in Companies F, I and M began packing their equipment on the 29th. On the 30th, half of Company F disembarked at Fort Huger and half disembarked at Fort Tracy. The men from Companies I and M arrived at Mobile at 4 P.M. They got their guns and equipment unloaded about dark and set out to find their camping area somewhere in the western limits of the city. Company M encamped on Massachusetts Street in the suburbs of the city, and the other companies camped nearby. The exact date of Companies' H, K and L moving to Mobile and where they camped is unknown.

What with the surrender of this army and the dismantling of the defenses of Mobile, the comrades of the 1st Indiana Heavies were hard at work hauling in all of the captured artillery from the numerous fortifications ringing Mobile. They had over 108 heavy guns, numerous field pieces, ammunition, equipment, etc. to catalogue, disassemble and haul to the wharf for shipment to various U.S. arsenals for storage.

When the men had some time to enjoy the city they viewed many beautiful gardens full of spring blooms. The fact that these gardens also had pretty female faces admiring the flowers was certain to capture the men's attention. They made several acquaintances, and very often a uniformed Federal soldier promenaded with a lady as if he were at home. The boys also had plenty of money to spend on diversions offered by the city. Nine paymasters had arrived to pay the men. Many of the soldiers spoke of their good fortune in being in a city that was spared from the ruin suffered by other southern cities. Mobile had plentiful quantities of food and goods which were scarce in cities like Atlanta, Columbia, Petersburg, and Richmond. This plenitude encouraged the troops to spend their money locally for personal items and sweet treats, which in turn helped maintain a thriving economy in Mobile.[2]

General E.R.S. Canby, U.S.A., met with General Richard Taylor, commander of all Confederate forces in the Army of the Mississippi, during the latter part of April to discuss terms of surrender for General Taylor's forces. The reports from the meeting indicated that Taylor's army would soon turn in its arms. What with General Robert E. Lee surrendering the Army of Northern Virginia on April 9, and General Joseph E. Johnston surrendering his army on April 26, it was only a matter time before General Richard Taylor surrendered, which he did on May 4, 1865. Taylor surrendered the largest Confederate army yet in the field. The Federals went to work issuing paroles to the surrendered men and paroling and releasing prisoners of war.

The Hoosiers continued in their routine clean up of the fortifications. They hauled siege platforms and lumber to an ordnance storage area and hauled wagon loads of ammunition from Confederate magazines all around the Mobile area. There were also the weapons and ammunition aboard the surrendered gunboats that were brought down the Alabama River to Mobile. Their work was interrupted when disaster struck the waterfront of Mobile on the 25th of May. At 3 P.M. a warehouse near the railroad terminus at the waterfront exploded. It was filled with captured ammunition, and its explosion destroyed nearly a third of the city. Four square city blocks were destroyed, two ships sunk, many others damaged, and every building within a half mile radius was damaged by the blast. The exact cause of the explosion was unknown, but a later court of inquiry determined that a worker dropped a percussion shell he was unloading from a train. As a precaution, the commanding general immediately issued orders that all paroled Confederates must have a pass to be allowed on the streets. This meant they must appear at the provost general's office with a copy of their parole and get a pass to be on their own street. Further, all able-bodied men were to report to clean up the debris.

General Granger sent out men to determine the number of homeless and injured among the civilian population. Based upon this information, rations were ordered to be distributed among them and to otherwise provide for those who had been dependent upon those killed or disabled in the disaster. Further, Granger received orders from General Canby to obtain and provide all medical assistance to the survivors of the blast that was possible. No one in the 1st Indiana was injured in the tragedy. The Hoosiers helped to clean up the rubble.[3]

On May 26, 1865, General Kirby Smith surrendered all Confederate forces west of the Mississippi River to the Federals. There were not too many regular forces, but there were many irregular and independent groups that the Confederate government had recognized. The business of accepting the surrender and giving parole documents to the small Confederate commands left in the field far and wide began. While these units were ordered by their commanders to remain at their posts until the Federal officers arrived to give them their documents, many of the intended recipients got tired of waiting and went home. The effect of this hasty action was not felt until years later when the soldiers' widows had difficulty in getting their late husbands' veteran pensions. Often, there was no record of his prior service, and the parole papers could have provided that proof.

Back in Louisiana, Companies E and G were ordered to embark up the Red River with such of the staff as was present at Baton Rouge. On June 1, they set out for Alexandria, Louisiana, with the 6th Missouri Cavalry aboard the gunboats *Benton*, *Ouachita*, and *Fort*

Hindman. Upon arrival at Alexandria, they took possession of the public property and Forts Buhlow and Randolph. They set about cataloguing the artillery, ammunition, caissons, wagons and dismantling it for shipment to U.S. arsenals like their comrades at Mobile. On June 3, paroles were given to the thirty-three men and officers of Boone's Louisiana Artillery Company who had remained at the forts awaiting parole. The parolees hurried to their homes, and the terms of surrender were carried out without problems.

A few weeks later the detachment of the Jackass Regiment at Alexandria came under the command of General George A. Custer when he and his cavalry were sent to administer the military rule of the area. The District of Morganza was discontinued, and the soldiers there would now report to Port Hudson which was consolidated with Baton Rouge as the new District of East Louisiana. This put Company D in another administrative district but still in Baton Rouge.[4]

The army was maintained in a state of readiness amidst of rumors that the troops may be needed further south. President Johnson had requested that the French emperor Maximilian leave Mexico. Armed intervention on behalf of the Mexican people was being considered by the United States government to drive the French out of that country. The bully boys of the 1st Indiana were of a mind to help drive the French emperor out if he declined to leave voluntarily. Dooley wrote: "Woe be to Mexico when he opposes American soldiers. We will teach the frog eaters what fighting is. They have been playing with the Mexicans long enough." Matters quieted down with the Mexican government, and the services of the Jackass Regiment were not needed to fight the French in Mexico.

The Hoosiers' stay in Mobile soon ended. A new military District of Mobile was established on June 12, under the command of General T. Kilby Smith. This district included Forts Morgan and Gaines. The siege train was officially disbanded, and except for infantry arms and equipment, the Indiana Jackass Regiment at Mobile turned over all their ordnance, ordnance stores and mules to the ordnance depot at Mobile. On the 15th, Colonel Benjamin F. Hays, commanding the 1st Indiana Heavies received orders to move his regimental headquarters and Companies H and K to Fort Gaines, Alabama. Major James W. Connelly was ordered to report for duty at Fort Morgan, Alabama, with Companies B and C. Major John W. Day was ordered with Companies F and L to report for duty at Fort Barrancas, Pensacola, Florida. Major Isaac C. Hendricks was ordered to report with Companies I and M to Fort Pickens, Santa Rosa Island, Florida across the bay from Fort Barrancas and Pensacola.[5]

The artillerists turned in their guns, gun carriages, caissons, limbers, mules, harness, wagons, forges, quartermaster stores, ammunition and other heavy artillery implements by June 21 under the assumption they were to be mustered out. Surprise! They were ordered aboard steamers bound for their new garrison posts. In only a week, the Hoosiers felt they were exiles. They were now cut off from the cities and the comradeship of the other army units, and they were isolated on hot, sandy shores, manning the heavy guns of lonely coastline forts.

The privates wondered as to why they were still on duty. After all, the war was over. Already they had thoughts of deserting, and a few had taken French leave while in Mobile. They sent petitions to Governor Morton requesting to be mustered out, especially, since he had worked so hard to get them into the volunteer army. The hoped for response with an immediate discharge and muster-out did not come. The esteemed governor of Indiana sent them a copy of an order from the War Department outlining the names of the regiments subject to being mustered out and under what conditions. While the 1st Indiana Heavy Artillery was on the list, the muster-out applied only to those who had enlisted for three years *prior* to October 1, 1862, and those men enlisting, drafted or as substitutes for one year *prior* to October 1, 1864. No orders applied to the mustering out of any *reenlisted veterans*! They were subject to the U.S. War Department, not Indiana, like it or not!

At Fort Gaines, the men had deep sand and lots of fleas. Even in their isolation, they had illness usually due to fever and diarrhea from contaminated food. Depression and stress over not being discharged also contributed to a lot of the men's ailments. On August 26, Rufus Dooley celebrated a melancholy twenty-third birthday at Fort Gaines. This was his fifth birthday since being mustered into the service of his country. He wrote home about the morale of his company: "Our Captain [William P. Wimmer] starts home on the first boat on a leave of absence. He is a man of discipline, and he now says he don't care if the boys all go home, and Lieutenant Snow says he wishes they would all desert. Now when the officers talk so, it is getting to be dangerous news and something will be done. I hope it will be done quick." Two hundred forty-nine men would eventually take french leave of the service from these desolate outposts before being discharged or mustered out in these final months of the regiment's service. However, the ones to whom the muster-out applied took advantage of it, which depleted the ranks to about 80 enlisted men per company from between 120 to 140 men.[6]

About two weeks later, an event occurred that broke the tedium of life on Dauphin Island. The boys heard that a ship was to land and put ashore four men ill with yellow fever for treatment in the post hospital. The regimental surgeon had approved of the transfer of the sick men to the island, because he was to receive $4.00 a day per patient. Rufus Dooley summed up the men's feelings about the surgeon quite well: "That old imp of Satan, who to do justice to humanity should be hung as high as Haman, done all he possibly could to get it [yellow fever] here." (This was before anyone knew that yellow fever was transmitted by mosquitoes.) The thought of yellow fever being brought among them was the proverbial straw that broke the camel's back.

The men of Companies H and K grabbed their rifles and stationed themselves along the beaches and on the wharves ready to repel with bullets any attempt to land the sick men. At 9 P.M. flames from the post hospital erupted into the sky where they could be seen from most any place on the island. While an armed guard kept anyone away who would attempt to extinguish the flames, the building burned to the ground. The loss of the hospital plus the armed demonstration resulted in the sick men being landed at Fort Morgan, where Companies B and C would deal with them. A few officers in companies H and K were unhappy about the actions of their men, but while they watched the anarchists, they did not interfere with their men's determined efforts. Most officers tacitly approved of the men's actions, and wisely remained in their quarters, keeping silent about the demonstration.

The men stayed on alert, and on the 16th of September, a ship's boat coming ashore for water narrowly avoided being blown away by the fort's artillery. Luckily for the crew of the boat, the Hoosiers recognized the water cask in the boat for what it was and let the boat land. They then learned from the boat's crew that the yellow fever cases had been taken to Fort Morgan. They also learned from this same crew that some sort of action was to be taken against them, but of what nature they could not determine. So, they remained vigilant for offensive movements against them, which did not happen. They had heard a rumor that a man had been hanged in one of the northern cities for the offense of bringing the yellow fever among the populace, and they resented the fact that they, being soldiers, were expected to put up with being purposely exposed to the fever. Further, several Hoosiers loudly vented their frustration against the general who had ordered the sick men to be sent among them saying that he should be hanged alongside of the surgeon who had requested the fever cases.[7]

The only action that was eventually taken against the two companies was to remove Company K from the island. The men of K were exiled a few miles north of Mobile to a post at the arsenal in the town of Mt. Vernon, Alabama. Evidently, the general-who-should-be-hanged" thought that splitting up these two rowdy companies would be sufficient punishment to restore order at Fort Gaines. Before long, the men in Company H settled into a routine garrison life on the island and even began to enjoy some of the recreational pursuits that are enjoyed on the island today. Dooley wrote that John Yelton, his roommate, had been hunting different shells along the beach. Besides hunting for unusual or pretty shells, the men tried new recipes such as oyster pie, a good tasting treat from the fort's brick ovens.

The men described their living quarters at Fort Gaines as cramped but adequate. The newly promoted Sergeant Rufus Dooley described his non-commissioned officer's quarters: "We are very comfortably fixed here. John Yelton and myself have a small room here about the size of a chicken office, one desk which holds our writing material, another table neatly covered with an oilcloth, which I am writing on; It generally supports a small looking glass, a comb, the housewife [a small sewing kit] you gave, and a musty old candlestick." The room also held a bunk bed with two straw-ticking mattresses.[8]

In November the regiment received orders to gather at Port Hudson to be mustered out. It took a while for the men to report in from their far-flung outposts. It was not until December 14, that Company M departed Fort Pickens on the steamer *Heroine*. The company arrived the next day at Camp Distribution at New Orleans where it spent the night. The next day they steamed up to Baton Rouge and landed that evening. Upon the arrival of the company from Florida, the Jackass Regiment was once again complete, and the mustering-out process could begin. While waiting in Baton Rouge, Rufus Dooley bought a tombstone for his brother's grave and paid his last respects at the new Federal military graveyard, located on the southern part of their Baton Rouge battlefield in the rear of their former camp. On December 26, 1865, Major Isaac C. Hendricks, commanding the regiment, cancelled the daily drill. At last, on January 10, 1866, the mustering out process was complete and 780 men and officers took their mustering out pay at Baton Rouge. Another 241 men and officers under command of Captain William Bough of Company C chose to travel to Indianapolis to be mustered out. Those who chose to be released in Louisiana made their own way home by various and sundry routes. Many stayed behind to marry and raise families in Louisiana or Alabama.[9]

At their official mustering out ceremony at Baton Rouge, Doctor Sherrod gave a lengthy farewell address to the men of the First Indiana Heavy Artillery Regiment, part of which is quoted because it reflects the sentiments of the regiment:

> You are about to return to the walks of civilian life.... How important the change — how fearful the responsibility ... if you would discharge your duty aright. As soldiers you have made a record for efficiency and bravery that will last as long as your Government holds a place among the civilized nations of the earth; let not that record be tarnished by any act of yours as citizens. And here permit me to remark that those who engaged you upon the battlefield were "foemen worthy of your steel." They have certainly presented to the world an example of courage under adversity and suffering seldom witnessed in the history of warfare.... To the last they rallied to their defenses or accepted battle in the open field.... At this time the most significant and gratifying fact is the disposition on the part of those who engaged us on the field of battle ... to forget the horrors and wickedness of war, and unite with us in all honorable efforts.... Some may feel that it is folly for me to speak of forgiveness at a time when the Southern homes are shrouded in the habiliments of mourning. God knows that we have had enough of these dark and hellish spirits of hatred and unforgiveness [sic]. We have them North as well as South. Let us swear here today, and let Heaven record the vow forever, that these disturbers of the country must cease their agitation.
>
> One other remark and I am done. Standing here as we do today, in full view of the bloody field of Baton Rouge, where many of your gallant comrades sleep the long sleep of death; on that memorable day you snatched victory from the very jaws of defeat, you stood like a stone wall, holding the columns of the enemy in check, while the cowards who had fled from the field were pouring deadly fire into your rear. Men who have conducted themselves so well as soldiers cannot but make good and respectable citizens.[10]

Eighteen. The War Is Over. When May We Go Home?

During its four years and six months of service, the regiment had traveled more than 15,000 miles. It had served more than three and one-half years in the Deep South, spending that time in the heartland of the enemy. The Hoosiers had received one furlough in their years of active duty. Besides their official designations as infantry and heavy artillery, they had also unofficially served as marines, cavalry, and light artillery. Three hundred seventy three men lost their lives through combat or illness during their time of service. The regiment had participated in the following battles, campaigns, skirmishes, or actions:

East Shore, Virginia	Brashear City, Louisiana
Forts Jackson and St. Philip, Louisiana	Port Hudson, Louisiana
New Orleans, Louisiana	LaFourche Crossing, Louisiana
Steamer Fox, Grand Caillou, Louisiana	Sabine Pass, Texas
Houma, Louisiana	Red River, Louisiana
Red Church, Louisiana	Blair's Landing, Louisiana
Grand Lake, Louisiana	Monette's Ferry, Louisiana
Donaldsonville, Louisiana	Mansura Plains, Louisiana
Baton Rouge, Louisiana	Yellow Bayou, Louisiana
Bayou Des Allemands, Louisiana	Fort Gaines, Alabama
Corni's [Cornay's] Bridge, Louisiana	Fort Morgan, Alabama
Camp Bisland, Louisiana	Spanish Fort, Alabama
Irish Bend, Louisiana	Fort Blakely, Alabama
Gunboat *Cotton*, Louisiana	Mobile, Alabama
Bayou Teche, Louisiana	

This ends the Civil War story of the Indiana Jackass Regiment. While little notice was given it by the Eastern political establishment, the regiment had an effect upon the lives of more than three thousand men who passed through its ranks and upon the tens of thousands of southern citizens and southern fighting men who they encountered in Maryland, Virginia, Louisiana, Texas, Alabama and Arkansas. A proper close to their story is found in this paragraph from page 13 of the "Memoirs," of Nelson Seybold, Company H, First Indiana Heavy Artillery: "The northern soldier returned to his home of peace and plenty, The southern soldier to a home of desolation from which all was gone but honor ... and they had the sympathy of our men for the hardships they had endured and for the poverty they were to face. These men surrendered in good faith and returned to their homes to become as good citizens as the country has ... a grateful people will remember to strew our graves with flowers as long as the country lasts."[11]

Epilogue

The Indiana Jackass Regiment's story is not quite finished. After their discharges at Baton Rouge many of the soldiers and officers remained in the general area around Baton Rouge and New Orleans. Colonel William Roy married a Baton Rouge maiden and went into business in New Orleans. He worked with the 9th Connecticut to raise money and build a monument to fallen Union soldiers in the Chalmette National Cemetery. He later moved to Arizona.

Colonel Keith returned to his successful law practice in Bedford, Indiana.

Former colonel and brigadier general James W. McMillan found employment as a government pension official.

Two members of Company D entered the business of petty thievery and stole two U.S. Army mules to ride back to Indiana. The army Provost Guard caught and jailed them at Port Hudson. They dug a hole under the log foundation and escaped. They arrived back in Indiana riding two stolen mules.

Others, tired of their wandering, took steamers to Indiana where several married and moved west to homestead. Most of those who did not move west remained in Indiana where they farmed and worked at their various specialties: carpentry, engineering, iron working, law, mercantile business, preaching, etc.

A couple of officers went into law enforcement as marshals or sheriffs in small towns in the West. Sergeant Rufus Dooley became a well-known businessman in Rockville, Indiana. Several of the men returning to north became farmers or hired farmhands in Indiana and Illinois. One such 25-year-old hired hand worked at this occupation for a short time, and then he eloped with a girl in her mid-teens, ten to twelve years his junior. Late at night, she tossed her valise out of her bedroom window into his waiting arms. He helped her down a ladder from the second floor and into his buggy. They quietly moved away from her home headed for the Illinois state line. Crossing it safely a couple of hours ahead of a posse raised by the girl's father, they married in Paris, Illinois. The bride and groom moved on to Kansas where they homesteaded. But that is another story.

Part II: Regimental Roster

21st Indiana Volunteer Infantry / 1st Indiana Heavy Artillery Regiment

1. This listing is based upon records obtained from "The Report of the Adjutant General of the State of Indiana" prepared under the auspices of W.H.H. Terrell, adjutant general, Indiana, hereinafter referred to as Terrell, Terrell's, or Terrell's Reports. The records were compared with Ancestry.com: "Military Records: Civil War Service Records" and certain National Archives records. The first spelling of names are as shown in Terrell, spellings in parentheses are other spellings contained in the Ancestry.com records. Names not found in Terrell's and not verified in the National Park Service-National Archives records but found in the Ancestry.com records are placed after the Unassigned Recruits at the end of this list.

2. Because the war was over, most desertions occurred during and after May 1865. Several were termed "French Leave" with no stigma attached by the enlisted men and some officers.

3. Company F's records were incomplete as published in the regimental listing in Terrell. The author has reconstructed these records from two other corrective sections or volumes of Terrell. Corrections and additions are welcomed by the author.

All persons are shown by last name, first name (*including known aliases and misspellings*)**, rank at entering service, date of muster-in, rank at leaving service, reason for end of service, date of leaving service and cause for leaving** (*if other than end of enlistment*).

Company A

Acton, John H., Recruit, 1864/03/26, Private, Discharged 10/07/1864, Disability.

Aingken, Samuel, Private, 1861/07/24, Private, Wounded at Battle of Baton Rouge, LA, 08/05/1862; Transferred 1st U.S. Arty. 11/21/62.

Anderson, William, Recruit, 1862/10/12, Artificer, Mustered Out 10/12/65.

Apple, Lewis, Sergeant, 1861/07/24, Sergeant, Discharged 04/15/1862, Disability.

Ashley, Ralph, Recruit, 1864/03/12, Private, Veteran, Mustered Out 01/13/1866.

Attinburg, Casper, Recruit, 1864/03/26, Private, Mustered Out 01/13/1866.

Bachelor, Henry T., Private, 1861/07/24, Private, Killed In Action at Battle of Baton Rouge, LA, 08/05/1862.

Bachus, Frank H., Private, 1861/07/24, Private, Trans. to 1st U.S. Arty. 11/21/62.

Baker, Hamilton T., Recruit, 1864/02/26, Private, Mustered Out 02/25/65.

Barr, Jacob, Private, 1861/07/24, Private, Veteran, Mustered Out 01/13/1866.

Barr, Robert N., Private, 1861/07/24, Private, Veteran, Mustered Out 01/13/1866.

Bart, John, Recruit, 1863/05/13, Private, Died at Indianapolis, IN 03/18/1864.

Batchelder, Ivora H., Recruit, 1864/03/12, Private, Mustered Out 01/13/1866.

Baughman, Isaiah, Recruit, 1964/04/01, Private, Mustered Out 01/13/1866.

Beagle, Noah, Recruit, 1864/03/26, Private, Mustered Out 01/13/1866.

Beagle, Thomas, Recruit, 1864/10/01, Private, Discharged 09/30/1865.

Bender, Harmon S., Recruit, 1862/02/26, Corporal, Discharged 02/25/1865.

Bernethy, George W., Recruit, 1864/09/26, Private, Mustered Out 08/05/1865.

Blackstone, Charles C., Recruit, 1864/09/06, Private, Mustered Out 08/05/1865.

Blanchard, Amos D., Private, 1861/07/24, Promoted 2nd Lieutenant 03/19/1865; Veteran; Mustered Out 01/10/1866 as 1st Sergeant.

Blue, David, Recruit, 1864/10/04, Private, Discharged 10/19/1865, Disability.

Bosier, Samuel J., Recruit, 1864/09/26, Private, Mustered Out 08/05/1865.

Bovington (aka Bevington), John A., Sergeant, 1861/07/24, First Sergeant, Killed In Action at Battle of Baton Rouge, LA, 08/05/1862.

Braugher, Manius, Recruit, 1862/02/26, Private, Wounded at Battle of Baton Rouge 08/05/1862; Killed In Action at Port Hudson, LA, 6/14/63.

Breslin, Henry, Recruit, 1861/07/24, Private, Veteran, Mustered Out 01/13/1866.

Breslin, William, Recruit, 1861/07/24, Private, Discharged 10/26/61, Disability.

Brink, Oliver, Private, 1861/07/24, Private, Trans. 1st U.S. Arty. 11/21/62

Brothwell, David, Recruit, 1864/09/26, Private, Mustered Out 08/05/1865.

Brown, Lewis, Recruit, 1864/09/17, Private, Mustered Out 08/05/1865.

Bryan, Henry, Recruit, 1864/03/12, Private, Mustered Out 01/13/1866.

Burns, (aka Burris), Peter A., 2nd Lieutenant, 1864/01/12, Promoted 1st Lieutenant 03/30/1864; Mustered Out 01/10/1866.

Butler, Dunn A., Recruit, 1864/04/02, Private, Mustered Out 01/13/1866.

Cady, David A. (aka Davis A.), Recruit, 1864/03/21, Private, Died 07/09/1864 at Morganza, LA.

Campbell, George, Recruit, 1864/03/21, Private, Mustered Out 01/13/1866.

Carmien, Jesse F., Corporal, 1861/07/24, Sergeant, Mustered Out 08/31/1864.

Carr, Leander T., Recruit, 1863/05/25, Private, Mustered Out 01/13/1866.

Carroll, Elias, Private, 1861/07/24, 1st Lieutenant [Private], Wounded at Battle of Baton Rouge, LA, 88/05/1862; Veteran, Mustered Out 1/13/1866.

Case, Elwin W., Musician, 1861/07/24, Bugler, Mustered Out 08/31/1864.

Cathcart, John, Recruit, 1863/05/08, Private, *Deserted 05/21/1864.*

Cause, James, Recruit, 1864/09/06, Private, Mustered Out 08/05/1865.

Chamberlain, Dorsey S., Private, 1861/07/24, Private, Veteran, Mustered Out 01/13/1866.

Charter, Alfred E., Private, 1861/07/24, Private, Veteran, Mustered Out 01/13/1866.

Coats, Charles W., Private, 1861/07/24, Corporal, Veteran, Mustered Out 01/13/1866.

Cole, Thomas, Private, 1861/07/24, Private, Wounded at Battle of Baton Rouge, LA, 08/05/1862; Wounded at Port Hudson, June 1863; Discharged 07/18/1865, Disability.

Conger, Pembroke S., Recruit, 1863/05/17, Private, Mustered Out 01/13/1866.

Conger, Selwin L., Recruit, 1862/10/25, Private, Mustered Out 10/24/1865.

Conley, Lewis, Recruit, 1864/09/26, Private, Mustered Out 08/05/1865.

Conover, William, Recruit, 1864/04/08, Private, Mustered Out 01/13/1866.

Cramer, William, Recruit, 1864/03/21, Private, Mustered Out 01/13/1866.

Crosby, Joel S., Recruit, 1864/04/04, Corporal, Discharged 07/18/1865, Disability.

Culbertson, Benjamin F., Private, 1861/07/24, Bugler, Veteran, Mustered Out 01/13/1866.

Culbertson (aka Albertson), Enoch R., Private, 1861/07/24, Sergeant, Veteran, Mustered Out 01/13/1866.

Culbertson, James K., Recruit, 1864/03/21, Private, Mustered Out 01/13/1866.

Daugherty, Sidwell, Private, 1861/07/24, Private, Discharged 10/14/1862, Disability.

Dickenson, Levant B., Recruit, 1864/09/25, Private, Mustered Out 08/05/1865.

Dickenson, Newell, Recruit, 1864/10/04, Private, Mustered Out 10/04/1865.

Dixon, Owen, Recruit, 1864/09/25, Private, Mustered Out 08/05/1865.

Draygoe, James, Recruit, 1864/03/26, Private, Mustered Out 01/13/1866.

Driskol, Dennis, Private, 1861/07/24, Private, Veteran, Mustered Out 01/13/1866.

Driskol (aka Driscol), Patrick, Private, 1861/07/24, Private, Discharged 10/31/1862.

Dryer, Bennis, Private, 1861/07/24, Private, Died in Hotel Dieu at New Orleans, 09/10/1862.

Dukes, Isaac, Recruit, 1864/04/01, Private, Died 10/01/1865 at Baton Rouge, LA.

Dunning, Jesse L., Recruit, 1863/04/18, Private, Mustered Out 01/13/1866.

Everts, Perry O., Private, 1861/07/24, Private, Veteran, Mustered Out 01/13/1866.

Ferguson (aka Furgeson), James, Private, 1861/07/24, Sergeant, Veteran, Mustered Out 01/13/1866.

Ferguson, John H., Recruit, 1864/04/28, Private, Mustered Out 01/13/1866.

Field, Daniel W., Recruit, 1864/09/26, Private, Mustered Out 08/05/1865.

Fisher, Albert W., Recruit, 1864/03/12, Private, Died 08/24/1864 at Cairo, IL.

Fisher, Eden H., First Sergeant, 1861/07/24, Promoted 2nd Lieutenant 01/10/1862; Promoted 1st Lieutenant 08/05/1862; Wounded at Berwick Bay, LA, Promoted Captain 03/10/1863; Resigned 11/20/1863; Disability from wounds.

Fitts, William, Recruit, 1863/06/03, Private, *Deserted 05/21/1864.*

Francis (aka Francis), Wilton (aka Welton), Recruit, 1862/10/25, Private, Mustered Out 10/25/1865.

Frink, Augustus P., Recruit, 1862/10/26, Private, Mustered Out 02/25/1865.

Gaby, Nelson V., Recruit, 1864/09/26, Private, Mustered Out 08/05/1865.

Gillett, Harvey J., Private, 1861/07/24, Private, Veteran, Mustered Out 01/13/1866.

Graham, John, Recruit, 1864/10/24, Private, Discharged 09/18/1865.

Grimm, Jacob, Recruit, 1864/09/07, Private, Mustered Out 08/05/1865.

Gunder, John W., Private, 1861/07/24, Private, Veteran, Mustered Out. 01/13/1866.

Gunnett, Samuel W., Recruit, 1864/09/26, Private, Mustered Out 08/05/1865.

Gunnett, Seth, Recruit, 1864/09/26, Private, Mustered Out 08/05/1865.

Gurnsey, Marvin, Private, 1861/07/24, Private, Discharged 09/20/1861, Disability.

Hall, Harvey B., Sergeant, 1861/07/24, Capt., Wounded at Battle of Baton Rouge, LA, 08/05/1862; Promoted 2nd Lieutenant 10/14/1862; Promoted 1st Lieutenant 03/10/1863; Promoted Captain 11/21/1863; Died 01/11/1864.

Hall, Martin V., Recruit, 1864/09/26, Private, Discharged 04/22/1865, Disability.

Hamlet, William L., Private, 1861/07/24, Corporal, Veteran, Mustered Out 01/13/1866.

Hamlin, Franklin W., Recruit, 1864/09/20, Private, Mustered Out 08/05/1865.

Hane, John, Private, 1861/07/24, Private, Veteran, Mustered Out 01/13/1866.

Harding, Martin V., Recruit, 1863/06/03, Private, *Deserted 05/21/1864.*

Harris, William C., Recruit, 1862/10/21, Private, Died 08/17/1863 at Baton Rouge.

Harrison, William, Private, 1861/07/24, Private, *Deserted 01/10/1862.*

Harvey [Hervy], Oscar P., Sergeant Major, 1861/07/24, Private, Transferred from non-comm. staff to Company A, 10/01/1862.

Haskins, Charles, Private, 1861/07/24, Private, Veteran, Mustered Out. 01/13/1866.

Hay, George, Recruit, 1864/03/26, Private, Mustered Out 01/13/1866.

Hayes, John H., Private, 1861/07/24, Private, Wounded at Battle of Baton Rouge, LA, 08/05/1862; Veteran, Mustered Out 01/13/1866.

Hersh, William F., Recruit, 1864/10/04, Private, Mustered Out 10/02/1865.

Hodges, Frank, Recruit, 1864/09/20, Private, Mustered Out 08/05/1865.

Holford, Daniel, Recruit, 1863/12/17, Private, Died 07/24/1864 at Baton Rouge, LA.

Homan, John, Recruit, 1864/09/06, Private, Veteran, Mustered Out 01/13/1866.

Hostetter, DeWitt C., Recruit, 1864/03/26, Private, *Deserted 04/18/1864.*

Houston, William J., Recruit, 1864/09/20, Private, Mustered Out 08/05/1865.

Howell, James R., Musician, 1861/07/24, Sergeant, Veteran, Mustered Out. 01/13/1866.

Hubbell, Edward T., Sergeant, 1861/07/24, 2nd Lieutenant. Discharged 10/14/1862 as Sergeant; Disability.

Hughey, Stephen F., Recruit, 1864/09/07, Private, Mustered Out 08/05/1865.

Humbert, Simon, Private, 1861/07/24, Private, Veteran, Mustered Out. 01/13/1866.

Ingram, George, Private, 1861/07/24, Private, Discharged 10/16/1862, Disability, wounds received at Battle of Baton Rouge.

Ingram, James, Private, 1861/07/24, Private, Wounded at Battle of Baton Rouge. LA, 08/05/1865; Veteran, Mustered Out. 1/13/1866.

Irish, Jonathan, Private, 1861/07/24, Private, Discharged 08/15/1862.

Jackson, Thaddeus P., Private, 1861/07/24, 2nd Lieutenant, Resigned 01/08/1865.

Johnston, Albert N., Private, 1861/07/24, Private, *Deserted 12/10/1861.*

Jones, John, Recruit, 1864/03/15, Corporal, Mustered Out 01/13/1866.

Jones, John W., Recruit, 1864/03/15, Private, Mustered Out 01/13/1866.

Kelly, Almon W., Private, 1861/07/24, Private, Veteran, Mustered Out. 01/13/1866.

Kennedy, Joseph, Recruit, 1864/04/08, Private, Mustered Out 01/13/1866.

Kerling, John, Recruit, 1864/03/12, Private, Mustered Out 01/13/1866.

Knepper, Daniel, Recruit, 1864/09/28, Private, Died 08/12/1865 on Hospital Boat.

Knight, Isaac, Private, 1861/07/24, Corporal, Killed In Action at Battle of Baton Rouge, LA, 08/05/1862.

Knight, Osborn, Recruit, 1864/03/26, Private, Died 09/28/64 on Steamer Olive Branch.

Knox, Robert B., Recruit, 1864/04/07, Private, *Deserted 04/18/1864.*

Kropstone, John, Recruit, 1864/04/21, Private, Mustered Out 01/13/1866.

LaDow, Frank, Recruit, 1864/03/03, Private, Mustered Out 01/13/1866.

Lane, George A., Corporal, 1861/07/24, Private [?], Discharged 08/31/1864.

Lane, Josiah, Recruit, 1862/02/26, Private, Mustered Out 02/25/1865.

Law, Oscar, Private, 1861/07/24, Private, Veteran, Mustered Out 01/13/1866.

Lee, Mathias, Recruit, 1862/06/03, Private, *Deserted 03/03/1864.*

Markham (aka Muskham), David E., Private, 1861/07/24, Private, Veteran, Mustered Out 01/13/1866.

Mason, Luther F., Private, 1861/07/24, Private, Transferred to 1st U.S. Art'y. 11/21/1862.

McCalla, Christopher G., Recruit, 1863/11/11, Private, Mustered Out 01/13/1866.

McConnell, Thomas B., Recruit, 1862/02/26, Private, Wounded at Port Hudson; June 1863; Mustered Out 02/25/1865.

McCord, William, Private, 1861/07/24, Private, Discharged 10/16/62, Disability, wounds rec'd. at Baton Rouge. Wounded at Battle of Baton Rouge, 8/5-1862, Mustered Out 02/05/1865.

McLain, Leonard N., Private, 1861/07/24, Private, Veteran, Mustered Out 01/13/1866.

McLean, George, Private, 1861/07/24, Corporal, Veteran, Mustered Out 01/13/1866.

McMeans, David, Recruit, 1864/10/04, Private, Mustered Out 10/02/1865.

Meek, Adam W., Private, 1861/07/24, Corporal, Discharged 09/29/1862, Disability, wounds received at Baton Rouge Port Hudson, June 1863.

Meinhart, Philip, Recruit, 1863/11/21, Private, Died 03/21/1864, New Orleans, LA.

Merriman, Judson J., Recruit, 1864/04/08, Private, Mustered Out 01/13/1866.

Meyers, John W., Private, 1861/07/24, Private, Veteran, Mustered Out. 01/13/1866.

Miller, Henry S., Recruit, 1862/02/26, Private, Mustered Out 02/25/1865.

Miller, Jacob S. (aka Jacob C., Jacob L.), Recruit, 1862/02/26, Private, Died at New Orleans, LA, 07/17/1863.

Minehart (aka Mimhart), Philip, Recruit, 1863/11/21, Private, Died at New Orleans, LA, 03/21/1864.

Modie (aka Moodie), George W., Private, 1861/07/24, Private, *Deserted 12/10/1861.*

Moore, Robert, Recruit, 1864/09/26, Private, Mustered Out 08/25/1865.

Mordaunt (aka Mordant), Ralph, Recruit, 1864/06/07, Private, Mustered Out 08/25/1865.

Morris, John, Private, 1861/07/24, Private, Discharged 1862/10/21, Disability.

Morton, James E., Recruit, 1864/04/08, Private, Discharged 10/12/1864, Disability.

Myers, John W., Private, 1861/07/24, Private, Veteran, Mustered Out 01/13/1866.

Nash, James, Private, 1861/07/24, Private, Mustered Out 07/13/1864.

Newman, Henry W., Recruit, 1864/09/26, Private, Mustered Out 08/25/1865.

Oliver, Josephus, Recruit, 1864/04/11, Private, *Deserted 10/21/1861.*

Omsted (aka Umstead), Harvey, Private, 1861/07/24, Private, Discharged, 10/14/1862, Disability.

Paulus, William H., Private, 1861/07/24, Corporal, Veteran, Mustered Out 01/13/1866.

Peirce, Dewitt, Private, 1861/07/24, Private, Veteran, Mustered Out 01/13/1866.

Perew (aka Peru, Pereu, Perue), David H., Recruit, 1864/09/26, Private, Mustered Out 08/25/1865.

Perkins (aka Pirkins), Enoch, Private, 1861/07/24, Private, Transferred to 1st U.S. Artillery 11/21/1862.

Perry, William A., Recruit, 1864/04/16, Private, Mustered Out 01/13/1866.

Pickets (aka Pickels, Pickles), Joseph, Recruit, 1864/09/26, Private, Mustered Out 08/25/1865.

Pierce, Dewitt M., Private, 1861/07/24, Private, Veteran, Mustered Out 01/13/1866.

Pippenger (aka Peppenger, Peppinger), Daniel F., Private, 1861/07/24, 2nd Lieutenant, Promoted 2nd Lieutenant 03/30/1864; Mustered Out 01/10/1866..

Pippinger, David, Private, 1861/07/24, Private, Discharged 10/26/1861, Disability.

Pitcher (aka Pitcer), Frederick, Recruit, 1863/08/11, Private, *Deserted 05/21/1864.*

Pitman, Eli, Private, 1861/07/24, Private, Died at Baltimore, MD 11/15/1861.

Poland (aka Polland), Samuel, Recruit, 1862/02/26, Private, Mustered Out 02/25/1865.

Pontius (aka Pountius), Benjamin F., Recruit, 1864/03/26, Private, Mustered Out 01/13/1866.

Potts, James M., Recruit, 1864/03/26, Private, Mustered Out 01/13/1866.

Potts, William, Recruit, 1863/04/28, Private, Mustered Out 01/13/1866.

Powell, Benjamin M., Private, 1861/07/24, Private, Mustered Out 07/31/1864.

Powers, Joseph, Recruit, 1864/04/21, Private, Died 06/06/1864 at Baton Rouge, LA.

Raber (aka Rober), Joel D., Recruit, 1864/09/26, Private, Mustered Out 08/05/1865.

Raber, Levi, Recruit, 1864/09/26, Private, Mustered Out 08/05/1865.

Rapine (aka Repine), John C., Recruit, 1864/09/26, Private, Mustered Out 08/05/1865.

Reed (aka Read), John C. (aka Jonathan T.), Recruit, 1864/03/27, Private, Mustered Out 01/13/1865. Discharged 04/15/1862, Disability.

Rheubottom (aka Remberton, Rhierbottom, Rhubottom), James R., Corporal, 1861/07/24, Corporal, Mustered Out 08/31/1864, Term Expired.

Riddle (aka Reddel), William W., Private, 1861/07/24, Sergeant, Veteran, Mustered Out 01/13/1866.

Ritter, Andrew J., Private, 1861/07/24, Corporal, Veteran, Mustered Out 01/13/1866.

Ritter, David, Private, 1861/12/28, Private, Veteran, Mustered Out 01/13/1866.

Ritter (aka Reiter), William, Recruit, 1864/03/28, Private, Mustered Out 01/13/1866.

Robbins (aka Robins), George J. (aka George G.), Private, 1861/07/24, Corporal, Veteran, Mustered Out 01/13/1866.

Roy (aka Ray), David M., Recruit, 1864/03/12, Private, Mustered Out 01/13/1866.

Roy (aka Ray), Leonard, Recruit, 1864/03/19, Private, Died 09/15/1864, Morganza, LA.

Roy, William, Captain, 1861/07/24, Promoted Major 03/10/1863; Promoted Lieutenant-Colonel 02/03/1865; Resigned 07/11/1865.

Salladay, George W. (aka George M.), Recruit, 1864/09/26, Private, Mustered Out 01/13/1865.

Sands, Henry, Private, 1861/07/24, Sergeant, Veteran, Mustered Out 01/13/1866.

Sargent (aka Sargeant, Sergant, Sergent, Sergeant), Alfred, Corporal, 1861/07/24, Private, Mustered Out 08/31/1864.

Saulsbury (aka Saulsberry), William, Recruit, 1863/11/30, Private, Discharged 05/25/1865, Disability.

Scripture, Samuel F., Recruit, 1864/09/26, Private, Mustered Out 08/05/1865.

Seely (aka Seeley), Charles D., 1st Lieutenant, 1861/07/24, 1st Lieutenant, Killed In Action at Battle of Baton Rouge, LA 08/05/1862.

Segnor (aka Segar), Edward B., Recruit, 1863/04/28, Private, Died, Baton Rouge, LA, 05/20/1864.

Segnor (aka Segner, Signor), George, Recruit, 1864/03/30, Private, Discharged 10/26/65, Disability.

Self, George W., Private, 1861/07/24, Sergeant, Veteran, Mustered Out 01/13/1866.

Self, Michael W., Recruit, 1864/03/29, Private, Mustered Out 01/13/1866.

Shaffer, Vital (aka Vetal), Recruit, 1864/04/02, Private, Discharged 03/21/1865, Disability.

Shaffstal (aka Shafstall), Adam, Private, 1861/07/24, Sergeant, Mustered Out 07/31/1864..

Shefler (aka Sheffler, Shiffler), John C., Recruit, 1864/09/26, Private, Mustered Out 08/5-1865.

Shemberger, Samuel, Private, 1861/07/24, Private, Wounded at Battle of Baton Rouge, LA, 08/05/1862; Discharged 10/27/1862 (due to wounds?).

Shoffstall (aka Shaffstal, Shafstall), Franklin, Recruit, 1862/10/25, Private, Mustered Out 10/24/1865.

Sibert (aka Seibert), John, Recruit, 1864/03/26, Private, Died on steamer *Olive Branch*, 10/01/1864.

Simmons, Abram W., Corporal, 1861/07/24, Captain, Promoted 2nd Lieutenant 03/10/1863; Promoted 2nd Lieutenant 11/21/1863; Promoted Captain 01/12/1864; Mustered Out 01/10/1866..

Simmons (aka Simmon), Isaac A., Recruit, 1865/11/03, Corporal, Veteran, Mustered Out 01/13/1866.

Simpson, Robert K., Private, 1861/07/24, Sergeant, Veteran, Mustered Out 01/13/1866.

Sitterfin (siderwell), John F. (Frederick, Frederick J.), Private, 1861/07/24, Private, Wounded at Battle of Baton Rouge. LA, 08/05/1862; Died 10/17/1862 at New Orleans (of Wounds?).

Skadden (aka Shadden, Skaven), Halsey F., Private, 1861/07/24, Private, Veteran, Mustered Out 01/13/1866.

Skinner, Merritt C., Corporal, 1861/07/24, 1st Lieutenant, Wounded at Battle of Baton Rouge, LA, 08/05/1862; Mustered Out 01/10/1866.

Smith, Barton (aka Barton), Private, 1862/02/26, Private, Died New Orleans, LA, 09/12/1862.

Smith, Daniel T. (aka Daniel F., Daniel P), Private, 1861/07/24, Private, Wounded at Battle of Baton Rouge, LA, 08/05/1862; Veteran, Mustered Out. 1/13/1866.

Smith, David, Private, 1861/07/24, Private, Died at Corunna, 03/14/1864.

Smith, John C. (aka John A.), Wagoner, 1861/07/24, Wagoner, Veteran, Mustered Out 01/13/1866.

Smith, Peter, Private, 1861/07/24, Private, Mustered Out 07/31/1864.

Smith, William H., Recruit, 1864/09/14, Private, Mustered Out 08/5-1865.

Smurr, William S., 2nd Lieutenant, 1861/07/24, 2nd Lieutenant, Resigned 01/08/1862.

Snyder, Isaac W., Private, 1861/07/24, Private, Wounded at Battle of Baton Rouge, LA, 08/05/1862; Veteran, Mustered Out 01/13/1866.

Spangal (aka Spangle), John A., Recruit, 1862/02/25, Private, Mustered Out 02/25/1865.

Spidell (aka Spidle), Daniel, Recruit, 1864/04/02, Private, Mustered Out 01/13/1866.

Steinbarger (aka Stienberger, Steenberger, Stinberger, Stineberger, Stuberger), Joseph A., Recruit, 1864/04/01, Private, Mustered Out 01/13/1866.

Stevenson (aka Stroman), Samuel, Recruit, 1864/03/26, Private, Mustered Out 01/13/1866.

Talmage (aka Talmadge), Joseph W., Corporal, 1861/07/24, Sergeant, Veteran, Mustered Out 01/13/1866.

Tantsman (aka Timstman, Tintsman, Tinstman), Joseph, Private, 1861/12/28, Private, Died, New Orleans, LA, 03/28/1864.

Taylor, Stephen P. (aka Stephan), Recruit, 1864/09/26, Private, Mustered Out 01/13/1866.

Temple (aka Timple), Edwin R. (aka Edward), Private, 1861/07/24, Sergeant, Veteran, Mustered Out 01/13/1866.

Thomas, Andrew W., Corporal, 1861/07/24, Corporal, Discharged, 04/15/1862, Disability.

Tinstman (aka Trustman. Twistman), Albert B. (aka Albert R), Private, 1861/07/24, Sergeant, Veteran, Mustered Out 01/13/1866.

Trump, William, Recruit, 1864/09/26, Private, Mustered Out 01/13/1866.

Vanarmon (aka Vanarman), George W., Private, 1861/07/24, Private, Discharged 10/26/1861, Disability.

Vanpelt (aka Vanfelt), Samuel, Private, 1861/07/24, Private, Mustered Out 07/31/1864.

Warren (aka Warner), William B., Private, 1861/07/24, Private, Discharged 10/14/1862, Disability.

Wartsbaugh (aka Vurstbaugh, Warstbough, Wertsbaugh, Westsbaugh Worstbaugh, Wurstbaugh), Daniel, Recruit, 1863/04/27, Private, Mustered Out 01/13/1866.

Wayburn (aka Waybem, Weybunn, Weybum), Albert H., Recruit, 1864/03/14, Private, Mustered Out 01/13/1866.

Wayburn (aka Waybem, Weybunn, Weybum), Oscar M., Recruit, 1864/03/12, Private, Died on steamer *Atlantic*, 10/28/1864.

Windell (aka Wendall, Wendell), Abram L., Recruit, 1864/04/01, Private, Mustered Out 01/13/1866.

White, Wilson W., Recruit, 1864/09/26, Private, Mustered Out 08/05/1865.

Widner (aka Wedder, Widens), Cornelius, Recruit, 1864/03/12, Private, Died at Baton Rouge, LA, 06/30/1864.

Williamson, Asher, Recruit, 1864/11/01, Private, Mustered Out 09/30/1865. Discharged 10/26/1861, Disability.

Woodford, John C., Recruit, 1864/03/08, Private, Mustered Out 01/13/1866.

Woodworth, Ira J. (aka Ira G.), Private, 1861/07/24, Private, Wounded at Battle of Baton Rouge, LA 08/05/1862; Mustered Out 07/31/1864.

Yard, Benjamin R., Private, 1861/07/24, Private, Discharged 10/26/1861, Disability.

Young, Jacob L., Private, 1861/07/24, Corporal, Veteran, Mustered Out 01/13/1866.

Wangramaker (aka Wannamache, Wannamaker, Waunnamaker, Winemaker, Winamaker), Peter, Recruit, 1863/11/28, Private, Mustered Out 01/13/1866.

Wellman (aka Welleman), Robert P., Recruit, 1863/12/08, Private, Mustered Out 01/13/1866.

Zinn (aka Yain), George E., Private, 1861/07/24, Private, Died at Baltimore, MD 09/26/1861.

Company B

Acuff, Luke, Private, 1861/07/24, Private, Mustered Out 07/31/1864.

Acuff, Wesley, Corporal, 1861/07/24, Sergeant Corporal, Mustered Out 07/31/1864.

Alberts, William, Recruit, 1862/05/26, Private, Died in St. James Infirmary at New Orleans, LA, 09/06/1862.

Alexander, Christopher H., Recruit, 1864/09/21, Private, Mustered Out 01/13/1866.

Allison, John W., Recruit, 1864/02/29, Private, Mustered Out 01/13/1866.

Anderson, Vincent, Private, 1861/07/24, Private, Discharged 07/10/1863, Disability.

Anderson, William H.H., Private, 1861/07/24, Private, Mustered Out 07/31/1864.

Arnett (aka Annet), Martin V., Private, 1861/07/24, Private, Discharged 04/10/1862, Disability.

Ashley (aka Ashly), Thomas J., Private, 1861/07/24, Corporal Private, Veteran, Discharged 11/01/1865, Disability.

Bailey (aka Baily), John (aka Jehu), Recruit, 1863/11/25, Private, Deserted 04/01/1864.

Baker (aka Backer), Isaac N., Recruit, 1864/02/18, Private, Mustered Out 01/13/1866.

Baker, Robert D., Recruit, 1862/01/31, Private, Mustered Out 02/01/1865.

Baker, Thomas F.S., Private, 1861/07/24, Corporal, Veteran, Died at New Orleans, LA, 02/19/1865.

Ballinger, Ner. B. (aka A.B.), Recruit, 1864/02/29, Private, Mustered Out 01/13/1866.

Baxter, Alonzo H.H., Recruit, 1863/11/28, Private, Mustered Out 01/13/1866.

Baxter, Franklin, Recruit, 1863/11/23, Private, *Deserted 06/06/1865*.

Beaman (aka Beeman, Beman), Eli C., Private, 1861/07/24, Private, Mustered Out 07/31/1864.

Beaman (aka Beman), John, Recruit, 1863/12/31, Private, Mustered Out 01/13/1866.

Bennett (aka Burnett), Franklin, Recruit, 1864/09/26, Private, Mustered Out, date not reported.

Bennett, William H., Recruit, 1864/09/08, Private, Died at New Orleans, LA, 01/26/1865.

Best, Thomas E., Private, 1861/07/24, Sergeant, Veteran, Mustered Out 01/13/1866.

Bickle (aka Bickel), William H., Recruit, 1863/11/25, Corporal, Mustered Out 01/13/1866.

Billingsley (aka Billingsly), James, Recruit, 09/23/1864, Private, Mustered Out, date not reported.

Blankenship (aka Blankinship), Philip H., Recruit, 1864/08/24, Corporal, Mustered Out 01/13/1866.

Blankenship (aka Blankinship), William H., First Sergeant, 1861/07/24, Captain, Mustered Out 01/10/1866.

Blockley (aka Blackley, Blockly), Charles, Recruit, 1864/03/18, Private, Mustered Out, date not reported.

Blunk (aka Blaunk), Goolsby, Private, 1861/07/24, Private, Died at Cairo, IL, while on sick leave.

Bock, Thomas J., Recruit, 1863/12/05, Private, Died at New Orleans, LA, 01/24/1865.

Bonsal (aka Bonsall, Bonsel), John D. (aka John E.), Recruit, 1863/11/28, Private, Mustered Out 01/13/1866.

Bower (aka Bowers), Philip, Recruit, 1864/01/12, Private, Mustered Out 01/13/1866.

Braze (aka Blaize, Brace, Braize), Frederick, Recruit, 1863/12/26, Private, *Deserted 07/01/1865*.

Brim, Andrew J., Private, 1861/07/24, Private, Veteran, Mustered Out 01/13/1866.

Brown, John M., Recruit, 1864/02/29, Corporal, Mustered Out 01/13/1866.

Brown, Tilghman H. (aka Tilghman A), Sergeant, 1861/07/24, Sergeant, Discharged 12/04/1863, Disability.

Brown, William A., Sr. (William A.), Recruit, 1863/11/23, Private, Mustered Out 01/13/1866.

Buckley (aka Buckly), Jeremiah, Recruit, 1863/12/23, Private, Mustered Out 01/13/1866.

Burns (aka Burnett), James, Recruit, 1864/10/07, Private, Mustered Out 10/07/1865.

Burt, Thomas P., Corporal, 1861/07/24, Corporal, Mustered Out 07/31/1864.

Butler, Tobias D. (aka Tobias C.), Private, 1861/07/24, Private, Mustered Out 07/31/1864.

Cambridge, John, Recruit, 1864/10/08, Private, Mustered Out 10/07/1865.

Card, Benjamin F. (aka B. Frank), Sergeant, 1861/07/24, 1st Lieutenant, Promoted to 1st Lieut. Co.L 10/21/1863; Discharged 09/28/1863.

Castor (aka Caster), Lewis, Recruit, 1863/11/02, Private, Mustered Out 01/13/1866.

Chambers, George W. (aka Grorge W.), Private, 1861/07/24, Corporal, Veteran, *Deserted 07/07/1865.*

Chambers, Harris L., Recruit, 1963/11/28, Private, Deserted, 09/09/1864.

Chenoweth (aka Chenwith, Cheworth, Chinnoweth, Chinoweth), James E., Recruit, 1864/08/05, Private, Mustered Out 01/13/1866.

Cherry, James, Recruit, 1864/09/19, Private, Mustered Out, Date Not Reported.

Chrisman, George E., Private, 1861/07/24, Private, Mustered Out 07/31/1864.

Colgan, John, Recruit, 1862/05/26, Private, Mustered Out 05/26/1865.

Conley (aka Connelly), Samuel, Private, 1861/07/24, Private, Died, Port Hudson, LA, 07/28/1863.

Conner, William M., 2nd Lieutenant, 1861/07/24, Lieutenant, Honorable Discharged 10/31/1864.

Coole, John G., Recruit, 1864/09/12, Private, Mustered Out, Date Not Reported.

Cooper, William, Recruit, 1862/05/26, Corporal, Died, Baton Rouge, LA, 06/18/1864.

Copenhaver (aka Copenhaven, Copenhigen), Adam A., Private, 1861/07/24, Private, Discharged 12/18/1861, Disability.

Cozine, Samuel L., Private, 1861/07/24, Private, Mustered Out 07/31/1864.

Cozine, William H., Private, 1861/07/24, Private, Mustered Out 07/31/1864.

Craig, Alonzo, Recruit, 1863/11/23, Private, *Deserted, 04/01/1864.*

Cromwell (aka Cromuell), John M., Recruit, 1863/12/31, Private, Mustered Out 01/13/1866.

Cummins (aka Cummings), Charles W., Recruit, 1862/05/15, Private, Died 10/23/1864 at New Orleans, LA. *Deserted 08/11/1865.*

Dagley, Joseph, Private, 1861/07/24, Private, Veteran, Mustered Out 01/13/1866.

Dagley (aka Dayley), William R. (aka William A., William L.), Private, 1861/07/24, Private, Mustered Out 07/31/1864.

Daniels (aka Daniel), Henry L., Private, 1861/07/24, Private, Transferred to Co. H, 04/01/1864; Mustered Out 07/31/1864.

Davis, Robert A. (aka Robert V.), Private, 1861/07/24, Private, Dishonorably Discharged by G.C.M., 12/29/1864. Mustered Out 01/17/1866. (Confined rather than Discharged?).

Day, John W., 1st Lieutenant, 1861/07/24, Major, Promoted Major 12/07/1864; Promoted Lieutenant-Colonel at Muster Out.

Demott (aka Dematt, Demote), Henry, Corporal, 1861/07/24, Private, Mustered Out 07/31/1864.

Dix (aka Dicks), George W., Private, 1861/07/24, Private, Mustered Out 07/31/1864.

Donovan (aka Donavan, Donovon, Dunivan), Ephraim, Recruit, 1864/10/01, Private, Mustered Out 01/13/1866.

Dowling (aka Douling, Doweling), Edward, Recruit, 1863/11/28, Private, Mustered Out 01/13/1866.

Duncan (aka Dunkin), Freeborn, Private, 1861/07/24, Private, Died, Baltimore, MD, 12/25/1861.

Edwards (aka Eduards), Newton, Private, 1861/07/24, Private, Veteran, Mustered Out 01/13/1866.

Estus (aka Ester, Estes, Estis), Joseph F. (aka Joseph T.), Recruit, 1864/03/15, Private, Died at New Orleans, LA, 10/19/1864.

Evans (aka Ivans, Nahan), Nathan (aka Evans), Private, 1861/07/24, Private, Deserted 10/12/1865.

Fielding, Charles, Recruit, 1864/11/28, Private, Mustered Out 01/13/1866.

Finchum (aka Fichan, Finchman, Finchim, Fenchum), William R. (aka William C.), Private, 1861/07/24, Private, Deserted, 07/31/1861.

Fishback, William, Private, 1861/07/24, Private, Died, Baton Rouge, LA, 06/15/1862.

Fisher, Leonard, Recruit, 1864/11/28, Private, Mustered Out 01/13/1866.

Fisher, William (aka William R.), Private, 1861/07/24, Private, Transferred to Co, K 04/01/1864; Mustered Out 07/31/1864.

Fletcher, John D., Recruit, 1863/12/31, Artificer, Mustered Out 01/13/1866.

Fulty (aka Fultz), Solomon, Private, 1861/07/24, Private, Veteran, Mustered Out 01/13/1866.

Gains (aka Gaines), William, Recruit, 1864/09/21, Private, Discharged, 06/10/1865, Disability.

Garretty (aka Garerty, Garratty, Garrerty), Patrick, Recruit, 1863/12/31, Private, Drowned at New Orleans, LA, 07/31/1864.

Gibbs, Simon P., Recruit, 1863/12/31, Private, Died at Indianapolis, IN, 12/24/1864.

Goss (aka Gass), William P., Corporal, 1861/07/24, 1st Lieutenant, Wounded at Battle of Baton Rouge, LA; Promoted 1st Lieutenant 11/01/1864; Mustered Out 01/10/1866..

Green, John W., Recruit, 1863/12/31, Private, Mustered Out 101/13/1866.

Grimsley (aka Grimsby, Grimsly, Grinsley), James, Captain, 1861/07/24, Major, Wounded at Battle of Baton Rouge, LA; Promoted Major 10/01/1863, Mustered Out, September, 1864.

Hagerty, John, Recruit, 1864/10/07, Private, Mustered Out 10/07/1865.

Hamilton, Jesse G., Private, 1861/07/24, Private, Discharged 04/04/1862, Disability.

Hamilton, John W., Private, 1861/07/24, Private, Discharged, 07/02/1863, Disability.

Hancock, Benjamin F., Recruit, 1863/12/31, Sergeant, Mustered Out 01/13/1866.

Harshbarger (aka Harshberger, Harshburger, Hartsboer), Parrott G. (aka Parrott, P.G.), Corporal, 1861/07/24, Corporal, Veteran, Mustered Out 01/13/1866.

Hartsock (aka Hartstock), George W., Private, 1861/07/24, Private, Veteran, Mustered Out 01/13/1866.

Hays (aka Hayes), Jesse A., Recruit, 1863/12/31, Musician, Mustered Out 01/13/1866.

Henry, James R., Corporal, 1861/07/24, 2nd Lieutenant, Promoted 2nd Lieutenant 11/01/1864; Mustered Out 01/10/1866.

Hill, Henry, Recruit, 1863/11/28, Private, *Deserted, 05/17/1864.*

Holden, Daniel, Recruit, 1864/10/08, Private, Mustered Out 10/07/1865.

Hollick, Thomas M., Recruit, 1862/01/06, Private, Mustered Out 01/06/1865.

Huffman, Jacob, Private, 1861/07/24, Private, Discharged 11/01/1861, Disability.

Hurt (aka Hunt), Nathan, Recruit, 1864/03/13, Private, Discharged, 06/16/1865, Disability.

Hurt, Robert B., Recruit, 1863/03/01, Private, Mustered Out 01/13/1866.

Hutton, Elijah, Private, 1861/07/24, Private, Veteran, Mustered Out 01/13/1866.

Jamison (aka Jameson, Jaminson), Joseph L., Recruit, 1864/09/23, Private, Mustered Out 08/05/1865.

Jearls (aka Jearles, Jerels, Jerles), Henry, Recruit, 1864/03/18, Private, Mustered Out 01/13/1866.

Jester, Harrison H., Recruit, 1863/11/28, Private, Mustered Out 01/13/1866.

Jewell (aka Jeuel, Jewel, Jewett), James E., Recruit, 1864/03/08, Private, Died at New Orleans, LA, 02/08/1865.

Johns, William H., Recruit, 1864/10/05, Private, Mustered Out 10/04/1865.

Johnson, John L, Recruit, 1863/11/28, Private, Mustered Out 01/13/1866.

Johnson, Silas, Recruit, 1862/01/31, Private, Mustered Out 02/01/1865.

Keeley (aka Keely, Kerley), John, Private, 1861/07/24, Private, Wounded at Battle of Baton Rouge, LA; Mustered Out 07/31/1864.

Kegley, Nelson A., Private, 1861/07/24, Private, Died, Baton Rouge, LA, 07/07/1862.

Kennedy, Sylvester F. (aka Sylvester T.), Recruit, 1863/11/23, Private, *Deserted, 08/15/1865.*

Kenworthy (aka Henworthy, Kenworth, Kenworthey, Kentworthy), Milas D. (aka Miles D., Wilson D.), Private, 1861/07/24, Private, Mustered Out 07/31/1864.

Kerr (aka Keer), John M., Private, 1861/07/24, Private, Mustered Out 07/31/1864.

King, Noah W., Private, 1861/07/24, Private, Mustered Out 07/31/1864.

Kiphart, Henry, Recruit, 1864/03/29, Private, Discharged, 05/18/1865, Disability.

Kiphart (aka Kephart), Jacob, Recruit, 1863/12/31, Private, Mustered Out 01/13/1866.

Kirk, Mason H., Private, 1861/07/24, Private, Mustered Out 07/31/1864.

Lamb, Albert, Recruit, 1864/09/19, Private, Mustered Out 08/05/1865.

Lamb, Henry M., Recruit, 1864/09/28, Private, Mustered Out 08/05/1865.

Little (aka Littell, Littelle), Milo F. (aka Milo T.), Private, 1861/07/24, Corporal, *Deserted 10/12/1865.*

Logan, John M., Recruit, 1864/10/03, Private, Mustered Out 10/04/1865.

Logan, Joseph H., Recruit, 1863/11/31, Private, Mustered Out 01/13/1866.

Long, Isaiah, Musician, 1861/07/24, Musician, Discharged 10/11/1861, Disability.

Loofborrow (aka Loffborrow, Loofburrow, Loofenborrough, Luffburrow), Jacob H., Recruit, 1863/11/23, Private, *Deserted 07/01/1865.*

Marksbury (aka Markesberry, Markesby, Marksberry), George W., Private, 1861/07/24, Private, Mustered Out 07/31/1864.

Massey, John W., Private, 1861/07/24, Private, Veteran, Mustered Out 01/13/1866.

Maulsby (aka Maulsbey), Samuel A., Private, 1861/07/24, Private, Mustered Out 07/31/1864. Discharged 10/22/18963, Disability.

May, Charles, Recruit, 1862/05/26, Private, *Deserted, 02/19/1863.*

McBride (aka McBende, McBridy), Jesse L., Recruit, 1864/09/14, Private, Mustered Out 08/05/1865.

McCollum (aka McCullum), John, Recruit, 1864/02/29, Corporal, Mustered Out 01/13/1866.

McCord, David, Recruit, 1864/10/06, Private, Mustered Out 10/04/1865.

McDaniels (aka McDaniel), Eli H., Private, 1861/07/24, Sergeant, Wounded at Battle of Baton Rouge, LA; Veteran, Mustered Out 01/13/1866.

McGinnis, Jacob D., Recruit, 1864/02/29, Private, Mustered Out 01/13/1866.

McMillan (aka McMillian, Mcmullun), Henry F. (aka Henry P.), Sergeant, 1861/07/24, Adjutant, Promoted Adjutant 08/05/1862; Honorably Discharged 04/21/1865.

McVey (aka McVay), Enoch V., Recruit, 1863/11/23, Sergeant, Mustered Out 01/13/1866.

McVey, William R., Recruit, 1864/09/30, Private, Mustered Out 08/05/1865.

Melbourme (aka Milbourn, Milbourne, Millbourm, Wilbourn), Charles F. (aka Charles T.), Recruit, 1863/11/23, Corporal, Mustered Out 01/13/1866.

Mills, George W., Recruit, 1863/11/28, Private, Mustered Out 01/13/1866.

Moore (aka More), James R., 2nd Lieutenant, 1861/07/24, 2nd Lieutenant, Resigned March 1862.

Moore (aka More), St. Claire (aka Sinclair), Recruit, 1863/11/28, Private, Died at New Orleans, LA, 09/16/1864.

Morris, Samuel, Private, 1861/07/24, Private, Discharged, 07/01/1862, Disability.

Mull, William M., Private, 1861/07/24, Private, Mustered Out 07/31/1864.

Murray (aka Muny), Daniel, Recruit, 1864/09/14, Corporal, Mustered Out 08/05/1865.

Myers, Charles, Private, 1861/07/24, Private, Discharged 08/28/1863, Eyes burned out at Port Hudson by premature discharge of his cannon.

Neyman (aka Neymon), Joseph, Recruit, 1864/09/21, Private, Mustered Out 08/05/1865.

Nicholas (aka Nicholds, Nichols), William H. (aka William N.), Recruit, 1864/03/03, Private, Mustered Out 01/13/1866.

Nicholson (aka Nicholdson), Isaac G., Recruit, 1864/09/26, Private, Mustered Out 08/05/1865.

Perkins, George W., Private, 1861/07/24, Private, Mustered Out 07/31/1864.

Pettus (aka Pettes,), John M. (aka John A., John W.), Recruit, 1863/11/28, Private, Mustered Out 01/13/1866.

Petty, Joseph, Private, 1861/07/24, Private, Died 08/29/1862 of Wounds Received at Battle of Baton Rouge, LA..

Phifer (aka Piper, Pipher), Joseph, Recruit, 1863/11/23, Corporal, Mustered Out 01/13/1866.

Phillips (aka Philips), James A., Private, 1861/07/24, Private, Veteran, Mustered Out 01/13/1866.

Phillips (aka Philips), James J., Private, 1861/07/24, Private, Mustered Out 07/31/1864.

Pierson (aka Pastron, Peirson), James, Recruit, 1864/09/19, Private, Mustered Out 08/05/1865.

Porter, Philip, Recruit, 1863/12/31, Private, Mustered Out 01/13/1866.

Poston (aka Posten), James, Recruit, 1863/11/23, Private, *Deserted 05/24/1865.*

Pritchet, Joseph J., Private, 1861/07/24, Private, Discharged 11/01/1861, Disability.

Pruett (aka Pruitt), John R., Private, 1861/07/24, Private, Veteran, Mustered Out 01/13/1866.

Quinn, James, Recruit, 1864/09/23, Private, *Deserted, 03/01/1865.*

Raper, Thomas J., Sergeant, 1863/11/21, 1st Lieutenant, Promoted 1st Lieutenant 10/01/1864; Mustered Out 01/10/1866..

Redman (aka Redmon, Redmond), Alfred P. (aka Alfred F, Alfred T, Albert P.), Recruit, 1863/12/31, Corporal, Mustered Out 01/13/1866.

Redman (aka Redmon), Collin M., Recruit, 1864/10/05, Private, Mustered Out 10/04/1865.

Robinson, Abner N. (aka Abraham N, Abraham U.), Recruit, not shown, Private, Died at Franklin, LA, 03/01/1864.

Rogers (aka Rodgers), Marcus L.(aka Marquis L), Private, 1861/07/24, Private, Veteran, Mustered Out 01/13/1866.

Rouse, George N. (aka George W.), Recruit, 1864/09/14, Private, Mustered Out 08/05/1865.

Runnion (aka Runion, Runyan, Runyon), Alfred, Recruit, 1864/01/27, Private, Died at New Orleans, LA, 12/13/1864.

Russel (aka Russell), James M., Recruit, 1864/09/30, Private, Mustered Out 08/05/1865.

Ruth (aka Reuth), William H. (aka William A.), Recruit, 1864/02/29, Private, Died at Baton Rouge, LA, 03/01/1864.

Ryan, James G. (aka James S), Private, 1861/07/24, Wagoner, Discharged 03/31/1862, Disability.

Saltcorn, Frederick, Private, 1861/07/24, Sergeant, Veteran, Mustered Out 01/13/1866.

Sanders, Cyrus, Recruit, 1864/09/30, Private, Mustered Out 08/05/1865.

Sargent (aka Sargant, Sargeant), James L. (aka James S.), Recruit, 1863/11/28, Wagoner, Mustered Out 01/13/1866.

Scott, Franklin H., Recruit, 1864/02/29, Private, Mustered Out 01/13/1866.

Scott, William J., Recruit, 1863/11/23, Sergeant, Mustered Out 01/13/1866.

Seay (aka Slay), James M., Private, 1861/07/24, Private, Veteran, Mustered Out 01/13/1866.

Seay (aka Slay), William B., Private, 1861/07/24, Private, Mustered Out 07/31/1864.

Shear (aka Shearer, Sheerer, Sherer), John J., Sergeant, 1861/07/24, Sergeant, Discharged 04/10/1862.

Shuler, Henry, Private, 1861/07/24, Sergeant, Veteran, Mustered Out 01/13/1866.

Shuler (aka Schuller), John A., Recruit, 1864/03/08, Private, Mustered Out 01/13/1866.

Shumaker (aka Shewmaker, Shoemaker), William H., Private, 1861/07/24, Private, Mustered Out 07/31/1864.

Simmons (aka Simmonds), Henry, Private, 1861/07/24, Wagoner, Mustered Out 07/31/1864.

Sink, Andrew J., Private, 1861/07/24, Private, Discharged 12/18/1861, Disability.

Smith, Benjamin F., Recruit, 1863/11/23, Private, Mustered Out 01/13/1866.

Smith, Elias R., Private, 1861/07/24, Private, Discharged 11/01/1861, Disability.

Smith, Henry, Recruit, 1863/11/28, Private, Discharged, 06/13/1865, Disability.

Smith, James M., Recruit, 1864/02/29, Private, Mustered Out 01/13/1866.

Smith, Jonathan G., Private, 1861/07/24, Private, Died at Baltimore, MD, 10/14/1861.

Smith, Robert S., Recruit, 1862/05/01, Private, Wounded at Battle of Baton Rouge, LA; Mustered Out 04/30/1865.

Smith, William C., Private, 1861/07/24, Private, Veteran, Mustered Out 01/13/1866.

Spangler, Isaac N., Private, 1861/07/24, Private, Veteran, Mustered Out 01/13/1866.

Stailey (aka Staley, Staly), James E., Recruit, 1864/03/03, Private, Mustered Out 01/13/1866.

Stamper, Richard M., Corporal, 1861/07/24, 2nd Lieutenant, Promoted 2nd Lieutenant 10/01/1864; Mustered Out 01/10/1866..

Stark, John, Private, 1861/07/24, Musician, Veteran, Mustered Out 01/13/1866.

Steckler, Simon, Recruit, 1862/05/26, Private, Wounded at Battle of Baton Rouge, LA; Mustered Out 05/26/1865.

Steel (aka Steele), Joseph H., Recruit, 1864/11/23, Private, Mustered Out 01/13/1866.

Stelts (aka Stellts, Steltz), Levi, Recruit, 1863/11/28, Private, *Deserted, 07/01/1865.*

Stines (aka Sims), Alexander, Private, 1861/07/24, Private, Killed at Port Hudson, LA, 06/14/1863.

Stines, Usebius (aka Eusebius, Ensiliner), Private, 1861/07/24, Private, Veteran, Mustered Out 01/13/1866.

Stivers, George M., Recruit, 1864/09/21, Private, Mustered Out 08/05/1865.

Stone, William, Private, 1861/07/24, Private, Died 08/24/1862, Wounds Received at Baton Rouge, LA.

Stout, Samuel, Private, 1861/07/24, Private, Veteran, Died at New Orleans, LA, 11/16/1864.

Strong, John T. (aka John G, John J.), Private, 1861/07/24, Private, Died 08/23/1862, Wounds received at Baton Rouge.

Sullivan (aka Silivan), John O. (aka John R.O., John I.), Recruit, 1864/09/22, Private, Mustered Out 01/13/1866.

Tabor (aka Taber), Abner, Private, 1861/07/24, Private, Wounded at Battle of Baton Rouge, LA; Mustered Out 07/31/1864.

Taylor, Thomas E., Recruit, 1863/11/23, Private, Mustered Out 01/13/1866.

Thomas, John H., Private, 1861/07/24, Private, Discharged 05/13/1864, Wounds.

Thomas, John W., Recruit, 1863/12/18, Corporal, Wounded at Battle of Baton Rouge, LA; Mustered Out 01/13/1866.

Thomas, William, Private, 1861/07/24, Private, Mustered Out 07/31/1864.

Thomas, William A., Recruit, 1863/06/01, Private, Mustered Out 05/31/1865.

Thompson, David C., Private, 1861/07/24, Private, Mustered Out 07/31/1864.

Thompson, Demarcus C., Private, 1861/07/24, Private, Discharged 03/03/1862, Disability.

Todd, George W., Recruit, 1864/01/10, Private, Mustered Out 01/13/1866.

Van Valkenburg (aka Van Valkerburgh, Vansalehenbush, Vanvalkinburgh, Vanvalkenberg), John J. (aka John H.), Recruit, 1864/11/28, Private, Mustered Out 01/13/1866.

Vannida (aka Vanide), Philip, Recruit, 1864/09/18, Private, Mustered Out 08/05/1865.

Vest, John W., Private, 1861/07/24, Private, Mustered Out 07/31/1864.

Walters (aka Walker), William H., Recruit, 1864/09/28, Private, Mustered Out 08/05/1865.

Wampler, Thomas B., Recruit, 1864/10/07, Private, Mustered Out 10/06/1865.

Ward (aka Word), Henry H., Private, 1861/07/24, Private, Killed at Battle of Baton Rouge, LA, 08/05/1862.

Wardlow (aka Wardelow, Wardlaw), James A., Recruit, 1862/06/01, Private, Mustered Out 05/31/1865.

Westfall, William H. (aka William N.), Private, 1861/07/24, Private, Mustered Out 07/31/1864.

Wheeler, Jason, Private, 1861/07/24, Private, Mustered Out 07/31/1864.

White, Jasper H. (aka Jose, Joseph H.), Private, 1861/07/24, Private, Died 08/06/1862, Wounds received at Baton Rouge, LA.

Wible (aka Weble, Woble), John W. (aka John), Private, 1861/07/24, Private, Veteran, Mustered Out. 1/13/1866.

Wilhite (aka Willhite), Eli, Private, 1861/07/24, Private, Veteran, Mustered Out. 1/13/1866.

Wilhite (aka Willhite), Jefferson H., Private, 1861/07/24, Private, Veteran, Mustered Out. 1/13/1866.

Wilhite (aka Willhite), John, Musician, 1861/07/24, Musician, Discharged 10/16/1862, Disability.

Wilhite (aka Wilhile, Willhite), Thomas J., Corporal, 1861/07/24, First Sergeant, Veteran, Mustered Out. 1/13/1866, 0

Wilkins (aka Wilkeson, Wilkison), William (aka Williams), Recruit, 1862/06/01, Private, *Deserted in the Face of The Enemy, Battle of Baton Rouge, 08/05/1862.*

Willison (aka Wilison, Wilson), Carrollton W. (aka Carlton W., Carleton W.D., Carleton W.G., Carolton W.G., Carlton D.), Recruit, 1864/01/07, Corporal, Mustered Out 01/13/1866.

Willmoth (aka Willmouth, Wilmath, Wilmoth, Wilmouth), James W., Recruit, 1863/11/23, Private, Died at New Orleans, LA, 12/17/1864.

Wilson, Christopher, Wagoner, 1861/07/24, Wagoner, Discharged, 12/18/1861, Disability.

Wilson (aka Willson), James M., Recruit, 1864/09/23, Private, Mustered Out 08/10/1865.

Company C

Alexander, James, Private, 1861/07/24, Private, Veteran, Mustered Out 01/13/1866.

Alexander, John M. (aka John W.), Private, 1861/07/24, Private, Discharged 1862; re-enlisted as recruit 03/25/1864; Mustered Out 01/13/1866.

Anderson, Sylvester S., Corporal, 1861/07/24, Private, Veteran, Mustered Out 01/13/1866.

Arthur, Aaron, Recruit, 1863/10/07, Musician, Mustered Out 01/18/1864.

Athens, Alfred (aka Alford D.), Private, 1861/07/24, Private, Veteran, Mustered Out 01/13/1866.

Axe, Thomas J., Private, 1861/07/24, Private, Discharged 09/21/1863.

Baker, William A., Recruit, 1863/10/07, Private, Mustered Out 01/13/1866.

Ballard, Thomas, Corporal, 1861/07/24, Corporal, Discharged, Died 08/07/1862, Wounds received in Battle of Baton Rouge, LA.

Barnes (aka Barns), John H., Recruit, 1864/03/28, Private, Mustered Out 01/13/1866.

Barrow (aka Barron, Burrow), Samuel C., Recruit, 1864/08/13, Private, Deserted 05/30/1865.

Bartlett, John B., Private, 1861/07/24, Private, Died 06/14/1862.

Bemount, William R., Private, 1861/07/24, Private, Veteran, Mustered Out 01/13/1866.

Benham, Andrew, Private, 1861/07/24, Private, Veteran, Mustered Out 01/13/1866.

Benham, William T., Corporal, 1861/07/24, Corporal, Died 08/31/1861.

Bennet, Horton, Private, 1864/04/09, Private, Mustered Out 01/13/1864.

Bennett, John, Private, 1864/06/30, Private, Mustered Out 01/13/1866.

Bensinger, John, Private, 1864/03/25, Private, Deserted 05/31/1865.

Berry, Joseph, Private, 1864/04/07, Private, Died 06/27/1864 at Baton Rouge, LA..

Berry, Martin, Private, 1864/04/14, Private, Died 08/25/1864.

Booker, John, Private, 1861/07/24, Private, Veteran, Mustered Out 01/13/1866.

Booker (aka Brooks), Perry R., Private, 1862/01/28, Private, Veteran, Mustered Out 01/13/1866.

Bough, William, 1st Lieutenant, 1861/07/24, Captain, Promoted Captain 12/09/1863; Mustered Out 01/10/1866..

Brandt, Lucas, Private, 1864/03/30, Corporal, Mustered Out 01/13/1866.

Brookshaven (aka Brookshare, Brookshaw, Brookshear), Benjamin L., Private, 1864/10/06, Artificer, mustered Out 10/06/1865.

Brookshear (aka Brookshare), John, Private, 1861/07/24, Corporal, Veteran, Mustered Out 01/13/1866.

Brown, George C., Private, 1864/04/19, Private, Mustered Out 01/13/1862.

Bryan, Spencer L., 2nd Lieutenant, 1861/07/24, 2nd Lieutenant, Resigned 1862; Re-entered Service as Captain of 115th Regiment (6-months service).

Bullenbaugh (aka Bullabaugh, Bullenbaugh), Abraham, Private, 1864/07/29, Private, Deserted 05/31/1865.

Burge (aka Burch), Charles, Private, 1861/07/24, Private, Veteran, Mustered Out 01/13/1866.

Burge, Nicholas C., Private, 1864/03/01, Private, Mustered Out 01/13/1866.

Campbell, Charles, Private, 1864/03/28, Private, Died, 09/19/1864.

Carmichael, Joseph T., Private, 1864/03/01, Private, Mustered Out 01/13/1866.

Carroll, Thomas, Private, 1864/09/21, Private, Died 11/20/1865.

Clark (aka Clarke), John, Private, 1861/07/24, Private, Died 11/21/1861.

Collins, Chauncy, Recruit, 1864/03/24, Transferred to Company I 05/21/1864; Never Joined Company.

Collins, David, Private, 1864/08/31, Private, Discharged, 01/07/1865, by order of War Department. Mustered Out 02/05/1865.

Combs, Francis M., Private, 1861/07/24, Corporal, Veteran, Mustered Out 01/13/1866.

Conkle, Jacob, Private, 1864/04/06, Private, Mustered Out 01/13/1866.

Cooper, Lewis A., Private, 1863/10/04, Private, Mustered Out 01/13/1866.

Corbley (aka Corbly), Richard J. A., Private, 1864/10/06, Private, Mustered Out 10/06/1865.

Cox, Alexander, Private, 1861/07/24, Private, Died 10/22/1862.

Crabtree (aka Crabbtree), Job W., Private, 1864/04/12, Private, Mustered Out 01/13/1866.

Crawley, Newton, Private, 1861/07/24, Private, Discharged, 12/04/1861, Disability.

Crock, James, Private, 1864/04/06, Private, Mustered Out 01/13/1866.

Cross (aka Cress), Andrew J., Private, 1864/03/01, Private, Mustered Out 01/13/1866.

Crouch, William A., Private, 1864/04/01, Private, Died 12/15/1864.

Dean (aka Deem), Thomas, Private, 1864/03/18, Private, Mustered Out 01/13/1866.

Denton, Robert J., Private, 1864/10/10, Private, Mustered Out 10/10/1865.

Donally (aka Danally, Danelley, Danelly, Danely), Alfred M. (aka Alford M.), Private, 1861/07/24, Private, Mustered Out 07/31/1864.

Dover, Asbury, Private, 1861/07/24, Private, Mustered Out 01/13/1866.

Dover, Jarvis, Private, 1861/07/24, Private, Discharged, 10/15/1862, Disability.

Dover, Wesley, Private, 1861/07/24, Private, Veteran, Mustered Out 01/13/1866.

Dyer (aka Dyar), John H., Private, 1862/01/30, Private, Discharged 10/26/1864, Disability.

Eccles, George, Private, 1864/09/21, Private, Died, 01/01/1865.

Elgan, Jesse, Private, 1861/07/24, Sergeant, Veteran, Mustered Out 01/13/1866.

Elgan (aka Edgan), Reason, Private, 1864/03/28, Private, Mustered Out 01/13/1864.

Evans (aka Eans), Armstead, Private, 1864/03/29, Private, Mustered Out 01/13/1866.

Farmer, Aaron E., Sergeant, 1861/07/24, Sergeant, Died 03/21/1862.

Fearnot, William, Private, 1861/07/24, Bugler, Veteran, Mustered Out 01/13/1866.

Fender, Samuel, Private, 1861/07/24, Private, Veteran, Mustered Out 01/13/1866.

Ferguson, Benjamin B. (aka Benjamin F.), Private, 1864/10/06, Private, Mustered Out 10/06/1865.

Forbes (aka Forbis), John, Private, 1864/03/17, Private, Mustered Out 01/13/1866.

Fortner, Jonas R., Private, 1861/07/24, Sergeant, Veteran, Mustered Out 01/13/1866.

Foster, Samuel, Private, 1861/07/24, 2nd Lieutenant, Promoted 2nd Lieutenant 06/18/1864; Veteran; Mustered Out 01/10/1866, Absent Sick..

Gadsbury (aka Gadsberry), John A. (aka John), Private, 1864/03/18, Private, Deserted 05/01/1864.

Gambill (aka Gamble), Wiley H., Private, 1864/03/29, Private, Died 05/03/1864.

Gardner, William [Milton], Private, 1864/04/16, Private, Mustered Out 01/13/1866.

Garrard (Gerard, Gerrard), Jeremiah, Private, 1864/03/30, Corporal, Mustered Out 01/13/1864.

Garret (aka Garritt), Reuben (aka Ruben), Private, 1864/02/29, Private, Discharged 11/02/1864, Disability.

Glenn, James, Private, 1861/07/24, Private, Veteran, Mustered Out 01/13/1866.

Glover, William B., First Sergeant, 1861/07/24, 1st Lieutenant, Promoted to 1st Lieutenant 12/09/1863; Died 06/17/1864.

Glover, William J., Sergeant, 1861/07/24, Sergeant, Veteran, Mustered Out 01/13/1866.

Goliday (aka Galliday, Golliday), Robert C., Private, 1864/03/01, Private, Mustered Out 01/13/1866.

Gordon (aka Garden, Gordan), John, Private, 1684/03/01, Sergeant, Mustered Out 01/13/1866.

Greer (aka Greet), James, Private, 1861/07/24, Private, Veteran, Mustered Out 01/13/1866.

Grice, Robert S., Private, 1864/10/20, Private, Mustered Out 01/13/1866.

Guisler (aka Gaisler), Mathias, Private, 1861/07/24, Private, Killed In Action at Baton Rouge, LA, 08/05/1862.

Hagerty (aka Hagarty), Richard, Private, 1964/03/03, Private, Mustered Out 01/13/1866.

Hall, Asa, Private, 1864/10/10, Private, Mustered Out 07/20/1865.

Hamersley (aka Hamersly, Hammersly, Kamersley), James, Private, 1861/07/24, Wagoner, Veteran, Mustered Out 01/13/1866.

Hamilton, John, Private, 1864/03/31, Corporal, Mustered Out 01/13/1866.

Harper, John, Private, 1864/03/29, Private, Mustered Out 01/13/1866.

Harrell, Ephraim, Private, 1861/07/24, Private, Veteran, Mustered Out 01/13/1866.

Harvey, Albert, Private, 1861/07/24, Private, Discharged, 11/01/1863, Disability.

Hayes (aka Hays), Horatio, Private, 1864/02/29, Private, Died 10/10/1864.

Haynes, Walter W., Private, 1864/03/30, Private, Mustered Out 01/13/1866.

Hays (aka Hay), Howard R., Sergeant, 1861/07/24, Sergeant, Died 12/13/1861.

Hays (aka Hayes), Nelson, Private, 1861/07/24, Private, Veteran, Mustered Out 01/13/1866.

Hays (aka Hayes), Henry (aka Henry Y.), Private, 1861/07/24, Private, Discharged 1862; Reenlisted 02/02/1964; Mustered Out 01/13/1866.

Hays, Howard R., Sergeant, 1861/07/24, Sergeant, Died 12/13/1861.

Haywood, Calvin, Private, 1861/07/24, Private, Died, 08/13/1862, Wounds Received At Baton Rouge, LA.

Haywood, Elias, Private, 1861/07/24, Corporal, Veteran, Mustered Out 01/13/1866.

Haywood, Joel, Private, 1861/07/24, Private, Killed In Action at Baton Rouge, LA 08/05/1862.

Hazelrigg (aka Hazlerig), Preston, Private, 1864/10/10, Private, Mustered Out 10/10/1865.

Heaton, Amos T., Private, 1864/04/16, Private, Mustered Out 01/13/1866.

Hendley (aka Hendly), James M., Private, 1864/10/06, Private, Mustered Out 10/06/1865.

Hill, Hiram (aka William), Recruit, 1864/04/06, Private, Transferred to Co. D 05/21/1864; Drowned at Baton Rouge 07/21/1865.

Hill, Nathan, Private, 1864/10/06, Private, Mustered Out 10/06/1865.

Hoag (aka Hague, Hogue, Houge), John, Private, 1861/07/24, Private, Veteran, Mustered Out 01/13/1866.

Hogland (aka Hoagland), Henry, Private, 1864/03/28, Private, Mustered Out 01/13/1866.

Hogue (aka Hogne), William, Private, 1864/10/07, Private, Killed at Spanish Fort, AL, 04/01/1865.

Huey, Philander, Private, 1861/07/24, Private, Veteran, Mustered Out 01/13/1866.

Huffman, Daniel B., Private, 1861/07/24, Private, Veteran, Mustered Out 01/13/1866.

James, William, Private, 1864/03/28, Private, Mustered Out 01/13/1866.

Johnson, Robert, Private, 1864/03/24, Private, Died, 08/22/1864.

Jordan (Jordon), Anthony, Private, 1861/07/24, Private, Discharged, 11/01/1863, Disability.

Kennedy (aka Kenedy), Daniel (aka David), Private, 1864/04/28, Private, Died, 01/22/1865..

King, James A., Private, 1864/03/30, Private, Died, 12/08/1864.

King, Jesse H. (aka Jesse K., Jesse N.), Musician, 1861/07/24, Private, Mustered Out 07/31/1864.

Kissill (aka Kissel, Kissle), Austin, Private, 03/15/1865, Private, Mustered Out 01/13/1866.

Klinger (aka Klaiger), Asa, Private, 1861/07/24, Private, Veteran, Mustered Out 01/13/1866.

Klinger (aka Klaiger), David, Private, 1861/07/24, Corporal, Veteran, Mustered Out 01/13/1866.

Layman (aka Lehman), David, Private, 1861/07/24, Private, Veteran, Mustered Out 01/13/1866.

Lee, Richard E., Recruit, 1864/08/13, Private, Mustered Out 07/29/1865, Substitute..

Lehman, Coley (aka Ooley), Recruit, 1864/04/07, Private, Discharged 07/29/1865, Disability. Mustered Out 10/10/1865..

Lehman (aka Lehmon), Simon, Corporal, 1861/07/24, Private, Discharged 1862; Re-enlisted 1864; Mustered Out 10/06/1865.

Leman (aka Lemar), Henry H., Private, 1861/07/24, Private, Mustered Out 09/07/1864.

Lisle (aka Lyle, Lysle), James, Recruit, 1864/04/18, Private, Mustered Out 01/13/1866.

Lloyd, John G., Recruit, 1864/10/10, Private, Mustered Out 10/10/1865.

Love, William, Recruit, 1864/03/28, Private, Mustered Out 01/13/1866.

Lowe (aka Love, Low), John F., Recruit, 1864/03/09, Private, Died, 02/08/1865.

Martin, William W., Recruit, 1864/10/10, Private, Mustered Out 10/10/1865.

May, Stephen D., Recruit, 1864/02/29, , Transferred to Co. I 05/21/1864; Never Reported to Company..

Mayfield, Richard, Recruit, 1864/08/26, Private, Transferred to Co. D 05/21/1864; Mustered Out 01/13/1866.

McAllister (aka McAlister), Henry, Recruit, 1864/08/25, Private, Deserted, 02/24/1865.

McClaren (aka McClairan, McClarren), Alfred B., Corporal, 1861/07/24, 1st Lieutenant, Promoted 2nd Lieutenant 12/09/1863; Promoted 1st Lieutenant 03/31/0864; Mustered Out 01/10/1864..

McClaren (aka McClairen, McClarren), Samuel, Recruit, 1862/01/30, Corporal, Veteran; Died 08/02/1864.

McCutchin (aka McCutchon), William S. (aka William), Recruit, 1864/03/23, Private, *Deserted to Enemy, 06/14/1864*..

McGath (aka Magath), Andrew, Private, 1861/07/24, Private, Veteran, Died 06/26/1864.

McIntire, Daniel, Private, 1861/07/24, Private, Mustered Out 07/31/1864.

Middleton, Alfred, Private, 1861/07/24, First Sergeant, Veteran, Mustered Out 01/13/1866.

Moats (aka Motz, Moutz), Ananias W., Private, 1861/07/24, Private, Veteran, Mustered Out 01/13/1866.

Moore, Thomas R., Private, 1861/07/24, Private, Died 03/29/1863.

Myers (aka Myres), Isaac H. (aka Isaac N.), Recruit, 1864/03/19, Private, Discharged 05/31/1865, Disability.

Myers (aka Myres), William H., Recruit, 1864/03/19, Private, Mustered Out 01/13/1866.

Nash, George W., Private, 1861/07/24, Private, Veteran, Discharged 08/21/1865, Disability.

Neighda, John, Private, 1861/07/24, Private, *Veteran, Deserted to the Enemy 06/16/1864.*

Nelson, William A., Recruit, 1864/10/10, Private, Mustered Out 10/10/1865.

Neville (aka Nevill), Erwin (aka Ervin, Irvin, Irwin), Private, 1861/07/24, Private, Veteran, Mustered Out 01/13/1866.

Newsome (aka Neusom, Newsom), William J., Private, 1861/07/24, Private, Discharged, 01/30/1864, Disability.

Norman, Ephraim, Recruit, 1864/03/28, Private, Mustered Out 01/13/1866.

O'Conner (aka O'Connor), Thomas, Private, 1861/07/24, Private, Killed In Action at Baton Rouge, LA, 08/05/1862. Died 09/15/1863 of Disease.

Oder, William R., Recruit, 1864/03/03, Private, Mustered Out 01/13/1866.

Osborn (aka Osbon, Osborne), Isaac N., Musician, 1861/07/24, Musician, Mustered Out 07/31/1864.

Parsley, James M., Private, 1861/07/24, Sergeant, Discharged 1862; Re-enlisted 03/26/1864; Mustered Out 01/13/1866.

Parsley, Jonathan R., Private, 1861/07/24, Private, Died while on furlough; date not reported..

Pingry (aka Pingrey), Isaac, Recruit, 1864/03/15, Private, Died 07/17/1864.

Plummer, John, Private, 1861/07/24, Private, Veteran; Died at Home, Bloomfield, IN; Date Not Reported.

Plusky (aka Pluckey, Plucky), William, Private, 1861/07/24, Private, Mustered Out 07/31/1864.

Priest (aka Preist), Leroy, Recruit, 1864/03/18, Private, Discharged 06/20/1865, Disability.

Pugh, Henry D., Recruit, 1863/10/07, Private, Discharged 02/03/1865, Disability.

Quillen, James H., Recruit, 1863/10/07, Private, Mustered Out 01/13/1866.

Quillen, Josephus, Private, 1861/07/24, Private, Died, 06/12/1864.

Quillen, Thomas J., Private, 1861/07/24, Sergeant, Veteran, Mustered Out 01/13/1866.

Ramsey (aka Ramsay), Franklin, Private, 1861/07/24, Sergeant, Veteran, Mustered Out 01/13/1866.

Reed, Isaac N., Private, 1861/07/24, Private, Mustered Out 07/31/1864.

Reynolds, Robert M., Recruit, 1864/04/16, Private, Mustered Out 01/13/1866.

Robertson, Jacob, Corporal, 1861/07/24, Private, Veteran, Mustered Out 01/13/1866.

Rodgers (aka Rogers), Davis E. (aka David E.), Private, 1861/07/24, Private, Mustered Out 07/31/1864.

Rodgers (aka Rogers), William B., Private, 1861/07/24, Private, Mustered Out 07/31/1864.

Rose, Elihu E., Captain, 1861/07/24, Captain, Resigned 12/08/1863.
Sanders (aka Saunders), Robert, Recruit, 1864/03/18, Private, Mustered Out 01/13/1866.
Sanders, Wesley, Corporal, 1861/07/24, Sergeant, Mustered Out 07/31/1864.
Scott, Joseph, Private, 1861/07/24, Artificer, Mustered Out 07/31/1864.
Seely, Enoch, Recruit, 1864/02/29, Private, Discharged 11/01/1865, Disability.
Shearer, David M. I(aka David W.), Recruit, 1864/04/25, Private, Mustered Out 01/13/1866.
Shouse, Joseph H., Private, 1861/07/24, Private, Died 06/16/1862.
Shryer (aka Shryar), Tobias, Private, 1861/07/24, Private, Discharged 10/15/1862, Disability.
Simpson, Benjamin, Private, 1861/07/24, Private, Discharged 09/21/1863, Disability.
Simpson, Sanford, Private, 1861/07/24, Private, Veteran, Mustered Out 01/13/1866.
Sisil, Elias, Private, 1861/07/24, Corporal, Veteran, Mustered Out 01/13/1866.
Smith, Augustus, Recruit, 1864/10/17, Private, Discharged 05/31/1865, Disability.
Smith, James P., Private, 1861/07/24, Private, Died 02/19/1863.
Smith, Josiah T., Recruit, 1864/04/18, Private, Mustered Out 01/13/1866.
Smith, Richard, Private, 1861/07/24, Corporal, Veteran, Mustered Out 01/13/1866.
Soward (aka Seward), Henry J., Private, 1861/07/24, Corporal, Veteran, Discharged 11/12/1864, Disability.
Spainhour (aka Spainhous, Spainhower), George E., Private, 1862/02/01, Private, Veteran, Mustered Out 01/13/1866.
Spainhower, James, Private, 1861/07/24, Corporal, Veteran, Mustered Out 01/13/1866.
Spencer, John, Recruit, 1864/04/14, Private, Died 06/05/1864.
Spencer, William T., Recruit, 1864/04/06, Private, Mustered Out 01/13/1866.
Stafford, Burlin (aka Berlin), Private, 1861/07/24, Private, Discharged 1015/1862, Disability.
Staggs, Edward W. (aka Edward), Recruit, 1864/03/15, Private, Transferred to Co. I 05/21/1864; Discharged 10/27/1865, Disability.
Stahl (aka Stall, Stohl), George, Wagoner, 1861/07/24, Wagoner, Veteran, Mustered Out 01/13/1866.
Stallcup (aka Stalcup), Stephen, Private, 1861/07/24, 2nd Lieutenant, Promoted 2nd Lieutenant 03/20/1865; Mustered Out 01/10/1866, Absent Sick..
Stamper (aka Slamper), Jonathan D., Recruit, 1863/10/07, Private, Died 11/30/1864.
Stamper (aka Slamper), Reid J. (aka Reed J.), Recruit, 1864/04/08, Private, Deserted 05/01/1864.
Stamper (aka Slamper), Wilburn (aka William), Recruit, 1863/10/07, Private, Deserted 11/12/1864.
Sullivan, Jesse O., Recruit, 1864/10/20, Private, Mustered Out 01/13/1866.
Tally (aka Talley), Aaron, Private, 1861/07/24, Private, Veteran, Mustered Out 01/13/1866.
Tally, James, Private, 1861/07/24, Private, Mustered Out 07/31/1864.
Tarver, Samuel W., Recruit, 1864/10/10, Private, Mustered Out 01/13/1866.
Taylor, Fielden E., Recruit, 1864/13/01, Private, Mustered Out 01/13/1866.
Taylor, Joseph, Private, 1861/07/24, Private, Mustered Out 07/31/1864.
Templeton, Wallace (aka William W.), Sergeant, 1861/07/24, 1st Lieutenant, Promoted 2nd Lieutenant 04/19/1864; Promoted 1st Lieutenant 03/20/1865; Mustered Out 01/10/1866..
Terrell, Hezekiah, Private, 1861/07/24, Private, Discharged 10/20/1864, Disability.
Thomas (aka Thomason), Walter W., Recruit, 1864/03/18, Private, Died 11/30/1864.
Thompson, William M. (aka William H.), Recruit, 1864/04/19, Private, Mustered Out 01/13/1866.
Tibbetts (aka Tibbett, Tibbitt, Tibbitts), William F., Private, 1861/07/24, Private, Veteran, Mustered Out 01/13/1866.
Travis, William J., Recruit, 1864/10/10, Private, Deserted 05/30/1865.
Tuttle, Charles, Recruit, 1864/03/18, Private, Deserted 05/31/1865.
Tuttle, George, Recruit, 1864/02/29, Private, Deserted 05/31/1865.
Waggoner, Henry V., Recruit, 1864/02/29, Private, Mustered Out 01/13/1866. Died 12/10/1865 at Bloomfield, IN, of Disease..
Wagoner (aka Waggoner), Hilton, Private, 1861/07/24, Private, Veteran, Mustered Out 01/13/1866.
Wiley (aka Willey), Simon, Private, 1861/07/24, Private, Died 06/30/1862.
Williams, Theodore, Recruit, 1864/03/26, Private, Mustered Out 01/13/1866.
Willis, Shephard (aka Shepherd), Recruit, 1864/03/01, Corporal, Mustered Out 01/13/1866.
Wolf (aka Wolfe, Woolf), David (aka David S.), Recruit, 1864/04/25, Private, Mustered Out 01/13/1866.
Woodard (aka Woodward), Philip (aka Phillip), Recruit, 1864/04/016, Private, Mustered Out 01/13/1866 [reported as transferring to Co. G in error].
Woodey (aka Wooddy, Woody), Nelson, Private, 1861/07/24, Private, Veteran, Mustered Out 01/13/1866.
Yoder, John G., Recruit, 1864/03/27, Private, Transferred to Co. I 05/21/1864; No record in Co. I.

Young, Lycurgus, Recruit, 1864/03/27, Private, Mustered Out 01/13/1864.

COMPANY D

Able, Cornelius, Recruit, 1864/10/05, Private, Mustered Out 10/05/1865.

Adams (aka Addams), Eleazar (aka Eleazer), Recruit, 1864/09/05, Private, Mustered Out 07/05/1865.

Anderson, Lemuel, Private, 1861/07/24, Private, Discharged, 08/11/1863, Disability.

Ashley (aka Ashly), John, Recruit, 1862/02/07, 1st Lieutenant, Promoted 2nd Lieutenant 03/31/1864; Promoted 1st Lieutenant 08/11/1864; Mustered Out 01/10/1866..

Atkinson (aka Adkins), William, Private, 1861/07/24, Corporal, Veteran; Discharged, 12/05/1864, Disability.

Barcus (aka Barcas), Samuel A., Private, 1861/07/24, Private, Mustered Out 08/01/1864.

Barkdall (aka Barkdale), Wesley, Recruit, 1864/09/05, Private, Mustered Out 07/05/1865.

Barrett, James, Recruit, Never Reported To the Company.

Bartley (aka Barley), Henry, Private, 1861/07/24, Private, Discharged, 11/21/1861, Disability.

Beam, John M. (aka John W.), Musician, 1861/07/24, Musician, Discharged 04/19/1862, Disability.

Beck, Jesse, Private, 1861/07/24, Private, Mustered Out 08/01/1864.

Beck (aka Best, Buck), Thomas C. (aka Thomas E.), Private, 1861/07/24, Private, **Wounded at Battle of Baton Rouge, LA;** Mustered Out 08/01/1864.

Bensinger, Adam (aka Adam F.), Private, 1861/07/24, Private, Died, 07/14/1862 in St. James Hospital at New Orleans, LA..

Berry, John, Private, 1861/07/24, Private, Veteran; Mustered Out 01/13/1866.

Berry, Mathew, Recruit, 1861/07/24, Private, Discharged 08/03/1864, Disability

Blackwell, William T., Recruit, 1864/09/26, Private, Mustered Out 07/05/1864.

Blevins (aka Blevine), James, Private, 1861/07/24, Private, Discharged, 10/13/1862, Disability.

Blevins (aka Blevines, Blivins), James M. (aka James H.), Recruit, 1863/10/05, Private, Mustered Out 01/13/1866.

Blevins (aka Blevines, Blivins), Thomas J., Recruit, 1862/02/07, Private, Veteran; Discharged 01/13/1866.

Bowlin (aka Bowlen, Bowling), William D., Recruit, 1864/09/05, Private, Mustered Out 09/04/1865.

Brock (aka Barker, Bock), George W., Private, 1861/07/24, Private, Discharged, 11/11/1861, Disability.

Brock, Phillip, Private, 1861/07/24, Private, Died, Baton Rouge, LA, 06/28/1862.

Brodie (aka Bodie, Bradiie), William M. (aka William A.), Recruit, 1864/03/26, Private, Mustered Out 01/13/1866.

Brown, Edward, Private, 1861/07/24, Private, Veteran, Mustered Out 01/13/1866.

Bryant (Briant), John A., Private, 1861/07/24, Private, Died, Baltimore, MD, 01/21/1862.

Buck, John W., Private, 1861/07/24, Private, Discharged, 10/13/1862, Disability.

Buckly, James F., Recruit, 1864/03/24, Private, Mustered Out 01/13/1866.

Buff, Benjamin F., Recruit, 1864/09/28, Private, Mustered Out 07/05/1865.

Buff, George W., Private, 1861/07/24, Private, Mustered Out 10/04/1865.

Burnett (aka Bennett), John W., Private, 1861/07/24, Corporal, Veteran; Mustered Out 01/13/1866.

Bush, William, Recruit, 1862/12/18, Musician, Mustered Out 12/17/1865.

Canover, Cornelius, Recruit, 1864/03/24, Private, Mustered Out 01/13/1866.

Cartwright, James, Recruit, 1864/03/24, Private, Mustered Out 01/13/1866.

Catlin (aka Cathline), William F. (aka William H., William T.), Private, 1861/07/24, Private, Discharged, 03/03/1862, Disability; Re-enlisted 04/02/1864; Mustered Out 01/13/1866.

Christman (aka Chrisman), Nicholas S., Recruit, 1863/12/16, Corporal, Transferred to Co. C 05/21/1864; Mustered Out 01/13/1866.

Clark, Oscar, Private, 1861/07/24, Private, Mustered Out 01/13/1866.

Clouser (aka Clowser), George W., Recruit, 1864/09/08, Private, Mustered Out 07/05/1865.

Cochran, Richard, Recruit, 1864/03/29, Private, Mustered Out 01/13/1866.

Collins, George, Recruit, Never Reported to Company.

Conary, George (aka Thomas), Recruit, Never Reported to Company.

Conner (aka Connery), Thomas E., Recruit, Never Reported to Company.

Conover, Cornelius G., Recruit, 1864/10/05, Private, Mustered Out 10/05/1865.

Cox, Israel P. (aka Israel B.), Recruit, 1864/03/24, Private, Died at Baton Rouge, LA, 07/03/1864.

Crance (aka Crouse), Peter, Private, 1861/07/24, Private, Veteran; Mustered Out 01/13/1866.

Creager, John, Recruit, 1864/10/07, Private, Mustered Out 10/07/1865.

Curry, Andrew A., Sergeant, 1861/07/24, Sergeant, Discharged 10/13/1862, Disability. Mustered Out 08/01/1864..

Curtner (aka Custner), Paul H., Private, 1861/07/24, Sergeant, Veteran; Mustered Out 01/13/1866.

DaHuff (aka Dayhoff, Dayhuff, Samuel, Recruit, 1864/03/24, Artificer, Mustered Out 01/13/1866.

Davis, Augustus C., Musician, 1861/07/24, Musician, Veteran; Discharged 06/1865, Disability. Mustered Out 07/05/1865..

Davis, Henry B., Corporal, 1861/07/24, Sergeant, Discharged 02/16/1862, Disability. Mustered 08/1-1864..

Davis, Homer, Recruit, 1864/03/24, Private, Discharged 01/24/1865, Disability.

Davis, William J., Private, 1861/07/24, Private, Discharged, 02/06/1862, Disability.

Dedman (aka Deadman, Deadwood, Deadmon, Dedmond), Mason, Private, 1861/07/24, Private, Discharged, 10/13/1862, Wounds received at Battle of Baton Rouge, LA.

Dooley (aka Dooly), James K., Recruit, 1864/04/11, Private, Mustered Out 01/13/1866.

Drummon (aka Drummond), George, Private, 1861/07/24, Private, Mustered Out 08/01/1864.

Drummond, Roman S. (aka Rowand), Private, 1861/07/24, Private, Mustered Out 01/13/1866.

Dunn, James A., Recruit, 1864/04/18, Private, Mustered Out 01/13/1866.

Earnest (aka Ernest), Jacob, Private, 1861/07/24, Private, Mustered Out 08/01/1864.

Edmiston, David, 2nd Lieutenant, 1861/07/24, Captain, Promoted Captain 06/01/1862; Resigned 01/21/1863.

Elswick, Joseph H., Recruit, 1864/04/30, Private, Mustered Out 01/13/1866.

Evans, Cyrus S., Recruit, 1864/10/06, Private, Mustered Out 09/09/1865.

Evans, George W., Recruit, 1864/02/29, Private, Mustered Out 01/13/1866.

Ferree (aka Ferrece), George D. (aka John D.), Recruit, 1864/04/11, Private, Mustered Out 01/13/1866.

Floyd, James, Recruit, Never Reported to Company.

Foote (aka Foot), William S., Recruit, 1864/10/07, Private, Discharged 09/19/1865.

Francis, Theodore, Recruit, 1864/03/26, Private, Died at Baton Rouge, LA, 05/21/1864.

Froment (aka Fromant, Fromeant, Froments), James, Private, 1861/07/24, Private, Veteran; Discharged 12/01/1865, Disability.

Gannon (aka Gammon), George, Private, 1861/07/24, Private, Veteran; Mustered Out 01/13/1866.

Gannon (aka Gannor), Samuel, Private, 1861/07/24, Artificer, Wounded at Battle of Baton Rouge, LA; Veteran; Mustered Out 01/13/1866.

Garber (aka Girber), Valentine E., Recruit, 1864/0905, Private, Mustered Out 10/03/1865.

Garrett, James H., Captain, 1861/07/24, Captain, Resigned May 1862.

Gettinger (aka Gettenger, Gittenger), Henry, Recruit, 1864/09/28, Private, Mustered Out 07/05/1865.

Giles, Andrew J., Recruit, 1864/10/05, Private, Mustered Out 10/05/1865.

Giles, Bennett W., Recruit, 1864/10/05, Private, Mustered Out 10/05/1865.

Giles, David H., Recruit, 1864/10/05, Private, Mustered Out 10/05/1865.

Gill, Thomas, Recruit, 1864/09/28, Private, Mustered Out 07/05/1865.

Glick, Monroe J., Recruit, 1864/03/04, Private, Mustered Out 01/13/1866.

Gobin, James M., Recruit, 1862/02/07, Private, Discharged 10/13/1862, Disability.

Good, Cyrus S. (aka Ceazer S, Cyrus L.), Recruit, 1864/09/05, Private, Mustered Out 08/03/1865.

Gott (aka Golt), Greenup, Private, 1861/07/24, Private, Mustered Out 08/01/1864.

Gregg, Lot B., Recruit, 1862/02/07, Private, Discharged 10/13/1862, Disability.

Gregg, Oliver P., Recruit, 1862/02/07, Private, Mustered Out 02/07/1865.

Gregg, William H., Private, 1861/07/24, Corporal, Discharged, 09/04/1862, Disability.

Hackney, William, Private, 1861/07/24, Private, Veteran; Mustered Out 01/13/1866.

Haddon (aka Hadden), Jesse, Corporal, 1861/07/24, Captain, Promoted 2nd Lieutenant 06/01/1862; Promoted 1st Lieutenant, 07/30/1863; Promoted Captain 08/11/1864; Wounded in Right Arm at Port Hudson, LA; Mustered Out 01/10/1866..

Huddon (aka Haddon, William R., Private, 1861/07/24, Private, Mustered Out 08/01/1864.

Hail (aka Hale), Nathan (aka Nathan T.), Private, 1861/07/24, Private, Discharged 10/13/1862, Disability.

Hall, John F., Recruit, 1864/03/24, Private, Mustered Out 01/13/1866.

Harper, Tobias (aka Tobias E.), Private, 1861/07/24, Private, Veteran; Died; Baton Rouge, LA, 03/04/1864.

Harper, William B., Private, 1861/07/24, Private, Veteran; Mustered Out 01/13/1866.

Harper (aka Hasper), William, First Sergeant, 1861/07/24, 1st Lieutenant, Promoted 1st Lieutenant 06/01/1862; Resigned 07/29/1863.

Harrington (aka Herrington), Francis M., Recruit, 1864/03/24, Private, Mustered Out 01/13/1866.

Hassell (aka Hussell), Raymond, Private, 1861/07/24, Private, Discharged 11/21/1861, Disability.

Hauke (aka Houk, Houke, Howk, Honk), Joseph, Private, 1861/07/24, Private, Veteran; Died, Baton Rouge, LA, 04/07/1865.

Haytey (aka Hagtey), John, Never Reported To Company.

Helms (aka Helm), Benjamin R., Private, 1861/07/24, 2nd Lieutenant, Promoted 2nd Lieutenant 11/01/1864; Mustered Out 01/10/1866..

Henning (aka Heming, Hening, Hennings, Hensing), Henry, Recruit, 1864/04/06, Private, Mustered Out 01/13/1866.

Hicks, William, Private, 1864/02/29, Private, Transferred to Company C 06/19/1864; Mustered Out 01/13/1866.

Hinkle, William S., Recruit, 1861/07/24, Regimental Q.M., Promoted to Regimental Quartermaster; Promoted Captain of Co. D; Discharged 8/10/1864..

Hitchcock (aka Hitchkocck), Alfred, Recruit, 1864/04/29, Private, Discharged, June, 1865, Disability.

Hopewell, Francis M., Recruit, 1864/09/07, Private, Mustered Out 07/05/1865.

Hopewell, Martin V. (aka Martin N.), Recruit, 1864/10/06, Private, Mustered Out 10/06/1865.

Hopper, Francis (aka Frank), Recruit, 1864/09/07, Private, Mustered Out 07/05/1865.

Hunt, Alsimus, Wagoner, 1861/07/24, Corporal, Veteran, Discharged 09/02/1864, Disability.

Hunter, Benjamin F., Recruit, 1864/04/11, Corporal, Mustered Out 01/13/1866.

Huntsinger (aka Huitsinger), William, Recruit, 1864/10/06, Private, Mustered Out 10/06/1865.

Jackson, Samuel, Private, 1861/07/24, Private, Veteran; Discharged 08/14/1864, Disability.

Jean (aka Jeans), Wesley S., Recruit, 1862/02/07, Private, Died at Newport News, VA, 03/26/1862.

Jenkins, Thomas, Private, 1861/07/24, Corporal, Veteran; Mustered Out 01/13/1866; Supposedly transferred to Company C — No Record of it.

Jewel, James R., Private, 1861/07/24, Sergeant, Veteran; Mustered Out 01/13/1866.

Jones, David E. (aka David P.), Recruit, 1864/09/28, Private, Mustered Out 07/05/1865.

Jones, George W., Recruit, 1864/03/26, Private, Mustered Out 01/13/1866.

Jones, James (aka James F.), Private, 1861/07/24, Sergeant, Veteran; Mustered Out 01/13/1866.

Jones, Nathan, Recruit, 1864/04/11, Private, Discharged 11/11/1865, Disability.

Kennerley (aka Kenerly, Kennedy, Kennerly), Robert F., Corporal, 1861/07/24, Sergeant, Veteran, Mustered Out 01/13/1866.

Kimberland (aka Kimberlain, Kimberlin), George (aka George W.), Private, 1861/07/24, Private, Veteran; Mustered Out 01/13/1866.

Knotts, William M., Recruit, 1864/04/11, Private, Discharged 04/01/1865, Disability.

Lake, Christopher M., Private, 1861/07/24, Private, Veteran; Mustered Out 01/13/1866.

Lamb, David, Recruit, 1864/03/24, Private, Died at Baton Rouge, LA 07/14/1864.

Lander (aka Lauder), Marshall, Private, 1861/07/24, Corporal, Veteran; Wounded at Port Hudson; Mustered Out 01/13/1866.

Lanigan (aka Lanagan), John, Recruit, 1864/03/24, Private, Died at Baton Rouge, LA, 12/13/1864.

Lauderdale, William, Recruit, 1864/03/24, Private, Mustered Out 01/13/1866.

Lisman (aka Lissman), William P., Corporal, 1861/07/24, Quartermaster Sergeant, Veteran, Mustered Out 01/13/1866.

Loyd (aka Lloyd), John, Private, 1861/07/24, Corporal, Mustered Out 08/01/1864.

Marks (aka Mart, Marts, Matts), John S., Sergeant, 1861/07/24, Private, Reduced, Mustered Out 08/01/1864.

Mason, Thomas, Recruit, 1864/04/11, Private, Mustered Out 01/13/1866.

Mathews, Jesse (aka Jessee), Private, 1861/07/24, Private, Discharged 11/21/1861, Disability.

Mayfield, Richard, Recruit, 1864/03/26, Private, Mustered Out 01/13/1866.

McArthur (aka McArther, McArthor), Harrison, Private, 1861/07/24, Private, Received furlough for 60 days, 09/1863, and never reported back. Discharged 09/22/1864, Disability..

McClung (aka McCluny, McClurg, McClury), Robert B., Private, 1861/07/24, Corporal, Veteran, Mustered Out 01/13/1866.

McClure, Gabriel, Private, 1861/07/24, Private, Killed In Action, Baton Rouge, LA, 08/05/1862.

McConnell, Benton, Private, 1861/07/24, Private, Veteran, Mustered Out 01/13/1866.

McConnell, John, Private, 1861/07/24, Private, Discharged, 04/10/1862, Disability.

McCormick (aka McCormack, McCormic), George, Private, 1861/07/24, Private, Discharged 01/16/1864, Disability from Wounds Received at Port Hudson.

McCormick (aka McCommick, McCormack, McCormic), James M., Recruit, 1862/09/19, Private, Mustered Out 07/05/1865.

McGowen (aka McGowan), Absalom S. (aka Absalom), Corporal, 1861/07/24, Corporal, Died 09/01/1862, Wounds Received at Battle of Baton Rouge, LA.

McGowen (aka McGovn, McGowan), John, Recruit, 1864/03/24, Private, Mustered Out 01/13/1866.

McNary, George, Recruit, 1864/03/08, Private, Mustered Out 01/13/1866.

Melam (aka Milam), John S. (aka John B.), 1st Lieutenant, 1861/07/24, 1st Lieutenant, Resigned, June 1862.

Miller, George W., Private, 1861/07/24, Private, Died, Carlisle, IN, 11/14/1863.

Mithoff, William, Recruit, 1862/10/06, , Promoted to 1st Lieutenant of 1st New Orleans Volunteers 01/27/1865.

Morice (aka Moris, Morris), Philip (aka Phillip), Recruit, 1864/10/06, Private, Mustered Out 10/06/1865.

Morice (aka Moris), Thomas, Recruit, 1864/04/25, Private, Mustered Out 01/13/1866.

Neely (aka Neeley), Joshua, Recruit, 1864/03/24, Private, Mustered Out 01/13/1866.

Neff, Leander, Recruit, 1864/03/08, Private, Mustered Out 01/13/1866.

Nickles (aka Nickels), John, , 1864/10/14, Never Reported to Company.

Norman, Francis, Private, 1861/07/24, Private, Veteran, Mustered Out 01/13/1866.

Norman, John, Recruit, 1864/03/24, Private, Mustered Out 01/13/1866.

Owen (aka Owens), Samuel C., Private, 1861/07/24, Private, Discharged 11/21/1861, Disability.

Parker, John, Private, 1861/07/24, Private, Veteran; Died at Baton Rouge, LA, 12/31/1865.

Parker, John G., Corporal, 1861/07/24, Private, Discharged 01/20/1863, Disability.

Pierce (aka Pearce), Elliott H., Recruit, 1864/03/24, Private, Mustered Out 01/13/1866.

Phillip (aka Philips, Phillips), Joseph, Recruit, 1864/09/05, Private, Mustered Out 09/05/1865.

Polk, Benjamin F., Recruit, 1864/03/24, Private, Mustered Out 01/13/1866.

Polk, Charles, Sergeant, 1861/07/24, 2nd Lieutenant, Promoted 2nd Lieutenant 04/01/1864; Veteran; Mustered Out 01/10/1866..

Power aka Powers), George, Private, 1861/07/24, Private, Died 08/23/1862, Wounds Received at Battle of Baton Rouge, LA.

Purcell (aka Percell), William, Corporal, 1861/07/24, Quartermaster Sergeant, Mustered Out 08/01/1864. Discharged 02/15/1862, Disability..

Pushee (aka Pashee), George R., Recruit, 1864/03/26, Private, Mustered Out 01/13/1866.

Raily (aka Raley, Raly), George B., Recruit, 1864/10/05, Private, Mustered Out 10/04/1865.

Raily (aka Raley, Raly), Joseph J., Recruit, 1864/10/05, Private, Mustered Out 10/04/1865.

Raily (aka Raley, Raly, Ruley), Samuel G., Recruit, 1864/10/05, Private, Mustered Out 10/04/1865.

Rector, John B., Recruit, 1864/10/30, Private, Mustered Out 07/05/1865.

Reece, John, Private, 1861/07/24, Private, Veteran; Discharged 06/10/1865, Disability.

Reese (aka Rees), John H., Private, 1861/07/24, Private, Veteran; Discharged 06/10/1865, Disability. Mustered Out 06/20/1865..

Richardson, James, Private, 1861/07/24, Private, Mustered Out 08/01/1864.

Roach, George W., Recruit, 1864/09/26, Private, Mustered Out 07/05/1865.

Robinson (aka Robison), Lorenzo D., Recruit, 1864/09/26, Private, Mustered Out 07/05/1865.

Salter, Calvin, Recruit, 1864/09/07, Private, Mustered Out 07/05/1865.

Sandusky (aka Sanduskey), Anthony, Private, 1861/07/24, Private, Veteran; Mustered Out 01/13/1865.

Shannon (aka Shanon, Sharon), Charles, Private, 1861/07/24, Corporal, Mustered Out 08/01/1864. Discharged 09/02/1864, Disability..

Shannon (aka Shannot), John T., Recruit, 1864/03/24, Private, Mustered Out 01/13/1866.

Sherman, Willis G., Private, 1861/07/24, Private, Discharged 04/10/1862, Disability.

Shown (aka Shawn), Arthur, Private, 1861/07/24, Private, Mustered Out 08/01/1864.

Simoral (aka Simerell, Simrell), John D., Recruit, 1864/03/30, Private, Discharged 06/18/1863, Disability. Mustered 01/14/1865..

Slagel (aka Slagbe, Stazel), Seymour, Private, 1861/07/24, Private, Died at New Orleans, LA, 03/26/1864.

Smith, Francis, Private, 1861/07/24, Private, Veteran; Mustered Out 01/13/1866.

Smith, George, Recruit, 1864/09/13, , Mustered Out 09/08/1865.

Smith, James J., Recruit, 1864/09/13, Private, Mustered Out 01/13/1866.

Smith, Philip W., Private, 1861/07/24, Private, Veteran; Mustered Out 01/13/1866.

Soloman (aka Solomon), William, Private, 1861/07/24, Corporal, Veteran; Died at Port Hudson, LA, 10/15/1865.

South, Thomas O., Recruit, 1864/03/24, Private, Mustered Out 01/13/1866.

Stark, Benjamin F., Recruit, 1864/10/10, Corporal, Mustered Out 10/10/1865.

Steward (aka Steuart, Stewart), Valentine, Private, 1861/07/24, Private, Killed In Action at Battle of Baton Rouge, LA 08/05/1862.

Stinson, Robert, Recruit, 1864/04/06, Private, Mustered Out 01/13/1866.

Stover, Benjamin F., Recruit, 1864/09/05, Private, Mustered Out 10/04/1865.

Strain (aka Strause), Thomas M. (aka Thomas. Thomas S.), Private, 1861/07/24, Private, Veteran; Mustered Out 01/13/1866.

Terwilliger, John N. (aka John A.), Recruit, 1864/10/05, Private, Mustered Out 10/05/1865.

Tewalt (aka Tewarlt), John, Private, 1861/07/24, Private, Veteran; Mustered Out 01/13/1866.

Tincher (aka Tucker), Samuel R., Recruit, 1864/10/10, Private, Mustered Out 10/10/1865.

Tucker, Malverd C., Sergeant, 1861/07/24, Sergeant, Mustered Out 08/01/1864.

Turner, Henry, Recruit, 1864/08/30, Private, Mustered Out 10/05/1865.

Vester, Andrew, Recruit, 1864/03/26, Private, Discharged 040/17/1865, Disability.

Wade (aka Waid), George A., Recruit, 1864/03/29, Private, AWOL since 11/27/1865; Dishonorably Discharged 01/28/1866..

Wallace, Martin, Recruit, 1862/02/07, Private, Mustered Out 02/07/1865.

Wallace, William, Private, 1861/07/24, Private, Veteran; Mustered Out 01/13/1866.

Walls, Bonaparte D., Private, 1861/07/24, Private, Discharged 11/21/1861, Disability.

Walls, Oliver H.P., Private, 1861/07/24, Corporal, Veteran; Mustered Out 01/13/1866.

Warner, Abraham, Recruit, 1864/10/10, Private, Mustered Out 10/10/1865.

Watson, George, Private, 1861/07/24, Private, Mustered Out 08/01/1864.

Wielderman (aka Weiderman, Welliman, Wilderman, Williman), Jacob, Recruit, 1864/03/29, Private, Discharged May 1865, Disability.

Weir (aka Wier), James A., Private, 1861/07/24, First Sergeant, Veteran; Mustered Out 01/13/1866.

Wells, John L., Recruit, 1864/03/24, Private, Mustered Out 01/13/1866.

Westner (aka Wesner), Eli, Private, 1861/07/24, Private, Wounded at Battle of Baton Rouge, LA; Veteran; Mustered Out 01/13/1866.

Whalen, John W. (aka John N.), Recruit, 1863/10/05, Corporal, Mustered Out 01/13/1866.

Whalen, Joseph O. (aka Joseph E.), Private, 1861/07/24, 1st Lieutenant, Wounded at Battle of Baton Rouge, LA; Promoted 2nd Lieutenant 07/30/1863; Promoted 1st Lieutenant 03/31/1864; Mustered Out 01/10/1866..

Whitaker (aka Whittaker), Henry S., Recruit, 1864/10/10, Private, Transferred to Company F, 04/01/1865. Died 07/17/1865 at Fort Barrancas, FL (Pensacola)..

Whitaker (aka Whitiker, Wittaker), John, Recruit, 1864/10/06, Private, Mustered Out 10/06/1865.

White, Andrew L. (aka Andrew S.), Recruit, 1864/09/28, Private, Mustered Out 07/05/1865.

Whitesal (aka Whitesel, Whitezel, Whitsel, Whitzer), Leander, Recruit, 1864/09/07, Private, Mustered Out 07/05/1865.

Whitlock (aka Whittock), Robert B., Private, 1861/07/24, Corporal, Veteran; Mustered Out 01/13/1866.

Whitman (aka Whiteman), Jacob, Recruit, 1864/04/14, Private, Mustered Out 01/13/1866.

Widener (aka Widner, Willener), Jacob A., Corporal, 1861/07/24, ?, Died, Baton Rouge 06/25/1862.

Wilkerson, Ezekiel F., Private, 1861/07/24, Private, Veteran; Discharged 11/04/1865, Disability.

Willis, Tilman (aka Tilghman), Recruit, 1864/0906, Private, Mustered Out 09/05/1865.

Wilson, Anson, Recruit, 1862/02/07, Private, Mustered Out 02/07/1865.

Wilson, James K. (aka James R.), Recruit, 1864/03/24, Private, Mustered Out 01/13/1866.

Wilson, Joseph, Private, 1861/07/24, Private, Died at Baton Rouge, LA, 07/20/1862.

Wilson, William, Private, 1861/07/24, Sergeant, Veteran; Mustered Out 01/13/1866.

Wisely (aka Wirseley, Wiseley, Wisley), George, Recruit, 1863/02/20, Private, Mustered Out 01/13/1866.

Wolfe (aka Wolf, Woolfe), John S., Recruit, 1864/03/24, Private, Mustered Out 01/13/1866.

Wood, Amos, Recruit, 1864/10/08, Private, Mustered Out 10/05/1865.

Woolen (aka Woollen), Mathew S., Recruit, 1864/03/29, Corporal, Mustered Out 01/13/1866.

Wortman (aka Worstman), John P., Private, 1861/07/24, Private, Veteran; Discharged 12/13/1864, Disability.

Wortman (aka Warstman, Worstman), John W., Recruit, 1863/05/12, Private, Mustered Out 01/13/1866.

Wortman (aka Worstman), Phillip, Private, 1861/07/24, Private, Discharged 10/13/1862, Disability.

Yocum, John, Recruit, 1864/10/21, Private, Mustered Out 10/21/1865.

Yocum, Simeon, Private, 1861/07/24, Corporal, Veteran; Mustered Out 01/13/1866.

Young, John, Recruit, 1864/08/30, Private, Transferred to Company F, 04/01/1865. Mustered Out 07/27/1865..

Yowell (aka Zowell), William, Recruit, 1864/10/04, Private, Mustered Out 10/04/1865.

COMPANY E

Albin (aka Albian), William W., Private, 1861/07/24, 1st Lieutenant, Promoted 2nd Lieutenant 09/07/1864; Promoted 1st Lieutenant 03/20/1865; Mustered Out 01/10/1866..

Baker (aka Balner), George, Recruit, 1864/09/22, Private, Deserted 07/01/1865.

Ball, Joseph B., Private, 1861/07/24, Private, Discharged 11/01/1863, Disability.

Barton, Wait R., Private, 1861/07/24, Private, Died at New Orleans, LA, 06/09/1862.

Barton (aka Baston), William, Recruit, 1864/08/30, Private, Deserted 09/18/1864.

Beason (aka Beeson), John, Recruit, 1864/09/27, Private, Mustered Out 07/22/1862 (1865?).

Beech (aka Beach, Beash, Beesh, Bush), Albert H., Private, 1861/07/24, Private, Mustered Out 07/31/0864.

Beem, John W., Recruit, 1863/11/10, Principal Musician, Mustered Out 01/13/1866.

Berry, Sergeant M., Private, 1861/07/24, Private, Mustered Out 07/31/1864.

Bidd (aka Bed, Bird), William, Recruit, 1864/03/24, Private, Died at Baton Rouge, LA, 05/05/1865.

Biddle, George A., Recruit, 1864/09/13, Private, Mustered Out 07/22/1865.

Blacketer (aka Batchelor, Blackiter, Blanckiter), John, Recruit, 1864/03/28, Private, Mustered Out 01/13/1866.

Bladen (aka Bladin), Franklin, Recruit, 1862/01/11, Private, Veteran; Died of Disease 10/22/1864.

Bladen (aka Bladin), Henry C., Private, 1861/07/24, Private, Mustered Out 07/31/1864.

Bohannon (aka Bohamon, Bohanan), James M. (aka James N.), Recruit, 1864/03/29, Private, Mustered Out 01/13/1866.

Bohannon (aka Bohamon, Bohanon), William H., Private, 1861/07/24, Corporal, Veteran; Mustered Out 01/13/1866.

Boone (aka Boon, Bron), Moses, Recruit, 1864/09/02, Private, Mustered Out 07/22/1865.

Bradshaw, Alexander, Recruit, 1864/03/24, Private, Died at Baton Rouge, LA, 08/15/1864.

Brann (aka Braun), James A., Recruit, 1864/09/05, Private, Mustered Out 07/22/1865.

Branson, George W., Private, 1861/07/24, Captain, Wounded at Battle of Baton Rouge, LA; Promoted 2nd Lieutenant 03/31/1864; Promoted 1st Lieutenant 1864/09/07; Promoted Captain 11/22/1864; Mustered Out 01/10/1866..

Bratton (aka Brattain, Bratten), Jabez (aka Jabus), Recruit, 1864/09/25, Private, Mustered Out 07/22/1865.

Bright, James E. (aka James C.), Recruit, 1864/08/31, Private, Deserted 07/01/1865.

Buddin (aka Budden), Solomon P. (aka Solomon F.), Private, 1861/07/24, Corporal, Wounded at Battle of Baton Rouge, LA; Discharged, Disability, Date Not Reported; Re-enlisted 03/24/1864; Mustered Out 01/13/1866.

Burnap, George, Recruit, 1862/01/30, Private, Deserted 02/23/1863.

Burnett, Isam (aka Isom), Recruit, 1862/01/25, Private, Veteran; Mustered Out 01/13/1866.

Burns, Martin, Recruit, 1864/12/24, Private, Mustered Out 01/13/1866.

Burton, James K., Corporal, 1861/07/24, Corporal, Discharged 02/07/1862, Disability.

Busby, Hiram, Recruit, 1864/04/01, Private, Mustered Out 01/13/1866.

Butcher, John C., Private, 1861/07/24, Private, Veteran; Discharged, Disability, Date Not Reported.

Byrum (aka Byram), Emanuel, Recruit, 1864/09/05, Private, Mustered Out 07/22/1865.

Carmichael (aka Carmichel), Jefferson, Recruit, 1864/03/24, Private, Mustered Out 01/13/1866.

Carter, Jasper N., Private, 1861/07/24, Sergeant, Veteran; Mustered Out 01/13/1866.

Chadwick (aka Chadwic), Ebonezer (aka Abenezer, Eboneezer), Recruit, 1864/09/29-, Private, Mustered Out 09/29/1865.

Chase, Benjamin F., Recruit, 1864/08/23, Private, Mustered Out 01/13/1866.

Coffman, Hiram L. (aka Luther), Recruit, 1864/09/02, Private, Mustered Out 09/02/1865.

Coffman (aka Coffaman), Solomon A., Recruit, 1864/09/02, Private, Died at Baton Rouge, LA, 09/03/1863.

Comstock, James C., Private, 1861/07/24, Private, Died at Fort McHenry, Baltimore, MD, 11/27/1861.

Cook, Zachariah T., Recruit, 1864/08/29, Private, Mustered Out 07/22/1865.

Cooper, Charles S., Recruit, 1864/03/15, Private, Mustered Out 01/13/1866.

Copple (aka Capple, Coople, Coppee), Newton, Recruit, 1864/10/10, Private, Mustered Out 10/10/1865.

Craig, James, Private, 1861/07/24, Private, Died at Fort McHenry, Baltimore, MD, 11/22/1861.

Craig (aka Creaig), Oscar (aka Osker), Recruit, 1864/08/31, Private, Mustered Out 07/27/1865.

Crawford, Taylor, Recruit, 1864/03/24, Private, Died at Memphis 10/25/1864.

Dailey (aka Daily, Dayly), Nathaniel H., Recruit, 1862/01/25, Private, Discharged 10/31/1862, Disability.

Danhour (aka Danhar), Nathan, Recruit, 1864/01/12, Private, Deserted 11/09/1865.

Davis, Henry, Private, 1861/07/24, Corporal, Veteran; Discharged 01/03/1865, Disability.

Dawson (aka Dowson), William L., Wagoner, 1861/07/24, Wagoner, Veteran; Died at Philadelphia 02/01/1865.

Devers (aka Deavers), Joseph, Recruit, 1864/08/31, Private, Transferred to Company C 10/16/1864; Substitute; Died 09/24/1865.

Devore (aka Deveore, Devon, Devour), Alfred, Recruit, 1864/03/24, Private, Mustered Out 01/13/1866.

Dilworth (aka Dillworth), William M., Private, 1861/07/24, Private, Mustered Out 07/31/1864.

Dix, Ostrander, Recruit, 1862/01/04, Private, Discharged 10/21/1862, Disability.

Douglas, Harrison, Private, 1861/07/24, Corporal, Veteran; Died at Quincy, IN, 02/06/1865.

Douglass, John F., Recruit, 1862/04/14, Private, Discharged 09/30/1865, Disability.

Duty, William F., Private, 1861/07/24, Private, Killed In Action at Battle of Baton Rouge, LA, 08/05/1862.

Eaglesfield (aka Eaglefield), William J., Private, 1861/07/24, Private, Mustered Out 07/31/1864.

Edson, Andrew J., Recruit, 1864/04/14, Private, Discharged 09/29/1865, Disability.

Edwards, Ephraim D., Recruit, 1864/08/31, Private, Transferred to Company C 10/16/1864; Discharged 07/20/1865, by order of War Department.

Erastus (aka Easter, Eastus, Estes), Henry J. (aka Henry), Recruit, 4/18/1864, Private, Transferred to Company C 10/16/1864; Discharged 10/26/64, Disability.

Evans, Allen C., Recruit, 1864/03/04, Corporal, Mustered Out 01/13/1866.

Evans, James M., Recruit, 1864/04/14, Private, Mustered Out 01/13/1866.

Evans, Mathias, Recruit, 1864/09/26, Private, Mustered Out 07/22/1865.
Fisher, Charles W., Private, 1861/07/24, Private, Discharged 04/10/1862, Disability.
Flinn (aka Flin), John W. (aka John H.), Recruit, 1864/09/06, Private, Mustered Out 07/22/1865.
Fox, Thomas A., Recruit, 1864/08/31, Private, Mustered Out 07/22/1865.
Frakes, Jesse, Sergeant, 1861/07/24, Sergeant, Killed near Houma, LA, by Guerrillas, 05/10/1862.
Fritts (aka Fritz), William E., Corporal, 1861/07/24, Private, Reduced; Veteran; Mustered Out 01/13/1866.
Frokes (aka Frakes), Parker, Private, 1861/07/24, Private, Mustered Out 07/31/1864.
Garrett, Monroe, Recruit, 1864/09/19, Private, Mustered Out 07/31/1864.
Gasway (aka Gasaway, Gosaway), James M., Recruit, 1863/06/10, Private, Died at Baton Rouge, LA, 07/26/1864.
Gasway (aka Gasaway, Gasoway, Gosaway), Smith L., Recruit, 1863/05/06, Private, Mustered Out 01/13/1866.
Gates, Austin B., Recruit, 1864/03/29, Private, Mustered Out 01/13/1866.
Gibbs, Thomas J., Private, 1861/07/24, Private, Veteran; Mustered Out 01/13/1866.
Glidewell (aka Gildwell, Gledewell), Marion (aka Marion F., Francis M., Francis Marion), Recruit, 1864/09/066, Private, Mustered Out 07/22/1865.
Goddard, Warren R., Recruit, 1864/09/06, Private, Mustered Out 07/22/1865.
Goodwin, Tilman B., Private, 1861/07/24, Sergeant, Veteran; Mustered Out 01/13/1866.
Gorham (aka Ghoram), George D., Recruit, 1864/03/24, Private, Mustered Out 01/13/1866.
Gorham (aka Garham, Ghoram), Silas W., Private, 1861/07/24, Private, Veteran; Died at Quincy, IN, 06/01/1865.
Gorham, Thomas T., Recruit, 1864/03/26, Private, Died at Greencastle, IN, 03/01/1865.
Gosaway (aka Gasaway, Gaseway, Gasoway, Gasway), John S., Private, 1861/07/24, Private, Veteran; Discharged 09/24/1864, Disability.
Gray (aka Grey), Alexander, Private, 1861/07/24, Private, Veteran; Discharged 06/01/1864, Disability.
Gray (aka Grey), Jacob S. (aka Jacob L., Jacob T.), Private, 1861/07/24, Private, Mustered Out 07/31/1864.
Gray, Robert A., Private, 1861/07/24, Private, Mustered Out 07/31/1864.
Grooms, Ransom H., Musician, 1861/07/24, Principal Musician, Promoted to Principal Musician 09/16/62; no additional information given.
Grubb, Henry, Recruit, 1862/12/10, Private, Mustered Out 12/10/1865.
Grubb (aka Grubbs), Joseph, Private, 1861/07/24, Corporal, Veteran; Mustered Out 01/13/1866.
Gwin (aka Gwinn, Guinn), Seth, Recruit, 1864/03/28, Private, Discharged 05/10/1865, Disability.
Hadley (aka hadly), George W., Private, 1861/07/24, Private, Died at New Orleans, LA, 09/07/1862.
Haley (aka Healey, Healy), Peter, Recruit, 1863/12/31, Private, Deserted 05/22/1864.
Hammond (aka Hammon), Eden, Recruit, 1864/03/28, Private, Deserted 11/09/1865.
Hamrick, James W. (aka James M.), 1st Lieutenant, 1861/07/24, Captain, Promoted Captain 12/24/1862; Honorably Discharged 11/21/1864.
Hardin (aka Harden), Granville M. (aka Greenville M), Recruit, 1864/03/23, Private, Discharged 09/20/1865, Disability.
Harlan (aka Harland, Harlin), Harrison, Recruit, 1864/09/06, Private, Mustered Out 07/22/1865.
Harlan (aka Harland, Harlin), Preston H., Recruit, 1864/09/07, Private, Mustered Out 07/22/1865.
Harlan (aka Harland, Harlin), Samuel, Recruit, 1864/09/29, Private, Mustered Out 07/22/1865.
Harney, David R., Sergeant, 1861/07/24, Corporal, Reduced; Died of Wounds (Rec'd at Port Hudson, LA) 07/06/1863.
Harney, Joshua T., Private, 1861/07/24, Private, Died at Baton Rouge, LA, 07/01/1862.
Harper, William, Private, 1864/08/29, Private, Transferred to Co. C 10/16/1864; Mustered Out 07/29/1865, Substitute.
Harris, John W., Recruit, 1864/09/13, Private, Mustered Out 01/13/1866.
Harris, William B., Private, 1861/07/24, Private, Discharged 12/03/1861, Disability.
Harrison, Manuel W. (aka Manuel H.), Recruit, 1864/03/15, Private, Died at Alexandria, LA, 07/03/1865.
Harrison, Thomas, Recruit, 1864/08/30, Private, Mustered Out 01/13/1866.
Hartley (aka Hartly), Samuel, First Sergeant, 1861/07/24, 1st Lieutenant, Promoted 2nd Lieutenant 12/20/1861; Promoted to 1st Lieutenant 12/24/1862; Resigned 08/25/1864.
Hartweg (aka Hartwig, Hartwigs), John, Private, 1861/07/24, Private, Veteran; Mustered Out 01/13/1866.
Henry, John H., Private, 1861/07/24, Private, Discharged 11/01/1863, Disability.
Henton, George W., Private, 1861/07/24, Private, Veteran; Mustered Out 01/13/1866.
Hice, H. Samuel (aka Samuel), Private, 1861/07/24, Sergeant, Veteran; Mustered Out 01/13/1866.
Hickson, Albert, Recruit, 1864/08/29, Private, Deserted 05/22/1864.
Hillis, John L., Private, 1861/07/24, Sergeant, Veteran; Mustered Out 01/13/1866.

Hines (aka Hiens), Jacob, Private, 1861/07/24, Private, Wounded at Battle of Baton Rouge, LA; Veteran; Mustered Out 01/13/1866.

Hines, John W., Recruit, 1863/04/01, Private, Died at Baton Rouge, LA, 06/29/1863.

Hodges, Daniel, Recruit, 1864/08/23, Private, Died at Baton Rouge, LA, 10/14/1864.

Hogue (aka Hague), George, Corporal, 1861/07/24, Corporal, Veteran; Mustered Out 01/13/1866.

Hood, James, Private, 1861/07/24, Corporal, Veteran; Mustered Out 01/13/1866.

Hood, John J., Private, 1861/07/24, Private, Died at Baton Rouge, LA, 08/01/1863.

Hood, Washington, Recruit, 1864/03/30, Private, Died at Baton Rouge, LA, 05/24/1864.

Horne (aka Harn, Horn), Nathan I. (aka Nathan J.), Recruit, 1864/09/07, Private, Mustered Out 07/22/1865.

Hough, Orson E., Recruit, 1864/03/18, Bugler, Mustered Out 01/13/1866.

Hudson, William, Private, 1861/07/24, Private, Mustered Out 07/31/1864.

Hunt, Martin D., Private, 1861/07/24, Private, Discharged 12/03/1861, Disability.

Huntzenger (aka Huntsinger, Huntzinger), James W. (aka James M.), Private, 1861/07/24, Private, Wounded at Battle of Baton Rouge, LA; Discharged 11/15/1862, Disability.

Hutcheson (aka Hutchinson, Hutchison), Ambrose D. (aka Dudley, Albert), Recruit, 1864/09/02, Private, Mustered Out 09/02/1865.

Jackson, Jesse, Private, 1861/07/24, Private, Died of disease on Steamer 08/05/1862.

Jarboe (aka Jarbo, Jorboe), Stanishlow (aka Stanishbelon, Stanishlaws), Private, 1861/07/24, Private, Killed In Action at Bayou Teche, LA, 11/03/1862.

Johnson (aka Johnston), Thomas (aka Thomas F., Thomas G.), Recruit, 1864/08/23, Private, Transferred to Co. C 10/16/1864; Mustered Out 07/21/1865..

Jones, Benjamin F., Private, 1864/03/08, Regimental Commissary Sergeant, Promoted Commissary Sergt. Mustered Out 01/13/1866.

Jones, John W., Recruit, 1864/03/15, Private, Died 06 25/1864.

Jordon (aka Jordan, Harry L. (aka Henry L.), Recruit, 1864/03/15, Private, Discharged 11/22/1864. Mustered 01/22/1865..

Keller (aka Kellar, Kreler), John, Recruit, 1864/04/01, Private, Mustered Out 01/13/1866.

Kemper, Elias, Recruit, 1864/03/31, Private, Mustered Out 01/13/1866.

Kennard, Adolphus, Recruit, 1864/08/23, Private, Mustered Out 07/22/1865.

Kennedy (aka Kenneda, Kennida), James H. (aka John H.), Private, 1861/07/24, Corporal, Veteran; Mustered Out 01/13/1866.

Kennedy (aka Kenneda, Kennedey), John, Recruit, 1863/06/03, Private, Mustered Out 01/13/1866.

Kennedy (aka Kenneda, Kennida), Milton, Private, 1861/07/24, Private, Discharged 12/03/1861, Disability.

King, John (aka John F.), Private, 1861/07/24, Private, Veteran; Mustered Out 01/13/1866.

King, Jonathan (aka John), Recruit, 1864/09/26, Private, Died at New Orleans, LA, 04/13/1865.

Lamb, Michael, Recruit, 1864/01/20, Private, Discharged 02/09/1865, Disability.

Landes (aka Landers, Landis), William, Recruit, 1864/08/25, Private, Mustered Out 07/22/1865.

Landes (aka Landers, Landis), John W., Recruit, 1864/09/06, Private, Mustered Out 09/06/1865.

Lane, Marshall W., Recruit, 1864/04/02, Private, Mustered Out 01/13/1866.

Lee, Green (aka Greene), Recruit, 1864/05/26, Private, Transferred to Co. C 10/16/1864; Mustered Out 01/13/1866.

Lee, Richard E., Recruit, 1864/08/31, Private, Transferred to Company C 10/18/1864.

Lemon, Lucien, Recruit, 1864/04/01, Private, Died at Baton Rouge, LA, 09/15/1864.

Lemon, Wickliff, Sergeant, 1861/07/24, Private, Reduced; Mustered Out 07/31/1864.

Lewis, Edward M., Recruit, 1866/03/30, Private, Died at Baton Rouge, LA, 07/26/1864.

Lilly, Eli, 2nd Lieutenant, 1861/07/24, 2nd Lieutenant, Resigned 12/09/1861; Re-entered Service as Captain of 18th Battery Light Artillery.

Lisby (aka Lasby, Lisbey), Howard, Recruit, 1864/09/27, Private, Mustered Out 07/22/1865.

Mahoney, Theobald J., Recruit, 1863/12/30, Private, Mustered Out 01/13/1866.

Marshall, Johnathan S., Recruit, 1863/06/09, Corporal, Transferred to Co. L 01/29/1864; Mustered Out 01/10/1866.

Martin, Allison (aka Alfred), Recruit, 1864/08/30, Private, *Deserted 09/18/1864.*

Martin, James, Recruit, 1864/08/30, Private, *Deserted 09/18/1864.*

Martin, James E. (aka James M.), Recruit, 1864/10/17, Private, Mustered Out 10/17/1865.

Masterson, David W., Recruit, 1864/08/20, Private, Mustered Out 07/22/1865.

Mathews (aka Matthews), Francis M., Private, 1861/07/24, Private, Killed In Action at Bayou Teche, LA, 11/03/1862.

McCallister (aka McAllister, McCallaster), James, Recruit, 1864/08/24, Private, Mustered Out 07/22/1865.

McCawley (aka McCaully, McCawly, McCowley), William, Private, 1861/07/24, Private, Transferred to 5th U.S. Artillery, November 1862.

McCookle (aka McCorkle), Robert T., Private, 1861/07/24, Private, Died at New Orleans, LA, 09/11/1862.

McCowen (aka McCowan, McCown), George J., Private, 1861/07/24, Private, Died at New Orleans, LA, of Wounds received at Battle of Baton Rouge, LA, 09/16/1862.

McGee, William, Recruit, unknown, unknown, Died at Baton Rouge, LA, 12/14/1864.

McHargue (aka McCurgue, McHergue), James M., Recruit, 1864/03/30, Private, Mustered Out 01/13/1866.

McHargue (aka McHergue), Stephen (aka Steven), Private, 1861/07/24, Private, Mustered Out 07/31/1864.

McVay (aka McVey), Joseph, Recruit, 1864/03/29, Private, Mustered Out 01/13/1866.

Melvin, John W., Recruit, 1863/12/30, Private, *Deserted 06/07/1864.*

Mershon, John N., Private, 1861/07/24, Private, Discharged 10/21/1862, Disability.

Mershon (aka Nershon), John W., Private, 1861/07/24, Private, Died at Camp Parapet, Carrollton, LA, 10/16/1863.

Miller (aka Millor), Henry S., Recruit, 1864/08/23, Private, Mustered Out 07/22/1865.

Moore (aka Moor), Thomas, Private, 1861/07/24, Private, Discharged 10/26/1862, Disability; Re-enlisted 04/09/1864; Mustered Out 01/13/1866.

Morgan, William J., Recruit, 1864/03/10, Private, *Deserted 06/09/1864*. Died 11/04/1864 at New Orleans, LA..

Moses (aka Moss), Newton J., Private, 1861/07/24, Private, Discharged 04/01/1862, Disability.

Murphy, James H., Recruit, 1864/09/06, Private, Mustered Out 07/22/1865.

Murphy, John W. (aka John H.), Recruit, 1864/04/01, Private, Mustered 01/13/1866.

Nelson, Perry T. (aka Perry F.), Private, 1861/07/24, Private, Veteran; Died at Baton Rouge, LA, 05/25/1865.

Nolen (aka Nolan), John B., Private, 1861/07/24, Private, Died at Camp Parapet, Carrollton, LA, 10/13/1862.

Norton, Isaac N., Private, 1861/07/24, Private, Veteran; Mustered Out 01/13/1866.

O'Neal, Bailey, Recruit, 1864/09/26, Private, Mustered Out 07/22/1865.

Palmer, Joseph W., Corporal, 1861/07/24, Sergeant, Wounded at Battle of Baton Rouge, LA; Mustered Out 07/31/1864.

Paris (aka Parris), John A., Recruit, 1864/09/09, Private, Mustered Out 07/22/1865.

Paris (aka Parris), Lorenzo D., Recruit, 1864/09/09, Private, Mustered Out 07/22/1865.

Parker, Thomas, Private, 1861/07/24, Private, Veteran; Died at Baton Rouge, LA, 07/25/1864.

Payne (aka Payn), Almond L. (aka Almon L.), Private, 1861/07/24, Corporal, Veteran; Mustered Out 01/13/1866.

Payne, Bennett, Recruit, 1864/10/17, Private, Mustered Out 10/16/1865.

Pearcy (aka Pearcey), James, Recruit, 1864/03/24, Private, Mustered Out 01/13/1866.

Perine (aka Perrine), Tobias E., Recruit, 1864/08/23, Private, Mustered Out 07/22/1865.

Phillips (aka Philips), William, Recruit, 1862/01/25, Sergeant, Veteran; Mustered Out 01/13/1866.

Polk, William H., Corporal, 1861/07/24, Sergeant, Veteran; Discharged 01/28/1865, Disability.

Postal (aka Pastal, Postall, Postell), William M. (aka William, William H., William N.), Recruit, 1863/12/09, Private, Transferred to Co. C 10/21/1864; *Deserted 12-xx-1864.*

Poteet, Mark M. (aka Mark N.), Private, 1861/07/24, Private, Killed In Action at Battle of Baton Rouge, LA, 08/05/1862.

Pottorff (aka Pattorff, Potorff), George H., Musician, 1861/07/24, Musician, Died 08/05/1862, at Baton Rouge, LA, (Of disease or Killed in Action?).

Pruett (aka Pruitt), Edmund, Private, 1861/07/24, Private, Discharged 10/21/1862, Disability.

Railsback, William L., Recruit, 1864/09/05, Private, Mustered Out 07/22/1865.

Redpath (aka Ridpath), William M., Recruit, 1864/09/08, Private, Mustered Out 07/22/1865.

Reeves (aka Reves), Henry C., Recruit, 1864/09/07, Private, Mustered Out 07/22/1865.

Reitzel (aka Rietzel, Ritzel, Ritzle), Martin L, (aka Morton L.), Private, 1861/07/24, Sergeant, Veteran; Mustered Out 01/13/1866.

Richardson, Joseph R. (aka Joseph K.), Recruit, 1864/03/28, Private, Mustered Out 01/13/1866.

Richardson (aka Richerdson, Richordson), William H., Private, 1861/07/24, Corporal, Discharged 10/30/1863, Disability; Re-enlisted 03/30/1864; Mustered Out 01/13/1866.

Riddle, John, Private, 1861/07/24, Bugler, Veteran; Mustered Out 01/13/1866.

Riddle, Paris G., Private, 1861/07/24, Corporal, Veteran; Mustered Out 01/13/1866.

Robbins, Robert, Recruit, 1864/09/19, Private, Mustered Out 09/19/1865.

Roublain (aka Raublau, Roublau, Roublaw, Roublow), Joseph, Recruit, 1864/09/09, Private, Mustered Out 01/13/1866.

Roupe (aka Roup), John T., Recruit, 1864/04/15, Private, Mustered Out 01/13/1866.

Rudisil (aka Rudisill, Rudissil, Rudissel), Philip (aka Phillip), Recruit, 1864/09/06, Private, Mustered Out 07/22/1865.

Ryner (aka Riner), John A., Recruit, 1864/09/05, Private, Died at Baton Rouge, LA, 01/11/1865.

Sears (aka Seares), Samuel R., Recruit, 1864/09/02, Private, Mustered Out 09/02/1865.

Shaw, Lewis F., Private, 1861/07/24, Private, Discharged 12/21/1861, Disability.

Shearer, John W., Recruit, 1864/08/19, Private, Mustered 08/19/1865.

Shearer (aka Scherer, Sherer), Loami E., Private, 1861/07/24, Private, Mustered 07/31/1864.

Shirley (aka Shely, Sherley), James A., Private, 1861/07/24, 1st Lieutenant, Promoted 2nd Lieutenant 03/31/1864; Promoted 1st Lieutenant 09/07/1864; Mustered Out 01/10/1866..

Shoemaker, James A., Corporal, 1861/07/24, Private, Wounded at Battle of Baton Rouge, LA; Reduced; Veteran; Mustered Out 01/13/1866.

Siddens (aka Siddins, Siddons, Siddens), John H. (aka John A., John W.), Recruit, 1864/03/28, Private, Mustered Out 01/13/1866.

Siddons (aka Siddens, Siddins), Joseph W., Sergeant, 1861/07/24, 1st Lieutenant, Promoted 1st Lieutenant 03/31/1864; Killed on Steamer *Empress* 08/10/1864.

Siddens (aka Siddins), William A., Recruit, 1864/03/28, Private, Mustered Out 01/13/1866.

Skelton, William M., Captain, 1861/07/24, Captain, Wounded at Battle of Baton Rouge, LA; Resigned 12/22/1862.

Snider, Calvin, Private, 1861/07/24, Private, Died at Baton Rouge, LA, 08/23/1863.

Spurgin (aka Spurgen, Spurgeon, Spurgon), Simon, Private, 1861/07/24, Private, Veteran; Died at Mansfield, IN, 09/22/1865.

Steinbrenner (aka Steinbreener, Steinbrener, Steinbrinner, Stunbrener), Jacob, Recruit, 1862/11/11, Private, Mustered Out 11/11/1865.

Stevens (aka Stephens), James H., Recruit, 1864/09/03, Private, Mustered Out 07/22/1865.

Stoner, Lycurgus, Recruit, 1862/01/25, Sergeant, Veteran; Mustered Out 01/13/1866.

Stoner, Peter S., Recruit, 1864/03/24, Private, Mustered Out 01/13/1866.

Stoner, William P., Recruit, 1864/08/31, Private, Mustered Out 07/22/1865.

Sullivan (aka Sulivan), Dennis, Private, 1861/07/24, Private, Mustered Out 07/31/1864. Veteran; Discharged 06/01/1865, Disability.

Sylvey (aka Silvey, Sylva), John J., Recruit, 1864/09/13, Private, Mustered Out 07/22/1865.

Talbot (aka Talbut), Arthur, Recruit, 1864/09/13, Private, Mustered Out 09/13/1865.

Taylor, James M., Private, 1861/07/24, Private, Veteran; Discharged 06/01/1865, Disability.

Taylor, Leonard O., Private, 1861/07/24, Private, Wounded at Battle of Baton Rouge, LA; Killed by Provost Guard in Mobile, AL, 05/24/1865.

Thornburg (aka Thornburgh, Thornberg), William E., Recruit, 1864/09/02, Private, Mustered Out 07/22/1865.

Tindall (aka Tindel), Alexander C., Recruit, 1863/11/10, Private, Deserted 07/01/1865. Transferred to Veteran Reserve Corps; Discharged 08/01/1865, Disability.

Tinder, Jeremiah W. (aka Jeremiah M.), Recruit, 1864/03/17, Private, Died at Baton Rouge, LA, 06/25/1865.

Tinder (aka Tindler), Samuel M., Private, 1861/07/24, First Sergeant, Promoted 2nd Lieutenant 03/20/1865; Veteran; Mustered Out 01/13/1866 as 1st Sergeant.

Todd (aka Tood), Wesley, Recruit, 1864/09/26, Private, Died at Baton Rouge, LA, 12/16/1864.

Turner, Edwin C. (aka Edward C.), Recruit, 1864/03/18, Private, Died at Greencastle, IN, 01/11/1865.

Tyler, William F., Recruit, 1864/04/09, Private, Mustered Out 01/13/1866.

Vancleve (aka Vancleave), Newton I, (aka Albert N., Newton J.), Recruit, 1864/04/01, Private, Mustered Out 01/13/1866.

Vansickle, James M., Recruit, 184/08/19, Private, Mustered Out 07/22/1865.

Vaughan (aka Vaughn), Hiram T., Recruit, 1864/06/16, Private, Died at Baton Rouge, LA, 02/13/1865.

Waples, John T., Recruit, 1862/10/15, Private, Transferred to Co. C 10/16/64; Mustered Out 10/21/1865.

Warsdall (aka Warsdell, Warsdoll, Woosdell, Worsdal, Worsdell, Worsdoll), William, Corporal, 1861/07/24, Private, Reduced; Veteran; Discharged 11/11/1864, Disability.

White, Caleb F., Recruit, 1864/08/23, Private, Mustered Out 07/22/1865.

White, Elisha, Recruit, 1864/03/26, Private, Mustered Out 01/13/1866.

White, William D., Recruit, 1864/08/26, Private, Died at Baton Rouge, LA, 02/15/1865.

Wigginton (aka Waggington, Wiggenton, Wiggington), Timothy, Recruit, 1864/02/06, Blacksmith, Mustered Out 07/22/1865.

Williams (aka William), John, Recruit, 1864, Private, *Deserted 09/18/1864.*

Williams, John W., Corporal, 1861/07/24, Corporal, Veteran; Discharged 08/02/1864, Disability.

Wilson (aka Willson), Henry P. (aka Harvey P.), Private, 1861/07/24, 1st Sergeant, Died of Wounds received at Battle of Baton Rouge, LA 08/07/1862.

Wilson (aka Willson), James R., Recruit, 1864/08/22, Private, Died at Baton Rouge, LA, 03/13/1865.

Winkler (aka Winklar, Winklor), Harvey, Private, 1861/07/24, Private, Discharged 10/21/1862, Disability. Discharged 11/11/1864, Disability.

Winkler (aka Winklar), Levi, Private, 1861/07/24, Private, Died at St. James Hospital, New Orleans, LA, 08/01/1863.

Winstead (aka Wenstead, Winsted), James, Private, 1861/07/24, Private, Mustered Out 07/31/1864. Discharged 10/21/1862, Disability.

Wright, Harrison, Recruit, 1862/01/25, 2nd Lieutenant, Promoted to 2nd Lieutenant 03/20/1864; Veteran; Mustered Out 01/10/1866..

Wright, Philbert S. (aka Philbard S., Philburg S.),

Recruit, 1864/03/15, Private, Died at Baton Rouge, LA, 11/12/1864.

Wynegar (aka Winegar, Wineger, Wyneger, Wynegor), John F., Private, 1861/07/24, Private, Veteran; Mustered Out 01/13/1866.

Zenor (aka Taylor, Zenar, Zener), Squire, Recruit, 1864/09/26, Private, Mustered Out 07/22/1865.

Company F

Adams, Andrew J., Private, 1861/07/24, Private, *Deserted July, 1861.*

Amel (aka Armel, Arnel), Albert, Recruit, 1862/02/07, Private, Mustered Out 01/10/1866.

Anderson, James W., Private, 1861/07/24, Sergeant, Veteran; Mustered Out 01/10/1866.

Arnold, John, Private, 1861/07/24, Private, Discharged October, 1861, (disability?).

Ashton, Charles, Recruit, 1864/09/09, Private, Mustered Out 07/28/1865.

Atcherson (aka Etchason), Jesse, Private, 1861/07/24, Private, Discharged; Date Not Stated. (Disability?).

Bailey (aka Baily), Commodore C., Private, 1861/07/24, Private, Mustered Out 01/10/1866.

Bailey (aka Baily), Benoni B. (aka Benony), Recruit, 1864/09/08, Private, Mustered Out 07/20/1865.

Baker, Abraham M., Sergeant, 1861/07/24, First Sergeant, Died in Marine Hospital at New Orleans, LA, 09/06/1862.

Baker, Esaw (aka Esau), Private, 1861/07/24, Private, Mustered Out 07/28/1865.

Baker, James W., Recruit, 1864/08/27, Private, Mustered Out 07/27/1865.

Beal, William, Recruit, 1864/04/08, Private, Mustered Out 01/10/1866.

Beaver, James R., Recruit, 1864/03/26, Private, Mustered Out 01/10/1866.

Beck, Jacob, unknown, Mustered Out 01/10/1866.

Bell, John, Private, 1861/10/31, Private, Mustered Out 07/31/1864.

Bellamy (aka Bellemy), Frederick W., Recruit, 1864/09/09, Private, Mustered Out 07/27/1865.

Benadune (aka Benadum, Benerdine), Francis H., Private, 1861/07/24, Private, Mustered Out 01/10/1865.

Beoah (aka Beoch, Block), John W.A., Recruit, 1864/10/06, Private, Died 08/14/1864 at New Orleans, LA.

Bishop, John, Recruit, 1863/06/19, Private, *Deserted 07/30/1865.*

Blackman (aka Blackburn), William H., Recruit, 1863/04/28, Private, Died 04/23/1864 at Baton Rouge, LA.

Blair, William, Private, 1861/07/24, Private, Discharged October, 1861, (disability?).

Bowden (aka Banden, Bawden, Bondean, Bowdin), Reney (aka Renney, Runy), Private, 1861/07/24, Sergeant, Mustered Out; Term Expired.

Brewer, William J., Recruit, 1864/09/08, Private, Mustered Out 07/28/1865.

Bridges, Henry J., Private, 1861/07/24, Private, Discharged 1862, (disability?).

Brock, Jacob, Private, 1861/07/24, Private, Veteran; Dishonorable Discharge 01/22/1866.

Brown, George J., Private, 1861/07/24, Captain, Promoted 2nd Lieutenant 12/31/1863; Promoted 1st Lieutenant 01/26/1864; Promoted Captain 08/12/1864; Mustered Out 01/10/1866..

Brown, James H., Private, 1861/07/24, 1st Lieutenant, Promoted 1st Lieutenant 07/01/1862; Dismissed 01/25/1864.

Buchal (aka Buchel, Buckel), Jacob, Recruit, 1864/09/17, Private, Mustered Out 01/10/1866.

Burgess, Benjamin, Recruit, 1864/09/01, Private, Mustered Out 01/10/1866, absent sick.

Burkhalter, James G., Recruit, 1864/09/02, Private, Mustered Out 01/10/1866.

Burns, James, Recruit, 1864/09/06, Private, Mustered Out 07/27/1865.

Calvin, Nathan P. (aka Nathan T.), Private, 1861/07/24, Sergeant, Mustered Out 01/10/1866.

Calvin, Samuel, Private, 1861/07/24, Private, Mustered Out 07/31/1864.

Caswell (aka Dooper), R. Cooper (aka Caswell R., Coswell R.), Private, 1861/07/24, Private, Discharged November, 1862 (Disability?).

Chapman, Francis, Private, 1861/07/24, Private, Died — Wounds Received at Battle of Baton Rouge, LA, 08/05/1862.

Clark, Drury C., Recruit, 1864/04/01, Private, Mustered Out 07/18/1865.

Clark, James, Recruit, 1864/09/27, Private, Died 01/05/1865 at New Orleans, LA.

Cole, William, Private, 1861/07/24, Private, Died 08/14/1862 at New Orleans, LA (of wounds received at Battle of Baton Rouge, LA?).

Cook, Isaac, Recruit, 1864/04/12, Private, Mustered Out 01/10/1866.

Cook, William, Private, 1861/07/24, Private, Discharged November, 1862 (Disability?).

Coulter, Richard H., Recruit, 1864/09/08, Private, Mustered Out 07/27/1865.

Crist, Robert H, Private, 1861/07/24, Private, Promoted 2nd Lieutenant of Company L 10/21/1863; Promoted 1st Lieutenant, Co. L 09/09/1864; Promoted Captain of Co. L 03/01/1865..

Crook, Alfred H., Private, 1861/07/24, Private, Discharged at Baton Rouge, LA 1863; Died after Reaching Home..

Crook, Garrison P. (aka Garrison B.), First Sergeant, 1861/07/24, First Sergeant, Veteran.

Crow, Joseph, Private, 1861/07/24, Private, Veteran; Mustered Out 01/10/1866.

Dailey (aka Daily), William, Private, 1861/07/24,

Private, Killed In Action at Battle of Baton Rouge, LA, 08/05/1862.

Davenport, Albert (aka Alvert), Private, 1861/10/31, Private, Mustered Out 10/30/1864.

Davis, David (aka David E.), Recruit, 1864/09/08, Private, Mustered Out 07/27/1865.

Davis, James H., Recruit, 1864/09/17, Private, Mustered Out 07/31/1865.

Delamater, Everet A., Sergeant, 1861/07/24, First Sergeant, Accidently Killed aboard the N.O.O. & G.W. R.R. near New Orleans, LA, 1862.

Denny (aka Denney), George, Recruit, 1864/09/08, Private, Died 02/26/1865 in New Orleans, LA.

Deshazo (aka Deshaze), Erastus W., Recruit, 1864/04/18, Private, Mustered Out 01/10/1866.

Doan, George, Private, 1861/07/24, Private, Discharged 1863 (disability?).

Dorsett, Isaac, Recruit, 1864/03/24, Private, Died 10/09/1864 in Indiana.

Dorsett, John, Private, 1861/07/24, Private, Veteran; Mustered Out 01/10/1866.

Douthett (aka Douthitt), Robert, Private, 1861/07/24, Corporal, Discharged 1862, (disability?).

Dudley, Preston, Recruit, 1864/09/30, Private, Mustered Out 07/31/1865.

Duncan, David I. (aka David J.), Recruit, 1864/09/02, Private, Mustered Out 07/31/1865.

Elkins, John W. (aka John A.), Private, 1861/07/24, Private, Mustered Out 07/31/1864.

Elligood (aka Ellegood), Benjamin F., Recruit, 1864/09/15, Private, Mustered Out 07/27/1865.

Elliott (aka Eliot), Jesse, 2nd Lieutenant, 1861/07/24, 2nd Lieutenant, Resigned 1861.

Ewing, Oliver H. P., 1st Lieutenant, 1864/03/20, 1st Lieutenant, Transferred to Company C; Resigned 11/17/1864.

Fairchild (aka Fairchilds), Jacob, Recruit, 1864/08/31, Private, Mustered out 08/31/1865.

Farris (aka Fairis), James W. (aka James H.), unknown, Died at Home, 1862.

Farris (aka Fairis), Milton, unknown, Mustered Out 01/10/1866.

Fields, Hugh, Private, 1861/07/24, Private, Mustered Out 01/10/1866.

Fisher, Jacob A., Private, 1861/07/24, Private, Discharged, 1862.

Forbes (aka Forbs, Forbus), Stephen W (aka Stephen H., Stephen N., Stephen V.), Private, 1861/07/24, Private, Transferred to Co. H 01/01/1864; Veteran; Mustered Out 01/13/1866.

Fox, George, Corporal, 1861/07/24, Corporal, Mustered Out 07/27/1865.

Freeman, Charles H., Recruit, 1864/09/08, Private, Mustered Out 07/27/1865.

Freeman, Henry O., Private, 1861/07/24, Sergeant, Discharged 06/15/1865, Disability.

Funderburk (aka Funderbush), William H., Recruit, 1864/09/07, Private, Mustered Out 09/06/1865.

Garrett (aka Guarrett), Duane (aka Daum), Recruit, 1864/10/07, Private, Mustered Out 10/26/1865.

Griffin, George W., Private, 1861/07/24, Private, Veteran; Mustered Out 01/10/1866.

Griner (aka Gruner, Ginery), Daniel, Recruit, 01/01/1864, Private, Transferred to Company K, 01/01/1864; Mustered Out 01/10/1866.

Grooms, Ransom H., Private, Mustered Out 07/31/1865.

Grubbs (aka Grubb), John W., Recruit, 1864/09/15, Private, Mustered Out 07/27/1865.

Grubbs, Richard A., Recruit, 1864/09/15, Private, Mustered Out 07/27/1865.

Hall, Horace P. (aka Horace T.), Recruit, 1864/09/23, Private, Mustered Out 05/13/1865.

Hamerley (aka Hamersley, Hamersly, Hammersley, Hamsley), William H. (aka William A.), Private, 1861/07/24, Private, Veteran; Mustered Out 01/10/1866.

Harding, George C., Regimental Quartermaster Sergeant, 1861/07/24, 2nd Lieutenant, Promoted 2nd Lieutenant 07/01/1862; Resigned 12/30/1863.

Hart (aka Heart), Frederick, Private, 1861/07/24, Private, Mustered Out 01/10/1866.

Hartey (aka Harty), Elisha, Recruit, 184/09/08, Private, Mustered Out 07/27/1865.

Hartup (aka Hartress), George W. (aka George D.), Recruit, 1864/09/08, Private, Mustered Out 07/27/1865.

Hatch, Henry T., Recruit, 1864/02/29, Private, Mustered Out 01/10/1866.

Head, George, Private, 1861/07/24, Private, Veteran; Mustered Out 01/10/1866.

Head, Joseph, Recruit, 1864/09/29, Private, Mustered Out 07/27/1865.

Hendershot (aka Hundershot), Ithamar, Recruit, 1864/03/24, Private, Discharged 11/16/1865, Disability.

Herrin (aka Herin, Herron), Daniel, Private, 1861/07/24, Private, Died 08/25/1862 in Charity Hospital at New Orleans, LA.

Heslip (aka Hisslip, Hyslip), James (aka James W.), Private, 1861/07/24, Corporal, Veteran; Discharged 11/10/1865, Disability.

Heslip (aka Hislip, Hyslip), Joseph, Private, 1861/07/24, Private, Mustered Out 01/10/1866.

Hibben (aka Hibbon), James, Recruit, 1864/03/24, Private, Mustered Out 01/10/1866.

Hill, Harrison, Recruit, 1864/09/08, Private, Mustered Out 07/27/1865.

Hines (aka Hynes), William, Private, 1861/07/24, Private, Mustered Out 07/31/1864.

Hogan (aka Hagan), Atlas M., Recruit, 1864/09/10, Private, Mustered Out 07/27/1865.

Holmes (aka Holms, Homes), John, Private, 1861/07/24, Private, *Deserted 11/04/1865.*

Hooker, John A., Recruit, 1864/04/18, Private, Mustered Out 01/10/1866.

Hutchinson (aka Hutchison, Hudson), Hezekiah, Recruit, 1864/09/02, Private, Unaccounted for per Terrell.

Hutton, William H. (aka William M.), Recruit, 1864/09/02, Private, Mustered Out 01/10/1866.

Irvin, John, Private, 1861/07/24, Private, Discharged 1862.

Irvin (aka Ervin, Irwin), Joseph, Private, 1861/07/24, Private, Mustered Out 07/31/1864.

Irvin (aka Ervin, Irwin), William T. (aka William F., Williamson F., Williamson T.), Private, 1861/07/24, Private, Veteran; Discharged 03/23/1865, Disability.

Jamison (aka Jameson, Jemmison), James, Recruit, unknown, Dishonorably Discharged 02/05/1866.

Jeter, James M. (aka James N, James U.), unknown, Mustered Out 07/31/1864.

Justice, Frederick, Recruit, 1864/09/08, Private, Mustered Out 07/27/1865.

Keck (aka Keek), Christian, Private, 1861/07/24, Private, Mustered Out 07/31/1864.

Keck (aka Keek), John, Private, 1861/07/24, Private, Mustered Out 07/31/1864.

Kennedy (aka Kenedy), Cyrus, Corporal, 1861/07/24, Private, Mustered Out 07/31/1864.

Kimbrell (aka Kimbrill), Joseph, Private, 1861/07/24, Private, Mustered Out 01/10/1866.

Kimbrell (aka Kimbrill), William, Corporal, 1861/07/24, Private, Veteran; Mustered Out 01/10/1866.

Kinnaman (aka Kiniman, Kinneman), Alfred, unknown, Mustered Out 01/10/1866.

Kinnaman (aka Kimmiman), James H., Recruit, 1864/04/07, Private, Mustered Out 01/10/1866.

Kinnaman (aka Kinneman), William H., unknown, Bugler, Mustered Out 01/10/1866.

Knight, Aaron (aka Heron), Recruit, 1864/03/24, Corporal, Mustered Out 01/10/1866.

Laha, Daniel, unknown, Died July 1862, at Baton Rouge, LA.

Lawler, John, Recruit, 1864/03/24, Private, Mustered Out 01/10/1866.

Layton, Andrew J. (aka Andrew T.), Recruit, 1864/03/03, Sergeant, Discharged 06/15/1865, Disability.

Lee, Whitfield, Recruit, 1864/09/02, Private, Mustered Out 01/10/1866.

Lee, William H., Recruit, 1864/02/08, Corporal, Mustered Out 01/10/1866.

Lewis, George S., Wagoner, 1861/07/24, Private, *Deserted January 1862.*

Long (aka Lang), Abraham, Private, 1861/07/24, Private, Veteran; Mustered Out 01/10/1866.

Loyd, Martin, Recruit, 1864/03/24, Private, Mustered Out 01/10/1866.

Lundy (aka Lindey, Londy, Lunday), George, Private, 1861/07/24, Private, Veteran; Mustered Out 01/10/1866.

Malott (aka Maloth), Eli, Private, 1861/07/24, Sergeant, Veteran; Mustered Out 01/10/1866.

Malott (aka Matott), Henry W. (Henry N.), Recruit, 1864/11/24, Private, Mustered Out 01/10/1866.

Marshall, Joseph, Recruit, 1863/05/29, Private, *Deserted 06/01/1864.*

Martin, Jacob W. (aka Jacob A.), Recruit, unknown, 1st Lieutenant, Commissioned 08/12/1864 as 1st Lieutenant; Mustered Out 01/10/1866.

Massa (aka Massey, Mussa), John S., Private, 1861/07/24, Private, Veteran; Mustered Out 01/10/1866.

McAfee, Robert C., 1st Lieutenant, 1861/07/24, 1st Lieutenant, Resigned 1862.

McClain, William, Recruit, 09/29/1864, Private, Mustered Out 07/27/1865. (Note — Found "Unattached. in "Unassigned Recruits" but with Muster Out Date; Because Most of These Persons Were Assigned to Company F, He Is Placed in Co. F.

McConnell (aka McConnel), Frank E. (aka Frank C.), Recruit, 1864/09/05, Private, Died 03/14/1865 at Baton Rouge, LA.

McCullough (aka McCullough), George A., Recruit, 1864/02/07, Private, Mustered Out 01/18/1865.

McQuiston (aka McQueston), William J. (aka William G.), Recruit, 1864/09/15, Private, Mustered Out 07/27/1865.

McWherter (aka McWheirter, McWhiter), Samuel, Private, 1861/07/24, Corporal, Died September, 1862, Accidental Wounds.

Miller, George W., Private, 1861/07/24, Corporal, *Deserted 10/10/1865.*

Miller, John, Private, 1861/07/24, Wagoner, Mustered Out 07/27/1965.

Mincer (aka Minces, Mucer), John, Recruit, 1864/10/07, Private, Mustered Out 10/07/1865.

Minich (aka Minick, Minnich, Minnick), Isaac, Sergeant, 1861/07/24, Sergeant, Discharged 11/16/1865, Disability.

Mooney, William A., Recruit, 1864/04/21, Private, Mustered Out 01/10/1866.

Nail (aka Vail), Eli, Private, 1861/07/24, Corporal, Veteran; Mustered Out 01/10/1866.

Noblet (aka Noblett, Noblette), Francis W., Captain, 1861/07/24, Captain, Discharged 08/11/1864.

Northcraft, James G., Recruit, unknown, 1st Lieutenant, Promoted 2nd Lieutenant 03/31/1864, Promoted 1st Lieutenant 08/12/1864; Mustered Out 01/10/1866.

Oats, Abraham, Recruit, 1864/09/02, Private, Mustered Out 01/10/1866.

Oldham, Charles W., Recruit, 1864/03/24, Private, Mustered Out 01/10/1866.

Owen (aka Owens), Benjamin F., Recruit, 1864/09/02, Private, Mustered Out 01/10/1866.

Owen (aka Owens), James W., Recruit, 1864/09/02, Private, *Deserted 10/04/1865.*

Palmer, John, Recruit, 1864/03/24, Sergeant, Mustered Out 01/10/1866.

Paton (aka Payton), Samuel, Recruit, 1864/09/02, Private, Mustered Out 01/10/1866.

Payne, Isaac, Recruit, 1864/03/24, Private, Discharged 04/06/1864.

Payne, Isaac, Private, 1861/07/24, Private, Mustered Out 01/10/1866.

Peter, James M. (aka William M.), Private, 1861/07/24, Private, Mustered Out 07/31/1864.

Phipps, James, Private, 1861/07/24, Private, Mustered Out 07/31/1864.

Phipps, Julius, Corporal, 1861/07/24, Corporal, Discharged, 1862.

Pittman (aka Pitman), Isaac N., Recruit, 1864/03/24, Private, Died 06/09/1864 at Baton Rouge, LA.

Pollom (aka Pollow, Pollum, Polum), John S., Recruit, 1862/02/07, Private, Mustered Out 01/18/1865.

Porter, Cyrus, Private, 1861/07/24, Private, Mustered Out 01/10/1866.

Porter, Robert, Private, 1861/07/24, Corporal, *Veteran; Deserted 10/10/1865.*

Porter (aka Porter), Samuel, Recruit, 1864/10/03, Never Reported To Company.

Pough (aka Paugh), Henry, Private, 1861/07/24, Private, Discharged, 1862.

Prow, Charles, Private, 1861/07/24, Private, Veteran; Mustered Out 01/10/1866.

Prowel, Joel, Private, 1861/07/24, Private, Unaccounted For As Per Terrell.

Pruett (aka Pruitt), Daniel, Corporal, 1861/07/24, Private, Discharged, 1862.

Rashbacher (aka Hashbarger, Rashbarge, Rashbarger, Rashburgh), Leonard, Recruit, 1864/09/20, Private, Mustered Out 01/10/1866.

Rawlings (aka Rallins, Rawlins, Rowlings), Jeremiah, Recruit, 1864/09/08, Private, Mustered Out 07/27/1865.

Redinger (aka Ridenger, Ridinger, Ridingur), Samuel, Recruit, 1864/03/24, Private, Mustered Out 01/10/1866.

Richardson (aka Richadson), Thomas, Private, 1861/07/24, Private, Mustered Out 07/31/1864.

Riley (aka Reily), George D., Corporal, 1861/07/24, Corporal, Mustered Out 07/31/1864.

Riley (aka Rieley, Riely), John M., Musician, 1861/07/24, Musician, Died 11/03/1863 at Baton Rouge, LA.

Robbins (aka Robinson), Marcus L., Recruit, 1864/09/09, Private, Mustered Out 07/27/1865.

Roberts, Aaron, Recruit, 1863/12/24, Corporal, Mustered Out 01/10/1866.

Roberts, Joseph, Recruit, 1864/09/12, Private, Mustered Out 07/27/1865.

Robinson, William M. (aka William L.), unknown, Mustered Out 01/10/1866.

Rodman, Francis H., Recruit, 1864/03/17, Corporal, Mustered Out 01/10/1866.

Roland, Mathias L., Recruit, unknown, Never Reported To Company.

Satterfield (aka Sadfield, Statterfield, Sutterfield), Augustus (aka Agustus, Gus), Recruit, 1864/09/07, Private, Mustered Out 09/07/1865.

Sears, Barton R., Private, 1861/07/24, Private, Veteran; Mustered Out 01/10/1866.

Sears, James R.W., Recruit, Private, Veteran; Mustered Out 01/10/1866.

Sears, Peter, Recruit, 1862/02/28, Private, Killed In Action at LaFourche Crossing, LA, 06/23/1863.

Shilling, Joseph J., Recruit, 1864/09/06, Private, Mustered Out 01/10/1866.

Shlott, William H., Recruit, 1864/09/10, Private, Mustered Out 07/27/1865.

Sipes (aka Sipse), Henry, Private, 1861/07/24, Corporal, Veteran; Mustered Out 01/10/1866.

Smith, Benjamin F., Recruit, 1861/07/24, Private, Mustered Out 07/31/1864.

Smith, James A. (aka James S.), Recruit, 1863/05/25, Private, Mustered Out 01/10/1866.

Smith, Jones (aka Jonas), Recruit, 1864/03/11, Private, Discharged 11/02/1864, Disability.

Smith, Nicholas C., Recruit, 1864/09/17, *Deserted 11/25/1864.*

Smith, William, Recruit, 1864/09/17, Private, Dishonorably Discharged 01/16/1866.

Spurgen (aka Spegeon, Spergen, Spurgeon, Charles, Private, 1861/07/24, Private, Discharged, 1861 (disability?).

Stalling (aka Stallings, Statling), David W., Recruit, 1864/03/24, Corporal, Mustered Out 01/10/1866.

Stanley (aka Stanly), Jonathan, Private, 1861/07/24, Private, Transferred to 4th U.S. Artillery.

Steel (aka Steele), Hamilton, Musician, 1861/07/24, Private, Mustered Out 07/31/1864.

Stephens (aka Stevens), Sanford A., Recruit, 1864/09/08, Private, Mustered Out 07/27/1865.

Strader (aka Staler), Patrick, Recruit, 1864/09/09, Private, Mustered Out 07/27/1865.

Strahan (aka Strahn), Samuel P., Recruit, 1864/09/08, Corporal, Mustered Out 07/31/1864.

Street, Mannon, Recruit, 1864/09/08, Private, Unaccounted For As Per Terrell.

Street, Samuel, Recruit, 1864/09/18, Private, Mustered Out 07/27/1864.

Suffler (aka Seefal, Sufal), William J., Recruit, 1864/09/09, Private, Mustered Out 07/27/1865.

Sullivan, William, Private, 1861/07/24, 2nd Lieutenant, Promoted 2nd Lieutenant 01/26/1864; Died at Indianapolis, IN, 1864.

Swift, Oliver P., Recruit, 1864/09/07, Private, Mustered Out 01/10/1866.

Taggard (aka Taggaart), William S., unknown, unknown, Promoted in U.S. Colored Troops.

Terrell (aka Terrill), John, Private, 1861/07/24, Private, Veteran; Deserted 10/04/1864.

Thomas, Madison M., Recruit, 1864/09/02, Private, Deserted 09/06/1865.

Thomason (aka Thomasson), John W., Private, 1861/07/24, Private, Mustered Out 10/26/1865.

Thornberg (aka Thornburg, Thornburgh), Thomas W., Recruit, 1864/09/30, Artificer, Mustered Out 07/27/1865.

Tincher, James, Recruit, 1864/09/14, Private, Mustered Out 07/27/1865.

Todd, David, Private, 1861/07/24, Private, Died October 1861, Baltimore, MD.

Townsend, Charles A., Private, 1861/07/24, Private, Unaccounted For As Per Terrell.

Trig (aka Teague), Solomon, Recruit, 1864/03/24, Private, Unaccounted for as per Terrell.

Vainman (aka Wainman), Levi, Private, 1861/07/24, Private, Veteran.

VanCleve (aka Vancleave, Vancleve), Robert C., Recruit, 1864/09/20, Private, Mustered Out 07/27/1865.

Vestal, William, Private, 1861/07/24, Corporal, Veteran; Discharged 09/02/1862. (reason unknown).

Walker, John, unknown, unknown, unknown, Died 03/11/1865 at Baton Rouge, LA.

Walton (aka Waltan), Truman (aka Freeman), Recruit, 1864/09/27, Private, Mustered Out 07/27/1865.

Ward, Zachariah T., Recruit, 1864/03/21, Bugler, Mustered Out 01/10/1866.

Warwick, Daniel, Private, 1861/07/24, Sergeant, Mustered Out 01/10/1866.

Washburn (aka Washburne), Joseph L. (aka Joseph H.), Recruit, 1861/07/24, 2nd Lieutenant, Promoted 2nd Lieutenant 08/12/1864; Mustered Out 01/10/1866..

Wayman (aka Waymen), Willet, Private, 1861/07/24, Corporal, Mustered Out 08/03/1865.

Webb (aka Wepp), Jesse F. (aka John F.), Recruit, 1864/03/24, Artificer, Mustered Out 07/27/1865.

Whitaker (aka Whittacker), William C., Recruit, 1864/08/29, Private, Mustered Out 07/27/1865.

Wildman (aka Wildiman), Jesse, Private, 1861/07/24, Sergeant, Mustered Out 01/10/1866.

Wilkes (aka Wilks), James M., Private, 1861/07/24, Private, Missing In Action at Battle of Baton Rouge, LA, 08/05/1862.

Williams, John B., Recruit, 1864/09/27, Private, Mustered Out 07/27/1865.

Williams, Seth M., Recruit, 1864/10/04, Private, Mustered Out 10/04/1865.

Winter (aka Winters), Edwin, Recruit, 1864/03/21, Private, Unaccounted for as per Terrell.

Wood, William, Private, 1861/07/24, 2nd Lieutenant, Promoted 2nd Lieutenant 03/20/1865; Mustered Out 01/10/1866.

FIELD AND STAFF

Black, Edward, Private, 1861/07/24, Musician Third Class, Mustered Out August 1862. (Youngest Drummer-boy in Service, age 8).

Brakeman, Nelson L., Chaplain, 1861/07/24, Chaplain, Appointed Hospital Chaplain, U.S.A.

Bremster, Albins W., Recruit, 1862/02/22, Hospital Steward, Mustered Out.

Brown (aka Browne), William H., Private, 1861/07/24, Musician Third Class, Mustered Out August 1862.

Campbell, John C. L., Assistant Surgeon, 1863/10/17, Assistant Surgeon, Resigned 06/30/1864.

Carter (aka Caster), John, Private, 1861/07/24, Musician, Mustered Out August 1862. Discharged 10/24/1861, Disability.

Colton, Edwin R., Private, 1861/07/24, Musician, Died at Algiers, LA June 1862.

Conn, Isaac T., Assistant Surgeon, 1865/06/05, Assistant Surgeon, Mustered Out 01/10/1866.

Crigler, William H., Hospital Steward, 1861/07/24, Hospital Steward.

Crowder (aka Crowdes), William B., Private, 1861/07/24, Musician, Mustered Out August 1862.

Dale, Samuel P., Private, 1861/07/24, Musician, Mustered Out August 1862.

Davis, John B., Assistant Surgeon, 1861/07/24, Assistant Surgeon.

Dunn, Williamson D. (aka William D.), Assistant Surgeon, 1862/09/26, Assistant Surgeon, Resigned 09/03/1863.

Gainey, Edward B., Private, 1861/07/24, Musician, Discharged 1861.

Geldsburg (aka Goldsberry), John A. (aka John R.), Assistant Surgeon, 1864/04/16, Assistant Surgeon, Resigned 07/11/1865.

Hawn (aka Haun), Emanuel R., Assistant Surgeon, 1862/10/24, Assistant Surgeon, Promoted Surgeon of the 49th Regiment 02/20/1864.

Hays, Benjamin F., Major, 1861/07/24, Colonel, Promoted to Lieut. Colonel 03/09/1863; Promoted Colonel 02/08/1865; Mustered Out 01/10/1866.

Hervey (aka Harvey), Oscar P., Sergeant Major, 1861/07/24, Private, Transferred to Company A 10/01/1862.

Hiffeman, Frast H., Private, 1861/07/2 Quartermaster Sergeant.

Hilmer (aka Helmer), Jerry W., Private, 1861/07/24, Musician Third Class, Mustered Out August 1862.

Hinds, Andrew B., Private, 1861/07/24, Musician Second Class, Mustered Out August 1862.

Hinkle, William S., Regimental Quartermaster / Lieutenant, 1861/07/24, Captain, Promoted Captain of Co. D; Discharged 08/10/1864..

Horn, Emmanuel R., Assistant Surgeon, 1861/07/24, Assistant Surgeon.

Johns, James S., Hospital Steward, 1861/07/24, Hospital Steward, Discharged 11/11/1861, Disability.

Keith (aka Kirth), John A., Lieutenant Colonel, 1861/07/24, Colonel, Wounded at Battle of Baton Rouge, LA, Promoted Colonel 03/09/1863; Hon. Discharge 02/02/1865.

Keen (aka Kenn), Daniel, Band Musician, 1861/07/24, Principal Musician, Mustered Out 09/11/1862.

Kissel, Alexander, Private, 1861/07/24, Musician, Mustered Out August 1862.

Kissel (aka Kipsel), Austin, Private, 1861/07/24, Private, Mustered Out August 1862.

Latham, Matthew A., 1st Lieutenant / Adjutant, 1861/07/24, Adjutant, Killed In Action at Battle of Baton Rouge, LA, 08/05/1862.

Malott, William P., Private, 1861/07/24, Private, Mustered Out 09/11/1862.

Margusette, Horatio, Private, 1861/07/24, Hospital Steward.

Matthews (aka Mathews, Matthens), Seth, Private, 1861/07/24, 1st Lieutenant, Promoted to 1st Lieutenant 02/17/1865 of Company K.

McCoy, George K., Acting Surgeon, 1864/08/05, Assistant Surgeon, Died 12/18/1864.

McMillan, James W., Colonel, 1861/07/24, Brigadier-General, Promoted Brigadier-General U.S.V. 11/29/1862; Assigned to Brigade in 19th Army Corps.

Mitchell, Thomas J., Private, 1861/07/24, Musician Third Class, Mustered Out 09/11/1862.

Mongiarottia (aka Margusette, Maurgiaratte, Mongairotti, Mongaizotti, Mongiarroth, Mongiuratti), Horatio, Private, 1861/12/20, Hospital Steward, Discharged, 10/22/1863, Disability.

Moody (aka Moodie), Charles, Principal Musician, 1861/07/24, Private, Transferred to Company G.

Mooney, Michael, Private, 1861/07/24, Sergeant Major.

Moss, Jasper J., Chaplain, 1861/07/24, Chaplain, Mustered Out 01/10/1866.

Northcroft (aka Northcraft), James G., Private, 1861/07/24, 1st Lieutenant, Transferred to Company F.

Osborn (aka Osborne), Wines W., Private, 1861/07/24, Musician Third Class, Mustered Out 09/11/1862.

Owen (aka Owens), Alexander G., Private, 1861/07/24, Musician First Class, Mustered Out 09/11/1862.

Owen (aka Owens), Alvin W., Private, 1861/07/24, Musician First Class, Mustered Out 09/11/1862.

Owen (aka Owens), Francis M., Private, 1861/07/24, Musician, Mustered Out 09/11/1862.

Owen, Henry C., Private, 1861/07/24, Private, Not Given.

Peterson, Christopher D., Quartermaster Sergeant, 1861/07/24, Quartermaster Sergeant, Dishonorably Discharged 11/11/1861.

Probst, Jacob, Private, 1861/07/24, Principal Musician, Mustered Out 01/10/1866; Veteran.

Read (aka Reed), Ezra, Surgeon, 1861/07/24, Surgeon, Resigned 12/15/1862; re-entered Service as Surgeon of 11th Cavalry.

Rhodius (aka Rhodieus, Rhodims, Rhodins), George, (aka Andrew), Principal Musician, 1861/07/24, Private, Discharged.

Seaward (aka Seaword, Seward), Irwin, Private, 1861/07/24, Musician, Mustered Out August 1862.

Sherrod, William F., Surgeon, 10/22/1862, Surgeon, Mustered Out 01/10/1866.

Sherwood, James S., Private, 1861/07/24, Musician, Mustered Out August 1862; Discharged 10/24/1861, Disability.

Whitted, Francis M., Private, 1861/07/24, Musician, Not Given.

Woods, Daniel L., Assistant Surgeon, 1865/09/19, Assistant Surgeon, Mustered Out 01/10/1866.

Company G

Abbernathy (aka Abbernethy, Abernathy, Abernethy), Alexander, Private, 1861/07/24, Private, Discharged 10/16/1862, Disability.

Adams, Benjamin F., Recruit, 1864/01/18, Private, Mustered Out 01/13/1866.

Adams, John M., Sergeant, 1861/07/24, 1st Lieutenant, Promoted 1st Lieutenant 01/01/1864; Mustered Out 07/31/1864.

Aiken (aka Aikin, Aken, Akin), Jackson, Private, 1861/07/24, Private, Wounded at Battle of Baton Rouge, LA.; Veteran; Deserted; Returned; Mustered Out 01/13/1866.

Alexander, Rufus, Recruit, 1863/06/15, Private, *Deserted 07/10/1865.*

Anderson, Frank, Private, 1861/07/24, Private, Discharged 04/01/1862, Disability.

Anderson, John F. (aka John L.), Recruit, 1863/03/08, Private, Mustered Out 01/13/1866.

Anderson, William H., Recruit, 1864/10/06, Private, Mustered Out 10/05/1865.

Baker, James, Recruit, 1864/03/03, Private, Mustered Out 01/13/1866.

Baker, Joseph, Recruit, 1864/03/17, Private, Mustered Out 01/13/1866.

Ball, John, Private, 1861/07/24, Private, Discharged 10/16/1862, Disability.

Beard, John, Recruit, 1863/05/05, Private, *Deserted 06/25/1863.*

Belden (aka Beldin), Henry, Recruit, 1866/10/10, Private, Mustered Out 10/16/1865.

Benson, Henry, Recruit, 1862/02/11, Private, Wounded at Battle of Baton Rouge, LA; Veteran; Deserted 12/04/1864.

Benson, James, Recruit, 1864/04/08, Private, Mustered Out 01/13/1866.

Bivins (aka Bevins, Bivans, Bivens), Levi P., Recruit, unknown, Private, Never Reported To Company.

Bivins (aka Bivens), Shepard (aka Elisha T.S.), Recruit, unknown, Private, Never Reported To Company..

Black, Richard T., Recruit, 1864/04/06, Private, Died at Baton Rouge, LA 06/12/1862 1864.

Blanchard, Charles V., Private, 1861/07/24, Private, Discharged; Disability.

Blanchard (aka Blanchar), Joseph, Recruit, 1864/09/22, Private, Mustered Out 10/21/1865.

Bollinger (aka Bolinger), David, Recruit, 1864/10/28, Private, Mustered Out 10/27/1864.

Bonney (aka Barney, Barny, Benney, Boney, Booney), Andrew, Recruit, 1863/04/21, Corporal, Veteran; Mustered Out 01/13/1866.

Bown (aka Bowen), William, Recruit, unknown, Never Reported To Company.

Bozer (aka Bozier), Truman (aka Freeman), Recruit, 1864/09/26, Private, Discharged 07/21/1865.

Brazier (aka Brashear, Brozier), James, Recruit, 1863/08/18.

Brinin (aka Brannen, Brannon, Brenan, Brennan), John, Recruit, 1863/08/07, Private, Mustered Out 01/13/1866.

Brewer (aka Brener), John A., Private, 1861/07/24, Sergeant, Veteran; Mustered Out 01/13/1866.

Brewster (aka Breuster), Albinus W., Recruit, 1862/02/22, Hospital Steward, Mustered Out, date unknown.

Brown, Charles, Recruit, 1864/09/04, Private, *Deserted 12/10/1865.*

Bummerstein (aka Bomechine, Bomechune, Bomerchine, Bomeschine), Thomas, Recruit, 1863/04/21, Unknown — No record in Terrell or Nat'l. Park Service / Nat'l Archives.

Burdine (aka Berdine), William, Recruit, 1863/04/21, Unknown — Unassigned.

Burgess, Benjamin, Recruit, 0864/09/13, Private, Discharged 07/21/1865.

Burke (aka Burk), George, Recruit, 1864/10/04, Private, Mustered Out 10/03/1865.

Butsch (aka Butch), Adam, Private, 1861/07/24, Private, Discharged 11/30/1861, Disability.

Campbell, Michael, Private, 1861/07/24, Private, Mustered Out 07/31/1864.

Cannaday (aka Kennedy), Horace W., Recruit, 1864/09/05, Private, Died at Baton Rouge, LA, date unknown.

Carr, Lafayette, Recruit, 1864/10/05, Private, Mustered Out 10/04/1865.

Chapman, Thomas, Private, 1861/07/24, Private, Died at Home in Knox County, IN, 07/06/1862.

Charleston, John, Private, 1861/07/24, Private, Discharged 10/02/1861, Disability.

Cleveland (aka Cleaveland), George W., Private, 1861/07/24, Corporal, Mustered Out 07/31/1864.

Coffey (aka Coffee, Coffin), John T., Recruit, 1863/03/30, Private, *Deserted; date not reported.*

Colin (aka Coleir, Colier, Collier), Jesse, Private, 1861/07/24, Private, Discharged 10/02/1891, Disability.

Colman (aka Coleman), William, Recruit, 1863/06/06, Private, *Deserted 01/01/1864.*

Con (aka Conn), Thomas E., Recruit, 1863/08/03, Private, Transferred to Department of the Northwest 09/06/1864.

Conner (aka Connor), John, Recruit, 1863/12/08, Private, in confinement for term of enlistment sentenced by General Court Martial..

Conner (aka Conners), Michael, Private, 1861/07/24, Private, Veteran; Discharged 12/30/1864, Disability.

Conway, Frank, Private, 1861/07/24, Sergeant, Wounded at the Battle of Baton Rouge, LA; Veteran; Mustered Out 01/13/1866.

Copmire (aka Capsenner, Cepsneer, Copsenire, Copsmire), Jacob, Recruit, 1863/04/21, Private, Died 11/26/1863 at Baton Rouge, LA.

Count (aka Court), James, Recruit, 1863/10/05, Private, Mustered Out 10/04/1865.

Cowgill (aka Cawgill, Congill), Benjamin W., Recruit, 1964/04/09, Corporal, Mustered Out 01/13/1866.

Coyle, Matthew, Private, 1861/07/24, Private, Shot by private Washington Cramer at Kenner's Landing, LA, 08/02/1862.

Crabtree, William, Recruit, 1863/09/05, Private, *Deserted 10/25/1864.*

Cramer, Washington, Private, 1861/07/24, Private, Taken by Rebels at Battle of Baton Rouge, LA, while under arrest; Returned; Veteran; Mustered Out 01/13/1866.

Craw, Richard K. L. (aka Richard H.L.), Recruit, 1863/05/05, Private, *Deserted 07/20/1865.*

Crawford, Simon P., Recruit, 1864/10/17, Private, Mustered Out 10/16/1865.

Crosby, Michael, Recruit, 1862/05/01, Private, Killed in Action at Battle of Baton Rouge, LA, 08/05/1862.

Daily (aka Dailey), Michael, Recruit, 1862/02/16, Artificer, Veteran; Mustered Out 01/13/1866.

Darnley (aka Danley, Donaly, Donaley, Doneley, Donley), John, Recruit, 1863/04/21, Private, *Deserted 10/08/1864.*

Dardee (aka Daidee, Dardeen, Dardene, Dardenne), Zeodore, Private, 1861/07/24, Corporal, Veteran; Mustered Out 01/13/1866.

Dashwood (aka Dashword, Deaschwood), George, Recruit, 1862/05/01, Private, *Deserted 11/01/1862.*

Daugherty (aka Dougherty), Charles, Recruit, 1862/05/01, Private, *Deserted 08/21/1862.*

Davis, George W., Recruit, 1864/10/25, Private, Mustered Out 10/24/1865.

Davis, John, Corporal, 1861/07/24, Corporal, Discharged 10/07/1861, Disability.

Davis, Robert W., Private, 1861/07/24, Private, Mustered Out 07/31/1864.

Daw, Patrick, Recruit, 1863/05/05, Private, Died at Baton Rouge, LA, 04/02/1864.

Dean, John, Recruit, 1862/09/21, Private, Deserter from 174th New York Regiment; Returned to His Regiment. .

Debly (aka Debley, Delbey, Delby), Eugene, Recruit, 1863/03/23, Private, *Deserted 12/04/1864.*

Denton (aka Denten), William, Private, 1861/07/24, Private, Discharged; Disability.

Dewey, Delemer (aka Delemar), Recruit, 1863/05/27, Private, *Deserted 07/20/1865.*

Donahue (aka Donehue, Donnohue, Dunahue), James, Recruit, 1863/04/21, Private, *Deserted 02/09/1865.*

Dunaven (aka Donavan, Donaven, Donavon Donovan), John, Recruit, 1862/05/01, Private, Mustered Out 05/01/1865.

Edwards, Daniel, Recruit, 1864/03/13, Private, *Deserted 07/25/1865.*

Edwards, Jacob, Private, 1861/07/24, Private, Veteran; Mustered Out 01/13/1866.

Eisler (aka Eissler), John W., Private, 1861/07/24, Private, Mustered Out 07/31/1864.

Elkins (aka Elkin), John C., Private, 1861/07/24, Private, *Deserted 07/31/1861.*

Elkins, William, Private, 1861/07/24, Private, Discharged 10/16/1862. Wounds Received at Battle of Baton Rouge, LA..

Ellsworth (aka Elsworth), Daniel, Recruit, 1863/07/21, Private, *Deserted 07/20/1865.*

Engle, William, Private, 1861/07/24, Quartermaster Sergeant, Veteran; Mustered Out 01/13/1866.

Erne (aka Ernie), George, Private, 1861/07/24, Private, Wounded at the Battle of Baton Rouge, LA; Mustered Out 07/31/1864.

Everett (aka Evereth, Evertt), Edward, Recruit, 1863/04/21, Private, *Deserted 10/25/1864.*

Farmer, John, Private, 1861/07/24, Private, Veteran; Discharged 01/10/18665, Disability.

Field (aka Feld), William, Private, 1861/07/24, Private, Mustered Out 07/31/1864.

Finch (aka French), John, Recruit, 1863/08/07, Private, *Deserted 10/08/1864.*

Foulk (aka Foulk, Foulke, Foulks, Fowlks), John, Private, 1861/07/24, Corporal, Mustered Out 07/31/1864.

Fox, George W., Private, 1861/07/24, Corporal, Wounded at Battle of Baton Rouge, LA. Drowned 08/16/1862. Died 08/16/1862 from Effect of Two Musket Balls in His Abdomen.

France (aka Franc), David B., recruit, 1864/03/03, Private, Mustered Out 01/13/1866.

Franklin, John, Recruit, 1863/04/21, Private, Deserted 01/11/1865.

Freeman, Charles H., Recruit, 1864/09/08, Private, Unknown — Unassigned.

Fuller, Robert, Corporal, 1861/07/24, 2nd Lieutenant, Promoted Sergeant by June, 1863, Promoted 2nd Lieutenant 01/04/1864; Mustered Out 01/10/1866..

Fuller, Stephen, Private, 1861/07/24, Private, Mustered Out 07/31/1864.

Gantran (aka Gantreau, Gautrau, Gautraw, Gautrea, Gautrean, Gautreau, Gautreem, Gawtrau, Gawtraw, Grantran), Adam F. (aka Adam T.), Recruit, 1863/06/06, Sergeant, Discharged 06/14/1865.

Geisendorffer (aka Gegsendorffer, Guysendoffer, Guyondoffer, Gysendorffer, Gysendrffer), Charles L., Private, 1861/07/24, Private, Killed by Guerrillas near Houma, LA, 05/09/1862.

Genine (aka Green), Patrick, Private, 1861/07/24, Private, Died at Ship Island, MS, 04/02/1862.

George, James, Private, 1861/07/24, Private, Discharged 10/02/1861, Disability.

George, Jesse, Private, 1861/07/24, Private, Veteran; Mustered Out 01/13/1866.

Graff, Jacob, Private, 1861/07/24, Private, Discharged 10/04/1862, Disability.

Grayson, Henry W., Recruit, 1864/10/06, Private, Mustered Out 10/05/1865.

Grayson, John W., Recruit, 1864/09/26, Private, Mustered Out 10/05/1865.

Grey (aka Guy), Harrison E., Private, 1861/07/24, Private, Killed In Action at Siege of Port Hudson, LA, 05/27/1863.

Haines (Haynes), Edward W., Recruit, 1863/09/05, Private, *Deserted; Date Not Reported.*

Hall, Samuel E., Recruit, 1864/01/04, Private, Mustered Out 10/03/1865.

Hamlin, Henry S., Recruit, 1864/09/26, Private, Mustered Out 07/22/1865.

Hanner (aka Hammer), Daniel, Private, 1861/07/24, Private, Mustered Out 07/31/1864.

Harcourt, Thomas J. (aka Thomas G.), Corporal, 1861/07/24, Quartermaster Sergeant. Veteran; Mustered Out 01/13/1866; Promoted 2nd Lieutenant of 89th Regiment U.S. Colored Troops.

Harp (aka Horp), Albert A. (aka Albert P.), Recruit, 1864/03/24, Private, Died 07/29/1864 at Morganza, LA.

Harrower (aka Hanower), Benjamin S. (aka Benjamin T.), First Sergeant, 1861/07/24, Captain, Promoted 2nd Lieutenant.

Harrower (aka Hanower), James, Private, 1861/07/24, Sergeant, Veteran; Mustered Out 01/13/1866.

Harsh (aka Harsch), Jacob, Recruit, 1864/10/25, Private, Mustered Out 11/17/1865.

Hart, John, Bounty Jumper (?), 1864/00/00, Bounty Jumper (?), Enlisted in 1864.

Hartley (aka Hartly), John D., Private, 1861/07/24, Corporal, Veteran; Mustered Out 01/13/1866.

Harveston (aka Herveston, Hurveston), Uriah, Recruit, 1863/06/15, Private, Mustered Out 01/13/1866.

Hatch, Levi, Private, 1861/07/24, Private, Mustered Out 07/31/1864.

Hatten, Mitchell (aka Michael), Private, 1861/07/24, Private, Died at Cairo, IL, 02/04/1864.

Hays (aka Hayes, Hayse), Thomas, Recruit, 1863/04/27, Private, Transferred to U.S. Navy 06/30/1864.

Heller, John A., Recruit, 1862/09/04, Private, Discharged 12/06/1863, Disability.

Hendricks, Elias, Recruit, 1864/10/04, Private, Mustered Out 10/03/1865.

Henry, Patrick, Private, 1861/07/24, Private, Mustered Out 07/31/1864.

Hill, Barney, Private, 1861/07/24, Corporal (?), Mustered Out 07/31/1864.

Hill, Camden L., Private, 1861/07/24, Private, Mustered Out 07/31/1864.

Hill, David H. (aka David M.), Recruit, unknown, unknown, *Deserted; Date not Reported.*

Hinshaw (aka Henshaw), Henry B., Recruit, 0864/09/08, Private, Mustered Out 07/22/1865.

Hoffman, Frederick (aka Frank), Recruit, 1862, Private, Killed In Action at Battle of Baton Rouge, LA, 08/05/1862.

Horace (aka Harris), George, Recruit, 1863/04/21, Private, Deserted 12/21/1864.

Houston (aka Housten, Huston), James G. (James J., James P.), Recruit, 1863/09/05, Private, Mustered Out 01/13/1866.

Howe (aka How), James, Recruit, 1863/08/18, Private, *Deserted 12/27/1864.*

Hunt, John W., Recruit, 1864/03/31, Private, Died 06/04/1864 at Baton Rouge, LA.

Hunt, Joseph, Private, 1861/07/24, Private, *Deserted 02/19/1862.*

Jackson, John W., Recruit, 1864/04/08, Private, Mustered Out 01/13/1866.

Johnson (aka Johnston), Austin, Private, 1861/07/24, Corporal (?), Killed In Action at Battle of Baton Rouge, LA, 08/05/1862.

Johnson (aka Johnston), Richard, Corporal, 1861/07/24, Sergeant, Died 08/03/1862.

Jones, Judson, Private, 1861/07/24, Corporal, Veteran; Mustered Out 01/13/1866.

Joyce (aka Joice), William, Private, 1861/07/24, Private, Mustered Out 07/31/1864.

Joyner (aka Jayner, Joiner), Thomas, Recruit, 1864/04/21, Private, Mustered Out 01/13/1866.

Kelly, Charles, Recruit, 1863/07/21, Private, Mustered Out 01/13/1866.

Kelly (aka Kelley), James, Recruit, 1863/06/25, Private, Discharged 09/27/1865, Disability.

Kesler (aka Kessler, Kesslor, Kissler), William, Recruit, 1864/09/26, Private, Mustered Out 01/13/1866.

Labby (aka Labbey, Labbly, Labey, Lobby, Lobey), Levi, Private, 1861/07/24, Corporal, Veteran; Mustered Out 01/13/1866.

Lanigan (aka Langan, Lanagan), John, Recruit, 1862/05/01, Private, Transferred to U.S.A. 11/01/1862.

Larathin (aka Larathier, Larothier), Charles, Sergeant, 1861/07/24, Sergeant, Discharged 11/30/1861, Disability.

Lawler (aka Lauler), Michael, Recruit, 1863/05/26, Private, Missing since 05/25/1865; Supposed to have been murdered.

Leasure (aka Lasure, Lazure, Leashure), Andrew, Recruit, 1863/05/28, Private, *Deserted 07/25/1865.*

Lebon (aka Loben), Gregory (aka Gregoire), Recruit, 1863/0528, Private, Died at New Orleans, LA, 02/25/1864.

Lee, John E. (aka John C.), Recruit, 1864/04/25, Private, Died at Morganza, LA, 07/26/1864.

Lenhart (aka Lenhardt), Joseph, Recruit, 1863/04/23, Private, *Deserted 10/03/1864.*

Leveron (aka Levering), Nos, Private, 1861/07/24, Private, Discharged 06/24/1862, Disability.

Lindsey (aka Lindsay), Mathew, Recruit, 1864/10/01, Private, Mustered Out 01/13/1866.

Louis, Henry A., 1st Lieutenant, 1861/07/24, 1st Lieutenant, Dismissed by General Court Martial 09/04/1861.

Lowe (aka Love, Low), Samuel, Private, 1861/07/24, Corporal, Veteran; Mustered Out 01/13/1866.

Lynch, William, Private, 1861/07/24, Private, Died 10/12/1863.

Lyons, Michael, Private, 1861/07/24, Corporal, Veteran; Mustered Out 01/13/1866.

Magal (aka Magie, Mayal, Mayol, Moyal), Martin, Private, 1861/07/24, Private, Mustered Out 07/31/1864.

Maguire (aka McGuire, McAguire), Richard, Private, 1861/07/24, Private, Mustered Out 07/31/1864.

Manly (aka Manley), John, Private, 1861/07/24, Private, Died at Baton Rouge, LA, 07/14/1864.

Manwaring (aka Mananning, Manwarring, Menwaring), John A., Recruit, 1863/04/27, Private, Discharged 01/10/1864, Disability.

Marsh (aka Masch, Morsch), Blacius (aka Blasius, Blacuise), Recruit, 1864/10/05, Private, Mustered Out 10/04/1865.

Martin, Charles, Recruit, 1864/10/25, Private, Mustered Out 10/25/1865.

McCann (aka McLean), Owen, Recruit, 1863/05/30, Private, Transferred to Co. L 05/30/1863; Mustered Out 01/13/1866.

McCartney (aka McCartny), Jasper, Recruit, 1864/03/03, Private, Mustered Out 05/26/1865.

McCormick (aka McCormack), Michael, Recruit, 1863/04/27, Private, *Deserted 10/08/1864.*

McDonald, Robert C., Recruit, 1863/09/05, Private, *Deserted, Date Not Reported.*

McKinsey (aka McKinny, McKincier, McKinney), Michael, Recruit, 1862/05/01, Private, Killed in Action at the Battle of Baton Rouge, LA 08/05/1862.

McKinsey (aka McKinzey, McKenzie), Sylvester, Recruit, 1864/03/17, Private, Mustered Out 01/13/1866.

McLaflin (aka McLaughlin, McLoflin), Edward, Captain, 1861/07/24, Major, Promoted Major 04/01/1864; Mustered Out; Term Expired.

McLaflin (aka McLoflin), William, Recruit, 1863/10/02, Private, Discharged 08/10/1864, Disability.

McLaughlin, Cordon, Private, 1861/07/24, Private, Discharged 10/02/1861, Disability.

McLaughlin (aka McLaflin, McLamplin), James H., Private, 1861/07/24, Private, *Deserted 07/31/1861.*

McMurray (aka McMurry), William, Recruit, 1864/09/07, Private, Mustered Out 07/22/1865.

Milligan, David, Recruit, 1864/10/05, Private, Mustered Out 10/04/1865.

Minick (aka Minich, Minnick), John, Private, 1861/07/24, Private, Discharged 06/24/1866, Disability.

Money (aka Mooney), John, Private, 1861/07/24, Corporal (?), Died on Ship Island, MS, 04/20/1862.

Monroe (aka Munroe), Thomas F., Recruit, 1863/07/21, Sergeant, Mustered Out 01/13/1866.

Moody, Charles, Musician, 1861/07/24, Private, Mustered Out 07/31/1864.

Moore (aka More), David, Recruit, 1863/11/24, Private, Mustered Out 01/13/1866.

Moran (aka Moren), Thomas, Recruit, 1864/09/23, Private, Mustered Out 07/22/1865.

Morgan, Samuel W., Recruit, 1863/09/05, Private, *Deserted 07/20/1865.*

Morris, Aaron, Private, 1861/07/24, Corporal, Veteran; Mustered Out 01/13/1866.

Morris (aka Moores), George, Private, 1861/07/24, Private, Killed In Action at Siege of Port Hudson, LA, 05/27/1863.

Mulholland (aka Mulholand), Francis, Recruit, 1863/04/21, Private, *Deserted 06/20/1865.*

Mulroy (aka Mahoy), Michael, Recruit, 1863/04/21, Private, *Deserted 07/20/1865.*

Murphy, William, Recruit, 1864/03/24, Private, Mustered Out 01/13/1866.

Myers (aka Mayer, Meyers), George, Recruit, 1864/10/05, Private, Mustered Out 10/04/1865.

Myers (aka Meers), John, Private, 1861/07/24, Private, Discharged 10/02/1861, Disability.

Nelson (aka Nellson), John, Recruit, 1863/04/21, Private, Unknown — No record in Terrell or Nat'l. Park Service / Nat'l Archives.

Nugent (aka Nugant), William, Recruit, 1863/11/24, Private, *Deserted 07/20/1865.*

O'Hair (aka O'Hara, O'Hare), James, Recruit, 1863/04/23, Private, *Deserted 12/14/1864.*

Oxley (aka Onley, O'Soley), William, Recruit, 1863/04/12, Private, *Deserted; date not reported.*

Pastheumers (aka Pasthenmers, Postamus, Postdums, Posthumons, Posthumous, Posthumus), John, Private, 1861/07/24, Private, Discharged 10/16/1862, Disability; Re-enlisted in Co. L 08/12/1863; Transferred to Co. G; Found Dead Near Baton Rouge, LA 05/30/1865..

Pifley (aka Peffley, Pefley), Thomas, Private, 1861/07/24, Private, Discharged 10/02/1861, Disability.

Perry, Lewis M., Recruit, 1863/08/16, Private, Mustered Out 01/13/1866.

Peters, John, Private, 1861/07/24, First Sergeant, Veteran; Mustered Out 01/13/1866.

Phillips (aka Philips), Jeremiah, Recruit, 1864/10/05, Private, Mustered Out 10/04/1865.

Plew (aka Plean, Plen), Louis, Recruit, 1863/04/27, Private, Deserted from 21st Mass Volunteers; Returned to his regiment.

Plumley (aka Plumely), Samuel J. (aka Samuel I., Samuel T.), Recruit, 1864/10/05, Private, Mustered Out 10/04/1865.

Powers, Vincent S., Private, 1861/07/24, Private, *Deserted in face of the enemy at Port Hudson, LA, 06/01/1863.*

Quigley (aka Quigly), James, Recruit, 1863/04/03, Private, Discharged 09/27/1865, Disability.

Rankins (aka Rankin), Charles, Corporal, 1861/07/24, Corporal, Veteran; Mustered Out 01/13/1866.

Reed, David N., Recruit, 1864/10/12, Private, Mustered Out 10/15/1865.

Reynolds (aka Reynolas), William A., Recruit, 1864/04/14, Private, Mustered Out 01/13/1866.

Rigney (aka Rigner), John B. (aka John E.), Recruit, 1864/03/30, Hospital Steward, Mustered Out 01/13/1866.

Riley, John, Recruit, 1863/05/05, Private, Deserted 10/10/1864.

Ripley, Moody, Recruit, 1864/10/17, Private, Mustered Out 10/16/1865.

Robbins (aka Robbes), Wallace (aka Wallis), Recruit, 1864/10/19, Private, Mustered Out 10/24/1865.

Rogers (aka Rodgers), William, Recruit, 1862/05/01, Private, Mustered Out 05/01/1865.

Rowden (aka Rawdon, Rowdon), John, Recruit, 1863/04/21, Private, *Deserted 12/12/1864.*

Rowe (aka Rawe), William, Recruit, 1864/10/10, Private, Mustered Out 10/16/1865.

Sackett, George W., Recruit, 1862/09/04, Private, Killed In Action at Port Hudson, LA, 06/04/1863.

Sample, William B. (aka Benjamin F, Benjamin

W.), Recruit, 1864/04/08, Private, Deserted 10/04/1865.

Schmidt (aka Smith), Charles, Recruit, 1863/06/30, Corporal, Deserted 01/07/1865.

Schmidt (aka Schmith), Christian, Private, 1861/07/24, Private, Wounded at Battle of Baton Rouge, LA; Discharged 10/13/1862 (due to wounds).

Scott, John, Recruit, 1863/05/30, Private, Deserted 06/14/1865. Died 06/26/1865..

Shatel (aka Hadel), David R., Private, 1861/07/24, Corporal, Veteran; Mustered Out 01/13/1866.

Shean (aka Spean), Daniel, Recruit, 1863/08/19, Private, Mustered Out 01/13/1866.

Sibert, Thomas (aka John), Corporal, 1861/07/24, 1st Lieutenant, Promoted to 2nd Lieutenant of Co. M; 01/21/1864; Promoted 1st Lieutenant Co. G 07/30/1864; Acting Regimental Adjutant during March and April, 1865; Mustered Out 01/10/1866..

Skinner, James, Recruit, 1864/10/17, Private, Mustered Out 10/16/1865.

Smith, Calendar J (aka Calvin J.)., Corporal, 1861/07/24, Corporal, Died 05/12/1864.

Smith, Cyrus A., Recruit, 1863/04/27, Private, Deserted from 174th N.Y. Vols. Returned to His Regiment.

Smith, James A., Private, 1861/07/24, Private, Died In St James Infirmary at New Orleans, LA, 08/24/1862..

Smith, John, Recruit, 1863/10/10, Private, *Deserted; Date not Reported..*

Smith, Solomon C., Recruit, 1864/03/11, Private, Died 07/31/1864 at Baton Rouge, LA..

Smith, Thomas, Recruit, 1863/03/15, Private, *Deserted; Date Unknown..*

Smith, William, Recruit, 1863/08/23, Private, *Deserted 12/17/1864.*

Sondriett (aka Saudriett, Sonderitt, Soudriett, Soudriette), John, Musician, 1861/07/24, Corporal, Veteran; Mustered Out 01/13/1866.

Sparks, James, Recruit, 1864/04/18, Bugler, Mustered Out 01/13/1866.

Spear (aka Spar), Robert B., Recruit, 1864/03/16, Private, Mustered Out 01/13/1866.

Spickenkoetter (aka Speakerkortter, Speckenkoetter, Speikerkoetter, Spekinkoetter, Spiekenkitter, Spoekerketter, Spokerkoetter, Spukenkotes), Charles, Recruit, 1863/08/11, Private, Mustered Out 01/13/1866.

Sponsell (aka Sporsell), Frederick, Private, 1861/07/24, Corporal, Veteran; Mustered Out 01/13/1866.

Sponsell (aka Sporsell), Henry, Private, 1861/07/24, Private, Discharged 10/16/1862, Wounds Received at Battle of Baton Rouge, LA.

Stacy, Thomas, Recruit, 1863/05/26, Private, *Deserted; Date Unknown..*

Stanley (aka Stanly), John C., Recruit, 1864/03/26, Private, Mustered Out 01/13/1866.

Still, James, Recruit, 1864/09/19, Private, Mustered Out 07/22/1865.

Sutton, George W., Private, 1861/07/24, Private, Died at Home in Knox County, IN, Date Unknown.

Swank, John, Recruit, 1864/03/24, Private, Mustered Out 01/13/1866.

Talkington (aka Tarkington), Anderson (aka Andrew), Recruit, 1864/01/01, Wagoner, Deserted 10/04/1865.

Tarver (aka Traver), John (aka John G.), Recruit, 1863/06/10, Private, Died 04/12/1865 at New Orleans, LA.

Thomason, John B. (aka John V.), Recruit, 1864/08/28, Private, Mustered Out 07/22/1865.

Thompson, Andrew, Private, 1861/07/24, Sergeant, Veteran; Mustered Out 01/13/1866.

Tomes (aka Thoms, Toms), Charles, Sergeant, 1861/07/24, 2nd Lieutenant, Promoted 2nd Lieutenant Co. M.

Trumppeller (aka Ttrumfeller, Trumpfeller, Trumpheller, Trumphelter, Trumppfeller, Truppfeller), Adam, Private, 1861/07/24, Corporal, Mustered Out 07/31/1864.

Tudrick (aka Tetirick, Tidrick), George, Recruit, 1864/12/03, Private, Mustered Out 01/13/1866.

Turner, William H. H., Sergeant, 1861/07/24, 1st Lieutenant, Promoted 2nd Lieutenant 01/01/1864; Promoted 1st Lieutenant 04/01/1864; Mustered Out 01/10/1866..

Ubert, John, Private, 1861/07/24, 2nd Lieutenant, Promoted 2nd Lieutenant 04/01/1864; Veteran; Resigned 11/15/1865.

Vanosdal (aka Vanarsdal, Vanarsdel, Varnesdall), Francis M. (aka Francis W.), Recruit, 1864/09/29, Private, Mustered Out 07/22/1865.

Vanroy (aka Vanwy), Enoch, Corporal, 1861/07/24, Sergeant, Veteran; Mustered Out 01/13/1866.

Vanroy (aka Vanwy, Varnoy), William T. (aka William F.), Wagoner, 1861/07/24, Wagoner, Mustered Out 07/31/1864.

Vine, Samuel H., Recruit, 1864/09/17, Private, Mustered Out 07/22/1865.

Walters (aka Watters), James, Recruit, 1863/11/24, Private, *Deserted 06/14/1865.*

Warren, Daniel, Recruit, 1864/04/01, Private, Mustered Out 01/13/1866.

Warren, Edwin (aka Edin, Edmund, Edward), Recruit, 1863/04/21, Private, Deserted 10/16/1864.

Weakly (aka Weekley, Weekly), Andrew J. (aka Andrew G.), Recruit, 1864/03/30, Private, Deserted in Indiana, Date Unknown..

Westcott (aka Wescott), John B., Recruit, 1863/04/20, Private, *Deserted 12/27/1864.*

Whitehead, Jonathan, Recruit, 1864/10/04, Private, Mustered Out 09/30/1865.

Widenhorn (aka Wedenhorn, Wiedenhorn, Weidinhorn), Joseph, Private, 1861/07/24, Private, Discharged 10/16/1862, Disability.

Wilkerson (aka Wilkinson, Wilkison), James, Recruit, 1863/04/21, Private, Transferred to Veteran Reserve Corps, 06/15/1864.

Wilkerson (aka Wilkeson, Wilkinson, Wilkison), Robert C., Recruit, 1863/05/15, Private, Deserted 12/04/1864.

Willard, John H. (aka John A.), Recruit, 1863/08/21, Private, *Deserted 01/11/1865.*

Williams, Isaiah, Recruit, 1864/04/05, Private, Mustered Out 01/13/1866.

Williams, James T. (aka James F.), Recruit, 1863/05/15, Private, Transferred to Company I 12/15/1863; Mustered Out 01/13/1866.

Williams, John, Recruit, 1863/06/05, Private, *Deserted 06/20/1865.*

Willis, Amos R. (aka Amasa R., Amos A.), Recruit, 1864/03/30, Private, Mustered Out 06/14/1865.

Willis, Levi W., Private, 1861/07/24, Private, Veteran; Mustered Out 01/13/1866.

Wilson (aka Willson), Cornelius H., Private, 1861/07/24, Private, Killed In Action along Bayou Teche, LA, 11/03/1862.

Wilson (aka Willson), Hugh M., Private, 1861/07/24, Private, Discharged 10/02/1861, Disability.

Wilson, James, Recruit, 1864/04/09, Private, Mustered Out 01/13/1866.

Wilson, Martin (aka Mathew), Recruit, 1864/03/24, Private, Mustered Out 01/13/1866.

Wilson (aka Willson), Robert P., Recruit, 1864/04/20, Private, Mustered Out 01/13/1866.

Wilson (aka Wilton), James D., Recruit, 1863/09/07, Private, Deserted 01/30/1864.

Wittman (aka Wettman, Willman), William, Private, 1861/07/24, Bugler, Veteran; Mustered Out 01/13/1866.

Wolf, Henry, Recruit, 1863/04/21, Private, Died 01/01/1864 at New Orleans, LA.

Wood, George, 2nd Lieutenant, 1861/07/24, 2nd Lieutenant, Promoted 1st Lieutenant 09/12/1862; Resigned 07/13/1863..

Wycoff, Eli, Private, 1861/07/24, Corporal, Veteran; Mustered Out 01/13/1866.

Wycoff, William, Musician, 1861/07/24, Private, Mustered Out 07/31/1864.

Yocum (aka Yochum), Michael, Recruit, 1864/10/04, Private, Mustered Out 10/05/1865.

Company H

Abbott, Francis M. (aka Francis W.), Private, 1861/07/24, Private, Veteran; Mustered Out 01/13/1866.

Adams, Isaac, Recruit, 1864/09/30, Private, Mustered Out 07/20/1865.

Adams, Samuel M., Recruit, 1864/03/12, Private, Mustered Out 01/13/1866.

Allen, George W., Private, 1861/07/24, Private, Discharged 08/01/1865, Disability.

Anderson, John, Private, 1861/07/24, Private, Transferred to Regular Army 11/21/1862; Reentered 1st Heavy Artillery (?); Mustered Out 01/13/1866.

Armstrong, Alexander G., Recruit, 1864/03/01, Private, Mustered Out 01/13/1866.

Aydelott, Matthew B., Corporal, 1861/07/24, Corporal, Died in Marine Hospital at New Orleans, LA, 08/15/1862.

Aydelott (aka Aydlott), William B. (aka William R.), Private, 1861/07/24, 2nd Lieutenant, Promoted 2nd Lieutenant 10/01/1864; Veteran; Mustered Out 01/10/1866..

Baccus (aka Bacus), William, Private, 1861/07/24, Private, Mustered Out 07/31/1864.

Back, Aaron, Private, 1861/07/24, Private, Veteran; Mustered Out 01/13/1866.

Back, Jackson, Private, 1861/07/24, Private, Died at Fort Gaines, AL, 08/08/1865.

Baker, George W., Recruit, 1864/03/17, Private, Veteran; Mustered Out 01/13/1866.

Baker, Nicholas, Recruit, 1864/09/24, Private, Mustered Out 07/20/1865.

Ballard, Jesse H., Recruit, 1864/09/05, Private, Mustered Out 07/20/1865.

Banard (aka Baynard), Mitchell, Recruit, unknown, Private, Mustered Out 01/13/1866.

Banta (aka Bonta, Bonty), Thomas, Private, 1861/07/24, Private, Discharged 03/06/1863 due to Wounds Received in Battle of Baton Rouge, LA.

Bard, Alfred F., Recruit, 1864/09/26, Private, Mustered Out 07/20/1865.

Bard, James W., Recruit, 1864/09/15, Private, Mustered Out 07/20/1865.

Benson, William S., Recruit, unknown, Private, Mustered Out 01/13/1866.

Bishop, John V., Private, 1861/07/24, Corporal, Veteran; Mustered Out 01/13/1866.

Blake, Isaac (aka Thomas), Private, 1861/07/24, Private, Wounded at Battle of Baton Rouge, LA; Mustered Out 07/31/1864.

Boord (aka Board), John W. (aka John A.), Recruit, 1864/10/19, Private, Mustered Out 10/18/1865.

Boord (aka Board), Lorenzo L., Recruit, 1864/10/19, Private, Mustered Out 10/18/1865.

Boos (aka Boose), Henry, Recruit, 1864/03/30, Private, Mustered Out 01/13/1866.

Boos (aka Boose), Thomas E., Private, 1861/07/24, Private, Veteran; Mustered Out 01/13/1866.

Boswell, George H., Private, 1861/07/24, Corporal, Mustered Out 07/31/1864.

Branham, John D., Recruit, 1864/10/01, Private, Mustered Out 07/20/1865.

Bristow (aka Bristo), Harlan (aka Nathan), Private, 1861/07/24, Private, Veteran; Mustered Out 01/13/1866.

Brown, Joseph B., Private, 1861/07/24, Private, Mustered Out 07/31/1864.

Brown, Joseph H., Recruit, none, deserted 05/21/1864 at Indianapolis, IN.

Brown, William A., Jr., Recruit, 1864/03/08, Private, Transferred to Company B 10/01/1864; Mustered Out 01/13/1866.

Bryant, Thomas D., 1st Lieutenant, 1861/07/24, 1st Lieutenant, Died 08/16/1862 from Wounds Received at Battle of Baton Rouge, LA.

Buckler, Mitchell, Recruit, 1864/03/01, Private, Mustered Out 01/13/1866.

Burch (aka Burtek), Alexander, Private, 1861/07/24, Private, Veteran; Deserted 09/25/1864.

Butcher, Simpson, Private, 1861/07/24, Private, Discharged 11/11/1861, Disability.

Cahill, Andrew, Recruit, 1864/03/22, Private, Died 04/09/1864 in Indiana.

Cahill, Henson E., Recruit, 1864/03/12, Private, Mustered Out 01/13/1866.

Cahill, Jesse F (aka Jesse T., John F.), Recruit, 1864/03/12, Private, Mustered Out 01/13/1866.

Campbell, John T. (aka John F.), Captain, 1861/07/24, Captain, Wounded at Battle of Baton Rouge, LA; Mustered Out 07/31/1864.

Campbell, Thomas A., Private, 1861/07/24, Corporal, Veteran; Mustered Out 01/13/1866.

Campbell, William S. (aka William T.), Recruit, 1864/04/08, Private, Mustered Out 01/13/1866.

Carmichael, Thomas W., Recruit, 1864/08/30, Private, Mustered Out 07/20/1865.

Carson, John, Recruit, 1864/03/01, Private, Died 02/12/1865 at New Orleans, LA.

Carter, James P., Recruit, 1864/09/17, Private, Mustered Out 07/20/1865.

Case, Francis M., Private, 1861/07/24, Private, Mustered Out 01/13/1866.

Chezem (aka Cherum, Chezen, Chezum), Samuel, Recruit, 1864/03/15, Private, Died 07/22/1865 at Mobile, LA.

Clark, Thomas N. (aka Thomas W.), Recruit, 1864/03/01, Private, Mustered Out 01/13/1866.

Coleman, James H., Private, 1861/07/24, Private, Veteran; Discharged 11/08/1864, Disability, Thigh Wound received 6/12/1863 at Port Hudson, LA..

Connelly, James W., 2nd Lieutenant, 1861/07/24, Lieut. Colonel, Promoted Captain 01/01/1863; Promoted Major October 1864; Promoted Lieutenant-Colonel 07/12/1865; Mustered Out 01/15/1866 as Major..

Coon (aka Kuhn), David E, Sergeant, 1861/07/24, Sergeant, Died at Algiers, LA, 05/31/1862.

Cox, Jesse, Recruit, 1864/09/24, Private, Mustered Out 07/20/1865.

Cummings (aka Cummins), Charles W., Recruit, 1862/05/15, Private, Transferred to Co. B, 10/01/1864; Deserted, 08/11/1865.

Dailey (aka Daily), Charles, Recruit, 1864/10/04, Private, Mustered Out 01/13/1866.

Dale, Albert P., Private, 1861/07/24, Private, Killed In Action at Battle of Baton Rouge, LA, 08/05/1862.

Daniels, Henry L., Private, 1861/07/24, Private, Mustered Out 07/31/1864.

Darroch (aka Darrock), Johnson R., Recruit, 1864/03/01, Private, Wounded at Fort Blakely, AL, Mustered Out 01/13/1866.

Davenport, William, Recruit, 1864/09/15, Private, Mustered Out 07/20/1865.

Davis, Gilbert, Recruit, 1964/03/30, Private, Mustered Out 01/13/1866.

Davis, James, Private, 1861/07/24, Corporal, Veteran; Mustered Out 01/13/1866.

Davis, Josiah R., Sergeant, 1861/07/24, Sergeant, Died at Ship Island, MS, 04/30/1862.

Davis, Julius H., Private, 1861/07/24, Private, Discharged 11/05/1863, Disability.

Davis, Samuel T. (aka Samuel G.), Private, 1861/07/24, Corporal, Veteran; Mustered Out 01/13/1866.

Deverter (Aka Diverter), George T., Corporal, 1861/07/24, Sergeant, Mustered Out 07/31/1864.

Dickinson (aka Dickenson), David M. (aka David W.), Recruit, 1864/10/01, Private, Mustered Out 09/30/1865.

Dike, James W., Private, 1861/07/24, Private, Died 08/31/1861 at Baltimore, MD.

Dill (aka Dille, Dilly), Henry, Recruit, 1864/09/30, Private, Mustered Out 07/20/1865.

Dooley, Atelus, Recruit, 1864/03/17, Private, Died 07/19/1864 at Baton Rouge, LA, Buried in Baton Rouge National Cemetery.

Dooley, George H., Recruit, 1864/01/21, Private, Mustered Out 01/13/1866.

Dooley (aka Dooly), Rufus, Private, 1861/07/24, Sergeant, Veteran; Mustered Out 01/13/1866.

Dowden, Kent M., Recruit, 1864/09/05, Private, Discharged 06/15/1865, Disability.

Dunton, John, Recruit, 1864/09/05, Private, Killed 06/09/1865 While Engaged in Larceny at Mobile, AL.

Durman (aka Dorman, Durmon), Thomas J., Private, 1861/07/24, Private, Wounded at Battle of Baton Rouge, LA; Mustered Out 07/31/1864.

Duzan (aka Deusan, Dugan), Nelson C., Private, 1861/07/24, Sergeant, Veteran; Mustered Out 01/13/1866.

Duzan (aka Dugan), William H. (aka William W.), Private, 1861/07/24, Corporal, Killed In Action at Battle of Baton Rouge, LA, 08/05/1862.

Earnest (aka Ernest), Nathaniel, Private, 1861/07/24, Private, Died 06/14/1862 at Algiers, LA.

Easterday, Jacob, Recruit, 1864/10/01, Private, Mustered Out 10/30/1865.

Edwards (aka Willis), Willis (aka Edwards), Recruit, 1862/01/14, Private, Veteran; Discharged 10/13/1865, Disability.

Engalls, Manly, Private, 1861/07/24, Private, Discharged 10/13/1865, Disability.

Enlow, Charles G., Recruit, 1864/09/15, Private, Mustered Out 07/20/1865.

Ermey (aka Ermes, Ermy), John E., Recruit, 1864/03/24, Private, Died 09/25/1864 at Baton Rouge, LA.

Eubanks (aka Ewbanks, Ewebanks), Martin V., Private, 1861/07/24, Private, Mustered Out 07/31/1864.

Evans, Anderson T (aka Andrew I.), Recruit, 1864/03/09, Private, Transferred to Company B, 10/01/1864; Died at New Orleans, LA, 01/21/1865.

Faith, Jacob H., Recruit, 1864/10/03, Private, Mustered Out 10/07/1865.

Filson (aka Tillson, Tilson), Davisson (aka Davison), Private, 1861/07/24, Corporal, Veteran; Mustered Out 01/13/1866.

Floyd, Laborn I., Recruit, 1864/09/15, Private, Mustered Out 07/20/1865.

Funkhouser (aka Funksouser), Young, Recruit, 1864/03/04, Private, Mustered Out 01/13/1866.

Garrigus (aka Garngus, Garragus), Samuel, Recruit, 1864/10/29, Private, Mustered Out 01/13/1866.

Goss, Lucius, Recruit, 1864/05/17, Corporal, Mustered Out 01/13/1866.

Gray (aka Grady), David B., Recruit, 1864/09/20, Private, Wounded at Spanish Fort, AL; Mustered Out 07/20/1865.

Green, Nathan S., Recruit, 1864/10/04, Private, Mustered Out 10/07/1865.

Hall, Martin V., Private, 1861/07/24, Private, Veteran; Deserted 09/25/1865.

Hamilton (aka Huselton), Andrew J. (aka Andrus), Recruit, 1862/01/14, Private, Discharged 06/27/1864, Disability.

Hamilton, Warren, Recruit, 1861/07/24, Corporal, Wounded and Commended for Bravery at Battle of Baton Rouge, LA; Mustered Out 07/31/1864.

Hammond, James, Recruit, none, Private, Deserted 05/21/1864 at Indianapolis, IN.

Heffleman, Frost H., Private, 1861/07/24, Quartermaster Serg't., Veteran; Mustered Out 01/13/1866.

Highnote (aka Hynote), Peter, Recruit, 1864/09/30, Private, Mustered Out 07/20/1865.

Holt, Joseph S., Recruit, 1864/10/04, Private, Discharged 08/26/1865 due to Wounds Received at Siege of Spanish Fort, AL. Wounded at Spanish Fort, AL; Mustered Out 08/11/1865..

Housand (aka Honsand), James P., Recruit, 1864/03/01, Private, Deserted 09/25/1865.

Huff (aka Hough), James R., Private, 1861/07/24, Private, Died of disease (smallpox) 12/06/1864 at New Orleans, LA.

Hunt, Cyrus E., Private, 1861/07/24, Sergeant, Veteran; Mustered Out 01/13/1866.

Jarvis, Alexander W., Private, 1861/07/24, Private, Discharged 10/20/1862, Disability.

Jerome, James N. (aka James M.), Corporal, 1861/07/24, Corporal, Commended for Bravery at Battle of Baton Rouge, LA; Mustered Out 07/31/1864.

Johns (aka Jons), Francis M., Recruit, 1864/03/24, Private, Mustered Out 01/13/1866.

Jones, Bettle, Private, 1861/07/24, Private, Veteran; Deserted 09/27/1865.

Jones, George S., Sergeant, 1861/07/24, Sergeant, Discharged 11/11/1861, Disability.

Jones, John F., Recruit, 1864/03/24, Private, Mustered Out 01/13/1866.

Jordan, James, Recruit, none, Private, *Deserted 05/21/1864.*

Kiphart (aka Kepart, Kiphar), Francis M. (aka Francis W.), Recruit, 1864/03/08, Private, Transferred to Company B 10/01/1864; Mustered Out 01/13/1866.

Kiphart (aka Kepart, Kiphar), William, Recruit, 1864/03/08, Private, Transferred to Company B 10/01/1864; Deserted, 08/18/1865..

Koons, James H., Recruit, 1864/10/08, Private, Mustered Out 10/09/1865.

Kuykendall (aka Kirkendall), John, Recruit, 1864/03/01, Private, Mustered Out 01/13/1866.

Lambert, Jerome, Recruit, 1864/01/21, Private, Died 08/14/1864 at Baton Rouge, LA.

Lambert, Josiah, Recruit, 1864/01/21, Private, Died 05/28/1864 at Baton Rouge, LA.

Larrance (aka Lawrence), Richard, Recruit, 1864/03/24, Private, Mustered Out 01/13/1866.

Lewis, Stephen C., Recruit, 1864/09/07, Private, Mustered Out 07/20/1865.

Little, Thomas J., Corporal, 1861/07/24, 2nd Lieutenant, Promoted 2nd Lieutenant 03/31/1864; Resigned 08/28/1865.

Little, William G., Recruit, 1864/03/24, Private, Mustered Out 01/13/1866.

Lough, George W., Musician, 1861/07/24, Bugler, Mustered Out 07/31/1864.

Lough, Jacob L., Recruit, 1864/03/29, Private, Died 09/27/1864 at Baton Rouge, LA.

Lough, John H., Private, 1861/07/24, Private, Discharged 11/11/1861, Disability. Died 08/17/1864 at New Orleans, LA..

Lough, Thomas J., Private, 1861/07/24, Corporal, Wounded and Commended for Bravery at Battle of Baton Rouge, LA; Veteran; Mustered Out 01/13/1866.

Lough (aka Loush), Thomas W., Private, 1861/07/24, Private, Veteran; Mustered Out 01/13/1866.

Lowderback (aka Louderback), Andrew, Private, 1861/07/24, Private, Veteran; Mustered Out 01/13/1866.

Maddock, James, Recruit, 1864/04/13, Private, Mustered Out 01/13/1866.

Maris (aka Maros), Enos J., Recruit, 1864/03/17, Private, Died 01/13/1864 on Steamer Groesbeck.

Martin, George P., Recruit, 1863/03/30, Private, Mustered Out 01/13/1866.

Martin, John W., Recruit, 1864/03/01, Private, Mustered Out 01/13/1866.

Mater, Hiram C., Private, 1861/07/24, Private, Discharged 10/20/1862, Disability.

Mater, Josiah D., Recruit, 1862/01/14, Private, Commended for Bravery at Battle of Baton Rouge, LA; Veteran; Mustered Out 01/13/1866.

Mater, Thomas W., Recruit, 1863/10/29, Private, Mustered Out 01/13/1866.

McCants, William, Private, 1861/07/24, Private, Veteran; Mustered Out 01/13/1866.

McClure, Allen A. (aka Alfred A.), Private, 1861/07/24, Private, Veteran; Deserted 09/25/1865.

McFarland, William J., Recruit, 1864/03/30, Private, Deserted 05/21/1864.

Melvin, Levi A., Recruit, 1864/09/24, Private, Mustered Out 07/20/1865.

Miller, Reuben, Private, 1861/07/24, Private, Mustered Out 07/31/1864.

Milliman (aka Millimon), James, Recruit, 1864/01/21, Private, Mustered Out 01/13/1866.

Mitchell (aka Nichel), Eli, Recruit, 1864/03/30, Corporal, Transferred to Co. B 10/01/1864; Mustered Out 01/13/1866.

Mitchell, Henry L., Private, 1861/07/24, Private, Transferred to Regular Army 11/21/1862. **Correction:** Died 08/24/1862 in Marine Hospital at New Orleans, LA.

Moody (aka Moodey), Foster M., Private, 1861/07/24, Private, Wounded at Battle of Baton Rouge, LA; Mustered Out 07/31/1864.

Moore, John A., Recruit, 1864/08/30, Private, Mustered Out 07/20/1865.

Moss (aka Mass), Thomas, Recruit, 1864/03/11, Private, *Deserted 05/21/1864.*

Musgrave, Jesse C., Recruit, 1864/03/17, Private, Mustered Out 01/13/1866.

Musgrove, John A., Private, 1861/07/24, Private, Killed at Battle of Baton Rouge, LA 08/05/1862,.

Newlin (aka Newton), Samuel H., Private, 1861/07/24, Private, Discharged 08/19/1862, Disability.

Newman, William B., Recruit, 1864/09/26, Private, Wouded at Spanish Fort, AL, Mustered Out 12/01/1865.

Noggle, John M., Private, 1861/07/24, Private, Died 07/15/1862 at Baton Rouge, LA.

Nolen (aka Nolan), James, Recruit, 1864/03/17, Artificer, Mustered Out 01/13/1866.

Orvis, Charles, Private, 1861/07/24, Private, Veteran; Discharged 08/23/1865, Disability.

Orvis, Joseph, Private, 1861/07/24, Private, Veteran; Deserted 10/05/1865.

Oug (aka Ong), John D., Private, 1861/07/24, Corporal, Discharged 1862; Re-entered Service as Recruit 08/10/1863; Discharged 11/01/1865, Disability.

Overman, William R., Recruit, 1864/04/08, Private, Died 06/24/1865 at New Orleans, LA.

Pavy (aka Pavey), Samuel A., Recruit, 1864/10/17, Private, Mustered Out 10/18/1865.

Peterson, Alfred, Recruit, 1864/10/05, Private, Mustered Out 10/07/1865.

Phelon (aka Phelan), Alexander C., Recruit, 1864/11/03, Private, Mustered Out 01/13/1866.

Phelon, George W., Private, 1861/07/24, Sergeant, Veteran; Mustered Out 01/13/1866.

Phelon, James M., Private, 1861/07/24, Private, Discharged 04/12/1862, Disability.

Phelon (aka Phelan), William H., Recruit, 1864/10/06, Private, Died 07/25/1865 at Fort Gaines, AL.

Phillips (aka Philips), James, Recruit, 1862/01/14, Private, Wounded at Battle of Baton Rouge, LA; Mustered Out 01/14/1865.

Pickett, George, Private, 1861/07/24, Private, Died in St. James Infirmary at New Orleans, LA, 08/17/1862.

Pierce, William J., Recruit, 1864/08/30, Bugler, Mustered Out 01/13/1866.

Pierson, Warren P., Recruit, 1864/03/08, Private, Transferred to Co.B 10/01/1864; Mustered Out 01/13/1866.

Pittman (aka Pitman), John, Private, 1861/07/24, Private, Wounded at Battle of Baton Rouge, LA; Died at New Iberia, LA, 10/10/1863 of accidental wounds..

Pollom (aka Pollum), Samuel, Recruit, 1864/09/21, Private, **Wounded at Spanish Fort,** AL; Mustered Out 07/20/1865.

Purcell, William M., Recruit, 1864/10/03, Private, Mustered Out 10/07/1865.

Ramsay (aka Ramsy), John A., Recruit, 1864/10/19, Private, Mustered 10/18/1865.

Ratcliffe (aka Radcliffe, Ratcliff), Samuel (aka Simon), Private, 1861/07/24, Private, Mustered Out 07/31/1864.

Reddish, Jesse, Corporal, 1861/07/24, Sergeant, Wounded at Battle of Baton Rouge, LA; Died in Indiana 05/14/1864.

Reed, John W., Recruit, 1864/03/24, Private, Mustered Out 01/13/1866.

Reeder (aka Reader), John G. (aka John P.), Private, 1861/07/24, Private, Discharged 02/14/1863, Disability.

Rivers, Frank, Recruit, 1864/09/27, Private, Mustered Out 07/20/1865.

Roads (aka Rhodes, Roods), William, Recruit, 1864/04/09, Private, Died 04/01/1865 at Fort Morgan, AL

Robbins, Eli N. (aka Eli V.), Private, 1861/07/24, Corporal, Veteran; Mustered Out 01/13/1866.

Roberds (aka Roberts), Sylvanus L., Recruit, 1864/03/03, Sergeant, Mustered Out 01/13/1866.

Rodman, James, Private, 1861/07/24, Private, Discharged 06/02/1863, Disability.

Rubottom (aka Robertson), Zeno, Private, 1861/07/24, Private, Wounded at Blair's Landing, LA. Mustered Out 07/31/1864.

Rumbaugh (aka Ranbaugh), Bartin, Recruit, 1864/03/01, Private, Died of disease, smallpox, 12/09/1864 at New Orleans, LA.

Samuels, Smith H. (aka Smith A.), Private, 1861/07/24, Bugler, Veteran; Mustered Out 01/13/1866. Deserted 04/27/1865; Dishonorably Discharged 09/13/1867.

Scott, George M., Private, 1861/07/24, Corporal, Veteran; Mustered Out 01/13/1866.

Scott, William H., Private, 1861/07/24, First Sergeant, Commended for Bravery at Battle of Baton Rouge, LA; Veteran; Mustered Out 01/13/1866.

Searing, Chauncey W., Recruit, 1864/05/17, Private, Discharged 02/20/1865, Disability.

Searing, James B., Recruit, 1864/10/06, Private, Mustered Out 10/07/1865.

Seybold, John M., Recruit, 1864/03/17, Private, Mustered Out 01/13/1866.

Seybold, John N., Recruit, 1864/03/01, Private, Mustered Out 01/13/1866.

Seybold, William H.H., Recruit, 1864/03/17, Private, Mustered Out 01/13/1866.

Shelby, James W., Recruit, 1864/08/25, Private, Mustered Out 07/20/1865.

Sherfey (aka Sherfy, Shirfy), Jacob F., Sergeant, 1861/07/24, 1st Lieutenant, Promoted 2nd Lieutenant 01/01/1863; Promoted 1st Lieutenant 03/31/1864; Mustered Out 01/10/1866..

Shirk, David, Private, 1861/07/24, Private, Discharged 11/12/1861, Disability.

Singleton, William H., Recruit, 1863/10/29, Private, Mustered Out 01/13/1866.

Sliger, Jacob C., Recruit, 1864/10/04, Private, Mustered Out 10/07/1865.

Smock, Randolph A., Recruit, 1864/03/24, Private, Wounded at Spanish Fort, AL; Mustered Out 01/13/1866.

Snow, Madison M. (aka Mattison), Private, 1861/07/24, 1st Lieutenant, Promoted 2nd Lieutenant 03/31/1864; Promoted 1st Lieutenant 10/01/1864; Veteran; Mustered Out 01/10/1866..

Spencer, John J., Corporal, 1861/07/24, Sergeant, Killed In Action at Battle of Baton Rouge, LA 08/05/1862.

Spencer, William A., Recruit, 1864/11/03, Private, Mustered Out 01/13/1866.

Stark, Albert S., Wagoner, 1861/07/24, Private, Veteran; Deserted 06/01/1865.

Stark, Hiram T. (aka Hiram J.), Recruit, 1864/03/24, Private, *Deserted 08/07/1865.*

Starke, William A., Private, 1861/07/24, Private, Discharged 09/22/1863, Disability.

Stevenson (aka Stephenson), Archibald J., Recruit, 1864/04/08, Private, Mustered Out 01/13/1866.

Strange, Daniel H., Recruit, 1864/03/07, Private, Mustered Out 09/04/1865.

Street, William S., Recruit, unknown, Deserted 05/31/1864.

Sublett, James, Recruit, 1864/09/30, Private, Mustered Out 07/20/1865.

Sutherland, Asa, Private, 1861/07/24, Private, Veteran; Mustered Out 01/13/1866.

Thomas, Don R. (aka Dunn R.), Private, 1861/07/24, Private, Mustered Out 07/31/1864.

Thomas, Henry M., Private, 1861/07/24, Private, Veteran; Mustered Out 01/13/1866.

Thomas, William H., Recruit, 1864/09/24, Private, Mustered Out 07/20/1865.

Thompson, David J., Recruit, 1864/03/30, Private, Died 11/17/1864 in Indiana.

Thompson, Henry, Private, 1861/07/24, Artificer, Wounded at Battle of Baton Rouge, LA; Veteran; Mustered Out 01/13/1866.

Thompson, Henry C., Private, 1861/07/24, Private, Veteran; Mustered Out 01/13/1866.

Thompson, Marion, Private, 1861/07/24, Private, Discharged 10/20/1862, Disability.

Thompson, Thomas, Recruit, 1864/09/06, Private, Mustered Out 07/20/1865.

Towell, Jonathan, Recruit, 1864/11/17, Private, Discharged 11/22/1864, Disability.

Towell, William, Recruit, 1864/03/17, Private, Died 10/17/1865 at Fort Gaines, AL.

Turner, Charles R., Recruit, 1862/01/14, Private, Veteran; Mustered Out 01/13/1866.

Tyler, John S., Recruit, 1864/10/10, Private, Mustered Out 10/09/1865.

Underwood, Daniel, Private, 1861/07/24, Private, Mustered Out 07/31/1864.

Vessels, Thomas J., Private, 1861/07/24, Private, Veteran; Deserted 09/25/1865.

Wallace, Henry, Recruit, 1864/10/03, Private, Mustered Out 10/07/1865.

Wam (aka Wann, Warm), John H., Recruit, 1864/03/24, Private, Mustered Out 01/13/1866.

Wampler, Joseph, Recruit, 1864/04/03, Private, Transferred to Co.B 10/01/1864; Mustered Out 10/05/1865.

Ward, Jordan, Recruit, 1864/02/29, Transferred to Company B 10/01/1864; No record in Co. B.

Watt, William, Private, 1861/07/24, Corporal, Veteran; Mustered Out 01/13/1866.

Weaver, Philip W., Private, 1861/07/24, Private, Discharged 10/15/1862 due to Wounds Received in Battle of Baton Rouge, LA.

Wells, Charles A. (aka Charles H.), Recruit, 1864/10/01, Private, Mustered Out 10/30/1865.

Wilkey (aka Wilky), William H. (aka William C.), Private, 1861/07/24, Sergeant, Veteran; Wounded at Fort Blakely, AL, Mustered Out 01/13/1866.

Wilkins (aka Wilkerson), Michael H., Private, 1861/07/24, Private, Discharged 10/26/1862, Disability.

Wilkins, Henry C., Private, 1861/07/24, Private, Wounded at Battle of Baton Rouge, LA; Mustered Out 07/31/1864.

Wilkinson, Michael, Musician, 1861/07/24, Private, Veteran; Discharged 11/01/1865, Disability.

Wilson, Isaac N., Private, 1861/07/24, Private, Discharged 09/08/1862, Disability.

Wilson, Thomas B., Private, 1861/07/24, Private, Died 03/05/1864 at Franklin, LA.

Wimmer (aka Weimmer), Perry W., Corporal, 1861/07/24, Corporal, Discharged 10/20/1862, Disability.

Wimmer (aka Wimner, Winner), William P., First Sergeant, 1861/07/24, Captain, Promoted 1st Lieutenant 01/01/1863; Promoted Captain 10/01/1864; Mustered Out 01/10/1866, Absent Sick..

Wolf (aka Wolfe), William C., Corporal, 1861/07/24, First Sergeant, Wounded and Commended for Bravery at Battle of Baton Rouge, LA; Killed in Action at Atchafalaya Bayou, LA, 10/23/1863.

Wood, Henry, Recruit, unknown, Private, *Deserted 05/21/1864.*

Wood, Herman A., Recruit, 1864/03/17, Private, Mustered Out 01/13/1866.

Wood, John Q., Recruit, 1864/10/07, Private, Mustered Out 01/13/1866.

Yelton (aka Welton, Yeton), John B., Private, 1861/07/24, Sergeant, Veteran; Mustered Out 01/13/1866.

Young, George, Recruit, 1864/09/30, Private, Mustered Out 07/20/1865.

Company I

Akers (aka Ackers, Akens), Abner, Recruit, 1863/06/19, Never Reported to the Company.

Albin (aka Albion), Benjamin F., Recruit, 1863/08/31, Private, Died 06/01/1864 at New Orleans, LA.

Andrews (aka Andrew), Samuel, Private, 1861/07/24, Private, Discharged; Disability.

Armstrong, Samuel E. (aka Samuel M.), 2nd Lieutenant, 1861/07/24, Major, Promoted to Captain of Company M 10/21/1863; Promoted Regimental Major 07/12/1865; Mustered Out 02/03/1866 as Captain.

Axford, William, Recruit, 1964/01/20, Private, Transferred 07/30/1864 to 21st Iowa Infantry.

Baker, Andrew, Private, 1861/07/24, Private, Mustered Out 01/10/1866.

Baker, George, Recruit, 1864/09/22, Corporal, Mustered Out 07/27/1865.

Baker, James H., Corporal, 1861/07/24, Sergeant, Veteran; Mustered Out 01/10/1866.

Baldwin, Thomas, Recruit, 1864/03/29, Private, Mustered Out 01/10/1866.

Ball, George W., Recruit, 1864/03/19, Private, Mustered Out 01/10/1866.

Barley (aka Barby, Borley), Francis M., Private, 1861/07/24, Private, Veteran; Mustered Out 01/10/1866.

Barton, John M., Private, 1861/07/24, Private, Veteran; Mustered Out 01/10/1866.

Basstick (aka Bosstic, Bosstick, Bostic, Bostick, Bostwick), William, Private, 1861/07/24, Private, Veteran; Mustered Out 01/10/1866.

Bates, Silas, Corporal, 1861/07/24, Captain, Promoted 2nd Lieutenant 10/21/1863; Promoted 1st Lieutenant 01/31/1864; Promoted Captain 04/27/1865; Mustered Out 01/10/1866.

Baum, Michael O., Private, 1861/07/24, Private, Died 08/07/1862, on Steamer.

Bayless (aka Baylees, Baylers), Alexander, Recruit, 1863/05/23, Private, Never Reported to the Company.

Benson, Robert P., Private, 1861/07/24, Private, Discharged 10/15/1862, Disability.

Berger (aka Burger), Solomon, Private, 1861/07/24, Private, Died 05/05/1862 at Pilot Town, LA.

Bilderback, Thomas, Private, 1861/07/24, Private, Discharged 04/14/1862, Disability.

Blythe (aka Blyth), Julius, Private, 1861/07/24, Private, Veteran; Mustered Out 01/10/1866.

Boling (aka Bodley, Bowling), James W. (aka James W.), Recruit, 1864/03/29, Corporal, Mustered Out 01/10/1866.

Boothe (aka Booth), Thompson M., Recruit, 1864/03/28, Corporal, Mustered Out 01/10/1866.

Brann (aka Braun), Daniel K., Private, 1861/07/24, First Sergeant, Veteran; Mustered Out 01/10/1866.

Brann (aka Bram, Braun, Brown), Richard W., Private, 1861/07/24, Sergeant, Mustered Out 07/24/1864.

Bruden (aka Breeden, Brenden), William O. (aka William C.), Recruit, 1864/01/20, Private, Transferred 07/20/1864 to 21st Iowa Infantry.

Brothers (aka Brathers), Thomas, Recruit, 1864/10/05, Private, Mustered Out 01/10/1866.

Burk, John, Recruit, 1864/09/26, Private, Died 06/29/1865 at Mobile, AL.

Burk (aka Burke, Burks), Samuel J. (aka Samual Z.), Private, 1861/07/24, Private, Veteran; Mustered Out 01/10/1866.

Butcher, John L., Private, 1861/07/24, Private, Veteran; Mustered Out 01/10/1866.

Butcher, William H., Private, 1861/07/24, Private, Veteran; Mustered Out 01/10/1866.

Cahill, Walter G., Private, 1861/07/24, Private, Died 03/07/1862 of Wounds Inflicted by a Camp Guard (Shot in Throat).

Cain (aka Cane), Milton J. (aka Milton), Recruit, 1864/10/05, Private, Mustered Out 01/10/1866.

Campbell, Enoch, Corporal, 1861/07/24, Sergeant, Discharged 1861, Disability.

Campbell, John, Private, 1861/07/24, Private, Discharged December, 1861, Accidental Wounds.

Campbell, Reed, Private, 1861/07/24, Private, Mustered Out 07/24/1864.

Campbell, Richard, Captain, 1861/07/24, Captain, Died 04/26/1865 of Disease..

Campbell, Stukely (aka Stukeley), Sergeant, 1861/07/24, 2nd Lieutenant, Promoted 2nd Lieutenant 07/01/1865; Veteran; Mustered Out 01/10/1866..

Church, Eli E., Private, 1861/07/24, Corporal, Veteran; Mustered Out 01/10/1866.

Church, James L. (aka James D.), Private, 1861/07/24, Private, Discharged 10/02/1861, Disability; Re-enlisted 04/02/1864; Mustered Out 01/10/1866.

Clark, Nimrod F., Private, 1861/07/24, Private, Discharged November, 1861, Disability.

Clymer, Henry F., Recruit, 1864/10/05, Private, Mustered Out 01/10/1866.

Cokenhour, Solomon, Private, 1861/07/24, Private, Died 06/11/1862 at New Orleans, LA.

Cole, George, Recruit, 1862/01/30, Private, Mustered Out 01/30/1865.

Cole, Jacob, Recruit, 1862/01/30, Private, Mustered Out 01/30/1865.

Cole, John, Recruit, 1862/01/30, Private, Mustered Out 01/30/1865.

Coleman, John, Recruit, Never Reported to the Company.

Collins, Chauncey, Recruit, Never Reported to the Company.

Comstock, Jeremiah, Recruit, 1864/03/08, Private, Died 11/03/1864 at New Orleans, LA.

Cooprider, Francis M., Recruit, 1864/10/05, Private, Mustered Out 01/10/1866.

Cooprider, Jackson, Recruit, 1864/10/05, Private, Mustered Out 01/10/1866.

Cooprider, Jasper, Recruit, 1863/06/23, Private, Mustered Out 01/10/1866.

Cooprider, John, Recruit, 1864/10/05, Private, Mustered Out 01/10/1866.

Cooprider, Newton, Recruit, 1862/01/20, Private, Died 09/13/1863 at Baton Rouge, LA.

Cooprider, Wilfred (aka W.F., Alford F.), Private, 1861/07/24, Private, Discharged 04/14/1862, Disability.

Cooprider, William, Corporal, 1861/07/24, Private, Veteran; Mustered Out 01/10/1866.

Cox, Josiah, Recruit, 1864/10/17, Private, Mustered Out 01/10/1866.

Cox, Lawrence N. (aka Lawrence B.), Private, 1861/07/24, Private, Mustered Out 07/24/1864.

Cox, William K. (aka William H.), Recruit, 1864/04/14, Private, Mustered Out 01/10/1866.

Cozine, John R., Recruit, 1862/02/01, Corporal, Mustered Out 02/01/1865.

Crews (aka Crewse), Josiah, Recruit, 1864/09/02, Private, Mustered Out 07/27/1865.

Cromwell, Granville P. (aka Granville H.), Recruit, 1864/03/25, Private, Mustered Out 01/10/1866.

Cromwell, Levi, Private, 1861/07/24, Corporal, Mustered Out 07/24/1864.

Cromwell, Marshall W., Private, 1861/07/24, Private, Mustered Out 07/24/1864.

Culler (aka Culer), Andrew, Recruit, 1864/03/28, Private, Died 02/09/1865 at Brashear City (now Morgan City), LA.

Cullifer, William R., Corporal, 1861/07/24, Private, Veteran; Mustered Out 01/10/1866.

Cully (aka Culley), Joseph, Recruit, 1864/10/05, Private, Mustered Out 01/10/1866.

Curts, Michael A., Recruit, 1864/09/28, Private, Mustered Out 07/27/1865.

Davis, John, Recruit, 1864/10/05, Private, Mustered Out 01/10/1866.

Dean, John, Private, 1861/07/24, Private, Discharged November, 1861, Disability.

Devenport (aka Davenport), Henderson, Recruit, 1864/09/30, Private, Mustered Out 07/27/1865.

Dick, Edward, Recruit, 1864/09/24, Private, Discharged 06/14/1864, Disability.

Dickey, Jacob, Private, 1861/07/24, Private, Mustered Out 07/24/1864.

Duty (aka Diety), William, Recruit, unknown, Private, Discharged 06/16/1864, Disability.

Eckard (aka Ekard), Harvey G., Private, 1861/07/24, Sergeant (?), Veteran; Mustered Out 01/10/1866.

Edwards, Albert, Recruit, 1864/10/07, Private, Mustered Out 01/10/1866.

Elkin (aka Elkins), Walker C., 1st Lieutenant, 1861/07/24, 1st Lieutenant, Resigned 10/20/1863.

Elwell (aka Ellwell), William, Recruit, 1864/03/29, Private, Mustered Out 01/10/1866.

Fetters, Daniel, Recruit, unknown, Private, Mustered Out 01/10/1866.

Fields, James, Recruit, 1862/08/20, Private, Discharged 11/02/1863, Disability.

Fields, Reuben, Recruit, 1862/08/20, Private, Died 01/22/1863 at Brashear City (now Morgan City), LA.

Fields, Samuel, Recruit, 1862/08/20, , Promoted to 1st Lieutenant of Co. M 10/21/1863; Resigned 01/20/1864.

Fields, Thomas M. (aka Thomas W.), Recruit, 1862/08/20, Private, Mustered Out 07/27/1865.

Florence (aka Florrence), James C., Recruit, Never Reported to the Company.

Fridley (aka Friedley, Friedly, Frietley), Samuel P., Recruit, unknown, Private, Died 10/17/1864 at New Orleans, LA.

Fulmer (aka Fedmer, Fulmen), Aaron, Recruit, 1864/01/20, Corporal, Transferred to 21st Iowa Infantry Regiment, 07/30/1864.

Gainey (aka Gainie, Ganney), Elijah N., Recruit, 1864/08/20, Private, Mustered Out 07/27/1865.

Gannon, Michael, Recruit, 1864/12/20, Private, Mustered Out 01/10/1866.

Garrigus (aka Garrigas), Jeptha, Private, 1861/07/24, Private, Mustered Out 10/15/1862.

Gay, Jackson, Recruit, Never Reported to the Company.

Gibbs, George, Recruit, Never Reported to the Company.

Gilbrich (aka Gilbrech, Gilbreck), Jacob, Private, 1861/07/24, Sergeant, Veteran; Mustered Out 01/10/1866.

Gildersleeve (aka Gildersleve), Francis I, Recruit, 1863/01/20, Private, Transferred to 21st Iowa Infantry Regiment 07/30/1864.

Gladden, George G., Recruit, 1864/09/14, Private, Mustered Out 01/10/1866.

Gladden, John W. (aka John M.), Recruit, 1864/09/14, Corporal, Mustered Out 07/27/1865.

Goder, John G., Recruit, Never Reported to the Company.

Grass (aka Grasse, Gross), Charles L. (aka Charles S.), Private, 1861/07/24, Private, Mustered Out 07/24/1864.

Graves (aka Grans), Timothy H., Recruit, 1862/01/30, Corporal, Discharged 02/08/1864, Disability.

Guinn (aka Gevinn), Daniel T. (aka Daniel F.), Private, 1861/07/24, Sergeant, Veteran; Mustered Out 01/10/1866.

Gulbrandson (aka Guldbrandson), Gilbert, Recruit, 1863/01/20, Private, Transferred to 21st Iowa Infantry Regiment 07/30/1864.

Hall, Martin V, Private, 1861/07/24, Private, Died 10/24/1862 at Camp Parapet near Carrollton, LA.

Hall, William S., Recruit, 1864/01/20, Private, Transferred to 21st Iowa Infantry Regiment 07/30/1864.

Harbaugh (aka Harbough), Thomas, Recruit, 1864/10/04, Private, Died 05/14/1865 at Mobile, AL.

Harden (aka Hardin), James, Private, 1861/07/24, Corporal, Veteran; Mustered Out 01/10/1866.

Harden (aka Hardin), William, Private, 1861/07/24, Corporal, Veteran; Mustered Out 01/10/1866.

Harding, Charles N., Musician, 1861/07/24, Private, Transferred to 4th U.S. Artillery, January, 1863.

Harris, Eli, Corporal, 1861/07/24, Corporal, Died 09/15/1862 at Carrollton, LA.

Harris, Samuel S., Recruit, 1864/09/23, Corporal, Mustered Out 07/27/1865.

Harrod (aka Herrod), Jesse M., Corporal, 1861/07/24, Private, Reduced; *Deserted 02/05/1863 to the Enemy at Brashear City, LA.*

Hart (aka Heart), George W., Recruit, 1864/01/20, Arrested by Civil Authority 02/09/1864.

Hartley (aka Hartly), Sylvester, Private, 1861/07/24, Sergeant, Veteran; Mustered Out 01/10/1866.

Hasket, Caswell W., Recruit, 1864/09/15, Private, Mustered Out 07/27/1865.

Haymaker, Benjamin F., Recruit, 1864/09/12, Private, Mustered Out 07/27/1865.

Hetser, John W., Recruit, 1864/04/14, Private, Mustered Out 01/10/1866.

Hobbs (aka Fox), James L., Recruit, 1864/01/30, Private, Died 10/07/1865 at Baton Rouge, LA.

Hogue (aka Hoge), Charles F., 2nd Lieutenant, 1861/07/24, 1st Lieutenant, 2nd Lieutenant 03/31/1864; Promoted 1st Lieutenant 05/01/1865; Mustered Out 01/10/1866..

Holmes (aka Homs), William B., Private, 1861/07/24, Private, Mustered Out 07/04/1864.

Housh (aka Haush, Housch), William P., Recruit, 1864/09/27, Private, Mustered Out 07/27/1865.

Hughs (aka Hughes), George W., Recruit, 1864/09/13, Private, Mustered Out 07/27/1865.

Isaacs, Matthew, Recruit, 1864/04/07, Private, Mustered Out 01/10/1866.

Jackman, James, Recruit, Never Reported to the Company.

Jacks, Anderson M, Private, 1861/07/24, Private, Discharged October, 1861, Disability.

James, George W., Sergeant, 1861/07/24, 1st Lieutenant, Promoted 2nd Lieutenant 03/31/1864; Promoted 1st Lieutenant 05/01/1864; Mustered Out 01/10/1866..

Kane (aka Cane), John, Recruit, 1864/01/20, Private, Died 09/10/1864 at Brashear City (now Morgan City), LA.

Kauble, Isaac, Private, 1861/07/24, Private, Mustered Out 07/24/1864.

Kennedy, John H., Recruit, 1864/10/04, Private, Mustered Out 01/10/1866.

Kinchen (aka Kinche), Ervin A. (aka Irvin A., Irwin A.), Recruit, 1863/08/30, Private, Mustered Out 01/10/1866.

Kinchen, Henry C. (aka Henry M.), Recruit, 1862/08/20, Private, Discharged 03/10/1864.

Kinchen, Oran M. (aka Oran W., Owen M.), Recruit, 1862/08/20, Private, Discharged 05/23/1865, Disability.

Kinchen, William A., Recruit, 1862/08/20, Private, Discharged 11/02/1863, Disability.

Kress (aka Kuess), William R., First Sergeant, 1861/07/24, First Sergeant, Discharged 05/04/1863, Disability.

Lankford, Ivy (aka John), Private, 1861/07/24, Private, Discharged 10/15/1862, Disability.

Lankford, John R., Private, 1861/07/24, Private, Discharged 10/15/1862, Disability.

Lankford, Sylvester, Private, 1861/07/24, Private, Mustered Out 07/24/1864.

Livesley (aka Livesly, Livisley, Livsley), David, Private, 1861/07/24, Sergeant, Veteran; Mustered Out 01/10/1866.

Lloyd, William M. (aka William L.), Private, 1861/07/24, Private, Veteran; Mustered Out 01/10/1866.

Long (aka Lomg), Benjamin F., Private, 1861/07/24, Private, Discharged November, 1861, Disability.

Lucas, George G., Private, 1861/07/24, Private, Died 07/17/1862 at Baton Rouge, LA.

Lucas, Jasper, Recruit, 1864/03/17, Private, Mustered Out 01/10/1866.

Lucas, Reuben, Recruit, 1864/10/10, Private, Mustered Out 01/10/1866

Lucas (aka Lucus), Thomas, Private, 1861/07/24, Private, Veteran; Died 11/13/1865 at Fort Pickens, FL.

Lucas, William S., Private, 1861/07/24, Corporal, Mustered Out 07/24/1864.

Markle, Theodore, Private, 1861/07/24, 1st Lieutenant, Transferred to Company M 01/30/1864; Promoted 2nd Lieut. of Co. M 09/09/1864; Promoted 1st Lieut. Of Co. M 03/01/1865; Mustered Out 01/10/1866.

Marsh, Thomas, Private, 1861/07/24, Private, Discharged November, 1861, Disability.

May, Stephen D., Recruit, Never Reported to the Company.

McCafferty, Hugh, Recruit, 1864/01/20, Private, Transferred to 21st Iowa Infantry Regiment 07/30/1864.

McCann, Owen, Recruit, 1863/05/30, Private, Mustered Out 01/10/1866.

McClure, George W., Private, 1861/07/24, Corporal, Veteran; Mustered Out 01/10/1866.

McCullough, John R., Recruit, 1864/03/29, Private, Mustered Out 01/10/1866.

McDougall, Neil J., Recruit, 1864/09/24, Private, Discharged per Order; Date Not Reported.

McKinley (aka McKinly), William S., Private, 1861/07/24, Private, Veteran; Mustered Out 01/10/1866.

McLaughlin (aka Lauglin, McLaflin), Edward, Recruit, 1863/12/26, Private, *Deserted 03/23/1864.*

McMann, Thomas (aka James), Recruit, unknown, Private, Mustered Out 01/10/1866.

McNett, Elisha, Rcruit, 1864/04/30, Private, Mustered Out 01/10/1866.

Merrell (aka Merrill), Abijah, Recruit, 1864/10/17, Private, Mustered Out 01/10/1866.

Merrell (aka Merrill), Edward, Recruit, 1864/10/17, Private, Mustered Out 01/10/1866.

Miller, Andrew, Recruit, 1864/10/17, Private, Mustered Out 01/10/1866.

Miner, Henry M., Recruit, 1864/01/20, Private, Transferred to 21st Iowa Infantry Regiment 07/30/1864.

Mishler (aka Michler), Cornelius, Private, 1861/07/24, Private, Veteran; Died 10/11/1864 at Brashear City (Morgan City), LA.

Molar, Andrew J., Recruit, 1864/04/14, Private, Mustered Out 01/10/1866.

Moore, William A., Private, 1861/07/24, Private, Discharged 04/14/1862, Disability.

Morgan, Benjamin D. (aka Benjamin F.), Recruit, 1864/03/28, Private, Mustered Out 01/10/1866.

Morris (aka Maurice), Josephus, Private, 1861/07/24, Private, Mustered Out 07/24/1864.

Mullen, James, Recruit, Never Reported to the Company.

Muncie (aka Mincie, Moncee, Moncie, Muney), Noah, Private, 1861/07/24, Private, Veteran; Mustered Out 01/10/1866.

Myers (aka Meyers), Dewitt, Recruit, 1864/01/20, Private, Transferred to 21st Iowa Infantry Regiment 07/30/1864.

Nance, William, Private, 1861/07/24, Private, Veteran; Mustered Out 01/10/1866.

Nelson (aka Netson), Josiah, Recruit, 1863/03/10, Private, Died 03/25/1865 at New Orleans, LA.

Nolen (aka Nolan), John, Recruit, 1864/01/20, Private, Transferred to 21st Iowa Infantry Regiment 07/30/1864.

Oswalt (aka Oswall), George W., Recruit, 1864/03/23, Private, Mustered Out 01/10/1866.

Owen (Owens, Owns), Daniel D. (aka Daniel B.), Private, 1861/07/24, Private, Veteran; Deserted 09/12/1865.

Owen (Owens), David W., Private, 1861/07/24, Private, Veteran; Mustered Out 01/10/1866.

Owen, Wyatt, Recruit, 1864/10/05, Private, Mustered Out 01/10/1866.

Patch (aka Parch, Partch), Augustus J., Recruit, 1864/01/30, Private, Transferred to 21st Iowa Infantry Regiment 07/27/1864.

Patton (aka Patten, Pattin), Lewis, Recruit, Never Reported to the Company.

Perry, Thomas, Recruit, 1864/09/17, Private, Mustered Out 07/27/1865.

Pinkerton, John, Recruit, 1864/10/05, Private, Mustered Out 01/10/1866.

Poland (aka Oland), Henry, Private, 1861/07/24, Corporal, Veteran; Died 09/27/1864 at Brashear City (now Morgan City), LA.

Polsen (aka Polson), Erick (aka Werick), Recruit, 1864/01/20, Private, Transferred to 21st Iowa Infantry Regiment 07/27/1864.

Poole (aka Pool), Oscar, Recruit, 1864/09/26, Private, Mustered Out 07/27/1865.

Pruitt (aka Prewitt, Pruett), William C., Recruit, 1864/04/21, Private, Mustered Out 01/10/1866.

Quartman, Herman H., Recruit, 1864/03/01, Private, Mustered Out 01/10/1866.

Ray (aka Roy), Abner P., Private, 1861/07/24, Corporal, Veteran; Mustered Out 01/10/1866.

Ray (aka Roy), George D. (aka George G.), Private, 1861/07/24, Private, Mustered Out 07/24/1864.

Ray (aka Roy), George G., Private, 1861/07/24, Private, Mustered Out 07/24/1864.
Reeder, Jonathan, Wagoner, 1861/07/24, Private, Veteran; Mustered Out 01/10/1866.
Roberts, James T., Private, 1861/07/24, Private, Mustered Out 07/24/1864.
Roberts, John, Recruit, unknown, Private, Mustered Out 01/10/1866.
Robertson, Russell P., Private, 1861/07/24, Corporal, Discharged 04/14/1862, Disability.
Rodenberger (aka Rosemberger), John, Recruit, 1864/04/12, Private, Mustered Out 01/10/1866.
Rodgers (aka Rogers), Jeffrey (aka Jeffrew), Sergeant, 1861/07/24, 2nd Lieutenant, Promoted 2nd Lieutenant 10/01/1861; Resigned 10/14/1865.
Rose, Ralph W., Private, 1861/07/24, Private, Veteran; Mustered Out 01/10/1866.
Sawdy (aka Sawdey), Henry C., Recruit, 1864/01/30, Private, Transferred to 21st Iowa Infantry Regiment 08/07/1864.
Seery (aka Seevery), William, Private, 1861/07/24, Corporal, Died 04/20/1862 at New Orleans, LA.
Selby, John R., Recruit, Never Reported to the Company.
Shall (aka Sholl), Isaac, Musician, 1861/07/24, Private, Discharged June, 1862, Disability.
Sherman, Thomas, Recruit, 1862/10/01, Private, Mustered Out 01/10/1866.
Simonson, Isaac M., Private, 1861/07/24, Corporal, Veteran; Mustered Out 01/10/1866.
Sink, Henry M., Private, 1861/07/24, Private, Mustered Out 07/24/1864.
Smith, John F. (aka John H.), Recruit, 1864/01/20, Private, Died 02/20/1864 at Indianapolis, IN.
Smith, Solomon, Recruit, 1864/03/28, Private, Died 05/15/1864 at Baton Rouge, LA.
Snellenberger (aka Snelenberger, Snelenborg, Snellenbarger, Sullenberger), Conrad, Private, 1861/07/24, Private, Mustered Out 07/24/1864.
Spangler, Elias, Private, 1861/07/24, Corporal, Veteran; Mustered Out 01/10/1866.
Spencer (aka Spenser), Moses, Recruit, 1862/08/20, Private, Died 11/03/1862 at Camp Parapet (Carrollton), LA.
Spengler (aka Spangler), Charles, Recruit, 1863/12/26, Private, *Deserted 03/23/1864.*
Staggs, Edward, Recruit, 1864/03/15, , Discharged 10/27/1865, Disability.
Starkey (aka Starky), Jasper N. (aka Jasper W.), Recruit, 1863/03/10, Private, Mustered Out 01/10/1866.
Stephenson (aka Stevenson), Francis F. (aka Frances M., Francis I.), Recruit, 1864/01/20, Private, Drowned 02/09/1864 in the Mississippi River.
Stewart (aka Steward), Charles, Recruit, , , Never Reported to the Company.
Stewart, William A., Private, 1861/07/24, Private, Veteran; Mustered Out 01/10/1866.

Stivender (aka Stevender), John, Recruit, 1863/03/20, Private, *Deserted 03/23/1864.*
Stores, John, Recruit, 1863/12/19, Private, Mustered Out 01/10/1866.
Stonn (aka Storm, Stormes), Adam, Recruit, 1864/09/26, Private, Mustered Out 07/27/1865.
Stonn (aka Storm, Stormes), John, Recruit, 1864/10/05, Private, Mustered Out 01/10/1866.
Stroud (aka Strood, Strown), Wilson, Recruit, 1864/10/05, Private, Mustered Out 01/10/1866.
Stuckey, Archibald, Recruit, 1862/08/20, Private, Died 01/13/1863 at New Orleans, LA.
Stuckey, Lewis E., Recruit, 1862/08/20, Private, Died 11/13/1863 at New Orleans, LA.
Stuckey, William, Recruit, 1862/08/20, Private, Died 09/11/1862 at Carrollton, LA.
Summerville (aka Somerville, Sommerville, Sumerville), James B., Recruit, 1864/03/27, Private, Mustered Out 03/05/1865.
Summerville (aka Somerville, Sommerville), John L., Recruit, 1864/03/21, Private, Mustered Out 01/10/1866.
Tarvin, Cornelius H. (aka William H.), Recruit, 1864/03/17, Private, Mustered Out 01/10/1866.
Taylor, Thomas, Private, 1861/07/24, Private, Veteran; Mustered Out 01/10/1866.
Thomas, Solomon M., Recruit, 1864/03/28, Corporal, Mustered Out 01/10/1866.
Thorlton, Robert C., Private, 1861/07/24, Private, Mustered Out 07/24/1864.
Thorlton, William A., Private, 1861/07/24, Private, Mustered Out 07/24/1864.
Thornberg (aka Thornberge, Thornburg, Thornburgh), Marcus M. (aka Marcus N.), Private, 1861/07/24, Private, Veteran; Mustered Out 01/10/1866.
Tipton, William, Corporal, 1861/07/24, Private, Died 07/13/1862 at Baton Rouge, LA.
Triplett (aka Triplett, Triplitt), James B., Private, 1861/07/24, Corporal, Veteran; Died 10/05/1865 at Fort Pickens, FL.
VanHorn (aka Vanhorn), Robert A., Recruit, 1864/10/05, Private, Mustered Out 01/10/1866.
Wallace, William, Recruit, Never Reported to the Company.
Ward (aka Waid), Alexander, Recruit, 1864/05/03, Private, Mustered Out 01/10/1866.
Warner, William M., Private, 1861/07/24, Private, Veteran; Died 02/11/1864 at New Orleans, LA.
Webster, Andrew B., Private, 1861/07/24, Private, Veteran; Mustered Out 01/10/1866.
Wendell (aka Wendall), Theodore, Private, 1861/07/24, Private, *Deserted 09/24/1861.*
White, Edward, Sergeant, 1861/07/24, Sergeant, Discharged 11, 1861, Disability.
Williams, James F., Recruit, 1863/03/15, , Mustered Out 01/10/1866.
Williams, Samuel D., Recruit, 1863/03/01, Private, Mustered Out 06/10/1865.

Williams, William H., Private, 1861/07/24, Sergeant, Veteran; Mustered Out 01/10/1866.
Young, James, Private, 1861/07/24, Private, Veteran; Mustered Out 01/10/1866.
Zenor, Berlin, Recruit, 1862/01/30, Corporal, Veteran; Mustered Out 01/10/1866.
Zenor, Commodore P., Recruit, 1864/03/28, Corporal, Mustered Out 01/10/1866.
Zenor, Merryman H. (aka Marrimon H.), Private, 1861/07/24, Sergeant, Veteran; Mustered Out 01/10/1866.

Company K

Abel (aka Ables), Branson (aka Brunson), Recruit, 1864/09/15, Private, Mustered Out 07/20/1865.
Agen (aka Agan), Michael, Private, 1861/07/24, Private, Mustered Out 07/31/1864.
Agen (aka Agan), Michael, Recruit, unknown, Private, Died 10/15/1865 at Fort Gaines, AL.
Albertson, Jacob, Corporal, 1861/07/24, Private, Reduced; Mustered Out 07/31/1864.
Albertson, Joab, Private, 1861/07/24, Private, Mustered Out 07/31/1864.
Anderson, John W., Recruit, 1864/09/28, Private, Mustered 07/20/1865.
Applegate (aka Aplegate), William H., Recruit, 1864/01/12, Private, Mustered Out 01/10/1866.
Bailey (aka Baile, Baily), Adonijah M., Recruit, 1864/03/27, Private, Mustered Out 01/10/1866.
Bailey, David, Private, 1861/07/24, Sergeant, Veteran; Died 03/03/1865 at New Orleans, LA.
Bailey, Enos, Private, 1861/07/24, Corporal, Veteran; Died 06/26/1865 at Mobile, AL.
Bailiff, David, Private, 1861/07/24, Private, Discharged 10/29/1861, Disability.
Baker, Thomas F. (aka Thomas J.), Private, 1861/07/24, Private, Veteran; Mustered Out 01/10/1866.
Balka (aka Balky), Ernest, Recruit, 1864/01/12, Private, Died 09/23/1864 at Mound City.
Beeson (aka Buson), Stephen, Recruit, 1862/01/14, Private, Mustered Out 01/14/1865.
Bennett, William, Private, 1861/07/24, , *Deserted at Baltimore, MD, 12/12/1861.*
Black, William, Corporal, 1861/07/24, First Sergeant, Veteran; Mustered Out 01/10/1866.
Blackburn, John W., Recruit, 1863/07/08, Private, Died 03/31/1864 at New Orleans, LA.
Blakely (aka Blakely), James R., Private, 1861/07/24, Private, Veteran; Mustered Out 01/10/1866.
Blunk, Adam G. (aka Adam Y.), Private, 1861/07/24, Private, Discharged 11/14/1861, Disability.
Bollar (aka Ballar, Bollor), James M., Private, 1861/07/24, Private, Veteran; Mustered Out 01/10/1866.
Botkin (aka Bockin), John, Recruit, 1864/09/17, Private, Mustered Out 07/20/1865.
Bowman, George W., Recruit, 1864/10/04, Private, Mustered Out 10/05/1865.
Bowman, William, Private, 1861/07/24, Private, Veteran; Mustered Out 01/10/1866.
Brandon (aka Branden), Robert, Recruit, 1863/12/26, Musician, Discharged 08/21/1864 by Order.
Bray, Solomon, Private, 1861/07/24, Private, Wounded at Battle of Baton Rouge 08/05/1862; Mustered Out 07/31/1864.
Breece (aka Brees, Breese), Andrew, Private, 1861/07/24, Private, Veteran; Mustered Out 01/10/1866.
Britton, Josiah, Recruit, 1864/03/03, Private, Mustered Out 01/10/1866.
Brown, Edward, Recruit, 1864/03/28, Private, Mustered Out 01/10/1866.
Brown, Thomas, Recruit, 1863/08/19, Private, Mustered Out 01/10/1866.
Brubaker (aka Brabaker), Hiram, Recruit, 1864/09/05, Private, Mustered Out 07/20/1865.
Bryant, John, Private, 1861/07/24, Private, Died 07/30/1862 at Baton Rouge, LA.
Campbell, Lewis E., Recruit, 1863/06/22, Corporal, Mustered Out 01/10/1866.
Campbell, William A. or William, Recruit, 1863/06/09, Private, Mustered Out 10/05/1865.
Carpenter, Robert, Recruit, 1863/07/08, Private, Mustered Out 10/05/1865.
Carter, Jasper, Private, 1861/07/24, Private, Veteran; Mustered Out 01/10/1866.
Coffeen, George N., Recruit, 1864/03/21, Corporal, Mustered Out 01/10/1866.
Collier, Caleb L., Recruit, 1863/09/13, Private, Died 10/08/1864 at New Orleans, LA.
Colvin (aka Calvin), Daniel, Recruit, 1863/06/29, Private, Died 05/08/1864 at New Orleans, LA.
Compton, Jonathan, Private, 1861/07/24, Private, Mustered Out 07/31/1864.
Compton, Samuel M., Private, 1861/07/24, Corporal, Mustered Out 01/10/1866.
Compton, Thomas M., Private, 1861/07/24, 2nd Lieutenant, Veteran; Promoted 2nd Lieutenant 07/26/1864; Resigned 07/24/1865.
Cosby, John W., Recruit, 1863/12/32, Private, Mustered Out 01/10/1866.
Cox, Chambers, Private, 1861/07/24, Captain, Promoted 2nd Lieutenant 01/01/1863; Promoted 1st Lieutenant 06/26/1863; Promoted Captain 07/26/1864; Mustered Out 01/10/1866..
Cox, Clayton, 2nd Lieutenant, 1861/07/24, Captain, Promoted Captain 01/01/1863; Mustered Out 07/25/1864.
Cox, Green, Private, 1861/07/24, Private, Veteran; Mustered Out 01/10/1866.
Cox, William R., Recruit, 1864/03/03, Private, Mustered Out 01/1.

Crank, William, Recruit, 1863/07/14, Private, Mustered Out 01/10/1866.

Daniels (aka Daniel), William A., Recruit, 1863/12/29, Private, Died 05/01/1864 at New Orleans, LA

Davis, Levi H., Recruit, 1864/10/05, Private, Mustered Out 10/05/1865.

Davis, Russell P., Recruit, 1864/02/29, Corporal, Mustered Out 01/10/1866.

Day, David F. (aka David T.), Private, 1861/07/24, Private, Mustered Out 07/31/1864.

Dickenson, James L., Recruit, 1864/10/05, Private, Mustered Out 10/05/1865.

Dooley, Moses, Musician, 1861/07/24, Musician, Discharged 10/20/1862, Disability.

Duncan, Martin V. (aka Martin N.), Recruit, 1864/01/02, Bugler, Mustered Out 01/10/1866.

Duncan, William E., Corporal, 1861/07/24, Corporal, Discharged 04/10/1862, Disability.

Eakin (aka Eaken), Leander, Recruit, 1864/03/18, Private, Mustered Out 01/10/1866.

Eggers, William, Private, 1861/07/24, Sergeant, Veteran; Mustered Out 01/10/1866.

Elkin (aka Ekins, Elkens, Elkins), Elijah M., Recruit, 1863/08/08, Private, *Deserted 08/14/1865.*

Elliott, Charles, Private, 1861/07/24, Private, Died 08/15/1862 of Wounds Received at Battle of Baton Rouge, LA.

Elliott, William R., Private, 1861/07/24, 2nd Lieutenant, Veteran; Promoted 2nd Lieutenant; Mustered Out 01/10/1866..

Faulkner, Lemuel, Private, 1861/07/24, Private, Transferred to 1st U.S. Artillery 03/01/1863.

Faurote (ala Faurot), Jacob H., Recruit, 1863/10/28, Private, Mustered Out 01/10/1866.

Faux (aka Fawx, Fox), Charles P. (aka Charles B.), Recruit, 1864/09/03, Private, Mustered Out 07/20/1865.

Feasel (aka Feazel, Frazel), James, Private, 1861/07/24, Private, Died 09/01/1861 at Baltimore, MD.

Feathering (aka Fethering), Obediah, Recruit, 1864/09/05, Private, Mustered Out 07/20/1865.

Fellows, Henry, Recruit, 1864/09/05, Private, Mustered Out 07/20/1865.

Finn, Jeremiah, Recruit, 1862/06/01, Private, Mustered Out 06/01/1865.

Fisher, Lewis D. (aka Lewis O.), Private, 1861/07/24, Private, Veteran; Discharged 08/19/1865, Disability.

Fisher, William H. or W.H., Private, 1861/07/24, Private, Veteran; Mustered Out 01/10/1866.

Fox, Joseph, Private, 1861/07/24, Private, Died 07/03/1862 at Baton Rouge, LA.

Fox, Lewis T. (aka Taylor), Private, 1861/07/24, Private, Discharged 10/20/1862, Disability.

Fry, Fountain M., Recruit, 1864/03/08, Private, Mustered Out 01/10/1866.

Fry, William, Corporal, 1861/07/24, Sergeant, Veteran; Mustered Out 01/10/1866.

Fry, George W., Corporal, 1861/07/24, Corporal, Died of Wounds Received at Battle of Baton Rouge, LA, 08/05/1862.

Gamble, James O., Recruit, 1864/03/13, Private, Died 03/26/1965 at New Orleans, LA.

Garrison, William, Private, 1861/07/24, Private, Discharged 09/18/1861 by Order of War Department.

Gooch, Claibourne (aka Claiboune), Private, 1861/07/24, Private, Wounded at Battle of Baton Rouge, LA; Veteran; Mustered Out 01/10/1866.

Gooch, Francis M., Recruit, 1863/06/09, Private, Died 03/29/1864 at New Orleans, LA.

Gooch, James, Recruit, 1863/06/08, Private, Died 10/24/1864 at Indianapolis, IN.

Gooch, John H., Recruit, 1863/06/08, Private, Mustered Out 01/10/1866.

Gooch, Philip, Recruit, 1863/12/02, Private, Mustered Out 01/10/1866.

Goolman, Jacob H., Private, 1861/07/24, Sergeant, Veteran; Died 07/05/1865 at Mobile, AL.

Griffin, John, Private, 1861/07/24, Private, Wounded at Battle of Baton Rouge, LA; Veteran: Deserted while on Veteran Furlough, March 1864.

Griggs, John M., Private, 1861/07/24, Private, Mustered Out 07/31/1864.

Griggs, Richard W., Sergeant, 1861/07/24, Private, Wounded at Battle of Baton Rouge, LA; Reduced; Mustered Out 07/31/1864.

Grinstead (aka Grimstead, Grinsteed), Thomas, 1st Lieutenant, 1861/07/24, 1st Lieutenant, Died at New Orleans, LA, in 1862 of Wounds Received at Battle of Baton Rouge, LA.

Grinstead (aka Grimstead), Thomas F. (aka Thomas Frank), Private, 1861/07/24, Private, Wounded at Battle of Baton Rouge, LA; Veteran: Mustered Out 01/10/1866.

Hadley, Eli, Recruit, 1864/03/03, Corporal, Mustered Out 01/10/1866.

Hall, Zachariah, Private, 1861/07/24, Sergeant, Died 07/23/1864 at New Orleans, LA.

Hammons (aka Hammeons, Hammon, Hammonds), Lemuel, Private, 1861/07/24, Private, Discharged 04/10/1862, Disability.

Haney, Henry, Recruit, 1864/09/28, Private, Mustered Out 07/20/1865.

Harlan (aka Harlen), Jesse R. (aka Jasper R., Jesse K., Joseph R.), Private, 1861/07/24, Private, Killed in Action at Battle of Baton Rouge, LA, 08/05/1862.

Harmon (aka Harman, Hameon), Jacob, Recruit, 1864/09/17, Private, Mustered Out 07/20/1865.

Harris, Allen W. (aka Allen H.), Recruit, 1863/08/20, Private, Discharged 11/01/1865, Disability.

Hastings (aka Hasting), John R., Private, 1861/

07/24, Private, Died 08/01/1862 at Baton Rouge, LA.

Hendricks (aka Hendrick), John J., Private, 1861/07/24, Sergeant, Veteran; Mustered Out 01/10/186.

Hess, Jacob, Captain, 1861/07/24, Captain, Resigned April, 1862.

Hill, Harmon, Wagoner, 1861/07/24, Wagoner, Discharged 10/26/1861, Disability.

Hobbs, William C., Recruit, unknown, Private, Died 04/23/1864 at New Orleans, LA.

Hobson, Aaron, Recruit, 1864/01/14, Private, Died 01/14/1865 at New Orleans, LA.

Hoover, Henry, Private, 1861/07/24, Private, Veteran; Mustered Out 01/10/1866.

Horner, Joseph M., Recruit, 1864/01/07, Private, Died 04/09/1864 at Pleasant Hill, LA.

Hudson, George, Private, 1861/07/24, Private, Veteran; Mustered Out 01/10/1866.

Hutchison (aka Hutcheson, Hutchinson), Alexander, Private, 1861/07/24, Private, Discharged 10/20/1862, Disability.

Ingle, John K. (aka John R.), Recruit, 1864/02/04, Private, Accidentally Drowned 03/15/1865 in Mobile Bay, AL.

Jackman, William A., Recruit, 1863/03/09, Private, Died 11/09/1864 at Andersonville, IN.

Johnson, Albert, Recruit, 1864/02/04, Private, Mustered Out 01/10/1866.

Jones, Cyryl C. (aka Cyrus), Recruit, 1864/03/26, Corporal, Mustered Out 01/10/1866.

Jones, Jesse M., Private, 1861/07/24, Private, Wounded at Battle of Baton Rouge, LA; Discharged 04/20/1863, Disability.

Keener (aka Kivner), John A., Recruit, 1864/03/23, Private, Mustered Out 01/10/1866.

Kelly, Samuel, Recruit, 1863/10/31, Private, Mustered Out 01/10/1866. Died 07/06/1865 at New Orleans, LA.

Kelly (aka Kelley), Timothy, Recruit, 1863/12/01, Private, Discharged 06/15/1865, Disability.

Kent, Thomas, Private, 1861/07/24, Private, Veteran; Mustered Out 01/10/1866.

Kepley (aka Kiply), John, Recruit, 1864/03/23, Private, *Deserted 08/04/1865.*

Kerr, Andrew J., Recruit, 1863/03/09, Private, Deserted and Returned; Mustered Out 01/10/1866.

Kersey (aka Korry), Jonathan, Private, 1861/07/24, Private, Discharged 01/26/1862 Disability.

Keveney (aka Keeveny, Keoney, Keveny), John, Recruit, 1863/05/20, Private, Transferred to Company L 03/23/1865; Mustered Out 01/10/1866.

Kiphart (aka Kipheart), Isaac, Private, 1861/07/24, Private, Died 08/24/1862 of Wounds Received at Battle of Baton Rouge, LA.

Kirkendall, Elias, Recruit, 1863/06/20, Private, Mustered Out 01/10/1866.

Kiser, William, Private, 1861/07/24, Corporal, Veteran: Mustered Out 01/10/1866.

Knowland, David, Private, 1861/07/24, Musician, Discharged 09/30/1865, Disability.

Lacy (aka Lacey), Jesse, Recruit, 1864/01/02, Private, Mustered Out 01/10/1866.

Larimore (aka Laramore), William, Private, 1861/07/24, Corporal, Discharged 09/23/1862, of Wounds Received at Battle of Baton Rouge, LA..

Leitzman (aka Lutzman), William (aka William L., Corporal, 1861/07/24, Corporal, Discharged 04/10/1862, Disability.

Little, Halstead, Recruit, 1864/03/17, Private, Transferred to Company F 05/05/1864; Mustered out 01/10/1866.

Majors (aka Major), James, Private, 1861/07/24, Private, Discharged 11/14/1861, Disability.

Marion, Harrison R., Recruit, 1864/09/09, Private, Mustered Out 07/20/1865.

Mathews, Seth, Private, 1861/07/24, 1st Lieutenant, Promoted 2nd Lieutenant 06/11/1864; Promoted 1st Lieutenant 02/17/1865; Veteran; Mustered Out 01/10/1866..

Matthews (aka Mathews), Hiram B., Recruit, 1864/03/28, Private, Mustered Out 01/10/1866.

Maxwell, William C., Private, 1861/07/24, Corporal, Mustered Out 07/31/1864.

McCarty (aka McCarthy), Lemuel, Private, 1861/07/24, 2nd Lieutenant, Promoted 2nd Lieutenant 02/17/1865; Veteran; Mustered Out 01/10/1866..

McClay, Zachariah T., Recruit, 1864/09/17, Private, Mustered Out 07/20/1865.

McCown (aka McCowan), Jacob, Private, 1861/07/24, Corporal, Veteran; Mustered Out 01/10/1866.

McCown (aka McCowan), James, Private, 1861/07/24, Private, Veteran; Mustered Out 01/10/1866.

McGlothlin (aka McGlauglin, McGlothlen, McLothlin, McLaughlin), Robert A. (aka Robert W.), Recruit, 1864/01/18, Private, Mustered Out 01/10/1866.

McPherson, Henry, Recruit, 1864/03/04, Corporal, Mustered Out 01/10/1866.

Miller, James, Recruit, 1862/01/14, Private, Discharged 11/01/1864, Disability.

Miller, Lewis, Recruit, 1864/09/03, Private, Mustered Out 07/20/1865.

Mills, Nelson T., Recruit, 1864/09/22, Private, Mustered Out 07/20/1865.

Monical, James W. (aka James M.), Sergeant, 1861/07/24, Sergeant, Discharged 12/15/1861, Disability.

Moore (aka More), James D. (aka James I., James T.), Recruit, 1863/12/24, Sergeant, Mustered Out 01/10/1866. Discharged 06/15/1865, Disability.

Mority (aka Morialty), John, Recruit, 1864/09/05, Private, Mustered Out 01/10/1866.
Morrow, William, Recruit, 1864/03/01, Private, Mustered Out 01/10/1866.
Mosier (aka Masier, Moriet), Adam B., Private, 1861/07/24, Private, Veteran; Mustered Out 01/10/1866.
Mosier (aka Moriet), James R., Recruit, 1864/03/29, Private, Mustered Out 01/10/1866.
Murray, Charles, Recruit, 1863/08/10, Corporal, Mustered Out 01/10/1866.
Napier, William, Recruit, 1864/01/18, Private, Mustered Out 01/10/1866.
Nelson, John W., Recruit, 1864/03/14, Private, Mustered Out 01/10/1866.
Newton, Martin V., Recruit, 1863/09/13, Private, Mustered Out 07/20/1865.
Northern, George R., Recruit, 1863/08/18, Private, Died 03/08/1864 at New Orleans, LA.
O'Brien (aka O'brian), Michael, Recruit, 1864/09/22, Private, Mustered Out 07/20/1865.
Olds, Francis M., Private, 1861/07/24, Private, Discharged 03/31/1862, Disability.
Olds, Harrison (aka Harrison W., H. Harrison, Henry H., Henry Harrison), Corporal, 1861/07/24, 1st Lieutenant, Promoted 2nd Lieutenant 01/26/1863; Promoted 1st Lieutenant 03/30/1864; Honorably Discharged 06/11/1864, due to Disability from Wounds Received at Battle of Baton Rouge.
Parker, Joseph, Private, 1861/07/24, Private, Discharged 10/26/1861, Disability.
Pearce (aka Pierce), Alfred V., Private, 1861/07/24, Corporal, Mustered Out 07/31/1864. Discharged 10/03/1864, Disability.
Pierce, Thomas V. (aka Thomas N.), Recruit, 1864/09/14, Private, Mustered Out 07/20/1865.
Pitcher, William, Private, 1861/07/24, Private, Killed in Action at Battle of Baton Rouge, LA 08/05/1862.
Pogue (aka Pogul, Pougue), Isaac, Recruit, 1863/12/27, Private, Mustered Out 01/10/1866.
Powell (aka Pomell), Osias, Recruit, 1963/07/11, Private, Mustered Out 01/10/1866.
Powers, Silas, Private, 1861/07/24, Private, Veteran; Mustered Out 01/10/1866.
Rasure (aka Razure), Amazar (aka Amazor), Private, 1861/07/24, Corporal, Veteran; Discharged 10/31/1864, Disability.
Rasure (aka Rasner, Razure), George W., Recruit, 1864/03/01, Private, *Deserted 06/23/1864.*
Record, Perry, Private, 1861/07/24, Sergeant, Veteran; Mustered Out 01/10/1866.
Rhea, Robert H., Private, 1861/07/24, 1st Lieutenant, Promoted 2nd Lieutenant, Company L 06/30/1863; Promoted 1st Lieutenant Company L 12/23/1863; Discharged 07/26/1863 (?).
Rhea, William L., Sergeant, 1861/07/24, 1st Lieutenant, Promoted 2nd Lieutenant 03/31/1864; Promoted 1st Lieutenant 07/26/1864; Resigned 12/28/1865..
Risley, Benjamin, Private, 1861/07/24, Corporal, Veteran; Discharged 05/12/1864, Disability.
Robbins, Theodore, Private, 1861/07/24, Private, Discharged 03/26/1862, Disability.
Robertson, James T., Recruit, 1864/07/07, Private, Discharged 05/19/1865, Disability.
Rooker, William A. (aka William N.), Recruit, unknown, Private, Died 05/26/1864 at Baton Rouge, LA.
Rosier (aka Rozier), William A., Recruit, 1864/09/23, Private, Mustered Out 07/20/1865.
Ruhe (aka Ruhes), Charles (aka Jacob), Recruit, unknown, Private, Mustered Out 01/10/1866.
Sailors, Jacob S., Recruit, 1864/03/09, Artificer, Mustered Out 01/10/1866.
Scott, John W., Recruit, 1864/01/30, Private, Discharged 06/15/1865, Disability.
Sears, William B., Recruit, 1864/03/08, Private, Mustered Out 01/10/1866.
Sellars (aka Sillans), Abyijah, Recruit, 1864/03/08, Private, Mustered Out 01/10/1866.
Sellers (aka Sellars), Richard, Private, 1861/07/24, Private, Veteran; Discharged 11/01/1865, Disability.
Seward, Albert B., Recruit, 1863/11/18, Sergeant, Mustered Out 01/10/1866.
Sheets (aka Sheetz), Harrison, Corporal, 1861/07/24, Corporal, Transferred to 1st U.S. Artillery 03/01/1863.
Shell, Charles, Private, 1861/07/24, Corporal, Veteran; Mustered Out 01/10/1866.
Shepherd (aka Shepard, Sheperd, Sheppard), Joel, Private, 1861/07/24, Private, Veteran; Mustered Out 01/10/1866.
Shoemaker, Harrison, Private, 1861/07/24, Private, Mustered Out 07/31/1864.
Simpson, William C., Private, 1861/07/24, Private, Discharged 10/26/1861, Disability.
Skelton, Allen H., Recruit, 1864/09/19, Private, Mustered Out 07/20/1865.
Skelton, Samuel W., Recruit, 1864/09/03, Private, Mustered Out 07/20/1865.
Small, John, Recruit, 1864/03/23, Private, Mustered Out 01/10/1866.
Smith, Charles, Recruit, 1863/07/06, *Deserted 09/28/1865.*
Snoddy (aka Shoddy, Snaddy), Harvey M., Private, 1861/07/24, Private, Wounded at Battle of Baton Rouge, LA; Died 04/22/1864 at New Orleans, LA.
Spoor (aka Sors), William O. (aka William B.), Recruit, 1864/03/09, Artificer, Mustered Out 01/10/1866.
Spurling (aka Spulin. Spurlin), Joshua, Recruit, 1863/12/29, Private, Mustered Out 01/10/1866.
Stacy (aka Stacey), Edgar, Private, 1861/07/24, Private, Mustered Out 07/31/1864.

St. Cloud, Edgar, Recruit, 1864/03/26, Private, *Deserted 06/17/1865.*

Stafford, Benjamin B., Recruit, 1863/11/29, Private, Mustered Out 07/20/1865.

Stafford, William H., Private, 1861/07/24, Sergeant, Veteran; Mustered Out 01/10/1866.

Stark, Hiram S. (aka Hiram T.), Recruit, 1862/02/25, Private, Discharged 10/12/1862, Disability.

Stiner (aka Stimer), Jacob H., Recruit, 1864/03/16, Private, Mustered Out 01/10/1866.

Stines, Andrew, Recruit, 1863/06/23, Private, Died 04/04/1864 at New Orleans, LA.

Stout, William A., Recruit, 1864/09/15, Private, Mustered Out 07/20/1865.

Strader, Brantley, Private, 1861/07/24, Private, Veteran; Discharged 08/07/1865, Disability. Mustered Out 07/31/1864.

Swain, Clinton D., Recruit, 1864/03/03, Private, Mustered Out 01/10/1866.

Tharp (aka Thorp), Nathan, Recruit, 1863/09/17, Private, Mustered Out 07/20/1865.

Tharpe (aka Tharp, Thorp), Lorenzo, Private, 1861/07/24, Private, Transferred to 1st U.S. Artillery 03/01/1863.

Thomas, Allen, Private, 1861/07/24, Private, Veteran; Mustered Out 01/10/1866.

Thomas, George W., Recruit, 1864/03/01, Private, Mustered Out 01/10/1866.

Townsend (aka Townsand), James M., Recruit, 1862/06/01, Private, Mustered Out 06/01/1865.

Treon (aka Treeon, Trerow, Trevie), Francis J., Recruit, 1863/12/08, Private, Mustered Out 01/10/1866.

Trusty, John A., Recruit, 1863/08/01, Private, Mustered Out 01/10/1866.

VanLeu (aka Vanlew), William T., Recruit, 1864/01/15, Private, Died 04/21/1864 at New Orleans, LA.

Vanvalkenburgh (aka Vanvalkenburg), Alfred H., Musician, 1861/07/24, Private, Died 04/29/1862 at Ship Island, MS.

Voss, William D., Recruit, 1864/01/07, Private, Discharged 06/18/1864, Disability.

Wagal (aka Wigal, Wigel), John W., Private, 1861/07/24, Private, Mustered Out 07/31/1864.

Walker, Phillip, Recruit, 1864/08/09, Private, Mustered Out 05/15/1865.

Wall, Garret, Sergeant, 1861/07/24, 1st Lieutenant, Promoted 1st Lieutenant 06/11/1864; Honorably Discharged 02/16/1865.

Ward, Lewis B., Recruit, 1864/03/23, Private, Mustered Out 01/10/1866.

Welsham (aka Welshans, Welshnes), William, Recruit, 1864/10/03, Private, Mustered Out 10/05/1865.

West, Fletcher (aka John F., John T), Recruit, 1864/09/14, Private, Died 10/18/1865 at Fort Gaines, AL.

Wexler, George B., Recruit, 1864/10/03, Private, Mustered Out 10/05/1865.

Whited (aka Whiten, Whitted), William C., Recruit, unknown, Private, Mustered Out 01/10/1866.

Whitney, Francis H. (aka Francis X.), Recruit, 1864/01/30, Private, *Deserted 08/04/1865.*

Wilcox (aka Willcox), William H., Recruit, 1864/09/15, Private, Mustered Out 07/20/1865.

Wilcoxon (aka Wilcoxan, Wilcoxen, Wilcoxen), John S., Recruit, 1864/03/23, Private, Mustered Out 01/10/1866.

Williams, William R., Recruit, 1864/09/17, Private, Mustered Out 07/20/1865.

Wilson, Calvin J., First Sergeant, 1861/07/24, 1st Lieutenant, Resigned 06/25/1863.

Winters, Hannibal, Private, 1861/07/24, Private, Mustered Out 07/31/1864.

Wood, John, Private, 1861/07/24, Sergeant, Veteran; Mustered Out 01/10/1866.

Worle (aka Worl), Henry C., Recruit, 1864/03/23, Private, Mustered Out 01/10/1866.

Worle, Joseph, Recruit, 1864/09/07, Private, Mustered Out 07/20/1865.

Wright, James M., Private, 1861/07/24, Corporal, Veteran; Mustered Out 01/10/1866.

Wright, Joseph H., Recruit, 1864/09/13, Private, Mustered Out 07/20/1865.

Wright, Richard, Private, 1861/07/24, Quartermaster Serg't., Veteran; Mustered Out 01/10/1866.

Yates, Spencer W., Recruit, 1863/08/10, Private, Mustered Out 01/10/1866.

Company L

Achenback (aka Achenbach), Herman, Private, 1863/08/12, Private, Discharged 12/04/1863, Disability.

Aldridge, John L., Private, 1863/08/12, Private, Mustered Out 01/10/1866.

Alford, James, Private, 1863/08/12, Private, Mustered Out 01/10/1866.

Antis (aka Austis), Jacob, Recruit, 1864/10/03, Private, Mustered Out 10/12/1865.

Arbuckle (aka Arbucle), James, Recruit, 1864/10/03, Private, Mustered Out 08/12/1865.

Baird, William, Private, 1863/08/12, Private, Mustered Out 01/10/1866.

Ballard, William, Private, 1863/08/12, Private, Discharged 09/05/1865, Disability.

Barker, George W., Private, 1863/08/12, Private, Mustered Out 01/10/1866.

Bedsaul, John H. (aka John S.), Recruit, 1864/10/30, Private, Substitute; Deserted 09/05/1865.

Benson, Levi G., Quartermaster Sergeant, 1863/08/12, 1st Lieutenant, Promoted 2nd Lieutenant 09/09/1864; Promoted 1st Lieutenant 03/01/1865; Mustered Out 01/10/1866..

Black, George H., 1st Lieutenant, 1863/08/12, 1st Lieutenant, Resigned 12/23/1863.
Bookwalter, John W. (aka George W.), Private, 1863/08/12, Private, Discharged 12/31/1863, Disability.
Booth (aka Boothe), Daniel J., Private, 1863/08/12, Private, *Deserted 10/11/1865.*
Bradford (aka Brooford), Joseph, Private, 1863/08/12, Private, *Deserted 09/05/1865.*
Brady, Carthon J., Recruit, 1864/03/09, Private, Mustered Out 01/10/1866.
Brady, Edward W., Recruit, 1864/02/25, Private, Mustered Out 04/20/1865.
Branham (aka Branhan), James, Private, 1863/08/12, Private, Mustered Out 01/10/1866.
Brewer, Thomas J., Private, 1863/08/12, Corporal, Mustered Out 01/10/1866.
Bridges, Lycurgus, Private, 1863/08/12, Private, *Deserted 08/01/1865.*
Bridges, Virgil, Private, 1863/08/12, Private, *Deserted 08/01/1865.*
Brown, Asbury, Recruit, 1864/10/07, Private, Mustered Out 10/12/1865.
Brown (aka Broun), John, Private, 1863/08/12, Private, Discharged 05/28/1865, Disability.
Brown, Peter T., Private, 1863/08/12, Private, Mustered Out 01/10/1866.
Brown, William T. (aka William F.), Recruit, 1864/09/09, Private, Died at Indianapolis, IN; Date Unknown.
Browning, Jeremiah, Private, 1863/08/12, Private, *Deserted 08/01/1865.*
Busby, James W., Recruit, 1864/02/02, Corporal, Discharged 11/21/1865, Disability.
Butler, William M., Private, 1863/08/12, Private, Mustered Out 01/10/1866.
Cashner, John, Private, 1863/08/12, Private, *Deserted 08/03/1864.*
Chambers, Joseph, Private, 1863/08/12, Private, Mustered Out 01/10/1866. Crist (aka Christ), Robert H., Private, 1863/08/12, Captain, Promoted 2nd Lieutenant 10/21/1863; Promoted 1st Lieutenant 09/09/1864; Promoted Captain 03/01/1865; Mustered Out 01/10/1866..
Clark, Ephraim, Recruit, 1864/06/08, Private, Discharged 11/27/1865, Disability.
Clary (aka Cleary), Tipton D., Private, 1863/08/12, 1st Lieutenant, Promoted 2nd Lieutenant 12/23/1863; Promoted 1st Lieutenant 09/09/1864; Mustered Out 01/10/1866..
Coble (aka Cable), William, Private, 1863/08/12, Corporal, Mustered Out 01/10/1866.
Collins, Jerome B., Private, 1863/08/12, Private, *Deserted 08/01/1865.*
Colvin (aka Calvin), Henry M., Recruit, 1863/08/12, Private, Mustered Out 01/10/1866.
Conklin, Morton G. (aka Martin G.), Private, 1863/08/12, Private, Discharged 08/03/1864, Disability.
Conner (Conery), Thomas E., Recruit, 1863/12/24, Private, Unaccounted For..
Crane, Franklin, Private, 1863/08/12, Private, Mustered Out 01/10/1866.
Crawford, Nathaniel J., Private, 1863/08/12, Corporal, Mustered Out 01/10/1866.
Dailey (aka Daily), Patrick, Private, 1863/08/12, Private, Deserted 08/18/1863. Mustered Out 09/08/1865.
Daulby, Wesley, Private, 1863/08/12, Private, Mustered Out 01/10/1866.
Davis, Edward, Recruit, 1864/10/06, Private, Mustered Out 10/12/1865.
Davis, James W., Private, 1863/08/12, Private, *Deserted 08/18/1863.*
Davis, Lloyd, Recruit, 1864/10/03, Private, Mustered Out 10/12/1865.
Davis, Nicholas, Private, 1863/08/12, Private, Mustered Out 01/10/1866.
Davis, Temple S., Private, 1863/08/12, Private, Mustered Out 01/10/1866.
Davison, Joseph, Private, 1863/08/12, Private, Died 10/14/1864 of disease.
Day, Libbeus, Recruit, 1864/10/03, Private, Mustered Out 10/12/1865.
Dempsey, Harbud (aka Harbred), Private, 1863/08/12, Private, Died 11/04/1863.
Denney (aka Denny), Ransom, Recruit, 1864/10/04, Private, Mustered Out 10/12/1865.
Dennis, Charles A., Private, 1863/08/12, Private, Died 03/29/1864.
Dermit (aka Durmit), Josiah, Private, 1863/08/12, Private, Discharged 11/20/1865, Disability.
Deyo, Aaron, Private, 1863/08/12, Private, Died 09/11/1863.
Dinkens (aka Dinkins), James, Private, 1863/08/12, Private, Mustered Out 01/10/1866.
Dorn, Richard, Private, 1863/08/12, Private, Discharged 12/10/1863.
Dower, James, Private, 1863/08/12, Private, Died 10/06/1864.
Driskill, Andrew J., Recruit, 1864/09/18, Private, Mustered Out 10/12/1865.
Edwards, Jeremiah, Private, 1863/08/12, Private, Died 01/17/1865 of disease.
Elliott, William W., Corporal, 1863/08/12, Private, *Reduced; Deserted 08/18/1865.*
Emerson (aka Emmerson), William, Recruit, 1864/09/07, Private, Mustered Out 10/12/1865.
Eves, William D., Private, 1863/08/12, Sergeant, Discharged 11/20/1865, Disability.
Farrell, Patrick, Private, 1863/08/12, Private, *Deserted 08/18/1863.*
Ferris (aka Farris), John, Private, 1863/08/12, Private, Mustered Out 01/10/1866.
Finegan (aka Finnegan, Finnigan), John, Recruit, 1864/10/03, Private, Mustered Out 10/12/1865.
Forsythe, Thomas J., Musician, 1863/08/12, First Sergeant, Mustered Out 01/10/1866.

Gaston (aka Goston, Guston), Asbury H., Private, 1863/08/12, Private, Mustered Out 01/10/1866.

Golliher, John D., Recruit, 1864/09/08, Private, Mustered Out 07/27/1865.

Graviley (aka Graveley), James H. (aka James M.), Recruit, 1863/05/25, Private, Unaccounted For..

Graves (aka Gravis), Irving, Recruit, 1864/05/17, Corporal, Mustered Out 01/10/1866.

Greer (aka Gree), John H., Private, 1863/08/12, Private, Died 05/08/1864 at Indianapolis, IN.

Gregory, John, Recruit, 1864/02/03, Private, Mustered Out 01/10/1866.

Gunn, William S., First Sergeant, 1863/08/12, Q'-master Serg't., Discharged 02/28/1865, Disability.

Guy, Leonard, Private, 1863/08/12, Private, Not Recorded.

Hall, James E., Recruit, 1864/10/04, Private, Mustered Out 10/24/1865.

Hallam, Thomas, Recruit, 1864/09/005, Private, Mustered Out 01/10/1866.

Hancock, Milton, Private, 1863/08/12, Private, Mustered Out 01/10/1866.

Harding, William H., Private, 1863/08/12, Private, *Deserted 08/18/1863.*

Harrold (aka Harold, Herolld), Jacob W., Private, 1863/08/12, Private, Mustered Out 01/10/1866.

Harry, Daniel, Private, 1863/08/12, Private, *Deserted 07/28/1864.*

Hays (aka Hayse), Charles W., Corporal, 1863/08/12, Private, *Reduced; Deserted 06/25/1865.*

Heath, George A. (aka George H.), Private, 1863/08/12, Private, Mustered Out 01/10/1866.

Hellwig (aka Helwig), William H., Private, 1863/08/12, Private, Mustered Out 01/10/1866.

Hendricks, Caleb G., Private, 1863/08/12, Bugler, Mustered Out 01/10/1866.

Hendricks, Isaac C., Captain, 1863/08/12, Major, Promoted Major 02/03/1865; Mustered Out 02/03/1866.

Hensley, Adolphus H., Private, 1863/08/12, Private, Died 09/16/1863 of disease.

Hewitt, Frank, Recruit, 1864/09/16, Private, Mustered Out 07/27/1865.

Highfield, Benjamin, Private, 1863/08/12, Private, *Deserted 08/13/1863.*

Hosier, Joshua, Private, 1863/08/12, Private, Mustered Out 01/10/1866.

Howard, Henry C., Private, 1863/08/12, Sergeant, Mustered Out 01/10/1866.

Jackson, Marshall, Private, 1863/08/12, Private, Died 07/06/1864.

Jacobs, Milton C., Private, 1863/08/12, Private, *Deserted 02/26/1865.*

Johnson, Timothy D, Private, 1863/08/12, Private, Drowned 11/18/1863 at Baton Rouge, LA.

Joseph, Mark, Corporal, 1863/08/12, 2nd Lieutenant, Promoted 2nd Lieutenant 03/01/1865; Mustered Out 09/15/1865, Disability.

Kelley (aka Kelly), John W., Private, 1863/08/12, Private, *Deserted 11/01/1865.*

Kinsley, Noah, Recruit, 1863/11/12, Private, Mustered Out 12/19/1865.

Kirby, Franklin, Private, 1863/08/12, Private, Mustered Out 01/10/1866.

Kirk, Edward S., Private, 1863/08/12, Corporal, Mustered Out 01/10/1866.

Knauner (aka Knauer, Krauer), John, Recruit, 11863/10/03, Private, Mustered Out 10/12/1865.

Koon, Calvin, Private, 1863/08/12, Private, *Deserted 08/01/1865.*

Kratzer (aka Krotzer), Samuel, Private, 1863/08/12, Private, Mustered Out 01/10/1866.

Leach, Charles H., Private, 1863/08/12, Bugler, Mustered Out 01/10/1866.

Lemaitre (aka LeMair), Victor, Private, 1863/08/12, Private, *Deserted 08/18/1865.*

Leonard, Calvin, Recruit, unknown, Private, Mustered Out 10/12/1865.

Leonard (aka Lenard), Guy, Sergeant, 1863/08/12, Private, *Reduced; Deserted 09/05/1864.*

Leonard, John C., Recruit, 1864/09/08, Private, Unaccounted For..

Lewis, Moses, Private, 1863/08/12, Private, *Deserted 08/01/1865.*

Lien (aka Lieus), Jackson, Recruit, 1864/09/08, Private, Unaccounted For..

Linsday (aka Lindsay), William, Recruit, 1864/02/05, Private, Mustered Out 10/12/1865.

Lively, William R., Corporal, 1863/08/12, Private, Died 03/03/1864 at Matagorda Island, TX.

Long (aka Lang), Francis, Corporal, 1863/08/12, Private, Reduced; Mustered Out 01/10/1866.

Ludlow, Levi N., Private, 1863/08/12, Private, Mustered Out 01/10/1866.

Luzader, Barton, Private, 1863/08/12, Private, Mustered Out 01/10/1866.

Lyons (aka Liens, Lions), Andrew J., Recruit, 1864/09/08, Private, Mustered Out 10/12/1865.

Mann (aka Manns), George W., Private, 1863/06/19, Private, Transferred to Company K 06/19/1863; Mustered Out 01/10/1866.

Marshall (aka Martiall), Jonithan S., Private, 1863/08/12, Corporal, Mustered Out 01/10/1866.

Massena, Adam H., Musician, 1863/08/12, Sergeant, Mustered Out 01/10/1866.

Matthews (aka Mathews, Matthew), John T., Recruit, 1864/10/09, Private, Mustered Out 10/12/1865.

McCarty, James, Private, 1863/08/12, Private, *Deserted 12/20/1863.*

McClure, Jacob S., Private, 1863/08/12, Private, Mustered Out 01/10/1866.

McClure (aka McLure), James R., Private, 1863/08/12, Corporal, Discharged 08/25/1865, Disability.

McCormack (aka McCormick), James A., Private, 1863/08/12, Sergeant, Mustered Out 01/10/1866.

McGarvin (aka McGarran, McGavern, McGavran, McGavren, McGovran), Francis, Private, 1863/08/12, Private, *Deserted 08/01/1865.*

McMillan (aka McMillen, McMillin), Charles, Private, 1863/08/12, Private, Mustered Out 01/10/1866.

Miller, Eli, Private, 1863/08/12, Private, *Deserted 08/01/1865.*

Miller, Eli, Private, 1863/08/12, Private, *Deserted 08/18/1865.*

Miller, William, Sergeant, 1863/08/12, Artificer, Mustered Out 01/10/1866.

Mobley, John L., Private, 1863/08/12, Corporal, Mustered Out 01/10/1866.

Morgan, Andrew C., Private, 1863/08/12, Private, Discharged 11/20/1865, Disability.

Morgan, George W., Private, 1863/08/12, Private, Mustered Out 01/10/1866.

Morgan, Martin L., Private, 1863/08/12, Private, Died 12/09/1865 at Fort Pickens (Pensacola), FL.

Nash, John S., Private, 1863/08/12, Private, *Deserted June, 1865, While on Furlough.*

Newby (aka Newly), John, Private, 1863/08/12, Private, Died 12/07/1863 of Disease.

Norton, Isaac N., Private, 1863/08/12, Corporal, Mustered Out 01/10/1866.

Parker, James, Private, 1863/08/12, Private, Mustered Out 01/10/1866.

Parker, James C., Private, 1863/08/12, Private, *Deserted 06/25/1865.*

Parker, John G., Sergeant, 1863/08/12, 2nd Lieutenant, Promoted 2nd Lieutenant 09/09/1864; Mustered Out 01/10/1866..

Phillips (aka Philips), Asa, Recruit, 1864/09/29, Private, Mustered Out 01/10/1866.

Pibbles (aka Pibles), Charles, Recruit, 1864/10/06, Private, Mustered Out 10/12/1865.

Posthumous (aka Postdums, Posthumnus, Posthumus), John, Private, 1863/08/12, Private, Transferred to Company G; Found Dead Near Baton Rouge, LA 05/30/1865.

Powell, Charles, Recruit, 1864/09/10, Private, Mustered Out 07/27/1865.

Powers, Thomas, Recruit, 1863/05/28, Private, Mustered Out 01/10/1866.

Pugh, Evan, Private, 1863/08/12, Private, Mustered Out 01/10/1866.

Reusch (aka Rensch), William, Recruit, 1864/10/15, Private, Mustered Out 01/10/1866.

Richwine, James H. (aka James L., James P.), Recruit, 1864/09/07, Private, Mustered Out 10/12/1865.

Rigney, Willis G., Recruit, 1863/07/22, Private, *Deserted 07/27/1865.*

Roback, Albert G., Private, 1863/08/12, Corporal, Mustered Out 01/10/1866.

Robbins (aka Robins), Christopher C., Private, 1863/08/12, Sergeant, Mustered Out 01/10/1866.

Roberts, Carroll K., Private, 1863/08/12, Private, *Deserted 06/25/1865.*

Roberts, Logan W., Corporal, 1863/08/12, Private, Reduced; Discharged 03/28/1865, Disability.

Rollins, Andrew, Private, 1863/08/12, Private, Mustered Out 01/10/1866.

Sanders (aka Saunders), William R., Private, 1863/08/12, Private, Transferred to Company K, March 1865; Mustered Out 01/10/1866.

Schwenheart (aka Schuienhart, Schweinhart, Schweinheart, Schweinhort), Andrew, Private, 1863/08/12, Private, Mustered Out 01/10/1866.

Seagraves, Mark C., Corporal, 1863/08/12, Corporal, *Deserted 08/03/1864.*

Seay, Jeremiah, Private, 1863/08/12, Private, Discharged 11/20/1865, Disability.

Server, Elliott S., Private, 1863/08/12, Private, Mustered Out 01/10/1866.

Seward (aka Steward), Augustus N., Recruit, 1864/02/05, Private, Mustered Out 01/10/1866.

Sharp (aka Sharpe), James L., Private, 1863/08/12, Private, Mustered Out 01/10/1866.

Slider (aka Slyder), George W., Wagoner, 1863/08/12, Private, *Reduced; Deserted 06/25/1865.*

Smith, Charles A., Private, 1863/08/12, Private, Transferred to Company K, 12/23/1864.

Smith, James, Private, 1863/08/12, Private, *Deserted February, 1865.*

Springer, Thomas W., Musician, 1863/08/12, Private, *Reduced; Deserted 08/02/1865.*

Sprow (aka Sporr, Spow), George W., Private, 1863/08/12, Private, Mustered Out 01/10/1866.

Spurrier (aka Spurrer), Dennis (aka Denis), Private, 1863/08/12, Corporal, Mustered Out 01/10/1866.

St. John, Robert, Private, 1863/08/12, Private, Mustered Out 01/10/1866.

Stanley (aka Standley), Lewis F., Private, 1863/08/12, Private, Mustered Out 01/10/1866.

Steambarger (aka Steamborger, Steenbarger, Steinburger, Stenbarger), Alexander, Private, 1863/08/12, Private, Died 10/24/1864 of Disease.

Steward, Henry B., Sergeant, 1863/08/12, Private, Mustered Out 01/10/1866.

Stider (aka Slider), Peter, Recruit, 1864/10/08, Private, Mustered Out 10/12/1865.

Stirk, David P., Artificer, 1863/08/12, Artificer, Mustered Out 01/10/1866.

Stumpf, Joseph, Recruit, 1864/10/07, Private, Mustered Out 10/12/1865.

Swing, Simpson, Recruit, 1864/10/03, Private, Mustered Out 10/12/1865.

Thomas, Richard W. (Richard M.), Recruit, 1864/02/03, Private, Discharged 06/18/1865, Disability.

Thornburg (aka Thornberg), Theophilus, Recruit, unknown, Private, Mustered Out 07/27/1865.

Todd, John H., Recruit, 1863/06/03, Private, *Deserted 06/25/1865.*

Tousey (aka Towsey), Omer, Private, 1863/08/12, 2nd Lieutenant, Promoted 2nd Lieutenant of Company C, 04/18/1864; Discharged 02/07/1865 for the Good of the Service.

Trogdon (aka Trogden), Benjamin F., Recruit, 1864/02/09, Private, Mustered Out 01/10/1866.

Vroman (aka Vrooman, George A., Recruit, 1864/09/27, Private, Mustered Out 10/12/1865.

Ward, Alexander, Private, 1863/08/12, Private, Mustered Out 01/10/1866.

Ward, James E., Private, 1863/08/12, Private, Mustered Out 01/10/1866.

Waterman, William T., Private, 1863/08/12, Private, Died 04/24/1865 of Disease.

Weaver, Andrew, Private, 1863/08/12, Private, Died 04/07/1864 of disease.

Weaver, Edwin M., Private, 1863/08/12, Private, Discharged 08/26/1865, Disability.

Weston, Thomas, Recruit, 1863/06/01, Private, Discharged 11/23/1864, Disability.

White, Oliver B., Private, 1863/08/12, Private, Mustered Out 01/10/1866.

Whitenger (aka Whitinger), John, Private, 1863/08/12, Private, *Deserted 07/27/1865.*

Williams (aka Willians), Arthur H., Private, 1863/08/12, Sergeant Major, Mustered Out 01/10/1866.

Williams, Joseph B. (aka James B.), Recruit, 1864/09/05, Private, Mustered Out 07/27/1865.

Wilson, John, Private, 1863/08/12, Private, *Deserted 08/18/1863.*

Wilson, John A., Private, 1863/08/12, Corporal, Mustered Out 01/10/1866.

Wilson, Thomas, Private, 1863/08/12, Private, Mustered Out 01/10/1866.

Wires, Columbus H., Recruit, 1864/10/03, Private, Mustered Out 10/12/1865.

Wires, Robert H., Recruit, 1864/10/03, Private, Mustered Out 10/12/1865.

Wise, Christopher, Private, 1863/08/12, Private, Mustered Out 01/10/1866.

Wise, Joshua M., Private, 1863/08/12, Private, Mustered Out 01/10/1866.

Wooten (aka Woolen, Wooton, Worton), Enoch, Private, 1863/08/12, Private, Mustered Out 01/10/1866.

Wooten (aka Wooton), James H., Private, 1863/08/12, Private, Discharged 12/04/1863, Disability.

Worle (aka Worl), John, Private, 1863/08/12, Private, Mustered Out 01/10/1866.

Young, David, Private, 1863/08/12, Sergeant, Died 08/12/1865 of Disease.

Yount, Thomas J., Corporal, 1863/08/12, Quartermaster Sergeant, Mustered Out 01/10/1866.

Company M

Altenburg (aka Alltenburg, Altonburg), Daniel W., Private, 1863/11/01, Private, Mustered Out 10/23/1865.

Altenburg (aka Alltenburg, Altonburg), Henry E., Private, 1863/11/01, Private, Mustered Out 10/23/1865.

Altenburg (aka Alltenburg, Altonburg), Isaac L., Private, 1863/11/01, Private, Mustered Out 10/23/1865.

Andrews, James H., Private, 1863/11/01, Private, Mustered Out 01/10/1866.

Andrews, William C., Recruit, 1863/12/07, Private, Mustered Out 01/10/1866.

Ashley, Joseph, Private, 1863/11/01, Private, Mustered Out 01/10/1866.

Austill (aka Anstill, Austell), William H., Private, 1863/11/01, Private, Mustered Out 01/10/1866.

Banman (aka Bauman), Andrew L. (aka Andrew S.), Private, 1863/11/01, Private, Discharged 09/20/1864, Disability.

Barnes (aka Barns), Abraham, Recruit, 1864/09/23, Private, Mustered Out 07/27/1865.

Barnhill (aka Burnhill), Anderson J. (aka Andrew J.), Recruit, 1864/09/20, Private, Mustered Out 07/27/1865.

Bastnagel (aka Bactnagel, Bastnagle), Joseph, Private, 1863/11/01, Private, Mustered Out 01/10/1866.

Bates, James E., Private, 1863/11/01, Private, Discharged 11/01/1865 by Civil Authority.

Bilby (aka Belby), Thomas F., Corporal, 1863/11/01, 2nd Lieutenant, Promoted 2nd Lieutenant 03/01/1865; Promoted 1st Lieutenant 07/03/1865; Mustered Out 01/10/1866 as 2nd Lieutenant..

Bindschadler (aka Bindschandler), John, Private, 1863/11/01, Q'master Serg't., Mustered Out 01/10/1866.

Boyd, Albert, Recruit, 1864/09/29, Private, Mustered Out 01/10/1866.

Boyd, Robert J., Private, 1863/11/01, Private, *Deserted 11/05/1864 at Indianapolis, IN.*

Bright, James C., Recruit, 18654/08/31, Private, Mustered Out 01/10/1866.

Britton (Britten), Alfred D., Private, 1863/11/01, Private, Died 09/07/1864 by Incision of Neck, Made by Himself.

Browne (aka Brown), George W., Private, 1863/11/01, Private, Mustered Out 01/10/1866.

Browning, William, Corporal, 1863/11/01, Private, Reduced; Mustered Out 01/10/1866.

Bullock, William W., Private, 1863/11/01, Private, Mustered Out 01/10/1866.

Calhoun, Joseph A., Recruit, 1864/09/19, Private, Mustered Out 07/27/1865.

Campbell, Alexander, Private, 1863/11/01, Private, Mustered Out 01/10/1866.

Carpenter, Allen, Private, 1863/11/01, Private, Mustered Out 01/10/1866.

Carr, Roland T., Private, 1863/11/01, Private, Mustered Out 01/10/1866. Cart, George W., Private, 1863/11/01, Corporal, Mustered Out 01/10/1866.

Coffer (aka Coffen), Joseph, Private, 1863/11/01, Private, Mustered Out 01/10/1866.
Compton, Alpheus G. (aka Alpheus C.), Private, 1863/11/01, Sergeant, Mustered Out 01/10/1866.
Cooper, John R., Private, 1863/11/01, Private, Discharged 08/29/1864, Disability.
Crull, Abner D. (aka Albert D.), Private, 1863/11/01, Private, Mustered Out 01/10/1866.
Curry (aka Currey), John L. (aka John C.), Private, 1863/11/01, Corporal, Mustered Out 01/10/1866.
Cutsinger, Edmond, Private, 1863/11/01, Private, Deserted 07/05/1865, from Confinement at Fort Pickens, FL.
Daniels, Edward B., Private, 1863/11/01, Private, Mustered Out 01/10/1866.
Davis, George M. D., Private, 1863/11/01, Private, Mustered Out 01/10/1866.
Devol, Clark, Private, 1863/11/01, Private, Discharged 12/01/1864, a Minor.
Dickey, Alfred, Private, 1863/11/01, Private, Mustered Out 01/10/1866.
Dines, William, Private, 1863/11/01, Private, Mustered Out 01/10/1866.
Dodds (aka Dods), Thompson, Private, 1863/11/01, Private, Mustered Out 01/10/1866.
Ellis, William, Private, 1863/11/01, Private, Discharged 06/12/1865.
Ellison, Franklin, Corporal, 1863/11/01, Private, Reduced; Mustered Out 01/10/1866.
Fahrion (aka Fabrion), Christian, Private, 1863/11/01, Private, Mustered Out 01/10/1866.
Finney, Charles D., Corporal, 1863/11/01, Corporal, Mustered Out 01/10/1866.
Fisher (aka Fistin), Charles, Private, 1863/11/01, Sergeant, Mustered Out 01/10/1866.
Frey, John, Private, 1863/11/01, Private, Discharged 06/12/1865, Disability.
Furguson (aka Ferguson), Harvey P. (Harry R.), Private, 1863/11/01, Private, Mustered Out 01/10/1866.
Gaines, William C., Recruit, 1864/09/21, Private, Discharged 06/10/1865, Disability.
Gaines, William H., Private, 1863/11/01, Private, Died 09/26/1864 on Train Near Terre Haute, IN.
Galloway (aka Gallaway), Harvey, Recruit, 1864/03/02, Sergeant, Mustered Out 01/10/1866.
Gard, James F., Sergeant, 1863/11/01, Private, Reduced; Mustered Out 01/10/1866.
Gibbons, Joseph, Sergeant, 1863/11/01, Private, Reduced; Mustered Out 01/10/1866.
Gimbel (aka Gimble), Jacob, Private, 1863/11/01, Private, Died 09/02/1864 at New Orleans, LA.
Golding, Andrew J., Private, 1863/11/01, Corporal, Mustered Out 01/10/1866.
Golding, Thomas, Recruit, 1864/09/05, Private, Mustered Out 07/27/1865.
Graves, Highland, Recruit, 1864/09/12, Private, Mustered Out 07/27/1865.
Green, Alfred, Private, 1863/11/01, Private, Mustered Out 01/10/1866.
Gunning, Alfred M., Private, 1863/11/01, Private, Mustered Out 01/10/1866.
Harney, Lewis C., Private, 1863/11/01, Private, Mustered Out 01/10/1866.
Harsh, George W., Private, 1863/11/01, Private, *Deserted 05/23/0864.*
Hart, Oliver S. (aka Oliver L.), Private, 1863/11/01, Private, Mustered Out 01/10/1866.
Hey, Jacob, Private, 1863/11/01, Private, Mustered Out 01/10/1866.
Higer (aka Higher), Martin V. (aka Martin H.), Private, 1863/11/01, Private, Transferred to V.R.C., 1864.
Hilligoss (aka Hillegoss), Daniel W., Private, 1863/11/01, Private, Mustered Out 01/10/1866.
Holden, John L., Corporal, 1863/11/01, Sergeant, Mustered Out 01/10/1866.
Holsten (aka Holston), John B. (aka John R.), Private, 1863/11/01, Private, Mustered Out 01/10/1866.
Hoover, John B., Private, 1863/11/01, Private, Died 04/02/1865.
Hughes, James, 1st Lieutenant, 1863/11/01, 1st Lieutenant, Promoted Captain 07/13/1865; Mustered Out 01/10/1866..
Hull, Absalom D., Recruit, 1864/10/04, Private, Mustered Out 10/10/1865.
Humphrey (aka Humphry), Lewis M., Private, 1863/11/01, Private, Mustered Out 01/10/1866.
Hunt, John S. John L.), Private, 1863/11/01, Private, Discharged 09/06/1865, Disability.
Hyatt, Milton, Private, 1863/11/01, Private, Died 10/25/1864 at New Orleans, LA.
Jaycox (aka Jacox), George, 2nd Lieutenant, 1863/11/01, 2nd Lieutenant, Resigned.
Jennings, Nelson C. (aka Wilson C.), Musician, 1863/11/01, Musician, Mustered Out 01/10/1866.
Johnson (aka Johnston), Squire, Private, 1863/11/01, Private, Mustered Out 01/10/1866.
Jones, Daniel S., Private, 1863/11/01, Private, Mustered Out 01/10/1866.
Karel (aka Karl, Karrel, Krael), William, Recruit, 1864/08/01, Private, Mustered Out 01/10/1866.
Kennedy (aka Kenedy), Napoleon B., Private, 1863/11/01, Artificer, Mustered Out 01/10/1866.
Keppel, John, Corporal, 1863/11/01, Private, Reduced; Mustered Out 01/10/1866.
Kinney (aka Kinny), Cornelius, Private, 1863/11/01, Private, Died 08/10/1864 on Steamer Empress.
Krietz (aka Kreity, Kreitz, Kritz), Peter, Private, 1863/11/01, Private, Mustered Out 01/10/1866.
Larimore (aka Laramore, Larrimore), Silas, Private, 1863/11/01, Private, Deserted 06/24/1865. Mustered Out 01/10/1866..

Lathrop, Jesse, Private, 1863/11/01, Private, Mustered Out 01/10/1866.

Leach, James, Private, 1863/11/01, Private, Mustered Out 01/10/1866.

Lodge, Oliver, Private, 1863/11/01, Private, Mustered Out 01/10/1866.

Luker (aka Laker), John, Private, 1863/11/01, Private, Mustered Out 01/10/1866.

Lyman (aka Lynman, Lynan), Robert, Private, 1863/11/01, Private, *Deserted 06/24/1865.*

Lyons (aka Farrell, Laynes), John A., Private, 1863/11/01, Private, *Deserted 08/08/1864.*

Maholm (aka Maholn, Maholen), John R., Corporal, 1863/11/01, Corporal, Mustered Out 01/10/1866.

Maier (Mair), William G., Sergeant, 1863/11/01, Q'master Sergeant., Discharged 10/24/1865, Disability.

Marcy (aka Marcey), David, Private, 1863/11/01, Private, Mustered Out 01/10/1866.

Markland (aka Marklind), Mathew, Private, 1863/11/01, Private, Mustered Out 01/10/1866.

McBurney, Jacob, Private, 1863/11/01, Private, Mustered Out 01/10/1866.

McCalla, Thomas P., Recruit, 1864/09/14, Private, Mustered Out 07/27/1865.

McCoombs, James, Private, 1863/11/01, Private, Mustered Out 01/10/1866.

McCoy, William H., Private, 1863/11/01, Private, Died 06/07/1864 of typhoid at Baton Rouge, LA.

McDaniel (aka McDaniels), William, Private, 1863/11/01, Private, Died 12/29/1863 at New Orleans, LA.

McDaniels (aka McDaniel), Harvey, Recruit, 1864/10/05, Private, Mustered Out 10/12/1865.

McGee (aka Migee), William (aka William H.), Private, 1863/11/01, Private, Discharged 09/28/1865, Disability.

McKee, William E., Private, 1863/11/01, Private, *Deserted 06/24/1865.*

McKenney (aka McKinney, McKinsey), George, Recruit, 1864/10/08, Private, Mustered Out 10/12/1865.

McKinney, Abraham, Private, 1863/11/01, Private, Mustered Out 01/10/1866.

McKinney, William, Private, 1863/11/01, Private, Discharged 06/12/1865, Disability.

McKinney Jr., John, Private, 1863/11/01, Private, Mustered Out 01/10/1866.

McKinney Sr., John, Private, 1863/11/01, Private, Mustered Out 01/10/1866.

McMachon (aka McMachan, McMahon, McMahan), David J., Private, 1863/11/01, Private, Mustered Out 01/10/1866.

Miller, George W. (aka George N.), Private, 1863/11/01, Private, Died 05/02/1864 of typhoid at Baton Rouge, LA.

Miller, James M., Private, 1863/11/01, Private, Mustered Out 01/10/1866.

Miller, Phillip, Private, 1863/11/01, Private, *Deserted 02/24/1865.*

Miller, Robert H., Corporal, 1863/11/01, Corporal, Mustered Out 01/10/1866.

Mitchell, David G., Private, 1863/11/01, Private, Mustered Out 01/10/1866.

Mitchell, Hezekiah, Private, 1863/11/01, Private, Mustered Out 01/10/1866.

Mixon (aka Nixon), James, Artificer, 1863/11/01, Artificer, Mustered Out 01/10/1866.

Moore, Edward, Private, 1863/11/01, Corporal, Mustered Out 01/10/1866.

Morgan, Oliver A., Private, 1863/11/01, Private, *Deserted 11/05/1863.*

Murray (aka Murry), Jesse C., Corporal, 1863/11/01, Sergeant, Mustered Out 01/10/1866.

Myers, Alfred W., Private, 1863/11/01, Private, Died 09/08/1864 at New Orleans, LA.

Nelson, George F., Private, 1863/11/01, Private, Mustered Out 01/10/1866.

Newcomer, Henry D., Private, 1863/11/01, Private, Died 04/07/1864 of typhoid at Baton Rouge, LA.

Newell, Jason L., Private, 1863/11/01, Private, Mustered Out 01/10/1866.

Newman, James, Private, 1863/11/01, Private, Mustered Out 01/10/1866.

Parrett, Baptist (aka Battest, Battiste), Recruit, 1863/09/22, Private, *Deserted 08/08/1864.*

Payton, William, Private, 1863/11/01, Private, Mustered Out 01/10/1866.

Petri (aka Petry), John, Private, 1863/11/01, Private, Discharged 09/27/1865, Disability.

Petry, William, Private, 1863/11/01, Private, Discharged 11/15/1865, Disability.

Phelps, John W., Private, 1863/11/01, Private, Mustered Out 01/10/1866.

Pinney (aka Penney, Penny), Edward M., Sergeant, 1863/11/01, 2nd Lieutenant, Promoted 2nd Lieutenant 03/02/1865; Mustered Out 01/10/1866.

Polk, James T., Private, 1863/11/01, Corporal, Mustered Out 01/10/1866.

Pollitt (aka Pollett), Erastus Q. (aka Erastus N.), Private, 1863/11/01, Private, Mustered Out 01/10/1866.

Pope, James, Private, 1863/11/01, Private, Died 09/11/1864 at New Orleans, LA.

Pounds, Anderson, Private, 1863/11/01, Private, Mustered Out 01/10/1866.

Priest, Benjamin L., Private, 1863/11/01, Private, Mustered Out 01/10/1866.

Pugh, Rue, Private, 1863/11/01, Private, Mustered Out 01/10/1866.

Rhodes (aka Rhoads), William H., Private, 1863/11/01, Wagoner, Mustered Out 01/10/1866.

Rice, James M., First Sergeant, 1863/11/01, Private, *Reduced; Deserted 01/07/1865.*

Richards, Lewis, Private, 1863/11/01, Corporal, Mustered Out 01/10/1866.

Ritchey (aka Richey), William, Private, 1863/11/01, Private, Mustered Out 01/10/1866.

Robinson (aka Robbinson, Robison), Andrew J., Recruit, 1864/10/04, Private, Died 06/28/1865 at Mobile, AL.

Runshe (aka Reushe), Abraham, Private, 1863/11/01, Private, Mustered Out 01/10/1866.

Runyon, John, Private, 1863/11/01, Private, Mustered Out 01/10/1866.

Ryan (aka Ryon), William P., Private, 1863/11/01, Private, Mustered Out 01/10/1866.

Sanders, William H.H., Private, 1863/11/01, Private, Discharged 02/01/1864, Disability.

Shurrum (aka Sherman, Sherrem, Sherrum, Shurum, George, Recruit, 1864/10/13, Private, Mustered Out 07/27/1865.

Simmons, Albert A., Corporal, 1863/11/01, Private, Reduced; Mustered Out 01/10/1866.

Simonson, William C., Recruit, 1864/09/19, Private, Mustered Out 07/27/1865.

Sloan (aka Sloane), Abner, Private, 1863/11/01, Private, Died 01/02/1865 at New Orleans, LA.

Smith, Daniel M. (aka Daniel N.), Private, 1863/11/01, Private, *Deserted 06/24/1865*.

Smith, John G., Private, 1863/11/01, Private, Mustered Out 01/10/1866.

Smithers, Joseph, Private, 1863/11/01, Private, Mustered Out 01/10/1866.

Smock, Simon V. (aka Simon H.), Private, 1863/11/01, Wagoner, Died 10/03/1864 at Home (Greenwood, IN?).

Smoot, Benjamin F., Private, 1863/11/01, Private, Mustered Out 01/10/1866.

Sparks, William H., Private, 1863/11/01, Private, Mustered Out 01/10/1866.

Stapleton, Thomas A., Private, 1863/11/01, Private, *Deserted 08/09/1864*.

Stewart (aka Stewert), James, Private, 1863/11/01, Private, Mustered Out 01/10/1866.

Stiner (aka Stener), Daniel J., Private, 1863/11/01, Private, Mustered Out 01/10/1866.

Stiner (aka Stener), Thomas L., Private, 1863/11/01, Private, Mustered Out 01/10/1866.

Stivers (aka Stevens), George W., Private, 1863/11/01, Private, Died 10/14/1864 at New Orleans, LA.

Stott (aka Sotte, Stottes), Jacob, Private, 1863/11/01, Private, Mustered Out 01/10/1866.

Swanger (aka Swauger), Henry T., Musician, 1863/11/01, Musician, Discharged 11/01/1865, Disability.

Thomas, Lewis, Private, 1863/11/01, Private, Mustered Out 01/10/1866.

Thompson, Joseph W., Private, 1863/11/01, Private, Deserted 07/25/1865 from Confinement at Fort Pickens, FL (Pensacola).

Tindel (aka Tindle), John W. (aka John M.), Private, 1863/11/01, Sergeant, Mustered Out 01/10/1866.

Treese (aka Trees, Truce), Caleb, Private, 1863/11/01, Private, Discharged 06/17/1865, Disability.

Trickett, Mont, Q'master Sergeant, 1863/11/01, Private, Reduced; Mustered Out 01/10/1866.

Vannetten (aka Vanetten), John, Private, 1863/11/01, Private, *Deserted 11/05/1863*.

Vanpelt, Aaron F., Sergeant, 1863/11/01, Private, Reduced; Mustered Out 01/10/1866.

Walker, James A., Sergeant, 1863/11/01, First Sergeant, Promoted 2nd Lieutenant 07/13/1865; Mustered Out 01/10/1866 as 1st Sergeant. Mustered Out 01/10/1866.

Warner, John C., Private, 1863/11/01, Private, Mustered Out 01/10/1866.

White, Thomas, Recruit, 1864/09/28, Corporal, Mustered Out 01/10/1866.

Wilcoxon (aka Wilcox, Wilcoxen, Willcoxen, Willcoxon), Thomas, Private, 1863/10/02, Private, Mustered Out 01/10/1866.

Williams, Henry (aka Harry), Private, 1863/11/01, Private, Deserted 10/20/1865.

Williamson, Stephen, Recruit, 1864/09/14, Private, Mustered Out 07/27/1865.

Wilson, Thomas, Private, 1863/11/01, Private, Mustered Out 01/10/1866.

Wolf (aka Wolfe), William, Corporal, 1863/11/01, Private, Reduced; Mustered Out 01/10/1866.

Woodard (aka Woodward), John, Private, 1863/11/01, Private, Died 09/02/1864 at New Orleans, LA.

Workman, George A. (aka George W.), Private, 1863/10/07, Private, *Deserted 06/24/1865*.

Zimmerman, Jacob B.F., Corporal, 1863/11/01, Private, Reduced; Mustered Out 01/10/1866.

Unassigned Recruits

Albaugh, Philip M., Recruit, No Record In Terrell.

Armstrong, John, Recruit, 1864/08/31, Unaccounted For as per Terrell.

Austin, Thomas, Recruit, 1864/09/29, Unaccounted For as per Terrell.

Bailey (aka Bagley), Willis, Recruit, 1864/09/02, Unaccounted For as per Terrell.

Benefiel, William, Recruit, 1864/09/05, Unaccounted For as per Terrell.

Benjamin, John, Recruit, 1864/09/07, Unaccounted For as per Terrell.

Benton, George A., Recruit, 1864/09/03, Unaccounted For as per Terrell.

Beussenmeiller, Chas. Fred, Recruit, No Record In Terrell.

Bois, William H., Recruit, 1863/08/25, Unaccounted For as per Terrell.

Bolin, Allan, Recruit, No Record In Terrell.

Booher, Alpheus, Recruit, No Record In Terrell.

Booher, James A., Recruit, No Record In Terrell.

Bostner, Andrew, Recruit, No Record In Terrell.
Bowden, John, Recruit, No Record In Terrell.
Brennan (aka Bremen), Robert, Recruit, 1864/09/26, Unaccounted For as per Terrell.
Britton, Erasmus, Recruit, 1864/09/02, Unaccounted For as per Terrell.
Brown, Peter, Recruit, 1864/10/01, Unaccounted For as per Terrell.
Brown, William, Recruit, 1864/09/15, Unaccounted For as per Terrell.
Brown, William E. G., Recruit, No Record In Terrell.
Brown, William F., Recruit, 1864/09/09, Private, Died at Indianapolis, IN, date not stated.
Buff, Nathaniel G., Recruit, 1864/10/04, Private, Mustered Out 05/15/1865.
Burdy (aka Burdge), Eli, Recruit, 1864/10/03, Unaccounted For as per Terrell.
Burns, Julius, Recruit, No Record In Terrell.
Butler, Thomas, Recruit, 1864/09/02, Unaccounted For as per Terrell.
Byers, James C., Recruit, 1864/02/07, Unaccounted For as per Terrell.
Calvin, Daniel, Recruit, No Record in Terrell.
Clarke, Joseph, Recruit, No Record in Terrell.
Coles, Charles, Recruit, 1864/10/04, Unaccounted For as per Terrell.
Cougleton, Newton H., Recruit, No Record in Terrell.
Cowgill, Tarvin W., Recruit, 1864/10/01, Unaccounted For as per Terrell.
Cretors, Milton, Recruit, No Record in Terrell.
Crichfield, David, Recruit, No Record in Terrell.
Cunningham, John, Recruit, 1864/09/13, Unaccounted For as per Terrell.
Dale, George W., Recruit, No Record in Terrell.
Davis, Edwin, Recruit, No Record in Terrell.
Davis, George W., Recruit, 1864/09/07, Unaccounted For as per Terrell.
Davis, William R., Recruit, No Record in Terrell.
Dimon (aka Dimion), Arthur, Recruit, 1863/09/05, Private, Died 09/28/1863 at Baton Rouge, LA.
Doe, Henry W., Recruit, 1864/10/06, Unaccounted For as per Terrell.
Dowden, Morris R., Recruit, 1864/10/07, Unaccounted For as per Terrell.
Duncan, John, Recruit, No Record in Terrell.
Dwyer, Michael, Recruit, No Record in Terrell.
Edmondson, James, Recruit, No Record in Terrell.
Farmer, Isaac, Recruit, No Record in Terrell.
Fisher, John R., Recruit, 1862/11/13, Unaccounted For as per Terrell.
Fisher, William, Recruit, No Record in Terrell.
Fitzgerald, Patrick, Recruit, 1864/09/07, Unaccounted For.
Forkner, Jesse, Recruit, No Record in Terrell.
Forrister (aka Forrester), George, Recruit, 1864/09/17, Unaccounted For as per Terrell. Fritz, Patrick, Recruit, No Record in Terrell.
Fuller, Stephen, Recruit, 1864/09/17, Unaccounted For as per Terrell.
Furguson (aka Ferguson), James, Recruit, 1864/09/05, Unaccounted For as per Terrell.
Gay, Joseph, Recruit, No Record in Terrell.
Golden, William, Recruit, 1864/09/22, Unaccounted For as per Terrell.
Goodwin, Isaiah, Recruit, 1863/08/10, Unaccounted For as per Terrell.
Green, John, Recruit, 1864/09/07, Unaccounted For as per Terrell.
Greene, Charles, Recruit, 1864/09/29, Unaccounted For as per Terrell.
Guthrie, James, Recruit, 1864/09/17, Private, Mustered Out 05/15/1865.
Hall, Samuel W., Recruit, No Record In Terrell.
Hamor (aka Hanor, Harior), David, Recruit, 1863/06/11, Unaccounted For as per Terrell.
Harris, Thomas B., Recruit, 1864/09/17, Unaccounted For as per Terrell.
Harrison, James, Recruit, 1864/09/29, Unaccounted For as per Terrell.
Henkel, Joseph, Corporal, No Record in Terrell.
Henry, John G., Recruit, 1864/09/17, Unaccounted For as per Terrell.
Hess, Loren, Recruit, 1865/09/30, Unaccounted For as per Terrell.
Hicks, Graham, Recruit, Unaccounted For as per Terrell.
Higgins, Williams, Recruit, No Record in Terrell.
Hire, William, Recruit, No Record In Terrell.
Hollern, William, Recruit, 1864/09/07, Unaccounted For as per Terrell.
Holtman, John H., Recruit, No Record In Terrell.
Hood, Lamar, Recruit, No Record In Terrell.
Horn (aka Harn), John D., Recruit, 1864/09/29, Unaccounted For as per Terrell.
Howard, Charles, Recruit, No Record In Terrell.
Howard, James, Recruit, 1862/11/15, Unaccounted For as per Terrell.
Howard, Thomas L. Recruit, 1863/09/09, Unaccounted For as per Terrell.
Howard, William, Recruit, No Record In Terrell.
Hough (aka Hughs), John D., Recruit, 1864/09/02, Unaccounted For as per Terrell.
Huckabay (aka Huckabery), John A., Recruit, 1864/09/17, Unaccounted For as per Terrell.
Hunt, George, Recruit, 1864/09/20, Unaccounted For as per Terrell.
Idding (aka Iddings), James H., Recruit, 1864/09/22, Unaccounted For as per Terrell.
Jessup, Samuel, Recruit, 1864/09/24, Unaccounted For as per Terrell
John, James J., Recruit, No Record in Terrell
Johnson, Smith, Recruit, 1863/06/02, Unaccounted For as per Terrell

Johnson, William, Recruit, 1864/09/29, Unaccounted For as per Terrell

Jolliffi, Stephen I., Recruit, 1864/09/24, Unaccounted For as per Terrell.

Jones, John, Recruit, 1864/09/17, Unaccounted For as per Terrell.

Jones, John T., Recruit, No Record in Terrell.

Jones, John W., Recruit, 1863/08/15, Unaccounted For as per Terrell.

Jones, William M., Recruit, 1864/09/29, Unaccounted For as per Terrell

Jordan (aka Jordon), William, Recruit, 1864/10/06, Unaccounted For as per Terrell

Kelly (aka Kelley), Alva C., Recruit, 1864/09/30, Unaccounted For as per Terrell

Kelly, John, Recruit, 1863/08/10, Unaccounted For as per Terrell

Kemper, John L., Recruit, No Record in Terrell

Kendy (aka Kenedy), Morris, Recruit, 1864/09/29, Unaccounted For as per Terrell

Kernan, Edward, Recruit, No Record in Terrell

King, Thomas, Recruit, 1864/09/17, Unaccounted For as per Terrell.

King, William S., Recruit, unknown, Unaccounted For as per Terrell.

Knable, John, Recruit, No Record in Terrell.

Lambert, Henry, Recruit, 1864/09/17, Unaccounted For as per Terrell.

LaWell (aka Lawell), Frank, Recruit, 1864/09/17, Unaccounted For as per Terrell

Lewis, Henry, Recruit, 1864/10/07, Unaccounted For as per Terrell.

Long, Henry J., Recruit, 1864/10/25, Unaccounted For as per Terrell.

Lough, Jackson, Recruit, No Record in Terrell.

Louthan, James, Recruit, No Record in Terrell.

Lucas, Benjamin W., Recruit, No Record in Terrell.

Lynch, Robert, Recruit, Unaccounted For as per Terrell.

Mahan, William A., Recruit, No Record in Terrell.

Martin, John, Recruit, 1864/09/03, Unaccounted For as per Terrell.

Mathews, Thomas, Recruit, No Record in Terrell.

McFarland, William, Recruit, 1864/09/17, Unaccounted For as per Terrell.

McGrath (aka McGath), Thomas, Recruit, 1864/09/24, Unaccounted For as per Terrell.

Mead, George, Recruit, No Record in Terrell.

Medsker, William, Recruit, 1863/10/02, Unaccounted For as per Terrell.

Metz, George, Recruit, 1863/09/22, Unaccounted For as per Terrell.

Miller, David E., Recruit, No Record in Terrell.

Miller, Frederick, Recruit, 1864/10/03, Unaccounted For as per Terrell.

Miller, John C., Recruit, No Record in Terrell.

Mills, Charles A., Recruit, No Record in Terrell.

Monty, John, Recruit, No Record in Terrell.

Moore, Charles C. (aka Charles H.), Recruit, 1863/05/29, Unaccounted For as per Terrell.

Morrison, Henry, Recruit, 1863/05/15, Unaccounted For as per Terrell.

Morton, Isaac M., Recruit, No Record in Terrell.

Murphy, Benjamin W., Recruit, No Record in Terrell.

Nash, James, Recruit, 1864/09/14, Unaccounted For as per Terrell.

Newcomer, William, Recruit, 1864/09/24, Unaccounted For as per Terrell.

O'Brian, John, Recruit, 1864/10/06, Unaccounted For as per Terrell.

Owen, Austin W., Recruit, No Record in Terrell.

Owen, Daniel D., Recruit, No Record in Terrell.

Parker, Thomas, Recruit, 1864/09/17, Unaccounted For as per Terrell.

Petree, James A., Recruit, No Record in Terrell.

Polute (aka Pottut), Jesse, Recruit, 1864/02/19, Unaccounted For as per Terrell.

Price, James, Recruit, No Record in Terrell.

Prichard, James, Recruit, 1864/08/31, Unaccounted For as per Terrell.

Reece, George E., Recruit, 1864/09/06, Unaccounted For as per Terrell.

Reed, George (aka George D., George I.), Recruit, 1864/09/24, Private, Mustered Out 05/15/1865.

Reynolds, Joseph H., Recruit, 1864/09/29, Unaccounted For as per Terrell.

Riggs, Staley D., Recruit, No Record in Terrell.

Riley, Peter, Recruit, No Record in Terrell.

Riley, Thomas, Recruit, No Record in Terrell.

Robinson, Henry E., Recruit, 1863/12/30, Unaccounted For as per Terrell.

Rosenbury, Clement F., Recruit, 1863/06/29, Unaccounted For as per Terrell.

Rushton, Leander, Recruit, 1863/06/09, Unaccounted For as per Terrell.

Russell, William P., Recruit, No Record in Terrell.

Ryan, William, Recruit, 1863/04/29, Unaccounted For as per Terrell.

Saiters, Henry, Recruit, No Record in Terrell.

Schaefer, Henry, Recruit, No Record in Terrell.

Schliter, Christian, Recruit, No Record in Terrell.

Shafer, William H., Recruit, 1863/01/20, Unaccounted For as per Terrell.

Smith, Henry W., Recruit, No Record in Terrell.

Snider, Alonzo M.C., Recruit, No Record in Terrell.

Snoddy, Reufus, Recruit, No Record in Terrell.

Spellman (aka Speelman), Soloman, Recruit, 1864/10/06, Unaccounted For as per Terrell.

Stall, Lewis, Recruit, 1863/09/08, Unaccounted For as per Terrell.

Stark, David P., Recruit, No Record in Terrell.

Strain, John, Recruit, No Record in Terrell.

Sullivan, Henry, Recruit, 1864/09/27, Unaccounted For as per Terrell.

Sullivan, James, Recruit, 1864/09/09, Unaccounted For as per Terrell.
Thompson, Charles, Recruit, No Record in Terrell.
Thompson, James, Recruit, 1864/09/24, Unaccounted For as per Terrell.
Tomlinson, James W., Recruit, 1864/09/02, Unaccounted For as per Terrell.
Ward, Amos H., Recruit, No Record in Terrell.
Watkins, William H., Recruit, No Record in Terrell.
Watson, William H., Recruit, 1864/08/31, Unaccounted For as per Terrell.
Wells, Jacob, Recruit, 1864/10/07, Unaccounted For as per Terrell.
West, Thomas J., Recruit, No Record in Terrell.
White, James, Recruit, Unaccounted For as per Terrell.
White, Lewis D., Recruit, 1864/09/08, Unaccounted For as per Terrell.
Wier, Thomas M., Recruit, No Record in Terrell.
Wiese, Anthony, Recruit, No Record in Terrell.
Wilcox, Lovet, Recruit, 1864/10/03, Unaccounted For as per Terrell.
Wilder, Benjamin F., Recruit, No Record in Terrell.
Wilgus, Levi, Recruit, No Record in Terrell.
Williams, John, Recruit, 1864/09/15, Unaccounted For as per Terrell.
Williams, Randolph E., Recruit, 1864/09/30, Unaccounted For as per Terrell.
Williams, William, Recruit, No Record in Terrell.
Wilson, Albert, Recruit, 1864/09/05, Unaccounted For as per Terrell.
Wilson, Thomas, Recruit, 1864/09/10, Unaccounted For as per Terrell.
Winchester, Thomas, Recruit, 1863/09/05, Unaccounted For as per Terrell.
Wright, Hamilton (aka Hamilton), Recruit, 1863/04/21, Unaccounted For as per Terrell.
Wright, William, Recruit, 1864/09/08, Unaccounted For as per Terrell.

NOT RECORDED BY THE INDIANA ADJUTANT GENERAL'S OFFICE OR THE NATIONAL PARK SERVICE / NATIONAL ARCHIVES

Alexander, William J., Private, unknown, Private, Co.E. Unknown — No record in Terrell or Nat'l. Park Service / Nat'l. Archives.
Anderson, Joseph B., Private, unknown, Private, Co.G, Unknown — No record in Terrell or Nat'l. Park Service / Nat'l Archives.
Beach, James C.W., Private, unknown, Private, Co.F. Known — No record in Terrell or Nat'l. Park Service / Nat'l. Archives.
Bernard (aka Burnard), Joseph, Recruit, 1863/08/08, Co.G, Unknown — No record in Terrell or Nat'l. Park Service / Nat'l Archives.
Bryant, William, Recruit, 1863/08/08, Co.G. Unknown — No record in Terrell or Nat'l. Park Service / Nat'l Archives.
Connover (aka Conover), Cornelius (aka Cornelius G), Private, unknown, Private, Co.F, Unknown — No record in Terrell or Nat'l. Park Service / Nat'l. Archive.
Doan, Riley, Private, unknown, Private, Co.F. Unknown — No record in Terrell or Nat'l. Park Service / Nat'l. Archives.
Dunn (aka Donn), John, Recruit, 1863/11/24, Private, Co.G. Unknown — Not recorded in Terrell or National Park Service / National Archives.
Fincher, James G., Private, unknown, Private, Co.G. Unknown — No record in Terrell or Nat'l. Park Service / Nat'l. Archives.
Forsyth, Thomas J., Musician, unknown, First Sergeant, Co.F. Unknown — No record in Terrell or Nat'l. Park Service / Nat'l. Archives.
Frakes, Sarket, Private, unknown, Private, Co.D. Unknown — No record in Terrell or Nat'l. Park Service / Nat'l. Archives.
Gilbert, Ossian A., Private, unknown, Corporal, Co.F. Unknown — No record in Terrell or Nat'l. Park Service / Nat'l. Archives.
Goldsmith, Wilson, Private, unknown, Private, Co.F. Unknown — No record in Terrell or Nat'l. Park Service / Nat'l. Archives.
Goodall (aka Goodell, Goodhull), Alfred, Recruit, 1863/05/05, unknown, Co.G, Unknown — No record in Terrell or Nat'l. Park Service / Nat'l Archives.
Gray, Charles, Recruit, Recruit, 1863/08/08, Private, Co.G, Unknown — No record in Terrell or Nat'l. Park Service / Nat'l Archives.
Grayson, George, unknown, Co.G. Unknown — No record in Terrell or Nat'l. Park Service / Nat'l Archives.
Hall, Edward, Private, unknown, Private, Co.L. Unknown — No record in Terrell or Nat'l. Park Service / Nat'l. Archives.
Herbert, Elsinas, unknown, Co.C. Unknown — No record in Terrell or Nat'l. Park Service / Nat'l. Archives.
Hogan, John, Recruit, 1863/04/21, Private, Co.G, Unknown — No record in Terrell or Nat'l. Park Service / Nat'l Archives.
Howard (aka Houard), Charles F. (aka Charles T.), Recruit, 1864/10/05, Private, Co.B. Unknown — No record in Terrell or Nat'l. Park Service / Nat'l. Archives.
Hughey, Stephen F., Private, unknown, Private, Co.I. Unknown — No record in Terrell or Nat'l. Park Service / Nat'l. Archives.
Hurkle, John, Private, unknown, Private, Co.D. Unknown — No record in Terrell or Nat'l. Park Service / Nat'l. Archives.
Johnson (aka Johnston), Robert F, Recruit, 1863/05/05, unknown, Co.G, Unknown — No record in Terrell or Nat'l. Park Service / Nat'l Archives.

Lambert, Lewis, Recruit, 1863/08/08, Private, Co.G, Unknown—No record in Terrell or Nat'l. Park Service / Nat'l Archives.

Leach (aka Leech), Zedick, Private, unknown, Private, Co.F, Unknown—No record in Terrell or Nat'l. Park Service / Nat'l. Archives.

Maxwell (aka Maxwill), William, Recruit, 1863/04/27, unknown, Co.G, Unknown—No record in Terrell or Nat'l. Park Service / Nat'l Archives.

Michael, H.C., Corporal, unknown, Corporal, Co.A. Unknown—No record in Terrell or Nat'l. Park Service / Nat'l. Archives.

Nortman, Phillip (aka Phillip A.), Private, unknown, Private, Co.D. Unknown—No record in Terrell or Nat'l. Park Service / Nat'l. Archives.

O'Hair (aka O'Hare), Patrick, Recruit, 1863/04/27, Unknown, Co.G, Unknown—No record in Terrell or Nat'l. Park Service / Nat'l Archives.

Popel (aka Pople), John, Ordnance Sergeant, 1863/11/01, Co.M, Unknown—No record in Terrell or Nat'l. Park Service / Nat'l. Archives.

Segnor, John A., Recruit, 1863/04/28, Artificer, Co.A. Unknown—No record in Terrell or Nat'l. Park Service / Nat'l. Archives.

Small, Thomas, Private, unknown, Private, Co.G. Unknown—No record in Terrell or Nat'l. Park Service / Nat'l Archives.

Smith, Calvin J., Corporal, unknown, Sergeant, Co.G, Unknown—No record in Terrell or Nat'l. Park Service / Nat'l Archives. [Probably another name for Calendar J. Smith.]

Spangel (aka Spangle), John A., Private, unknown, unknown, Co.I, Unknown—No record in Terrell or Nat'l .Park Service / Nat'l. Archives.

Stamford, William, Recruit, 1863/08/18, unknown, Co.G, Unknown—No record in Terrell or Nat'l. Park Service / Nat'l Archives.

Stevens, David, Private, unknown, Private, Co.K. Unknown—No record in Terrell or Nat'l. Park Service / Nat'l. Archives.

Taylor, Charles A., unknown, unknown, unknown, Co.L. Unknown—No record in Terrell or Nat'l. Park Service / Nat'l. Archives.

Taylor, John C., Private, unknown, Private, Co.C. Unknown—No record in Terrell or Nat'l. Park Service / Nat'l. Archives.

Temple, William B., Recruit, 1864/04/08, Private, Unknown, Co.G, No record in Terrell or Nat'l. Park Service / Nat'l Archives.

Thomas, John A., Private, unknown, Private, Co.F, Unknown—No record in Terrell or Nat'l. Park Service / Nat'l. Archives.

Water (aka Walters, Waters), Franklin, Recruit, 1863/04/21, unknown, Co.G, Unknown—No record in Terrell or Nat'l. Park Service / Nat'l Archives.

Welch (aka Walsh), Thomas, Recruit, 1863/04/21, Co.G, Unknown—No record in Terrell or Nat'l. Park Service / Nat'l Archives.

Winer, Daniel, unknown, unknown, Private, Co.B. Unknown—No record in Terrell or Nat'l. Park Service / Nat'l. Archives.

PART III: APPENDICES, NOTES, BIBLIOGRAPHY, INDEX

A—Ship Island

INDIANA JACKASS REGIMENT'S LOSSES DUE TO PRIVATION AT SHIP ISLAND

Dead: Josiah R. Davis, 4/30/1862, Patrick Genine, 4/2/1862, John Money (Mooney), 4/20/1862, Alfred H. Vanvalkenburgh, 4/29/1862. Disabled: John M. Alexander, Frank Anderson, Lewis Apple, Martin V. Arnett, Jesse Beck, Thomas Bilderback, Wilfred Cooprider, Jesse G. Hamilton, Lemuel Hammons (Hammonds), Henry Hays, John McConnell, Newton J. Moss (Moses), Francis M. Olds, James M. Phelon, Theodore Robbins, James T. Robertson, Russell P. Robertson, James G. Ryan, Isaac Shell (Sholl, Shull), John J. Shearer (Shear), Willis G. Sherman and Andrew W. Thomas.

B—The Battle of Baton Rouge

UNITS ENGAGED IN BATTLE OF BATON ROUGE, AUG. 5, 1862.
CONFEDERATE ORDER OF BATTLE

FIRST DIVISION (Clark)
Hunt's Brigade
4th Alabama Battalion
31st Alabama
4th Kentucky
5th Kentucky
31st Mississippi
Hudson's battery

Smith's Brigade
15th Mississippi
22nd Mississippi
19th Tennessee
20th Tennessee
28th Tennessee
45th Tennessee
Cobb's battery

SECOND DIVISION (Ruggles)
Thompson's Brigade
35th Alabama
3rd Kentucky
6th Kentucky
7th Kentucky
Sharpshooter battalion

Allen's Brigade
4th Louisiana
9th Louisiana (Boyd's battalion)
30th Louisiana
39th Mississippi, Co. I
Semmes' battery

Source: *Official Records of the Union and Confederate Armies, Series I, Vol. 15*

FEDERAL ORDER OF BATTLE

INFANTRY

9th Connecticut Regiment
14th Maine Regiment
6th Michigan Regiment
4th Wisconsin Regiment

21st Indiana Regiment.
30th Massachusetts Regiment
7th Vermont Regiment

ARTILLERY

2nd Massachusetts (Nims') Battery (six 3.67rifled" bronze guns)
4th Massachusetts (Manning's) Battery (four rifled heavy 12-pounder [4.62" bore] bronze guns, two 12-pounder howitzers)

6th Massachusetts (Everett's) Battery (two 3.67" rifles, four 6-pounder guns)
Improvised Indiana Jackass (Brown's) Battery (three 6-pounder guns)

CAVALRY
2nd Company Massachusetts Cavalry (Magee's)

List of the 21st Indiana Regiment's Casualties at the Battle of Baton Rouge

FIELD OFFICERS
Killed: Adjutant Mathew Latham
Wounded: Lieutenant-Colonel John A. Keith, severely, shoulder.
Major Benjamin F. Hays, in foot.

COMPANY A
Killed:
- 1st Lieut. Charles D. Seely
- Orderly Sergt. John A. Bovington
- Corporal Isaac Knight
- Private Henry T. Bachelor

Wounded:
- Sergt. Harvey B. Hall, severely
- Sergt. Merritt C. Skinner, slightly
- Corporal Elias I. Carroll, severely

Privates:
- Samuel Aingken, severely
- Thomas Cole, severely
- Manias Braugher, slightly
- John N. Hays, slightly
- James Ingram, slightly
- William McCord, severely
- Frederick Sitterlin, severely
- Isaac W. Snyder, slightly
- Daniel T. Smith, severely
- Samuel Shemberger, severely
- Ira I. Woodworth, slightly

Respectfully, E. N. Fisher, 2nd Lieut., Comdg., Company

COMPANY B
Killed: Private Henry H. Ward
Wounded:
- Capt. James Grimsley, Slightly, in Thigh
- Sergt. William Goss, Slightly, in Knee

Privates:
- Joseph Petty, Severely, in Thigh
- Jasper F. White, (Since Died) Mortally, in Thigh
- William Stone, Severely, in Back
- John Keely, Severely, in Mouth
- Abner Tabor, Severely, in Leg
- Eli McDaniels, Severely, in Leg
- John H. Thomas, Slightly in Hip
- Robert G. Smith, Severely in Back
- Simon Steckler, Severely in both Thighs.
  [He was a New Orleans recruit.]
- William Wilkins, Deserted in the Face of the Enemy.

COMPANY C
Whole number engaged:
Lieuts.   2
Enlisted men   42
Killed: Privates: Joel Haywood

	Thomas O. Connor
	Mathias Guisler
Wounded, Mortally:	Corpl. Thomas Ballard
	Private Calvin Haywood.

The Company occupied or were engaged on the right of the Battalion as skirmishers, and assisted in holding in check a flanking regiment of the enemy.

Respectfully, Lieut. William Bough, Comndg. Co.

[Corporal Thomas Ballard was in the Battalion Color Guard and saw action in the center of the regiment. He was shot in the back as the colors withdrew during the Rebel charge against the 21st Indiana's camp. After the battle and before he died, he told his friend, Alfred Danely, Company C, that the advancing Confederates did not step on him as they passed by, but they commented that he was dead or would be dead soon. His spine severed by a bullet, Ballard died on August 7, choking to death on his clotted blood and phlegm. (Danely, Alfred, letter, September 18, 1862.)]

COMPANY D

Commanded by 1st Lieut. William Harper. Capt. Edmiston being in charge of the Guard.

Killed:	Private Gabriel McClure
	Private Valentine Steward
Missing:	Corp. William Purcell [Found 8-6-62; mustered out August 1864, Sgt.]
Wounded:	Orderly Sergt. Joseph Whalen, a flesh wound in thigh
	Corp. Absalom McGowen, in leg, slightly
Privates:	Eli Westner, badly wounded in the face
	Mason Dedman, shot through both thighs (bad)
	Samuel Gannon, in leg, not serious
	George Power, in foot, slightly [died of wounds, August 23, 1862.]
	Thomas Beck, in the arm, slightly.

COMPANY E

Killed:	Private William F. Duty
	Private Mark M. Poteet
Wounded:	Capt. William Skelton, Slightly
	Sergt. George W. Branson, Severe in Back
	Corp. J. W. Palmer, Slightly
	Corp. J. A. Shoemaker, Slightly in Back
Privates:	Sol. P. Buddin, right Arm
	Jacob Hines, Slightly
	George J. McCowen, Slightly. [Died Sept. 16, 1862, from wounds.]
	J. W. Huntzenger, Ankle, Badly. [Discharged Nov. 15, 1862, disability.]
	Harry P. Wilson, Mortally
	Leonard O. Taylor, Slightly
Missing: Privates:	Dennis Sullivan
	Joseph Grubb
	Isaac N. Norton.

[All found, one found by 8-6-62; all mustered out in 1864 and 1865.]
Respectfully, Lieut. James W. Hamrick, Commanding Co.

COMPANY F

[Only limited information from Indiana Adjutant General's Report.]
Killed:	Private William Dailey
Wounded:	Private Francis Chapman
Missing:	Private James M. Wilks

[The Morning Report of August 7, 1862, shows two men killed in action, one man missing, and seven men wounded.]

COMPANY G

Killed: Corporal Austin Johnson, Fell while nobly discharging his duty.
Private Michael Crosby,   "   "   "   "   "   "
Private Michael McKinsey, "   "   "   "   "   "

Wounded: Co. Q.M. Sergt. Charles Tomes, Severely wounded in Hip
Corporal George W. Fox, Mortally wounded, Abdomen, Two Ball. [Died August 16, 1862.]

Privates: Jackson Aiken, Severely, wounded in Hip.
Henry Benson, Slightly wounded.
Frank Conway, Severely wounded in the Arm.
George Erne, Severely wounded in the Arm.
William Elkins, Mortally wounded in the Abdomen.
Fredrick Hoffman, Mortally wounded in the Abdomen. [Died later, Aug. 5]
Martin Magal, Seriously wounded in both legs and one ear shot off
Henry Sponsell, Seriously wounded in Abdomen. [Discharged October 16, 1862, for wounds.]
Christian Schmidt, Severely wounded by bayonet in Side. [Discharged October 13, 1862, for wounds.]

Missing: None [Private Washington Cramer, under arrest, was taken by the retreating Rebels.]

"The men fought Bravely until the last & when they were lost from the Co., they fell in with other companies & done their duty nobly."

COMPANY H

Killed: Sergt. John J. Spencer
Corpl. William H. Duzan

Privates: Albert P. Dale
John A. Musgrove

Wounded: Capt. John T. Campbell, Slightly, in right lower leg.
Lieut. Thomas D. Bryant, Badly, in the left arm [Died, August 18, 1862, of wounds.]
Sergt. William Wolfe, finger shot off.
Corpl. Jesse Reddish, flesh wound in left thigh.

Privates: Thomas Banta, shot through the left side.
Thomas Blake, shot through the foot.
Nelson Duzan, slightly, in the back of his head.
Warren Hamilton, Slightly, right hip, ankle and side.
Foster M. Moody, in the face, by the bursting of his own gun.
Thomas J. Lough, flesh wound in the thigh.
James Phillips, slightly, left side.
John Pittman, finger shot.
Henry Thompson, badly, but we don't know where.
Philip W. Weaver, badly, right wrist.
Henry C. Wilkins, flesh wound in right thigh.

"Co. H all fought well, and several of its members distinguished themselves for coolness and bravery among who are the following: Sergeant William C. Wolfe; Privates: Warren Hamilton, James Jerome, William H. Scott, Thomas J. Lough and J. D. Mater."

COMPANY I

[No deaths listed in the Indiana Adjutant General's Report; the August 7th Regimental Morning Report shows 3 men wounded.]

COMPANY K

Killed: Corpl. George W. Fry
Private Jesse R. Harlan
Private William Pitcher

Wounded: Lieut. Thomas Grinstead, Mortally in the Leg

B—The Battle of Baton Rouge

Privates:
Sergt. John [Richard] W. Griggs, Slightly in the Arm
Corpl. Henry Harrison Olds, Slightly, Thigh. [Lower leg; Discharged 1864, disability from this non-healing fractured bone wound.]
Jesse M. Jones, Mortally wounded in the Thigh. [Discharged, April 20, 1863, disability.]
John Griffin, Slightly wounded in the Arm
Solomon Bray, Flesh wound in the Thigh
Harvey M. Snoddy, Slightly Wounded in the Hip
Claibourne Gooch, Flesh wound in the Hip
Isaac Kiphart, Severely wounded in the Knee and Hand. [Died of wounds, August 24, 1862.]
Thomas Frank Grinstead, Slightly wounded in the Hip.
Charles Elliot, Severely wounded in the Shoulder. [Died of wounds August 15, 1862.]
William Larimore, Flesh wound in the leg [Discharged, September 23, 1862, for wounds.]

Confederate and Federal Casualties at Baton Rouge
(only dead and wounded counted)

Confederate:		Federal:	
Hudson's battery	6	General officers	1
Semmes' battery	15	Magee's cavalry	1
4th Alabama Battalion	25	Nims' battery†	4/2
31st Alabama	11	Manning's battery†	7/6
35th Alabama	25	Everett's battery	13
3rd Kentucky	17	9th Connecticut	10
4th Kentucky*	18/48	7th Vermont	10
5th Kentucky	33	30th Massachusetts	18
6th Kentucky	25	6th Michigan	59
7th Kentucky	13	14th Maine†	107/119
4th Louisiana	30	21st Indiana	124
9th Louisiana Battalion	32		
30th Louisiana	40		
22nd Mississippi	47		
31st Mississippi	47		
39th Mississippi, Co. I	3		
19th Tennessee	1		
20th Tennessee	2		
28th Tennessee	3		
45th Tennessee	3		
Cobb's battery	0		
Sharpshooters	2		
Total	398/428	Total	353/365

*Two reports of casualties exist. The author does not know which one contains the transcription error; therefore, both numbers are given for the reader's information.

†SOR, Part II, Volume 25, page 502 shows 36 KIA, 71 wounded and 12 missing. 119 total casualties in the 14th Maine; Part II, Volume 27, pages 360 and 372.

(The 31st Mississippi claimed the highest number of casualties in proportion to the total number of men present for battle; the 22nd Mississippi claimed the second highest proportionate number of casualties.)

Sources: Grimsley, James, miscellaneous papers; Rowland, Dunbar, "Military History of Mississippi, 1803–1898, pages 245 and 290; SOR, Part II, Volume 23, page 249. Southern Historical Society Papers, Vol. 16, page 135.

Writings Attesting to the Valor of the 21st Indiana at the Battle of Baton Rouge

Captain James Grimsley, 21st Indiana, Company B wrote to his wife on August 8, 1862: "We fought them from the beginning to the end. [We] were in the hottest and thickest of all the danger, in fact we fought the battle with the assistance of the 6th Michigan Regiment and the two batteries of the brigade. The battlefield was our camp and the grounds surrounding. The other regiments came to the engagement, but as a general thing, retired under the first fire. This was particularly the case with the eastern extreme Yankee regiments.

"We took prisoners who fought at Mill Springs, Kentucky and at Pittsburgh Landing [Shiloh]. They say that this was the bloodiest engagement they have met.... They would not at first believe that we had only one Indiana regiment; they thought that they had met three different Indiana regiments; they are only mistaken, they met us at three different places."[1]

Eli Griffin, 6th Michigan, Company A, wrote his wife on August 10, 1862: "I tell you the 6th Michigan Regiment and the 21st Indiana won the battle of Baton Rouge.... Well, the 6th Mich. and the 21st Indiana drove off the rebels. The Wis. 4th was held as a reserve. The 9th Connecticut, 7th Vermont, and 14th Maine gave way and retreated. The 30th Massachusetts did pretty well but did not fight much. The Vermont 7th ran like a lot of sheep and lay on the levee along the river and could not be coaxed out or driven to fight. Our brave Western men fought like heroes and won the Battle, and the Eastern cowards will get the praise as General Butler is from Mass."[2]

I. J. W. Shaffer wrote to Colonel McMillan on August 9, 1862: "I cannot help writing and saying to you that your Regiment has more than sustained the reputation of the Western Troops. The wounded rebels that came down swear that your regiment had more than 2,000 men in it. It was a glorious victory, and while all did well, your regiment appears to have been the mainstay.

"Accept from me for your fine regiment, the gratitude of about the only Western Man in New Orleans. Colonel Turner joins me in this, and I hope that all of the wants of the sick and wounded in the entire brigade will be made known, and as far as is in my power, they shall be supplied.

"I am, Colonel, truly your friend, I. J. W. Shaffer. Could I do anything for Colonel Keith?"

"I, as another Western Man, endorse all of the above. G. Weitzel, Lt., U.S. Engineers, Chief, Engineering Dept. of the Gulf." This comment from Manning's Battery gives the most honor to the 21st Indiana: "But the last charge of the Twenty-First Indiana decided the fate of the day, and the Battle of Baton Rouge proved a victorious day to the forces of the Union."[3]

General Butler's official commendation, stated in part: "To the Twenty-first Indiana high mead of praise is awarded...'Honor to whom honor is due.'"

At a later reunion of the 21st Indiana, General Butler wrote them a letter which contained the following praise: "For the Twenty-first Indiana, I have the highest regard. Their conduct at Baton Rouge in August, 1862, was beyond all praise, and doubtless saved the day."[4]

Reference Notes:
1. Grimsley, James, letter to wife, August 8, 1862.
2. Griffin, Eli, letter to wife, August 6, 1862.
3. Grimsley, James, misc. papers. [Lieutenant Godfrey Weitzel was one of the few Regular Army officers the Westerners were fond of. Perhaps it was due to his being a "Western Man."]. "Public Documents of Massachusetts," page 403
4. Dooley, Rufus, "Speech," page 105. OR, Volume 15, page 43.

C—The Battle of Bisland

List of Land Artillery Engaged at Bisland and Irish Bend, LA, April 12–14, 1863

CONFEDERATE ARTILLERY

Valverde Battery (Texas), two 12-pdr. guns and four 6-pdr guns.
1st Regular Confederate Light Artillery (Louisiana), two 12-pdr. guns and six 6-pdr. guns.
St. Mary's Cannoneers (1st Louisiana), two 12-pdr. guns and two 12-pdr. howitzers.
Pelican Light Artillery (5th Louisiana), two 3-inch banded rifles, two 6-pdr. guns and two 12-pdr. howitzers.

FEDERAL ARTILLERY

EMORY'S:
1st Maine Light Artillery, four 3.67-inch bronze rifled guns and two 12-pdr. Napoleons.
1st U.S. Light Artillery, Company F, six 12-pdr. Napoleons.

C—The Battle of Bisland / D—The Battle of Port Hudson

WEITZEL'S:
1st Indiana Heavy Artillery, Companies A, G and K.
Four 20-pdr. Parrott rifles, four 30-pdr. Parrott rifles and two 12-pdr. (4.62-inch) rifled brass guns.
6th Massachusetts Light Artillery, four 12-pdr. Napoleons and two 12-pdr. howitzers.
18th New York (Mack's Black Horse Artillery), four 20-pounder Parrott rifles.
1st U.S. Light Artillery, Company A, four 12-pdr. Napoleons and two 3-inch Ordnance rifles.
GROVER'S:
2nd Massachusetts Light Artillery, six 3.67-inch bronze rifled guns.
1st U.S. Light Artillery, Company L, four 12-pdr. Napoleons and two 10-pdr. (2.9-inch) Parrott rifles.
2nd U.S. Light Artillery, Company C, six 12-pdr. Napoleons.

D—The Battle of Port Hudson

What follows is a descriptive list of armament and ranges from each river battery. Positions are about January 1863. Copied from a period map drawn by J. Fremaux, Confederate engineer at Port Hudson. (Courtesy University of North Carolina at Charlotte.)

No. of Battery	GUNS	Calibre	Rifled	Smooth Bore	How Mounted	Elevation Above Water in Feet	Description of Points of Location	Van Winkle's (upstream from Port Hudson)	Ferry Landing (below Port Hudson)	Mr. Ware's Water's Edge (Below)	Roberson's Water's Edge (Below)	Dr. Egan's Water's Edge (Below)
										Yds.		
I						85	Bluff in town of Port Hudson	4440	1514	2662	4169	5276
II	1	42		1	Barbette		Bluff North of	4455	1209	1507	3257	4850
	1	24	1		Siege Carr.	85	Rail Road Depot	4455	1209	1507	3257	4850
	1	24	1		Barbette			4455	1209	1507	3257	4850
III	1	32	1		Barbette	36.3	Water's Edge North of Rail	4711	1947	1386	3058	4620
	2					41.8	Road Depot	4711	1947	1386	3058	4620
IV	1	64		1	Columbiad	85	Bluff South of Rail Road Depot	4223	834	1012	2750	
V	1	128		1	Columbiad	85	Bluff at Mr. W. Ranaldson's		835	1155	2662	4092
VI	1	32		1	Barbette	85	Ditto		836	1155	2662	4092
VII						85	Ditto		836	1155	2662	4092
VIII	2	24	2		Barbette	57.5	Second Bluff at J.H. Gibbon's		965	561	2090	2788
IX						40.4	Plateau at Gibbon's			649	1661	1215
X	2	24		2	Siege Carr.	319	Gibbon's Landing		1320	660	1340	1985
	1	32	1		Barbette	319			1320	60	1340	1985
XI	2	24	2		Siege Carr.	516	End of River		1766	1781	1122	2090
	1	20	1		Parrott Rifle	45.8	Bluff		1766	1781	1122	2090

Artillery Engaged at Port Hudson, LA, May 27, 1863

CONFEDERATE ARTILLERY

STEEDMAN'S:

Battery B, 1st Mississippi: Captain Herod, four 6-pdr. (3.67") guns and two 12-pdr. (4.62") howitzers.
Battery F, 1st Mississippi (one section) Captain J. L. Bradford, two 6-pdr. (3.67") guns.
1st Tennessee Battalion Heavy Artillery, one company: Captain James M. Sparkman, two 3.5" Blakely rifles.
Company A, 1st Alabama Infantry: Lieutenant Harman, one 24-pdr. (5.82") rifled siege gun; Lieutenant Sanford, one 24-pdr. (5.82") rifled siege gun.
Watson Battery, (one section) Lieutenant E. A. Toledano, two 6-pdr. (3.67") guns.
Company K, 39th Mississippi Infantry, Lieutenant J. D. Dalliet, one 2-pdr. (2") breechloading gun. (Possibly Hughes gun)
Wingfield's Battalion, 9th Louisiana Partisan Rangers (dismounted cavalry), detachment with two small breechloading guns. (Probably Hughes or Williams guns; referenced by Fred Y. Dabney as "Whitfield" (Whitworth?) guns.)

BEALL'S:

Company K, 1st Alabama Infantry, Lieutenant Frank, one 12-pdr. (4.62") bronze rifled gun.
Battery F, 1st Mississippi (one section), two 6-pdr. (3.67") guns.
Battery K, 1st Mississippi, Captain George Abbay, five 12-pdr. (4.62") howitzers. (Possibly three 6-pdr. (3.67") guns and two 12-pdr. (4.62") howitzers; however, within the defenses of Port Hudson Abbay's men crewed seven cannons.) The only written record on Abbay's armament states that they were armed with six 12-pounder howitzers when organized; the same person never mentioned receiving any different cannons. (Abbay had one gun disabled at Plains Store; it may or may not have been repaired in time to give him six guns for his battery by this date.)
Watson's battery, (two sections), Lieut. J. E. Nores and Sergeant-Major H. L. Nichols, two 6-pdr (3.67") guns and two 12-pdr. (4.62") howitzers.
Company D, 12th Louisiana Heavy Artillery Battalion (detachment), Captain W. Norris Coffin, one 24-pdr. (5.82") rifled siege gun.
1st Tennessee Battalion Heavy Artillery, Rock City Artillery Company, (detachment), Captain F. J. Weller and Lieut. Lahey, two 24-pounder smoothbore siege guns.

MILES':

Roberts' Seven Stars Battery, Captain Calvit Roberts, two 3" banded rifles, two 6-pdr. (3.67") guns.
Boone's battery, Captain R. M. Boone, four 6-pdr. (3.67") guns, one 3.3" bronze rifle, and two 12-pdr. (4.62") howitzers.
Lieutenant Watts Kearney, one 20-pdr. (3.67") Parrott rifle.
(Other small pieces such as 2-pounder breechloaders and 3" banded rifles were on hand, but not yet mounted on carriages. At least two were mounted on whatever would support them and used by both infantry and artillery units against the enemy. Two exist as trophies at the United States Military Academy at West Point, NY.)

P. F. DeGournay's and M. J. Smith's River Batteries
(Coming UP the River from River Battery XI)

Battery XI:	Company K, 1st Alabama, Lieutenant Pratt, 4.62" Gibbon and Andrews single-banded siege rifle.
Battery X:	empty
Battery IX	Company B, 12th Louisiana Battalion Heavy Artillery, one 8" shell gun one 32-pdr. (6.4") smoothbore siege gun.
Battery VIII:	Company D, 12th Louisiana Battalion Heavy Artillery (detachment), one rifled 24-pdr. (5.82") rifled siege gun.
Battery VII:	empty
Battery VI:	Company A, 12th Louisiana Battalion Heavy Artillery, two 24-pdr. (5.82") rifled siege guns.
Battery V:	Company B, 1st Alabama Infantry, one 10" Columbiad, one 42-pdr. (7") smoothbore siege gun, one 32-pdr. (6.4") smoothbore siege gun.
Battery IV:	Company E, 12th Louisiana Battalion Heavy Artillery, one 8" Columbiad one 10" Columbiad.

D—*The Battle of Port Hudson*

Battery III: Company G, 1st Alabama Infantry, one 32-pdr. (6.4") rifled siege gun, one 42-pdr. (7") smoothbore navy gun.
Battery II: Company A, 1st Alabama Infantry, one 42-pdr. smoothbore
Battery I: Company K, 1st Alabama Artillery, Lieutenant Tuttle, one 24-pdr. (5.82") rifled siege gun.

LOGAN's Cavalry (outside of Port Hudson — in enemy's rear):
Roberts' Seven Stars Battery, one section, two 6-pdr. iron howitzers.

FEDERAL ARTILLERY

WEITZEL'S:
1st Maine Battery, Lieutenants Albert Bradbury, John E. Morton and Eben Haley; six 3.67-inch bronze rifled guns.
2nd Massachusetts Battery, Captain Ormond F. Nims; six 3.67" bronze rifled guns.
4th Massachusetts Battery, Captain George G. Trull and Lieutenant Frederick W. Reinhard; four 12-pdr. Napoleon guns and two 3" Ordnance rifles (in reserve for General Augur).
6th Massachusetts Battery, Captain William Carruth and Lieutenant Phelps; four 12-pdr. Napoleon guns and two 12-pdr. howitzers (two of these Napoleon guns were on the west bank of the Mississippi with cavalry).
Company A, 1st U. S., Captain Edmund C. Bainbridge; four 12-pdr. Napoleon guns and two 3" Ordnance rifles.
Company F, 1st U. S., Captain Richard C. Duryea and Lieutenants Norris and Haskin; six 12-pdr. Napoleon guns.

GROVER'S:
Battery L, 1st U.S.: Captain Henry W. Closson and Lieutenants Taylor and Appleton; four 12-pdr. Napoleon guns and two 10-pdr. (2.9") Parrott rifles.
Company C, 2nd U.S.: Captain John I. Rodgers and Lieutenant Theodore Bradley; six 12-pdr. Napoleon guns.

AUGUR'S:
Indiana Jackass Regiment (1st Indiana Heavy Artillery):
  Company B, Captain James Grimsley, two 30-pdr. (4.2") Parrott rifles;
  Company E, Captain James Hamrick, four 20-pdr. (3.67") Parrott rifles;
  Company G, Captain Edward McLaflin, three 3-pdr. (4.2") Parrott rifles;
  Company H, Captain James Connelly, two 30-pdr. (4.2") Parrott rifles;
  Company K, Captain Clayton Cox, two 12-pdr. (4.62") bronze rifled guns.
18th New York: Captain Albert Mack, six 20-pdr. (3.67") Parrott rifles.
Company G, 5th U.S., Captain Jacob Rawles, six 12-pdr. Napoleon guns.
2nd Vermont Battery, Captain Pythagoras E. Holcomb, six 12-pdr. (3.67") Sawyer guns.

SHERMAN'S:
Indiana Jackass Regiment (1st Indiana Heavy Artillery):
  Company A, Captain [Major] William Roy; four 20-pdr. (3.67") Parrott rifles.
21st New York Battery: Captain James Barnes, four 3" Ordnance rifles.
1st Vermont Battery: Captain George Hebard, six 3" Ordnance rifles.

SOURCES:
Freret, James, "Fortification and Siege."
Mississippi State Archives, R.G. 9, Volume 21, F.11 and Volume 22, F.13.
NARG 393, 1799; NARG 393, 1802; NARG 393, Volume 44.
O. R., Volume 26, Parts 1 and 2;
Port Hudson State Commemorative Area, Austen Diary; Reports from F.Y. Dabney, P.F. DeGournay, J. Shelby and M.J. Smith.
Smith, Daniel J., Diary, Alabama State Archives.
Wright, Howard, "Port Hudson, Its History," page 27.

Artillery engaged at Port Hudson, Louisiana, June 14, 1863

CONFEDERATE

STEEDMAN'S:
Battery B, 1st Mississippi: Captain Herod, three 6-pdr. (3.67") guns and one 12-pdr. (4.62") howitzers.

Battery F, 1st Mississippi (one section) Captain J. L. Bradford, two 6-pdr. (3.67") guns.
1st Tennessee Battalion Heavy Artillery, one company: two 3.5" Blakely rifles.
Company A, 1st Alabama Infantry: Lieutenant Harmon, one 24-pdr. (5.82") rifled siege gun; Lieutenant Tuttle, Lt. Sanford, one 24-pdr. (5.82") rifled siege gun.
Watson's battery (one section), Lieutenant E. A. Toledano, two 6-pdr. guns.
Company K, 39th Mississippi Infantry, Lieutenant J. D. Dalliet, one 2-pdr. (2") breechloading gun.

BEALL'S:
Company K, 1st Alabama Infantry, Lieutenant Frank, one 12-pdr. (4.62") bronze rifled gun.
Battery F, 1st Mississippi (one section), two 6-pdr. (3.67") guns.
Battery K, 1st Mississippi, Captain George Abbay, four 6-pdr. (3.67") guns and two 12-pdr. (4.62") howitzers [possibly all of Abbay's pieces were 12-pounder howitzers].
Watson's battery, (one sections), Lieut. J. E. Nores and Sergeant-Major H. L. Nichols, two 6-pdr (3.67") guns.
Company D, 12th Louisiana Heavy Artillery Battalion (detachment), Captain W. Norris Coffin, one 32-pdr. (6.4") smoothbore siege gun.
1st Tennessee Battalion Heavy Artillery, Rock City Artillery Company, (detachment), Lieut. Lahey, one 24-pounder smoothbore siege gun.

MILES':
Roberts' Seven Stars Battery, Captain Calvit Roberts, two 3" banded rifles, two 6-pdr. (3.67") guns.
Boone's battery, Captain R. M. Boone, four 6-pdr. (3.67") guns, two 12-pdr. (4.62") howitzers and one 3.3" bronze rifle.
Lieutenant Watts Kearney, 20-pdr. (3.67") Parrott rifle.
[Several disabled guns were strapped to supports, loaded with scrap iron and readied to sweep the parapets should the enemy come over in force.

LOGAN'S Cavalry (outside of Port Hudson — in enemy's rear):
Roberts' Seven Stars Battery, one section, two 6-pdr. iron howitzers.

P. F. DeGOURNAY'S and M. J. SMITH'S RIVER BATTERIES:

Battery XI:	Company K, 1st Alabama, Lieutenant Pratt, one 24-pdr. (5.82") rifled siege gun ("Virginia").
Battery X	one 32-pdr. (6.4") rifled siege gun.
Battery IX:	Company D, 12th Louisiana Battalion Heavy Artillery (detachment), one 24-pdr. (5.82") rifled siege gun.
Battery VIII:	Company B, 12th Louisiana Battalion Heavy Artillery, one 8" shell gun.
Battery VII:	Empty.
Battery VI:	Empty. (One gun in upper portion of battery fell into the river due to a cave-in; surviving gun moved to land Battery VII.)
Battery V:	Company B, 1st Alabama Infantry, one 10" Columbiad, one 42-pdr. (7") smooth-bore siege gun, and one 32-pdr. (6.4") smoothbore siege gun.
Battery IV:	Company E, 12th Louisiana Battalion Heavy Artillery, one 8" and one 10" Columbiad.
Battery III:	Empty.
Battery II:	Company G, 1st Alabama Infantry, one 42-pdr. (7") smoothbore naval gun.
Battery I:	Company A, 1st Alabama Infantry, one 42-pdr. smoothbore.

FEDERAL ARTILLERY

AUGUR'S:
Indiana Jackass Regiment (1st Indiana Heavy Artillery):
　Company C, Captain Elihu E. Rose, four 8" siege howitzers;
　Company D, Captain William S. Hinkle, four 24-pounder (pdr.) smoothbore siege guns;
　Company E, Captain James Hamrick, four 20-pdr. (3.67") Parrott rifles;
　Company G, Captain Edward McLaflin, three 3-pdr. (4.2") Parrott rifles;
　Company K, Captain Clayton Cox, two 12-pdr. (4.62") bronze rifle guns.
1st Maine Battery, Lieutenants Albert Bradbury, John E. Morton and Eben D. Haley; four 12-pdr. Napoleon guns and two 12-pdr. howitzers.
6th Massachusetts Battery, Captain William Carruth and Lieutenant Phelps; four 12-pdr. Napoleon guns and two 12-pdr. howitzers.
18th New York Battery, Captain Albert Mack, six 20-pdr. (3.67") Parrott rifles.

Company A, 1st U. S., Captain Edmund C. Bainbridge; four 12-pdr. Napoleon guns and two 3" Ordnance rifles.
Company G, 5th U. S., Captain Jacob Rawles, six 12-pdr. Napoleon guns.

PAINE'S:
4th Massachusetts Battery, Captain George G. Trull and Lieutenant Frederick W. Reinhard; four 12-pdr. Napoleon guns and two 3" Ordnance rifles.
2nd Vermont Battery, Captain Pythagoras E. Holcomb, six 12-pdr. (3.67") Sawyer guns.
Company F, 1st U. S., Captain Richard C. Duryea and Lieutenants Norris and Haskin; six 12-pdr. Napoleon guns.

GROVER'S:
2nd Massachusetts Battery, Captain Ormond F. Nims; six 3.67" bronze rifled guns.
Company C, 2nd U.S., Captain John I. Rodgers and Lieut. Theodore Bradley; six 12-pdr. Napoleon guns.
Detachment, Co. L, 1st U.S. Light Artillery, Lieut. F. E. Taylor, four (total) of 8-inch and 10-inch siege mortars.

DWIGHT'S:
Indiana Jackass Regiment (1st Indiana Heavy Artillery):
Company A, Captain Eden Fisher; four 20-pdr. (3.67") Parrott rifles.
Company B, Captain James Grimsley, two 30-pdr. (4.2") Parrott rifles;
Company H, Captain James Connelly, two 30-pdr. (4.2") Parrott rifles.
13th Massachusetts Battery, Captain Charles H.J. Hamlin, four 10-inch siege mortars.
1st Vermont Battery, Captain George Hebard, six 3" Ordnance rifles.
Battery L, 1st U.S., Captain Henry W. Closson and Lieutenants Taylor and Appleton; four 12-pdr. Napoleon guns and two 10-pdr. (2.9") Parrott rifles.
21st New York Battery, Captain James Barnes, four 3" Ordnance rifles.

SOURCES:
Freret, James, "Fortification and Siege."
Mississippi State Archives, RG 9, Volume 21, F.11 and Volume 22, F.13.
NARG 393, 1799; NARG 393, 1802; NARG 393, Volume 44.
O. R., Volume 15 and Volume 26, Parts 1 and 2.
Port Hudson State Commemorative Area, Austen Diary; Reports from F. Y. Dabney, P. F. DeGournay, W. Shelby and M. J. Smith
Smith, Daniel J., Diary, Alabama State Archives.
Wright, Howard, "Port Hudson, Its History," page 27.

TABLE OF INDIRECT FIRE FROM FEDERAL SIEGE BATTERIES AT PORT HUDSON
(The listing is copied from the National Archives RG 393–1802)

[Author's Note — based upon battery locations and descriptions, this table was prepared between June 16 and June 20, 1863. The batteries were originally numbered from the south to north, not from north to south as batteries later appear on all known Federal maps. The bracketed battery number is the number that will correspond with the battery number on the maps used in this work. The aiming points that are not identified targets are to salient points (saw-tooth shaped angles) of the Confederate defenses.]

[Luce, Oltmanns and Robbins were all members of the engineering staff in the Department of the Gulf. As of this date no copies of their Port Hudson sketches or their photographs are known to exist. The author concludes that both direct and indirect fire was being used against the defenders of Port Hudson.]

Battery 1 [21]
four — 30-pounder Parrott rifles
    N — 27-¾° W -   980 yds. }
    N — 6-¾° E -   870 yds. } Mr. Oltmanns' sketch [reference to authority
    N — 19 ° E -   1012 yds. } by which the distance &
    N — 36-¾° E -   1650 yds. } bearing were estimated.]
    N — 9-½° W -   1925 yds, — To 10-inch Columbiad at Landing (water batt.)

    N— 7° W—   4840 yds.— To N.W. salient (opposite Nelson)
    N— 1-½° W—   2860 yds.— To Church
    N— 5° E—   4378 yds.— To Commissary buildings
    N— 6-¾° E—   4862 yds.— To Work opposite Bainbridge
    N—13-½° E—   4620 yds.— To Salient opposite 9-inch gun Battery.

Battery 2 [20]
four — 20-pounder Parrott rifles
    N— 53° W—   1110 yds.— To 2nd Salient   }
    N— 39° W—   1012 yds.—   } Oltmanns' sketch
    North—   1133 yds.—   }
    N— 10-½° E— 1331 yds.—   }
    N— 38° W—   2134 yds.— To 10-inch Columbiad }
    N— 22-¼° W— 3838 yds.— To Church   } Oltmanns'— Pos.
                                                           Bat. transferred
    N— 8-½° W— 4180 yds.— To Commissary buildings }

Battery 3 [19]
Six — 3-inch rifles
    West—   2046 yds. }
    West—   1452 yds } Oltmanns'
    N— 84-½° W— 1232 yds. } sketch
    N— 52-½° W— 748 yds. }
    N— 29-½° W— 726 yds. }
    N— 62-½° W— 2200 yds.—} 10-inch Columbiad } Oltmanns'
    N— 42° W—   2596 yds.— To church }   trans. Bat.

Battery 4 [18]
Four Mortars
    S— 81-½° W— 2398 yds. }
    S— 79° W—   1848 yds. }
    S— 81-½° W— 1584 yds. } Oltmanns' sketch
    N— 84° W—   924 yds. }
    N— 67-½° W— 748 yds. }
    N— 41° W—   1045 yds. } Position Bat. Oltmanns.' trans.
    N— 35° W—   1122 yds. }
    N— 30-½° W— 1210 yds. } Position Salients— Robbins
    N— 74° W—   2400 yds } To Columbiad Lady Davis } Oltmanns' trans
    N— 51-½° W— 2620 yds. } To Church   } Bat.

Battery 5 [17]
8-inch Howitzers
    S— 49-½° W— 1067 yds. To S.E. Salient   }
    S— 55-¼° W— 1243 yds.   }
    S— 76-½° W— 902 yds.   } Robbin's sketch
    S— 85° W—   858 yds.   }
    N— 85° W—   836 yds.   }
    N— 59-½° W— 820 yds.   }
    S— 65-½° W— 2860 yds to 10-inch Columbiad } Robbin's trans.
    S— 84-¼° W— 2519 yds to Church   } bat.
    S— 70-¼° W— 2574 yds. to 10-inch Columbiad } Photograph
    N— 89-¼° W— 2310 yds. to Church   }

Battery 6 [15]
Two 20-pounder Parrott rifles; two 24-pounder siege guns
    S— 37-½° W— 1188/ yds. to 1st Salient North of S.E. }
    S— 41-½° W— 1068 yds.   }Robbin's sketch
    S— 46° W—   957 yds.   }
    S— 61° W—   629 yds   }
    S— 51-½° W— 3146 yds. to S.W. Salients [in line (?)]   }
    S— 67-½° W— 2600 yds. to 10-inch Columbiad   }Robbin's trans. bat.

D—The Battle of Port Hudson

    S — 88–½° W -   2180 yds. to Church   }
    S — 55° -   3322 yds. to N. W. Salient   }

Battery 7 [13]
Three 24-pounder guns
    S — 37–½° W -   550 yds. to 1st Salient South of Plains Road   }
    S — 46–½° W -   3102 yds. to 10-inch Columbiad   } Photograph
    S — 59° W -   2354 yds. to Church   } Bat.
    S — 79° W -   570 yds. to Salient   } Luce's
    West -   636 yds. to Salient   } Salients
    N — 78–¼° W -   680 yds. to Salient   }
    N — 73° W -   2684 yds. to N. W. Salient   }
    N — 60° W -   792 yds. to Salient   }
    N — 56–½° W -   1264 yds. to Work opposite Bainbridge [Fort Desperate] }

Battery 8 [11]
Four 20-pounder Parrotts
    S — 22–½° W -   1300 yds. to Salient South of Plains Road   }
    S — 36–½° W -   1130 yds. to Salient   } Luce's trans.
    S — 50° W -   1023 yds. to Salient   } sketch
    S — 64–½° W -   900 yds. to Salient   }
    S — 74° W -   1760 yds. to Commissary buildings   }

Battery 9 [10]
Four 9-inch Dahlgren guns
    S — 10° W -   1320 yds. to Salient at Plains Road   }
    S — 22° W -   1080 yds to Salient   }
    S — 34–½° W -   3696 yds. to 10-inch Columbiad   } Luce's trans. bat.
    S — 34–½° W -   920 yds. to Salient   }
    S — 41–½° W -   2805 yds. to Church   }
    S — 46–½° W -   959 yds. to Salient   }
    S — 67–½° W -   1340 yds. to Commissary buildings   }
    S — 82–½° W -   1022 yds. to Work opposite Bainbridge   }
    S — 87° W -   2420 yds. to N. W. Bastion   }

Battery 10 [9]
Two 12-pounder rifled [Model 1841 heavy 12-pounders rifled for 4.62" shells]
    S — 4° E -   1440 yds. to Salient south of Plains Road   }
    S — 3–½° W -   1144 yds. to Salient   }
    S — 11–½° W -   913 yds. to Salient   } Photograph
    S — 16° W -   700 yds. to Salient   }
    S — 34–¾° W -   2706 yds. to Church   }

Battery 11 [7]
Two 30-pounder Parrotts (Bainbridge) [McLaflin's 1st IN, Co. G]
    S — 24° E -   748 yds. to Salient   }
    S — 20° W -   3410 yds. to 10-inch Columbiad   }
    S — 20° W -   330 yds. to work in front   } Photograph
    S — 25–½° W -   2440 yds. to Church   }
    S — 34° W -   770 yds. to work near Commissary   }

Battery 12 [4]
One 30-pounder Parrott
    S — 37° E -   374 yds. to work opposite Bainbridge   }
    S — 8–½° W -   660 yds. to work at Commissary bld'gs.   } Photograph
    S — 15° W -   3310 yds. to 10-inch Columbiad   }
    S — 15° W -   2354 yds. to Church   }

Battery 13 [1 (on 1864 map)]
One 30-pounder Parrott
    S — 35° E -   1048 yds. to Commissary buildings   }
    S — 3–½° E -   2354 yds. to Church   } Photograph

S — 1-½° W -	3300 yds. to 10-inch Columbiad	}
S — 47° W -	542 yds. to N. W. Salient interior	}

Battery 14 [3 (on 1864 map)]
Four Mortars

S — 42° E -	1120 yds. to Commissary buildings	}
S — 8° E -	2376 yds. to Church	} Photograph
S — 2° W -	3300 yds. to 10-inch Columbiad	}
S — 32-½° W -	473 yds.. to Interior of N. W. Salient	}

FEDERAL BATTERY POSITIONS AT PORT HUDSON AT END OF SIEGE

Corrected list of Federal batteries compiled from Ordnance records at National Archives compared with Batteries on map of Port Hudson with positions as numbered from 1864 map prepared for General Banks; also, corrected as to location of Battery Bailey in properly numbered spaces and sequence on that map. Battery commanders are corrected, as well as type of guns used at the end of siege.

Position	# of guns & type	Commander and Unit
1	one 30-pounder Parrott rifle	Lt. William H. Blankenship, B 1st IN
2	two 12-pdr. Howitzers	Lt. John F. Phelps, 6th MA.
3	four 8" & 10" siege mortars	Lt. F. E. Taylor, L, 1st U.S.
4	one 30-pounder Parrott rifle	Lt. Benjamin S. Harrower, G, 1st IN
5	four 6-[pounder] bronze rifles	Lt. Eben D. Healy, 1st ME
6	six 12-pounder Napoleons	Capt. Richard C. Duryea, F, 1st U.S.
7	two 30-pounder Parrott rifles	Capt. Edward McLaflin, G, 1st IN
8	four 12-pounder Napoleons	Capt. William W. Carruth, 6th MA.
8	four 12-pounder Napoleons	Capt. Bainbridge, A, 1st U.S.
8	two 3-inch Ordnance rifles	Lt. H. P. Norris, A [F], 1st U.S.
9	two 12-pounder bronze rifles	Capt. Clayton Cox, K, 1st IN
10	two 9-inch Dahlgren guns	Lt. Comm. Ed. Terry, U.S.N.
11	six 20-pounder Parrott rifles	Capt. Albert Mack, 18th N.Y.
12	six 12-pounder Napoleons	Capt. Richard C. Duryea, F, 1st U.S.
12	one 20-pounder Parrott rifle,	" " "
13	three 24-pounder smooth bores	Lt. Jesse Hadden, D, 1st IN
14	six 6-pounder Sawyers	Capt. Pythagoras E. Holcomb, 2nd VT.
15	two 20-pounder Parrotts	Capt. James W. Hamrick, E, 1st IN
15	two 24-pounder smooth bores	Lt. William Harper, D, 1st IN
16	four 3-inch rifles	Capt. James Barnes, 21st NY
16	six 12-pounder Napoleons	Lt. J. Rawles, G, 5th U.S.
17	four 8-inch siege howitzers	Capt. Elihu Rose, C, 1st IN
18	two 10" siege mortars and two 8" siege mortars	Capt. R.M. Hill, Ordnance Dept.
19	six 3-inch Ordnance rifles	Capt. George T. Hebard, 1st VT.
20	four 20-pounder Parrotts	Capt. Eden H. Fisher, A, 1st IN
21	four 12-pounder Napoleons	Lt. Theodore Bradley, C, 2nd U.S.
22	one 8-inch siege howitzer	Lt. William Bough, C, 1st IN
23	one 10-inch siege mortar	Lt. Ellis L. Motte, 13th MA.
24	two 20-pounder Parrotts	Lt. Samuel Hartley, E, 1st IN
24	three 24-pounder smooth bores	Capt. William Hinkle, D, 1st IN
24	two 9-inch Dahlgrens	Ensign R. Swann, U.S.N.
24	one 8-inch howitzer	Lt. William Glover, C, 1st IN
24	two 12-pounder Napoleons	Capt. Henry Closson, L, 1st U.S.
24	two 10-pounder Parrott rifles	Lt. Appleton, L, 1st U.S.
24	two 30-pounder Parrott rifles	Capt. James B. Grimsley, B, 1st IN
25	two 10-inch siege mortars	Capt. Charles H. J. Hamlin, 13th MA.
26	trench cavalier at Priest Cap.	
27	two 30-pounder Parrott rifles,	Capt. James W. Connelly, H, 1st IN.
28	two 12-pounder Napoleons Section of Nims' Battery, 2nd MA, or a two	

D—The Battle of Port Hudson

Position	# of guns & type	Commander and Unit
	3-inch rifle section of Capt. Closson's L, 1st U.S., under Lieut. Theo. Bradley.	

Source: National Archives Map files and NARG 393—1799, & NARG 393—1802.

CAPTURED CONFEDERATE ORDINANCE AT PORT HUDSON

Copies of two reports follow to illustrate the difficulty in establishing accuracy of information in this book. Author's corrections are bracketed.

Fifteen heavy guns, in good condition; five complete field-batteries, thirty-one guns in good condition, besides disabled guns; 1,911 shot and shell for heavy guns, various calibres; 775 cartridges, 12,000 pounds of powder, made up in cartridges, for heavy guns, various calibres; 32,000 pounds cannon powder; 150,000 cartridges, small arms; 5,000 muskets." [46 guns]

Source: "The Rebellion Record," 1864, Vol. 7, page 207:

(Undated memo):
Field Work, Louisiana, Port Hudson, **CAPTURED**—
2—10" Columbiads
1—8" Columbiad
3—42 Pdr. Smooth bore
1—32 Pdr. Smooth bore
3—24 Pdr. Rifled—Siege Carriages
6—12 Pdr. Howitzers
6—6 Pdr. Howitzers [Guns]
2—Napoleons—**Not** Captured
1—20 Pdr. Parrott
3—10 Pdr. Parrott
~~14—light Battery~~" [this entry was crossed out in the original].

[Author's note: 26 captured heavy and light guns remained. The 6-pounder *guns* were mislabeled as 6-pounder *howitzers* in the original report. Also the 10-pounder Parrots were 3.5-inch Blakely rifles (see October 2, 1863 letter below). I have excluded the 14 light battery guns and the 2 Napoleons (Federal guns) from the total.]

Source: NARG 393—1802

Oct. 2, 1863: letter from Office Chief of Artillery, Port Hudson:

"The three 24-Pdr. Rifled guns are in my opinion good and serviceable guns; but being adapted for a projectile not fabricated for our use, and of which but a limited quantity are on hand, I question whether it be policy to consider them a part of the permanent armament, unless a further supply of the projectiles adapted to them can be relied on. The 20-Pdr. Parrott Gun is in good Condition and Entirely serviceable.

Three guns of foreign make stated to be 10 pdr. Parrotts (by Engr. Dept.) are not such, but are what is called the Blakely Gun, and like the 24-Pdr. Rifle cannot be relied upon as Permanent Armament. Fourteen field guns (the three light batteries now here) are included in the armament of the defenses."
Source: NARG 393—1802

LIST OF CANNONS TAKEN UP AT PORT HUDSON, LOUISIANA, AND SENT AS TROPHIES TO WEST POINT MILITARY ACADEMY, NEW YORK

Original Trophy ID Marking	Description of Cannon	
I	3-inch Confed. Parrott Rifle	Display at USMA
II	3-inch Confed. Parrott Rifle	Display at USMA
III	6-pounder Bronze Gun, Barrel Broken	Missing since 1914
IV	6-pounder Bronze Gun	Scrapped, 1943
V	12-pounder Bronze Field Howitzer	Scrapped, 1943
VI	6-pounder Bronze Gun	Display at USMA
VII	6-pounder Bronze Gun "Johnson"	Display at USMA

Original Trophy ID Marking	Description of Cannon	
VIII	6-pounder Bronze Gun "Jeff Davis"	Display at USMA
IX	6-pounder Bronze Gun	Display at USMA
X	5.82-inch Rifled Siege Gun	Scrapped, 1843
XI	3.3-inch Bronze Rifle by Leeds	Display at USMA
XII	32-Pdr. Short Navy Gun	Display at Port Hudson, LA, SHA
XIII	4.62-inch Cast Iron Rifle	Scrapped, 1943
XIV	24-pounder Smooth-bore Siege Gun	Scrapped, 1943
XV	24-pounder Smooth-bore Siege Gun	Scrapped, 1943
XVI	5.82-inch rifled siege gun	Display at USMA
XVII	8-inch Navy Shell Gun	Display at Port Hudson. LA SHA

Names in quotes are inscribed on barrel of cannon. USMA means United States Military Academy at West Point, NY. SHA means State Historic Area" Leeds is the name of a New Orleans foundry.

Buildings Surviving the Siege

Three of the surviving buildings were open sheds used for storing grain and food, which the Federals continued to use for the same purpose.

The Yankees turned the three room Clinton & Port Hudson Railroad depot into an 80-foot by 55-foot storehouse.

The two-story four-room 40-foot by 35-foot Port Hudson Hotel became a storehouse for the Federal Ordnance Department.

A one-room 60-foot by 40-foot one-story frame building (maybe the church) became another Ordnance Department storehouse.

Among the other houses and buildings, the Federals listed:
  a three-room former Post Headquarters house,
  a two-room storehouse,
  a seven-room house used for the post's print-shop and storehouse,
  a two-story four-room office and storehouse,
  a two-room house used as a quartermaster's issuing room,
  a six-room 49-foot by 40-foot house used as officer's quarters and
  a two-room 85-foot by 26-foot wheelwright and blacksmith shop building were repaired and put into similar use by the Federals.

E—Spanish Fort and Blakely

Number of Rounds Expended by Heavy Artillery During the Sieges by Unit

During the sieges of Spanish Fort and Blakely, the Indiana Jackass Artillery (First Indiana Heavy Artillery) fired more than 105 tons of shot and shell at their targets. Each company's contribution was as follows:

Company B fired 570 rounds of 10-inch shell and 639 rounds of 8-inch shell from their mortars.
Company C fired 286 rounds of 8-inch shell from their howitzers.
Company H fired 701 rounds of 30-pounder shot and shell: 475 while at Bay Minette and 226 fired at Blakely.
Company I fired 411 rounds total of 30-pounder and 20-pounder shot and shell as well as 24-pounder coehorn mortar shells.
Company K fired 720 rounds of 30-pounder shot and shell.
Company L fired 643 rounds of 30-pounder shot and shell.
Company M fired 400 rounds of 30-pounder shot and shell.
Other heavy batteries fired as follows:
18th New York fired 2000 rounds of 20-pounder Parrott shot and shell.
6th Michigan Heavy Artillery, Company K, 10-inch mortars, 495 rounds
(Sharing the Bay Minette Battery with Companies H and K, a 26th New York Battery section with two 12-pounder Napoleons fired 250 rounds and the Whitworth rifle fired 136 rounds.)
Source: Andrews, C.C., op.cit., page 151. "Records," Hays and Wimmer Battle Reports.

Chapter Notes

The Formation

1. American Heritage, *American Heritage Civil War Chronology*, Part 1; Pierre G. T. Beauregard, "Official Report," April 16, 1861, from Mississippi State Archives, Jackson, MS; William C. Davis and the Editors of Time-Life Books, *Brother Against Brother*, pp. 35, 39, 40.
2. W.H.H. Terrell, *Indiana in the War of the Rebellion*, vol. 1, pp. 6, 11, 12, 564.
3. *Indianapolis Journal*, July 24, 1861; Terrell, *Indiana in the War of the Rebellion*, pp. 14–16, 20 and 564.
4. American Heritage, *American Heritage Civil War Chronology*, Part I; *Indianapolis Journal*, July 24, 1861; Terrell, vol. 1, pp. 9, 14–16, 20, 564.
5. Thomas Ballard, letter to Bill [?], October 7, 1861; Funk, Arville L., *Hoosiers in the Civil War*, page 106; Bruce L. Hackett, "Hoosier Freemen: Harboring Negroes in Parke County Indiana," *Traces of Indiana and Midwestern History*, vol. 21, no. 3 (Summer 2009): Indiana Historical Society, 36–37.
6. John R. Rowell, *Yankee Artilleryman*, p. 7; Terrell, vol. 2, pp. 194–199, vol. 4, pp. 447–476.
7. William C. Davis, *Rebels and Yankees: Fighting Men of the Civil War*, p. 17; *Parke County Republican*, June 19, July 3 and August 7, 1861; *The Proceedings of 13th Annual Reunion of Co. A, 21st Indiana Regiment Indiana Volunteers*, p. 6 (hereafter cited as *13th Annual Reunion of Company A*).

One

1. Thomas Ballard, to sister, July 21, 1861; Rufus Dooley, letter, July 14, 1861; *Indianapolis Journal*, July 24, 1861; Theo. T. Scribner, *Indiana's Roll of Honor*, vol. 2, p. 375.
2. *Indianapolis Journal*, July 31, 1861; *LaGrange Standard*, August 1, 1861; photograph in author's collection.
3. *LaGrange Standard*, August 1, 1861.
4. *Indianapolis Journal*, July 24, 1861; Catharine Merrill, *The Soldier of Indiana in the War for the Union*, vol. 1, p. 544.
5. *Indianapolis Journal*, August 1, 1861; *LaGrange Standard*, August 1, 1861.
6. *Indianapolis Journal*, August 1, 1861; *Official Records of the War of the Rebellion* (hereafter cited as *O.R.*), Ser. 1, vol. 51, Part 1, p. 432; *O.R.*, Ser. 3, vol. 1, p. 368.
7. George C. Harding, *The Miscellaneous Writings of George C. Harding* (hereafter cited as *Misc. Writings*, p. 190; Merrill, vol. 1, p. 544; *13th Annual Reunion of Company A*, p. 7.
8. *Parke County Republican*, August 14, 1861. The phrase "in a horn" means in rut, in heat, or "horny."
9. Rufus Dooley, to mother, August 7, 1861.
10. Ibid.
11. Ibid; *Parke County Republican*, August 14, 1861.
12. *Parke County Republican*, August 14, 1861.
13. Dooley, letter to mother, August 7, 1861; Harding, p. 192; Merrill, vol. 1, p. 544; Scribner, pp. 376–377.
14. Norman Rukert, *Fort McHenry, Home of the Brave*, pp. 55, 59.
15. Alexander Abernathy, *Memoirs*; James Grimsley, to wife, September 8, 1861; Harding, p. 192; Merrill, vol. 1, p. 544; *O.R.*, vol. 5, pp. 556, 566, 570–571; Rowell, *Yankee Artillerymen*, pp. 7, 8; *13th Annual Reunion of Company A*, pp. 7–8.
16. Kirkpatrick Family Papers, published letter from Chaplain Nelson Brakeman, August 1861; Merrill, vol. 1, pp. 544–545.
17. Grimsley, Papers, copies of orders dated August 22, September 11, 1861; Grimsley, letter to wife, September 12, 1861; Harding, pp. 194, 197–99; *O.R.*, Ser. 2, vol. 1, p. 295.
18. Kirkpatrick Family Papers, published letter from Chaplain Nelson Brakeman, August 1861; *Parke County Republican*, September 25, 1861.
19. Merrill, vol. 1, p. 545.
20. Harding, letter to wife, August 11, 15, 1861.
21. Thomas Ballard, to Bill, October 7, 1861; Harding, letter to wife, August 19, 1861; Harding, *Misc. Writings*, pp. 195–96; *Parke County Republican*, September 4, 1861.
22. Harding, *Misc. Writings*, p. 201; Merrill, vol. 1, pp. 544–545.
23. Harding, letters, August 11, 19, 1861; Harding, *Misc. Writings*, pp. 201–202, 214.
24. Rufus Dooley, Papers, letter from John B. Yelton to Silas Dooley, September 21, 1861; Harding, letter to wife, September 27, 1861; Harding, *Misc. Writings*, p. 214; S.E. Armstrong, Diary, January 2, 1862.
25. Harding, *Misc. Writings*, pp. 215–216; Rufus Dooley, letter to mother, October 18, 1861.
26. Dooley, letter to mother, October 18, 1861; Harding, letter to wife, October 16, 1861; Harding, *Misc. Writings*, pp. 207, 217, 244–245; John D. McAulay, *Civil War Breechloading Rifles*, p. 61. The Merrill breechloading system allowed the weapon to be loaded from the breech end by the insertion of a paper cartridge containing the powder and bullet. The conventional muzzle-loading system used powder poured down the muzzle and the bullet or ball rammed down the barrel with a ramrod to load it. The breech-loading rifle could be loaded and fired in about

one-half the time it took to load and fire a muzzle-loading rifle. The Federal War Department purchased only 769 Merrill rifles of which 566 were designated for the 21st Indiana. The 21st Indiana privately purchased more than 140 of these weapons prior to the U.S. War Department's purchases. This regiment had more of these weapons than any other regiment. It still listed 293 of these rifles on hand in its June 30, 1864, ordnance report. Rifles with a small "7" or an "L" stamped into the wood inside of the toolbox generally were not issued; 350 were stored in the Washington, D.C., arsenal for the balance of the war. These rifles were in the 9,000, 10,000 and 14,000 serial numbers. (Per the author's research for "A Treatise on Merrill Rifles and Carbines," *The Gun Report*, July-August 2001.)

27. Harding, letter to wife, October 16, 1861; Harding, *Misc. Writings*, pp. 220–221; Merrill, vol. 1, p. 545; Rowell, *Yankee Artillerymen*, p. 7; Scribner, p. 377.

28. *Parke County Republican*, December 4, 1861.

29. Dooley, letter, November 28, 1861; Grimsley, letter to wife, November 6, 1861; Merrill, vol. 1, p. 545; *13th Annual Reunion of Company A*, p. 8; Scribner, p. 377.

30. Harding, *Misc. Writings*, pp. 225, 228, 230; *LaGrange Standard*, December 26, 1861; *Parke County Republican*, December 18, 1861.

31. Dooley, letter, December 8, 1861; Harding, *Misc. Writings*, pp. 229, 236; Michael J. Martin, *A History of the 4th Wisconsin Infantry and Cavalry in the Civil War*, pp. 33–34 (hereafter cited as *History of the 4th Wisc.*); Merrill, vol. 1, p. 545; *Parke County Republican*, December 18, 1861; Ethel Ellis, oral history of John Yelton as told to author.

32. Dooley, letter, November 28, 1861; Grimsley, letter to wife, November 29, 1861; Harding, *Misc. Writings*, p. 233; *Parke County Republican*, December 18, 1861; *O.R.*, vol. 5, p. 435. Thomas P. Southwick, *A Duryea Zouave*, p. 48.

33. Harding, *Misc. Writings*, pp. 235, 242; *O.R.*, vol. 5, p. 428.

34. Dooley, letter, November 28, 1861; Harding, *Misc. Writings*, p. 249; Merrill, vol. 1, p. 545.

35. *American Tribune*, February 18, 1899; Dooley, letter to mother, January 2, 1862; Harding, letter to wife, October 16, 1861.

36. Mitchell Hatten, letter to sister, Catherine, January 29, 1862.

37. Dooley, letter, February 8, 1862; William H. Price, *Civil War Handbook*, p. 16; John D. McAuley, *Civil War Breechloading Rifles*, p. 61. When Private Dooley wrote concerning payment of $15.00 for his Merrill rifle, it was more than two weeks after he had received his January 21 pay, and he still had $10.00 left to spend after loaning out $10.00. Private Yelton had received about $22.00 in December for one month's pay. The going pay was $13.00 per month as of May 4, 1861. Therefore, it appears that the 21st Indiana was getting enlistment bounty per the July 21, 1861, Federal legislation plus state and county bonuses (Emma Lou Thornbrough, *Indiana in the Civil War Era*, p. 136.)

38. Grimsley, letter to wife, February 1862; McAuley, pp. 61, 62.

39. Grimsley, letter to wife, February 1862; Harding, *Misc. Writings*, p. 250; *LaGrange Standard*, February 13, 1862.

40. Armstrong, Diary, February 4, 1862; Dooley, letter, February 8, 1862.

Two

1. James Grimsley, letter to wife, February 1862; George Harding, *Misc. Writings*, p. 250; *Parke County Republican*, December 4, 1861.

2. Rufus Dooley, letter to father, February 27, 1862; Grimsley, letter, February 19, 1862; Harding, *Misc. Writings*, p. 251; *Parke County Republican*, March 5, 1862.

3. *American Tribune*, December 24, 1898; S.E. Armstrong, Diary, February 19–20, 1862; Harding, *Misc. Writings*, p. 251; Merrill, vol. 1, pp. 547, 548; *Parke County Republican*, March 5, 1862.

4. Armstrong, Diary, February 21, 1862; Harding, *Misc. Writings*, p. 252; *O.R.*, Ser. 1, vol. 6, Part 1, p. 694.

5. *American Tribune*, December 24, 1898; Armstrong, Diary, March 2–5, 1862; Grimsley, Papers, ordnance report; Merrill, p. 548; *O.R.*, Ser. 1, vol. 6, p. 687; *O.R.*, Ser. 2, vol. 3, pp. 341–342; *Parke County Republican*, April 16, 1862; Scribner, *Roll of Honor*, pp. 377–378.

6. Armstrong, Diary, March 6, 1862; Dooley, letter, March 14, 1862; Grimsley, letter to wife, March 11, 1862; Merrill, vol. 1, p. 548; *Parke County Republican*, April 16, 1862; Scribner, p. 378.

7. *American Tribune*, December 24, 1898; Merrill, vol. 1, pp. 548–549; *Parke County Republican*, April 16, 1862; Scribner, p. 378.

8. *O.R.*, Ser. 1, vol. 6, pp. 466–468.

9. Armstrong, Diary, March 13, 1862; Grimsley, letter to wife, March 14, 1862; Scribner, p. 378.

10. Grimsley, letter, March 14, 1862; Merrill, vol. 1, p. 549.

11. Armstrong, Diary, March 14–15, 1862; Grimsley, letter, March 14, 1862; *Parke County Republican*, April 16, 1862; Scribner, p. 378.

12. Rufus Dooley, speech, *Indiana Historical Commission Bulletin*, No. 15, p. 101 (hereafter cited as Dooley, Speech); *Parke County Republican*, April 16, 1862.

13. *Parke County Republican*, April 16, 1862; Grimsley, letter to wife, April 4, 1862; Thomas H. Murray, *History of the Ninth Regiment, Connecticut Volunteer Infantry*, p. 63 (hereafter cited as *History of the 9th CT.*)

14. *Parke County Republican*, April 16, 1862.

15. Armstrong, Diary, drawing inside back cover of 1862 edition; Edward Bacon, *Among the Cotton Thieves*, pp. 16–21; Cathie Falls, *The Eaton Rifles: The Men of Company H*; Michael J. Martin, *History of the 4th Wisconsin*, p. 50; *O.R.*, vol. 6, p. 706; Scribner, p. 379.

16. Harding, *Misc Writings*, pp. 259–260.

17. *O.R.*, vol. 6, p. 705.

18. Armstrong, Diary, March 30, 31, 1862; Grimsley, letter to wife, April 4, 1862; *O.R.*, vol. 6, pp. 708–709; *O.R.*, vol. 53, Part 1, pp. 517, 521.

19. Armstrong, Diary, April 3, 1863; Dooley, Speech, pp. 101, 102.

20. Armstrong, Diary, April 7 and 8, 1862.

21. *American Tribune*, unknown date; Armstrong, Diary, April 11, 1862; *Company Journal*, 21st Indiana Regiment, April 8, 1862.

22. Grimsley, to wife, April 4 and April 9, 1862.

23. *American Tribune*, unknown date; Armstrong, Diary, April 11, 1862; Dooley, letter, April 13, 1862; Falls, Cathie, *The Eaton Rifles: The Man of Company H*; Fawcett, Francis W., 31st Massachusetts Infantry, Diary, April 12, 1862.

24. Martin, *History of the 4th Wisconsin*, p. 55; *O.R.*, vol. 6, p. 708; *Parke County Republican*, May 21, 1862.

25. Benjamin Butler Papers, "List of Invalids to Be Sent Away from Ship Island Aboard the *Undaunted*," Library of Congress.

Three

1. S.E. Armstrong, Diary, April 15, 1862; George C. Harding, *Misc. Writings*, p. 254; Michael J. Martin, *His-

tory of the 4th Wisc., p. 54; Catharine Merrill, vol. 1, pp. 549, 550; *Parke County Republican*, May 21, 1862.

2. Armstrong, Diary, April 16–18, 1862; Harding, *Misc. Writings*, p. 255; *Parke County Republican*, May 21, 1862.

3. Rufus Dooley, Speech, p. 102; Harding, *Misc. Writings*, p. 260.

4. *American Tribune*, unknown date; Harding, *Misc. Writings*, p. 260; A. T. Mahan, *The Gulf and Inland Waters*, pp. 52–53.

5. *O.R.*, Ser. 1, vol. 6, Part 1, pp. 695, 710.

6. John Dimitri, "Louisiana," *Confederate Military History*, vol. 10, Part 1, p. 36 (hereafter cited as "Louisiana"); Grimsley, Papers, clipping from the *New Orleans Picayune* dated April 5, 1862; Mahan, *Gulf and Inland Waters*, pp. 64–66.

7. Grimsley, Papers, clipping from the *New Orleans Picayune* dated April 5, 1862; Mahan, *Gulf and Inland Waters*, pp. 61–62.

8. Mahan, *Gulf and Inland Waters*, pp. 61–62.

9. "The Night the War Was Lost," *Journal of the Louisiana Historical Association* 2, no. 2, pp. 161–165; Dick Nolan, *Benjamin Franklin Butler: The Damnedest Yankee*, p. 149.

10. *American Tribune*, January 8, 1899; Armstrong, Diary, April 21, 1862; Dooley, Speech, p. 102; Harding, *Misc. Writings*, p. 255.

11. *American Tribune*, January 8, 1899; Armstrong, Diary, April 23, 24, 1862; Harding, *Misc. Writings* page 261; Merrill, vol. 1, p. 550.

12. *O.R.*, vol. 6, p. 713; Reed, *Combined Operations*, p. 193.

13. *Daily Picayune*, May 30, 1862; Mahan, *Gulf and Inland Waters*, pp. 66–68; *O.R.*, vol. 6, pp. 713–714; John D. Winters, *The Civil War in Louisiana*, p. 93.

14. Armstrong, Diary, April 25–28, 1862; *Daily Picayune*, May 30, 1862; Dooley, Speech, p. 102; Harding, *Misc. Writings*, pp. 261–262; Merrill, vol. 1, p. 550; *O.R.*, vol. 6, p. 504, 505; Scribner, pp. 379–380.

15. *Daily Picayune*, May 30, 1862; Dooley, Speech, p. 102; Wyckham Hoffman, *Camp, Court and Siege*, p. 21; Winters, p. 100.

16. "Personal Sketches: John Keith," *Bartholomew County Atlas*, p. 20; *Daily Picayune*, May 30, 1862; Hoffman, *Camp, Court, and Siege*, pp. 14, 15, 21; Merrill, vol. 1, p. 550; Dick, *Benjamin Franklin Butler*, p. 147; *O.R.*, vol. 6, p. 504; David D. Porter, "The Opening of the Lower Mississippi," in Robert U. Johnson, *Battles and Leaders of the Civil War*, vol. 3, pp. 36, 38; Rowena Reed, *Combined Operations in the Civil War*, p. 193.

17. Dimitry, "Louisiana," pages 43–44; Dooley, Speech, p. 102; Harding, *Misc. Writings*, pp. 262, 264–265; Katharine Jones, ed., *Heroines of Dixie: Spring of High Hopes*, p. 135.

18. *American Tribune*, January 8, 1899; Armstrong, Diary, May 1, 1862; Dimitry, "Louisiana," pages 46, 47; Harding, *Misc. Writings*, p. 263; *LaGrange Standard*, May 19, 1862; M. Myers, letter, April 29, 1862; Winters, p. 96.

19. Winters, p. 9; Benjamin Butler Papers, Amos Wheeler, Letter, May 17, 1862, and "Report of August 1, 1862, by J. M. J.," LOC; Harding, *Misc. Writings*, p. 267; James C. Hazlett, Edwin Olmstead, and M. Hume Parks, *Field Artillery Weapons of the Civil War*, pp. 228, 229; *LaGrange Standard*, May 19, 1862; Merrill, vol. 1, p. 551; *Minutes, Annual Reunion of the 21st Regiment, First Indiana Heavy Artillery, 1892*, p. 22; Reed, p. 195; Scribner, p. 380.

20. *American Tribune*, January 8, 1899; Alexander Abernathy, "Memoirs"; Dooley, Speech, p. 102; Hoffman, *Camp, Court, and Siege*, pp. 23–24. Merrill, vol. 1, pp. 551–552. *Minutes, Annual Reunion of the 21st Regiment, First Indiana Heavy Artillery, 1892*, p. 22.

Four

1. *American Tribune*, unknown date; S.E. Armstrong, Diary, May 2, 1862; G.G. Benedict, *Vermont in the Civil War*, vol. 2, p. 89; George C. Harding, letter to wife, May 4, 1862; C. Merrill, *Soldier of Indiana*, vol. 1, p. 552; *O.R.*, Ser. 1, vol. 6, Part 1, p. 506.

2. Rufus Dooley, Speech, p. 103; George C. Harding, *Misc. Writings*, p. 270; *LaGrange Standard*, June 23, 1862.

3. *O.R.*, vol. 6, p. 506; Harding, *Misc. Writings*, p. 269.

4. Harding, letter to wife, May 4, 1862; Merrill, vol. 1, p. 552.

5. *American Tribune*, January 29, 1899; Armstrong, Diary, May 2–4, 1862; Harding, *Misc. Writings*, p. 269.

6. Armstrong, Diary, May 5, 1862; *O.R.*, vol. 6, Part 1, p. 506; Merrill, vol. 1, p. 552.

7. Armstrong, Diary, May 6, 1862; Merrill, vol. 1, p. 552; *O.R.*, vol. 6, p. 506; Theo. Scribner, *Roll of Honor*, p. 381.

8. *American Tribune*, January 29, 1999; Armstrong, Diary, May 6, 1862.

9. Merrill, vol. 1, p. 553.

10. Armstrong, Diary, May 9, 1862; Benjamin Butler Papers, James W. McMillan, Letter, May 10, 1862, LOC; *Official Records of the Navy* (hereafter cited as *ORN*), vol. 17, p. 234; Scribner, p. 381.

11. Benjamin Butler Papers, McMillan, Letter, May 10, 1862, LOC; Harding, *Misc. Writings*, p. 276.

12. Benjamin Butler Papers, McMillan, Letter, May 10, 1862, LOC; Harding, *Misc. Writings*, pp. 277–278; Merrill, vol. 1, p. 555.

13. Harding, *Misc. Writings*, pp. 280–281; Merrill, vol. 1, p. 555.

14. Benjamin Butler Papers, McMillan, Letter, May 10, 1862, LOC; Harding, *Misc. Writings*, pp. 281–282; Merrill, vol. 1, p. 557; Nolan, *Benjamin Franklin Butler*, p. 192; *O.R.*, vol. 6, p. 657; *O.R.*, Ser. 3, vol. 2, pp. 259, 688, 689; Scribner, p. 381.

15. "Personal Sketches: John A. Keith," *Bartholomew County Atlas*, p. 20; Rufus Dooley, Speech, p. 103; Merrill, vol. 1, p. 555; *O.R.*, vol. 15, p. 451; Scribner, p. 381; *The Weekly Junior Register*, May 22, 1862. [This Confederate newspaper account states that the ambuscade was led by Confederate officers, one of them, Lieutenant T. A. Woods (who was the owner of the Houma newspaper, *The Ceres*), and that they had attacked the main body of McMillan's men — not four sick men. Emphasis added by the author.]

16. *Bartholomew County Atlas*, p. 20; *Minutes, Annual Reunion of the 21st Regiment, First Indiana Heavy Artillery, 1889*.

17. *O.R.*, vol. 15, p. 452.

18. Armstrong, Diary, May 11, 1862; *Bartholomew County Atlas*, p. 59; Merrill, vol. 1, p. 556; *O.R.*, vol. 15, p. 450.

19. *Bartholomew County Atlas*, p. 59; Merrill, vol. 1, p. 556; *O.R.*, Ser. 1, vol. 15, Part 1, p. 452.

20. Dooley, Speech, p. 104; Merrill, vol. 1, pp. 555–556; *Minutes, Annual Reunion of the 21st Regiment—1st Indiana Heavy Artillery, 1889*; *O.R.*, Ser. 1, vol. 15, Part 1, pp. 452, 453; Scribner, p. 382.

21. *Bartholomew County Atlas*, p. 59; Scribner, p. 381.

22. Merrill, vol. 1, p. 556; *New York Daily Tribune*, June 16, 1862; *O.R.*, vol. 15, pp. 453, 454.

23. *American Tribune*, February 13, 1899; *Bartholomew County Atlas*, p. 59; *O.R.*, vol. 5, p. 455; *Minutes, Annual Reunion of the 21st Regiment — 1st Indiana Heavy*

Artillery, 1891. Captain Connelly presented the regiment a "mammoth tin spoon" in honor of being "the spooniest regiment in the service." The ladies auxiliary corps of the veteran's organization presented all members with a miniature silver spoon to be carried in honor of their efforts and as a symbol of respect to their former commander, Benjamin F. Butler, and not as a symbol of opprobrium. In addition, a specially engraved spoon was sent to Butler expressing those sentiments. Terrell, W. H. H., *Indiana in the War of the Rebellion,* vol. 6, p. 158.

24. *O.R.,* vol. 15, p. 455; First Indiana Heavy Artillery Regiment Records, 1862–1865.

25. Grimsley, letter to wife, May 18, 1862.

26. Grimsley, letters to wife, May 22, 25, 1862; Grimsley, Papers, note from John A. Keith dated May 30, 1862.

27. Harding, *Misc. Writings,* pp. 286–287; Merrill, vol. 1, pp. 557, 568.

28. Armstrong, Diary, May 19 to 22, 1862; *O.R.,* vol. 15, p. 1102.

29. *American Tribune,* February 13, 1899; Armstrong, Diary, May 22, 1862; Harding, *Misc. Writings,* p. 271; Scribner, p. 382.

30. Armstrong, Diary, May 28 to 30, 1862; Merrill, vol. 1, p. 558; *O.R.,* vol. 15, p. 1102.

31. Hoffman, *Camp, Court, and Siege,* p. 32; *O.R.,* vol. 15, p. 426.

32. *The Daily Herald,* Newburyport, Mass., June 25, 1862; *Memphis Daily Appeal,* July, 1862; *O.R.,* vol. 15, pp. 504, 510, 511. Mrs. Philips and Mrs. Larue were sentenced to prison on Ship Island, Mississippi. Mr. Fidel Keller was sentenced to prison on Ship Island at the same time for putting a human skeleton labeled "Chickahominy" in his bookstore window and telling any who asked that it was "A Yankee Soldier." Mrs. Phillips' reputation must not have been the best. While Keller was confined on Ship Island, he was allowed to converse only with Mrs. Phillips and vice-versa. Keller declined the privilege to talk with, as he said: "*that woman!*" Mrs. Philips previously had been arrested and released at Washington, D.C., for "traitorous activities."

33. Armstrong, Diary, May 25, 1862; Grimsley, Papers, note from John A. Keith dated May 30, 1862.

34. Harding, *Misc. Writings,* p. 273; Merrill, vol. 1, p. 558; Scribner, p. 382.

35. *Parke County Republican,* July 2, 1862; Scribner, p. 383.

36. Armstrong, Diary, May 31, June 1–4, 1862.

Five

1. Mitchel Hatten, Letter to Sister, June 7, 1862. *Parke County Republican,* July 2, 1862; *O.R.,* Ser. 1, vol. 15, Part 1, p. 25.

2. George C. Harding, *Misc. Writings,* p. 284; *LaGrange Standard,* July 7, 1862; Catharine Merrill, *Soldier of Indiana,* vol. 1, p. 558.

3. Benjamin Butler Papers, Letters from General B. Butler and Colonel J. W. McMillan on June 1, and General T. W. Williams on June 6, 1862, LOC; James Grimsley, Letter to Wife, June 8, 1862; Harding, *Misc. Writings,* pp. 282–283; Merrill, vol. 1, p. 558. Camp Magnolia Grove was between present-day 19th and 17th streets and North Street and Florida Street.

4. Grimsley, letter to wife, June 8, 1862; Katharine M. Jones, ed., *Heroines of Dixie: Spring of High Hopes,* pp. 138, 140–142.

5. Grimsley, letter to ?, June 14, 1862, and to wife, July 17, 1862.

6. Tom Ballard, letter to sister, July 3, 1862.

7. Benjamin Butler Papers, Letters, General Butler to Williams, June 1, General T. W. Williams to Butler June 6, 1862, LOC; Jones, *Heroines of Dixie: Spring of High Hopes,* p. 143; Merrill, vol. 1, pp. 558–559; *13th Annual Reunion of Company A,* p. 9.

8. Merrill, vol. 1, p. 559.

9. Armstrong, Diary, June 10, 1862; A. P. Dale, letter to brother, July 4, 1862; Grimsley, letter to ?, June 14, 1862; *Parke County Republican,* July 2, 1862; Merrill, vol. 1, p. 559.

10. Grimsley, letter to [unknown], June 14, 1862; Harding, *Misc. Writings,* pp. 285–286; *LaGrange Standard,* June 30, 1862; *O.R.,* Ser. 2, vol. 4, p. 883; *Parke County Republican,* July 2, 1862.

11. Rufus Dooley, letter, June 28, 1863; *O.R.,* Ser. 2, vol. 4, p. 883; John D. Winters, *The Civil War in Louisiana,* p. 135.

12. Davis, et al., *Brother Against Brother,* p. 228; *O.R.,* Ser. 1, vol. 6, Part 1, pp. 25–29.

13. Armstrong, Diary, June 20, June 25–26, 1862.

14. "Personal Sketches: John A. Keith," *Bartholomew County Atlas,* p. 59; Dunbar Rowland, *Military History of Mississippi,* p. 409; *O.R.,* Ser. 1, vol. 15, Part 1, p. 36, 787–788; *Rebellion Record: A Diary of American Events,* vol. 5, p. 277.

15. *American Tribune,* February 13, 1899; Armstrong, Diary, June 28, 1862. *Bartholomew County Atlas,* p. 59; Dooley, Letter, July 5, 1862; *O.R.,* vol. 15, pp. 37, 788; *Rebellion Record,* vol. 5, p. 278.

16. Dale, letter to brother, July 4, 1862; Grimsley, letters to wife, June 21, June 30, July 5, July 7, July 15, 1862.

17. Ballard, letter to sister, July 3, 1862; Dale, letter to brother, July 5, 1862; Dooley, letter, June 28, 1862.

18. Dale, letter to brother, July 4, 1862; Grimsley, letter to wife, July 5, 1862; Hoffman, *Camp, Court, and Siege,* p. 38.

19. *American Tribune,* April 16, 1899; Armstrong, Diary, June 27, July 6, July 8, 1862.

20. Thomas H. Murray, *History of the Ninth CT,* pp. 111–112.

21. Rowena Reed, *Combined Operations in the Civil War,* pp. 218, 219.

22. *O.R.,* Ser. 1, vol. 15, Part 1, p. 31; Winters, pp. 109–110.

23. Armstrong, Diary, July 21, July 22, July 25, 1862; Grimsley, letter to wife, July 22, 1862. Scribner, pp. 383, 240.

24. Edward Bacon, *Among the Cotton Thieves,* p. 8; Grimsley, letter to wife, August 1, 1862; Ben Johnson, *A Soldier's Life,* pp. 38, 39.

25. A.T. Mahan, *The Gulf and Inland Waters,* p. 105; Rowena Reed, p. 220. *ORN,* vol. 19, p. 771.

26. Grimsley, letter to wife, August 1, 1862; Murray, *History of the Ninth CT,* p. 113.

27. William C. Davis, *The Orphan Brigade,* pp. 114–115. *O.R.,* vol. 15, p. 76; Eliza McHatton Ripley, *From Flag to Flag,* p. 31.

28. Herman Seebold, *Old Louisiana Plantation Homes and Family Trees,* pp. 139, 140.

29. *Mobile Register and Advertiser,* August 13, 1862; Seebold, pp. 144–145.

30. Seebold, pp. 145–147.

31. Ibid., pp. 145–146.

32. Ibid., pp. 139, 147–148; W.H.H. Terrell, *Adjutant General's Report,* vol. 4, p. 465.

33. *Bartholomew County Atlas,* p. 60; *Mobile Advertiser and Register,* August 13, 1862; *O.R.,* Ser. 1, vol. 34, Part 2, p. 277; Seebold, p. 149; Harrison Soule, letter to wife, August 3, 1862.

34. *American Tribune,* no date; Benjamin Butler Papers, Benjamin Butler to William, August 3, 1862, LOC; Irwin, Richard, *History of the 19th Corps,* p. 36; *Parke County Republican,* July 2, 1862.

35. Davis, *The Orphan Brigade,* p. 115; *O.R.,* Ser. 1, vol. 15, Part 1, p. 76; Eliza McHatton Ripley, *From Flag to Flag,* pp. 30–31; *Supplement to the Army Official Records,* Part 2, vol. 24, pp. 565–566 (hereafter cited as *SOR*).

36. *American Tribune,* no date; William C. Davis, p. 118; Merrill, vol. 1, pp. 559–560; *O.R.,* vol. 15, p. 77; *SOR,* Part 2, vol. 34, p. 44.

Six

1. George C. Harding, *Misc. Writings,* p. 294; John S. Kendall, "Recollections of a Confederate Officer," *Louisiana Historical Quarterly* 29, 1946: 1083; Merrill, *Soldier of Indiana,* vol. 1, p. 560; *O.R.,* Ser. 1, vol. 15, Part 1, pp. 77, 79; *Parke County Republican,* September 3, 1862. This edition of this newspaper published letters from the 21st Indiana's colonel James B. McMillan, surgeon Ezra Reed, and Captain John Campbell, describing the Battle of Baton Rouge. *Southern Historical Society Papers,* John B. Pirtle, "Defense of Vicksburg," Vol. 8, p. 329; *Rebellion Record,* vol. 5, "Documents," page 310, vol. 10, "Documents," page 699; John D. Winters, *The Civil War in Louisiana,* p. 112.

2. Grimsley, letter to wife, August 8, 1862; Merrill, vol. 1, p. 561; *Southern Historical Society Papers,* "Defense of Vicksburg," page 329. The march from *Norma* is a lilting happy melody; it is hardly what one would expect to hear for inspiration to go into battle.

3. Merrill, vol. 1, p. 560; National Archives Map, RG 77-Z-275: "Battlefield of Baton Rouge."

4. Benedict, *Vermont in the Civil War,* vol. 2, p. 25, 26; Ira B. Gardner, *Recollections of a Boy Member of Company I, Fourteenth Maine Volunteers* (hereafter cited as *Recollections of the 14th Maine*), pp. 15, 16; National Archives Map, RG 77-Z-275. *O.R.,* vol. 15, pp. 59–60, 63.

5. Charles Carleton Coffin, *Stories of Our Soldiers,* pp. 25–26; Sarah A. Dorsey, *Recollections of Henry W. Allen,* pp. 129, 389; Gardner, p. 13; Grimsley, letter to wife, August 8, 1862; Merrill, vol. 1, pp. 561–562; *O.R.,* vol. 15, p. 59; National Archives Map, RG 77-Z-275.

6. Kendall, *Recollections of a Confederate Officer,* p. 1083; Winters, p. 114.

7. A. W. Bergeron, *Guide to Louisiana Confederate Military Units,* p. 18; Sarah A. Dorsey, *Recollections of Henry W. Allen,* p. 133; *O.R.,* vol. 15, pp. 90, 104, 107; Rowland, *Military History of Mississippi,* pp. 482–483; E. P. Thompson, *History of the Orphan Brigade,* p. 125.

8. *American Tribune,* no date; Harding, *Misc. Writings,* p. 295; Merrill, p. 561.

9. Grimsley, letter to wife, August 8, 1862; *Bartholomew County Atlas,* "Personal Sketches: John A. Keith," page 59; Kendall, "Recollections of a Confederate Officer," page 1085; Harding, *Misc. Writings,* p. 296; Merrill, vol. 1, p. 562; *O.R.,* vol. 15, pp. 56, 73, 90; *Parke County Republican,* September 3, 1862.

10. Harding, *Misc* Writings, p. 296; Merrill, vol. 1, p. 562; *Parke County Republican,* September 3, 1862; Ethel Ellis, oral history John Yelton as told to author.

11. Dorsey, p. 133; Gardner, pp. 15–16; Merrill, vol. 1, p. 562; *O.R.,* vol. 15, pp. 69–70, 77, 104; Caroline Whitcomb, *History of the 2nd Massachusetts Battery,* p. 36; William E. S. Whitman, *Maine in the War for the Union,* p. 320.

12. Dooley, Speech, p. 105; Grimsley, Papers, letter from Captain Francis Noblet, August 6, 1862; Harding, *Misc. Writings,* p. 302; Merrill, vol. 1, p. 562; *O.R.,* vol. 15, pp. 64–65, 73. *Parke County Republican,* September 3, 1862; *Public Document of Massachusetts,* p. 411.

13. Gardner, p. 16; Grimsley, Papers, letter from Captain Francis Noblett, August 6, 1862; Kendall, "Recollections of a Confederate Officer," page 1083; *O.R.,* vol. 15, pp. 65, 104; George Taylor, *Recollections of the Battle of Baton Rouge;* Whitman, p. 321.

14. T. W. Gillette, "Memoir," page 25 (4th Wisconsin, Co. I); Harding, *Misc. Writings,* p. 304; *Parke County Republican,* September 3, 1862; Taylor, *Recollections of the Battle of Baton Rouge.*

15. Harding, letter to wife, August 9, 1862; *Rebellion Record,* vol. 5, "Documents," page 312.

16. Gardner, p. 16; Merrill, vol. 1, p. 562; *O.R.,* vol. 15, pp. 68, 105; *SOR,* Part 2, vol. 34, p. 44.

17. Alfred Danely, letter to Lot Owen, September 11, 1862; *Parke County Republican,* September 3, 1862.

18. Benedict, *Vermont in the Civil War,* vol. 2, pp. 26, 27; Eli Griffin, letter to wife, August 10, 1862; Harding, *Misc.* Writings, p. 197; William Holbrook, *A Narrative of the Services of the Officers and Enlisted Men of the 7th Regiment of Vermont Volunteers, Veterans, from 1862 to 1866,* pp. 43–45, 48; Merrill, vol. 1, p. 563; Taylor, *Recollections of the Battle of Baton Rouge.*

19. *Confederate Veteran* 20, p. 469; *Daily Picayune,* October 3, 1863; Merrill, vol. 1, p. 563.

20. *Parke County Republican,* September 3, 1862.

21. Gillette, *Reminiscences,* p. 28; Harding, *Misc. Writings,* p. 297; Merrill, vol. 1, p. 563; National Archives map, RG 77, Z-275; *Parke County Republican,* September 3, 1862; Taylor, *Recollections of the Battle of Baton Rouge.*

22. Merrill, vol. 1, p. 564; *Parke County Republican,* September 3, 1862.

23. Harding, *Misc. Writings,* p. 299.

24. Dimitri, "Louisiana," *Confederate Military History,* vol. X, Part 1, p. 69; Dorsey, pp. 129, 134–135; Kendall, p. 1084; Frank Moore, ed., *Rebellion Record,* vol. 5, p. 719.

25. *O.R.,* vol. 15, pp. 100–107; Winters, p. 118.

26. Dimitri, "Louisiana," *Confederate Military History,* vol. X, pp. 68–69; John Corden, letter to wife, August 8, 1862; Dorsey, pp. 138, 139; Harding, *Misc. Writings,* p. 299; Kendall, p. 1087; *O.R.,* vol. 15, pp. 100–107; A.P. Richards, *The Saint Helena Rifles,* p. 4; *SOR,* Part 1, vol. 3, p. 127; Winters, p. 118. [The author counted the number of balls in one of his Civil War 6-pounder canister relics.]

27. Corden, letter to wife, August 8, 1862; Harding, *Misc. Writings,* p. 307; Johnson, *A Soldier's Life,* p. 42; Kendall, p. 1087; Merrill, vol. 1, p. 563; *Parke County Republican,* September 3, 1862; Richards, *The Saint Helena Rifles,* pp. 4, 5; Winters, pp. 118, 119.

28. Arthur, W. Bergeron, Jr., *Guide to Louisiana Confederate Units, 1861–1865,* pp. 80, 142, 162; Charles Elliot, oral history of this grandfather, formerly in the 39th Louisiana; Griffin, letter to "John," August 26, 1862; Johnson, *A Soldier's Life,* pp. 42–44; *Memphis Daily Appeal,* August 11, 1862; *O.R.,* vol. 15, pp. 68, 103, 107. Taylor, *Recollections of the Battle of Baton Rouge;* Winters, p. 119. [Allen's brigade had 42 casualties in the 4th Louisiana Regiment, 49 casualties in the 9th Louisiana battalion, 58 casualties in the 30th Louisiana Regiment and 3 in Company I, 39th Mississippi. The Indiana Jackass Battery and four companies of the 6th Michigan inflicted most all of these 152 casualties.]

29. Kendall, p. 1088; *O.R.,* vol. 15, p. 108.

30. Dorsey, p. 140; Hoffman, *Camp, Court, and Siege,* p. 49; Merrill, vol. 1, p. 563.

31. Dimitri, "Louisiana," *Confederate Military History*, vol. X, pp. 68–69; Dooley, Speech, p. 105; Harding, *Misc. Writings*, p. 298; Hoffman, p. 49; Kendall, p. 1090, 1092; Michael J. Martin, *History of the 4th Wisc.*, p. 99, 101; Merrill, vol. 1, pp. 563–564.

32. Alfred H. Danely, letter, September 18, 1862; Dorsey, p. 141; Cathie Falls, *The Eaton Rifles, The Men of Company H*, p. 3; Grimsley, letter to wife, August 8, 1862; Merrill, vol. 1, p. 564; *Official Records of the Union and Confederate Navies in the War of the Rebellion* (hereafter cited as *ORN*), vol. 19, pp. 114, 117; *Public Records of Massachusetts*, pp. 319–320.

33. *O.R.*, vol. 15, p. 99; *Southern Historical Society Papers*, January 1905, p. 15.

34. *American Tribune*, April 16, 1899; *O.R.*, vol. 15, pp. 51, 82, 93; *ORN*, vol. 19, pp. 116, 118; *SOR*, Part 2, vol. 25, pp. 523–524, 531.

35. Armstrong, Diary, August 5, 1862; J. Stoddard Johnson, "Kentucky," *Confederate Military History*, vol. IX, p. 76. This page shows Confederate casualties to be 467; therefore, the author concludes the Confederate losses were 29 percent greater than Federal losses. *O.R.*, vol. 15, pp. 51, 82, 93, 804; *ORN*, vol. 19, pp. 116, 118; Eliza McHatton Ripley, *From Flag to Flag*, pp. 36–37, 39; Richards, p. 5; Rowland, p. 245; Southern Historical Society Papers, *The Confederate Veteran*, vol. 16, p. 135; *SOR*, Part 1, vol. 3, pp. 123–126.

Seven

1. Benedict, *Vermont in the Civil War*, vol. 2, p. 41; Henry Warren Howe, *Passages From the Life of Henry Warren Howe*, p. 124; *Memphis Daily Appeal*, August 11, 1862; *O.R.*, vol. 15, p. 79.

2. *Mobile Register & Advertiser*, August 15, 1862. Thomas H. Murray, *History of the Ninth CT*, pp. 115, 118, 122.

3. Murray, p. 122; *Rebellion Record*, vol. 5, p. 301.

4. Murray, p. 123.

5. *American Tribune*, April 16, 1899; James Grimsley, Papers, Muster Roll for August 7, 1862 (interpolated by Author); *O.R.*, vol. 15, p. 77.

6. *American Tribune*, April 10, 1899; Coffin, *Stories of Our Soldiers*, p. 26; Theodore W. Gillette, *Memoir*, pp. 27, 28; Griffin, letters, August 11, September 6, 1862; Harding, *Misc. Writings*, p. 304; Jones, *Heroines of Dixie: Spring of High Hopes*, p. 180.

7. Grimsley, Papers; *Harper's Weekly*, September 6, 1862; James W. McMillan, letter to Merrill, Thomas & Co., September 10, 1862.

8. *ORN*, vol. 19, pp. 121–122.

9. *Jackson Mississippian*, August 9, 1862; *ORN*, vol. 19, pp. 125, 131, 135–136; *Southern Historical Society Papers*, vol. 1, p. 361.

10. Ibid.

11. Edward Bacon, *Among the Cotton Thieves*, p. 30.

12. *American Tribune*, April 10, 1899; Armstrong, Diary, August 6–10, 1862; *O.R.*, vol. 15, pp. 544–546.

13. *The Daily Picayune*, August 9, 1862; *ORN*, vol. 19, pp. 138–139, 720.

14. *ORN*, vol. 19, pp. 138, 139, 720; *Parke County Republican*, September 3, 1862.

15. Armstrong, Diary, August 9, 1862; Grimsley, letter to wife, August 8, 1862.

16. Armstrong, Diary, August 11, 1862.

17. Grimsley, Papers; *O.R.*, vol. 15, p. 72.

18. *American Tribune*, April 16, 1899; Armstrong, Diary, August 13, 1862; *ORN*, vol. 19, pp. 144, 145.

19. Armstrong, Diary, August 15, 1862; Charles East, ed., *The Civil War Diary of Sarah Morgan*, pp. 234–235; *O.R.*, vol. 53, pp. 533–534.

20. *O.R.*, vol. 15, pp. 53, 552–553.

21. *O.R.*, vol. 15, pp. 550–551.

22. Arthur, W. Bergeron, Jr., in *Black Southerners in Gray*, p. 89; Editors of Combined Books, *The Civil War Book of Lists*, p. 170; Harding, *Misc. Writings*, p. 305; *Memphis Daily Appeal*, August 11, 1862; *Rebellion Record*, vol. 5, p. 307.

23. Armstrong, Diary, August 20–21, 1862; Benedict, vol. 2, p. 44; Murray, p. 127.

24. Armstrong, Diary, August 20–21, 1862; Murray, p. 127; *O.R.*, vol. 15, p. 130.

25. Armstrong, Diary, August 21–22, 1862; Bacon, *Among the Cotton Thieves*, p. 47; Benedict, vol. 2, p. 45.

26. Benedict, vol. 2, p. 44; *O.R.*, vol. 15, pp. 46–47.

27. Benedict, vol. 2, pp. 46, 47; *O.R.*, vol. 15, pp. 48–50.

Eight

1. Powell A. Casey, *Encyclopedia of Forts, Posts, Named Camps and Other Military Installations in Louisiana, 1700–1981*, pp. 145–147, 418–420; *O.R.*, vol. 53, p. 534.

2. *O.R.*, vol. 53, p. 534; *Lloyd's American Railroad Weekly*, April 27, 1861. Today all that remains of these earthworks is the powder magazine of the redoubt near the river. It stands between the levee and Ochsner Clinic in Metairie, Louisiana.

3. Armstrong, Diary, August 24, 1862; Harding, *Misc. Writings*, p. 309; Martin, *History of the Fourth Wisc.*, p. 110; *O.R.*, vol. 53, p. 535; *Parke County Republican*, October 14, 1862.

4. Casey, *Encyclopedia of Forts*, p. 146; Irwin, *History of the 19th Corps*, pp. 43, 44; *New Orleans Daily Picayune*, August 24, 1862; *O.R.*, vol. 53, p. 535.

5. Bennett, *Vermont in the Civil War*, pp. 98–100, 105, 106; George R. Morris, "The Battle of Bayou Des Allemandes," *Confederate Veteran* 34, pp. 15, 16; Richard Taylor, *Destruction and Reconstruction: Personal Experiences of the Late War*, pp. 131–132.

6. Armstrong, Diary, September 4–5, 1862; Benedict, vol. 2, pp. 99, 100, 104; Harding, *Misc. Writings*, p. 311; *LaGrange Standard*, October 6, 1862; Merrill, vol. 1, p. 566; *O.R.*, vol. 15, pp. 134–135; G. Ralston, letter to W. Withers, November 20, 1862, Mississippi State Archives, RG 9, vol. 112. [The howitzer lost by the 8th Vermont at Bayou Des Allemandes was sent to Captain G. Ralston's 1st Mississippi Artillery Regiment, Battery H.]

7. N. H. Chittenden, *History and Catalogue of the Fourth Regiment Wisconsin Volunteers* (hereafter cited as *History of the 4th Wisconsin*), p. 11; Harding, *Misc. Writings*, p. 311; *O.R.*, vol. 15, pp. 135–136. *ORN*, vol. 19, p. 187; Charles Spurlin, ed., *West of the Mississippi with Waller's 13th Texas Cavalry Battalion, CSA*, p. 3.

8. October 6, 1862; *O.R.*, vol. 15, p. 136.

9. *American Tribune*, no date; Harding, *Misc. Writings*, p. 312; *LaGrange Standard*, October 6, 1862; *O.R.*, vol. 15, p. 136; *ORN*, vol. 19, p. 244; Christopher Pena, *Touched by War*, p. 130; Spurlin, p. 48.

10. *American Tribune*, no date; Chittenden, p. 12; *LaGrange Standard*, October 6, 1862; Pena, p. 133; Spurlin, pp. 48–50, 67; Taylor, p. 133.

11. Rufus Dooley, letter, September 13, 1862; Harding, *Misc. Writings*, pp. 313–314; *LaGrange Standard*, October 6, 1862; *O.R.*, Ser. 1, Part 1, vol. 15, p. 138; *SOR*, Part 2, vol. 15, p. 527.

12. Alfred Danely, letter, September 18, 1862; Dooley, letter to mother, September 13, 1862; Grimsley, letter to

wife, September 11, 1862; Mitchel [Michael] Hatten, letter to sister, September 17, 1862; Elihu Rose, letter to Thomas O'Conner's father, September 18, 1862.

13. *American Tribune,* no date; Armstrong, Diary, September 20–23, 1862; *LaGrange Standard,* November 24, 1862; *O.R.,* vol. 15, p. 142.

14. *American Tribune,* no date; Armstrong, Diary, September 24, 1862; *LaGrange Standard,* November 24, 1862; *O.R.,* vol. 15, p. 142.

15. *American Tribune,* no date; Armstrong, Diary, September 25, 1862; Bergeron, *Guide to Louisiana Confederate Military Units, 1861–1865,* p. 19; *LaGrange Standard,* November 24, 1862; Merrill, vol. 1, p. 567; *O.R.,* vol. 15, p. 142.

16. *American Tribune,* no date; Armstrong, Diary, September 24–25, 1862 (Armstrong writes that Lieutenant Harding was captured because he was too drunk to keep up with the retreating troops.); Bergeron, *Guide to Louisiana Units,* pp. 41, 42; Harding, letter to wife, September 25, 1862; *LaGrange Standard,* November 24, 1862; Merrill, vol. 1, p. 567; *O.R.,* vol. 15, p. 142; *ORN,* vol. 19, p. 215, 244; Pena, pp. 136–142.

17. Harding, letter to wife, September 26, 1862; Harding, *Misc. Writings,* pp. 321–324.

18. Harding, *Misc. Writings,* p. 325; *Parke County Republican,* December 10, 1862.

19. *Parke County Republican,* December 10, 1862.

20. Grimsley, letters to wife, September 23, October 2, 1862; *LaGrange Standard,* November 24, 1862.

21. *American Tribune,* unknown date; Grimsley, letter to wife, October 2, 1862.

22. Grimsley, letters to wife, October 18, 22, 1862.

23. Indiana Historical Society, First Indiana Heavy Artillery Regiment Records.

Nine

1. S. E. Armstrong, Diary, October 26, 27, 28, 1862; Dooley, letter to mother, November, 11, 1862; Grimsley, letter to wife, October 30, 1862.

2. *O.R.,* vol. 15, pp. 167–171, 176–178; Winters, *The Civil War in Louisiana,* pp. 160–161.

3. Armstrong, Diary, October 29, 30, 1862; Dooley, letter to mother, November 11, 1862; Eden Fisher, military records, National Archives; Grimsley, letter to wife, November 11, 1862; *LaGrange Standard,* April 11, 1863; *Minutes, Annual Reunion of the 21st Regiment, First Indiana Heavy Artillery, 1892,* p. 24; *ORN,* vol. 19, p. 326, 333; Scribner, *Roll of Honor,* p. 385.

4. Armstrong, Diary, October 30–31, November 1–2, 1862; *O.R.,* vol. 15, p. 179; *ORN,* vol. 19, pp. 326–327.

5. Armstrong, Diary, November 2, 1862; *O.R.,* vol. 15, pp. 179, 184, 186; *ORN,* vol. 19, pp. 327, 332, 335, 337, 342.

6. Arthur W. Bergeron, Jr., ed., *The Civil War Reminiscences of Silas T Grisamore, C.S.A.,* p. 101; *ORN,* vol. 19, pp. 327, 331, 333, 336–337; *Rebellion Record,* vol. 6, p. 174.

7. Armstrong, Diary, November 3–4, 1862; *ORN,* vol. 19, pp. 328, 330, 332, 334; Scribner, p. 366; Terrell, *Indiana in the War of The Rebellion,* vol. 4, pp. 461, 466.

8. Armstrong, Diary, November 6, 1862; *ORN,* vol. 19, p. 328.

9. Armstrong, Diary, November 5, 1862; *ORN,* vol. 19, p. 332.

10. Armstrong, Diary, November 7–10; Benedict, *Vermont in the Civil War,* vol. 2, p. 109; *O.R.,* vol. 15, pp. 169–171; *ORN,* vol. 19, p. 328.

11. Armstrong, Diary, November 16, 17, 1862; Merrill, vol. 1, p. 567.

12. *O.R.,* vol. 52, Part 2, pp. 355–356.

13. Armstrong, Diary, November 18–19, 1862; *O.R.,* vol. 52, Part 2, pp. 355–356.

14. Armstrong, Diary, November 20, 1862; Theo. Noel, *A Campaign from Santa Fe to the Mississippi; Being a History of the Old Sibley Brigade* (hereafter cited as *Old Sibley Brigade*), p. 45; *O.R.,* vol. 15, p. 1088.

15. Armstrong, Diary, November 21–22, 1862; *O.R.,* vol. 15, p. 1088.

16. Armstrong, Diary, November 23–30, 1862; Merrill, vol. 1, p. 567; *O.R.,* vol. 15, p. 1088.

17. Armstrong, Diary, November 23, 28, December 4, 1862; Grimsley, letter to wife, December 4, 1862; Hoffman, *Camp, Court, and Siege,* pp. 38, 56; *O.R.,* vol. 15, p. 590. Morris Raphael, *Battle in the Bayou Country,* p. 62; Winters, p. 141.

18. Armstrong, Diary, November 31, December 1–3, 1862.

19. Armstrong, Diary, December 4–20, 1862.

20. *ORN,* vol. 19, p. 393; David C. Edmonds, *The Conduct of Federal Troops in Louisiana,* pp. 58, 59.

21. *Annual Reunion of the Twenty-first Indiana Volunteers, First Heavy Artillery, Minutes, 1892,* pp. 33–34.

22. *American Tribune,* March 13, 1899.

23. Armstrong, Diary, December 20, 21, 27, 31, 1862; Dooley, letter to mother, January 1, 1863. Grimsley, letter to wife, December 7, 16, 26, 1862; *O.R.,* vol. 15, p. 610; *ORN,* vol. 19, pp. 761–762; *Parke County Republican,* December 31, 1862.

Ten

1. *O.R.,* vol. 15, pp. 234, 636, 1088; War Department, General Orders, No. 5.

2. Rufus Dooley, letter to mother, January 18, 1863; Richard B. Irwin, *History of The Nineteenth Army Corps,* p. 73. *O.R.,* vol. 15, pp. 234, 655.

3. Dooley, letter to mother, January 18, 1863; *O.R.,* vol. 15, p. 237.

4. *American Tribune,* March, 1899; Dooley, letter to mother, January 18, 1863.

5. Dooley, letter to mother, January 18, 1863; James Grimsley, Ordnance Return. [The Official Records do not report that the 21st Indiana was engaged in the affair with the *Cotton,* but the 21st Indiana Company B's Ordnance Return shows this company fired 337 rounds during the engagement.] Grimsley, letter to wife, January 17, 1863; *Indianapolis Daily Journal,* letter dated January 19, 1863, from Benjamin F. Card, February 5, 1863; Irwin, p. 74; *Natchitoches Union,* January 29, 1863; *O.R.,* vol. 15, p. 236; Winters, *The Civil War in Louisiana,* p. 213.

6. *Natchitoches Union,* January 29, 1863.

7. Bergeron, *The Civil War Reminiscences of Silas T Grisamore, C.S.A.,* p. 105; Dooley, letter to mother, January 18, 1863; *Indianapolis Daily Journal,* February 5, 1863; *O.R.,* vol. 15, p. 235. Winters, p. 213.

8. Grimsley, letter to wife, January 17, 1863; *Indianapolis Daily Journal,* February 5, 1863; *O.R.,* vol. 15, p. 234.

9. *Minutes, Annual Reunion of the 21st Regiment, First Indiana Heavy Artillery, 1892,* p. 32; Grimsley, letter to wife, February 3, 1863.

10. Grimsley, letter to wife, February 5, 1863; *Indianapolis Daily Journal,* February 5, 1863. National Archives Record Group (hereafter cited as NARG) 94, E112–115, P1-P17, *Regimental Records, 1st Indiana Heavy Artillery* (hereafter cited as *Regimental Records*).

11. Dooley, letter to mother, February 7. 1863.

12. Dooley, letter to mother, February 8, 1863; NARG

94, E112–115, P1-P17, *Regimental Records*; Scribner, *Roll of Honor*, p. 386.

13. Dooley, letter, February 11, 1863.
14. Dooley, letter, March 2, 1863; Hatten, letter to sister, February 28, 1863.
15. Harding, letter to wife, February 12, 1863; NARG, E112–115, P1-P17, *Regimental Records*.
16. Johnson, *A Soldier's Life*, pp. 50–51; *Parke County Republican*, published letter dated February 15, 1863, from Cyrus Hunt, March 11, 1863; *Parke County Republican*, published letter from W. R. Aydelotte, May 13, 1863. [After the war, the 9th Connecticut and the 1st Indiana reconciled their differences. These two regiments sponsored the G.A.R. memorial in Chalmette National Cemetery outside of New Orleans.]
17. *O.R.*, vol. 15, pp. 240–243; *Port Hudson Tri-Weekly News*, February 27, 1863.
18. Grimsley, letter to wife, March 6, 1863; *Parke County Republican*, May 13, 1863.
19. Kendall, "Recollections of a Confederate Officer," pages 1108–1109; *O.R.*, vol. 15, pp. 251–256, 1032, 1033; *ORN*, vol. 19, p. 704.
20. L. J. Fremaux, chief engineer at Port Hudson, Map dated October 30, 1862; *O.R.*, vol. 15, p. 1027; Daniel Smith, *History of Company K*, pp. 40, 41, 45, 49; George S. Waterman, "Afloat — Afield — Afloat" (hereafter cited as "A-A-A"), *Confederate Veteran*, April 1898, p. 172.
21. *Confederate Veteran*, "Ships That Passed in the Night," June 1896; *Confederate Veteran*, "The Battleship Mississippi," March 1917, July 1918; *Confederate Veteran*, "Hot Shot at Port Hudson," July 1918; *Confederate Veteran*, "The Sinking of the Mississippi," May 1924; Kendall, pp. 1108–1109; *O.R.*, vol. 15, pp. 302, 693; *ORN*, vol. 19, pp. 669, 671, 673, 675, 680, 681, 688, 695; *Rebellion Record*, vol. 6, p. 456. [Based upon witness' descriptions of the rifled shot that hit the *Richmond* and the *Monongahela*, this "80-pounder rifle" was a 32-pounder smoothbore rifled to fire a 6.4-inch rifle projectile. This particular piece did not have a reinforcing band added to its breech for strength. Also, the navy referred to the "short" 6.4-inch rifle projectiles as 80-pounder and to 6.4-inch rifles as 6-inch rifles. See *ORN*, vol. 19, pp. 627–29, 632, 633, 675, and Warren Ripley's *Artillery and Ammunition of the Civil War*, p. 117.]
22. Unknown diarist writing from Fort Pike, Louisiana, March 14, 1863; Smith, Diary, January 19, February 15, March 16, March 23, 1863. Smith, *History of Company K*, pp. 52–53. Waterman, "A-A-A," *Confederate Veteran*, vol. 6, pp. 390–394.
22. Grimsley, to wife, March 19, 1863; NARG-393, report from Captain Richard Arnold, chief of artillery, Department of the Gulf, to General G. L. Andrews, chief of staff.
23. Ibid.
24. Dooley, letter, April 1, 1863; Grimsley, letter to wife, March 31, 1863; Irwin, *History of the Nineteenth Army Corps*, pp. 88–89. Noel, p. 45; *Parke County Republican*, May 13, 1863; *O.R.*, vol. 15, p. 258; *ORN*, vol. 20, pp. 108–113.
25. Dooley, letters to mother and father, April 10, 18, 1863; NARG, 393–1799, vol. 44.
26. Bergeron, *The Civil War Reminiscences of Silas T. Grisamore, C.S.A.*, p. 112; Irwin, pp. 92–93; Noel, p. 46; *O.R.*, vol. 15, pp. 320, 324, 328.
27. Irwin, p. 94; NARG 77, Maps 76, M111, M111-1, M111-2, Z33–144.
28. Bergeron, *Guide to Louisiana Confederate Units*, pp. 17, 19, 23, 130, 132, 163; J.L. Brent Collection, L.H.A.-55-L, folder #7, April 22, 1863, report; *O.R.*, vol. 15, pp. 320, 390, 1090–1093.

29. *American Tribune*, obscured date. Bergeron, *The Civil War Reminiscences of Silas T. Grisamore, C.S.A.* page 113; *Daily Picayune*, April 21, 1863; William Fowler, *Memorials of William Fowler*, pp. 34–36; Irwin, p. 96; Noel, p. 47; *O.R.*, vol. 15, pp. 320, 329, 390; *Parke County Republican*, May 20, 1863; *Rebellion Record*, vol. 6, p. 534; *SOR*, Part 2, vol. 15, p. 532.
30. *Daily Picayune*, April 21, 1863; Irwin, p. 98; *O.R.*, vol. 15, pp. 321–322, 334–335; *Rebellion Record*, vol. 6, pp. 535, 536; *Supplement to the Official Records*, Part 2, vol. 42, pp. 316, 318.
31. Irwin, pp. 97–100; Noel, p. 47; William H. Root, *Private Journal*, p. 642.
32. Artillery report from Cornay's battery found at the Archives of Miami University of Ohio. Dpecifically, this gun weighed 1,700 pounds and was marked on the breech: "Psh. St. Mary." Irwin, p. 101; *O.R.*, vol. 15, pp. 321, 391–392, 1091–1092.
33. Irwin, pp. 107–110, 113; Noel, p. 47; *O.R.*, vol. 15, p. 391; Root, p. 643.
34. *Daily Picayune*, April 21, 1863; Irwin, pp. 114–115; Noel, pp. 48–49; *O.R.*, vol. 15. pages 392–394; *Rebellion Record*, vol. 6, p. 541.
35. *Daily Picayune*, April 21, 1863; Irwin, p. 124; Noel, p. 49; *O.R.*, vol. 15, p. 393.
36. Irwin, pp. 124–125; Noel, p. 49.
37. Irwin, pp. 127–128; Claudius Rider, diary, April 19, 1863; Root, pp. 644–645.
38. Irwin, pp. 132–134; Root, p. 647.
39. *American Tribune*, unknown date. Dooley, to mother, April 18, May 8, 1863; Ethel Ellis, oral history of John Yelton as told to author; *Parke County Republican*, May 13, 1863.
40. Grimsley, to wife, May 19, 1863; *O.R.*, vol. 26, Part 1, pp. 492–493.

Eleven

1. *O.R.*, vol. 15, p. 1080.
2. Stoddard, "Kentucky," *Confederate Military History*, vol. IX, p. 77; Irwin, *History of the Nineteenth Corps*, p. 150; *O.R.*, vol. 15, p. 731.
3. Irwin, p. 152; *O.R.*, vol. 26, Part 1, pp. 486–489, 493; William Wilcox, letter to wife, May 4, 1863.
4. Irwin, pp. 153–154; *O.R.*, vol. 26, Part 1, pp. 493, 499, 500–502; *ORN*, vol. 20, p. 204; Henry A. Willis, *Fifty-Third Regiment Massachusetts Volunteers*, pp. 116, 117.
5. Fred Y. Dabney, *Report of Siege of Port Hudson*; James Freret, "Fortification and Siege of Port Hudson," *Southern Historical Society Papers*, vol. 14, p. 312; Irwin, pp. 154, 165; *ORN*, vol. 20, p. 220.
6. NARG 393, 1799, vol. 44; Terrell, *Report of the Adjutant General of State of Indiana*, vol. 4, p. 466.
7. Benedict, *Vermont in the Civil War*, vol. 2, p. 714; Dabney, *Report of Siege of Port Hudson*; Freret, pp. 313–314; Irwin, 161–162; McDonald, Robert, *Historical Data Record*, Mississippi State Archives, R.G. 9, vol. 21B, Folder 11; *O.R.*, vol. 26, Part 1, pp. 39, 121–122; Collection of Elizabeth Shaifer Hollingsworth, A. K. "Kell" Shaifer, notes on the Battle of Plains Store; *SOR*, Part 2, vol. 42, p. 318.
8. *OR*, Part 2, vol. 42, p. 318; Earl VanDorn Miller, *Historical Data Record*, Mississippi State Archives, R.G. 9, vol. 21B, Folder 11; Headquarters Book, Miles' Legion, May 22, 1863; Collection of Elizabeth Shaifer Hollingsworth, A. K. "Kell" Shaifer, miscellaneous notes and papers.
9. Confederate Map, NARG, Z33–141; Freret, pp. 314–315; Headquarters Book, Miles' Legion, May 22, 23, 1863; Mississippi State Archives, Confederate Civil

War Records, Record Group 9, vol. 21. Collection of Elizabeth Shaifer Hollingsworth, A. K. "Kell" Shaifer, miscellaneous notes and papers.

10. Austen Diary, May 21, 22, 1863; Arthur W. Bergeron Jr., and Lawrence L. Hewitt, *Boone's Louisiana Battery*, p. 14; Freret, *Southern Historical Society Papers*, pp. 315–316; Irwin, pp. 165–166; *O.R.*, vol. 26, Part 1, pp. 501, 503; J. G. W. Steedman, letter to uncle, July 1, 1863; Howard Wright, *Port Hudson, Its History*, p. 26.

11. Benedict, vol. 2, pp. 700–701. Irwin, p. 166; Merrill, vol. 2, *Soldier of Indiana*, pp. 344, 347. [Pages 344 through 350 are the 1st Indiana Heavy Artillery, Colonel John A. Keith's official report to Brigadier-General Richard Arnold, chief of artillery, Department of the Gulf. This report was otherwise lost, and it is missing from *The Official Records of the War of Rebellion*, etc.] *New Orleans Era*, July 21, 1863; *O.R.*, vol. 26, pp. 504, 526–527; George W Powers, *Thirty-Eighth Regiment Massachusetts Volunteers*, p. 91; W. B. Shelby, Report of action at Port Hudson, August 5, 1863; *SOR*, Part 1, vol. 4, pp. 742, 782–783; Harrison Soule, letter to father July 2, 1863; W.S. Turner, Diary, May 25–26, 1863 (39th Mississippi Regiment).

12. Freret, pp. 314, 315, 318; *O.R.*, vol. 26, Part 1, p. 145; Smith, *History of Company K*, p. 62; Wright, *Port Hudson, Its History*, p. 27.

13. Merrill, vol. 2, p. 345; NARG 393, 1799, vol. 44; *O.R.*, vol. 26, Part 1, p. 508.

14. *O.R.*, vol. 26, part 1, pp. 507–509; *O.R.*, vol. 26, Part 2, p. 10; *Rebellion Record*, vol. 6, p. 632.

15. Bergeron and Hewitt, *Boone's Louisiana Battery*, p. 15; L. J. Fremaux, chief engineer at Port Hudson, map dated October 30, 1862; Merrill, vol. 2, p. 345.

16. NARG, 393, 1799, vol. 44; Captain Jacob Rawles, report to Captain George Halstead, A.A.G., May 30, 1863; Kenneth E. Shewmaker, and Andrew K. Prinz, eds., "Notes and Documents, a Yankee in Louisiana: Selections From the Diary and Correspondence of Henry R. Gardner, 1862–1866," *Louisiana History* 5, no. 3 (1964): 277. (hereafter cited as Shewmaker and Prinz, *Notes and Documents*); *SOR*, Part 2, vol. 42, p. 318.

17. Willoughby Babcock, letter to wife, May 30, 1863; Albert F. B. Edwards, diary, May 25–26, 1863; Ira B. Gardner, *Recollections*, pp. 26–28; William H. Root, *Private Journal*, p. 658.

18. T. A. Dalring, letter to Col. J. L. Powers, November 4, 1900; P. F. DeGournay, report to Gardner, September 12, 1863; Freret, pp. 315, 318–319; Edward Young McMorries, Ph.D., *History of the First Regiment Alabama Volunteer Infantry*, p. 61; Colonel W.R. Miles, report to Gardner, July 23, 1863; *O.R.*, vol. 26, part 1, p. 165; J.B. Rawles, report of May 30, 1863; W. B. Shelby, report to Gardner, August 3, 1863; Daniel K. Smith, *History of Company K*, pp. 62–63.

19. Irwin, p. 169; *New Orleans Era*, July 18, 1863; ORN, vol. 20, pp. 211–213.

20. Henry A. Willis, *Fifty-Third Regiment Massachusetts Volunteers*, p. 122; Freret, p. 323; William L. Haskin, *The History of the First Regiment of Artillery*, pp. 192, 551–552; Irwin, pp. 170–171; Whitman and True, *Maine in the War for the Union*, p. 387; Willis, p. 122.

21. Colonel N A.M. Dudley, report to Capt. Halstead, A.A.G., May 30, 1863; Haskin, pp. 192, 551; Irwin, p. 172; Colonel Benjamin Whitfield Johnson, "Report on the Fifteenth Arkansas Infantry," dated September 12, 1863, Special Collections, Hill Memorial Library, Louisiana State University; Michael J. Martin, *The 4th Wisconsin Infantry*, p. 168; Caroline E. Whitcomb, *History of the 2nd Massachusetts Battery of Light Artillery*, p. 48.

22. *New Orleans Era*, July 11, 1863; Irwin, pp. 170–171; McMorries, p. 63; Winters, pp. 250–252.

23. Edward Bacon, *Among the Cotton Thieves*, pp. 160–161.

24 Bergeron and Hewitt, *Boone's Louisiana Battery*, pp. 15, 16; Freret, pp. 321–322; Irwin, pp. 173–174; *New York Daily Tribune*, June 9, 1863; Shelby to Gardner, August 3, 1863; *SOR*, Part 1, vol. 4, pp. 785–786; Turner, Diary, May 27, 1863, 39th Mississippi.

25. John W. DeForest, *A Volunteer's Adventures*, p. 113; Lawrence Hewitt, ed., *A Place Named Desperate*, pp. 11–12; Irwin, p. 172; "Port Hudson, Its History," *New Orleans Era*, August 9, 1863; *SOR*, Part 1, vol. 4, p. 746; Winters, p. 254.

26. Irwin, pp. 176–177; Henry T. Johns, *Life with the 49th Massachusetts Volunteers*, p. 253; *O.R.*, vol. 26, Part 1, pp. 509–510.

27. J. M. Bailey, *Memoirs of Captain J.M. Bailey*, p. 35; Albert F. B. Edwards, Diary, May 27, 1863; Falls, *The Eaton Rifles*, p. 8; Irwin, pp. 177–178; James M'Murray, "Heroism of Union Officer at Port Hudson," *Confederate Veteran* 16, p. 428; Wright, "Port Hudson, Its History," *The Daily True Delta*, August 8, 1863; *O.R.*, vol. 26, Part 1, p. 510; Soule, letter to father, July 2, 1863; Lawrence Van Alstyne, *Diary of an Enlisted Man*, pp. 113–115; Robert Wilkinson (128th New York Volunteers), letter dated June 3, 1863.

28. Bailey, pp. 35–36; Freret, p. 324; Irwin, p. 178; Kendall, p. 1114; Robert McDonald, report to J. Powers, no date; M'Murray, p. 428; "Port Hudson, Its History," *New Orleans Era*, July 18, 1863, August 9, 1863; *O.R.*, vol. 26, Part. 1, p. 511; Warren Ripley, *Artillery and Ammunition of the Civil War*, p. 379; Rowland, p. 466; Collection of Elizabeth Shaifer Hollingsworth: A. K. "Kell" Shaifer, miscellaneous notes on his map of Port Hudson; Soule, letter to father, July 2, 1863; Van Alstyne, p. 115; Wilkinson, letter dated 6-3-1863 (partial copy held by author).

29. Irwin, p. 178; Kendall, pp. 1115–1116; M'Murray, p. 428; *Rebellion Record*, vol. 7, "Humor and Incidents," page 83; Collection of Elizabeth Shaifer Hollingsworth: A. K. "Kell" Shaifer, miscellaneous notes; *SOR*, Part 1, vol. 4, p. 787; Soule, letter to father, July 2, 1863.

30. Edward, Diary, May 27, 1863; Irwin, pp. 178, 179; Jacob B. Rawles, report dated May 30, 1863, to George B. Halstead, A.A.G.; Collection of Elizabeth Shaifer Hollingsworth: A. K. "Kell" Shaifer, miscellaneous notes; Van Alstyne, p. 114.

31. Dooley, letter, June 16, 1863; Pythagoras E. Holcomb, report of May 30, 1863; Merrill, vol. 2, p. 347; Frederick W. Reinhard, report dated May 27, 1863; Shewmaker and Prinz, *Notes and Documents*, p. 277; William B. Stevens, *History of the 50th Regiment of Infantry* (Massachusetts), p. 135. [Most light artillery units (when detached) usually fought in two-gun sections; therefore, it was not uncommon to withdraw a sound piece from action along with its companion disabled piece.]

32. Dooley, letter, June 16, 1863; Freret, p. 325; Merrill, vol. 2, pp. 347–348; "Port Hudson, Its History," *The Daily True Delta*, August 8, 1863; *SOR*, Part 1, vol. 4, p. 787.

33. Irwin, pp. 179–180; Henry T. Johns, *Life with the 49th Massachusetts Volunteers*, pp. 228–235, 253; E. D. Johnson, report of May 29, 1863; Merrill, vol. 2, p. 347; George W. Powers, *The Story of the Thirty Eighth Massachusetts Volunteers* (hereafter cited as *The Thirty Eighth Massachusetts*), p. 94; Frederick W. Reinhard, report of May 27, 1863; Stevens, pp. 139, 279; Winters, pp. 254–255, 257–258.

34. Irwin, p. 181; *O.R.*, vol. 26, p. 145; Smith, *History of Company K*, pp. 63–65; Stevens, pp. 140–141.

35. Dooley, letter dated June 16, 1863; Holcomb, report of May 30, 1863; Merrill, vol. 2, pp. 345, 347–49; *Parke County Republican*, August 5, 1863; Rawles, report dated May 30, 1863 to George B. Halstead, A.A.G.; Reinhard, report of May 27, 1863; *SOR*, Part 1, vol. 4, p. 734.

36. Grimsley, letter to wife, dated June 5, 1863; McMorries, p. 64; Merrill, vol. 2, pp. 345–346, 348; Smith, *History of Company K*, pp. 64–65.

Twelve

1. Irwin, *History of the Nineteenth Corps*, p. 189; McMorries, *History of the First Alabama Regiment*, p. 65; Shelby, report to Gardner, August 3, 1863; *New Orleans Era*, July 16, 1863; Turner, Diary, May 28, 1863 (39th Mississippi Regiment).

2. Irwin, p. 186. NARG 393, Pt. 1, e1738, vol. 5, letter of May 28, 1863, from Banks to Emory; NARG 393: 802, 1837.

3. Irwin, pp. 187–189; Winters, *The Civil War in Louisiana*, p. 261.

4. David C. Edmunds, *The Guns of Port Hudson*, p. 114; William L. Haskin, *History of the First Regiment of Artillery*, pp. 193, 552, 553; *Rebellion Record*, vol. 7, "Documents," page 269; *SOR*, Part 2, vol. 25, p. 114; Willis, *The Fifty-Third Regiment of Massachusetts Volunteers*, p. 126; Winters, p. 261.

5. Austen, Diary, June 17, 1863; Smith, *History of Company K*, pp. 66–67; *O.R.*, Ser. 1, vol. 26, Part 1, pp. 145, 153; *ORN*, Ser. 1, vol. 20, p. 777.

6. Merrill, *Soldier of Indiana*, vol. 2, p. 346; *New Orleans Era*, July 11, 1863; *Rebellion Record*, vol. 7, "Documents," page 269; W.H.H. Terrell, *Indiana in the War for the Union*, vol. 4, p. 46; Turner, Diary, June 2–3, 1863.

7. Freret, *Fortification and Siege*, p. 330; Merrill, vol. 2, pp. 346–347; *SOR*, Part 1, vol. 4, pp. 791–792.

8. *ORN*, vol. 20, p. 797; NARG 393, Part 1, e1738, vol. 5; *The Daily True Delta*, "Port Hudson, Its History," August 8, 1863.

9. Merrill, vol. 2, pp. 345, 348; NARG 393, Part 1, e1738, vol. 5; *O.R.*, Ser. 1, vol. 15, pp. 845, 846; *Rebellion Record*, vol. 7, "Documents," page 338; *SOR*, Part 2, vol. 15, p. 532; Terrell, vol. 4, p. 468.

10. Kendall, p. 1118; *O.R.*, Ser. 1, vol. 26, part 1, p. 171; NARG, 393, part 1, e1738, vol. 5; NARG, 393–1802, note from Dwight to Arnold; *Rebellion Record*, vol. 7, "Documents," page 269; *SOR*, Part 1, vol. 4, pp. 727–728, 732; *O.R.*, Ser. 1, vol. 26, p. 141.

11. Austen, Diary, June 8, 1863; *O.R.*, Ser. 1, vol. 26, part 1, p. 172; Benedict, *Vermont in the Civil War*, vol. 2, p. 702; Dooley, letter to mother dated June 16, 1863; Irvin, p. 189; Merrill, vol. 2, pp. 346, 348; *New Orleans Era*, July 16, 1863; *Rebellion Record*, vol. 7, "Documents," page 269; Turner, Diary, June 9, 1863 (39th Mississippi Infantry).

12. Bell, Diary, June 8, 1863; Merrill, vol. 2, p. 346; NARG, 393–1802, telegram; *O.R.*, vol. 26, p. 172; *SOR*, Ser. 1, Part 1, vol. 4, p. 770; Turner, Diary, June 9, 1863; Wright, p. 39.

13. *O.R.*, Ser. 1, vol. 26, part 1, pp. 157–159; Lawrence L. Hewitt, and Arthur W. Bergeron, Jr., *Post Hospital Ledger, Port Hudson, Louisiana, 1862–1863*, Entry 2402, p. 97; Winters, pp. 265–266; Turner, Diary, June 10, 1863.

14. NARG, 393–1802, telegrams between Arnold and Armstrong; "Port Hudson, Its History," *The Daily True Delta*, August 8, 11, 1863.

15. Bacon, *Among the Cotton Thieves*, p. 134; Dooley, letter to mother, dated June 16, 1863; Freret, p. 330: National Archives Quarterly Ordnance Returns: *O.R.*, Ser. 1, vol. 26, Part 1, p. 155: *Parke County Republican*, August 5, 1863; *SOR*, Part 2, vol. 15, p. 528; Turner, Diary, June 12, 1863.

16. Dooley, letter to mother, June 16, 1863; Edwin Olmstead, Wayne E. Stark, and Spencer C. Tucker, *The Big Guns*, pp. 183, 184, 193; Merrill, vol. 2, p. 348; *O.R.*, Ser. 1, vol. 26, Part 1, p. 155. [This rifled cannon was *none* of the types described by the Confederates or the Federals. A study of a contemporary photograph of the rifle and comparison with dimensions of a surviving piece raised from a river in North Carolina led artillery experts Edwin Olmstead and Wayne Stark to conclude the Port Hudson piece was a 4.62-inch Gibbon & Andrews single-band siege rifle. Contemporary photographs show a much thicker, heavier, full-tapered piece than a 30-pounder Parrott, which has a smaller 4.2-inch bore. Trophy photographs from West Point Military Academy show this piece in relation to a 30-pounder Parrott, and this piece is obviously not a Parrott. Also, Daniel Smith, a member of the 1st Alabama, had served on this gun's crew and had also served on the crew of "The Baby." He describes this piece as having a *4.62-inch bore* the *same as* the *4.62-inch bore* of "The Baby," a bronze 12-pounder rifle. Smith goes on to state that both weapons "fired the same caliber projectile"; also, that they did not have the proper projectile for the heavy siege rifle, but were forced to use a lighter weight projectile of about twenty pounds.]

17. *New Orleans Era*, July 21, 1863; Bell, Diary, June 13, 1863; Dooley, letter to mother, June 16, 1863; Gardner, p. 280.

18. Austen, diary, June 13, 1863; NARG, 393–1802; NARG, 393, part 2, e2109; Benedict, vol. 2, p. 714; Port Hudson State Historical Site, Compilation of Movement of Heavy Guns in the River Batteries; Smith, p. 69; Whitcomb, p. 49; Robert Williamson, 128th New York, letter of July 7, 1863.

19. Bacon, pp. 170–171; *The Daily True Delta*, "Port Hudson, Its History," August 11, 12, 1863; *New Orleans Era*, July 19, 1863; Powers, p. 105; Willis, pp. 131, 132.

20. Edmonds, *The Guns of Port Hudson*, vol. 2, pp. 213, 229; Michael J. Martin, *The 4th Wisconsin Infantry*, pp. 190–191, 193–194; Powers, p. 106. Albert Plummer, *History of the Forty-Eighth Regiment, M. V. M.*, p. 65; E. B. Quiner, *The Military History of Wisconsin*, p. 505; Willis, pp. 137–138.

21. Bailey, *Memoirs*, pp. 40–41; Henry I. Clark (24th Connecticut), journal in letter form, June 14, 1863; Jerry E. Flint, letter dated June 23, 1863; Irvin, pp. 194, 196–197; Martin, pp. 195, 197, 205; Powers, p. 108; Smith, p. 71.

22. Bailey, pp. 41–42; Clark, journal, June 14, 1863; *The New Orleans Era*, August 12, 1863; Hewitt, and Bergeron, pp. 98–100; Irwin, pp. 198–199, 204; *Rebellion Record*, vol. 7, Documents, p. 47.

23. Bacon, pp. 173–179; Dooley, letter to mother, June 16, 1863; *New Orleans Era*, July 19, 1863; *O.R.*, Ser. 1, vol. 26, part 1, p. 174; Plummer, p. 43; Smith, p. 71; Soule, letter to father, July 2, 1863; Robert Wilkinson, 128th New York, letter of July 7, 1863 (partial copy held by author).

24. *American Tribune*, no date; Armstrong, telegrams to Richard Arnold, June 14, 1863; NARG 393–1802; Bacon, p. 190; Bailey, p. 41; Grimsley, letter to wife, June 30, 1863; Irvin, p. 201; Powers, p. 108; *Rebellion Record*, vol. 7: Documents: page 44; *SOR*, Part 2, vol. 15, p. 524; Terrell, vol. 4, p. 449 (death of Manius Braugher of Company A on June 14, 1863); Luther Tracy Townsend, *History of the Sixteenth Regiment, New Hampshire Volunteers*, p. 232; Willis, pp. 137, 138.

Thirteen

1. Bailey, *Memoirs*, pp. 41–42; Clark, journal, June 17, 1863; Bacon, p. 187; Irwin, pp. 204, 212; *Rebellion Record*, vol. 7, "Documents," p. 338; Smith, pp. 72–73; Willis, p. 186.
2. Irwin, pp. 210–212; *New Orleans Era*, July 19, 1863; O.R., Ser. 1, vol. 26, part 1, p. 176; Soule, letter to wife, June 17, 1863.
3. Bacon, pp. 189, 212, 215, 220, 222; Bailey, pp. 39–40; Soule, letter to wife, June 17, 1863. Turner, Diary, June 15, 1863; Wilkinson, letter home, July 7, 1863.
4. William Jefferson Bell, Diary, June 16, 1863; NARG 393–1802, S.E. Armstrong, telegrams to Richard Arnold, June 15, 1863, and E.W. Leymour, telegrams to Richard Arnold, June 15, 1863; NARG 393, part 1, e1738, vol. 5, Banks, N. P., signal to Farragut, June 15, 1863; NARG 393, part 2, e2109, Dwight to Irwin, telegram, June 16, 1863; O.R., Ser. 1, vol. 26, Part 1, p. 145; Turner, Diary, June 15, 1863.
5. NARG 94, E112–115, P1–17, Regimental Records; NARG, 393, part 1, e1738, vol. 5, Telegram from Banks' headquarters; O.R., Ser. 1, vol. 26, Part 1, pp. 36, 40, 127, 128; Turner, Diary, June 17, 1863; Willis, p. 142.
6. Armstrong, to Richard Arnold, June 20, 1863; Bacon, pp. 166, 201–202; NARG, 393, 1802, telegram from Dwight's headquarters; NARG, 393, chart of ranges and positions, from battery #1 of thirty-pounders on the left to position #14 of four mortars on the right, to targets within Port Hudson (numbered as written on document, not as written on maps); O.R., Ser. 1, vol. 26, Part 1, p. 141; Stewart Sifakis, *Who Was Who in the Civil War*, pp. 196–197.
7. Dooley, letters to mother, June 16, June 21, 1863; Edmonds, pp. 265–268; Haskin, p. 193; NARG, 393, part 1, e1738, vol. 5; *Parke County Republican*, August 5, 1863; *Rebellion Record*, vol. 7, "Documents," page 338.
8. Bacon, p. 137; O.R., Ser. 1, vol. 26, Part 1, pp. 145–146, 160; Wright, p. 44.
9. Merrill, vol. 2, pp. 345–348; SOR, Part 1, vol. 4, p. 799; Turner, Diary, June 22, 1863.
10. Bacon, pp. 224, 227, 228, 230; NARG, 393–1802; SOR, Part 1, vol. 4, pp. 799–800; Willis, p. 186.
11. Bacon, p. 227; Dooley, letter to mother, June 21, 1863, continued through July 10, 1863; Haskin, p. 193; NARG, 303–1799, vol. 44; NARG, 393–1802; SOR, Part 2, vol. 25, p. 527.
12. Dooley, letter to mother, June 21–July 10, 1863; SOR, Part 1, vol. 4, p. 799.
13. Bailey, pp. 43, 44; Turner, Diary, June 21–June 25, 1863; Willis, p. 186.
14. Fred Y. Dabney, Report to T. F. Wilson, Assistant Adjutant General of events on June 24 and 25; James Freret, "Fortification and Siege," pp. 333, 334; Lawrence Lee Hewitt, *A Place Named ... Desperate*, pp. 19, 20; Smith, p. 69, 73; SOR, Part 1, vol. 4, pp. 799–800, 805; Wright, pp. 44, 46, 52.
15. Bailey, p. 45; Bailey, p. 45; Grimsley, letter to wife, July 11, 1863; Kendall, p. 1121; Powers, p. 115; Daniel Smith, "History of Company K," p. 76; Turner, Diary, June 24, 1863; Wright, p. 44.
16. Austen, Diary, June 29, 1863; Dooley, letter to mother, June 21–July 10, 1863; *New Orleans Era*, July 15, 1863; Grimsley, letters to wife, June 30, 1863, July 11, 1863; Hewitt and Bergeron Jr., p. 101; SOR, Part 1, vol. 4, p. 800, Willis, p. 134.
17. Austen, Diary, June 29, 1863; Richard McClung, Diary, p. 29; NARG, 393, pt. 1, e1738, Vol. 5; O.R., Ser. 1, vol. 26, Part 1, pp. 141–142, 155–156; Smith, "History of Company K," pp. 76, 77; Wright, p. 48.
18. Bacon, p. 229; *LaGrange Standard*, August 8, 1863 (letter from James Rheubottom of 1st Indiana, Company A); Merrill, vol. 2, p. 349; Shelby, Report of August 6, 1863 to T. Friend Wilson, A. A. G; Soule, letter to father, July 20, 1863; Turner, Diary, June 25, 27, 1863.
19. Grimsley, letter, July 11, 1863; Haskin, p. 193; NARG, 393, part 1, e1738, vol. 5; NARG, 393–1802; Turner, Diary, June 28, 1863; O.R., Ser. 1, vol. 26, Part 1, p. 161.
20. Bacon, pp. 260–266, 274, 275; Kendall, p. 1119; *New Orleans Era*, July 15, 1863; Wright, p. 49.
21. Dooley, letter to mother, June 21–July 10, 1863; Haskin, p. 194; SOR, Ser. 1, Part 1, vol. 4, p. 805.
22. Austen, diary, July 4, 1863; Dooley, letter to mother, June 21, 1863 through July 10, 1863; Edwards, diary, July 1, 1863; Shewmaker and Prinz, *Notes and Documents*, p. 281; Hewitt and Bergeron, entry 2498, p. 101; O.R., Ser. 1, vol. 26, Part 1, p. 86; *Parke County Republican*, August 5, 1863; Turner, diary, June 30, July 1, 1863.
23. Dooley, letter to mother, June 21–July 10, 1863; O.R., Ser. 1, vol. 26, Part 1, pp. 85–87, 96–98, 156; *Parke County Republican*, August 5, 1863.
24. Edwards, Diary, July 1–2, 1863; SOR, Ser. 1, Part 1, vol. 4, pp. 803–806; Wright, *Port Hudson*, pp. 48, 49.
25. O.R., Ser. 1, vol. 26, Part 1, pp. 126, 182; Smith, p. 75; Wright, pp. 49–50.
26. Austen, Diary, July 4, 1863; Bell, Diary, July 3–4, 1863; Elliott, letter to parents, July 6, 1863; Kendall, p. 1123; O.R., Ser. 1, vol. 26, Part 1, p. 164; General I. G. W. Steedman, letter to uncle, events of July 1–7, 1863; Turner, Diary, July 4, 1863.
27. Austen, Diary, July 4, 1863; NARG, 393–1802; SOR, Ser. 1, vol. 4, Part 1, p. 807; Whitcomb, pp. 51–52.
28. Freret, p. 240; Merrill, vol. 2, p. 348; Sydney C. Kerksis, and Thomas S. Dickey, *Heavy Artillery Projectiles of the Civil War, 1861–1865*, pp. 248–250; *Parke County Republican*, August 5, 1863; Wright p. 52.
29. Irwin, pp. 222, 224; NARG, 393, Part 1, e1738, vol. 4; NARG, 393, Part 1, e1738, vol. 5; NARG, 1802.
30. Irwin, pp. 212–213, 225; NARG, 393, Part 1, e1738, vol. 5; NARG, 393, Part 2, e2109.
31. DeGournay, report to T. F. Wilson, A.A.G., September 12, 1863; Irwin, pp. 225–228; NARG, 393-Part 2, e2109.
32. Irwin, pp. 228–230; Kendall, p. 1128; Smith, pp. 78, 79; Wright, p. 55.
33. Irwin, p. 228–231; Kendall, pp. 1129–1130; NARG, 393, 1802; Wright, letter to mother, July 16, 1863; Wright, p. 56.
34. Irwin, p. 232; Kendall, pp. 1131, 1130; *Parke County Republican*, August 5, 1863; Wright, p. 57.
35. Freret, p. 347; Irwin, pp. 233–234; Kendall, p. 1132; NARG, 393, Part 1, e1738, vol. 5; NARG, 393–1802; O.R., Ser. 1, vol. 26, Part 1, pp. 67–70; Smith, p. 81; SOR, Ser. 1, Part 2, vol. 32, p. 560.
36. Grimsley, letter to wife, July 11, 1863; Kendall, pp. 1133–1134; Merrill, Vol. II, pp. 349–350; *Rebellion Record*, Vol. VI, p. 26; *Rebellion Record*, Vol. VII, "Documents," p. 207; Smith, p. 81.
37. NARG, 393, Part 1, e1738, vol. 5; NARG, 393–1802.

Fourteen

1. O.R., Ser. 1, vol. 26, Part 1, pp. 217, 567; Taylor, *Destruction and Reconstruction*, pp. 167, 149. General Sibley became very ill after reaching Louisiana and

turned over command of his mounted infantry and cavalry brigade and four light guns (the Valverde Battery) to Colonel Thomas Green.

2. *O.R.*, Ser. 1, vol. 26, Part 1, p. 218.
3. Harding, *Misc. Writings*, p. 274; *Indianapolis Daily Journal*, July 11, 1863; Irwin, pp. 238–239; *O.R.*, vol. 26, pp. 187, 193–197, 217–218; Taylor, p. 170; Terrell, vol. 8, p. 72.
4. Irwin, pp. 240–241; NARG 77, M116–2; Drawer 133, Sheet 63; NARG 94, E112–115, P 1–17, Regimental Records; *O.R.*, vol. 26, pp. 211–212, 215, 223–264, 266, 268–269, 911–914; Taylor, p. 170.
5. *O.R.*, vol. 26, pp. 211–15, 224–25, 912–14.
6. *Cincinnati Daily Commercial*, July 14, 1863; Bergeron, *The Civil War Reminiscences of Major Silas T. Grisamore, C.S.A.*, p. 123; *Daily Evening Gazette*, July 14, 1863; *O.R.*, vol. 26, pp. 216, 219; David C. Edmonds, ed., *Official Report Relative to the Conduct of Federal Troops in Louisiana*, pp. 115, 121.
7. *O.R.*, vol. 26, pp. 202, 204, 227–229; Taylor, pp. 172–174.
8. *Bartholomew County Atlas*, "Personal Sketches, John A. Keith," page 59; James Grimsley, letters to wife, July 16, July 30, 1863; Irwin, p. 255; *O.R.*, vol. 26, pp. 207–209; *O.R.*, vol. 53, p. 564; Isaac N. Osborn, letter.
9. Rufus Dooley, letter, August 10, 1863; Grimsley, letters to wife, August 3, 14, September 6, 1863; Scribner, *Indiana's Roll of Honor*, vol. 2, p. 387; NARG 94, Regimental Orders, August 9, 1863; *O.R.*, vol. 23, Part 2, p. 585; Vol. 30, Part 2, p. 556.
10. Scribner, vol. 2, p. 387; *O.R.*, Ser. 1, vol. 26, Part 1, pp. 287, 299; Vol. 53, Part 1, p. 552.
11. *Parke County Republican*, October 14, 1863; *O.R.*, vol. 26, pp. 294–295, 300.
12. *Parke County Republican*, October 14, 1863; *O.R.*, vol. 26, pp. 295, 300; "Records: First Indiana Heavy Artillery," Indiana Historical Society.
13. O.M. Roberts, "Texas," *Confederate Military History*, vol. XI, pp. 106–110; *SOR*, Part 2, vol. 25, "Maine," page 543.
14. Roberts, "Texas," *Confederate Military History*, vol. XI, pp. 107–110; Dooley, letter to mother, October 4, 1863; *Parke County Republican*, October 14, 1863.
15. Grimsley, letter to wife September 6, 1863, letter to father and mother, September 22, 1863; Harding, letter to wife, September 19, 1863.
16. Dooley, letter to mother, October 15, 1863; David C. Edmonds, *Yankee Autumn in Acadiana*, pp. 106, 164–69; "Records: First Indiana Heavy Artillery"; Indiana Historical Society; *O.R.*, vol. 26, pp. 369, 721.
17. Irwin, pp. 277–278; *O.R.*, vol. 26, p. 369; *Parke County Republican*, October 14, 1863.
18. Indiana Historical Society, "Records: First Indiana Heavy Artillery."
19. Dooley, letter to mother; Grimsley, Papers; Mitchell Hatten, Letters, Indiana Historical Society; *O.R.*, vol. 26, pp. 342, 357–358, 369, 394–395.
20. Dooley, letter to mother; Grimsley, Papers; Hatten, Letters, Indiana Historical Society; *O.R.*, vol. 26, p. 369; Ethel Ellis, oral history of John Yelton as told to author; Indiana Historical Society, "Records: First Indiana Heavy Artillery."
21. Harding, *Misc. Writings*, p. 330; Hillingoss, "Journal"; *O.R.*, vol. 26, pp. 481, 810, 876; Terrell, vol. 2, p. 207.
22. George W. Nash, Letter; NARG 156, microfilm Roll 1, vol. 3; *O.R.*, Ser. 1, vol. 26, Part 1, pp. 894–896.
23. NARG 94, "Regimental Orders," August 26, September 15, 22, 23, October 7, 9, 10, 23, 26, 28, November 2, 1863; *O.R.*, Ser. 1, vol. 26, Part 1, pp. 756, 895.

Fifteen

1. Rufus Dooley, letter to mother, December 28, 1863; Terrell, *Indiana in the War of the Rebellion*, vol. 1, pp. 412–413.
2. James Grimsley, letter to wife, December 25, 1863; Winters, *The Civil War in Louisiana*, p. 325.
3. Dooley, letter to mother, January 6, 1864; Irwin, p. 279.
4. Hilligoss, Journal; NARG 94, "Regimental Records," February 8, 1864; *O.R.*, Ser. 1, vol. 34, Part 2, pp. 38, 87.
5. Dooley, letter to father, January 18, 1864; NARG 94, "Regimental Records," Morning Reports, January 1864; Scribner, vol. 2, p. 388.
6. Dooley, letter to father, January 15, 1864, letter to mother January 27, 1864; Grimsley, letter to wife, December 14, 1863.
7. Dooley, letter from mother; *O.R.*, Ser. 1, vol. 34, Part 4, pp. 6, 7; Scribner, vol. 2, p. 388; Terrill, vol. 1, pp. 31, 122, 124.
8. Terrill, vol. 1, pp. 349–360.
9. Dooley, letter to mother, April 12, 1864; NARG 94, "Regimental Records," Morning Reports, April, 1864; *O.R.*, Ser. 1, vol. 32, Part 3, p. 231; *O.R.*, Ser. 1, vol. 34, Part 3, p. 114; John N. Seybold, *My War Experiences*, p. 5.
10. *O.R.*, Ser. 1, vol. 32, Part 3, pp. 254, 371–73, 435.
11. *Minutes, Annual Reunion of the 21st Regiment, First Indiana Heavy Artillery*, 1901, p. 10 (hereafter cited as *Minutes, 1901*); *O.R.*, Ser. 1, vol. 34, Part 2, pp. 513–516, 519–20, 543–45, 562–63, 611, 654–55; Irwin, pp. 292–295.
12. *Minutes, 1901*, p. 10; *O.R.*, Ser. 1, vol. 34, Part 1, p. 408; Irwin, pp. 294–296.
13. *Minutes, 1901*, pp. 10–12; Bergeron, *The Civil War Reminiscences of Major Silas T. Grisamore, C.S.A.*, pp. 145–149; Irwin, pp. 299–311; *O.R.*, Ser. 1, vol. 34, Part 1, pp. 263–268, 527; *SOR*, Part 1, vol. 6, p. 366; *SOR*, Part 2, vol. 27, pp. 359–60.
14. *Minutes, 1901*, p. 11; Irwin, pp. 313–22; *O.R.*, Ser. 1, vol. 34, Part 1, p. 309; Taylor, *Destruction and Reconstruction*, pp. 204–210; Terrell, vol. 4, p. 477.
15. *Confederate Veteran*, Vol. XXIII, 1915, "Service in the Trans-Mississippi," p. 32; *Minutes, 1901*, pp. 9–10; *Indianapolis Daily Journal*, April 26, 1864; *O.R.*, Ser. 1, vol. 34, Part 1, pp. 381–382, 388, 408–409; Part 3, p. 433; *ORN*, Ser. 1, vol. 26, pp. 49–50, 52, 54–55, 61–62, 781, 789–790; "Rubottom Reminiscin [sic]," Rootsweb.com/~dansge/rubch4.htm; *SOR*, Part 1, vol. 6, p. 353.
16. *Minutes, 1901*, p. 12; Bergeron, *The Civil War Reminiscences Major Silas T. Grisamore, C.S.A.*, p. 153; Irwin, pp. 331–332; *O.R.*, Ser. 1, vol. 34, Part 1, p. 406.
17. *Minutes, 1901*, pp. 12–13. Bergeron, *The Civil War Reminiscences Major Silas T. Grisamore, C.S.A.*, p. 153; Irwin, pp. 330, 332–333; *O.R.*, Ser. 1, vol. 34, Part 1, pp. 407, 460, 610–11; *SOR*, Part 1, vol. 6, p. 353.
18. *Minutes, Annual Reunion of the 21st Regiment—1st Indiana Heavy Artillery*, 1892, p. 32; *Minutes, 1901*, p. 13; Irwin, pp. 333–334, 337–342; *O.R.*, Ser. 1, vol. 34, Part 1, p. 408; *SOR* Part 1, vol. 6, p. 318.
19. *Minutes, 1901*, pp. 13–14; Irwin, pp. 344–345; "For Bales," The Florida Star website of Civil War Songs, *O.R.*, Ser. 1, vol. 34, Part 1, pp. 630–631; *O.R.*, Part 3, p. 514; *ORN*, Ser. 1, vol. 26, pp. 129–130; *SOR*, Part 1, vol. 6, pp. 347–348.
20. Bergeron, *The Civil War Reminiscences Major Silas T. Grisamore, C.S.A.*, pp. 156–157; *Confederate Veteran* 25, pp. 94–95, February 1917; Irwin, pp. 345–48; *Minutes, 1901*, pp. 14–16; *O.R.*, Ser. 1, vol. 34, Part 1, pp. 311, 594, 630–631; Edmonds, p. 184; Taylor, p. 232.

Sixteen

1. Danely, letter to friends, June 7, 1864; *O.R.*, Ser. 1, vol. 34, Part IV, pp. 6–7.

2. Danely, letter to friends, June 7, 1864; Dooley, letter to mother, May 28, and to Betsy Jane, June 16, 1864; NARG 94, "Regimental Orders," April 25, May 31, 1864; *O.R.*, Ser. 1, vol. 34, Part 4, pp. 18, 277, 322, 359; *Parke County Republican*, June 1, 1864.

3. Irwin, p. 353; *O.R.*, vol. 34, Part 4, pp. 358, 618.

4. Samuel E. Armstrong, Diary, July 4, 1864; Dooley, letter to mother, May 28, 1864.

5. *Minutes, Annual Reunion of the 21st Regiment— 1st Indiana Heavy Artillery, 1892*, p. 24; Armstrong, Diary, July 6–9, 1864; Dooley, letters to mother, July 9, 18, 1864; Hillingoss, Journal; NARG-94, "Regimental Orders," July 3, 5, 12, 1864; *O.R.*, vol. 41, Part 2, pp. 57, 83, 93, 370, 969–973.

6. Armstrong, Diary, July 20, 21, 1864; Dooley, letter to mother, July 18, 1864; Hilligoss, Journal; NARG 94, "Regimental Orders," June 25, 1864.

7. NARG 94, "Regimental Orders," July 25, 1864; *O.R.*, vol. 41, Part 2, pp. 280–281.

8. Dooley, letter to mother, August 10, 1864; *Philadelphia Inquirer*, August 17, 1864 (repeating excerpts from Richmond, VA newspapers); Seybold, pp. 6, 7.

9. Dooley, letter to mother, August 10, 1864; *O.R.*, Ser. 1, vol. 39, Part 1, p. 403; Seybold, p. 8.

10. *Confederate Veteran*, March 1913, "Served in the Army and Then in the Navy," p. 112; *O.R.*, Ser. 1, vol. 39, Part 1, pp. 406–08; Seybold, p. 8.

11. Dooley, letter to mother (including a sketch map of Dauphin Island showing where Company H had been and was) August 10, 1864; *O.R.*, Ser. 1, vol. 39, Part 1, pp. 403, 410; *O.R.* Vol. 39, Part 2, p. 306; *O.R.*, vol. 53, Part 2, pp. 743, 744; *Philadelphia Inquirer*, August 17, 1864 (repeating excerpts from Richmond, Virginia, newspapers); Seybold, p. 8.

12. Grimsley, letters to wife, June 3, August 14, 16, September 12, 1864; Terrell, vol. 2, pp. 199–206.

13. *O.R.*, Ser. 1, vol. 41, Part 2, p. 773; *O.R.*, vol. 41, Part 2, p. 784; *ORN*, Ser. 1, vol. 26, pp. 504–506; Terrell, vol. 2, pp. 199–206; Vol. 4, p. 481.

14. C.C. Andrews, *Campaign of Mobile*, p. 18; *Minutes, Annual Reunion of the 21st Regiment, First Indiana Heavy Artillery, 1892*, p. 24; *Atlas to Accompany the Official Records of the Union and Confederate Armies*, page 53 (hereafter cited as *Atlas*); Dooley, letter to mother, August 28, 1864; NARG-94, "Regimental Orders," August 13, 1864; *O.R.*, Ser. 1, vol. 41, Part 2, pp. 632, 646–47, 663; *O.R.*, Ser. 1, vol. 39, Part 1, pp. 411–412, 423–424; Seybold, p. 8.

15. *Atlas*, p. 63; Dooley, letter to mother, August 22, 1864; Ethel Ellis, oral history of John Yelton as told to author; *O.R.*, Ser. 1, vol. 39, Part 1, p. 412; Seybold, p. 9; Joseph B. Wilkinson, Jr., (1st Tennessee Heavy Artillery), Diary, August 15–16, 1864.

16. *Atlas*, p. 63; *O.R.*, Ser. 1, vol. 39, Part 1, p. 413; Wilkinson, Diary, August 17, 1864.

17. *Harper's Weekly*, September 24, 1864; *LaGrange Standard*, August 27, 1864; *O.R.*, Ser. 1, vol. 39, Part 1, p. 418; Part 2, pp. 423–424; Seybold, p. 10.

18. Dooley, letter to mother, August 28, 1864; *O.R.*, Ser. 1, vol. 39, Part 1, p. 414; *O.R.*, Part 2, pp. 423–424; Seybold, p. 10.

19. Andrews, pp. 18–19; Dooley, letter to mother, August 28, 1864; *O.R.*, Ser. 1, vol. 39, Part 1, pp. 422, 424; Seybold, p. 10.

20. *O.R.*, Ser. 1, vol. 39, Part 1, p. 414; Andrews, p. 18; Dooley, letter to mother, August 28, 1864.

21. *Parke County Republican*, September 28, 1864; *O.R.*, Part 2, vol. 39, pp. 336, 337.

Seventeen

1. Rufus Dooley, letter, September 6, 1864; Hillingoss, Journal; NARG 94, "Regimental Orders," August 29, 1864; *Parke County Republican*, September 28, 1864; *O.R.*, vol. 39, Part 2, pp. 336–337; *O.R.*, vol. 41, Part 2, p. 886; *SOR*, Part 2, vol. 1, pp. 142, 202, 208–209.

2. Dooley, letter dated October 20, 1864; NARG-94, "Regimental Orders," September 9, 10, 15, 20, 1864; *O.R.*, vol. 41, Part 3, pp. 601–602.

3. *O.R.*, vol. 41, Part IV, pp. 4, 450–451, 464, 485, 498, 532, 765, 766.

4. Dooley, letters of October 28, November 21, December 16, newspaper clipping of November 21, 1894; NARG 94, "Regimental Orders," November 3, 1894.

5. Armstrong, Diary, November 8, 14, 19, December 18, 1864; *Bartholomew County Atlas*, "Personal Sketches: John A. Keith," page 59; Dooley, letters of December 20, 1864, January 12, 1865; NARG 94, "Regimental Records," January 19 through February 21, 1865. Seybold, p. 11.

6. Andrews, p. 26; Armstrong, Diary, December 30, 1864; Dooley, letter, January 12, 1865; *O.R.*, vol. 48, Part 1, pp. 731, 846, 882; *SOR*, Part 2, vol. 30, pp. 284, 301; *SOR*, vol. 42, p. 317.

7. Armstrong, Diary, February 21, 1865; Dooley, letters, February 21, 26, 1865; Hillingoss, Journal; *O.R.*, Ser. 1, vol. 48, Part 1, p. 731; Seybold, p. 11.

8. Dooley, letter, March 8, 1865; NARG 94, "Regimental Orders," February 23, 1865; *O.R.*, Ser. 1, vol. 49, Part 2, pp. 14–16; Seybold, p. 11.

9. Andrews, pp. 29, 33–34; *O.R.*, Ser. 1, vol. 49, Part 2, pp. 8–9, 14–16.

10. Andrews, pp. 33–34; *O.R.*, Ser. 1, vol. 49, Part 2, pp. 23. 25–26, 41–42, 51, 56, 68, 78, 80, 85–89.

11. Andrews, pp. 35, 41, 46, 49; Armstrong, Diary, March 30, 31, April 1, 1865; *O.R.*, vol. 9, Part 2, pp. 114–115.

12. Armstrong, Diary, March 30–31, April 1, 1865; *O.R.*, vol. 49, Part 2, pp. 114–115; First Indiana Heavy Artillery Records, 1862–1865, "Battle Reports of Lieutenant Colonel Benjamin Hays, Regimental Commander, and Captain William Wimmer, Company H" (hereafter cited as "Records: Hays and Wimmer Battle Reports").

13. Andrews, pp. 68–69; George S. Waterman, *Confederate Veteran*, January 1900, vol. 8, "Afloat—Afield—Afloat" (hereafter cited as "A-A-A"), p. 22; P.D. Stephenson, "Journal," vol. 8, p. 75; "Records: Hays and Wimmer Battle Reports."

14. Andrews, pp. 67–72; *O.R.*, Ser. 1, vol. 49, Part 1, p. 231; *O.R.*, Ser. 1, Vol. 49, Part 2, pp. 147–149. "Southern Historical Society Papers," Vol. 39, p. 135.

15. *O.R.*, Ser. 1, vol. 49, Part 2, p. 150; Seybold, p. 12.

16. *O.R.*, Ser. 1, vol. 49, Part 1, pp. 229, 320, 823; *ORN*, vol. 22, pp. 225–226; "Records: Hays and Wimmer Battle Reports."

17. Waterman, p. 22; *O.R.*, Ser. 1, vol. 49, Part 2, p. 166; *Parke County Republican*, May 3, 1865; "Records: Hays and Wimmer Battle Reports."

18. *O.R.*, Ser. 1, vol. 49, Part 2, p. 166; "Records: Hays and Wimmer Battle Reports."

19. *O.R.*, Ser. 1, vol. 49, Part 2, pp. 182–183; "Records: Hays and Wimmer Battle Reports."

20. "Records: Hays and Wimmer Battle Reports."

21. Waterman, p. 490; Maury, Dabney, "Letter to P. G. T. Beauregard," June 1, 1865; *O.R.*, Ser. 1, vol. 49, Part 2, pp. 1185-1188; Stephenson, Journal, p. 65.

22. Andrews, pp. 130, 131; *O.R.*, vol. 49, Part 2, pp. 190–191, 235.
23. Andrews, p. 131; "Records: Hays and Wimmer Battle Reports."
24. Andrews, p. 166; Kerksis and Dickey, pp. 239–242; "Records: Hays and Wimmer Battle Reports."
25. Andrews, p. 13; Hillengoss, Journal, April 2, 1865; "Records: Hays and Wimmer Battle Reports"; Stephenson, Journal, page 81.
26. Andrews, p. 137; "Diary of a Confederate Officer," April 3, quoted in Andrews, *Campaign of Mobile*, p. 80, note 2; Waterman, p. 23; *O.R.*, vol. 49, Part 2, p. 221; "Records: Hays and Wimmer Battle Reports"; Seybold, Memoirs, p. 12; Stephenson, Journal, page 105.
27. Andrews, p. 138; *ORN*, vol. 22, p. 79; "Records: Hays and Wimmer Battle Reports."
28. Andrews, pp. 139–140; Armstrong, Diary, April 4, 1865; Caldwell Delaney, *Confederate Mobile*, pp. 353–355; Hillengoss, Journal, April 4, 1865; *O.R.*, Ser. 1, vol. 49, Part 2, p. 1199; *Southern Historical Society Papers* 21, pp. 220–221, quoted from the New Orleans, Louisiana, *Picayune*, October 1, 1893.
29. Andrews, pp. 140, 146; *O.R.*, Ser. 1, vol. 49, Part 2, pp. 226–227; *ORN*, vol. 22, p. 80.
30. Andrews, p. 141; "Records: Hays and Wimmer Battle Reports," April 5, 1865.
31. Andrews, p. 144; Armstrong, Diary, April 6, 1865; *O.R.*, Ser. 1, vol. 49, Part 2, pp. 255–256, 266; "Records: Hays and Wimmer Battle Reports," April 5, 1865; Seybold, Memoirs, p. 13.
32. *O.R.*, vol. 49, Part 1, pp. 296–297; Part 2, pp. 266–267.
33. Andrews, pp. 145–147; *O.R.*, Ser. 1, vol. 49, Part 2, pp. 283–84; "Records: Hays and Wimmer Battle Reports."
34. Andrews, pp. 149–150; Hillengoss, Journal; *O.R.*, Ser. 1, vol. 49, Part 2, p. 321; Stephenson, Journal, p. 91, 95, 97.
35. Andrews, pp. 151–53; Stephenson, Journal, pp. 99, 101, 103.
36. Andrews, pp. 154, 157–58, 160, 162, 164; Hillengoss, Journal; *O.R.*, vol. 49, Part 2, p. 305; *Southern Historical Society Papers*, vol. 4, 1877, p. 222; Stephenson, Journal, pp. 105, 109, 111.
37. National Archives, Maps, Drawer 121, Sheet 16, Map of Siege Operations, Spanish Fort and Mobile Bay; *O.R.*, vol. 49, Part 2, pp. 285–289; "Records: Hays and Wimmer Battle Reports."
38. Andrews, pp. 187–188; Ralph Donnelly, *The Confederate States Marine Corps: The Rebel Leathernecks*, pp. 84–85; *O.R.*, vol. 49, Part 1, pp. 283, 287, 296, 298, 321; *O.R.*, Part 2, p. 283; *ORN*, vol. 22, p. 86; "Records: Hays and Wimmer Battle Reports."
39. *O.R.*, vol. 49, Part 1, p. 321; *ORN*, vol. 22, p. 86, 100, 101; "Records: Hays and Wimmer Battle Reports."
40. Andrews, p. 190; *O.R.*, Ser. 1, vol. 49, Part 1, p. 248; "Records: Hays and Wimmer Battle Reports."
41. Andrews, pp. 189, 194–201; *Confederate Veteran* 23, October 1915, "Siege and Capture of Fort Blakely,", p. 457; *O.R.*, Ser. 1, vol. 49, Part 1, pp. 287, 289, 296; *O.R.*, Part 2, pp. 298–303, 305–306; *ORN*, vol. 22, p. 101.
42. Armstrong, diary, April 9–11, 1865; Hillengoss, Journal, April, 9–10, 1865; *O.R.*, vol. 49, Part 2, p. 312; *SOR*, Part 2, vol. 30, p. 301.
43. Andrews, p. 231; NARG 94, "Regimental Orders," April 14, 1865; *O.R.*, vol. 49, Part 1, pp. 99, 102, 110; "Records: Hays and Wimmer Battle Reports."
44. *O.R.*, vol. 49, Part 1, p. 153; "Records: Hays and Wimmer Battle Reports."

Eighteen

1. Armstrong, diary, April 16–21, 1865.
2. Dooley, letter, no date; Hillengoss, Journal, April 29, 30, 1865; *O.R.*, vol. 49, Part 2, p. 1283; Dabney Maury, Letter, April 15, 1865; NARG -94, E-112–115, "Company Records," April 23, 1865.
3. Armstrong, diary, May 2, 5, 1865; *O.R.*, Ser. 1, vol. 49, Part 2, pp. 907, 911–912, 914, 1283; Schmandt and Schulte, *A Civil War Diary*, May 25, 1865.
4. Bergeron and Hewitt, *Boone's Louisiana Battery*, pp. 33–4; *O.R.*, Ser. 1, vol. 48, Part 2, pp. 681, 747–748.
5. Armstrong, diary, April 21, 25–26, May 12, 15, 21, 24, June 4, 1865; Dooley, letter, June 8, 1865; Hillingoss, Journal; *O.R.*, Ser. 1, vol. 48, Part 2, p. 891; *O.R.*, vol. 49, Part 2, 987, 1038.
6. *Minutes, Annual Reunion of the 21st Regiment, First Indiana Heavy Artillery, 1892*, p. 24 (hereafter cited as *Reunion, Minutes, 1892*); Dooley, letters, July 1, August 6, 26, 1865; *LaGrange Standard*, June 10, 1865; NARG 94, E112–115, "Regimental Records, *Morning Reports*, 1st Indiana Heavy Artillery."
7. Dooley, letter, September 16, 1865.
8. *Reunion Minutes, 1892*, p. 24; Dooley, letter, October 3, 1865; NARG 94, "Regimental Records," October 1, 1865.
9. *Reunion Minutes, 1892*, p. 25; Dooley, undated letter; Hillengoss, Journal, December, 1865; NARG 94, "Regimental Records," December 26, 1865; *Parke County Republican*, January 24, 1866.
10. *Parke County Republican*, January 31, 1866.
11. Hillengoss, Journal; *Indiana Battle Flags*, pp. 568–71; Seybold, Memoirs, page 13.

Bibliography

PRIMARY SOURCES

Andrews, C.C. *History of the Campaign of Mobile.* New York: Van Nostrand, 1867. Reprint, Range, AL: Tyree, 1985.

Bacon, Edward. *Among the Cotton Thieves.* Detroit: Free Press Steam Book and Job Printing House, 1867. Reprint, Bossier City, LA: Everett, 1989.

Bailey, J. M. *Memoirs of Captain J. M. Bailey.* Edited by James Troy Massey. Harrison, AR: Massey, 1995.

Benedict, G.G. *Vermont in the Civil War: A History of the Part Taken by the Vermont Soldiers and Sailors in the War for the Union, 1861–65.* Vol. 2. Burlington, VT: The Free Press Association, 1888.

Bergeron, Arthur W. Jr., ed. *The Civil War Reminiscences of Major Salas T. Grisamore, C.S.A.* Baton Rouge: Louisiana State University Press, 1993.

____, and Lawrence Lee Hewitt. *Boone's Louisiana Battery.* Baton Rouge: Elliott's Bookshop Press, 1986.

Dimitry, John, A. M. *Confederate Military History.* Vols. 9, 10, 11. *Louisiana.* Atlanta: Confederate, 1899.

Dorsey, Sarah A. *Recollections of Henry Watkins Allen.* New York: Doolady, 1866.

Gardner, Ira B. *Recollections of a Boy Member of Co. I, Fourteenth Maine Volunteers, 1861 to 1865.* Lewiston, ME: Lewiston Journal, 1902.

Harding, George C. *The Miscellaneous Writings of George C. Harding.* Indianapolis: Carlton and Hollenbeck, 1882.

Haskin, William L. *The History of the First Regiment of Artillery.* Fort Preble, Portland, ME: Thurston and Company, 1879.

Hoffman, Wyckham. *Camp, Court and Siege.* New York: Harper and Brothers, 1877.

Irwin, Richard B. *History of the Nineteenth Army Corps.* 1892. Reprint, Baton Rouge: Elliott's Book Shop Press, 1985.

McMorries, Edward Young. *History of the First Regiment Alabama Volunteer Infantry, C.S.A.* Montgomery, AL: Brown, 1904.

Merrill, Catharine. *The Soldier of Indiana in the War of the Union.* Vols. 1 and 2. Indianapolis: Merrill, 1866.

Moore, Frank, ed. *Rebellion Record: A Diary of American Events.* Vols. 5 and 6. New York: Putnam, 1863.

____. *Rebellion Record: A Diary of American Events.* Vols. 7, 8, 9, 10. New York: Van Nostrand, 1864–1867.

The War of the Rebellion: A Compilation of the Official Records of the Union and Confederate Armies. Ser. 1, Vol. 5; Vol. 6; Vol. 15; Vol. 17, Pt. 2; Vol. 23, Pt. 2; Vol. 26, Pts. 1, 2; Vol. 30, Pt. 2; Vol. 34, Pts. 1, 2, 3, 4; Vol. 39, Pts. 1, 2; Vol. 41, Pts. 1, 2, 3, 4; Vol. 48, Pts. 1, 2; Vol. 49, Pts. 1, 2; Vol. 51, Pts. 1, 2; Vol. 53, Pt. 1; Ser. 2: Vols. 1, 4; Ser. 3, Vol. 1. Washington, DC: Government Printing Office, 1891.

Official Records of the Union and Confederate Navies in the War of the Rebellion. Ser. 1, Vols. 19, 20, 21, 26. Washington, DC: Government Printing Office, 1914.

Official Report Relative to the Conduct of Federal Troops in Western Louisiana During the Invasions of 1863 and 1864, Compiled From Sworn Testimony Under the Direction of Governor Henry W. Allen. 1865. Reprint, Lafayette, LA: Acadiana Press, 1988.

Powers, George W. *The Story of the Thirty-Eighth Regiment of Massachusetts Volunteers.* Cambridge, MA: Dakin and Metcalf, 1866.

Rowland, Dunbar. *Military History of Mississippi, 1803–1898.* Reprint with index by H. Grady Howell Jr. Spartanburg, SC: Reprint, 1988.

Scribner, Theo. T. *Indiana's Roll of Honor.* Vol. 2. Indianapolis: Streight, 1866.

Smith, Daniel K. *History of Co. K, First Alabama Regiment, or Three Years in the Confederate Service.* Prattville, AL: Smith, 1885.

Supplement to the Official Records of the Union and Confederate Armies. Vol. 1–95. Wilmington, NC: Broadfoot, 1995–1999.

Taylor, Richard. *Destruction and Reconstruction: Personal Experiences of the Late War.* New York: Appleton, 1879.

Terrell, W.H.H. *Indiana in the War of the Rebellion.* Vols. 1–8. Indianapolis: Douglass and Connor, 1869.

Willis, Henry A. *53rd Regiment Massachusetts Volunteers.* Fitchburg, MA: Blanchard & Brown, 1889.

Wright, Howard C. *Port Hudson: Its History from An Interior Point of View.* Reprint. Baton Rouge: Eagle Press, 1978.

SECONDARY BOOKS

American Heritage. *American Heritage Civil War Chronology.* New York: American Heritage, 1960.

Babcock, Willoughby M. Jr. *Selections from the Letters and Diaries of Brevet-Brigadier General Willoughby Babcock of the Seventy-Fifth New York Volunteers.* Albany: University of the State of New York, 1922.

Battles & Leaders of the Civil War, Volume II. Porter, David D., "The Opening of the Lower Mississippi," pp. 36 and 38. Secaucus, NJ: Reprint by Castle, a division of Book Sales, Inc.

Bergeron, Arthur W. Jr. *Guide to Louisiana Confederate Military Units, 1861–1865.* Baton Rouge: Louisiana State University Press, 1989.

Casey, Powell A. *Encyclopedia of Forts, Posts, Named Camps and Other Military Installations in Louisiana, 1700–1981.* Baton Rouge: Claitor's, 1983.

Chittenden, N. H. *History and Catalogue of the Fourth Regiment Wisconsin Volunteers: From June 1861, to March 1864.* Baton Rouge: Gazette & Comet Book and Job Office, 1864.

Coffin, Charles Carleton. *Stories of Our Soldiers, War Reminiscences.* Boston: Journal Newspaper, 1898.

Davis, William C. *Rebels & Yankees: The Fighting Men of the Civil War.* New York: Gallery Books, 1989.

_____, and the Editors of Time-Life Books. *Brother Against Brother.* New York: Prentiss-Hall Press, 1990.

DeForest, John W. *A Volunteer's Adventures.* New Haven, CT: Yale University Press, 1946.

Delaney, Caldwell. *Confederate Mobile.* Mobile, AL: The Haunted Book Shop, 1971.

Donnelly, Ralph. *The Confederate States Marine Corps: The Rebel Leathernecks.* Shippensburg, PA: White Mane, 1989.

Editors of Combined Books. *The Civil War Book of Lists.* New York: Book Sales, 2008.

Edmonds, David C. *Guns of Port Hudson.* Vols. 1 and 2. Lafayette, LA: Acadiana Press, 1984.

_____. *Yankee Autumn in Acadiana.* Lafayette, LA: Acadiana Press, 1979.

Fowler, William. *Memorials of William Fowler.* New York: Randolph, 1875.

Hewitt, Lawrence L., ed. *A Place Named...Desperate!* Baton Rouge: VAAPR, 1982.

_____, and Arthur W. Bergeron, Jr., eds. *Post Hospital Ledger, Port Hudson, Louisiana, 1862–1863.* Baton Rouge: Le Comité des Archives de la Louisiane, 1981.

Holbrook, William. *A Narrative of the Services of the Officer and Enlisted Men of the 7th Regiment of Vermont Volunteers, Veterans, From 1862 to 1866.* New York: American Bank Note, 1882.

Howe, Henry Warren. *Passages from the Life of Henry Warren Howe, consisting of Diary and Letters Written During the Civil War, 1861–1865.* Lowell, MA: Courier-Citizen, 1899.

Indiana Battle Flag Commission, Mindwell C. Wilson, ed. *Indiana Battle Flags.* Indianapolis: Indiana Battle Flag Commission, 1929.

Johns, Henry T. *Life with the 49th Massachusetts Volunteers.* Pittsfield, MA: Johns, 1864.

Johnson, Ben C. *A Soldier's Life.* Edited by Alan S. Brown. Kalamazoo: Western Michigan University Press, 1962.

Jones, Katharine M., ed. *Heroines of Dixie: Spring of High Hopes.* 1955. Reprint. St. Simons Island, GA: Mockingbird Books, 1986.

Kerksis, Sydney C., and Thomas S. Dickey. *Heavy Artillery Projectiles of the Civil War, 1861–1865.* Kennesaw, GA: Phoenix Press, 1972.

McAulay, John D. *Civil War Breechloading Rifles.* Lincoln, RI: Mowbray, 1987.

Mahan, A. T. *The Gulf and Inland Waters.* 1883. Reprint. Wilmington, NC: Broadfoot, 1989.

Martin, Michael J. *A History of the 4th Wisconsin Infantry and Cavalry in the Civil War.* New York: Savas Beatie, 2006.

Morgan, Sarah. *The Civil War Diary of Sarah Morgan.* Edited by Charles East. Reprint. Athens: University of Georgia Press, 1991.

Murray, Thomas H. *History of the Ninth Regiment, Connecticut Volunteer Infantry: The Irish Regiment, In The War of the Rebellion, 1861–65.* New Haven, CT: Price, Lee & Adkins, 1908.

Noel, Theo. *A Campaign from Santa Fe to the Mississippi; Being A History of the Old Sibley Brigade.* 1865. Reprint. Raleigh, NC: Sanders, 1961.

Nolan, Dick. *Benjamin Franklin Butler: The Damnedest Yankee.* Novato, CA: Presidio Press, 1991.

Olmstead, Edwin, Wayne E. Starke, and Spencer C. Tucker. *The Big Guns.* Alexandria Bay, NY: Museum Restoration Service, 1997.

Pena, Christopher. *Touched By War: Battles Fought*

in the LaFourche District. Thibodaux, LA: C.G.P. Press, 1998.

Plummer, Albert. *History of the Forty-Eighth Regiment, M.V.M. During the Civil War.* Boston: New England Druggist, 1907.

Public Documents of Massachusetts; Being the Annual Reports of Various Public Officers and Institutions for the Year 1862. Vol. 2. Boston: Wright & Potter, State Printers. 1863.

Reed, Rowena. *Combined Operations in the Civil War.* Annapolis, MD: Naval Institute Press, 1978.

Richards, A.P. *The Saint Helena Rifles.* Houston: Johnson, 1968.

Ripley, Warren. *Artillery and Ammunition of the Civil War.* Charleston, SC: Battery Press, 1984.

Ripley, Eliza McHatton. *From Flag to Flag.* New York: Appleton, 1888.

Rollins, Richard, ed. *Black Southerners in Gray.* Redondo Beach, CA: Rank and File, 1997.

Rowell, John W. *Yankee Artillerymen: Through the Civil War with Eli Lilly's Indiana Battery.* Knoxville, TN: University of Tennessee Press, 1975.

Seebold, Herman. *Old Louisiana Plantation Homes and Family Trees. Vol I.* Privately Published, 1941; reprinted, Gretna, LA: Pelican, 1971.

Sifakis, Stewart. *Who Was Who in the Civil War.* New York: Facts on File, 1988.

Smith, George G. *Leaves from A Soldier's Diary: The Personal Record of Lieutenant George G. Smith, Co. C, 1st Louisiana Regiment Infantry Volunteers (White) During the War of the Rebellion...* Putnam, CT: Smith, 1906.

Southwick, Thomas P. *A Duryee Zouave.* Brookneal, VA: Schroeder, 1995.

Spurlin, Charles, ed. *West of the Mississippi with Waller's 13th Texas Cavalry Battalion, CSA.* Hillsboro, TX: Hill Junior College, 1971.

Steedman, I. G. W. Report of His Defense of Port Hudson. See: Hewitt, *A Place Named ... Desperate!*

Stevens, William B. *History of the Fiftieth Regiment of Infantry.* Boston: Griffiths-Stillings Press, 1907.

Thompson, Edwin Porter. *History of the Orphan Brigade.* Reprint. Dayton, OH: Morningside Bookshop, 1973.

Thornbrough, Emma Lou. *Indiana in the Civil War Era, 1850–1880.* Indianapolis: Indiana Historical Bureau and Indiana Historical Society, 1965.

Townsend, Luther Tracey. *History of the Sixteenth Regiment, New Hampshire Volunteers.* Washington, DC: Elliott, 1897.

True, Charles H., and William E. S. Whitman. *Maine in the War for The Union: A History of the Part Borne by Maine Troops in the Suppression of the American Rebellion.* Lewiston, ME: Dingley, 1865.

Van Alstyne, Lawrence. *Diary of An Enlisted Man.* New Haven, CT: Tuttle, Morehouse & Taylor, 1910.

Whitman, William E. S. (See True, Charles H., above.)

Whitcomb, Caroline E. *History of the Second Massachusetts Battery (Nims' Battery) of Light Artillery, 1861–1865.* Concord, NH: Rumford Press, 1912.

Winters, John D. *The Civil War in Louisiana.* Baton Rouge: Louisiana State University Press, 1963.

Manuscript Collections

Alabama State Archives, Montgomery, AL.
  Smith, Daniel K. Diary.
American Antiquarian Society, Worcester, MA.
  Unknown diarist from 4th Massachusetts Battery stationed at Fort Pike, LA, 1863.
Bartholomew County Historical Society, Columbus, IN.
  Bartholomew County Atlas. "Personal Sketches Colonel John A. Keith." Chicago: Beers, 1879.
DePauw University, Greencastle, IN.
  Minutes, Annual Reunion of the 21st Regiment, First Indiana Heavy Artillery, 1892.
Fort Morgan, AL, Museum, Mobile Point, AL
  Wilkinson, Joseph B. Jr., Lieutenant, 1st Tennessee Artillery. Diary.
Indiana Historical Society, Indianapolis.
  Ballard, Thomas. Letter. E-506.
  Danely, Alfred. Letter. E-506.
  Dooley, Rufus. Papers; M 0383. (Mostly letters to and from his mother, other family members and friends; it also contains letters between other soldiers in his infantry company and his family.)
  First Indiana Heavy Artillery Regiment Records, 1862–1865; BV 3052–3054.
    A. Three ledger books of orders, receipts for commissary, quartermaster supplies and recipes.
    B. Firing Record of Company H, at Spanish Fort and Blakely.
    C. Battle report for Spanish Fort and Blakely by Captain William Wimmer.
    D. Battle report for Spanish Fort and Blakely by Colonel Benjamin Hays.
  Grimsley, James. Papers; M 0121. (Letters to his wife, newspaper clippings, casualty reports from the battle of Baton Rouge and ordnance reports.)
  Harding, George. Letters; E 506, 4C5.
  Hillingoss, Daniel. "Journal." (A letter narrative of events while he was in Company M of the 1st Indiana Heavy Artillery.)
  Indiana Historical Commission *Bulletin*, No. 15, February 1922.
  Indiana's Part in the Butler Expedition to New Orleans During the Civil War. Text of speech given by Rufus Dooley, Rockville, IN
  Nash, George W. Letter. E-506.
  Osborn, Isaac. Letter. E-506.
  Phillips, William. Letter. E-506.

Rose, Elihu. Letter. E-506
Underwood, Albert S. Diary.
Indiana State Library, Indianapolis.
   Abbernathy, Alexander. "Memoirs."
   Brakeman, Nelson. Published letter. (Kirkpatrick family papers)
   Minutes. Annual Reunion of the 21st Regiment, First Indiana Heavy Artillery, 1893.
      Correspondence of the 21st Regiment of Volunteers (Letters and miscellaneous forms mostly from James W. McMillan. Microfilm.)
Library of Congress, Washington, DC.
   Alvord, Jabez. Diary.
   Browning, Silas. Letters.
   Butler, Benjamin. Collection of letters, orders, etc.
   Graham, Henry. Journal.
   Van Dorn, Earl. Collection of letters and telegrams.
Lilly Library, Bloomington, IN
   Hatten, Mitchel. Letters.
Living History Association Museum, Wilmington, VT.
   Typed transcribed copy of diaries of W. H. Flint, 2nd Vt. Light Artillery Battery.
Louisiana State University, Department of Archives and Manuscripts (Hill Memorial Library), Baton Rouge.
   Edwards, Albert F. B. Diary.
   Johnson, Benjamin Whitfield.
   Maury, Dabney H. Letter.
   Paine, Halbert E. Letter.
   Stephenson, P. D. Autobiographical Journal.
   Tyson, Robert A. Diary.
Minnesota Historical Society, St. Paul, MN.
   Babcock, Willoughby, Letters.
Mississippi State Archives, Jackson, MS.
   Confederate Records, RG 9. First Mississippi Light Artillery. Muster Rolls and Historical Questionnaires.
   Johnson, Jonathan H. Letters.
Southern Historical Society Papers.
   The Confederate Veteran. Volumes 1 through 34. Nashville, TN, 1896 through 1924. Bound copies at the Mississippi State Archives, Jackson, MS. (See chapter notes for specific references, except for "Afloat, Afield, Afloat.")
National Archives, Washington, DC.
   Summary Statements of Quarterly Returns of Ordnance and Ordnance Stores on Hand in Regular and Volunteer Army Organizations 1862–1867. Record Group 156. Microfilm Rolls 1, 4 and 5.
   Record Group 94, E112–115, P 1–17. "Regimental Records, Twenty-first Indiana Infantry Regiment/First Indiana Heavy Artillery."
   Record Group 159, Ordnance Records, Department of the Gulf.
   Record Group 393, Continental Army Commands, Department of the Gulf.
   Record Group 393, Part I, Department of the Gulf, Entry 1756, letters received (John A. Kennedy, 1st Arkansas Regiment, Journal).
New York Historical Society, New York.
   Company A, 21st Regiment Indiana Volunteers.
   Proceedings of the 12th Annual Reunion (1901) and the 13th Annual Reunion, 1902.
Owens County Public Library.
   American Tribune. Indianapolis, Various issues—1899–1900. (A series of letters written by Vint Anderson of Company B, 21st Indiana Infantry/1st Indiana Heavy Artillery Regiment. Microfilm held by Spencer, IN–Owens County Public Library.)
Port Hudson State Commemorative Area, Zachary, LA
   Austen, John D. Diary.
   Bell, William Jefferson. Diary.
   Gillette, Theodore. Memoir.
   Rawles, Jacob. Miscellaneous letters.
Texas State Library and Archives Commission, Austin, TX.
   Bailey, J. M., *The Story of a Confederate Soldier, 1861–5.* (Typed copy.)
Tulane University Howard Tilton Library, Manuscript Department, Special Collections Division, Louisiana Historical Association Collection, New Orleans, LA.
   Dabney, Fred Y. Report of Siege of Port Hudson to Major T. F. Willson, A.A.G., August 24, 1863.
   DeGournay, Paul F. Report to Major T. F. Willson, A.A.G., September 12, 1863.
   "*Headquarters Book*, Miles' Legion, May 22 to July 9, 1863.
   Lewis, A.J. Report to Major T. F. Willson, July 9, 1863.
   Miles, William. F. Report to Major T. F. Willson, A.A.G., July 23, 1863.
   Myers, M., Letter to "Francis," April 29, 1862.
   Shelby. William B. Colonel, Report to Maj. T. F. Willson, A.A.G., August 5, 1863.
   Smith, Marshall J. Report to Major-General Franklin Gardner, October 28, 1863.
   RG 55-L, Joseph L. Brent Collection, Misc. Ordnance Reports and Letters.
   RG 55-B-41 (bound volumes)
University of Michigan, Bentley Historical Library, Michigan Historical Collections, Ann Arbor, MI.
   Corden, John. Letters
   Griffin, Eli. Letters.
   Moulton, Charles H. Letters.
   Spaulding, Wilbur F. Letters.
   Soule, Harrison. Letters.
University of Texas at Austin, The Center for American History, Austin, TX.
   McClung, Richard L., Diary, pages 25 through 30.
Wabash County Historical Society, IN.
   Dale, Albert P. Letter
Wisconsin State College, River Falls, WI.
   Flint, Jerry. Letters.

PRIVATE COLLECTIONS

Faller, Phillip E. Private Collection, LA.
   Minutes, Annual Reunion of the 21st Regiment, First Indiana Heavy Artillery (for the years 1887, 1888, 1889, 1891, 1892, 1901 and 1903).

Assorted Discharge papers and Court-Martial records of the 1st Indiana Heavy Artillery.
    Taylor, George A., Lieutenant. *Recollections of The Battle of Baton Rouge, August 5, 1862.* (Manuscript/ letter by Lieut. George Taylor of the 4th Massachusetts Light Artillery Battery. Currently being considered for private publication as an informative pamphlet by the author.)
    Clark, Henry I. Copy of letter-from journal of siege of Port Hudson, LA (24th Connecticut).
    Wilkinson, Robert. 128th N.Y. Volunteers. Partial copy of letter dated June 3, 1863.
    Armstrong, S. E., Lieutenant. Diaries: 1862, 1864 and 1865. (All transcribed by, decoded by and typed copy held by the author. Original owner deceased more than ten years and whereabouts of original diaries are unknown. Original owner gave the author permission to use the transcriptions of the diaries as he wished.)
Private Collection of Mrs. Elizabeth Shaifer Hollingsworth, MS.
    Miscellaneous notes and papers of Lieutenant A. K. Shaifer, Battery K, 1st Mississippi Light Artillery.
Private collection of William Rogers, Brandon, MS.
    Typed transcribed diary of Walter S. Turner, 39th Mississippi Infantry Reg't., May 21, 1863 through July 25, 1863.
Private collection of Mrs. Ann White, Indianapolis.
    Seybold, John N., *My War Experiences.* (Company H, 1st Indiana Heavy Artillery.) Typed narrative given to the author.

Newspapers

Daily Picayune. August 1862 through October 3, 1863.
Daily True Delta. June 1, 1862, and June 16 through September 5, 1863. Hill Memorial Library, Louisiana State University, Baton Rouge.
Indianapolis Daily Journal. February 1863 through April 1864. Indiana State Library, Indianapolis.
LaGrange Standard. May 1861 through June 1865. Indiana State Library, Indianapolis. (Mostly published letters from the 21st Indiana Infantry / 1st Indiana Heavy Artillery Regiment.)
The Jackson Mississippian. August 9, 1862. Mississippi State Archives, Jackson, MS.
Lloyd's American Railroad Weekly, April 27, 1861.
Memphis Daily Appeal. August 6 through August 11, 1862. Mississippi State Archives, Jackson.
Mobile Advertiser and Register. August 13 through 15, 1862, August 9, 1863. Alabama State Archives, Montgomery.
Natchitoches Union. January 29, 1863, Hill Memorial Library, Louisiana State University, Baton Rouge.
New Orleans Era. July 11, 15, 16, 17, 18, 19, 21, 24 and 25, 1863, Indiana Historical Society Library, Indianapolis (Grimsley Collection).
New Orleans Picayune. April 5, 1862, Indiana Historical Society Library, Indianapolis (Grimsley Collection).
New York Daily Tribune, June 16, 1862. Joseph Hawley Collection, Library of Congress, Washington, DC.
New York Daily Tribune. August 18 and 19, 1962, February 11, April 27, May 21, June 10, July 25, 1863. Author's collection.
Parke County Republican. August 1861 through February 1866. Indiana State Library, Indianapolis. (Published letters from the 21st Indiana Infantry / 1st Heavy Artillery Regiment.)
Philadelphia Inquirer. August 19, 1862, July 31, 1863, September 3, 1864. Author's collection.
_____. August 17, 1864. Joseph Hawley Collection, Library of Congress, Washington, DC.
Taunton Daily Gazette. Taunton, MA, July 23, 1863. Author's collection.
Tri-Weekly News. Port Hudson, LA, February 27, 1863. Mississippi State Archives, Jackson, MS.
The Weekly Junior Register. May 22, 1862. Mississippi State Archives, Jackson, MS.

Articles, Periodicals and Other Publications

Faller, Phillip E. "Port Hudson Siege Guns." *The Artilleryman*, Spring 1992: 8–10.
_____. "Port Hudson Trophy Gun." *The Artilleryman*, Winter, 1993.
_____. "A Treatise on Merrill Rifles and Carbines." *The Artilleryman*, July and August, 2001: 16–29, 41–50.
Falls, Cathie. *The Eaton Rifles: The Men of Company H (6th Michigan Volunteer Infantry Regiment).* Eaton County, MI: Eaton County Historical Commission. echc/EatonRif.htm).
"Fortification and Siege of Port Hudson." *The Southern Historical Society Papers.* Compiled by the Defenders of Port Hudson. Pages 305–348.
Kendall, John Smith. "Recollections of a Confederate Officer." *Louisiana Historical Quarterly* 29, 1946: 1041–1228.
Root, William H. "Private Journal..." *The Louisiana Historical Quarterly* 19, 1936: 635–667.
Shewmaker, Kenneth E., and Andrew K. Prinz, eds. "Notes and Documents, a Yankee in Louisiana: Selections From the Diary and Correspondence of Henry R. Gardner, 1862–1866." *Louisiana History* 5, no. 3 (1964): 271–295.
Waterman, George S. "Afloat, Afield, Afloat." *Confederate Veteran.* January, February, April, and August 1898; January, October, and November 1899; January and February 1900; January 1901; November 1902.

Drawings, Maps and Photographs

Alabama Department of Archives and History, Montgomery.

Atlas to Accompany the Official Records of the Union and Confederate Armies. Washington, DC: Government Printing Office, 1891–1895. Reprint by Arno Press and Crown, 1978; 1983 edition by Fairfax Press, Hong Kong.

Frank Leslie's Illustrated Newspaper. May 24, 1862; August 30, 1862; May 9, 1863; July 11, 1863; July 25, 1863. Author's collection.

Harper's Weekly. August 30, 1862; September 6, 1862; May 9, 1863; June 20, 1863; July 11, 1863; July 18, 1863; July 25, 1863; August 8, 1863; May 14, 1864; September 24, 1864; October 22, 1864; April 29, 1865; May 6, 1865. Author's collection.

Illinois State Historical Library, Springfield.

Library of Congress, Washington, DC
    Department of the Gulf, Map #2. Battle of Bisland.
    Nathaniel P. Banks Collection, Map #76.

Louisiana State Archives, Baton Rouge.
    Battle of Baton Rouge, Louisiana.

Historic Orleans Collection, New Orleans, Louisiana.
    Port Hudson sketch map by Major J. DeBaun, 9th LA Cavalry Battalion
    Military Order of the Loyal Legion of the United States, housed at US Army Military History Institute, Carlisle Barracks, PA.

National Archives, Washington, DC.
    Alabama: Fort Blakely, Fort Gaines, Fort Morgan and Spanish Fort.
    Louisiana: Alexandria, Baton Rouge, Bisland, Brashear City, Parapet Line, Port Hudson, A Portion of Southeastern Louisiana, and New Orleans to Vicksburg.

Index

Alexandria, LA 113–114, 205, 207, 212–213, 257–258
Algiers, LA 31–32, 36, 38, 93–94, 116
Allen, Col. Henry W., 4th LA Volunteers (Vols.), CSA 54, 63–65, 68
Appalachee River *see* Blakely River
USS *Arizona* (US gunboat) 116, 195–19
Arkansas 233
CSS *Arkansas* (ram-style gunboat) 46, 73–74, 78
Armstrong, Lt./Capt. Samuel E. "Ed," 21st IN Vols. 18, 20–21, 23, 37–39, 50, 81, 93–96, 150, 159, 162, 164, 199, 245, 247–248
Arnold, Brig.-Gen. Richard, (US) 106, 111, 116–117, 121, 140, 150, 153, 159, 162, 205
Ashland Plantation, Ascension Parish, Louisiana 47–48
Atchafalaya River, LA 32, 99, 190–192, 214–215
Augur, Brig.-Gen. Christopher, USA 116–118, 134, 137, 140, 154, 160, 163
(J.D.) Avery Salt Works on Avery Island, LA 94

Bailey, Maj. Joseph, Fourth Wisconsin Vol. Infantry 161, 212, 214
Bailey's Dam (named for Major Joseph Bailey) 212
Ballard, Pvt. Thomas, 21st IN Vols. 1, 61
Baltimore, MD 11–12, 16, 18
Banks, Maj.-Gen. Nathaniel P., United States Volunteers (USV) 97, 98, 101, 103, 106–107, 113–114, 121, 123, 129, 143, 151, 153–154, 160–161, 163, 173, 175, 182, 185–186, 190, 193, 195, 202, 207, 209, 215–216
Baton Rouge, LA 40, 44, 48, 65, 75, 76, 80, 98, 103, 113, 189, 194, 197, 203, 216–217, 244, 258, 260, 262; Battle of August 5, 1862 50–74

Battery Bailey 168, 172–174, 176–177, 184
Bay Minette, LA *see* Minette Bay (Civil War parlance)
Bayou Grand Caillou, LA 33
Bayou Rapides, LA 212
Bayou Robert, LA 212
Bayou Teche, LA 32, 99, 107–108, 110–112, 197
Beall, Brig.-Gen. William N. R., CSA 117, 119, 149, 184
Bee (river steamer [21st IN capture]) 37–38, 116
Bee, Brig.-Gen. Hamilton, CSA 207–209, 211–212
Benton's Texas Battery 214
Berwick, LA 99, 107, 191–192, 197
Bisland, LA, battle of 107–111
Black, Edward (musician, 21st IN Vols.) 8, 19, 51
Blair's Landing, LA, engagement at 210
Blakely River, AL 238, 240, 244
Blankenship, Capt. William, 1st IN Heavy Art'y. 239, 247, 250
Boone's Battery, Louisiana Vols. (CSA) 117, 124, 144, 150, 157, 258
Bough, Lt./Capt. William, 21st IN Vols. 33, 37, 166, 260
Brakeman, Chap. Nelson, 21st IN Vols. 13, 21
Brashear City (Morgan City), LA 31–32, 91, 93–97, 101, 106, 113, 116, 143, 190, 192–193, 197, 203, 217
Breckenridge, Maj.-Gen. John C., CSA 47, 49, 50, 69, 72–74, 80
Brown, Lt. James, 21st IN Vols. 37, 51, 66, 68, 191
Bryant, Lt. Thomas, 21st IN Vols. 10, 18, 36, 79
Butler, Andrew (so-called "colonel," Gen. Butler's brother) 23, 27, 95
Butler, Maj.-Gen. Benjamin, USV 19, 22–23, 26–27, 30, 33, 35, 36, 40–41, 46, 49, 80, 82, 95, 97

Cahil, Pvt. Walter G., 21st IN Vols. 16

Cahill, Col. Thomas, 30th MA, Vols. 72, 75
USS *Calhoun* (gunboat) 90–93
Camp Magnolia Grove, Baton Rouge, LA 41, 194
Camp Moore, LA, CSA 40, 47, 49, 74
Camp Morton, Indianapolis, IN 5, 9
Camp Murray (Druid Hill), Baltimore, MD 13–14
Camp Parapet (Camp Lewis), Carrollton, LA 81, 83, 86, 90, 98
Camp Pratt (Confederate prison camp near New Iberia, LA) 84, 88
Camp Sullivan, Indianapolis, IN 6, 9, 10
Campbell, Capt. John, Company H, 21st IN Vols. 10, 62
Campbell, Capt. Richard, Company I, 1st IN Heavy Art'y., 201, 248
Canby, Maj.-Gen. (USV)/Brig.-Gen. (USA) Edward R.S. 215–217, 219, 233, 235–238, 240–241, 246, 249, 257
Cane River, LA 207, 211–212
Carrollton, LA 81, 83
Chesapeake Bay 15
Chicago Mercantile Battery 208
Citadel 141–142, 146, 148, 151, 154, 157, 161–162, 168, 170, 172–173, 175, 177–178, 183; *see also* (River) Battery XI
Clark, Gen. Charles, CSA 47, 50, 52, 69, 70, 71, 72
USS *Clifton* (gunboat) 194–196, 200
Cobb's Kentucky Battery, CSA 50, 54
USS *Colorado* (frigate) 27
Commissary Hill 126, 133–135, 142, 183
Connelly, Lt./Capt./Maj. James, 21st IN Vols., Company H 36, 39, 88–89, 98, 101, 122, 133–134, 136, 151, 153, 165, 167, 176, 179, 223, 227, 229, 231, 235, 255, 258
Constitution (steam transport) 19–21

361

Cooke, Brig.-Gen. Philip St. George, (USA) 200, 205
"Copperheads" 204
Corden, Capt. John, 6th Michigan Vols. 25, 66, 163–164
Cornay's Battery, CSA 107–109, 111; see also St. Mary's Cannoneers
Corps de Afrique see "Native Guards"
Cotton (Confederate gunboat) 90–93, 100
Cotton Bale battery 162, 164, 166–168, 172–174, 177; see also Battery Bailey
Cox, Capt. Chambers, 1st IN Heavy Artillery, Company K 250, 255
Cox, Lt./Capt. Clayton, 21st IN Vols., Company K 39, 88–89, 98, 101, 110, 122, 134, 136, 153, 182, 184, 223
Coyle, Matthew, 21st IN Vols. 48
Cramer, Washington, 21st IN Vols. 48, 62

Dabney, Lt. Frederick Y., Engineer CSA 150, 169, 172
Dauphin Island, Alabama 219, 221–222, 235, 238, 259
Davis, Pres. Jefferson, CSA 5, 39, 43, 114, 124
Day, Lt./Capt./Maj. John 223, 235, 255, 258
DeGournay, Lt.-Col. Paul F. 140, 152; see also Twelfth Louisiana Heavy Artillery Battalion
Department of Arkansas 233
Department of the Gulf, USA 24, 99, 235; see also Nineteenth (XIX) Corps
DesAllemands, LA 31, 84, 88
Devil's Elbow 146, 148, 157, 170, 172
Diana (US steamer, converted to gunboat) 39, 91–96; captured by and used as CSA gunboat 106–109, 111
Donaldsonville, LA 86–89, 99, 174, 186, 189–190, 193–194
Dooley, Pvt./Corp./Sgt. Rufus, 21st IN Vols., Company H 13, 16, 18, 37, 86, 133, 152, 165, 168, 197, 199, 203, 216–217, 223, 230, 232, 234, 258–260, 262
Dow, Brig.-Gen. Neal, USA 129–130, 140, 178
Dowling, Lt. Richard "Dick," Davis Guards, Texas 195–196
Dudley, Col. Nathan A.M., 30th Mass. Vols. 72, 116–117, 144
Dwight, Brig.-Gen. William, USV 113, 119, 125–126, 128, 140, 148, 153–154, 157, 161, 163, 174–175, 208, 212

Eastern Shore Campaign, VA 15–16
Eighteenth New York (Mack's or Black Horse) Artillery 110–111, 117, 122, 124, 134, 147, 153, 170, 176, 183, 197, 235, 243–244, 247, 253
Eighth Louisiana Infantry (CSA) 108
Eighth New Hampshire Vol. Infantry 155–156, 158, 186
Eighth Vermont Vol. Infantry, USA 84, 93, 100
Emory, Brig.-Gen. William H., (US) 106, 114, 116, 190, 208–209
Empress (river steamer) 223
Essex (US gunboat) 46, 71, 78, 80, 116, 142, 151
Estrella (US gunboat) 90–93, 96, 116, 194

Farragut, Flag Off./Adm. David G., USA 26, 27, 30, 46, 103, 105, 140, 219–221, 233
Federal Hill, Baltimore, MD 14
Fifteenth Arkansas Infantry (Johnson's), CSA 120, 126, 128, 163, 169, 172, 182
Fifteenth New Hampshire Infantry 129, 133, 177
Fifth New York Volunteer Infantry 15
Fifth US Battery, Company G (Rawles') 122, 134, 138, 184, 211
Fifth Washington Artillery, CSA 240, 245, 247–248, 250
Fifty-third Massachusetts Vol. Infantry 155–156, 166, 169
First Alabama Heavy Artillery Battalion, CSA 232
First Alabama Infantry/Heavy Artillery, CSA 118, 124–125, 137, 142–143, 148–149, 157, 169, 187, 232
First Delaware Light Battery (Nields') 211
First Indiana Light Battery (Klaus') 208, 214
First Louisiana Regular Battery (Semmes'), CSA 54, 57–58, 68, 87–88, 92, 107–108, 191
First Maine Vol. Battery (Healy's) 85–86, 100, 110, 123, 125–126, 140, 148, 197
First Mississippi Infantry 169
First Mississippi Light Artillery, Company B (Herod's) 120, 123, 126–127
First Mississippi Light Artillery, Company F (Bradford's) 123, 124, 134
First Mississippi Light Artillery, Company K (Abbay's) 117, 129–132, 187
First Missouri Light Artillery, Company F (Foust's) 254, 256
First Tennessee Battalion Heavy Artillery 124, 126, 134, 136, 149, 182, 184, 187, 224
First US Artillery, Company A (Bainbridge's) 99, 107, 110, 123, 125–126, 140, 153, 197
First US Artillery, Company F (Duryea's) 110, 123, 125–126, 140, 153, 175, 186–187, 197
First US Artillery, Company L (Closson's) 123, 125–126, 147, 153, 166, 168, 174, 184, 197
First Vermont Battery (Hebard's) 119, 122, 129, 144, 148, 166, 174, 197
Fisher, Eden, Lieutenant, 21st IN Vols. 91
Fort Blakely, AL 237, 248, 251, 255; siege of 248–254
"Fort Desperate" 126–129, 156, 161, 163, 169, 178, 183
Fort Gaines, AL 221–224, 236, 238, 258–260
Fort Griffin, Texas 195–196
Fort Huger, AL 238–241, 245–246, 248–249, 251, 253–255
Fort Jackson, LA 25–27, 29, 38, 218, 244
Fort Livingston, LA 38
Fort Marshall (aka Murray Hill or Snake Hill) Baltimore, MD 14
Fort McDermott (aka Fort Alexis at south end of Spanish Fort defenses) 239, 242–243, 245–247, 250
Fort Morgan, AL 221, 224, 226, 230, 232, 236 238, 258–259; siege 223–230
Fort Pickens, FL 260
Fort St. Philip, LA 25–29, 218, 244
Fort Tracey, AL 238–239–240, 245–246, 248, 250, 253–255
Fort Williams (aka Camp Williams), Baton Rouge, LA 79, 103, 194, 200, 216–217
Fortress Monroe, VA 19
Forty-eighth Massachusetts Volunteer (Vol.) Infantry 149, 158
Fourteenth Maine Volunteer Vol. Infantry 51, 54–55, 57, 59, 73, 157–158, 167, 186, 196
Fourth Louisiana Vol. Infantry, CSA 65–66, 68, 81, 104, 132, 175
Fourth Massachusetts Vol. Battery (Manning's, Taylor's, Briggs,' Reinhard's) 51, 58, 61, 71, 102, 123, 134, 136, 138, 197
Fourth Massachusetts Vol. Infantry 155–156, 158
Fourth Wisconsin Vol. Infantry 15, 21, 24, 28, 30, 43, 51, 58, 69, 71, 126, 155–156, 158, 161, 186
Fox (blockade runner, 21st IN capture) 33–34
Frakes, Jesse, 21st IN Vols. 34
Franklin, Maj.-Gen. William B. 195, 197–198, 202, 205, 208
Freret, Lt./Eng. James, CSA 150

Gardner, Maj.-Gen. Franklin, CSA 103, 114, 117–119, 123, 153, 160, 173–174, 184–186
Geisendorffer, Charles, 21st IN Vols. 34
Gibson, Brig.-Gen. R.L., CSA 244
Grand Ecore, LA 207, 209

Granger, Maj.-Gen. Gordon 218, 221, 238, 248, 257
USS *Granite City* (gunboat) 195–196
Grayson, Capt. John B., CSA 242–243
Great Republic (US ocean transport) 24–28
Green, Col. Thomas, Texas Cavalry (CSA) 111–112, 190–193, 198, 207, 209–210
Grey Cloud (aka *Kinsman*; US gunboat) 91–96
Grimsley, Capt./Maj. James, 21st IN Vols., Company B 14, 17, 32, 35–36, 39, 44, 69, 79, 89–90, 106, 122, 134, 159, 166, 172–173, 189, 194, 197, 200, 202–203, 223
Grover, Brig.-Gen. Cuvier (US) 106, 110–112, 114, 118, 125, 128, 140, 153–154, 163, 193, 198–199

Hamrick, Capt. James, 21st IN Vols., Company E 110, 118, 122, 142, 165, 223
Harding, Regt. Q-master/2nd Lt. George C., 21st IN Vols. 88–89, 197
USS *Hartford* (sloop-of-war) 104, 105, 221
Hays, Maj./Col. Benjamin, 21st IN Vols. 14–39, 52, 55, 62, 101, 194, 217, 234–235, 255, 258
Hendricks, Capt. Isaac, Company L 1st IN Heavy Artillery 194, 250, 258, 260
Hervey, Sgt. O.P., 21st IN Vols. 31
Hinkle, QM/Capt. William, 21st IN Vols., Company D 10, 21, 36, 142, 166, 207, 209–212, 223
Hoosier Newsboy (21st IN newspaper in Algiers, LA) 31
Houma, LA 33–34
Hudson's Mississippi Battery, CSA 54, 57, 71
Hunt, Col. Thomas H., CSA 53, 55, 57–58, 69, 72
CSS *Huntsville* (casemated ram-style gunboat) 241, 249, 251, 253

Indiana Jackass Battery (Brown's, improvised) 51–52, 58, 63, 65, 68, 85–87, 90, 98–99, 204
Indianapolis, Indiana 5–6, 9, 10, 194, 204, 260
Indianola, Texas 203

USS *Jackson* (gunboat) 25

USS *Katahdin* (gunboat) 86, 88
Kearney, Lt. J. Watts, Miles Legion 104, 124, 144
Keith, Lt.-Col./Col. John, 21st IN Vols. 28, 34–37, 44, 48, 52, 55, 62, 69, 71, 75, 101, 121–122, 144, 187–188, 194, 200, 205, 216–217, 233–234, 262
USS *Kineo* (gunboat) 29–30

Landis, J.C. (steam transport) 195, 197
Latham, Adj./Lt. Mathew A., 21st IN Vols. 10, 42, 49, 69
Laurel Hill (river steamer) 116, 197
Lee, Brig.-Gen. Albert, USA 207–208
Lewis (steamer) 20–21
Liddell, Brig.-Gen. St. John R., CSA 237, 244, 254
Lilly, Lt. Eli, 21st IN Vols. 12
Lincoln, Pres. Abraham, USA 5, 10, 99, 202, 256
CSS *Louisiana* (gunboat) 26
Louisiana Belle (river steamer, 21st IN capture) 38–39

Magnolia Cemetery, Baton Rouge, LA 41, 52, 58–61, 65, 76
Major, Col. James P., CSA 190–191, 198, 211–214
Mansura, LA, engagement at 213–214
Matagorda, Texas 200, 216–217
Maury, Maj.-Gen. Dabney, CSA 244, 256
McClellan, Maj.-Gen. George, USA 19
McLaflin, Capt. Edward, 21st IN Vols., Company G 12, 35, 85, 92, 108, 122, 133–134, 142–143, 145, 153, 194, 217, 223
McMillan, Col. (21st IN Infantry)/Brig.-Gen. (USV) James W. 6, 10–11, 13, 17, 21–22, 26, 31, 33–34, 37, 40, 42–43, 62, 64, 75, 76, 80, 86, 89–90, 94–95, 97–98, 101, 208, 262
Merrill rifle 14, 16–18, 62, 78, 150–152, 174, 204, 216–217, 232
USS *Miami* (gunboat) 28, 30
Miles, Col. W.R., Louisiana CSA 119, 130, 149, 157, 168, 184
Miles' Legion, Louisiana Vol. Infantry 104, 117, 157
Military Division of West Mississippi 233
Minette Bay, AL 238, 240, 242, 246, 248, 250, 253–254
Mississippi (steamer) 40
USS *Mississippi* (side-wheel steam-powered frigate) 81, 85, 104, 105
Mississippi Dragoons (Terrell's), CSA 44
Mobile, AL 244, 251, 256–258
Mobile Bay, AL 236
Mobile Point, AL 223–224, 235–236
Monette's ferry, LA, engagement at 211–212
Moore, Gov. Thomas, LA 39
CSS *Morgan* (side-wheeler open deck gunboat) 221, 242, 248, 251–253
Morganza, LA 216–217
Morning Light (river steamer, 21st IN capture) 37–38, 84
Morris, Pvt. Josephus, 21st IN Vols. 34–35

Morton, Gov. Oliver P., Indiana 5–6, 10, 13, 204, 258
Mount Pleasant (LA) 157–158, 161, 168
Mouton, Brig.-Gen. Jean Jacques Alfred Alexander, Louisiana, CSA 90, 100, 107, 108, 112, 190, 207–208

CSS *Nashville* (open decked ram-style gunboat) 241, 248–249, 251–253
Natchitoches, LA 207, 211
Native Guards (Negro troops or "Engineers"/"Pioneers") 120, 126, 127–128, 137, 139, 143–144, 183; *see also* U.S. Colored Troops
New Iberia, LA 199–200, 202
New Orleans, LA 25–26, 29, 30, 38, 83, 89, 101, 113, 187, 197, 199, 201–202, 216–217, 231–233, 260, 262
New Orleans Opelousas & Great Western Railroad 31, 84, 91, 107, 191
Newport News, VA 19
Nickerson, Col. Frank, 14th Maine Infantry, USV 51, 57, 129, 130, 132, 157, 174
Nineteenth (XIX) Corps 99, 107, 150, 190, 194, 197–199, 204, 207, 211, 215, 217–218
Ninth Connecticut Infantry, USV 40, 43, 51–52, 71, 79, 103, 262
Ninth Louisiana Battalion Partisan Rangers (Wingfield's Battalion), CSA 44–45, 50, 54, 81, 118, 120, 127–128, 143, 187
Ninth Louisiana Infantry Battalion, CSA 64–66, 68
Noblett, Capt. Francis, 21st IN Vols., Company F 191–192, 223

Old Spanish Fort, AL (river-side of Spanish Fort defenses) 240, 247, 254
One-hundred Fourteenth Illinois Pontoniers 255
One-hundred Fourteenth New York Vol. Infantry 110
One-hundred Sixtieth New York Vol. Infantry 100, 128, 184
One-hundred Sixty-fifth New York Zouaves 132, 137, 158, 175
One-hundred Sixty-first New York Vol. Infantry 128, 146
One-hundred Thirty-third New York Vol. Infantry 155–156
One-hundred Twenty-eighth New York Vol. Infantry 130, 152, 158
"order of combat" 22, 48, 51

Paine, Col. (4th WI Vols.)/Bvt. Brig.-Gen. (USV) Halbert E. 22, 78–79, 80, 83, 110, 119, 125, 140, 154–156
Pattersonville, LA 99, 107

Pelican Light Artillery (aka Faries' or Winchester's), Louisiana, CSA 87, 92, 94, 108, 111, 214
Pemberton, Lt.-Gen. John C., CSA 114, 183
Plains, LA, Road and Store 116–118, 122
Pleasant Hill, LA 207–209
Polignac, Brig.-Gen. Camille Armand Jules Marie Prince de, CSA 211, 213–214
Port Hudson 74, 78, 103, 114–117, 190, 194, 201, 231, 260, 262; Siege of May 23 to July 9, 1863 118–189
Porter, Cmdr./Adm. David D., USN 26–28, 104, 205, 207, 213
Powers, Col. Frank, LA Cavalry 117
Priest Cap 141, 145, 154, 156–157, 160–161, 163, 166–167, 169, 174, 178–179, 182–184

Read, Surg. Ezra, 21st Indiana Vols. 62, 86–87
Red Fort (Redoubt in Spanish Fort defenses) 239–240, 242–245, 247, 249–250
Red River 205, 207, 211–212; Campaign 205–215
River Battery XI 104, 157, 172; *see also* Citadel
Rob Roy (river steamer) 207, 209–211
Rose, Capt. Elihu, 21st IN Vols., Company C 34–35, 91, 96, 142, 148–149
Roy, Capt./Maj./Col. William, 21st IN, Vols., Company A 8, 12, 32, 35, 42, 64, 85, 94–95, 133, 144, 150, 163, 174, 194, 200, 262
Rubottom, Pvt. Zeno, 21st IN Vols. Company H 11, 164
Ruggles, Maj.-Gen. Daniel, CSA 47, 52

Sabine Crossroads, LA 207
Sabine Pass, Texas 195–196
Sachem (US gunboat) 116, 195–196
St. Charles (steam transport) 195
St. Mary's (steam transport) 90–91, 94–96, 98, 150, 174
St. Mary's Cannoneers, LA 214; *see also* Cornay's Battery
Second Connecticut Light Artillery 218
Second Illinois Heavy Artillery, Company A 218, 224, 232
Second Illinois Light Battery (Lowell's) 253
Second Massachusetts Vol. Battery (Nims'), USA 12, 15, 23, 40, 43, 51–52, 68–69, 73, 123, 125–126, 152, 179, 197, 208
Second US Artillery, Company C 123, 144, 153, 166, 177
Second Vermont Battery (Holcomb's), USA 117, 122, 133–134, 138, 143, 147, 152

Seven Stars Artillery (Robert's) (Mississippi), CSA 124, 144, 170
Seventeenth Ohio Light Artillery (Rice's) 218, 253
Seventeenth provisional Red River Corps (XVII) 207, 214
Seventh Corps, Department of Arkansas 233
Seventh Massachusetts Battery 244
Seventh Vermont Vol. Infantry 43, 51, 61, 73, 82, 193
Seventy-fifth New York Vol. Infantry 100, 110, 186
Seybold, Nelson, 1st IN Heavy Art'y., Company H 261
Sherfey, Sgt. Jacob, 21st IN Vols. 37, 191–192
Sherman, Brig.-Gen. Thomas W., USA 116–117, 122, 124, 129–130, 135, 137, 140
Shields, Lt.-Col. Thomas, CSA 54, 57–58
Ship Island, MS 20–24, 234–235
Sibley, Brig.-Gen. Henry H. (CSA) 107–108, 111
Sixteenth Arkansas Vol. Infantry 155, 169, 171
Sixteenth Corps (XVI Corps) 205, 207, 212, 214, 235–236
Sixteenth New Hampshire Vol. Infantry 159
Sixth Kentucky Vols., CSA 59
Sixth Massachusetts Volunteer Battery (Everett's, Carruth's), USA 35, 43, 51, 52, 57, 58, 71, 110, 123, 125, 142, 153, 197
Sixth Michigan Volunteer Infantry/Heavy Artillery 15, 24, 30, 42, 43, 49, 51, 58–59, 65–66, 82, 100, 129, 130, 133, 151, 157–158, 162, 165, 175, 186, 235–236, 243–244, 254
Skelton, Capt. William, Company E, 21st IN Vols. 12, 35, 62
Slaughter's Field 130–131, 141
Slocumb, Capt. Cuthbert A, Fifth Washington Artillery, CSA 240, 246
Smith, Brig.-Gen. Andrew Jackson "A.J." 205, 209, 240, 249
Smith, Col. Thomas B., CSA 53–55, 58, 70, 71
Spanish Fort, AL 236–237, 240, 244, 246, 254; siege 237–251
Spencer, Pvt./Corp. John J., 21st IN Vols. 36
Springfield Landing, LA 140, 142–143, 145, 150, 152–153, 159, 164, 167–168, 174, 176, 178
Stamper, Lt. Richard, Company B 1st IN Heavy Artillery, commendation 249
Steedman, Col. I.G.W., Alabama (CSA) 118–119, 149, 156, 160, 165, 174, 184
Steele, Maj.-Gen. Frederick, USV 243, 249, 253
Stockdale, Thomas R., MS Cavalry Battalion 116–117

Taylor, Maj.-Gen./Lt.-Gen. Richard "Dick," CSA 84, 107, 111, 113, 174, 190, 194, 207, 213, 257
Tenth Louisiana Infantry Battalion (CSA) 108
Terre Bonne Parish, LA 35, 39
Terre Bonne Station, LA 33, 36, 191
Third Indiana Light Battery (Ginn's) 253
Thirteenth (XIII) Corps 197–198–199, 203, 207–208, 214–215, 217, 235–236, 245
Thirteenth Massachusetts Light Artillery 168
Thirteenth Texas Cavalry Battalion (Waller's), CSA 84–86, 106, 108
Thirtieth Louisiana Vol. Infantry, CSA 54, 66, 188
Thirtieth Massachusetts Vol. Infantry, USA 38, 40, 43, 51, 61, 64, 68, 69
Thirty-eighth Massachusetts Vol. Infantry 155–156
Thirty-first Massachusetts Vol. Infantry, USA 21, 23–24, 30, 155–156
Thirty-first Mississippi Vol. Infantry, CSA 59
Thirty-ninth Mississippi Vol. Infantry (Shelby's), CSA 65–66, 120, 127–128, 139, 143, 149, 153, 163, 165–166, 173, 187
Thompson, Col. A.P., CSA 53–55, 65, 69, 70, 71
Totten, Bvt. Brig.-Gen. James (chief of Artillery and chief of Ordnance, USV) 235, 238, 245
Twelfth Connecticut Vol. Infantry 100
Twelfth Louisiana Heavy Artillery Battalion 124, 141–142, 151, 173, 187; *see also* DeGournay, Paul F.
Twelfth Maine Infantry 149
Twenty-eighth Louisiana Vol. Infantry (CSA) 108
Twenty-first New York Battery (Barnes') 122, 129, 144, 174
Twenty-fourth Connecticut Vol. Infantry 156–158
Twenty-fourth Louisiana Vol. Infantry (CSA) 108
Twenty-second Maine Vol. Infantry 149
Twenty-second Mississippi Vol. Infantry, CSA 62
Twenty-sixth Massachusetts Vol. Infantry, USA 28
Tyler, Texas 193

U.S. Colored Troops (USCT) 193, 216, 218, 253–254; *see also* Native Guards

Valverde Battery (Texas, CSA) 106, 108, 110
Vicksburg, MS 43, 46, 74, 114, 183–184, 205, 214

Index

CSS *Virginia* 19
Walker, Lt. Gen. John G., CSA 207
Washburn, Maj.-Gen. Cadwallader C., USV 199–200
Washington, DC 6, 12
Watson Battery (Louisiana), CSA 124
Weitzel, Lt. (USA)/Capt./Chief Eng. (Dept of the Gulf, USA)/Brig. Gen. (USV)/Brig.-Gen. (USA)/Maj.-Gen. (USV) Godfrey 79, 90, 99, 106, 110, 114, 119, 125, 140, 154, 156, 186, 193–194, 198–199
Wharton, Maj.-Gen. John A., CSA 211, 213–214
"Whistling Dick" (Lieutenant Harrower's [Indiana Company G] 30-pounder Parrott rifle) 146, 148, 160, 174, 177
White River, Arkansas 223, 233
Williams, Brig.-Gen. Thomas, USA 19, 22–23, 25, 27–28, 40, 43, 46, 48, 52, 58, 61, 69, 70, 71, 79

Wimmer, Capt. William, Company H, First IN Heavy Artillery 242, 252–255, 259
Wingfield's Battalion *see* "Ninth Battalion Louisiana Partisan Rangers"

Yellow Bayou, LA, engagement at 214
Yelton, Pvt./Corp./Sgt. John B., 21st IN Vols., Company H 13, 36, 55, 86, 103, 113, 194, 216, 232, 245, 252, 260

www.ingramcontent.com/pod-product-compliance
Lightning Source LLC
Chambersburg PA
CBHW080803020526
44114CB00046B/2737